Transnational Crime and Public Security

U.S.–Mexico Contemporary Perspectives Series, 18
Center for U.S.–Mexican Studies
University of California, San Diego

Contributors

Peter Andreas
W. Carsten Andresen
Sigrid Arzt
John Bailey
Fernando Castillo
Jorge Chabat
Leonardo Curzio
Graham Farrell
José Z. García
Roy Godson
Dennis Jay Kenney
Brian Latell
Ernesto López Portillo Vargas
Viviana Macías
William F. McDonald
José M. Ramos
Jorge Regalado Santillán
Graham H. Turbiville, Jr.
Bruce Zagaris
Guillermo Zepeda Lecuona

This volume was published with the assistance of Georgetown University and the William and Flora Hewlett Foundation.

Transnational Crime and Public Security

Challenges to Mexico and the United States

edited by

John Bailey and Jorge Chabat

LA JOLLA

CENTER FOR U.S.–MEXICAN STUDIES
UNIVERSITY OF CALIFORNIA, SAN DIEGO

© 2002 by the Regents of the University of California. Published by the Center for U.S.–Mexican Studies at the University of California, San Diego. All rights reserved under International and Pan-American Conventions. No part of this publication may be reproduced or transmitted in any form or by any means, electronic or mechanical, including photocopy, recording, or any information storage or retrieval system, without prior permission in writing from the publisher.

Printed in the United States of America

Library of Congress Cataloging-in-Publication Data

Transnational crime and public security : challenges to Mexico and the United States / edited by John Bailey and Jorge Chabat.
p. cm. -- (U.S.-Mexico contemporary perspectives series ; 18)
Includes bibliographical references.
ISBN 1-878367-45-5 (paper)
1. Transnational crime—Mexico. 2. Transnational crime—United States. 3. National secuirty—Mexico. 4. National security—United States. 5. Law enforcement—Mexico—International cooperation. 6. Law enforcement—United States—Foreign relations. I. Bailey, John, 1944 Nov. 30- II. Chabat, Jorge. III. Series.

HV6252.5.M6 T73 2002
364.1'35—dc21

2001059874

CONTENTS

List of Tables and Figures

TABLES

FIGURES

Preface

Why would two otherwise respectable political scientists venture to organize a volume on crime, violence, corruption, and defective law enforcement in the Mexico–U.S. context? By convention, these topics belong to the realms of criminology, law, and journalism. Rare is the graduate program in political science that offers coursework on such themes. In our view, however, issues of public security are bedrock concerns in the establishment of political order, and political order is the foundation of a state that can engage its society to create rule of law. With rule of law comes the possibility of justice and democratic governability. Thus, until we have a clearer understanding of the dynamics of crime, violence, and corruption, and their effects on state and society, our comprehension of broader issues of democratic transition and consolidation will be limited.

The editors traveled parallel roads to arrive at this project. Jorge Chabat has been studying U.S.–Mexican relations since the 1980s. During the past decade he began to focus on drug trafficking as a key dynamic of the bilateral relationship. This became his dissertation topic at the University of Miami under the guidance of Bruce Bagley. From 1992 to 1994, he coordinated the Mexico team in a project on "Drug Trafficking in the Americas" of the North-South Center of the University of Miami. He has published various articles on drug trafficking in U.S.–Mexican relations and has also studied the links between national security and drug trafficking.

For his part, John Bailey spent the last decade or so in the study of "national security" in U.S.–Mexican relations. This began with a project, co-organized with Sergio Aguayo of the Colegio de México, which resulted in a volume also published by the Center for U.S.–Mexican Studies. One of the important findings of that study was that varieties of crime and domestic violence were emerging as preeminent concerns in the case of Mexico and the U.S.–Mexican border region. And one of these in particular—drug trafficking—was being perceived as a national security threat by Mexican and U.S. authorities. With this background, Bailey teamed up with Roy Godson, also of Georgetown's Government Department, to undertake a research project on the dynamics of organized crime in Mexico and the U.S.–Mexico borderlands.

The present collection expands the scope to consider issues of "common" crime, violence, corruption, and law enforcement as these interact with transnational crime and affect the domestic politics and bilateral relations of Mexico and the United States. We try as well to offer recommendations to improve knowledge, communications, and confidence related to public security.

One of our great pleasures in the project was to work with a task force of distinguished U.S. and Mexican policymakers and academics, along with an Argentine specialist included for additional perspective, whom we recognize in the acknowledgments. Based on two substantial meetings of the task force, and drawing especially on the working papers that were revised for publication in this volume, the editors produced a report, "Public Security and Democratic Governability: Challenges to Mexico and the United States," which is available in both Spanish and English at www.georgetown.edu/sfs/programs/clas/mexico/new.htm. This report was presented in Mexico City and Washington, D.C., in March and April 2001. It is important to emphasize that the conclusions to this volume are those of the editors, and although we benefited from the task force's advice and criticisms, these conclusions go beyond the report's conclusions in several respects.

Much of the project was conceived during the period when Mexico was still under the nearly seven-decade rule of the Institutional Revolutionary Party (PRI). Most of the chapters were written from the perspective of that period. At the time of writing (autumn 2001), much is undergoing rapid change with the administration of President Vicente Fox, who took power in Mexico in December 2000. President Fox has signaled a new spirit of cooperation with the United States on security and law enforcement matters. Similarly, the administration of George W. Bush in the United States has placed higher priority on relations with Mexico than was the case under the Clinton administration. In fact, the pace of reform and the new spirit of cooperation have gotten ahead of the expectations we brought to the subject. Even so, the roots of the problems of crime, violence, and corruption run deep into institutions and practices that have survived the old order.

The United States and Mexico are indeed divided by language. The editors jokingly asserted at their presentations of the report that a constant problem in this undertaking was not just two, but six, languages: social science, legalese, and bureaucratese, rendered in both Spanish and English. We have struggled to translate such basic terms as "law enforcement" in Spanish (for example, "*aplicación de la ley*" seems more accurate than "*procuración de justicia*"), or from Spanish to English ("*ministerios públicos*" as "prosecuting attorneys" is a reasonable but not precise equivalent, given that the Spanish term can also mean "investigating attorney"). One of our recommendations, in fact, is that a conveniently accessible source be made available that can provide precise, updated information in both languages about institutions, laws, policies, and issues related to public security in the two countries. We certainly wish such a source had been available to us!

As the Center for U.S.–Mexican Studies embarks on a significant research project on the reform of justice in Mexico, our hope is that this book can provide background, analysis, and policy ideas useful for understanding the crisis of public security as this affects Mexico and the United States.

Acknowledgments

The editors are enormously grateful to several colleagues, students, and institutions whose support made this book possible. Adriana Pérez Mina and Jorge Rebolledo Flores at Georgetown University attended to the overall administration of the project, including the flows of communications, drafts, and translations. Most of the actual book preparation fell to Mr. Rebolledo's care. Along with Yolanda Muñoz of the Centro de Investigación y Docencia Económicas (CIDE) in Mexico City, they coordinated the administration of meetings and presentations in Mexico City and Washington, D.C. In Mexico City, Ms. Angelina Peralta worked ably to help the editors bring the report to the attention of the media. Several Georgetown University students helped with research, translations, or interpretation at meetings or with the project papers: Mariana Cordera Rascón, Verónica Malo Guzmán, Enrique Morris Martínez, Abelardo Rodríguez Sumano, Ana Luisa Valle, Jeffrey Villaveces, Janelle Garret, Roberto Dondisch, and Cinthia Yadira López. Gabriel Farfán Mares, who also assisted with a previous volume on organized crime, was especially helpful in gathering data on the extradition issue and in editing the Spanish and English versions of the tables and figures. Pablo Paras provided and helped us interpret public opinion data. In addition to their fine contributions to this volume, Ernesto López Portillo Vargas and Sigrid Arzt gave us helpful advice and assistance with the volume.

As noted in the preface, we were privileged to work with a group of distinguished Mexican, U.S., and Argentine scholars and practitioners. In a field where the scholarship is thin, their advice and experience were invaluable. We thank Mr. Alan Bersin, Esq., Superintendent of Public Education, San Diego Unified School District; Ambassador Morris D. Busby, President, BGI International Consulting Services, Inc.; Dr. José Ramón Cossío, Director, Law Department, Instituto Tecnológico Autónomo de México; Mr. Larry Dever, Sheriff, Cochise County, Arizona; Dr. Eduardo E. Estévez, Citizen Security Program, Interior Ministry, Republic of Argentina, and Project Director, Instituto de Investigación sobre Seguridad y Crimen Organizado (ISCO)—Universidad Católica de Salta/Subsede Buenos Aires; Dr. Sergio García Ramírez, Secretary General, Institutional Revolutionary Party, and Researcher, Universidad Nacional Autónoma de México (UNAM); Lic. Antonio

Lozano Gracia, Visiting Researcher, Georgetown University; Lic. Moisés Moreno, President, Centro de Estudios de Política Criminal y Ciencias Penales; Dr. William Olson, Staff Director, U.S. Senate Narcotics Caucus; Congressman Silvestre Reyes, U.S. House of Representatives, (D-Texas, 16th District); Lic. Rafael Ruiz Harrell, Researcher, Universidad Nacional Autónoma de México, and Columnist, *Reforma* (Mexico City); and Dr. Francisco Thoumi, Senior Visiting Scholar, Latin American and Caribbean Center, Florida International University. Special thanks are owed Antonio Lozano, who—as a Visiting Researcher at Georgetown in 1997–2000—gave us continued advice and support.

Arturo Valenzuela, Director of Georgetown's Center for Latin American Studies, and Carlos Elizondo, Director of CIDE, lent their steady support. Wayne Cornelius, Director of the Center for U.S.–Mexican Studies at the University of California, San Diego advised and encouraged us, as the Center presently embarks on a significant project dealing with reform of justice in Mexico. Finally, we are most grateful for financial support and encouragement from the Smith Richardson Foundation, whose charge it is to contribute to research and public dialogue related to significant public policy issues.

List of Acronyms

AJCSD	Arizona Juvenile Court Services Division
AOC	Administrative Office of the Courts
ATF	Bureau of Alcohol, Tobacco and Firearms
BARF	Border Alien Robbery Force
BCIU	Border Crime Intervention Unit
BCPU	Border Crime Prevention Unit
BJS	Bureau of Justice Statistics
BLM	Border Liaison Mechanism
B.O.M.	Based of Mixed Operations
CENDRO	Centro de Planeación para el Control de las Drogas / National Drug Control Center
CFPP	Código Federal de Procedimientos Penales / Federal Code of Criminal Procedures
CIA	U.S. Central Intelligence Agency
CIDAC	Centro de Investigaciones para el Desarrollo / Research Center for Development
CIDE	Centro de Investigación y Docencia Económicas / Center for Economic Research and Teaching
CISEN	Centro de Investigación y Seguridad Nacional / Center for Research and National Security
CNDH	Comisión Nacional de Derechos Humanos / National Commission on Human Rights
CNESP	Consejo Nacional de Empresas de Seguridad Pública / National Council of Public Security Companies
CNSP	Consejo Nacional de Seguridad Pública / National Public Security Council
COTUME	Consejo para la Tutoría de Menores / Council for the Guardianship of Minors
CTAC	Counterdrug Technology Assessment Center

DARE	Drug Abuse Resistance Education
DCM	Differentiated Case Management
DDDT	Do Drugs, Do Time
DDT	Dedicated Drug Treatment
DEA	Drug Enforcement Administration
DFS	Dirección Federal de Seguridad / Federal Security Directorate
DIPD	División de Investigaciones para la Prevención de la Delincuencia / Division of Investigations for Crime Prevention
DISEN	Dirección General de Investigación y Seguridad Nacional / General Directorate of Research and National Security
DTAP	Drug Treatment Alternative-to-Prison Program
DYTR	Department of Youth Treatment and Rehabilitation
EPIC	El Paso Intelligence Center
EPR	Ejército Popular Revolucionario / Popular Revolutionary Army
ERPI	Ejército Revolucionario del Pueblo Insurgente / Insurgent People's Revolutionary Army
ESB	Effective School Battery
EZLN	Ejército Zapatista de Liberación Nacional / Zapatista Army of National Liberation
FASP	Fondo de Aportaciones para la Seguridad Pública / Special Fund for Public Security
FBI	Federal Bureau of Investigation
FCM	Family Case Management
FEADS	Fiscalía Especializada para la Atención de Delitos contra la Salud / Office of the Special Prosecutor for Crimes against Health
FINCEN	Financial Crimes Enforcement Network
FTA	Free Trade Agreement
GAFE	Grupo Aerotransportado de Fuerzas Especiales / Airborne Special Forces Group
GAFI	Grupo de Acción Financiera / Financial Action Group

GANFES	Grupos Anfibios de Fuerzas Especiales / Special Forces Amphibious Groups
GAO	U.S. General Accounting Office
GAT	Grupo Anti-Terrorista / Anti-Terrorist Group
GDP	gross domestic product
GED	General Educational Development
HIDTA	High Intensity Drug Trafficking Area
HLCG	High Level Contact Group
ICAC	Independent Commission Against Corruption
IMET	International Military Education and Training
INACIPE	Instituto Nacional de Ciencias Penales / National Institute for Criminal Sciences
INCD	Instituto Nacional para el Combate a las Drogas / National Institute to Combat Drugs
INS	U.S. Immigration and Naturalization Service
INEGI	Instituto Nacional de Estadística, Geografía e Informática / National Institute for Statistics, Geography, and Informatics
IOM	International Organization for Migration
IRCA	Immigration Reform and Control Act
IVU	intravenous drug user
JTF–6	Joint Task Force Six
LAPD	Los Angeles Police Department
LFCDO	Ley Federal Contra la Delincuencia Organizada / Federal Organized Crime Law
LG–SNSP	Ley General que Establece las Bases de Coordinación del Sistema Nacional de Seguridad Pública / General Law of the National Public Security System
LPFP	Ley de la Policía Federal Preventiva / Law of the Federal Preventive Police
MLAT	Mutual Legal Assistance Treaty
MOU	memorandum of understanding
MPF	Ministerio Público Federal / Public Ministry
MZ	military zone
NAFTA	North American Free Trade Agreement

NCSC	National Center for State Courts
NGO	nongovernmental organization
NIJ	National Institute of Justice
NSIC	National Strategy Information Center
NYADMC	National Youth Anti-Drug Media Campaign
OAS	Organization of American States
OCDETF	Organized Crime Drug Enforcement Task Forces
ONDCP	Office of National Drug Control Policy
OSS	Office of Strategic Services
PAN	Partido Acción Nacional / National Action Party
PDFA	Partnership for a Drug-Free America
PFP	Policía Federal Preventiva / Federal Preventive Police
PGJDF	Procuraduría General de Justicia del Distrito Federal / Attorney General's Office of the Federal District
PGR	Procuraduría General de la República / Attorney General's Office
PJE	Policía Judicial Estatal / State Judicial Police
PJF	Policía Judicial Federal / Federal Judicial Police
PME	Performance Measures of Effectiveness
PNSP	Programa Nacional de Seguridad Pública / National Public Security Program
PPT	Programa de Protección a Testigos / Witness Protection Program
PRD	Partido de la Revolución Democrática / Party of the Democratic Revolution
PRI	Partido Revolucionario Institucional / Institutional Revolutionary Party
SAT	Scholastic Assessment Test
SCJN	Suprema Corte de Justicia de la Nación / Supreme Court of Justice
SEBS	Secretario de Educación de Baja California / Baja California State Secretary of Education and Social Welfare

SEDENA	Secretaría de la Defensa Nacional / Ministry of National Defense
SHCP	Secretaría de Hacienda y Crédito Público / Treasury Ministry
SNSP	Sistema Nacional de Seguridad Pública / National Public Security System
SRE	Secretaría de Relaciones Exteriores / Foreign Relations Ministry
SSP	Secretaría de Seguridad Pública / Public Security Ministry
TASC	Treatment Alternatives to Street Crime
	Treatment Assessment Screening Center
TC	Therapeutic Community
TOPS	Treatment Outcome Prospective Study
UECLD	Unidad Especializada contra el Lavado de Dinero / Special Anti–Money Laundering Unit
UEDO	Unidad Especializada en Delincuencia Organizada / Special Organized Crime Unit
UNAM	Universidad Nacional Autónoma de México / National Autonomous University of Mexico
USAID	U.S. Agency for International Development
WHO	World Health Organization

1

Transational Crime and Public Security: Trends and Issues

John Bailey and Jorge Chabat

Inadequate public security presently ranks near the top of Mexico's political agenda and has become a central issue shaping U.S.–Mexico relations. There is much debate about the meaning of "public security," which is sometimes given as "citizen security," "human security," or "public safety." The debate concerns the boundaries of the concept and whether and how to include issues such as income inequality, poverty, education, popular culture, morality, and the like. Although we recognize the potential significance of such matters, we are concerned here with the core issues of crime, violence, corruption, and inadequate law enforcement, viewed as an integrated set of problems.

As noted in the preface, this introductory chapter grows out of a report that was prepared for a select group of distinguished citizens and was based primarily on the scholarly essays collected in this volume. These essays deal with the multiple challenges of crime, violence, and the associated problems of corruption with respect to Mexico and the United States and to the bilateral relationship. The goals of the project were: (1) to describe and assess the dimensions of the problems of insecurity and the governmental and societal responses, and (2) to propose initiatives to promote bilateral cooperation to improve public security. This chapter takes up the first of these goals; the concluding essay summarizes a series of recommendations to promote long-term strategic cooperation.

Our main arguments are that the governmental institutions, legal systems, and circumstances of public security are importantly different in the two countries. Reflecting this, the countries address the issues in different ways. In Mexico the term used is "national public security program," while in the United States the concept more often employed is "the criminal justice system." Mexico's law enforcement and judicial institutions have functioned inadequately for many years, and Mexico's current profound political and economic transition has exacerbated multiple problems of insecurity over the short period when the newly created institutions are not yet operating effectively. The United States is experiencing chronic but decreasing levels of insecurity, and it is currently focused on gun-related violence and the multiple problems surrounding drug trafficking and abuse. The shared U.S.–Mexico border region presents a more complex and more intense set of security-related problems, as well as opportunities for cooperative solutions.

The key point is that the security-related priorities of the two countries differ fundamentally, and the capacities of the two nations to address the problems, as currently defined, are insufficient. For the United States, the suppression of transnational criminal gangs, especially those involved with drug production and trafficking, is the top priority. For Mexico, the overriding security priority is to construct effective and professional law enforcement and judicial institutions that, in cooperation with civil society, can confront the multiple problems of crime, violence, and corruption. These problems are related to "common" crime as well as organized crime. Institution building will require substantial resource investments and a relatively long time horizon. But strong political pressures push for short-term solutions.

We should distinguish between the challenges of insecurity that are largely domestic and internal in nature (both common and organized crime) as opposed to transnational organized crime that traffics in varieties of goods and services. The former set of concerns can be addressed by each government and society individually. In Mexico's case, this sort of institutional and programmatic development will require time, resources, and vigorous leadership. The government of President Vicente Fox Quesada (December 1, 2000–November 30, 2006) is implementing a number of important initiatives to address domestic insecurity. In this respect, the United States can assist with technical support through either bilateral or multilateral channels. For its part, the United States operates a relatively institutionalized criminal justice system, which has seen significant increases in budget allocations, arrests, prosecutions, and incarcerations in the 1990s, resulting in the largest prison population per capita among industrialized nations.

Transnational organized crime is a qualitatively different challenge due to: (1) the quantities of money and other resources with which it can corrupt government and society, (2) its capacity for violence and intimidation, (3) the extent and sophistication of its organization and operations, which can overwhelm the capacity of regular police and law enforcement, and (4) the special challenges created by the need for international official and societal responses. The priority for U.S.–Mexican cooperation concerns transnational organized crime, particularly in the common border region.

Although differences in the two countries' priorities have created tensions in the bilateral relationship, recent developments suggest that conditions are emerging that may foster the creation of a strategic partnership to confront transnational organized crime. The administrations that took office in late 2000 and early 2001 are building on advances in bilateral cooperation from the 1990s. They have signaled an unusual willingness to expand cooperation still further in order to attack long-standing problems of drug trafficking and abuse, illegal migration, and corruption and inefficiency in public security agencies. The key to strengthening the partnership is fostering trust and communication at all levels. One step in this direction is to recast the security-related aspects of the drug and migration problems from the relatively narrow domain of law enforcement to the broader context of public safety. The Mexican and U.S. governments differ with respect to the criminal nature of undocumented migration. Where there is basis for agreement, however, is in repressing the transnational criminal organizations that traffic in illegal migrants. In all respects, government cannot address these issues alone. Civil society must assume a prominent and continuous role in promoting public security.

PUBLIC INSECURITY: NATURE OF THE CHALLENGES

The causes of public insecurity are multiple and imprecisely understood, and virtually all societies endure one or another degree of insecurity. In Mexico there are four interconnected aspects of public insecurity. First, rates of reported crime (official complaints or police reports, as opposed to crime measured by surveys) jumped significantly in 1995–1997 and remain at relatively high levels by historical standards (although not particularly high by international standards). Second, a series of high-profile murders beginning in 1993 shocked the public. Third, revelations of serious corruption at high levels in the government and security forces further undermined public confidence. Fourth, responses by government were seen as inadequate. Concerns about crime, violence, and corruption have become a central political issue, nearly on par with the top priority issues of economic growth and improved living standards. A more vocal and exigent public perceives that government is unable to guarantee citizen security. Even worse, law enforcement officers are perceived to be integral parts of the problem of insecurity, as recognized by top officials.[1]

In his inaugural address on December 1, 2000, President Vicente Fox emphasized that his government would make a fresh start to combat impunity and corruption. He also stressed the certainty of punishment as more important than the severity of the penalties.

> Corruption has exhausted society's belief in the government. Arrogance and arbitrariness have configured the remainder of its image. Such excesses maintain in the public agenda the demand to restore moral authority to the exercise of the government. The solution is not just more laws or harder laws. What is required above all is that the law be applied in a framework of complete certainty. That is the best alternative. I will fight these wrongs with the severity and the rule of law, with all the power of the president of the Republic, but also with the simple and powerful strength of example.[2]

In sum, the perception of crisis is based in realities, and the Mexican government and society are struggling to generate effective responses. Explanations for the upsurge in crime, discussed below, appear related to economic stagnation and income inequality, drug trafficking, and inefficient law enforcement. Also, there appears to be an inertial effect in crime rates in the sense that, once initiated, higher crime rates appear to persist over time. Apart from realities, we should also underline the subjective dimensions of insecurity. The citizenry's sense of insecurity appears more closely related to their perception of the government's ineffectiveness in enforcing the law than to perceptions of crime itself. Other factors may also come into play. The mass media can intensify insecurity by sensationalizing particular cases of crime and corruption. Politicians often seek to capitalize on public fears by exaggerating real problems.

Public insecurity in the United States, measured in terms of reported crime and perceptions of crime as a threat, appeared to moderate and even decline in the 1990s, but it still remained at relatively high levels. These trends hold for the United States at large as well as for the states and counties along the country's southwest border. For the United States, insecurity constitutes a relatively chronic, but manageable, set of concerns that manifests itself in different forms over time. In the context of the 2000 presidential campaign, the issue focused on gun-related violence, taking the form of debates over gun control in a variety of forums. Some fairly notorious cases of police brutality and corruption have received ample media coverage as well.[3]

Corruption, understood as the abuse of public trust for private gain, afflicts both Mexico and the United States, but its nature and consequences are different in the two countries. Corruption in Mexico tends to penetrate deeper into political institutions because the political system is highly centralized; the government lacks a professional career civil service (with some exceptions); and accountability, through such mechanisms as congressional oversight and audit, is only weakly developed. Furthermore, until very recently, the country's political system was dominated by one party (the Institutional Revolutionary Party, or PRI), which acted to inhibit the regular functioning of checks and balances. Recent developments, however, suggest that the Mexican government and civil society are taking steps to counter corrupt behavior. For example, stronger representation of various parties in the federal Chamber of Deputies after 1997 strengthened budgetary oversight and audit of executive branch agencies. This trend was continued by the July 2000 elections, in which the presidency was won by the candidate of the National Action Party (PAN) and in which no party won a majority in the Chamber. Greater freedom in the mass media has produced more aggressive investigative reporting. And leading intellectuals and public figures recently founded a Mexican chapter of Transparency International.

Historically, corruption in the United States has figured in important ways at all levels of government, especially since the post–Civil War period (1860s). At the present time, corruption appears more frequently at the state and local levels and typically involves individuals acting alone or in small groups. Corruption can penetrate a particular department or agency, and cases of towns or cities falling under corrupt control are not uncommon. But competitive parties, professional norms, federal oversight, aggressive litigation, and a variety of checks operate to contain corruption. The mass media at all levels also maintain a fairly steady surveillance of public agencies and activities.[4] Debates in the 2000 presidential election campaign about reforming campaign finance legislation reflected concerns about the ways in which contributions to parties and candidates may imply corrupt exchanges.

With respect to drug-related corruption, the differences between the two countries are marked. Mexico is largely a producer and conduit of illegal drugs, although problems related to consumption are rapidly growing. This means that Mexico serves rather like a funnel, with illegal activities channeled into and through the country and concentrating most sharply at the northern border. Associated corruption is thus focused and multiplied due to the institutional features such as centralization and one-party dominance noted above. Although the United States is a significant producer as well, it is largely a consumer of drugs. On the consumption side, drugs are distributed through a large number of local-level markets. These markets operate in a political system that is also highly decentralized. Thus drug-related violence and corruption is widely scattered among neighborhoods, small towns, and even the countryside.[5]

Mexico and the United States are closely integrated in a variety of ways, and the security situation of each country affects the other. For Mexico, U.S.–related insecurity takes three basic forms. First, the demand for illegal drugs is the basic engine that drives drug production and trafficking. Second, U.S. ambivalence about illegal migration (demand for cheap labor and relatively lax inspection of business employment practices versus aggressive hardening of the border) has stimulated a growing role for transnational organized crime related to migrant trafficking.

Third, the United States appears to be a principal source of north-south smuggling of weapons that strengthen criminal groups operating in Mexico and contribute to increased lethal violence.

For the United States, Mexico-related insecurity takes two interconnected forms. First, corruption and inefficiency in police and judicial institutions in Mexico allow transnational organized crime groups to operate without sufficient control. Second, the concentration of crime, corruption, and violence along the U.S.–Mexico border creates tensions and points of conflict between the countries. Reducing consumption of illicit drugs is of paramount interest, because drug trafficking and abuse are perceived to be leading causes of crime and corruption in both countries. Official U.S. policy calls for a balanced attack on both supply and consumption, and some progress has been made since the 1970s in reducing consumption. In this regard, experience shows that the relative time horizons of political institutions affect policy priorities.

Demand reduction is a complex, long-term undertaking. Supply reduction is also complicated and long-term, but it may offer the illusion of producing quicker payoffs. Strong public pressures to achieve results, coupled with short electoral cycles (two-year terms in the U.S. House of Representatives, for example), lead to an emphasis on short-term, visible results. The logical implication is a more visible and vigorous attack on supply, both at home and abroad. Thus rates of incarceration in the United States are among the highest in the world, with a substantial proportion of prisoners convicted for drug-related crimes. At the same time, the U.S. government pursues policies abroad to repress production and trafficking of illegal drugs and invests increasing quantities of resources in interdiction.

Money laundering also holds different priority positions in the two countries. Mexico is only recently emerging from the severe financial crisis of 1994–1995. Banks were reprivatized in the early 1990s, and a new regulatory framework is being implemented. However, the new agencies have not yet developed the resources and experience to effectively monitor the banking system.[6] U.S. banks also confront problems of effective regulation, and recent money-laundering cases suggest that the problem is significant on the U.S. side of the border as well.[7] Although comparatively larger quantities of illicit money are laundered in the United States than in Mexico (or elsewhere), the amounts as a proportion of U.S. gross domestic product (GDP) are quite small.

With regard to insecurity, the interests and capacities of Mexico and the United States both converge and diverge. This, in turn, has created points of cooperation and of friction in the bilateral relationship. For Mexico, the top priority is confronting multiple types of crime and corruption and constructing effective law enforcement and judicial institutions, all the while protecting civil and human rights and defending national sovereignty. Mexico is in the midst of a profound economic and political transition, and public insecurity has worsened precisely at a time when the long-standing problems of law enforcement institutions are increasingly exposed to public scrutiny. In this context, organized crime presents a particularly serious threat due to its capacity to penetrate and corrupt security forces and judicial institutions.

Organized crime can assume a multitude of forms—from a few individuals who form an ad hoc gang to assault taxi passengers, to a multistate organization of several dozen persons dedicated to cargo hijacking. Transnational organized crime usually operates at the more complex end of the continuum. The most menacing form of transnational organized crime is drug trafficking, which has been designated as the leading threat to both national and public security. In contrast to crimes against innocent victims, such as kidnapping or robbery, drug trafficking may operate as a consensual crime—that is, as a victimless business operation—which makes its repression more difficult. Due to the quantities of money generated, the scope and sophistication of the criminal organizations, and the intensity of the associated violence and corruption, drug trafficking represents the type of crime that Mexican authorities have been least able to repress.

The points of convergence of U.S. and Mexican interests lead to agreement and cooperation in a number of areas. The U.S. government recognizes that it is in its self-interest to reduce drug consumption, interdict arms trafficking, and prosecute money laundering. The Mexican government recognizes its self-interest in halting the production and trafficking of drugs and prosecuting money laundering and corrupt practices. The points of tension and frustration concern the United States' inability to reduce drug consumption and Mexico's inability to repress drug production and trafficking, both to an important degree and over the short term.

This noted, the enormous asymmetry in power between the two countries tips the scale toward repression of illegal migration and of drug production and trafficking. The results for Mexico have been the rapid introduction of laws and organizations to repress production and trafficking, along with an increasing tendency toward the militarization of police forces, accompanied by higher levels of violence between (and among) police forces and criminal gangs. Further, the power asymmetries and perceptions of Mexican authorities' lack of will to repress transnational crime occasionally tempt the United States to take unilateral initiatives, which create a negative climate for cooperation.[8]

As noted, the border region merits separate treatment. In this rapidly growing zone, the various types of insecurity converge on border governments and civil society and become magnified as more diverse and concentrated problems of crime, violence, and corruption. Human rights violations on both sides of the border, mainly against Mexican citizens, are a serious concern. Also, the growing militarization of police forces in Mexico and the buildup of security forces on the U.S. side, absent effective cross-border communication, create the risk of accidental confrontation. Thus a particular priority concerns the promotion of cross-border cooperation and communication between the two countries' security forces.

This volume deals with both governmental and societal responses to insecurity. It falls primarily upon government to ensure acceptable levels of public security for all citizens, including physical safety, protection of civil rights, and access to equitable and efficient administration of justice. Governments at all levels in both countries have taken significant steps in recent years to address challenges of insecurity. But government responses alone will be inadequate. Individual citizens and civil society—taken to mean civic organizations, service clubs, business and professional associations, labor unions, sports clubs, schools and religious organizations, and the like—have critical roles to play in instilling and protecting a culture of lawfulness. Governments make and attempt to enforce laws, but unless civil society is engaged and supportive, the process is difficult—if not impossible—to sustain.

To summarize, Mexico confronts problems of public insecurity that are of sufficient scale as to delay or distort the political and economic transition under way in that country. While recognizing that relevant social and economic conditions must be addressed, priority goes to building effective law enforcement and judicial institutions to deal with problems of common and organized crime. Transnational organized crime is one of several dimensions of insecurity. With respect to the United States, Mexico's concerns focus on drug consumption, the ambivalent policy about illegal migration, and conditions that foster gun trafficking. The United States is experiencing less severe overall problems of insecurity than was the case in the 1970s and 1980s. Public opinion and government policy focus primarily on issues of gun-related violence and drug abuse. With respect to Mexico, U.S. attention focuses on corruption, illegal migration, and drug trafficking.

These differences in conditions and perceptions lead to points of convergence and divergence between the two countries. The priority is to create a stronger, long-term basis for cooperation in the shared task of suppressing transnational organized crime. The key prerequisite for cooperation is building mutual trust and promoting communications at all levels.

CHALLENGES FACING MEXICO

How significant are problems of public insecurity in Mexico for the consolidation of democracy? Are the problems getting better or worse? What are the more significant governmental and societal responses?

Trends and Perceptions Concerning Insecurity

Crime statistics are notoriously difficult to gather and interpret. Corruption and violence are even harder to measure. This is decidedly the case in Mexico, where accurate data gathering lags perhaps farthest behind in the law enforcement field. An important requirement to gauge the dimensions of the problems of insecurity is the improvement of data collection, including the periodic use of national victimization surveys, following internationally accepted standards. Recognizing the data gaps, we offer two generalizations: (1) Mexico's overall reported crime rates jumped significantly in 1995–1997 but are not particularly high by international standards, and (2) the reported rates are much lower in relation to the rates measured in public opinion surveys.[9]

Using official data Ernesto López Portillo Vargas (this volume) reports that:

> At the national level, the number of alleged criminals grew by an average 14 percent per year between 1980 and 1996, compared with an overall population growth rate of just over 2 percent. In other words, reported crime increased about seven times faster than the population. According to the 1995–2000 National Public Security Program (PNSP), between 1980 and 1994 crime rates increased 102 percent in state and local jurisdictions (*fuero común*) and 286 percent in the federal jurisdiction (*fuero federal*). If we calculate crime rates by the number of sentences imposed, state and local crime increased by 112 percent, and federal crime by 209 percent.

Also working with official data from 1996, Rafael Ruiz Harrell notes that Mexico's overall national rate of 1,671 police reports (*denuncias*) per 100,000 was 42 percent above that of 1993. Even so, the 1996 rate was about the same as that of the United States in 1957. Put another way, Mexico's 1996 rate was about 30 percent of that reported for the European Union and about 33 percent that of the United States for the same year. The crime problem showed clear regional tendencies: rates were notably high in the Federal District, Baja California, Baja California Sur, Morelos, Sinaloa, Tabasco, and Yucatán. In terms of cities, Mexico City, Tijuana, and Ciudad Juárez stood out with high rates.[10] Theft (*robo*) is the most common crime; it is the one that has increased most since 1993 and the only type of crime that did not decline in 1997 and 1998. Overall, theft represented 42 percent of reported crimes in 1998. It, too, showed pronounced regional tendencies, with especially high rates in Mexico City, Baja California, Baja California Sur, Chihuahua, and Quintana Roo.[11]

There are indications that crime rates may have flattened out recently and begun to decline somewhat. In his fifth State of the Nation message

(September 1, 1999), President Ernesto Zedillo (1994–2000) reported that crime rates in state and local jurisdictions peaked in 1997 at 15.7 crimes reported per 1,000 inhabitants, increasing at a pace faster than population growth. That year about 1.5 million crimes were reported and 1.33 million preliminary investigations were opened. In 1998, the rate of reported crime dropped to 14.3 per 1,000 population, and in 1999 it fell to 13.4. In the federal jurisdiction, however, the rate remained constant at 8 crimes per 1,000 over 1997–1999.

Difficulties in the availability of comparable data make it impossible to put Mexico in comparative perspective with other countries in the hemisphere in terms of various forms of crime, violence, or corruption. One measure that may be comparable, however, is homicide rates. Table 1.1 suggests three points in this respect: (1) homicide rates in Mexico increased only slightly between 1984 and 1994, from 18.2 to 19.5 per 100,000; (2) rates of increase in homicides were substantially higher in Central America and the Spanish-speaking Caribbean, the Andean region, and Brazil; and (3) overall, Mexico's 1994 rates fell between those of the Southern Cone and the English-speaking Caribbean and the Andes, Central America, and Brazil. Table 1.2 puts the point even more clearly. In comparison with El Salvador, Colombia, Honduras, and Brazil, Mexico's homicide rate has been relatively lower and steadier over time.

Table 1.1 **Homicide Rates in Latin America and the Caribbean, 1984 and 1994 (per 100,000 inhabitants)**

	1984			1994		
Regions	Total	Men	Women	Total	Men	Women
Central America and Latin Caribbean	17.5	31.5	3.8	21.1	38.1	4.0
Andean region	25.2	46.6	4.0	51.9	96.6	7.7
Anglo Caribbean	5.2	7.6	2.8	8.7	13.1	4.2
Southern Cone	5.4	9.3	1.8	6.2	10.5	1.9
Brazil	23.2	42.4	4.0	30.1	54.8	5.2
Mexico	18.2	33.3	3.1	19.5	34.8	3.8

Source: Irma Arriagada y Lorena Godoy, *Seguridad ciudadana y violencia en América Latina: diagnóstico y políticas en los años noventa*. Serie Políticas Sociales (Santiago, Chile: División de Desarrollo Social, CEPAL/ONU, August 1999), p. 17.

Table 1.2 **Homicide Rates in Latin America (13 Countries), 1980, 1990, and 1995 (per 100,000 inhabitants)**

Countries	Late 1970s, Early 1980s	Late 1980s, Early 1990s	Last Data Available (about 1995)
El Salvador	...	138.2	117.0
Colombia	20.5	89.5	65.0
Honduras	...	...	40.0
Brazil	11.5	19.7	30.1
Mexico	18.2	17.8	19.5
Venezuela	11.7	15.2	22.0
Peru	2.4	11.5	10.3
Panama	2.1	10.9	...
Ecuador	6.4	10.3	...
Argentina	3.9	4.8	...
Costa Rica	5.7	4.1	...
Uruguay	2.6	4.4	...
Paraguay	5.1	4.0	...
Chile	2.6	3.0	1.8

Source: Irma Arriagada y Lorena Godoy, *Seguridad ciudadana y violencia en América Latina: diagnóstico y políticas en los años noventa*, Serie Políticas Sociales (Santiago, Chile: División de Desarrollo Social, CEPAL/ONU, August 1999), p. 17.

The data suggest that Mexico's problem of insecurity may be less related to rates of crime than to inadequate law enforcement. As Ruiz Harrell put it: "Without doubt, there is a national problem—and a grave one. It is not in the amount of crime, however, but rather in the clear inability of the authorities to enforce the law."[12] With regard to the perception of impunity, again using data from the Interior Ministry (Secretaría de Gobernación), in 1998 some 1.49 million criminal complaints were filed; 1.33 million preliminary inquiries were opened, but only 249,000 cases were decided. In these cases, 149,000 arrest warrants were issued, but only 85,000 were carried out. Further, as the government acknowledges, reported crimes represent a small fraction of committed crimes.

An important dimension of insecurity concerns the impacts of organized crime. Criminal organizations range from street gangs dedicated to one or another illegal activity—auto theft, robbery, assault, kidnapping, and so on—to large-scale multi-state and international gangs dedicated to trafficking in drugs or undocumented migrants. We do not have extensive data, but a recent report on Mexico City found that "the number of criminal gangs that violently prey upon Mexico City is about 750, which gather at least 20,000 delinquents on a daily basis, with an average per gang of about 26.7, using conservative estimates."[13] These criminal gangs are frequently protected, in some cases even organized and directed, by police. Certain neighborhoods—such as Buenos Aires, Doctores, Tepito, and Morelos—are especially affected by criminal gangs. Drug abuse and trafficking is common in these gangs, as is violence.

Drug-related violence is especially devastating in certain Mexican states. In Sinaloa, for example, 1.2 persons are murdered daily in gang-related violence; in Baja California, some 65 percent of homicides in 1999 were connected to drug trafficking; in Jalisco, about 17 percent of 344 violent homicides were so-called settling of accounts (*"ajustes de cuentas"*).[14]

Statistics convey only part of the crisis. Important as well are the high-level incidents of murder, assault, or revealed corruption which—when magnified by the media—contribute to a climate of insecurity. Examples include the murders of Cardinal Juan Jesús Posadas (May 1993), PRI presidential candidate Luis Donaldo Colosio (March 1994), PRI secretary general José Francisco Ruiz Massieu (September 1994), popular television entertainer Francisco Stanley (June 1999), and Tijuana police chief Alfredo de la Torre (February 2000). High-level scandals include army generals on active duty, state governors (in Morelos and Quintana Roo, for example), a director of the national antidrug agency, and a former director of the Federal Judicial Police (PJF), all accused of collaborating with drug traffickers. It is important to emphasize that the arrests and accusations do not constitute the guilt of those charged. Rather, the point is that the incidents create unease in the public mind about increasing violence along with government corruption and impunity.

What factors explain the increases in crime in Mexico? We find no concise explanation. A recent World Bank study notes that "very few empirical studies have addressed why crime rates vary across countries over time."[15] We know that crime rates (specifically homicide) for the world in general have been rising since the mid–1970s. Overall, the highest homicide rates are found in Latin America and the Caribbean, followed by sub-Saharan Africa. (See tables 1.1 and 1.2 with respect to subregions in the hemisphere.) The study found clear economic correlates for crime. Crime rates are countercyclical: "Stagnant economic activity induces heightened homicide rates." Further, there seems to be a clear correlation between economic inequality and crime, "so that countries with more unequal distributions of income tend to have higher crime rates than those with more equalitarian patterns of income distribution."[16] The study also found support for the popular view that violent crimes increase with drug trafficking, although it was not clear whether the increases were directly related to trafficking or whether criminal organizations established to traffic drugs also engaged in other forms of crime. Another important finding of the study is that crime rates show an inertial effect. That is, for reasons that are not well understood, once rates have increased significantly, they tend to take on their own momentum.

All of these factors are present in Mexico's case. The country has a relatively high rate of income inequality. Crime rates increased in the aftermath of the economic crisis of 1995. As noted above, crime and violence related to drug trafficking appear significant in certain states (including Baja California, Chihuahua, Jalisco, and Sinaloa). An additional factor with respect to Mexico may be related to the political transition itself. For example, as opposition parties come to govern in certain cities and states, they need time to assemble teams and acquire the knowledge and experience to administer law enforcement. In this same context, crime victims may feel more willing to file complaints before new authorities.[17] Also, mass media operate with fewer controls and stronger incentives to compete in a market environment. Crime coverage and investigative reporting may encourage crime victims to file reports.

The combined problems of higher crime rates, inadequate government responses, and high-profile incidents of crime and corruption—all magnified by the mass media—have contributed to the public's sense of insecurity, as reported in public opinion polls. Figure 1.1 reports survey results from Mexico City, which because of higher reported crime rates should not be generalized to the whole country. From December 1997 to June 2000, over 90 percent of survey respondents indicated that they considered the problem of public insecurity to be very or somewhat serious. With respect to perceptions of institutions, figure 1.2 reports results from a national survey conducted in 1999, which suggest that about 90 percent of the respondents indicated little or no trust in the police. Figure 1.3 reports findings from a 1998 national survey in which substantial majorities of all age groups report little or no trust in the courts.

Problems in Law Enforcement

Mexico's criminal justice system is complex, and we draw from Guillermo Zepeda's essay (chapter 3 in this volume) to touch on some of the more significant issues. The key actors are police forces, prosecuting attorneys (*ministerios públicos*), and technical experts. In general, much emphasis has been placed on expanding the size of police forces and on hardening penalties for crimes, to the relative neglect of improving judicial processes in a broader sense. Experience teaches that crime prevention, taken broadly to involve civil society, is the best long-term investment. Also, the relative certainty of punishment, even a moderate one, has a stronger deterrent effect than does the specter of harsh penalties coupled with a high expectation of impunity. As Zepeda demonstrates in his chapter, the Mexican judicial system suffers from inefficiency and corruption. Harsher penalties partnered with an ineffective judicial system and corrupt police is a perverse combination that contributes to human rights abuses and aggravates citizens' insecurity. The great majority of genuine criminals

Figure 1.1 **Insecurity in Mexico City**
(Question: "How Serious Do you Consider the Problem of Public Security in Mexico City?")

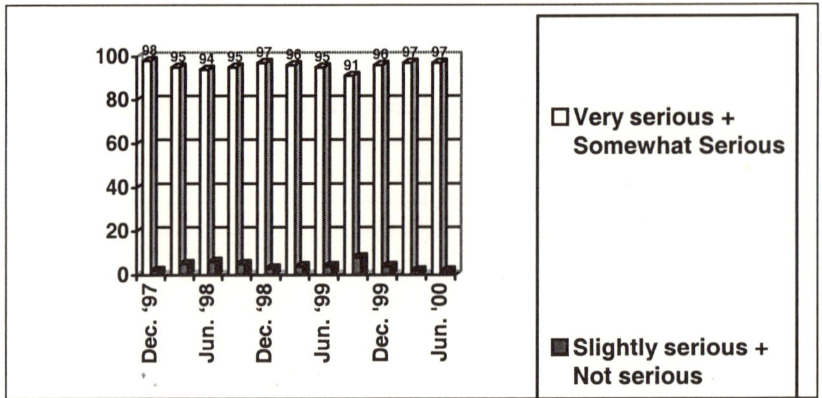

Source: Este País 101 (August 1999): 44 (sample of 1,587 adult home personal interviews in the Federal District); and Centro de Estudios de Opinión Pública (data from September 1999 to June 2000).

Figure 1.2 **Citizens' Trust in Institutions: The Police**
(Question: "Overall, how much do you trust the following institutions?")

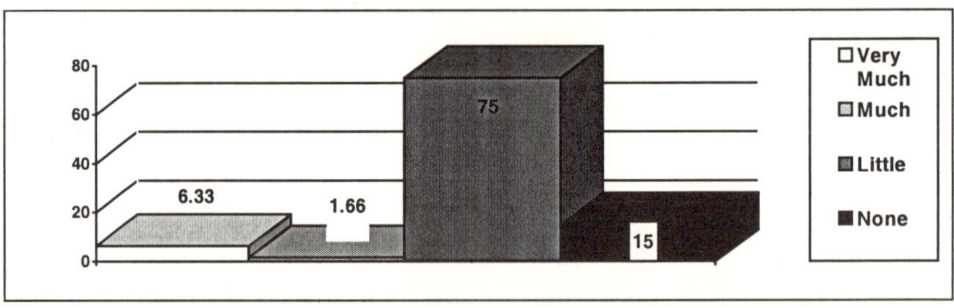

Source: Este País 101 (August 1999): 27 (sample of 1,000 nationwide telephone interviews done in January, February, and March 1999. Other institutions—the Catholic Church, the Federal Electoral Institute, and the Mexican army—were considered.

Figure 1.3 **Citizens' Trust in Institutions: The Courts (by Age Group)**

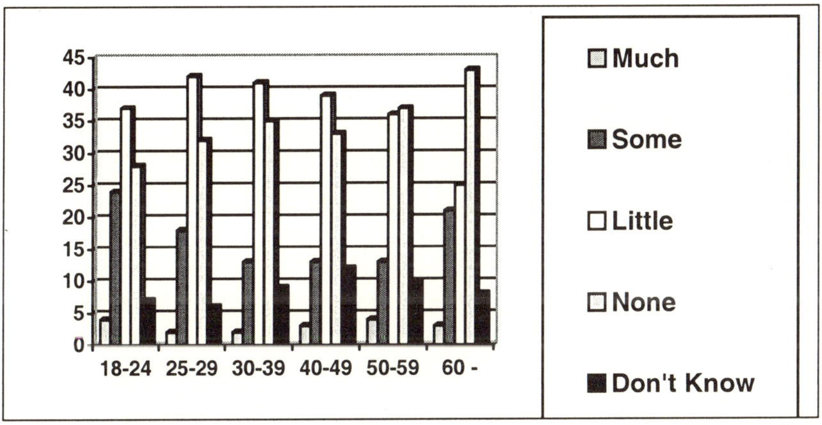

45
40
35
30
25
20
15
10
5
0

18-24 25-29 30-39 40-49 50-59 60 -

Much
Some
Little
None
Don't Know

Source: Este País 87 (June 1998): 29 (1,200 in-home personal interviews in eighty localities in the thirty-two states. Conducted by *Reforma* y *El Norte* between January 23 and 26, 1998).

elude justice altogether, and innocent persons who are caught up in the criminal justice system often suffer grave abuses.

Zepeda notes that public security is understood broadly to encompass citizen security (both crime prevention and police protection), the provision of justice (proper authorities undertake relevant inquiries in response to an apparent illegal act), the administration of justice (a judge determines if sufficient basis is shown to take action and proceeds accordingly), and, where necessary, imprisonment or social readaptation. There are two jurisdictions in Mexican penal law, federal and local (with "local" understood as "state" in the United States). Federal law has jurisdiction over drug-related crimes, which can create tensions with state and local authorities (see, for example, Ramos, chapter 13). The local jurisdiction, commonly called *fuero común*, or state criminal law, is more important for Mexico's overall security situation because it is the realm of some 95 percent of crimes committed and is the system that operates closest to the citizenry. This system suffers serious problems that have led to severe inefficiency and to low regard in public opinion. These problems begin with a severe overloading at the "front end" of the process: the work capacity of prosecuting attorneys and technical experts. The problems accumulate at subsequent points, and Zepeda offers a detailed analysis of their nature and effects on justice and human rights in Mexico.

The police are of critical importance, and Ernesto López Portillo Vargas (chapter 4) puts Mexico's police organization and behavior in broad perspective. Law enforcement agencies and practices generally reflect the political and social forces and institutions in which they were created. In the case of Mexico, grave problems of political instability and public disorder that grew out of the War of Independence (1810–1821) and marked the first decades of the new republic blurred important distinctions between criminals and political oppositions and between police and military forces. Military forces assumed police functions, and both types of forces typically acted as coercive instruments of political authorities to maintain control over the population in general and over potential oppositions in particular. This pattern was reproduced in the period of the Porfiriato (1876–1910), in which Profirio Díaz—like Benito Juárez before him—relied on the rural police (*los rurales*) to both fight crime and enforce political control. In exchange for political loyalty, the *rurales* enjoyed considerable organizational and operational autonomy and engaged in various criminal activities. The police themselves were poorly trained and equipped, and they suffered high rates of personnel turnover. This pattern survived the Mexican Revolution (1910–1917) and, according to López Portillo Vargas, reappeared in the construction of the PRI–government regime.

López Portillo Vargas describes the various types of police in Mexico's federal system and their roles in law enforcement as follows:

> The main problems confronted by police forces to one or another degree throughout the country, as indicated in the government's National Public Security Program (PNSP), include: lack of planning criteria to guide the organization and operation of police services, inadequate budgets, resource allocation not based on specific criteria, lack of adequate criteria in determining salaries, low pay, high rates of personnel turnover which, in turn, complicate efficient resource allocation over the medium and long term, and a lack of standard merit policies on promotions or dismissals.
>
> Police forces also suffer the constant shuffling of personnel between one or another agency across the country. Some former police officers leave public service to enter the "criminal labor market." There are considerable disparities across communities in terms of police presence in proportion to population. Coordination among police forces is inadequate. Educational backgrounds, pay and training, and working conditions for the police are below minimum professional and constitutional standards for the society.

In sum, a useful perspective on Mexico's law enforcement system emphasizes the roles of the *ministerios públicos* and technical experts. Training and resources devoted to these roles can pay larger dividends than can a narrow focus on the police. It also follows that improvements in law enforcement and judicial administration will have important preventive effects.

Governmental Responses to Insecurity

The mid–1990s saw the rapid deterioration of public security and the initial responses of the government of Carlos Salinas de Gortari (1988–1994). Along with greater reliance on the army for law enforcement, the Salinas administration also oversaw the introduction of legal-institutional changes. The reforms included human rights protection, especially in criminal processes; clarification of limits on authorities in investigative process; and the introduction of the PNSP, designed to professionalize police forces. The process of change was accelerated by the high-profile assassinations and guerrilla violence of 1994. In that context, in November 1994 Salinas created the National Public Security Council (CNSP), headed by former labor minister Arsenio Farell Cubillas.[18]

The Zedillo government (1994–2000) responded to the crisis of insecurity by further increasing reliance on the army for law enforcement, as described at length by Graham Turbiville (chapter 10). President Zedillo also took the unprecedented step in December 1994 of appointing as attorney general a prominent leader in the opposition National Action Party, Antonio Lozano Gracia, who in turn attempted to reform the Attorney General's Office (PGR). In addition, the Zedillo government adopted three main initiatives. First, in December 1994, reforms to Articles 21 and 73 of the Constitution elevated "the guarantee of public security" to a basic civil right and raised public security to the status of a "state policy."[19] Second, legislation was passed a year later to implement a National Public Security System (SNSP).[20] And third, a National Crusade against Crime and Delinquency was launched in August 1998 by then-secretary of the interior Francisco Labastida. We shall briefly characterize the SNSP and then focus on: (1) the involvement of the military in law enforcement, (2) the implementation of the law against organized crime, (3) the development of a civilian intelligence capacity, (4) the Crusade against Crime and Delinquency, and (5) the creation of the Federal Preventive Police (PFP).

The National Public Security System (SNSP)

The Zedillo government's overall strategic response to insecurity, the SNSP, was designed in a systems framework to integrate measures from crime prevention through law enforcement and judicial administration and on to social rehabilitation. A key decision was to locate the SNSP in the Interior Ministry rather than in the Attorney General's Office. The decision was based on Interior's legal responsibility to supervise internal security, which encompasses threats to public order taken more broadly than crime. A Subsecretariat of Public Security was created within the Interior Ministry to house the SNSP. The legislation created a National Public Security Council and a series of coordinating councils at the state and local levels, and it emphasized the central government's role in a federal system as one of coordination rather than control.

The placement of the SNSP in the Interior Ministry sparked concerns among some observers that, because political problems often blur into security matters, the agency would be influenced by the government's political priorities. Also, the decision recalled to memory the experience of the Federal Security Directorate (DFS), created in 1947, which was alleged to have formed corrupt alliances with criminal groups, including drug traffickers, before its dissolution in 1985.

Beginning in June 1996, the National Council undertook an assessment of personnel and resources available at the various levels of government to combat crime and delinquency. The most striking problem from the outset was the lack of reliable data. Much crime-relevant data at the national level simply did not exist. Partial data at the national and state levels were typically incompatible—that is, gathered with different methods. The situation was worse at the local level, where, in most cases, the police were focused on traffic management, and record keeping in other matters was largely neglected. Complicating the situation, states were reluctant to share information about police and law enforcement, citing the need to protect the integrity of ongoing investigations. The requirement for accurate data was driven by the need to link planning and program administration with the annual budget cycle. That is, the central government intended to allocate substantially more resources to anticrime programs, and it needed accurate data to determine where best to target the money. Complicating the introduction of more resources, the relatively understaffed and poorly trained budget divisions of the law enforcement agencies had trouble communicating effectively with national budget officials.

At the outset, the SNSP focused on developing databases about law enforcement personnel and improving communications among agencies at the national level and also among the federal, state, and local levels. Budgetary increases for the SNSP were unprecedented, according to President Zedillo. In 1996 the SNSP received about 25.3 million pesos. In

2000 the program was funded at 12.6 billion pesos (about US$1.28 billion), 23 percent over 1999 and 267 percent over 1997 (in real terms). The bulk of the money (about 10.4 billion pesos in 2000) came from federal sources, with the remainder drawn from states and municipalities.[21] To date, there has not been a public evaluation of the SNSP's effectiveness in crime prevention and law enforcement. The enormous outlays of resources, coupled with the apparent modest declines in reported crime, suggest that an evaluation is much needed.

The Mexican Military in Law Enforcement

Increasingly since the 1970s the Mexican military has been involved in various law enforcement functions, and this involvement gained momentum in the 1990s. By no means is Mexico distinctive in this respect. In the post–Cold War period, discussion in many countries concerns a variety of nontraditional challenges to national security and public safety and the implications of these changes for the armed forces. The discussion includes new military roles in counterterrorism, drug interdiction, border security, and other internal security functions in support of civil authorities. As in many countries, the Mexican military are tasked with several roles that go beyond national defense, strictly defined. These include civic action (in mostly rural areas), disaster relief, and, increasingly, anticrime operations. The problems—potential and real—with military involvement in police activities are many: human rights abuses by troops poorly trained for police roles, vulnerability of the armed forces to corruption, reduction of combat readiness as resources and time are devoted to police duties, and tensions and rivalries with civilian law enforcement agencies. Graham Turbiville's survey (this volume) suggests that the record of military success in police duties is a mixed one.

At the direction of civilian authorities, the Mexican military's response to the crisis of public insecurity in the 1990s took two basic forms: replacement of civilian police by military personnel, and increased use of military forces to support counter-drug and anticrime missions. Military forces replaced civilian police mainly because of a perception of endemic police criminality and inefficiency. As we have seen, these perceptions reinforced the public's starkly negative evaluation of police forces. Military replacement of civilian authorities in 1996 was most dramatic in Mexico City. The record proved mixed, however; reported crime continued to rise, and some army units were accused of human rights violations.

Military forces, whether technically on leave or on active duty, took prominent roles at the state and local levels throughout the country. By 1996, military were in charge of federal police forces in the border states of Baja California, Chihuahua, and Tamaulipas. Military officers also occupied key roles as head of the Federal Judicial Police and of the antidrug unit. Overall, by the end of 1996, some form of military involvement in law enforcement was seen in most of Mexico's thirty-one states and in the Federal District. By 1999, the military remained involved in major ways in twenty-eight states and in Mexico City.[22]

With regard to counter-drug operations, the Mexican military have been active since the 1970s in such tasks as crop eradication. The counter-drug role expanded in the 1990s, and army troops have been increasingly involved in tactical police operations. However, army involvement in police activity has been marred by serious problems of corruption. The most damaging of these involved General Jesús Gutiérrez Rebollo, appointed in February 1997 to head the National Institute to Combat Drugs (INCD). Within a few short weeks of his appointment, Gutiérrez Rebollo was arrested and charged with collaborating with Amado Carrillo Fuentes, then head of the Juárez drug cartel. The revelations regarding Gutiérrez seriously tarnished the image of the Mexican army and undermined foreign governments' willingness to collaborate. This was particularly true of the United States.[23]

Apart from the problems of military involvement in law enforcement already noted, a particularly troubling issue is identifying the effective lines of control and authority over military personnel (whether retired, on leave, or on active duty) acting in police roles. Is the effective control exercised by federal and state attorneys general and by civilian authorities? Or is the effective line of control exercised by the National Defense Ministry? If the latter is the case, the growing politicization of the army as an institution presents a troubling scenario.

The Organized Crime Unit of the PGR

The Federal Organized Crime Law (LFCDO), passed in November 1996, is aimed especially against drug trafficking, although it also covers other crimes—migrant smuggling, trafficking in arms and infant children, terrorism, and the like. As Sigrid Arzt notes (chapter 5), the implementation of the LFCDO coincided with the aforementioned scandal involving General Gutiérrez Rebollo. The National Institute to Combat Drugs, which Gutiérrez commanded, was renamed the Office of the Special Prosecutor for Crimes against Health (FEADS) and put under the direction of a civilian, Mariano Herrán. Three key units within the FEADS are the Border Rapid Response Groups (Grupos de Respuesta Rápida Fronteriza), the Special Organized Crime Unit (UEDO) and the Special Anti–Money Laundering Unit (UECLD), created in January 1998 to implement anti–money laundering legislation passed in 1990.

Among the innovative tools available to the UEDO are: witness protection, legally authorized wiretaps, confiscation of goods, incentives for cooperation in investigations (such as reducing or dropping charges), undercover agents, home detention (*arraigo*), and searches. A practical constraint is that the UEDO must employ personnel who are both technically qualified and specially vetted. That is, technical experts require training in their particular skills (wiretapping, for example), and all officers must pass background checks and a variety of tests, including a polygraph. All this takes time. As of August 2000, the UEDO listed a total of 191 personnel, which included 46 investigating officers (*agentes del ministerio público*) and 38 agents of the Federal Judicial Police. The selectivity helps prevent penetration by organized crime, but the small numbers of personnel also limit the UEDO's impact.

Arzt's analysis concludes that, in the short term, rather little has been accomplished. Three years after the implementation of the law, she notes, one can detect few concrete accomplishments that stand out with regard to its capacity to undermine the operation of organized crime in Mexico. Arzt also provides a rather skeptical assessment of UECLD.

Civilian Intelligence

Effective intelligence—taken to mean both information gathering and information processing as well as operational capacity to protect government and society and act against internal and external adversaries—is crucial to a successful governmental response to insecurity. Governments need a capacity to gather information and to evaluate and employ information for strategic and tactical purposes. At the heart of prevention is the capacity to gather and use information to anticipate and prevent crime. Intelligence activities are, by nature, a sensitive topic in democratic systems, particularly when they include covert operations. They are especially controversial in Mexico, due largely to an authoritarian legacy in which intelligence agencies acted to support the regime in power, often against opposition parties. As Leonardo Curzio puts it (chapter 6), the central question for Mexico with respect to developing an effective intelligence capacity is "how to ensure that intelligence services traditionally politicized in favor of the regime in power will be converted into an organ at the service of the state that will loyally and efficiently serve all those political forces traditionally considered as enemies, and therefore as targets of espionage." The necessary elements are to depoliticize and professionalize the intelligence capacity and to build effective democratic oversight. Most significantly, Mexico's intelligence gathering lacks a framework law to define its mission and to guide democratic oversight.

Curzio traces the origins and evolution of the Center for Research and National Security (CISEN), Mexico's principal civilian intelligence agency.[24] According to Curzio, two sets of concerns have influenced CISEN's organization and functioning: (1) the desirability of separating intelligence processing from operations, and (2) the power of drug-trafficking gangs to penetrate law enforcement agencies. CISEN's main job is to process information, although it performs a number of related functions. CISEN's director served as "technical secretary" for the National Security Cabinet (Gabinete de Seguridad Nacional) created by President Salinas in 1988. As noted earlier, Salinas created the National Public Security Council in 1994. The difference between the two offices was that the former was a standing staff office within the presidency while the latter was a special response to the upsurge in public security problems in 1994. As Curzio notes, "The fact that authority for coordination of public security was placed within the National Security Cabinet only underscored the interdependence of public security and national security as these two concepts were merged in the coordination machinery of the higher levels of government." That is, just as public insecurity was defined increasingly as a threat to national security, the corresponding administrative apparatuses began to merge as well. President Zedillo attempted to re-separate the two by creating the Public Security Council (Consejo de Seguridad Pública).

Among CISEN's main organizational achievements, Curzio notes an improvement in interagency cooperation and in the recruitment and vetting of intelligence and law enforcement personnel. As noted, President Zedillo initially sought to re-separate the apparatuses of national versus public security. In 1999, however, CISEN's operational arm (the protection directorate, later renamed the counterintelligence directorate) was transferred to the newly created Federal Preventive Police. That transfer, along with the assignment of personnel from the military police, appeared to reconnect national security with public security.

The National Crusade against Crime and Delinquency

Announced by President Zedillo in August 1998, the National Crusade against Crime and Delinquency can be characterized as a high-profile effort to articulate the multiple strategies and specific actions that governments at various levels were undertaking to combat crime. The emphasis was to show how the various anticrime components were developed in a National Public Security Program, which was the action strategy of the National Public Security System. The president presented some 26 strategies and 120 specific actions that dealt with training, crime prevention, data gathering and analysis, equipment and new technologies, coordinating mechanisms and processes, community involvement, legal reforms, and regulation of private security forces.[25] Although criticized for coming late in the president's term, the Crusade clearly reflected the political importance attached to responding to the public's demand for improved security.

The Federal Preventive Police

Authorized by the Mexican Congress in December 1998, the Federal Preventive Police was established as a national law enforcement body. It integrated existing police, intelligence, and military forces, and also recruited and trained new officers. The PFP brought into its ranks the Federal Highway Police (Policía Federal de Caminos), the Federal Fiscal Police (Policía Fiscal Federal), the Federal Migration Police (Policía Migratoria Federal), and about 4,900 soldiers from the Third Military Police Brigade and a special forces unit of unspecified origin. As noted above, the operational arm of CISEN (the counterintelligence directorate) was transferred to the PFP as well. The mandate of the new police in terms of functions and jurisdiction is quite broad, as discussed by López Portillo Vargas (this volume).

The formation of the PFP sparked controversy, primarily due to fears that the government would use it for political purposes. Spokespersons from the Party of the Democratic Revolution (PRD) were critical in this respect, and then–PAN presidential candidate Vicente Fox indicated his intention to disband the new police force. Critics' fears were borne out when the PFP was employed in February 2000 to forcibly remove students who for several months had occupied the main campus of the National University (UNAM) in Mexico City.

Whatever its future, the new PFP is a significant legal and organizational innovation designed to meet at least three different sets of needs: (1) for a force that is better organized, trained, and equipped than a traditional police force; (2) for a police that can combine both preventive and investigative functions; and (3) for a force that can more flexibly work with state and local police. The dangers are apparent as well: (1) it is a police with a strongly military origin and ethos, and (2) it can be employed for ends that are perceived to be political, as in repressing legal dissent or acting against lawful opposition parties and groups. The potential dangers suggest two implications. First, to be effective over the long term, the PFP needs a stronger political consensus in its favor. Second, part of the consensus will require effective congressional oversight with multi-party participation.

The thread that runs through the discussion of governmental responses is that priority should go to human capital formation in law enforcement and judicial processes. This implies attention to selective recruitment and intensive training. Along with professionalization comes the need for adequate oversight by government and involvement by civil society in order to promote accountability.

Societal Responses to Insecurity

In the context of Mexico's heightened insecurity since the mid–1990s, civil society has responded both individually and collectively, as discussed by Jorge Regalado Santillán in chapter 7. Individuals' responses consist basically of modifying personal conduct in ways to protect themselves from criminal aggression. These adjustments range from changing daily commuting routines to reducing or forgoing evening activities, avoiding certain urban areas, not carrying credit cards or large quantities of cash, not using questionable taxis, protecting one's home during extended absences, and the like. It is difficult to assess the effectiveness of such measures, but it is noteworthy that some of them have been promoted in announcements sponsored by banks and police departments. Also at the individual level, some wealthy Mexicans have hired private security and taken extra precautions such as armoring their cars or installing alarm systems.[26]

Given the evident failure of public security, companies and neighborhood groups have also begun contracting private security services. In fact, Mexico now ranks third worldwide in purchases of security equipment.[27] Between 1998 and 1999, the number of private security companies in Mexico rose some 40 percent.[28] Probably because of this rapid growth, the Mexican government has had problems regulating these companies, most of which lack the necessary legal permits. By late 1999, it was estimated that about 10,000 private security firms were operating in Mexico, but only some 2,000 had any kind of official permit.[29] According to official figures, by December 2000, 2,984 private security companies were registered in Mexico, together employing 153,885 workers.[30] The lack of legal control over these companies exacerbates the security situation. Because many of them are unregulated, it is possible that some will engage in criminal activities instead of protecting their clients. In fact, there are documented cases of private security guards' involvement in crime, which leads one to suppose that this risk will persist in private security firms in upcoming years. The fact that significant numbers of private security guards were formerly police officers contributes to this situation.[31]

In a more political vein, organizations have emerged in the last few years that try to pressure government to improve public security. A prominent example is Mexico United against Delinquency (México Unido contra la Delincuencia). This organization, which appeared in early 1998, has acquired a national presence through marches and high visibility in the media. It has attempted to join the various anticrime organizations, which to date number about fourteen. The group also promoted a meeting of the three major presidential candidates in Mexico City in 2000, which further enhanced its visibility.

A new response from the citizenry that may offer important long-term benefits is school-based education to raise awareness of personal and social ethical decision-making, the reasons to support rule of law, the dangers of crime, and techniques to resist involvement in criminality and corruption.[32]

CHALLENGES FACING THE UNITED STATES

This section provides background information about recent trends related to law enforcement in the United States. We find that crime rates flattened out and began to fall in the 1990s, though remaining at relatively high levels. The reasons are complex, but they appear to include a robust economy, an aging society, and a substantially increased investment in law enforcement, resulting in significant increases in arrests, prosecution, and imprisonment. Much more than Mexico, the United States' approach to public security emphasizes punishment. At a subjective level, public opinion surveys suggest that Americans report improvement in public safety.

The most contentious public security issue from the U.S. perspective is drug trafficking and abuse. Drug abuse continues to be a serious problem that generates enormous costs to U.S. society in terms of crime, lost productivity, and family and personal distress. The costs in terms of crime, violence, and corruption stem in good part from the ways in which drug trafficking and abuse have been criminalized and from an aggressive enforcement of the relevant laws. We should emphasize that the illicit drug market, estimated in 1995 at some US$57 billion, is equal to only a small percentage of licit drugs sales (including caffeine, alcohol, nicotine, and prescription and over-the-counter drugs). Objectively, one can argue that the public health costs of legal drugs, such as alcohol and tobacco, far outweigh the damage inflicted by illegal drugs. But the violence, corruption, and social disorganization sparked by illicit drugs stand out as leading causes of public insecurity. Furthermore, analysis cannot be limited to an "objective" assessment. The ways in which drugs-related issues are embedded in U.S. culture have linked the issue to national security and have reinforced policy responses that emphasize punishment and supply reduction over treatment and demand reduction. Therefore, the adoption by the U.S. government in its 1999 National Drug Strategy Report of quantitative targets for demand reduction is a significant step forward in the binational dialogue on drugs.

Crime Rates: Trends and Perceptions

Summarizing the main trends in the FBI Uniform Crime Reports since 1960, the overall rate of reported crime (both violent and property crimes) more than tripled, from 1,887 per 100,000 population in 1960 to a peak of 5,898 in 1991, after which it dropped steadily to 4,922 in 1997. Violent crimes (murder, forcible rape, robbery, and aggravated assault) make up a small fraction of the total and follow the general pattern, quadrupling from 161 per 100,000 in 1960 to 758 in 1991, before declining to 611 in 1997. Crime rates accelerated dramatically in the late 1960s and then rose rather steadily through the 1970s and 1980s before tapering off in the 1990s. Preliminary reporting indicates that crime rates continued to drop in 1998 and 1999.[33] The trends in reported crime are substantiated in the National Crime Victimization Survey, which showed violent crime down 10 percent in 1999, to the lowest level since the surveys were begun in 1973. Property crime dropped 9 percent in 1999, continuing more than twenty years of decline.[34]

The states along the United States' southwest border report overall higher rates of crime than the national average, but with significant variations. Arizona's crime rates on the whole have been consistently and substantially (about 60 percent) above the national trend, with property crimes accounting for all of the disparity. Violent crime generally followed the national average, with peaks in 1980 and 1993. California has ridden a roller coaster, beginning with an overall rate above the national average in 1960 (3,474 per 100,000 versus 1,887 nationally) and falling below the national rate in 1997. Both property crime and violent crime began well above the national average, and only property crime has fallen consistently. Violent crime in California remains above the national average. Texas's crime rate index has consistently tracked slightly above the national average, with the difference being attributable to property crime rates. New Mexico's overall crime index is lower than the other southwestern states, but it is still above the national average. New Mexico is the only state in the border region that is experiencing a continuing increase in reported crime.

Law Enforcement, Prosecutions, and Imprisonment

Police forces reflect the broader institutional environment in which they operate. Important features of the U.S. case are federalism, decentralization, and exclusion of the military from police functions. It is important to note that the professionalization of U.S. police forces is a relatively recent development, beginning in the Progressive period early in the twentieth century but only gathering momentum in the 1950s. The most important of the national police forces is the Federal Bureau of Investigation (FBI).

The FBI was founded in 1908 and was shaped into a modern organization beginning in the 1920s and 1930s. The idea of a strong national police has been consistently resisted in the United States. In 1996 there were approximately 738,000 full-time sworn law enforcement officers in the United States. Of these, only about 10 percent (74,493) were civilian, federal (national-level) officers authorized to carry firearms and make arrests. More than half of the total (410,956) worked in 13,578 local police departments, and 252,579 officers worked for 4,453 state, county, or special police departments.[35]

Similar to the Mexican case, law enforcement jurisdictions in the United States include federal, state, and local levels. The great bulk of prosecution activity is at the state and local levels. In 1996, 2,343 state court prosecutors employed about 71,000 attorneys, investigators, and support staff, a 25 percent increase from 1992 and up 9 percent from 1994. The trend is toward the employment of full-time prosecutors, up to three-quarters in 1996 from about half in 1990.[36]

Law enforcement received substantial increases in resources in the 1990s. The Bureau of Justice Statistics reports that:

> In fiscal 1996 Federal, State, and local governments spent more than $120 billion for civil and criminal justice, a 73 percent increase over 1995. For every resident, the three levels of government together spent $454. In fiscal 1996 State and local governments combined spent 85 percent of all justice dollars; the Federal Government spent the rest. The Federal Government alone spent more than $23 billion on criminal and civil justice in 1996, compared to almost $48 billion by State governments, $30 billion by counties, and $34 billion by municipalities.[37]

With increased investment in law enforcement came an increase in arrests and convictions at all levels of government. The number of felony convictions increased 14 percent in state courts and 11 percent in federal courts between 1994 and 1996. State courts convicted almost 998,000 adults of a felony in 1996, an average growth rate of about 5 percent every year since 1988, when adult felony convictions totaled 667,366. In 1996, for the first time, state and federal courts convicted a combined total of over one million adults of felonies.[38]

The result is a burgeoning prison population, the largest per capita among industrialized countries. "Between 1990 and 1999, the incarcerated population grew an average 5.7 percent annually. Population growth during 1999 was significantly lower in State prisons (up 2.1 percent) and local jails (up 2.3 percent) than in previous years. The population in custody of Federal prison authorities rose by 13.4 percent (up 14,889 prisoners, the largest 12–month gain ever reported)." At the end of 1999, 6.3 million persons—roughly 3.1 percent of all U.S. adult residents—were

Table 1.3. **Trends in Perceptions of Crime in the Respondents' Area, 1972–1998**
(Question: "Is there more crime in your area than a year ago or less?")

	1972	1975	1977	1981	1983	1989	1990	1992	1996	1997	1998
More	51%	50%	43%	54%	37%	50%	51%	54%	46%	46%	31%
Less	10	12	17	8	17	20	18	19	25	32	48
Same	27	29	21	29	36	25	24	23	24	20	16

Source: The Gallup Organization, 1999, at www.gallup.com/poll/indicators/indcrime.asp.

Note: Surveys began three days prior to the date listed.

on probation, in jail or prison, or on parole. State and federal prison authorities had 1,366,721 inmates under their jurisdiction; local jails held or supervised 687,973 persons awaiting trial or serving their sentence.[39]

Thus the U.S. approach to public safety leans heavily toward prosecution and imprisonment. If recent incarceration rates remain unchanged, an estimated one of very twenty persons (5.1 percent) will serve time in a prison during their lifetime. The chances for a prison term are higher for men (9 percent) than for women (1.1 percent). In terms of race and ethnicity, the chances are much greater for African Americans (16.0 percent) and Hispanics (9.4 percent) than for Anglos (2.5 percent). "Based on current rates of first incarceration, an estimated 28 percent of black males will enter State or Federal prison during their lifetime, compared to 16 percent of Hispanic males and 4.4 percent of white males."[40]

There is evidence that suggests an improvement in Americans' sense of public security. Based on Gallup poll findings, beginning in 1992 respondents indicate their perception that there is relatively less crime in their area (table 1.3). This trend also appears when respondents are asked, "Is there more crime in the United States than a year ago, or less?" (table 1.4).

Table 1.4 **Trends in Perceptions of Crime in the United States, 1990–1998** (Question: "Is there more crime in the U.S. than a year ago, or less?")

Survey date	More	Less	Same	No opinion
Sept. 25, 1998	52%	35%	8%	5%
Aug. 25, 1997	64	25	6	5
July 28, 1996	71	15	8	6
Oct. 18, 1993	87	4	5	4
Mar. 1, 1992	89	3	4	4
Sept. 10, 1990	84	3	7	6
July 1, 1989	84	5	5	6

Source: The Gallup Organization, 1999. http:www.gallup.com/poll/indicators/indcrime.asp.
Note: Surveys began three days prior to the date listed.

With respect to the drug problem, the U.S. Office of National Drug Control Policy (ONDCP) reports that:

> In 1997, there were 13.9 million current users of any illicit drug in the total household population aged twelve and older, down from the peak year of 1979, when 25 million (or 14.1 percent of the population) consumed illegal drugs. The 13.9 million number represents 6.4 percent of the total population and is statistically unchanged from 1996. Thirty-six percent aged twelve

> years and older have used an illegal drug in their lifetime. Of these, more than 90 percent used either marijuana or hashish, and approximately 30 percent tried cocaine. There are an estimated 4 million chronic drug users in the United States: 3.6 million chronic users of cocaine (primarily crack cocaine) and 810,000 chronic heroin users.[41]

In terms of the general population, findings from a 1997 National Household Survey on Drug Abuse show that 77 million (35.6 percent) of Americans aged twelve years and older reported use of an illicit drug at least once in their lifetime. Among those aged twelve or older, an estimated 1.5 million were current cocaine users and 11.1 million reported using marijuana at least once within the past month. In the same population, 2.5 percent reported using methamphetamine, and 5.7 percent reported using inhalants at least once in their lifetime. A 1998 study by the National Institute on Drug Abuse reported that 54.1 percent of high school seniors said they had used an illicit drug at least once, 41.4 percent reported such use within the past year, and 25.6 percent reported use within the past month. Apart from the general population, the number of drug-related episodes in hospital emergency departments rose slightly between 1995 and 1996 (from 513,633 to 514,347), and the number of drug-abuse deaths rose slightly as well over the same biennium (from 14,218 to 14,843).[42] These trends are consistent with the interpretation that smaller numbers of people are abusing larger volumes of drugs.

Drug and alcohol abuse remains a serious factor in crime. A 1997 Bureau of Justice Statistics (BJS) report found that 51 percent of prison inmates committed their offense under the influence of drugs or alcohol. (The report does not specify the relative percentages related to drugs or alcohol or both.) A 1996 BJS survey of inmates in local jails reports that 82 percent had used a drug at some point in their lives, about 60 percent reported being under the influence of drugs or alcohol at the time of their arrest, and 16 percent overall said they committed their offense to get money to buy drugs. In broad terms, annual drug-related arrests (for possession, manufacture, or sale) increased steadily between 1988 and 1997, rising from 1.155 million (8.4 percent of all arrests in 1988) to 1.584 million (10.4 percent of arrests in 1997).[43]

Estimates of government spending devoted to antidrug programs are problematic in the sense that coordinating agencies basically sum up the amounts that reporting agencies claim they are devoting to fight drug trafficking or abuse. Also, a significant portion of expenditures is targeted to several programs jointly. This noted, overall federal drug control spending reportedly increased (in nominal terms) from US$13.25 billion in 1995 to $17.89 billion in 1999. The usual breakdown of federal spending suggests that about two-thirds is supply related and the balance is demand reduction. But this may be misleading. The bulk of federal spending does not go toward foreign operations. The largest single share of the budget—on average, about half—is devoted to the U.S. criminal justice system. About one-third is devoted to treatment and prevention. And substantially less—about 20 percent on average—is spent on international operations and drug interdiction. With respect to interdiction, drug seizures of heroin, cocaine, and marijuana have increased as well over the same four-year period. By and large, however, the retail or "street" price and quality for these drugs over the 1996–1998 period remained more or less stable (cocaine), or the price has fallen while purity held about stable (heroin and methamphetamine).[44]

The statistics tell only part of the story, however. Recent history, public opinion, and political institutions interact to tilt public policy toward an emphasis on law enforcement and supply reduction. Briefly put, drug abuse increased sharply in the 1960s and continued at a high rate into the 1980s. Drug abuse became associated in political discourse with the 1960s counterculture, then with the trauma of the Viet Nam War, and also with the perception of rising crime rates in the 1970s and 1980s. Deeply ingrained public opinion is the key to understanding U.S. drugs policy. In surveys, the majority of Americans respond that drug abuse is a serious problem, that their government should do more to protect them from the influx of drugs from foreign countries, and, specifically, that Mexico is not doing enough to repress drug trafficking.[45] U.S. political institutions respond to public opinion. Elected officials must heed deep-seated public attitudes when shaping policies; and public bureaucracies, both military and civilian, respond to elected officials. Thus an enormous inertia has built up over time that responds to a military rhetoric of a "war on drugs" and commits the bulk of resources accordingly. So great is the inertia that there is a striking disconnect between the near-consensus in research that suggests putting more emphasis on treatment and demand reduction, as opposed to the continuing emphasis on a sanctions-supply approach.

Antidrugs Strategies: Challenges of Demand Reduction

A fairly widespread perception in Mexico is that government and society in the United States do rather little to reduce internal demand for illicit drugs and that the main thrust of antidrug policy goes toward supply reduction. Supply-reduction policies emphasize crop eradication and drug interdiction measures that, in turn, imply coercive law enforcement measures whose effects are felt most strongly in Mexico and other affected countries. The sense of frustration is that drug-related crime, violence, and corruption are suffered in greater measure by Mexico, and until and unless consumption is substantially reduced in the United States, Mexico (and other affected countries) are condemned by the realities of power asymmetries to long-term stress and even institutional decay. For their part, U.S. authorities emphasize that the antidrug policy is a balanced approach, including both supply-reduction and demand-reduction dimensions.

The dynamics of U.S. federalism, an institutional factor often overlooked by foreign observers, should be underlined: drug policy making in the United States is shared by local, state, and federal jurisdictions. Two implications follow. First, federal policies and budgets (which make up about half of general government spending) are fairly transparent, but much less is known about state and local practices and expenditures. Second, the federal government plays the dominant role in foreign policy, which is the supply-reduction field; state and local governments play greater roles in treatment and demand reduction. Thus Mexicans see the supply reduction rhetoric and programs of the U.S. federal government much more clearly than they do the demand reduction programs of state and local governments and civil society actors. The investments in and results of state and local demand reduction programs are not well known.

There have been significant, positive developments in recent U.S.–Mexico drug policy making. The *U.S./Mexico Bi-National Drug Threat Assessment* (1997) was the first joint effort to assess the common drug threat. Presidents Bill Clinton and Ernesto Zedillo announced the *Declaration of Alliance Against Drugs* (May 1997), followed in February 1998 by the *US/Mexico Bi-National Drug Strategy*. This was followed in 1999 by the *Bi-National Drug Control Strategy-Performance Measures of Effectiveness: Implementation and Findings*, which represents an important advance in setting out empirical measures by which to assess antidrug policies. Significantly, demand reduction is the first of sixteen "Alliance Points." As Andresen and Farrell suggest (chapter 9), the introduction of empirical measures may have the effect of increasing the factual basis of the policy dialogue and of giving each country more mechanisms by which it can monitor, and thereby influence, the activity of the other.

Overall U.S. policy as stated in the 1999 *National Drug Control Strategy* is a ten-year plan to cut present drug use in half, to 3.1 percent of the population by the year 2007.[46] This is an extraordinary goal. The measures encompass prevention, treatment, and rehabilitation, including a focus on illicit drug use in the criminal justice system. About $5.9 billion, or one-third of the overall federal drug control budget, is targeted for demand-reduction programs. The terms "supply" and "demand" need clarification as well. We are referring to "realized demand"—that is, actual consumption—as opposed to potential demand. Further, supply itself influences demand: "drug traffickers target profitable markets, which in recent history have been the U.S. and Western Europe.... Expanding opportunities for trafficking produce increased supply, which in turn produces increased opportunity for illicit consumption. Hence, although demand is undoubtedly influenced by other factors, the level of supply necessarily plays a role."[47]

"Prevention" also has specific meanings. Primary prevention is aimed at ensuring that a disorder or problem will not begin. Secondary prevention is aimed at identifying and terminating or modifying for the better a disorder or problem. Tertiary prevention is aimed at stopping or retarding the progress of a disorder even though the basic condition may persist; that is, tertiary prevention aims to minimize some effects of the most harmful drug abuse. U.S. demand-side policy focuses mainly on primary and secondary prevention.

Andresen and Farrell's assessment of demand-side drug policies and programs emphasizes two themes: (1) there are scores of different types of drug-reduction programs ongoing throughout the United States and aimed at either primary or secondary prevention; and (2) insufficient attention has been given to program evaluation. To illustrate, these authors examine media campaigns such as Partnership for a Drug-Free America and the National Youth Anti-Drug Media Campaign. In both cases, the campaigns were unscientifically evaluated in their failure to use randomization of subjects and control groups. The assessments of implementation fail to make, much less measure, a connection between awareness of the antidrug messages and abstention from or reduction in drug use. Similarly, most of the evaluations of the popular Drug Abuse Resistance Education program (DARE) were not rigorous. The most scientifically rigorous evaluation reported that DARE had no long-term effects on a wide range of drug use measures.

Overall, Andresen and Farrell conclude that the activities and expenditures in the United States aimed at demand reduction argue against the notion that nothing is being done in this regard.

> It may not be too inaccurate to say that there is little firm evidence that any of the current demand-reduction efforts ... have a substantial impact.... As of 2000, the United States could claim that it was at least making some effort—more than previously—to reduce demand. As a political bargaining chip, the United States could probably claim that it is making as much effort, or more, than Mexico had made in relation to reducing the illicit supply of drugs.
>
> Further, the United States could claim that the demand for illicit drugs, when measured in terms of prevalence, has been reduced over the long term within the U.S. population. This same claim could not be made in relation to frequent users or in relation to the overall instances of illicit drug use or the volume of drugs consumed.[48]

In sum, greater attention toward demand reduction requires more effective program design and evaluation.

DILEMMAS WITH MEXICO

Trade Facilitation versus Drug Interdiction

Peter Andreas (chapter 8) analyzes the unique dynamic that the United States confronts with Mexico in the interaction between commerce in legal and illegal goods and services. Mexico is the second market in importance (behind Canada) for U.S. imports and exports, and the rate of growth in trade has accelerated dramatically since the implementation of the North American Free Trade Agreement (NAFTA) in January 1994. Thus controversy over trade policy interacts with polemics over antidrug and illegal migration policies to produce a sometimes-harsh discourse in national-level politics. The Bush and Clinton administrations worked to mute the drugs-related problems with Mexico during the negotiations leading up to NAFTA. In the period following implementation, increased attention focused on the southwest border and problems of drug smuggling. The attention and controversy, in turn, played a role in complicating Clinton's subsequent trade policy initiatives, blocking his efforts in 1997 to secure renewal of fast-track negotiating authority.[49]

We can summarize the complexity of the trade facilitation–drug enforcement dilemma by reviewing key sequences. The U.S. initiative in the early 1980s to step up drug interdiction along the southeast border had the overall effect of shifting the bulk of drug flows from the Caribbean toward land routes in Mexico and thus to the United States' southwestern border. The subsequent success in building a "Maginot Line" of radar along the border forced drug smuggling from the air to the ground, and thus into the same transportation routes being used for the growing volumes of legitimate commerce. "Equally significant, grounding the cocaine trade made Colombian traffickers more reliant on their Mexican counterparts, who controlled the road smuggling networks across the border."[50] This dynamic, in turn, contributed to strengthening the Mexican drug gangs to the point that they have become a significant national security threat. Grounding the drug smuggling also exacerbated problems of violence and drug abuse in the border zone itself, especially on the Mexican side.

Drug interdiction along the 2,000–mile U.S.–Mexico border is a daunting task. An estimated 60 percent of the cocaine and 29 percent of the heroin sold in the United States in 1998 transited that border. As Andreas notes, "At the same time, the cross-border flow of legitimate commerce has more than doubled in the 1990s.... Indeed, the border is the busiest land crossing in the world: in 1998, 278 million people, 86 million cars, and 4 million trucks and railcars entered the United States from Mexico."[51] Put another way, on average, 220,000 vehicles cross the border daily into the United States. With respect to supply,

> It takes only nine large tractor-trailers loaded with cocaine to satisfy the United States' drug demand for one year. Thus the enforcement challenge is the equivalent of finding a needle in a haystack—and the haystack keeps getting bigger and the needle keeps getting better at hiding. U.S. border officials searched more than a million commercial trucks and railway cars crossing from Mexico in 1997 and found cocaine in only six of the searches.[52]

Yet hardening the border further—as, for example, by significantly increasing inspection of vehicles and persons—would seriously disrupt legitimate trade. A customs official estimated that an inspection of every truck entering the United States would produce unacceptable backups and delays. "Customs would back up the truck traffic bumper-to-bumper into Mexico City in just two weeks—15.8 days. In 15.8 days, there would be 95,608 trucks backed up into Mexico. That's 1,177 miles of trucks, end to end, or the distance from Mexico City to the city of Laredo in the United States."[53]

The result is a genuine dilemma. Barring some technological "silver bullet" (and U.S. authorities are investing significant resources to develop such technologies), drug interdiction along the border is unlikely to produce major reductions in drug supply. Given this reality, U.S. pressures will continue, or increase, for stronger efforts by Mexican authorities to repress trafficking. It is conceivable that hardening the border and increasing repression might reduce trafficking, but experience teaches us to expect two likely outcomes: (1) levels of violence and corruption in Mexico and the border region will escalate, with unpredictable results; and (2) the so-called balloon effect will push trafficking into new routes (or return them to old ones).

Problems of Weapons Trafficking

From Mexico's perspective, one worrisome ingredient in its recent rise in violent crime is the increasing availability of guns. The manufacture, sale, and use of firearms are, in principle, highly regulated within Mexico. These regulations have created a market for firearms smuggled into the country. Some unknown quantity of these weapons is smuggled from the United States, and there may be connections between gun smuggling and drug trafficking. The Mexican government has voiced its concern that the U.S. government should do more to repress weapons trafficking. Complicating the situation, due to law and custom, guns are much more widely available in the United States. Though gun-related violence is of increasing concern in the United States, and the manufacture, sale, and use of guns are regulated by laws at all levels of government, it remains fairly easy for individuals in the United States to purchase guns and smuggle them across the border.

We lack rigorous studies on the problem of weapons trafficking. A recent investigative report by the *Los Angeles Times* covered some examples of problems and some more general issues. The key problems, according to the *Los Angeles Times*, are factors that limit regulation of gun dealers and the lenient punishment for violations of law. A relatively small number of agents of the Bureau of Alcohol, Tobacco and Firearms (ATF) (about 200 field inspectors) inspect a large number of gun dealers (about 83,000). Further, ATF inspectors are limited by Congress from conducting more than one surprise inspection of a dealer per year. ATF also lacks intermediate sanctions, such as fines, to impose on problem dealers and must rely on the harsh measure of license revocation. The Bureau has never revoked more than forty-four licenses in a single year, and in many years it has revoked fewer than ten. With respect to sentencing, the guidelines that federal judges follow provide for tough penalties for the use of guns to commit crimes or for gun possession by felons. But the guidelines fail to treat most trafficking offenses as serious crime.[54]

One achievement of the U.S.–Mexico High Level Contact Group, formed in 1996, was the creation of the Bi-National Firearms Trafficking Working Group. A problem confronted by the Working Group has been the constant turnover of Mexican officials serving as points of contact for joint investigations. Personnel turnover has also affected the ability of the two governments to successfully trace recovered firearms, as trained personnel were frequently transferred to positions not requiring their expertise. A complicating factor was the lack of a central clearance mechanism to coordinate requests for weapons traces. This complication has been alleviated in part by the creation in 1997 of a Technical Subcommittee of the Firearms Trafficking Working Group, whose biweekly meetings in Mexico City serve as a forum for the exchange of intelligence information and for the resolution of specific problems. Also, the designation of the National Drug Control Center (CENDRO) as the lead agency of the Mexican government for all firearms traces has improved cooperation. CENDRO's efforts have contributed to a significant increase in successful trace requests, reaching a 42–percent success rate in 2000 (in contrast to a rate below 10 percent prior to 1996). The Technical Subcommittee also reports important advances in firearms-related training and in cooperation between the U.S. Bureau of Alcohol, Tobacco and Firearms and Mexico's Federal Preventive Police. More remains to be done, however, in curtailing the smuggling of guns. A problem noted is the need to establish better cross-border communication between officials dealing with preventing and investigating firearms trafficking.[55]

Prosecution versus Extradition

Although the prosecution-versus-extradition issue is particularly relevant to the borderlands, it has generated frictions at the overall binational level to the extent that it deserves separate treatment. With the two societies so densely integrated by trade, migration, travel, and communication, the issue of bilateral and multilateral cooperation in apprehending and processing fugitive suspects has become increasingly important. The two criminal justice systems are quite different, and standards of procedure are appropriately rigorous when individuals' liberties are at stake. Traditional procedures, such as mutual legal assistance treaties or letters rogatory, have proven slow, cumbersome, and rather easily manipulated. Needed are more flexible forms of cooperation that still meet procedural requirements as established by law.

With respect to extradition, Mexico's 1980 bilateral treaty with the United States was overridden by the Mexican Constitution and a statute prohibiting the extradition of a Mexican citizen to a foreign country, including the United States. In recent years, particularly during the Zedillo administration, Mexico has opted to extradite Mexican citizens in exceptional circumstances.

> The Mexican government is still refining the definition of "exceptional circumstances." At this time it is limited to crimes of violence, such as murder and rape, or organized crime figures, such as persons with long-standing convictions and/or multiple charges for high-level trafficking crimes. It has not yet been extended to include extradition for perjury [which is important to evidence gathering for U.S. purposes].[56]

The trend has been that Mexican courts increasingly find means to grant exemptions in order to extradite to the United States its own nationals accused of serious crime. As of April 2000, Mexico had extradited eleven Mexican citizens (eight born in Mexico and three naturalized) and another two with deferred delivery. In addition, Mexico granted the extradition of nine other Mexican citizens who found protection under injunctions (*amparos*). There were at least another half-dozen individuals whose extradition had been authorized.[57] In several cases, the extradition of Mexican nationals was blocked by the appellate courts *(cortes de apelación)* which ruled that the "exceptional cases" concept applied only where no bilateral treaty was in effect, and that the Mexican criminal code required that Mexican nationals wanted for crimes abroad had to be prosecuted in Mexico, according to Mexico's criminal code.[58] In January 2001, Mexico's Supreme Court ruled 10 to 1 that the extradition of Mexican nationals does not violate the Constitution, thus ending a legal debate that had blocked cooperation on extraditions for many years. The court's ruling confirmed that the executive branch has the authority to decide whether "exceptional circumstances" justify granting an extradition request.[59] The court's decision would appear to open the door to binational cooperation in the future, depending on executive branch decisions.

In principle, if due process requirements are met, U.S. courts routinely extradite suspects to Mexico. In fact, however, U.S. courts deny many extradition requests, even for Mexican nationals, because of problems they perceive with the Mexican criminal justice system. A high-profile example was the case of Francisco Ruiz Massieu, whose extradition was frustrated on four occasions. Overall, the numbers and rates of extradition during the past five years between the two governments are roughly comparable.

A number of conflicts have arisen over this issue. Mexico strongly protests "irregular rendition" (when a suspect Mexican national is delivered across the border by extra-official means for trial in the United States). A form of irregular rendition is the posting of bounties by U.S. authorities for the apprehension and delivery of suspects. For their part, U.S. officials complain that the regular procedures as covered in the 1980 extradition treaty are hampered by lax law enforcement and inefficient judicial procedures in Mexico. A particular bone of contention has been Mexico's reluctance to extradite Mexican nationals to the United States to face drug-related charges.

But the image of conflict and stalemate over extradition is misleading and rather limited to high-profile cases concerning the national governments. To be expected, private citizens and officials at various levels in both countries are continually seeking means to improve cooperation while maintaining legal standards and protection of national sovereignty. Bruce Zagaris's essay (chapter 14) on the Arizona-Sonora experiment in law enforcement cooperation documents such a case. Further, according to William McDonald (chapter 15), there is a rich but little known history of repeated efforts along the border to promote cooperation. Also, the Bi-National Commission at the national level, begun in 1981, has spun off a number of binational subgroups over the years to work on these issues. One of the most important initiatives, suggested in 1986 by Attorney General Sergio García Ramírez, became the U.S.–Mexico Border States Attorneys General Conference, which had met eighteen times as of 1999.

An important but largely unknown alternative to extradition is "foreign prosecution," a procedure by which Mexico will prosecute persons who commit crimes abroad and flee to Mexico.

> The circumstances under which Mexico will prosecute a defendant in Mexico with evidence developed and presented by U.S. law enforcement agencies are the following: (1) the defendant must be in Mexico, (2) the defendant must not have been tried in the country where the crime occurred, and (3) the act for which the defendant is charged must be a crime in both countries.[60]

This procedure has been used by the California Department of Justice since the 1980s. Its Mexican Liaison Unit became the Foreign Prosecution Unit, whose purpose was to assist all California law enforcement agencies with filing cases. The Los Angeles Police Department (LAPD) had so many cases that it established its own separate unit in 1985. San Diego and Orange counties in Southern California followed suit shortly thereafter. Interestingly, the procedure remained confined to use by California officials until 1992, when Texas Attorney General Dan Morales adopted the LAPD guidelines to open a foreign prosecution unit; attorneys general of Arizona and New Mexico subsequently established similar offices.

There are numerous problems with foreign prosecution. It is difficult to track cases through Mexican courts. Arrest warrants may be issued but go unserved for a variety of reasons. But Mexican courts have been cooperative on the whole, especially since the procedure has been endorsed by Mexico's attorney general. Overall, Americans believe the procedure represents a crucial opening to a new era in cooperation with Mexican law enforcement.[61]

In addition to foreign prosecution, another mechanism may prove useful in the future. In November 1997, Mexico and the United States adopted a Protocol to the 1980 extradition treaty that permits "temporary extradition." This Protocol provides that, while adhering to the treaty's procedures, each government can temporarily extradite to the other country an individual who has been sentenced or is serving a sentence. The benefit of the Protocol is that individuals can be temporarily extradited to stand trial or to provide testimony in trials under way in the other country, thus preventing loss of evidence and facilitating prosecution. The U.S. Senate approved the Protocol in October 1998, and President Clinton signed it in January 1999. The Protocol appears to have been blocked by the Mexican Senate, however, pending the U.S. Senate's approval of the Treaty Prohibiting Transborder Abductions, negotiated in November 1994.

U.S. Intelligence in the Bilateral Relationship

One of the most controversial but least examined topics in the bilateral relationship concerns the role of U.S. intelligence activities with respect to

Mexico and Latin America. Clearly, intelligence cooperation at a variety of levels is essential to develop strategies with which to confront threats to public security. Brian Latell (chapter 10) traces what he calls "the special strategic relationship" that the United States' Federal Bureau of Investigation and Central Intelligence Agency forged with Mexico's security agencies through the World War II and Cold War periods. "The special strategic relationship," he argues, "was an unusual arrangement that worked to the advantage of both countries for most of the five decades following Pearl Harbor." The end of the Cold War—along with the democratic transition in Mexico and the rise of new challenges, such as transnational criminal and terrorist organizations—may be fostering conditions for deeper bilateral cooperation. Although Latell is guardedly optimistic about possibilities for cooperation, he suggests that "U.S. policymakers will need to be especially sensitive to Mexican internal security priorities that are unique or may conflict with dominant U.S. approaches and policies." A key point that Latell does not develop concerns the time and resource requirements for building an effective and reliable intelligence capacity in Mexico.

CHALLENGES IN THE U.S.–MEXICO BORDERLANDS

If we adopt the definition of the borderlands established in the 1983 Agreement for the Protection and Improvement of the Environment in the Border Area, the region includes a fringe of territory 100 kilometers (62 miles) deep on either side of the 2,000–mile border. The area encompasses four U.S. and six Mexican states, forty-five border crossings, and fourteen twin cities, and it accounts for about 92 percent of the border population. By their nature, international boundaries create criminogenic conditions by dividing a market and restricting the exchange of goods and people, thus generating differentials in costs and incentives. Criminal enterprises typically emerge to take advantage of these opportunities. The range and complexity of criminal activities are impressive, encompassing, for example, petty larceny, auto theft, human smuggling, assault, white-collar fraud, and prostitution, as carried out by individuals or by gangs that vary between one-time, ad hoc encounters of a few persons to long-standing, complex organizations involving hundreds of members.[62]

Although crime statistics for Mexico's border states and counties (*municipios*) are difficult to obtain, it appears that overall rates in the mid–1990s were increasing at a faster pace than in the rest of the country. One study reported that the northern border states experienced a 9 percent annual average increase in criminal prosecutions in 1990–1995, compared with a 2.3 percent growth rate in the interior of Mexico.[63] In addition, drug-related social problems in the larger cities along the border appear to be worsening. Part of the cause is that traffickers pay some of their workers in kind rather than cash, which has meant that a certain quantity of illegal drugs has remained on the Mexican side of the border, creating a secondary market. Ciudad Juárez police in 1999 investigated 900 "*picaderos*" (places where drugs are sold or consumed), although other estimates suggest as many as 2,000 *picaderos* for this metropolitan area of nearly two million people. In Tijuana there were an estimated 4,000 to 4,500 *picaderos*. Although the data are difficult to locate, there appeared to be a sharply growing problem of heroin addiction in Ciudad Juárez and Tijuana, and cocaine addiction is the leading problem associated with troubled youth.[64]

As noted above, overall crime rates in the southwestern border states of the United States have run slightly above national trends since the 1960s. Uniform Crime Reports data for these states suggest that, by and large, crime indices in the counties along the border for the 1994–1997 period run slightly below the average rates for the states. The exception is Texas, where property crime rates are higher in the border counties and violent crime runs at the same rate along the border as in the rest of the state. In New Mexico's case, property crime in the border counties rose in 1997 to a rate equal to the statewide index.

Migration-related Crime

Illegal migration between Mexico and the United States is a difficult and controversial issue. We emphasize the distinction between individuals illegally crossing the U.S.–Mexico border and the professional criminal gangs that smuggle groups of illegal migrants across the border. It is unlikely that the U.S. and Mexican governments will agree on the criminal nature of individuals' migrating. Rather, it is the issue of transnational organized crime related to migration that is of greater concern and that requires bilateral cooperation.

Illegal migration between Mexico and the United States is a longstanding cause of tensions between the two countries. For fiscal year 1998, estimates are that between 278 and 351 million people legally crossed the border from Mexico to the United States, making this the world's busiest land border. The number of illegal crossings is not known. In the same fiscal year, more than 1.5 million persons were arrested for attempting to cross without inspection, and there were more than 1.1 million "voluntary returns," whereby the detainee returns to Mexico without formal deportation. Entering the United States without inspection has been defined as a crime since 1924. Unlawful reentry after formal deportation is a more serious offense, punishable by a harsh penalty (twenty years imprisonment). Illegal immigration of this magnitude reinforces a culture of lawlessness and imposes real costs, especially on the border communities themselves. In a broader context, illegal migration generates enormous illegal profits, strengthens organized crime groups, foments serious human rights abuses, and contributes to a climate of violence, corruption, and insecurity.[65]

Mexico and the United States share a common interest in preventing Mexico's becoming a transit country for the thousands of third-country nationals attempting to enter the United States. In response, the United States, Mexico, Canada, and the Central American countries are seeking ways to jointly address illegal migration.

Recent U.S. policies have made illegal immigration more difficult. In turn, the costs and profits in migrant smuggling have risen dramatically, and the numbers of criminal gangs engaged in migrant smuggling have increased. There are large-scale transnational gangs, most notably in China, that are dedicated to migrant smuggling and which target Mexico and Central America as transit zones. To illustrate the scope and profitability of migrant smuggling, the Gloria Canales organization, based in Costa Rica and dismantled in 1995, is believed to have moved some 10,000 aliens of various nationalities through Central America and Mexico. The gang's income was estimated at between US$60 and $80 million over eight years. Predictably, problems of corruption have worsened throughout these zones and have penetrated U.S. agencies, including the Border Patrol and Customs Service.[66]

What are the relationships between illegal migration and crime rates in the United States? U.S. law enforcement officials generally believe that Mexican nationals are involved in serious crime along the border and that the trend is toward greater involvement. But obtaining accurate data is problematic because none of the studies dealing with the criminality of Mexican immigrants has sufficient methodological rigor to support firm conclusions. Most of the studies are not focused on Mexican immigrants per se, but on illegal immigrants of whom varying proportions are Mexicans. None of the studies has positively identified the citizenship of the offenders.

Nevertheless, some contours of the problem can be estimated. It appears that the criminality of Mexican nationals in the United States differs from that of U.S. citizens, although this varies by region. It also appears that crime by Mexicans in the United States has shifted over time from property offenses to drug offenses and more violent crimes. Poor methodologies and a lack of data, however, hinder our ability to make precise statements about the relative criminality of Mexicans (or Mexican immigrants) as compared with U.S. citizens (or other immigrant groups).[67]

Institutional Dynamics and Interagency Cooperation

José Z. García (chapter 12) notes an extraordinary buildup of two parallel sets of law enforcement agencies (including military forces) with roughly similar functions operating in close juxtaposition along the U.S.–Mexico border. These buildups were not designed to counter potential government hostilities; rather, they are aimed at regulating and/or deterring individuals and groups that are often, but not always, engaged in cross-border activities. García finds that, rather than a border security *community*—that is, a convergence around security goals sufficient to generate cooperation—there is relatively little cross-border operational cooperation between law enforcement agencies at any level within the border region. Interagency cross-border cooperation is improving, but thus far it seems aimed more at reducing cross-border irritants and misunderstandings than inspiring coordinated operational efforts. At the local level, there is a variable degree of success in creating cross-border cooperative mechanisms. "Thus, although hostility in U.S.–Mexico relations is absent, a security community between the two countries cannot be said to exist, although long-term trends in that direction can be detected."[68]

The absence of a security community can be explained in part by the different strategic priorities in border security in the two countries. On the U.S. side of the border, priority goes to interdicting illegal persons and goods entering from Mexico or—failing this—to block the transportation of illicit cargo to the U.S. interior by seizures or by disruption of trafficking organizations near the border. As these systems fail and contraband enters the interior, other law enforcement systems attempt to disrupt distribution and sales of goods or the illegal employment of individuals. There have been significant improvements in interagency cooperation and the achievement of flexible joint operations since the buildups of the mid–1980s. Mechanisms have been developed to better coordinate city, state, and federal forces. Despite the improvements and the dramatic buildup of forces (federal law enforcement on the border nearly doubled from 1993 to 1998, from 7,487 to 12,738 officers), drug trafficking and illegal migration have continued at high rates.

The priority for Mexico is the physical security of persons living in the communities along the border. Emigration from Mexico is not illegal, illegal immigration from the United States is not a significant problem, and north-south contraband is not drug driven. Efforts remain labor intensive, centered on points of entry, and focused on enforcing restrictions on legal imports as well as on illegal imports such as firearms.

By the end of the 1990s, then, Mexico had created new administrative and operational configurations to deal with security issues. Antidrug components were initiated on the border, drug-related crime was targeted in the larger border cities through increases in municipal budgets, and efforts were made to increase protection for migrants increasingly vulnerable to predatory criminals. Interagency operation units like Grupo Orión and the "combined cells" (*células mixtas*) addressed relatively low-level drug-trafficking activities in the local context. The armed forces focused on interdicting drug en route and eradicating crops at the regional, largely rural, level. And the FEADS and some elements of the Federal Judicial Police investigated national crime syndicates. Unlike the U.S. border buildup, Mexican law enforcement has no parallel border interdiction machinery, and Mexico has much more readily deployed the armed forces in a number of law enforcement activities. Like their U.S. counterparts, Mexican security officials have experimented with a more integrated approach, combining local, state, and federal officers into flexible units.[69]

Efforts to improve cross-border cooperation increased in the 1990s, and they have borne modest fruits. A cabinet-level High Level Contact Group, established in 1996, has succeeded in improving communications and developing broad strategic goals, including the improvement of cross-border cooperation. The Border Liaison Mechanism (BLM) was created in 1993 to improve cross-border official communications. Consulates in twin cities along the border convene quarterly meetings to discuss problems of mutual concern, including law enforcement. By and large, law enforcement officers find the meetings useful in establishing personal ties. The meetings have not, however, led to exchanges of intelligence or other sensitive information, nor to long-term operational cooperation.

The United States' priority focus on halting or disrupting trafficking leads to repeated efforts to gain Mexico's cooperation in attacking Mexico-based organizations. On the Mexican side, the goal is to increase the security of persons living near the border. The dominant strategy is to improve police capabilities to combat growing crime rates. Antidrug operations seem aimed primarily against the lower end of the organizational hierarchy—local distribution and drug-related crime, rather than cross-border cartels. Also, significant efforts have been made—by Grupo Beta, among others—to protect potential emigrants from predators in the border region. When abuse occurs on the U.S. side, such efforts have relied on stronger consular activity. One gets a sense of the difference in priorities from the much greater federal government presence on the U.S. side of the border than on the Mexican side.

Given the differences in priorities, it is not surprising that a security community has failed to materialize between parallel agencies along the border. Nor is it surprising that the border security regimes of the two countries have failed to either provide safety or halt cross-border trafficking. Nevertheless, "drug trafficking, drug-related crime rates, and migration between the United States and Mexico are simply too bilaterally interconnected. Addressing these issues independently on each side of the border, with different goals and priorities, limited by 'supply-side' ideologies, and with virtually no operational interfacing—these are formulas for failure."[70]

José M. Ramos (chapter 13) offers the hypothesis that the formal legal, administrative ,and political agreements developed at the bilateral level to promote antidrugs cooperation need not complicate or obstruct efforts at the state and local levels to generate informal working agreements. He sees the possibility for cross-border cooperation, especially in cities where drug trafficking has led to high levels of public insecurity. The key, in his reasoning, is to connect drug trafficking with the broader issue of public safety at the community level.

Ramos argues that the nature of Mexican centralism needs to be revised. Drug trafficking is a transnational problem that hits hardest at the state and local levels. State-level authorities too often abstain from acting because drug trafficking belongs to the federal jurisdiction (*fuero federal*), but federal authorities have a weak and ineffective presence at the state and local levels. "The challenge," in Ramos's view, "is a more effective public handling and promotion (*gestión*) from an intergovernmental perspective."[71]

Societal Dynamics and Bilateral Cooperation

In general, the closer integration of the Mexican and U.S. economies and societies is reflected along the border with increased interaction among governmental, business, educational, and civic associations. However, societal cooperation has lagged behind security and law enforcement cooperation. With the national security imprimatur and the rapid buildup of federal agencies and personnel along the U.S. side of the border, the balance of influence has shifted toward federal priorities. On the Mexican side, public opinion seems focused on local problems of personal insecurity. In a subregion characterized by partisan sensitivities and given the danger associated with making drug-related accusations, protest tends to be muted. A dramatic exception concerns non–drug-related issues, such as the protest by women's groups in Ciudad Juárez that focused on the disappearance of over two hundred women in the metropolitan area over the past seven years.

On the U.S. side of the border, law enforcement issues are voiced more in terms of national problems of drugs and migration. Groups concerned about human rights violations by Border Patrol agents couch their arguments in national norms such as protest against "unreasonable search and seizure," rather than on the grounds of the relative benefits of law enforcement to public security in the border region itself. The opposite tends to characterize discourse on the Mexican side, where attention focuses on the relative ineffectiveness of public agencies to repress criminality. Seldom are broader national or international issues emphasized. In all, cross-border citizens groups that address the region-wide, cross-border security problematic have not yet emerged.[72]

The key to designing future cross-border security alignments is to create strong mechanisms of local, state, and national accountability with broad public involvement and support. The High Intensity Drug Trafficking Area mechanism has succeeded for the United States in part because it fostered interagency consultation and participation in goal setting. In this same vein, it would seem useful for public officials to seek public participation in the *definition* of security threats and priorities. This might broaden the relatively narrow national priorities about drugs and migration, and allow articulation and inclusion of local concerns. On the Mexican side as well, it is important for law enforcement authorities to seek strong public input in the initial discussions of security threats and priorities, and to have clear-cut lines of accountability. Finally, the obvious point to underline is that public security problems and communities vary considerably along the border, and issues and priorities will vary accordingly.[73]

These considerations hold two implications. First, although bilateral mechanisms should continue to operate, more attention should be paid to finding mutual definitions of security threats, as well as mutual goals, strategies, and tactics. This suggests a stronger effort by both countries to work together to consult with relevant publics to determine mutually acceptable security regimes. Second, border-specific law enforcement regimes should evolve from concrete efforts to promote security *communities*—that is, developing community-specific, cross-border interaction among law enforcement officials, local policymakers, and the public at large.

A specific way to involve society in the fight against crime is school-based education. As a pilot project, the Ministry of Education of Baja California and the San Diego County Office of Education began in 1998 to develop a school-based project to improve students' knowledge about crime and to strengthen their support for the rule of law. Selected teachers from both communities drew on the experiences of western Sicily and Hong Kong to develop a pilot curriculum, which was implemented in eleven high schools (eight in Mexico and three in the United States) in the fall of 1999. The results indicated that school-based education is a useful approach to preventing crime and corruption. After thirty-six hours of instruction, students' knowledge about and resistance to crime improved substantially. In addition, the project raised students' interpersonal competency and self-esteem, as well as their problem-solving ability to avoid lawless behavior.

Testing of the students, teachers, and focus groups involved in the project did suggest, however, that the curriculum and effectiveness of the approach can be improved. Something on the order of sixty hours of classroom instruction may be optimal. The curriculum and requisite teacher training might place a stronger focus on internalizing the rationale and legitimacy of rules and laws and on the rewards for law-abiding behavior and the remorse felt as a consequence of law-breaking behavior.

Plans are under way to make these revisions, and further testing of the project is envisioned in the border area in the near future.[74]

ORGANIZATION OF THE BOOK

The following chapters are grouped to follow the logic of the introduction. Part 1 takes up the challenges of transnational crime and public security as these affect Mexico. Part 2 considers these issues with respect to the United States. Part 3 focuses on the Mexico–U.S. border region. The main points are summarized in the concluding essay, and a series of recommendations is presented.

Notes

1. Leonardo Curzio (this volume) quotes President Zedillo and Interior Minister Francisco Labastida to this effect.

2. Vicente Fox Quesada, "Mensaje de Toma de Posesión," Mexico City, December 1, 2000, Sesión Solemne del H. Congreso de la Unión, at www.presidencia.gob.mx/?Art=4&Orden=Leer.

3. Highly publicized incidents of mass violence in public schools—such as the April 1999 shootings at Columbine High School in Colorado—have fueled public debate. Race-related police brutality in New York City and drug-related police corruption in Los Angeles also received considerable media coverage. "A federal judge recently ruled that the LAPD [Los Angeles Police Department] could be considered a criminal enterprise in upcoming lawsuits, an unprecedented decision against a law enforcement agency." The U.S. Department of Justice has intervened to oversee reforms of the LAPD, an action it has taken with respect to Pittsburgh, Pennsylvania; Steubenville, Ohio; and the New Jersey State Police. Federal investigations into patterns of misconduct are continuing in Washington, New Orleans, and five other municipalities. William Booth, "Outsiders to Oversee Reforms at LAPD," *Washington Post*, September 22, 2000.

4. Robert J. Kelly, "An American Way of Crime and Corruption," *Trends in Organized Crime* 5:2 (Winter 1999): 85–122.

5. Francisco Thoumi, "La relación entre corrupción y narcotráfico: un análisis general y algunas referencias a Colombia" (manuscript, 1999).

6. See Arzt, this volume, for an assessment of anti–money laundering policies.

7. U.S. Senate, *Minority Staff Report for Permanent Subcommittee on Investigations, Hearing on Private Banking and Money Laundering: A Case Study of Opportunities and Vulnerabilities* (November 9, 1999, at http://levin.senate.gov/issues/psirerport2.htm); and Minority Staff of the Permanent Subcommittee on Investigations, *Report on Correspondent Banking: A Gateway for Money Laundering* (Washington, D.C., February 5, 2001, mimeo).

8. The money-laundering sting "Operation Casablanca," described by Ramos (this volume), is a good example of unilateral initiatives.

9. A victimization survey carried out by the Mexican Health Foundation and World Bank in Mexico City in May 1999 reported that the crime rate for the six

months prior to the survey was thirty-eight per one hundred inhabitants. In 49 percent of the households surveyed, some member had been victimized during the period under study. Only 17 percent of the victims reported the crime to the police. Among the main reasons given, 44 percent thought it was pointless; 26 percent thought it a waste of time; 21 percent lacked proof or could not identify their aggressor; 15 percent were afraid to report the incident; and 8 percent indicated the paperwork was too tedious. The rate of reporting was slightly higher for violent as opposed to nonviolent crimes. See Mexican Health Foundation and World Bank, *Trends and Empirical Causes of Violent Crime in Mexico (Final Report)* (October 1999), 22, 24.

10. Rafael Ruiz Harrell, *Reforma, suplemento Enfoque*, March 28, 1999, 6, 8.

11. Rafael Ruiz Harrell, *Reforma*, April 8, 1999, 29.

12. Rafael Ruiz Harrell, *Reforma, suplemento Enfoque*.

13. Asamblea Legislativa del Distrito Federal, Comisión de Seguridad Pública, "Atlas delictivo de la Ciudad de México" (November 3, 1998), 1.

14. *Reforma*, January 31, 2000. Cited in Arzt, this volume.

15. Pablo Fajnzylber et al., *Determinants of Crime Rates in Latin America and the World: An Empirical Assessment* (Washington, D.C.: World Bank, 1998).

16. Ibid.

17. Ramos discusses this point in his chapter in this volume.

18. As discussed by Macías and Castillo and by Arzt, both in this volume.

19. A "state policy" is an unofficial designation that the policy carries more significance than ordinary legislation.

20. This was the Ley General que Establece las Bases de Coordinación del Sistema Nacional de Seguridad Pública (LG–SNSP). Our discussion draws on Macías and Castillo, this volume.

21. Ernesto Zedillo, "Sexto Informe de Gobierno" (September 1, 2000), 58–59.

22. Turbiville, this volume.

23. Ibid.

24. Note that "intelligence" does not appear in the agency's title.

25. *Suplemento* to *El Nacional*, August 28, 1998.

26. This section draws on Regalado Santillán, this volume.

27. Information provided by Horacio Cantú Díaz, president of the Asociación Mexicana de Sistemas Integrales de Seguridad Privada, in *La Jornada*, June 13, 1997.

28. "Las empresas de seguridad privada tienen un gran negocio," *La Jornada*, November 14, 1999.

29. Ibid.

30. Secretaría de Comercio y Fomento Industrial, Banco de Información Sectorial, Sistema de Información Empresarial. (Internet).

According to a study carried out by the committee on security of the Mexico City legislature, in 1998 there were an estimated 150,000 private security guards, more than the approximately 100,000 officers employed by the city's police department. "Las empresas de seguridad privada cuentan con una fuerza policiaca mayor que la contratada por la SSP," *La Jornada*, October 28, 1998 (internet edition).

31. See "La PGJDF y la SPP cumplen orden de aprehensión contra 53 elementos de cuerpos de seguridad," *La Jornada*, November 24, 1998; Francisco A. Morales, "Cae una banda de ladrones y narcos comandada por un elemento de seguridad privada," *Crónica*, January 9, 1999; and "Laboran en agencias de seguridad privada expolicías con antecedentes penales," *La Jornada*, January 8, 1999.

32. Godson and Kenney (this volume) describe one such experiment recently carried out along the U.S.–Mexico border.

33. The FBI reported that both violent and property crimes were down 7 percent in 1999 compared with the previous year. John Mintz, "Serious Crime Is Down for 8th Year," *Washington Post*, May 8, 2000; Peter Slevin, "Violent Crime Down 10 percent in 1999," *Washington Post*, August 28, 2000.

34. Bureau of Justice Statistics, "Crime and Victims Statistics," at www.ojp.usdoj.gov/bjs.cvict.htm.

35. Bureau of Justice Statistics, "Law Enforcement Statistics," at www.ojp.usdoj.gov/bjs/lawenf.htm.

36. Bureau of Justice Statistics, "Prosecution Statistics," at www.ojp.usdoj.gov/bjs/pros.htm.

37. Bureau of Justice Statistics, "Expenditure and Employment Statistics," at www.ojp.usdoj.gov/bjs/eande.htm.

38. Bureau of Justice Statistics, "Courts and Sentencing Statistics," at www.ojp.usdoj.gov/bjs/stssent.htm.

39. Bureau of Justice Statistics, "Corrections Statistics," at www.ojp.usdoj.gov/bjs/correct.htm.

40. Bureau of Justice Statistics, "Criminal Offender Statistics," at www.ojp.usdoj.gov/bjs/crimoff.htm.

41. ONDCP, "National Drug Control Strategy," May 1999, 59

42. ONDCP, "Drug Data Summary," April 1999, 1.

43. Ibid., 2.

44. Ibid., 4–5.

45. A Princeton Survey Research poll (January 1998) reported 80 percent of respondents "very concerned" about the drug problem, with 14 percent "somewhat concerned." A Hart & Teeter/NBC/Wall Street Journal survey (April 1998) found 71 percent believed the government is "doing too little" in regulating illegal drugs. A Fox News/Opinion Dynamics survey of May 1997 found 84 percent agreeing with the proposition that "the United States should get tougher with Mexico to try to stop the flow of drugs into this country." As to assigning blame for the drug problem, a Louis Harris and Associates poll (April 1999) found 43 percent assigned blame to U.S. consumption and 48 percent to Mexico's lax law enforcement.

46. ONDCP, *The National Drug Control Strategy: 1999 Annual Report*, 44, at www.whitehousedrugpolicy.gov/publications/policy/99ndcs/99ndcs.pdf.

47. Andresen and Farrell, this volume.

48. Ibid.

49. This section draws on Peter Andreas's essay in this volume.

50. Ibid.

51. Ibid.

52. Ibid.
53. Ibid.
54. Myron Levin, "Corrupt Dealers Expose Weakness in Gun Laws," *Los Angeles Times*, June 1, 2000.
55. U.S.–Mexico High Level Contact Group, Bi-National Firearms Trafficking Working Group, *Illegal Arms Trafficking Working Report* (August 2000), 1–2.
56. Zagaris, this volume.
57. See Rodrigo Labardini, "Developments in U.S.–Mexico Extradition," *International Enforcement Law Reporter* 16:4 (April 2000): 689.
58. Mary Lee Warren, Deputy Assistant Attorney General, *Statement before the Subcommittee on Criminal Justice, Drug Policy and Human Resources, Concerning the Importance of Extradition in International Crime Control* (Committee on Government Reform, U.S. House of Representatives, May 13, 1999).
59. Norma Jiménez, "Descartan ministros de la SCJN represalias de narcos," *Diario Milenio*, January 22, 2001, at www.milenio.com/frame.asp?url=http://www.mileniodiario.com.mx/index.asp.
60. Zagaris, this volume.
61. Ibid.
62. McDonald, this volume.
63. Alejandro Burgues et al., "Inseguridad pública en la frontera norte," *Ciudades* 40 (October–December 1998), cited in García, this volume.
64. Ibid.
65. McDonald, this volume.
66. Ibid.
67. William McDonald, "The Criminality of Mexican Immigrants," unpublished research note, October 9, 2000.
68. García, this volume.
69. Ibid.
70. Ibid.
71. Ramos, this volume.
72. García, this volume.
73. José M. Ramos (this volume) presents a useful discussion of the main twin-cities characteristics along the border.
74. Godson and Kenney, this volume.

PART 1

Challenges to Mexico

2

Mexico's National Public Security System: Perspectives for the New Millennium

Viviana Macías and Fernando Castillo

INTRODUCTION

Mexico entered the new millennium determined to reverse rising crime rates and to strengthen government agencies with public security responsibilities. In accord with these goals, Mexico has developed and begun implementing a national public security policy designed to satisfy three basic criteria. The first is to create a public policy where none previously existed and integrate all areas of government that relate to public security. The second is to fashion a judicial framework and regulatory system that fundamentally transform the work of the police. And the third is to restore the role of public security institutions in legitimizing the state and fostering the rule of law.[1]

A preliminary step, taken in December 1994, was the inclusion of justice and security reforms in the Mexican Constitution. Legislation passed in December 1995 identifies public security as a "state policy"—that is, as an essential and high-priority public policy. This legislation also specifies which authorities will participate, and it outlines the procedures for coordinating public security by jurisdiction and authority, effectively establishing the basis for the country's National Public Security System (SNSP).

The new SNSP model comprises the anticrime efforts of all police institutions and judicial authorities throughout Mexico in a fusion of forces that supports coordination of activities among uniformed preventive police, the judicial system, the penal system, and the citizenry. Guiding this judicial and operational coordination effort are the SNSP's executive secretariat and councils, a framework that also provides the system's theoretical and conceptual basis.

This chapter examines new ways to envision national public security, reviews the achievements of the new model, and outlines new perspectives on the important issue of public security.

WHAT GAVE RISE TO THE SNSP?

Prior to the late 1980s, matters of public security and law enforcement were low on the list of the Mexican state's priorities. The study of police organization and methods assumed new urgency, however, following the institutional crisis of government security agencies in the 1990s and the discovery that they were involved in the protection of drug traffickers. At the same time came the first visible signals of the deterioration of public security forces, including inadequate funding, poor organization and administration, low levels of professionalization, and an obsolete legal and administrative framework.[2]

Two separate efforts, by Presidents Miguel de la Madrid (1982–1988) and Carlos Salinas de Gortari (1988–1994), respectively, to make public security a national policy[3] resulted in the creation in 1994 of the National Office for Public Security Coordination.[4] During the Salinas administration, the government struggled to halt a national crime wave that included the assassinations of Cardinal Juan Jesús Posadas Ocampo and presidential candidate Luis Donaldo Colosio as well as the kidnappings of prominent bankers and businessmen. The judicial framework, adopted by executive decree, harmonized the powers of the Attorney General's Office (PGR) and the Ministries of Defense and the Navy in an administrative structure that reported directly to the president.

Despite this initiative, the government fell short of its aims, for two reasons. On the one hand, it failed to satisfy provisions of the Organic Law of Federal Public Administration regarding the jurisdiction and powers of the forces involved. On the other hand, the various agencies lacked the personnel and resources needed to formulate and support the work of the National Office for Public Security Coordination. Together, these circumstances meant that the National Office existed primarily on paper, without any real accomplishments

Given these antecedents, President Ernesto Zedillo (1994–2000) entered office advocating strongly for a public security system. He proposed a vision that would be both broader and more explicit than the Constitution's focus on the powers of municipalities to regulate public security and public transit. Under this systemic vision, outlined in reforms to constitutional articles 21 and 73, the concept of public security was expanded to encompass the preventive and judicial police, along with law enforcement and the judicial and penal systems. With these changes the government hoped to lay the groundwork for coordination efforts that could reap full advantage of the public security and justice powers vested in the state to strengthen the rule of law in Mexico.[5]

WHAT IS PUBLIC SECURITY?

According to Mexico's Constitution, "ensuring public security is the duty of the federal government, the Federal District, and the states and municipalities, according to their respective functions under the Constitution and as directed by law to establish a national system of public security."[6] This understanding of functions refers not only to Mexico's constitutional form of government but also to the federal and state penal systems and to the authorities included under the new systems concept.[7] Public security also gives recognition to the constitutional definition of Mexico "as a representative, democratic, federal republic, composed of free and sovereign states in everything related to their internal order, but united in a federation established according to the principles of this fundamental law."[8]

All of the aforementioned concepts are integrated within the General Law of the National Public Security System (LG–SNSP). This law regulates the constitutional function of public security and establishes the first steps to be taken in its implementation.

As noted earlier, one of most important incentives for the legal reforms was the institutional deterioration of government agencies responsible for enforcing laws related to crime prevention and the prosecution and punishment of criminals.[9] The police, for example, had become increasingly unable to deliver results, due both to low levels of professionalization and to corruption within the ranks.[10] Police operations tended to follow inefficient and informal norms and to respond primarily to the repressive and coercive needs of the political system. In the 1970s, when the corrosive influence of drug trafficking infiltrated the government structures created to fight the illegal drug trade, the institutional framework collapsed.[11] Moreover, this occurred in a context of increased criminal activity overall and a dangerous increase in organized crime's control over such activities.[12]

All of these factors converged at the beginning of the Zedillo administration to influence the incoming president's decision to design a public policy for security and justice issues, a policy structured within the framework of the Constitution.

WHAT IS THE NATIONAL PUBLIC SECURITY SYSTEM?

In the words of its primary architect, the National Public Security System "is an instrument to harness the efforts of the different spheres of government and society in the priority matter of public security. Its interlocking judicial, political, and social elements constitute the state's response to an emerging situation."[13] This new public policy integrates the powers of federal, state, and municipal authorities in police operations and combines the powers granted by law and by civil and criminal statutes to guide the work of courts, public prosecutors, and prisons.[14]

The General Law that structures the SNSP, contained in constitutional article 21, was the product of intense negotiations.[15] The Interior Ministry (Secretaría de Gobernación), which led the negotiations, invited representatives from various federal government institutions to participate, along with academics and legislators from Mexico's three major parties—the Institutional Revolutionary Party (PRI), National Action Party (PAN), and Party of the Democratic Revolution (PRD).

Their debates ranged widely, with participants stressing the need to avoid past failures on public security. In particular, they insisted that the new law not create additional authorities, that new mechanisms coordinate rather than control (out of respect for the sovereignty of state-level government), that the law adopt a systems concept of public security, that it emphasize a professional police force, that it privilege respect for human rights, and that it focus on crime prevention as well as punishment.

The LG–SNSP precisely defined the preventive focus of the new public security policy, as well as the various authorities' duties in carrying it out. In essence, by outlining the procedures for linking and coordinating powers, duties, and functions among all components of the system, the law integrates all of the necessary elements for a coherent public policy.[16] It establishes the system's collective coordinating bodies, including the National Public Security Council (CNSP, the top political coordinating body in the system), regional councils, state and Federal District councils, municipal and inter-city councils, crime prevention and rehabilitation councils, a law enforcement council, and the municipal participation council. As institutionally integrated within the National Public Security System, each of these parts contributes toward harmonizing, modernizing, and making more efficient the regulations, instruments, and actions that support public security.[17]

The coordinating bodies are classified as principals (councils) and auxiliaries (specialized commissions). Councils carry out coordination, regulation, planning, and supervision duties, while the commissions analyze, formulate proposals, and resolve issues regarding special subjects falling under their jurisdiction.

The CNSP is the highest coordinating forum within the system, and the most important national policy decisions are taken here. All authorities throughout Mexico must abide by the public security agreements reached by the CNSP. The CNSP's membership comprises the interior minister (presiding); the state governors and the mayor of Mexico City; the ministers of defense, the navy, and communications and transportation; the attorney general; and the executive secretary of the SNSP. This same authority structure is replicated at the state level, staffed by local officials who directly control public security functions and by the field office directors of the federal agencies that participate in the National Council.

The position of executive secretary within the SNSP (established under Article 17 of the LG–SNSP) was designed to guarantee an efficient channeling of agreements and resolutions to the various bodies within the SNSP and to ensure coordination of actions within the system.[18] The executive secretary administers information services and citizen protection and welfare services. He or she coordinates actions to promote national support for police academies and law enforcement as a career; harmonizes actions among the Federal Preventive Police (PFP) agencies; and promotes specialized studies and develops proposals for the further development of the SNSP. In effect, the executive secretary provides general oversight of SNSP activities.

The responsibilities of the national-level executive secretary are replicated at a more regional level in the responsibilities of the executive secretaries in the state councils. These individuals serve as key facilitators for the National Council and as pivotal coordination points in the National Public Security System.

WHAT HAS THE SNSP ACCOMPLISHED?

The implementation of Mexico's new public security policy passed through three stages prior to September 1999. The first stage began when the LG–SNSP went into effect in December 1995 and ended with the third meeting of the National Public Security Council in May 1997. This phase involved refining the SNSP's working strategy by separating it into four component parts: (1) formalizing coordination among state actors, (2) developing public security administrative policies with efficient, high-quality guidelines, (3) structuring and fully utilizing the capacities of public security forces, and (4) modifying existing perceptions of public security by increasing the professionalization of institutions and officials.

When Francisco Labastida was named minister of the interior in 1998, the public security focus shifted strongly to crime fighting. Escalating rates of crime, especially federal offenses such as drug trafficking, were harming Mexico's public image at home and abroad, despite the armed forces' strong support to law enforcement.[19]

To counter the crime trend, prosecutors' offices received additional personnel and equipment, along with updated technology. This second stage in the implementation of the SNSP formally began with the National Crusade against Crime in August 1998.[20] The Crusade attributed the growth in crime to the following factors: (1) insufficient law enforcement personnel and judges; (2) poor training of law enforcement personnel; (3) low salaries and poor benefits for workers in law enforcement, in combination with these workers' vulnerability to being corrupted by criminal elements; (4) technologically unsophisticated anticrime information and intelligence systems, as well as outdated communications and investigation tactics; (5) inadequate financial resources; (6) a mismatch between current problems and the country's legal framework and penalties; (7) insufficient coordination among security agencies; and (8) a low level of public involvement.

In response, the Crusade set for itself the following objectives:[21]

- Review the quality of law enforcement personnel. Excise and punish those who violate the law, and provide better training, salaries, and benefits to those remaining.
- Double the number of judicial police, investigators, and technicians in the Public Ministry (Ministerio Público) to improve the system's coverage and capacity to respond to crime.
- Develop a communications, information, and intelligence system using cutting-edge technology and encrypted channels, repeating stations, microwave and satellite technology, and fiber optics. Using appropriate cartography and vectorization, create a 066 emergency system that would store data on weapons, police, and crime, as well as information on current arrest warrants.
- Reinforce equipment and infrastructure.
- Strengthen coordination between the branches of government and federal institutions.
- Improve the legal framework and review current penalties for specific crimes.
- Regulate and supervise private security services, including their registration, personnel, and equipment.
- Promote citizen participation.

The National Crusade against Crime pledged to show results within two years of its creation, by which time it anticipated it would have installed a nationwide communications network, upgraded police forces, and developed intelligence systems for police operations. The Crusade gained strength with the addition of two new divisions within the Interior Ministry—the Undersecretariat of Public Security and the General Directorate for the Regulation and Supervision of Public Security—which augmented the Ministry's involvement in coordinating joint police operations. These additions gave the SNSP more weight in the Cabinet and facilitated its communications with state and municipal governments, which, in turn, enabled the SNSP to combat crime more directly and more efficiently.

Consistent with this focus, the Interior Ministry was assigned a more active role in countering drug trafficking. And from this followed the decision to create the Federal Preventive Police,[22] whose mission is to develop criminal intelligence, investigate the origins and basic structures of organized crime, and place anticrime responses under a single command to avoid situations in which jurisdictional limits might conflict with functional and operational responsibilities.

The third stage in the SNSP's implementation began with Diódoro Carrasco's appointment as interior minister in September 1999. Carrasco maintained the focus and strategies of his predecessor while further strengthening prosecuting agencies and the PFP.

WHAT ADVANCES WERE MADE?

The first difficulty that surfaced during the early stages of making the SNSP operational was the paucity of available information on crime in Mexico as a whole. What little information the Interior Ministry had in hand was of limited use because differences in methodology prevented comparison between data sets.[23]

State and municipal governments also lacked systematic, uniform methods to quantify and evaluate police work and the work of their own institutions. In almost no state were uniform criteria used to quantify crime rates by type of crime or type of preliminary investigation. In addition, analyses focused almost completely on transit services and the preventive police, failing to take into account any criteria to evaluate professionalization, salaries, or promotions within police forces. This situation was complicated by the vast contrasts between judicial frameworks from state to state and from municipality to municipality, and by similar inter-state and inter-municipality differences regarding police duties. Moreover, there was strong reluctance at the state level to provide whatever information did exist on police activities, prosecutors' offices, or preliminary investigations, purportedly because of these organizations' need for confidentiality and security. (The Interior Ministry had better data on the penal system because it is under federal government control. Although much of this information was stored in paper files and manual information systems—hence time-consuming to retrieve—the data were highly reliable.)

To resolve these problems, a major effort was made during the first and second stages of the SNSP's implementation to consolidate existing information, define a work plan, and set an appropriate budget. The first comprehensive analysis of public security was presented in draft form to the National Council, and its members were asked to respond.

The document was amended to reflect the members' input, and the National Program for Public Security (PNSP) was formally presented to the National Council on June 7, 1996, and published in the *Diario Oficial* on July 18, 1996.[24] After the Joint Finance Commission of the SNSP reviewed this document and evaluated budgetary requirements for public security nationwide, negotiations were launched to obtain appropriations from federal sources.[25]

The 1997 federal budget authorized 1.9 billion pesos (about US$200 million) for public security, supplemented by 500 million pesos in state contributions. Governors and members of the Joint Finance Commission agreed on a single formula, based on information provided by the states, for distributing these resources.[26] Beginning in 1998, a special fund was created to support federal and state governments by managing the resources earmarked for public security (see table 2.1 for resource distribution in 1998 and 1999). And also beginning in 1998, municipalities began to receive funds directly from the federal government to support their public security costs, as part of Mexico's general decentralization of resources and governmental authority.

In the seventh meeting of the National Council, Interior Minister (and council president) Diódoro Carrasco and the executive secretary of the SNSP made the following points regarding Mexico's public security challenges and achievements:

- Crime rates dropped by 7 percent in 1998. However, high-impact social crimes rose an average of 11 percent.
- The incidence of crime was 14 criminal acts per 1,000 inhabitants.
- Surveys had found that, by state, between 20 and 66 percent of the population identified insecurity as Mexico's foremost problem.
- Mexico employed 24,069 judicial police; 6,550 agents from the Public Ministry; 3,548 technicians; and 88,294 state preventive police. This total of 122,461 persons does not include municipal preventive police, auxiliary police, or prison wardens.
- Of this total, only 19,920 judicial police, 5,480 agents from the Public Ministry, and 2,960 investigators had been evaluated and trained.
- On examinations, 8.8 percent of these workers scored very high, 75.1 percent achieved a satisfactory score, and results for 16.3 percent were unsatisfactory.
- The 1999 federal budget for public security was 9.2 billion pesos, up 160 percent from 1998 and 270 percent from 1997.
- Thirty percent of the installation work on the national communications network had been completed.

- Construction of 47,523 prison cells was programmed for 1998–2000.
- Purchases in 1999 would include 4,500 vehicles, primarily for law enforcement agencies; 7,900 weapons for judicial and preventive police; more than 340,000 pieces of riot gear; and 14 helicopters.
- Construction was under way on five regional police academies and two police training centers.[27]

Table 2.1 **SNSP Budget, 1998–1999** (millions of current U.S. dollars)

Concept	Spent in 1998	Allocated for 1999	Real Variation (%)
INCOME			
Federal resources			
FASP	218.4	488.0	101.9
Federal agencies	79.5	267.9	204.6
Subtotal, federal	297.9	755.9	129.3
State resources	84.7	184.9	97.1
Total federal and state income	382.9	941.0	122.2
EXPENDITURES			
Federal and state resources intended for the states and the Federal District	303.3	672.9	100.6
Professionalization	41.9	39.5	-14.9
Coverage and response capacity	-	80.5	n.a.
Weapons, equipment, and technology	155.5	338.0	96.4
Construction and reinforcements of penitentiary infrastructure and public security	87.8	198.7	104.4
Coordination efforts	-	7.9	n.a.
Social communication and community participation	-	7.9	n.a.
Emergency legal situations	17.8	0.0	n.a.

Source: Interior Ministry, taken from the Fifth State of the Nation address, Federal Executive Branch, Mexico, September 1999.

WHAT PROBLEMS REMAINED?

Both President Zedillo and Interior Minister Carrasco acknowledged progress in the areas of updating penal codes, evaluating personnel, and equipping police forces with improved budgets, information technology, and communications tools. However, they also noted that the results were insufficient,[28] largely because the integration foreseen in the SNSP had not yet been able to penetrate all institutional structures.

It had been noted throughout the Salinas and Zedillo administrations that public security had to be envisioned as a system that begins with the reduction and prevention of risk factors for crime and ends with former prisoners' reincorporation into society. The prior emphasis on *reacting* to crime rather than preventing it—that is, focusing exclusively on the role of law enforcement agencies in public security—had failed. This approach had tended to encourage public prosecutors and police officials to downgrade crime prevention and instead to employ the reaction to crime as an ill-directed strategy to reduce crime.

The rationale for creating the Federal Preventive Police affirmed that "the guarantee of security cannot be limited to coercive state force. It is indispensable to support prevention. The use of preventive forces can efficiently achieve a reduction in crime by preventing violations of the law. In the criminal wave engulfing the country, public security requires an integrated focus and complementary programs to support these goals."[29]

These criteria reflect the spirit of Article 3 of the LG–SNSP, which states:

> In accord with Article 21 of the Constitution and in support of this law, public security is the responsibility of the State, which is invested with the role of safeguarding integrity and human rights, as well as preserving freedom, order, and public peace.
>
> The appropriate authorities will achieve the objective of public security through the prevention, prosecution, and punishment of violations and crimes, as well as the reincorporation of the criminal into society.
>
> The State will address the causes of crime and anti-social conduct, and will develop policies, programs, and actions to promote cultural and civic values in society that foment respect for the law.
>
> These objectives will be achieved by the preventive police, the Public Ministry, the courts, and prison staff; by the enforcement of penalties and the treatment of minors who break the law; by persons tasked with protecting strategic national sites and services; and by all authorities who can

> reasonably contribute, directly or indirectly, to the enforcement of this law.

Clearly, this vision of public security is broad, ambitious, and complex, but such a vision is crucial for putting together a public policy that accords with Mexico's constitutional structure.[30] Only in this way can state and municipal public security systems be integrated into the federal environment, to create a coordinated system capable of fighting crime.

The vision and practices that existed prior to the passage of the General Law still persist among some public security authorities, particularly in state and municipal environments. Police forces tend to undervalue the importance of information gathering for planning police operations and for assessing crime trends and enforcement performance, with obvious impacts on police organization, administration, and operations. Up to now, police operations have relied on "street smarts" gained through police work, and these are only passed on selectively to co-workers. These customs provide a unique historical and cultural memory, but this deeply rooted system of traditional habits must give way if the new SNSP model of public security is to succeed.

This fact was apparent in 1994, when President Zedillo noted:

> It is crucial that we invest in public security. But it is equally essential that the funds invested are accompanied by a scrupulous, honest, and efficient use of these resources.... I propose a radical change in the administration of public security, using efficiency as a basic criterion. Let us utilize the experience and knowledge of our highly qualified public administrators in the area of public security. There is no reason that public security forces should not rely on an efficient and modern administration of human, material, and financial resources.[31]

Even though much attention and public funding have been invested in public security, public security forces are in a weakened condition, and this makes it hard to combat crime efficiently (and to see results) simply by increasing allocations. Bottlenecks prevent the efficient use of budgetary resources that have already been allocated. There is also the problem of a shortage of trained personnel to work in the administrative and financial departments of public agencies responsible for public security, law enforcement, and the penal system. The result is that financial departments, state budget offices, and public security and law enforcement agencies sometimes appear to speak different languages.

All of these factors hinder the adoption of the new conceptual model and its operative methodology, delaying the day when police work is guided by criteria of quality and efficiency. This situation argues for a stepped-up effort to improve the administration of public security. Improved administration would enable the government to prevent a situation in which adding personnel and resources would only ratchet up police corruption and impunity, generating an even deeper institutional crisis than the one that currently exists.

Institution building is the best way to make police forces more efficient and more trustworthy at all levels. The same is true for all federal, state, and municipal agencies with a public security role. Only through institution building will the financial resources allocated for public security be used to their fullest potential. Public security can be strengthened as public policy only if administrative controls and assessments are in place to demonstrate that government funds are being used to produce results.

The SNSP's greatest achievements have come in identification, information, and communications systems. These systems will strengthen police work by giving police improved crime-fighting tools. However, this outcome could be hindered if there is no concurrent effort to study crime and its prevention. Updated statistics on crime by state, type of crime, and/or the presence of organized crime are not available from state investigative agencies or the Attorney General's Office. Also important is information on a key national crime problem—the rising incidence of violence in criminal acts. Violence has long been an element in federal crimes such as drug and weapons trafficking, but there has been a recent surge in the use of firearms in street muggings, corporate burglaries, and carjackings.

Perhaps the foremost public security challenge is to halt organized crime's infiltration of government agencies, something visible in most police ranks in Mexico. Organized crime—ranging from the petty theft of items peddled through street vendors to the sophisticated financial fraud perpetrated through banks and the stock market—is all too often "protected" thanks to payments to officials or through membership in large crime syndicates.

All of these factors have undermined the average Mexican citizen's view of security. The public's perception of insecurity as one of the most serious problems that Mexico currently faces will present a formidable challenge to the Mexican state in coming years.[32]

CONCLUSION

The SNSP is a highly appropriate state response to the crime trend that is jeopardizing public security in Mexico. The SNSP has managed to consolidate as one of the nation's most important public policies. It has established a base and a constitutional mandate, generated regulatory laws and new criminal laws, created a national program, and obtained resources to carry out policies that are national in scope and that integrate the efforts of the three branches of government. In addition, the SNSP has the power to pull together state governors, law enforcement agencies, the new Federal Preventive Police, and federal and state interior ministries to coordinate the responsibilities of police, Public Ministry agents, and prison wardens.

Although the challenges are considerable and the consolidation of a public security policy will take time and resources, the SNSP provides a strong foundation on which to build. There is wide support for the SNSP among public officials, including those recently appointed, and this broad consensus bodes well for the further strengthening of the public security model.

Nevertheless, from the perspective of the general citizenry, the new public policy has not yet translated into tangible benefits. Organized crime's formidable impacts on Mexico's economic and political systems and on the nation's foreign policy will help validate the continued implementation of public security policy to transform the current situation. Institution building and professionalization offer the best means to transform the police force and the rest of the nation's security agencies, but such institution building must proceed at a pace that allows current projects to mature if Mexico is to avoid the errors of previous failed antidrug initiatives.

Institution building must be accompanied by continuity in basic policies. The creation of a career civil service would prevent breaks in policies and protect against political pressure to produce quick results in a crisis that is, by nature, long term.

Mexico's antidrug strategy has yielded good results, but this has been accomplished at high cost due to the involvement of the armed forces.[33] Public security forces, and especially police forces, should gradually relieve the military of their current crime-fighting responsibilities. Public confidence can be maintained if the police adopt as their norm the institutional strength, professionalism, and service ethic that the army has displayed.

To achieve a thorough modernization of public security in Mexico requires amending the Constitution. Constitutional reforms would pave the way for instituting policies to fight drug traffickers with all the force of the state, revamping the Attorney General's Office and the judicial police, simplifying the prosecution of local or federal crimes, and streamlining the police system. Of these reforms, perhaps the most urgent are simplifying the judicial system and unifying the police system. The most significant challenge, however, will continue to be the fight against drug trafficking, which should receive top priority. All of these efforts could be supported by the SNSP.

An important footnote to this discussion is that professionalization, citizen participation, and crime prevention should not lead to a situation in which the fight against crime creates an authoritarian state and impedes the democratic forces at work in society. In the end, public security is intended to protect citizens, not to protect governments from their citizens.

POSTSCRIPT

Several important developments took place in the Mexican political system between fall 1999 and summer 2001, when this chapter was written. President Vicente Fox introduced important changes beginning in December 2000. He created the Ministry of Public Security, headed by Alejandro Gertz Manero, and assigned to it the Federal Preventive Police and the National Public Security System. Police matters are no longer handled by the Interior Ministry, which now focuses on issues dealing with political parties, Congress, and intergovernmental relations. Fox also created a National Coordinating Office for Order and Respect within the Office of the President to oversee security matters, specifically with respect to the new Ministry of Public Security and the Ministries of Defense and the Navy, as well as the Attorney General's Office.

As is the norm in the Mexican political system, the change of presidential administration meant the end of virtually all policies of the preceding government. In public security matters, however, the centralizing stamp that Interior Minister Labastida put on the security apparatus has remained, even though allocations of federal and state funds to this centralized vision have yet to yield the desired fruit. Inefficiency continues to characterize public security agencies' management of human, material, financial, and technological resources. The police continue to be guided by "street smarts" and have yet to generate the intelligence and planning indicators needed to permit more effective performance. Citizen participation remains a distant goal throughout most of the country. The national communications network and national telephone emergency service, promised in 1998, are not yet in operation. And drug trafficking continues to be the force driving public security concerns at the national level (which explains why an army general was appointed as attorney general).

Despite the recent changes in Mexico's political system, the evaluation of the National Public Security System presented in this chapter remains valid. In the area of public security, the Mexican state today has instruments for institutional transformation that it lacked six years ago. A reformed judicial infrastructure and budgetary support provide the bases for a long-term public policy. A new national police and a new sense of federalism now exist and should be further strengthened. A municipal-level vision that emphasizes local needs forms a core element of effective public security policy.

The administration of Mexico's public security policy needs to be made more professional, incorporating suitable methods for program evaluation that include appropriate indicators for quality and efficiency, all aimed toward a strategy of real change. In times of budgetary austerity, squandering public money is unacceptable to both society and government. This is why the management of public security has to be opened to professionals in public and private administration. The management of public security should not be left to the regular police, whether federal, state, or local. In sum, there will be no change in public security without administrative modernization.

It is possible to reduce the levels of public insecurity in Mexico. The bases on which to build are adherence to the policy coordination established in the SNSP General Law and the institutionalization of national, state, and municipal policies. These bases can support professionalization of the police and increase efficiency in the justice ministries, the courts, and the penal system. Coordination can help fulfill the functions of intelligence gathering and investigation, and thus support the country's anticrime efforts.

Notes

Translated by Ruth Urry.

1. Institutions, as understood in this essay, are public agencies that carry out government policies and programs with public resources.

2. See "Programa Nacional de Seguridad Pública 1995–2000," *Diario Oficial*, July 18, 1996.

3. These were under the direction, respectively, of National Program Coordinator Ignacio Morales Lechuga (1985) and National Public Security Coordinator Arsenio Farell Cubillas (1994).

4. *Diario Oficial*, April 26, 1994.

5. Amendments to Article 21 stipulate that federal, state, and municipal governments, as well as the Federal District, are constitutionally obligated to become integrated into a National Public Security System. Amendments to Article 73 facilitate congressional involvement in this issue area. It is worth reiterating that these measures did not exist before 1994.

6. Article 21 of the *Constitución Política de los Estados Unidos Mexicanos* (Mexico City: Secretaría de Gobernación, 1997). This definition marks a point of departure for Mexico's constitutional framework and should be understood in light of the country's judicial tradition. In most Latin American nations, descended from a Roman legal philosophy, the most important aspects of society should refer to a constitutional source.

7. Articles 10 through 21 of the Mexican Constitution lay out judicial and administrative functions, and identify the appropriate authorities to provide

individual security guarantees. Article 21 draws from all of these articles to establish the National Public Security System.

8. Article 40, *Constitución Política de los Estados Unidos Mexicanos.*

9. An analysis of this situation is found in "Programa Nacional de Seguridad Pública 1995–2000" and in the speech by former interior minister Francisco Labastida at the inauguration of the National Crusade against Crime, August 28, 1998.

10. One can find extensive analyses of this problem in the *Plan Nacional de Desarrollo 1995–2000* (Mexico City: Poder Ejecutivo Federal, 1995), in the "Programa Nacional de Seguridad Pública 1995–2000," and in the National Crusade. It also appears in President Zedillo's campaign speeches, especially his statements on justice and security.

11. This was the case with the Federal Security Directorate (DFS) and, later, the Federal Judicial Police (PJF), from whose ranks came many drug traffickers. Another stage of the crisis appeared during Arturo Durazo Moreno's administration of the Mexico City police (1976–1982), when corruption in police circles reached its highest levels.

12. Despite the lack of detailed information on crime rates by state or type of crime during the first half of the 1990s, by 1995 it was possible to integrate studies about the prevalence of organized crime in federal and local entities for kidnappings, bank robberies, drug crimes, and arms trafficking. In 1995, crime statistics began to be compiled at the state level using information from state prosecutors.

13. Juan Ramiro Robledo Ruiz, prologue to *Introducción al estudio del Sistema Nacional de Seguridad Pública,* edited by José G. Sandoval Ulloa (Mexico City: Secretaría de Gobernación, 1997).

14. According to Alejandro Medina and José Mejía Lira, eds., *El control de la implantación de la política pública* (Mexico City: Plaza and Valdez, 1987), public policies are what the government chooses to do or not to do. This refers to actions and not to what the government says it will do. There are five stages: creation, formulation, decision, implementation, and evaluation of results.

15. The most thorough study of the LG–SNSP is found in Robledo Ruiz, *Introducción al estudio del Sistema Nacional de Seguridad Pública.*

16. According to Medina and Lira (*El control de la implantación de la política pública,* 18), "state involvement under any definition is minimally constituted by (1) the acknowledgment of a public problem, (2) the definition of the nature of the problem, (3) a diagnosis of at least some of the causes of the problem and the proposal of some measures to solve or mitigate it, (4) the definition of a solution or a general objective, (5) the definition of certain objectives or strategies to achieve the general goal, and (6) the supervision of the execution of the strategy, which could be achieved by the same state."

17. The National Council has developed basic rules and procedures for the functioning of the National Public Security System. These rules and procedures have been adopted by local councils with a view to promoting effective operation of the National Office for Public Security Coordination.

18. Mayolo Medina Linares was executive secretary in February 2000. According to modifications to internal regulations in the Interior Ministry in 1998,

the executive secretary is a decentralized actor falling under the authority of the Interior Ministry, which coordinates daily with the undersecretary of public security, even if the executive secretary is not in the direct chain of command.

19. Roberto Zavala and Jesús Murillo Karam served, during different periods, as undersecretary of public security at the Interior Ministry. Alfonso Ontiveros and Mayolo Medina served as SNSP executive secretary. Omar Fayad served as the first commissioner of the Federal Preventive Police.

20. See www.seguridadpublica.gob.mx/phps/InstSideMenuV2.php@MenuEstrategiaAcciones&IdDocumento.html.

21. For a detailed analysis, see the speeches of President Zedillo and Interior Minister Francisco Labastida at the ceremony inaugurating the National Crusade against Crime, *El Universal*, August 29,1998.

22. The creation of the PFP had been contemplated since 1994, and it was approved as part of the new crime-fighting strategy. However, an opportune moment to implement it did not appear until Interior Minister Labastida determined that it was fundamentally important for the Interior Ministry to have its own police force.

23. It has been suggested that the Interior Ministry may have discarded information gathered in the past that would have helped create an overview of the current nature and distribution of crime in Mexico.

24. As noted previously, a similar national program was proposed in 1985 but was not implemented for a variety of reasons.

25. The Joint Finance Commission, created at the first meeting of the National Council, comprises five governors, the mayor of Mexico City, and the heads of the PGR and the Interior Ministry. The working documents prepared by the Commission reflect budgetary information contributed by other members of the National Council, as well as by state-level officials, law enforcement officers, and municipal presidents.

26. The formula took account of demographic factors, territorial area, crime rates, defined goals, and particular problems with organized crime, drug trafficking, kidnappings, bank robberies, and so on.

27. *El Universal*, August 19, 1999.

28. Ernesto Zedillo Ponce de León, *Quinto Informe de Gobierno*, September 1, 1999, and the speech by Diódoro Carrasco at the seventh meeting of the National Public Security Council, August 1999.

29. Cited in the speech outlining the reasons for establishing the Federal Preventive Police. At http://www.pfp.gob.mx/general/asps/fraMain.asp.

30. This assertion was confirmed by Samuel González, Ernesto López Portillo, and José Arturo Yáñez, who also noted that "the current state structure hinders a team vision of public security." *Seguridad pública en México: problemas, perspectivas y propuestas* (Mexico City: Coordinación de Humanidades, Universidad Nacional Autónoma de México, 1994), 175.

31. Speech by then PRI presidential candidate Ernesto Zedillo at the "National Forum on Justice and Security," Guadalajara, July 14, 1994.

32. González, López Portillo, and Yáñez, *Seguridad pública en México.*

---

33. Between 1989 and 1999, the government seized 362 tons of cocaine, 1,902 kilos of heroin, and more than 41,000 illegal weapons. It also arrested 147,875 individuals linked to drug trafficking. The Attorney General's Office spent 5.2 billion pesos to achieve these results. Zedillo, *Quinto Informe de Gobierno.*

3

Inefficiency at the Service of Impunity: Criminal Justice Organizations in Mexico

Guillermo Zepeda Lecuona

This chapter presents five performance standards that are useful in evaluating the effectiveness of institutions charged with prosecuting crime in Mexico. Empirical evidence presented in the analysis of these standards shows that organizational inertia distorts the formal objectives and legal mandates that were designed to guide these institutions in prevailing over the de facto interests of groups with which they interact during the criminal justice process.

THE MEXICAN CRIMINAL JUSTICE SYSTEM

We can simplify our discussion of the interaction of actors in the public security and justice arenas by dividing the Mexican criminal justice process into four stages: (1) public safety (crime prevention, police patrols); (2) the pursuit of justice (once a crime has been alleged, the Procuracy (Procuraduría de Justicia), assisted by police and crime experts, launches an investigation to support a legal suit); (3) the dispensing of justice (a judge reviews the prosecutor's case, issues arrest warrants, and determines if evidence for probable cause exists; after evidentiary hearings and the entering of pleas, the accused is either convicted or cleared of charges); and (4) incarceration or return to society (the set of organizations charged with implementing and administering sentences). The executive branch administers all stages but the third, which is administered by the court.

When agents from the Procuracy, an authority charged with both the investigation and prosecution of crime, receive a crime report (following the filing of a complaint), they begin a preliminary investigation (*averiguación previa*). If this investigation uncovers probable cause[1] and physical evidence ("a group of objective and external elements that constitute the materiality of an act that the law deems to be a crime"),[2] the prosecutor can ask a judge for an arrest warrant.

A suspect can be apprehended without an arrest warrant under two conditions. First, if a suspect is discovered during the commission of a crime or trying to flee (in flagrante delicto), any citizen may make the arrest, as long as the suspect is delivered immediately to the authorities. Second, in an "urgent case"—that is, when the crime is serious, when there is a risk that the suspect will flee, and when the "hour, place, or circumstance" make it impossible to obtain an arrest warrant (Article 16 of the Mexican Constitution)—the Procuracy can make an arrest without a warrant. In both cases, however, a judge must verify that the arrest was made in accord with constitutional requirements, and the suspect must be freed or the case remanded to a judge within forty-eight hours (ninety-six hours in organized crime cases).

Once a prisoner appears before a judge, the judge has a constitutionally mandated limit of seventy-two hours to review the prisoner's deposition to determine his or her legal status. The judge then issues a writ of constitutional limitations (*auto de término constitucional*), specifying whether the prisoner should be charged and sent to trial or freed for lack of evidence. If an arraignment (*auto de formal prisión*) or trial is ordered, evidence will continue to be heard from both the accused and the plaintiff.[3] The judge then decrees the end of the presentation of evidence, and the parties make closing statements. The judge subsequently declares the accused not guilty or remands him or her to prison.

The Mexican criminal justice system has two jurisdictions: the federal and the local (the latter is frequently—and incorrectly—called *fuero común*). Which jurisdiction has authority to prosecute a case depends on the nature of the crime and the suspects involved. This chapter focuses primarily on the procedures and performance of the local organizations at the second stage of the criminal justice process, during which the Procuracy carries out preliminary investigations and delivers findings to a judge. Because 95 percent of all crime in Mexico falls within the local jurisdiction and because local offices interact more closely with the public they serve, local offices shoulder a heavier workload, and they approach it with relatively fewer resources than their federal-level counterparts.[4]

Performance Standards in Mexico's Criminal Justice System

The organizations charged with criminal investigation and prosecution might be viewed as constituting an "open system." They both influence and are influenced by other factors in the criminal justice system and in society in general. In other words, social context (unemployment, social inequality) and other actors (criminal groups, police departments, private security organizations) affect the performance of prosecutorial departments—as does the effectiveness of the departments themselves—in terms of the scope of their investigations and their success in apprehending suspected criminals. Similarly, the conduct of persons associated with the Procuracy can affect other organizations in the criminal justice system (for example, an arrest made unconstitutionally or a flawed preliminary investigation will influence the outcome of a case that goes to trial). Moreover, the internal structures and procedures of the various organizations within the criminal justice system can provoke coordination and communication problems as the interests and agendas of the prosecuting attorneys, crime experts, police, social workers, psychologists, and administrative personnel collide.

Given this complex situation, how do we judge the Procuracy's effectiveness? And what do we mean by "effectiveness"? Is it effectiveness vis-à-vis other departments in the criminal justice system (measured by the degree to which crime is prevented or the rights of the accused are respected, and so forth)? Effectiveness for whom? Effectiveness measured in terms of institutional values and goals? The complexity and plurality of proposals and objectives defy comprehension.

There are three types of goals or objectives for organizations: formal, informal, and de facto.[5] Formal goals are those outlined in an organization's statutes or mission statement. Informal goals are those dictated by tradition, custom, or oral agreement. Finally, de facto goals are those that an organization's members construct as they go about their daily work. De facto goals generally appear as a result of employees' operational needs, or perhaps as anomalies derived from personal interest or erroneous interpretations of the organization's mission, combined with poor supervision. De facto objectives can distort or contradict the organization's official or formal mission, and they may even be illegal.

The powers and duties of the procuracies, as public service organizations, are defined by constitutional provisions and Mexico's legal framework. To facilitate a discussion of these duties as performance standards, they can be divided into four sets of formal/legal responsibilities and a fifth objective, related to informal motivations and expectations.

The first set of responsibilities includes prosecution of crimes (Article 21 of the Constitution). Procurators:

- receive reports of crimes committed and examine crime scenes (several articles in the penal code, circulars);
- gather material evidence of the crime and investigate the culpability of the suspect (Article 16 of the Constitution and the penal code);[6] and
- arrest suspects (Article 16 and statutes/codes).

Second, acting as the plaintiff in criminal proceedings (Articles 16 and 19), procurators comply with legal requirements to show probable cause before the court. The elements that fall under this rubric are:

- judicial independence;
- writs of constitutional limitation (Article 19); and
- sentencing (Article 14).

Third, the objectives of the Procuracy that pertain to crime victims (Articles 8, 17, and 21 of the Constitution; various statutes in the penal code and law) include:

- providing access to justice;
- assisting crime victims (with legal aid, case processing, psychological counseling); and
- ensuring the safety of victims, witnesses, and their families.

Fourth are the objectives relating to the rule of law, due process, and human rights (individual and procedural guarantees, Articles 14, 16, 17, 19, 20, and 22) and involving the interaction of criminal justice system officials with the general public.

Fifth are the informal goals, which are linked to the criminal justice system's political and social context. These include:

- portrayals of the criminal justice system's services in the media and public perceptions; and
- citizen demands for public safety, which carries over into competition among political parties and the actions of civil servants responsible for prosecuting criminal acts.

Strictly speaking, so many diverse—though not necessarily incompatible—goals in practice cause conflict and friction among the departments and agencies within the procuracies. Each section privileges its own objectives to the detriment of the others' goals. Competition exists with other social actors in general and with the criminal justice system in particular.

Ideally, criminal justice organizations should maximize their performance across all fronts without diminishing effectiveness in any one area. In other words, their goal should be to solve the greatest possible number of cases, but not at the cost of harming victims or the rights of the accused. Actors in the criminal justice system must recognize the need to integrate objectives, and the leadership should devise mechanisms to communicate this consensus to all branches of the system and to ensure that all departments and actors are working to advance the set of objectives as a whole.

The tensions that are set up by the diversity of goals should prove beneficial as a counterweight and control among departments and agencies in the justice system and among the actors who work within them. They may even increase efficiency by making the system more adaptable to societal change.[7]

Friction among formal objectives is commonplace in justice systems around the world. Nevertheless, most contradictions and performance inefficiencies within procuracies tends to arise from conflicts between formal and informal goals and, even more, a lack of congruence between formal and de facto objectives. The following section presents empirical evidence for each of the five standards outlined above.

"OKAY, WHO'S GOT THE CASE FILE?" CRIMINAL INVESTIGATION AND PROSECUTION

This section analyzes the procuracies' efficiency in taking crime reports, conducting preliminary investigations, and executing arrest warrants. Here lies the Achilles' heel of the criminal justice system. In Mexico, the enormous demand for legal services creates a workload that swamps the system and diminishes prosecutors' ability to respond and the quality of service they can deliver. The excessive workload, combined with the ample discretion accorded to criminal justice authorities, creates conditions for corruption in legal agencies throughout Mexico.

In Mexico, there is one Procuracy agent for every 16,200 individuals over twelve years of age.[8] (This is the age group used in studies and surveys of crime victims, because it closely approximates the age of potential victims and consumers of services provided by criminal justice institutions. The complete figures report one agent for every 23,415 individuals.) On average, each agent received 389 complaints in 1997, and those crimes were added to those still under investigation from prior years. There is marked state-to-state variation in workload: in 1997, on average, an agent in Yucatán received 1,955 complaints; in Baja California, 1,383; and in the state of México, 1,143. On the low end are Oaxaca and Sinaloa, with an average of 171 and 111 complaints, respectively.[9]

Although the number of complaints received declined almost 8 percent in 1998, there were 75 percent more crime reports in 1998 than in 1991 (see figure 3.1). It is important to note here that the number of reports authorities receive is much smaller than the number of crimes committed. In urban areas of Mexico at least,[10] reported crimes have declined as a proportion of crimes committed. In September 1999, a survey in Mexico City revealed that only 24 percent of crimes committed had been reported.[11] In this chapter, we use the proportion of crimes that are reported as a variable to measure the effectiveness of local procuracies in handling the cases brought to them by the public. During 1997, there were 2,276,216 preliminary investigations under way in local procuracies. Of these, 42 percent (964,582) were investigations begun during 1996. (Cases that were opened in 1995 or earlier and are yet to be completed are not included.)[12]

Figure 3.1 **Complaints Received by Local Procuracies (1000s)**

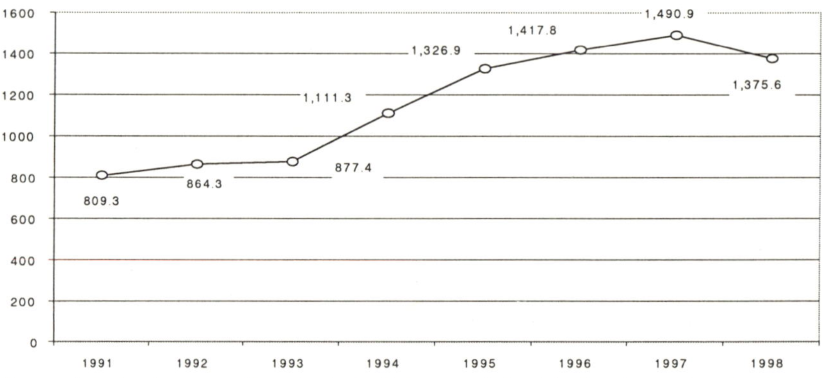

Source: Interior Ministry (Secretaría de Gobernación), with data from state-level procuracies.

The filing of a crime report initiates a preliminary investigation to gather facts and determine the crime's legal status. Investigators visit the crime scene, collect witnesses' statements, and call in experts to determine whether the two constitutionally mandated elements for initiating a criminal proceeding are present. On average, of every one hundred cases reported, seventy result in an investigation (see figure 3.2). In forty-seven of these seventy, on average, preliminary findings fail to prove that a crime has occurred or do not uncover probable cause, and the case is filed pending receipt of additional evidence or the expiration of the statute of limitations. That is, the right of the Procuracy to ask the court to try the case lapses. As shall be demonstrated below, this is the outcome more often than not. In only twenty-three of every one hundred cases are full investigations concluded (and, as we shall also see, concluding an investigation does not always imply that society's expectations for justice have been met).

Figure 3.2 **Preliminary Criminal Investigations in Mexico, 1997 (state & local level)**

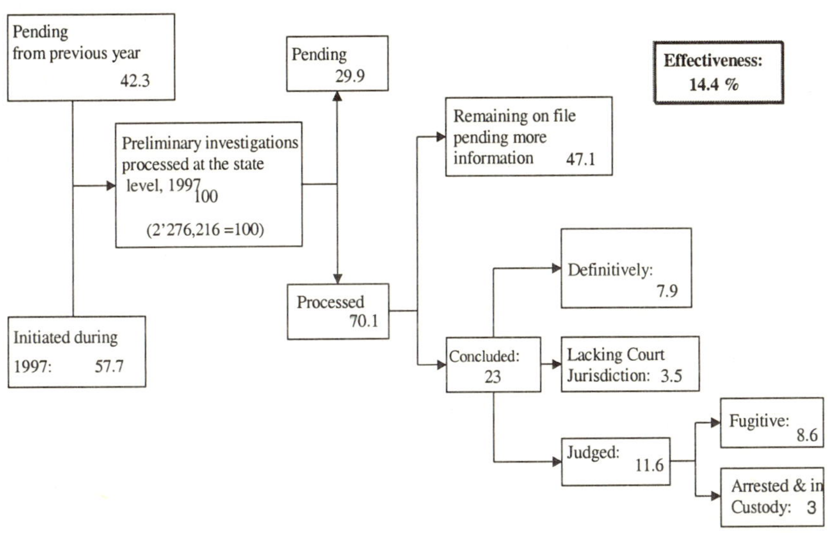

Source: Instituto Nacional de Estadística, Geografía, e Informática, *Anuarios estadísticos de los estados*, 1996, 1997, and 1998. (Durango has not been included, because its yearbook has data for the state capital only, and the government reports do not provide sufficient information.)

Clearly, not all preliminary investigations should end in the bringing of formal changes. In many cases, the facts fail to indicate the commission of a crime. There are, for example, instances involving disputes between neighbors or between vendors and consumers, and even instances in which litigants try to "criminalize" problems that are of an eminently civil nature (for example, reporting debts as fraud) in order to exert pressure on the other party. Consequently, it would be incorrect to measure effectiveness solely in terms of either the number of remanded inquiries (those that have led to a criminal proceeding) or the number of suspects. A better performance standard would be the degree of efficiency that procuracies demonstrate in handling preliminary investigations to compile sufficient evidence to initiate a criminal proceeding (physical evidence or *corpora delicti* and the presumed culpability of the suspect).

Thus a case may be considered "successfully concluded" after the Procuracy has: (1) remanded the investigation (recommending that the case be heard); (2) deemed that the case lies outside its jurisdiction (determining, for example, that it is a minor infraction or a federal crime, or that it corresponds to another state); or (3) determined that insufficient evidence exists to hear the case (no crime exists or the suspect holds no responsibility) and the investigation is closed. In these instances, one can claim that the authorities have responded appropriately to the citizen complaint. The case was channeled to the proper authorities, facts were gathered, and the decision whether to hear the case was duly made. In effect, justice was done. In contrast, remanded investigations with no prisoner in custody should not be considered effectively resolved or closed. The matter is pending the execution of the arrest warrant, which has been turned over to the police; hence the Procuracy has not finished its work.

The application of this performance standard to the handling of preliminary investigations in local jurisdictions yields an average effectiveness "score" of 14.4 percent (3 percent remanded with an arrest, 3.5 percent deemed to be out of the jurisdiction, and 7.9 are percent permanently filed [*archivado definitivamente*]). This is empirical evidence of poor performance. Seventy-seven percent of cases are never cleared up, and in 8.6 percent a criminal proceeding cannot be initiated because no one is in custody. In other words, in 85.6 percent of the cases, the measures taken to forward the investigation have not produced a satisfactory result.[13]

These statistics hold even more discouraging implications regarding local officials' handling of preliminary investigations. The most significant of the three categories that comprise the performance standard for the handling of preliminary investigations is "permanently filed." That label refers to cases that have been closed for a variety of reasons. For example, it may have been determined that there was no crime to prosecute (*no ejercicio de la acción penal*) and the Procuracy reviewed and approved that determination without challenge from the injured party. Or it may have been determined that there was cause to vacate the case—for example, if the suspect had died, amnesty was granted, the prisoner (generally a family member of the plaintiff) had been "pardoned" by his or her accuser, or new legislation had rendered the prisoner's act non-criminal. Some state-level procuracies, such as the one in Nuevo León, refer to cases as being resolved (and *archivado definitivamente*) as the result of an agreement or a "discontinuance."[14] Others, like that of Chihuahua, also refer to "conciliation."[15] Clearly, cases come under the rubric of "permanently filed" for a broad array of reasons, and these cases actually have only one thing in common—the investigation has been closed (see figure 3.3). Yet not all of these ways of legally closing the matter should be equated with a satisfactory resolution.

Figure 3.3 **Composition of Closed Inquiries**

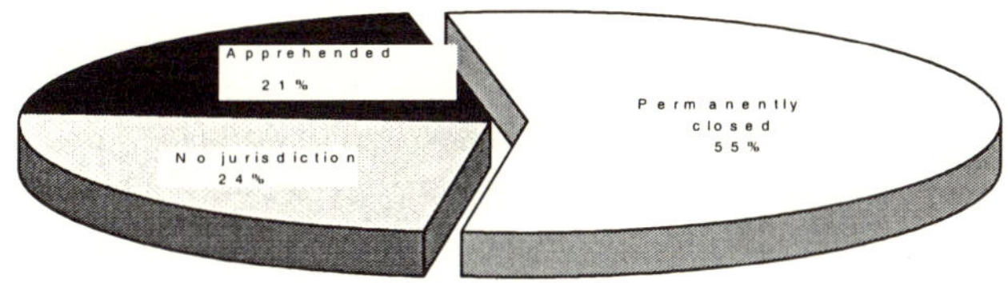

Source: Author's interpretation using data from the *Anuarios Estadísticos de los Estados* (Mexico City: INEGI).

Cases of limitation of action (*prescripciones*)—which in some states make up the bulk of permanently filed cases—are not the same as vacating a criminal proceeding, which assumes that the justice process has been set in motion by a citizen complaint concerning a supposed criminal act. Instead, a limitation of action, invoked when there is a lack of action on an unresolved case, is a penalty for a breach of procedural rules. In other words, it means that a file has died of procedural starvation. Sufficient evidence has not been gathered to persuade the Procuracy to remand the case to the courts and to find the alleged criminals and take them into custody. Given that procuracies have the duty to prosecute cases, a limitation of action resolution should not be considered an effective culmination to an investigation. The duty to prosecute is a formal obligation that prevails even when it runs counter to the wishes of the plaintiff or victim.

Unfortunately, most states lack disaggregated data, which makes it impossible to separate limitation of action cases from cases that are archived for other reasons. Only a few states list the reason for closing an investigation or offer the choice of selecting "no court proceeding initiated" (*no ejercicio de la acción penal*)—that is, that following the preliminary inquiry, the Procuracy could not show that there was a crime to prosecute. Data from these states reveal that such cases account for no more than 3 to 4 percent of all current investigations (a proportion similar to those remanded with a prisoner in custody). Thus the seventeen states that report more than 5 percent of all cases in their "permanently filed" category may very well be including under that rubric a considerable portion of limitation of action cases.

In other states, the "no court proceeding initiated" category may contain cases filed for other reasons. For example, Sonora placed 12 percent of its preliminary investigations in this category; and the Procuracy of the Federal District included 600,000 closed investigations under that rubric in 1993 and 1994, four times the number of investigations in the jurisdiction during 1991 and more than twice the number recorded during 1996.[16]

Nuevo León offers another example. This state, which also reports disaggregated statistics, has the second-highest proportion of permanently filed cases (37.9 percent). Only 3.2 percent of these filed cases fell into the "no court proceeding initiated" category (see figure 3.4). (Certain states, such as Tamaulipas and Nuevo León, use the label *inejercicios* or "unexercised.") Of the remainder, 24 percent were placed under the "discontinuances" category and 5.2 percent under "agreements." But two of every three cases (20,000) fell under a generic label of "archived" or permanently filed (in effect, closed). Given all the possible reasons for "archiving" a case, it seems unlikely that 20,000 investigations could be closed because the prisoner had died or was granted amnesty. This makes it reasonable to assume that the category may contain a high number of limitation of action cases. For this reason, the statistics on permanently closed cases should be viewed with caution when evaluating effectiveness, especially when those cases account for more than 5 percent of all investigations.[17]

Another important element in evaluating procuracies' performance is the percentage of issued arrest warrants that result in apprehensions. When a prosecuting attorney (*ministerio público*) successfully demonstrates probable cause, the judge is supposed to order an arrest so that the responsible party can be apprehended and sent to trial. In Mexico, however, only one in four warrants results in an apprehension. At any given time, the judicial police have pending approximately six out of every ten warrants they have received. Nearly 14 percent (13.6) of arrest warrants are canceled, with the main reasons being cancellation of the criminal suit; cases involving a minor, who must appear in juvenile court; or cases in which a writ of habeas corpus (*juicio de amparo*) has provisionally suspended the charges against the defendant. In this last instance, a recent legislative reform requires the accused person to appear within seventy-two hours before the judge who issued the warrant (*comparecencia espontánea*) in order for the warrant to be definitively canceled.

The effectiveness measure on executing arrest warrants is very low (figure 3.5). Mexico's procuracies tend to be impassive regarding evidence gathering—and largely inefficient in carrying out arrest warrants in cases in which it has been determined that a crime has occurred and should be prosecuted.

Figure 3.4 **Distribution of Permanently Closed Cases, Nuevo León, 1997**

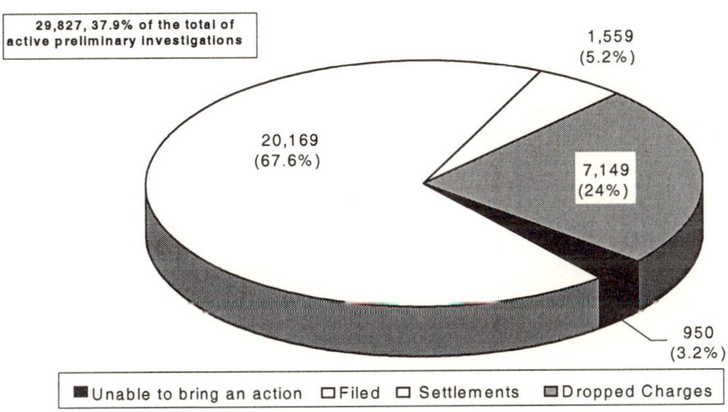

Source: Author's interpretation of data from the *Anuario Estadístico del Estado de Nuevo León* (Mexico City: INEGI, 1998).

Figure 3.5 **Arrest Warrants Issued at the Local Level, 1997**

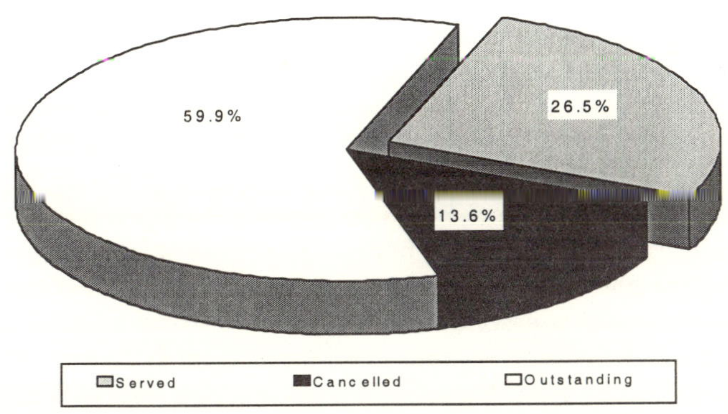

Source: Author's interpretation of information from the *Anuarios Estadísticos de los Estados de México* (Mexico City: INEGI).

Figure 3.5 demonstrates that procuracies are failing to respond satisfactorily to the public in general and to complainants in particular. These officials are deficient in handling complaints and conducting investigations, in gathering facts and delivering justice, and in locating and apprehending suspects. An assistant public attorney in the Federal District acknowledged that his office "is unable to investigate all the complaints it receives.... It can investigate only 8 percent of them."[18]

The inherent institutional limitations of the procuracies are also revealed in the number of suspects in custody compared to the number of crimes reported. Unlike the steady increase in the number of complaints filed, the number of suspects in custody sometimes rises and sometimes falls (it rose 8.5 percent in 1995 but declined 4 percent in 1997). It seems that procuracies' limited institutional resources make it impossible to apprehend and try more than some 150,000 people per year, regardless of the number of crimes committed. The gap between demand for services and the authorities' ability to respond is evident.[19]

In fulfilling its mission, the Procuracy is independent, irrecusable, and indivisible under the law. The law also gives the office broad powers, which make it the dominant actor in criminal proceedings. As noted previously, in "urgent" or flagrante delicto cases, this agency can detain a suspect without an arrest warrant for up to forty-eight hours (or twice that period in organized crime cases). It also has full discretion in conducting preliminary investigations; it is the principal initiator of criminal proceeding (it determines whether to free the suspect), and it has the exclusive right to request an arraignment.

The Procuracy supervises the police and technical experts involved in handling investigations. If the victim of a crime believes the inquiry is not being conducted properly, he or she can lodge an administrative appeal or complain to the investigator's superiors, though the latter option is rarely effective. When the Procuracy finds that the evidence presented is insufficient, it can close a case pending new evidence. It is the Procuracy that must initiate a criminal proceeding by bringing a suspect before the judge. Some scholars of Mexico's criminal proceedings law maintain that a peculiarity of this office is its "indispensable nature" (*imprescindibilidad*).[20]

For decades, the Procuracy held a "prosecutorial monopoly." It had exclusive authority to determine whether a case went to trial. If it was decided not to try a case, this decision was not subject to external review. The chief prosecutor alone could review the judgment of the subordinate who had handled the investigation. A 1994 constitutional reform opened up the possibility of challenging such decisions,[21] but there is still no recourse when cases are closed. The Procuracy may have lost its monopoly in the broadest sense, but it still retains monopoly control over the right to initiate criminal proceedings.

Seventy-seven percent of investigations in Mexico are either pending or have been filed (*archivadas con las reservas de ley*) while awaiting new evidence that would determine the case's legal status. Many of these investigations will never reemerge from the archives. Of the complaints received by state-level human rights commissions during 1997, 7 percent involved "delays in the administration of justice."[22]

Given the overwhelming demand for the Procuracy's services, this office's extensive discretionary power has created a set of incentives in Mexico's criminal justice system that lead to arbitrariness and corruption. Human rights commissions, the procuracies themselves, nongovernmental organizations, and the media have all documented cases of torture during investigations, irregularities in searches and detentions, and bribe taking in exchange for failing to execute arrest warrants, preventing a case from going to trial, closing an investigation, and even falsifying evidence.

The agencies within the Procuracy have long promoted objectives that parallel legal or de facto institutional goals: profiting from and illegal use of arbitrary powers by justice system functionaries and officials. These individuals abuse their authority with impunity. In a virtual "privatization" of civil service, deciding which cases will be processed has been turned into an auction, with court services going to the highest bidder.

"EVERYONE GETS A DRINK OF WATER AND AN ARRAIGNMENT": JUDGES AND THE ADMINISTRATION OF JUSTICE

When state-level public attorneys or state governors in Mexico want to present data on institutional efficiency, they turn to arraignment and sentencing figures.[23] With this shift in focus, the utter inefficiency and ineffectiveness characterizing preliminary investigations and the pursuit and apprehension of suspects suddenly give way to a model of efficacy.

The arraignment criterion evaluates the procuracies' ability to gather the evidence necessary to convince a judge to bring a suspect to trial and then to prove the case and win a conviction. This is a crucial stage because it moves the criminal proceeding to the judiciary. The independent and impartial judiciary reviews the actions of the Procuracy in order to ensure that the arrest and evidence gathering meet constitutional requirements, to safeguard the rights of the accused, and to determine whether the evidence to be presented suffices to demonstrate the accused's culpability.

This, at least, is how the system is supposed to work. In reality, the judiciary has little independence and tends to tolerate a high level of incompetence in prosecutorial investigations. Before, during, and after the court proceedings, the judiciary's powers are strictly limited. The court has no information beyond what the Procuracy presents, even though, as we have seen, the preliminary investigations by this office tend to be marred by incompetence and discretionary decisions. For every two cases investigated, only one is determined to be a prosecutable crime. In only one of every four remanded cases (those in which a crime does exist) is a suspect caught and brought to trial. In other words, the number of cases that go to trial represents only a miniscule fraction of potentially criminal acts committed.

Once a trial has begun, the judge can closely examine and evaluate the evidence. In criminal matters, the judge has broad latitude to admit circumstantial evidence. Nevertheless, legal reforms, proposed by the executive branch and approved by Congress, have created some safeguards. For example, the Code of Criminal Procedures of the Federal District reinforces the evidentiary value of the Procuracy's actions: "The procedures conducted by the public attorney and the police will have full evidentiary value as long as they accord with the rules of this law" (Article 286). There are even judicial precedents that reinforce the power advantages that local procuracies wield. For example, suspects' statements taken by officials in the Procuracy take precedence over those made before a judge.

These fundamentals of procedural law are incompatible with the judiciary's role as guardian of procedural guarantees. Clearly, the accuser (the public prosecutor's office) has the advantage, even though the presumption of innocence should favor the accused. As one procedural law scholar noted,

> The full proof, binding on the judge in his determination of whether ... proof, as defined in the code, has been met, is the legal evidence. In other words, the legislative branch has set precise and tangible rules beforehand—a veritable judicial standard—that the judge must follow in evaluating the evidence. Thus the judge is turned into a mechanical man, limited to abstract, pre-established rules and guidelines concerning the conclusions to be drawn in light of the evidence.[24]

Even after the trial has been concluded, the actions of the executive continue to sabotage the court's power. When the sentence is "final"—that is, if it is not appealed or, if appealed, it has been ratified by a superior court—personnel in the executive branch control its implementation. (These agencies are usually located within the state-level interior secretariats; the one in the Federal District is called the General Directorate for Crime Prevention and Social Rehabilitation [*Dirección General de Prevención y Readaptación Social*]).

These entities determine where a sentence is served, supervise its implementation, and grant (or deny) probation. They also control whether the sentence will be commuted or modified in any way. A better option would be to put these decisions in the hands of the judge who heard the case and imposed the sentence. Even if technical consultants advise the bureaucratic entities currently responsible for overseeing sentences, the latter are still subject to political and administrative constraints.[25]

Moreover, the Institutional Revolutionary Party's long hegemony in Mexico and the concentration of federal-level power in the executive branch—a pattern reproduced at the local level—have rendered null and void all counterweights designed to ensure a separation of political roles between the president, legislature, and judiciary. Even though procedures for raising individuals to the bench and the prohibition on removing judges from office have been respected, informal controls have made it impossible to form an independent and impartial judiciary. Judges—who in theory have "permanent" appointments—in practice resign every six years, coincident with the change in administration. The new administration fills judicial vacancies according to its pleasure. These practices hold at the local level as well, including during transitions between parties in power.[26]

The first point at which a judge can control the Procuracy's actions is when the judge reviews a prosecutor's request for an arrest warrant. Prosecutors must show material evidence of a crime and probable cause in order to obtain a warrant,[27] and judges grant most of these requests.[28]

When the Procuracy believes that a prosecutable crime exists and that the person in custody is responsible, it must initiate a criminal proceeding. After the prisoner appears before the judge, the court has seventy-two hours in which to determine the suspect's legal status (constitutional article 19). During this period, the judge can evaluate the prosecutor's evidence to confirm the presence of the *corpus delicti* and probable cause.[29] This stage should serve as a filter to ensure that there has been no arbitrariness on the part of the police and prosecutors, to guarantee respect for human rights, and to avoid harm to innocent citizens.[30] At this point, the judge evaluates the constitutionality of the arrest and examines the legality and quality of the evidence gathered during the Procuracy's investigation of the case.

The judge's evaluation determines whether a prisoner is sent to trial, which is accomplished by declaring formal charges or by issuing a writ of "subject to trial" (*sujeción a proceso*). (The latter occurs when the crime merits a lesser punishment than imprisonment.) When the Procuracy's agents have not provided sufficient material evidence to proceed to trial, the court releases the prisoner. Some judicial decrees (almost 2 percent) give other specific reasons for dropping charges (*extinción de la acción penal*). As mentioned previously, these can include pardons (in cases that come to trial), limitations (*prescipciones*), and amnesty, among others.

Selecting among various kinds of resolutions in bringing a criminal case to closure is very significant. It implies a substantive review of the case (verifying that a prosecutable crime exists and demonstrating evidence of probable guilt), as well as a judge's review to ensure that the arrest and criminal proceedings meet constitutional and legal requirements. In Mexico, where approximately 40 percent of all arrests are made without a warrant,[31] this "constitutional filter" is very important. Furthermore, the writ of constitutional limitations protects against pursuing someone against whom there is insufficient evidence and against imprisoning someone who is ultimately proven innocent. Even so, 89.9 percent of suspects on average receive a writ of constitutional limitations that submits them to a criminal proceeding (*auto de término constitucional*).[32]

As noted in the preceding section, the data on dropped charges are ambiguous. They could refer to instances in which the injured party exercised his or her legal right to pardon the suspect (in cases of sexual harassment, statutory rape, or defamation of character, among others). They could also indicate cases of limitation of action resulting from delayed action on the part of the investigating institutions. The states with the highest proportion of dropped charges are Sinaloa (8.3 percent), Tabasco (6.5 percent), and Morelos (5.9 percent).

Between 1993 and 1998, procuracies were required to present the same type of proof when requesting an arrest warrant or seeking to arraign a prisoner. Thus, if an individual was arrested, it usually followed that he or she was also arraigned. Exceptions arose when the suspect's statement to the judge or new evidence proved the suspect's innocence or cast doubt on the information the Procuracy had presented to the court. In the case of prisoners arrested without a warrant (approximately 40 percent of the cases, as noted previously), this is the point at which the judge views the evidence for the first time.

Nevertheless, the majority of suspects go to trial. The tendency to send suspects to trial may be attributable to a thorough investigation of crimes. On the other had, it may reflect the courts' tolerance for poorly executed investigations coupled with an incompetent defense.[33] In cases in which a prisoner is already in custody, some judges believe that the mandated period of forty-eight hours (twice that in organized crime cases) is too brief to gather sufficient evidence. Moreover, a released suspect may evade justice, so there is a logic for remanding the prisoner pending trial. The ease with which judges order suspects to stand trial has led to a legal idiom that paraphrases a rule of etiquette: "Everyone is entitled to a drink of water and an arraignment."

Following the presentation of evidence at trial and arguments from both sides in a case, the judge issues sentence. In this area, too, procuracies appear to be quite successful, with courts issuing guilty verdicts in 84 percent of their cases.[34] The states with the highest proportion of guilty verdicts are Nayarit (93 percent), Quintana Roo (92.6 percent), Baja California (92.5 percent), and Oaxaca (92 percent). The states with the lowest levels are Guerrero (68.5 percent), Morelos (70.25 percent), and México (70.9 percent).

There are also data that permit a qualitative appraisal of the Mexican courts' sentencing of prisoners. The data indicate that the courts find 72.5 percent of defendants guilty of minor crimes. In fact, in 4.7 percent of cases, the crimes involved are deemed to merit no prison time at all. Instead, the accused are either fined or assigned to community service. And of defendants who must serve time in prison, 71 percent are given sentences of less than two years.

Serious crimes receive a far different response. A serious crime is defined in Mexico's legal code as any crime for which the average of the lightest and heaviest applicable sentences exceeds five years in prison. In Mexico's justice system, 15 percent (14,706) of all prisoners receive prison sentences of five years or more.[35]

Serious crimes do not represent the largest portion of offenses reported. However, it is also true that more dangerous crimes are less frequently investigated and successfully prosecuted. For example, almost half of reported *robos* (thefts, robberies, and burglaries)[36] are cases of aggravated theft (*robo calificado*, which involves the use of weapons, theft from an inhabited building, bank theft, and other special cases).[37] Yet only 19 percent of prisoners sentenced for this crime receive more than five years imprisonment, the same sentence given, on average, to defendants found guilty of simple theft (*robo simple*),[38] even though the mean sentence set for aggravated theft is approximately eight years.[39]

In other words, the procuracies have little difficulty winning convictions with jail time for defendants accused of minor crimes or crimes of negligence, such as simple robbery, unintentional injury, personal threats, or property damage. The level of difficulty increases when they try to prove cases involving more serious crimes or crimes with aggravating circumstances.

"PEOPLE COOL DOWN": COSTS TO THE VICTIMS

Every crime has two legal consequences. One is the physical or emotional harm to the injured party and/or the loss of material possessions. The other is crime's impact as an attack against society at large. Whenever possible, the individual victim tries to get restitution for the losses sustained. The public's interest, in contrast, demands punishment—and the criminal's separation from the rest of society in order to prevent any future attack on other members of the community.

Consequently, Mexico's legal system endows public institutions with the power to seek punishment of a person responsible for a crime. Absent this institutional power, society would find itself enmeshed in a system ruled by private vengeance, where the victims of crime would themselves punish those who commit crimes against them. Instead, the state relieves the citizen of the tasks of investigating, gathering evidence, accusing, trying, and punishing the responsible party. Thus, when the appointed authorities learn of a possible crime, they are obliged as a matter of duty to launch an inquiry, whether or not someone asks them to do so.

The Mexican Constitution stipulates that the Procuracy is responsible for investigating and prosecuting crimes. That institution has a duty to press charges. Anyone who is aware of the commission of a crime is required to report it, and the victim has the right to seek reparations.

Thus, prosecuting crime is a duty that must be undertaken even when it counters the will of the person who reported the crime. Criminal policy requires the state to take action in order to prevent the crime from being repeated against other members of society. The only exceptions are crimes prosecuted as a result of a complaint (*querella*) in which the injured party may ask that the investigation be suspended (even following sentencing) because its continuance would bring further harm to the injured party. Such cases generally involve sexual harassment, statutory rape, adultery, and slander, among others. In these cases, it is essential to have the victim's consent to conduct an investigation. In all other cases, an investigation is obligatory.

Unfortunately, the principle of public prosecution of crime set forth in Mexico's Constitution and legal code is not upheld in the justice process itself. The very imperfect functioning of organizations charged with administering justice leads to de facto situations in which the victim has no access to justice and must press his or her case informally. Thus what exists in practice is closely akin to a system of "private vengeance."

This situation exists "on the ground" despite the fact that related discussions in Mexico tend to highlight the constitutional articles that protect victims' rights. Article 8 gives citizens the right to petition (in writing and in a peaceable, respectful manner), and authorities must respond to such petitions in writing. Article 17 states that individuals must not take the law into their own hands, but in exchange they are guaranteed swift and commensurate justice. The right of the victim or person reporting a crime, as established in Article 21, is the right to turn over the duty of investigating and prosecuting the crime to the Procuracy, the constitutionally mandated, autonomous entity charged with carrying out justice.

The injured party has the right to "legal representation, to damages when due, to assist the Procuracy, to urgent medical attention when required, and to whatever else the law demands. In turn, the victim will turn over to the investigators, public prosecutors, and instructing judge any and all information pertinent to the case, including material evidence, evidence of probable cause, and justification for reparations for damages."[40]

In criminal investigations, the primary source of evidence and information tends to be the victim or eyewitnesses. These individuals should provide any available evidence to the prosecutor, through whom the judge will become aware of it. This does not mean, however, that the victim is *responsible* for handling the investigation and gathering evidence. It falls to the Procuracy to direct the investigation. In practice, the victim's "right to assist" in the investigation has been twisted to make the victim an investigative assistant to the Procuracy's personnel.

Legislative changes and day-to-day practices of civil servants in the justice system have raised the costs for victims. Personnel within the procuracies—from administrative staff to directors—assert that their work should be reactive; that is, they should act only when pressed to do so.[41] These bureaucracies push their own private agendas, to the detriment of the general public and the law they are charged to uphold. By increasing the costs to the victim, they reduce their own workloads (fewer and fewer people are apt to file complaints), and they justify their own lack of initiative.

The fact that most offenses leading to formal complaints are minor crimes that pose little danger makes it easier for procuracies to justify overlooking them when the "interested party" does not insist on an investigation. There also exists a set of inadmissible offenses (*improcedencias*) that do not even reach the level of minor crime. Authorities generally do not bother to investigate these minor criminal acts. For example, the government of Baja California received 61,000 robbery reports in 1997.[42] Yet it reported that "in 1997, there were 19,662 robberies that merited a preliminary investigation."[43] In other words, no one bothered to pursue the majority of robbery reports. Only one of every four complaints received in Baja California in 1997 resulted in an investigation.

Reporting a crime is a trying undertaking. The injured party is first asked to pinpoint on a map the exact location where the crime occurred. If the location fall's within the agency's jurisdiction, the presiding official, unable to rid the office of the case, typically asks the person to take a seat in the waiting room (generally for ninety minutes or more) until a crime report can be taken.

The person reporting the crime is next asked to return in four days to the agency or another office to sign a formal complaint. Article 119 of the Federal Penal Code originally established such ratification of the complaint as mandatory. This provision was later struck from the code, and nothing in the Constitution states that ratification is necessary to initiate or conduct an investigation—only that the crime must be reported to the authorities. Yet the ratification requirement persists in some local codes, rules, and administrative guidelines. The requirement that the complainant appear twice is excessive; it suggests that failure to appear to sign the complaint could have consequences equivalent to a "discontinuance ... which is contrary to the meaning of Article 21."[44]

If the crime being reported was violent, the victim may still be upset at the time of making the report. He or she may not have documents at hand that could shed light on the events. Under these circumstances, the victim should be allowed to return at a later time to give more details or provide new evidence that did not appear in the original complaint. Nevertheless, in these cases, we are faced with an amplification of the complaint or providing evidence to prove ownership of goods, and so forth. Even in those cases, new information is no guarantee that officials will continue the investigation.

It seems clear that failure to ratify a complaint should not halt an investigation. Nevertheless, the personnel in many procuracies cite this requirement when presenting their view of the victim's role in the crime investigation: "if the plaintiff, the victim, and the witnesses are the principal sources of evidence and these parties do not come forward with more information, the obvious choice is to close the case." When these officials are asked why a complaint needs to be ratified, they respond that it is because new information might become available (which, as noted, is actually an amplification of the complaint) or "to prove the legal interest and to ensure the suit will not be closed." There appears to be broad consensus among civil servants that continuation of an investigation depends on its ratification.[45]

Because of a lack of material or human resources in local procuracies, or simply because it is the path of least resistance, the burden of gathering evidence, presenting testimonies, and identifying suspects has fallen to crime's victims. Civil servants tell the victims, "you have to bring us witnesses," "you have to show us an inventory," but only infrequently do they make their expertise or resources available to the victim. Instead, they tend to see in the victims the source of their agency's excessive workload. When a suspect is arrested, the judicial time clock increases the pressure on the victim, who now must gather evidence while responding to investigators' requests. It is not unusual for investigators to telephone an injured party at home, threatening that, if requested evidence is not delivered, the prisoner will be set free. In extreme cases, investigators have even sent police officers to ensure the victim's compliance.

Successive steps in the judicial process are repeatedly delayed, further exacerbating the strains on the victim. For example, hearings are regularly postponed, and a victim must often sacrifice his or her normal activities to be sure the case moves forward.[46] Few are willing to travel this road.

For civil servants wishing to lessen their workload, one quick and simple strategy is to question the veracity of statements made by the person reporting the crime. Authorities often rationalize their inaction by asserting that an offense was really "self-robbery" or some other fraudulent complaint filed to collect insurance money. Indeed, there have been kidnapping cases in which the authorities refused to accept the word of the person reporting the crime. By suggesting that the missing person was simply "late" and suggesting that friends and relatives be questioned first, the authorities allowed the trail to go cold.

The perception that the victim is the sole "interested party" is deeply rooted among procuracy personnel. For example, at offices located in airports and at other points of heavy tourist traffic, agents are charged with helping travelers who have been victimized by crime. Yet only 23 percent of the cases reported in these agencies resulted in a preliminary investigation. The remainder prompted only a written report and the issuance of a special report (*acta especial*) indicating that "the complainant is unwilling to pursue the case or cannot produce the evidence needed to begin a preliminary investigation."[47] Thus, if the victim shows little interest in pursuing the case, no investigation will begin and there are no further repercussions in the criminal justice system. In another example, an official from the state procuracy in Jalisco was asked to identify the cause of the enormous backlog in uninvestigated crime reports. He answered, "Well, people cool down, you know." That is, injured parties who initiate a process and appear once or twice eventually stop coming back. It apparently does not occur to officials that a sound policy would be to minimize the cost to the victim. Instead, these functionaries focus on the victim's willingness to maintain a constant level of rage—in other words, private vengeance.

A total absence of protection for victims and witnesses is another shortcoming of the procuracies. During hearings, lineups, and face-to-face encounters, suspects commonly insult, ridicule, and even threaten crime victims and witnesses while authorities turn a deaf ear. A suspect and the defense attorney have access to the case file, which includes the name, address, and telephone number of the individual who filed the report. Not surprisingly, complainants frequently receive intimidating telephone calls, yet the procuracies seem to have neither the will nor the resources to respond.[48]

In extreme cases of institutional corruption, functionaries may actually try to distance the injured parties from the process. With the victim out of the way, the officers can use their ample discretionary powers to set the prisoner free. It is not uncommon to hear reports of civil servants in the criminal justice system cutting a deal, allowing a suspect to escape before the victim's relatives or a superior officer can arrive. In other cases, complainants are restrained from taking action. One victim recounted that an officer at the police station asked him, "Do you really want to file a complaint? Be careful; these people are really nasty!"

In their public relations campaigns, the procuracies and the agencies charged with maintaining public security encourage citizens to file criminal complaints. Officials allege that Mexicans' sense of civic duty is so weak that they do not report crimes committed against them. However, after talking to victims, reviewing the empirical evidence, and observing the filing of a crime report, one comes away with a sense that what citizens are avoiding is involving themselves in the criminal justice process in any way. It is one thing to have a sense of civic duty, another to be so self-destructive as to come forward to present a complaint.

In this official environment of excessive workloads, incompetent personnel, corruption, infiltration of criminal elements into police departments, and day-to-day practices that make the victim responsible for pressing "his case," it is the injured party, not the criminal, who ends up powerless within the country's criminal justice system.

DUE PROCESS AND HUMAN RIGHTS

The state procuracies have also failed to observe procedural guarantees designed to protect suspects, victims, and other participants in the criminal justice process. This is due to these offices' ineptitude in handling investigations and proving cases in court. Moreover, authorities in the executive and legislative branches have adopted public safety policies that shrink the scope of citizens' rights, and the judiciary has relaxed its guard regarding due process and respect for human rights during criminal proceedings.

By its very nature, the state's role in investigating and prosecuting crime implies balancing citizens' freedoms and rights with the authorities' actions. This interaction tends to produce frictions. To reestablish the legal order, any inappropriate interference with individual rights by the state should be unlawful. Legal remedies must be made available for making restitution to the injured party and assigning responsibility to the official or government agency that acted inappropriately.

In Mexico, the writ of habeas corpus (*juicio de amparo*) is designed to defend the constitutional rights of the citizenry. In the same way, a series of appeals, clear definitions of the responsibilities of civil servants, and legal definitions of crimes against the administration of justice all attempt to establish a system of control, scrutiny, and sanctions over the exercise of official power.

Nevertheless, unmet demand for accessible ways to report human rights violations led to the establishment in the early 1990s of the National Commission on Human Rights (CNDH) and its state-level counterparts. These autonomous institutions investigate complaints to determine if constitutional rights have been violated and, when needed, make recommendations to the appropriate government agencies. The strength and legitimacy of their recommendations rest on the moral authority the commissions hold in public opinion.

The commissions' activities have made it possible to detect, quantify, document, and pursue reported rights violations. The complaints received show that the criminal justice institutions themselves are responsible for most of the alleged violations. Likewise, most recommendations the commissions have issued are directed to these organizations, principally to state-level procuracies. In 1997, human rights commissions in twenty-six Mexican states and the Federal District[49] reviewed 43,519 new complaints[50] and confirmed a likely violation of human rights in about two-thirds (28,710) of them.[51] In the remaining third, either no violation had occurred or the complaint was channeled to another jurisdiction. Most of the complaints were resolved or closed, principally as a result of conciliation, discontinuance, or lack of interest. Recommendations were sent to the responsible officials in only 999 cases.

Of the presumed violations that the human rights commissions detected, 31.2 percent held the state-level procuracies responsible (public prosecutors, 14.8 percent; judicial police, 13.5 percent; other offices, 2.9 percent).[52] Public security agencies were responsible for 9.1 percent. Almost half of the human rights commissions' recommendations were directed to procuracies and about 20 percent to the police and prisons.

The principal root of corroborated human rights violations was abuse of authority (see table 3.1). In criminal matters, this is expressed in the excesses committed by procuracy personnel, who deny services, interfere with the application of the law, and so forth. Unlawful detention—instances in which arresting agents did not properly identify themselves or failed to show an arrest warrant—was cited as the cause in almost 2,500 complaints. There were also cases of illegal raids in which police entered a home without a search warrant. The third most common complaint involved delays in the administration of justice,[53] including sluggishness or negligence in handling the crime investigation.

Table 3.1 **Types of Alleged Violations (percentages)**

Alleged Violation	Percent of Total
Abuse of authority	16.4
Unlawful detention	11.9
Delay in the delivery of justice	3.8
Torture	1.8
Illegal raids or searches	1.3
Denial of justice	1.1
Anomalies in handling of preliminary investigations	0.5

Source: *Statistical Yearbooks for the States, 1998* (Mexico City: INEGI, 1998).

Complaints of torture have declined nationwide (though holding steady in southeastern Mexico). Nevertheless, the national rate—369 complaints in 1997—is alarming.[54] Abuse of authority and other violations of suspects' and crime victims' rights reflect the impunity of official personnel who suppose they will incur no "cost" for committing abuses or even assume such practices are "necessary." Frequently the police and civil servants charged with combating crime view the legal or official regulations that supposedly guide their daily activities as unrealistic, opening a gap between expectations and directives for lawful conduct and "operational attitudes."[55] This helps explain the apathy—or negligence—of mid-level functionaries in controlling this type of abuse, and it also accounts for working personnel who resist, or are indifferent to, changes in public policy and legal reforms.

Another important cause of the disregard for human rights is a failure on the part of police and investigators to maintain their professionalism when investigating crimes. The reduction in the number of torture cases noted above may have resulted primarily from the passage in December 1991 of the Federal Law to Prevent and Punish Torture (Ley Federal para Prevenir y Sancionar la Tortura), which ruled out confessions as sufficient proof of a prisoner's guilt.

Officials' frequent failure to gather evidence at the crime scene immediately or soon after a crime takes place forces them to rely more on suspicion than evidentiary proof. Suspects are forced to confess to a crime, and victims and witnesses are forced to revise their testimonies to match those of the suspects. When suspicions are not supported by facts, police reports are "doctored" to match the investigators' hypothesis, and "evidence" is sometimes fabricated.

Courts have a duty to punish violations of citizen guarantees and to declare inadmissible any evidence obtained by coercion or without strict observance of due process. Yet, as noted previously, the scope of judicial authority sometimes leads judges to tolerate arbitrariness and incompetence in the judicial process even in cases that involve a violation of constitutional rights.

Even though the Mexican Constitution makes clear the inadmissibility of evidence obtained through violations of individuals' constitutional rights, judicial opinion has tolerated and even supported an abusive interpretation of authority. Furthermore, coercion in evidence gathering, arbitrary arrest, and detention exceeding the constitutionally mandated period are still legal. Such practices tend to rely on judicial negligence, which permits such measures to go unchallenged during trial.[56]

Despite complaints presented to human rights commissions and these commissions' recommendations, judges' decisions do not seem to take illegal arrest into account. Thus, although about 40 percent of indicted prisoners are apprehended without a warrant (in flagrante delicto crimes), only 10 percent of all prisoners receive release decrees (*autos de libertad*). There are two possible explanations for this; either the judges are failing in their duty to review the constitutionality of arrests made in the cases that come before them, or the procuracies are being scrupulous in their apprehension of suspects. A recent study of human rights in Mexico notes, "It is quite apparent that Mexican law and the court's interpretation of it leave wide open the possibility that judges are not taking into consideration human rights violations when issuing their decisions."[57]

Finally, executive power is on a trajectory, supported by the legislature's passing of amendments to laws and legal codes, that is detrimental to citizens' basic rights. The number of offenses for which suspects are denied bail is increasing, expanding the population of suspects in preventive custody. Furthermore, the period for which suspects can be held pending an investigation has been doubled for organized crime cases, and requirements for issuing arrest warrants have been eased.

At first glance, these steps might be seen as strengthening the instruments for combating crime. But given the institutional incompetence described above, they are more likely to result in reducing the burden of proof to show probable cause and weakening respect for human rights.[58] Denying the right to post bail reflects the system's inability to execute re-arrests. It also compensates for prosecutors' poor record in cases involving technical difficulties—or in cases in which defendants are represented by a competent defense lawyer (frequently the case in white-collar crime). By refusing bail, the authorities have the consolation of knowing that, even if the prisoner is freed, at least he or she has been imprisoned for the duration of the trial. Of course, denying bail also increases the number of cases that represent a miscarriage of justice. What is more, a suspect who is found innocent cannot appeal for economic compensation for the time spent in jail. The good faith of the Mexican authorities is assumed, and their incompetence or negligence is glossed over.

POLITICS, PUBLIC OPINION, AND THE ADMINISTRATION OF JUSTICE

In recent years, society's perception of a public security threat has exceeded the reality reflected in crime statistics. The media have heightened public security concerns by highlighting local crime stories and sensational trials, largely in an effort to hold their audience. Thus, although statistics show a decline in crime, surveys show that crime still tops the list of community concerns.

Despite a decline, crime statistics in Mexico remain high in comparison to figures from the early 1990s. Official data, in combination with the proliferation of police stories in the media, have made public safety a top government priority. On the other hand, frequent stories of corruption, abuse, and ineptitude on the part of bureaucrats and police have created a sense of helplessness among the general public, setting up a virtuous cycle of intense proposals and initiatives offered by elected officials and candidates to public office.

Campaign speeches and government initiatives attempt to respond to the public's demand for safety and justice. Cognizant of the media's strong impact on public opinion, politicians and officials turn to the media to argue the particular merits of their respective proposals and to register their achievements on the public safety front—or, in the absence of progress, to minimize the problem or to blame someone else. As one high-level official in the Procuracy of the Federal District put it in 1997, "policies are dictated by the media."[59]

Even though the number of crimes reported is beginning to drop, local procuracies still seem to be losing the battle against crime. In response, elected officials and civil servants charged with the administration of justice are trying to stem the loss of their credibility among the public. One strategy emerging in the public information policies of the procuracies is to excuse these organizations by placing the blame on entities outside the criminal justice system or at another level of government within the administration.[60] The preferred "villains" in these concocted arguments are the defenders of human rights: "idealistic" commissions and judges (identified as "legal technocrats") who are rigid in their application of the law but who supposedly miss the point when it comes to delivering justice and fulfilling the requirements of public safety policy.

Civil servants in the judicial system, the police, and even high-level officials claim that the human rights commissions impede justice by pleading on behalf of suspects (whom they call "guilty parties" or "criminals," although they have not yet been tried) and by recommending in certain cases that the suspect receive legal representation or be freed. On many occasions, procuracy agents have refused to admit to rights violations of which they have been accused, and have chosen to ignore commission recommendations. This strategy has proved largely successful in shaping public opinion. On the street, one frequently hears that the human rights commissions "defend criminals." Such accusations severely undermine the commissions, whose recommendations have weight only to the degree that the commissions can maintain their moral authority.[61]

Public policy measures reflect the views of the authorities. In their efforts to facilitate the operation of judicial institutions, they have implemented legislative reforms that weaken Mexico's legal institutions or seek to make them more flexible. The general public, meanwhile, has despaired of current efforts to solve the public security problem and now supports a "tightening of the law"—including institution of the death penalty. In joining the campaign to limit suspects' rights, some legal scholars have presented what they see as an unassailable syllogism: human beings have rights; criminals are not human beings; therefore, criminals do not have rights.[62]

This line of argumentation is false. It is not that the law is not "tight enough." Rather, criminal justice institutions are "too loose." Suspects' rights do not justify poor performance on the part of the procuracies. For example, the constitutional requirement to obtain an arrest warrant is not an obstacle to the effective performance of prosecutorial duties. In fact, most requests result in the issuance of a warrant; the problem is that only one in four is executed. Human rights concerns are not responsible for that shortcoming. Admittedly, due process and respect for a suspect's rights require a certain institutional infrastructure, and the prosecutor assumes the burden of proof. But none of these requirements is insurmountable, nor should they be considered "obstacles." Adherence to the law is a condition without which state action cannot be justified. It is the sine que non that endows institutions with legitimacy. Any other form of combating crime would be tantamount to wrongdoing by an outlaw state.

Furthermore, empirical evidence shows that human rights commissions are not defenders of "criminals." More than half of the complaints criticizing the procuracies' actions come from crime victims upset with case delays and the prosecutor's negligence. In the Federal District, for example, crime victims' complaints against judicial organizations (principally about delays) account for between 65 and 80 percent of all complaints filed with the human rights commission.[63] Clearly it is not only the suspected perpetrators of crime who seek to be protected from the procuracies.

As mentioned above, judges have also become targets of accusations coming from the procuracies. The judicial standards that are applied to the investigative work and courtroom performance of the public attorneys and their staff are not high. Yet the procuracies sometimes claim that, because judges are corrupt or base their decisions on legal "technicalities," they often set "criminals" free. Indeed, judges themselves are increasingly facing criminal proceedings on charges of crimes against the administration of justice. For example, in the Federal District (the jurisdiction with the lowest proportion [5 percent] of not-guilty decisions), such criminal suits have been entered against several judges. The fact that a number of these cases are pending has been viewed as reflecting efforts to intimidate the judges under investigation.[64]

The victims themselves are yet another scapegoat in prosecutors' explanations for the bad state of affairs. According to these officials, victims lack a sense of civic duty and therefore fail to report crime, fail to appear to sign their complaints, fail to participate fully in "their" process, or, as noted above, fail to maintain the hot rage of vengeance. The procuracies cite these faults as reasons for their own ineffectiveness. They claim that their "hands are tied" when the affected parties are unwilling to accept their part in the process.

These various arguments constitute more than a public relations strategy. They have been adopted as the official diagnosis of the public security situation in Mexico. The initiatives that government officials have sent to the federal Congress and state legislatures, as well as the policies that have been implemented as a result, stem from this interpretation. Thus a misguided interpretation of public security issues has become the guiding principle in developing public policy. At best, security policies have achieved meager successes. But politicians, eager to portray their effectiveness in resolving the problem, have created the impression of an all-out war on crime. In practice, it is more "virtual combat" than real battle. A decline of nearly 8 percent in reported crimes in 1998–1999 gave authorities the evidence they needed for continuing down the same road of bigger budgets, more legal instruments and personnel, and stiffer sentences.

CONCLUSION: IMPUNITY AND DISREPUTE

The evidence analyzed in this chapter indicates that, for the most part, procuracies in Mexico are ineffective.[65] Officials do not fully comply with their formal institutional mission and legal mandate to investigate criminal acts and apprehend criminal suspects.

What is more, justice system personnel make poor use of the powers and legal instruments at their disposal. These organizations have de facto goals that run counter to their formal institutional aims and objectives. The consequent failure to meet formal institutional objectives means that most crimes committed in Mexico are not punished. Hence society is not protected from criminals and criminal organizations that may again transgress against the social order, and potential offenders are not dissuaded from breaking the law.

Additionally, citizens who seek the procuracies' services do not receive appropriate attention. Victims of crime are forced to assume responsibility for filing a crime report and participating in the criminal proceeding. Consequently, these offices have lost credibility with the public, and this, in turn, has eroded the crucial links needed for citizen cooperation with, and participation in, public institutions' efforts to combat crime.

The huge numbers of criminal cases that go uninvestigated, the many investigations that are closed because of statute-of limitations restrictions, and the low number of executed arrest warrants are all suggestive of ineptitude on the part of Mexico's procuracies. In terms of their effectiveness in criminal proceedings, aggregate data at the national level show that prosecutors are able to evade most of the safeguards the courts have put in place to ensure compliance with the law. Approvals on requests for arrest warrants, writs of constitutional limitations, and sentencing all favor the prosecuting attorneys. It seems that on the very, very few complaints and investigations that reach the arraignment stage, the procuracies' performance is remarkable: 90 percent of all prisoners are tried and 84.3 percent are sentenced.

We must, however, consider two caveats in regard to these statistics. First, the time that elapses from arraignment (*auto de formal prisión or sujeción a proceso*) to sentencing is not a matter of hours or days. On average, criminal trials last between eight months and two years. To discover after two years of proceedings that a prisoner is innocent is a grave miscarriage of justice. Second, most sentences are for minor crimes and are levied in cases where the defendant is represented by a (generally poorly trained and overwhelmed) public defender. Obtaining a guilty decision in such cases is not a great challenge. In contrast, prosecutors fair far less well in serious crime cases in which the defendant is well represented.

Mexico's justice system is also characterized by impunity. Given arrest statistics (only 18 arrests are made for every 1,000 cases) and the likelihood of being sentenced (75.7 percent), the probability that the author of a crime (whether accused or not) will serve jail time is 14 in 1,000.

Another performance standard is access to the legal system, including services provided and security for victims, witnesses, and others involved in criminal proceedings. Victims incur high costs during legal proceedings and suffer marginalization and infringements of their rights as Mexican citizens. Although it is impossible to quantify the number of violations that go unreported, actions by criminal justice institutions and trends in recently implemented policies demonstrate a less than scrupulous respect for fundamental rights. On the contrary, authorities often view human rights as unrealistic and incompatible with the operational criteria that civil servants must follow in administering justice.

Public opinion polls indicate that the agencies charged with the administration of justice in Mexico have suffered a serious loss in credibility. Citizens have lost confidence in them as a result of their direct or indirect experience as consumers of these offices' services or as a result of their general perception of public security threats and police incompetence.

This is reflected in the substantial proportion of crimes that go unreported.[66] If we look only at estimates of reported crime, Mexico's rate of approximately 30 percent (three out of ten crimes are reported) is similar to rates in other countries. For example, only 37.4 percent of crimes are reported in the United States[67] and 36 percent in the United Kingdom.[68] Chile has one of the highest reporting levels, at 46.5 percent.[69]

However, the picture changes dramatically if we consider the reasons why people decide not to report crimes. The most frequent reason given for not reporting crimes in the United States, the United Kingdom, and Holland is that the victim feels that the incident is too trivial or that the crime does not deserve police attention.[70] In contrast, in Mexico, the primary reason (given in 44 percent of unreported crimes) is that "there is no point; it won't fix anything."[71] Mistrust and even outright fear of authorities were also mentioned frequently.

The analysis of performance standards outlined in this chapter reveals that the organizations involved in the administration of justice in Mexico present serious anomalies derived from lack of material and human resources, as well as from an inappropriate system of incentives and poor supervision of work performance. The most serious problems are those in which civil servants place their private interests above their civic duty and the legal objectives of their institutions. Because of these de facto priorities, the bureaucracies in the procuracies fail to perform their duties or perform them only perfunctorily. Worse, they sometimes extort their institutions' clients by means of corrupt or criminal practices.

The way to stop these practices and to improve service is to link the public interest and legal objectives of the justice organizations with the civil servants' private goals. This can be accomplished by instituting an appropriate system of incentives backed by effective supervisory mechanisms.

Although a detailed strategy goes beyond the scope of this chapter, Mexico's law enforcement system should take steps to halt operational irregularities, diminish excessive workloads, improve response capacity, reinforce judicial power during the trial stage, minimize the costs to victims, and guarantee respect for human rights. A purging of the organizations charged with public safety and the administration of justice is urgently needed. The country's procuracies should move quickly to implement effective systems for recruitment, tenure, promotion, supervision, and—when needed—discipline of its civil servants.

Notes

This chapter forms part of a larger study, "Justicia, crimen y derechos humanos en México," a product of the project on Institutions for the Rule of Law in Mexico, organized by the Centro de Investigación y Docencia Económicas (CIDE) in Mexico City and directed by Beatriz Magaloni and Guillermo Zepeda.

Translated by Patricia Rosas.

1. In the preliminary investigation, the suspect is referred to as the "*indiciado*" (presumed suspect) because he or she has yet to be formally accused, and there exist only "suspicions" of probable culpability.

2. *Código Federal de Procedimientos Penales,* Art. 168. *Diario Oficial,* May 18, 1999. This requirement is the outcome of a legal and constitutional reform (*Diario Oficial,* March 8, 1999) which reduces the requirements for criminal action. Previously the requirement called for evidence of all the elements of the crime ("*tipo penal*")—that is, not just the material evidence but also subjective evidence, such as motive. These requirements were incorporated into a legal reform in 1993. In the traditional "trial-and-error" style of the Mexican legislature, recent legislative changes have returned things to the status quo ante.

3. In cases where the legal nature of the crimes under investigation makes it possible to request provisional release (by posting a bail bond), the order can be requested from the Procuracy or from the judge, depending upon the stage at which the process stands.

For several years, the primary criterion for deciding if bail could be posted has been the gravity of the crime. At certain times, the list of "serious crimes" has contained as many as forty offenses. Reforms have recently been proposed that would return to a definition of "serious crime" that uses as a measurement the arithmetic mean of the shortest and the longest possible sentence for a given crime. Those crimes whose arithmetic mean is less than five years are bailable.

4. This distinction should not be taken as a denial that much local-level criminal activity—such as narco-trafficking—derives from or is associated with criminal activity at the federal jurisdiction.

5. For more on the complexity of criminal justice organizations in an open system, see Stan Stojkovic, David Kalinich, and John Klofas, *Criminal Justice Organizations: Administration and Management*, 2d ed. (Belmont, Calif.: West/Wadsworth, 1998).

6. As noted, the requirement that the prosecutor produce the *corpus delicti* (material evidence of a crime) comes from a recent constitutional reform. This chapter's empirical evidence is from 1997, when the prosecutor's burden of proof included all elements of *tipo penal* (even subjective things, such as motive).

7. Stojkovic, Kalinich, and Klofas, *Criminal Justice Organizations*, 11–12.

8. Author's interpretation of information from the statistical yearbooks for the Mexican states and from the final results of the 1995 population and household census, conducted by the Instituto Nacional de Estadística, Geografía e Informática (INEGI).

9. Ibid. These data may underestimate workload, since it is possible that some states reported employees of district attorney's offices who were assigned to civil courts to monitor compliance with the provisions of family law. In Guerrero, the only state that explicitly notes that the statistics are aggregated (that is, these reports do not differentiate between agents who work on criminal matters and those who do not), the average number of complaints received by each agent is eighty per year.

10. Most available surveys have been taken in urban areas. The proportion of crimes reported is low (between 20 and 35 percent of all offenses) and is getting lower.

11. *Reforma*, September 13 and 14, 1999. Statistics from the newspaper's quarterly survey on reported crimes as a portion of all crimes have varied from 36 percent (July 19, 1995) to less than 15 percent (October 20, 1997).

12. The state-level procuracies do not acknowledge this number of prior-year pending cases. They admit only to carrying over 430,936 cases. That figure, however, represents only 55 percent of the number recorded in the CIDAC databank, which compiles statistics from reports prepared by the local offices of public attorneys and by the governors' offices. Local-level public prosecutors tend to consider as "resolved" those investigations for which evidence has not yet been compiled to determine if the case should go forward or be dismissed. Such cases are "filed for technical reasons" (*archivadas con las reservas de la ley*). For that reason, these investigations disappear from the reports the following year. Several states (Baja California Sur, Chihuahua, Colima, Hidalgo, Querétaro, Quintana Roo, San Luis Potosí, Tamaulipas, Zacatecas) and the Federal District do not acknowledge that *any* cases have been carried over. Their reports either contain no category along the lines of "in process from last year" or they note that this information is "unavailable."

13. These figures are low compared with information available for other countries. In Europe (with the exception of Holland, which has an effectiveness of 25 percent), the average number of closed cases ranges between 45 and 55 percent. In Germany, for example, all investigations brought before the prosecutors must be completed, whether there is sufficient evidence (43.8 percent) or not (56.2 percent). In other words, there are no pending cases (Julia Fionda, *Public Prosecutors and Discretion: A Comparative Study* [Oxford: Clarendon, 1995]). The data are from 1991.

14. This may refer to cases in which the prisoner was pardoned or to instances where, at some point in the process, the Procuracy may have concluded that it did not err in its initial determination to send the investigation to trial, and it may have formulated non-accusatory conclusions. (However, in the case of Nuevo León, agreements and discontinuances accounted for 7,000 cases—more than the total number of criminal proceedings in the entire jurisdiction during 1997.)

15. A debate rages over the advisability of allowing parties to a crime to negotiate among themselves over culpability (even when a mediator is involved). Many argue that crimes are a matter of public safety. Besides the injury to the victim, there is the risk that the suspect might inflict further harm on other members of the community. On the other hand, negotiation is also recognized as a good way to resolve problems of lesser importance, and it has a role as a preventive measure to ameliorate minor controversies. Compare Fionda, *Public Prosecutors and Discretion*.

16. "The observed increase in the resolution of preliminary investigations for 1993 and 1994 is due to a review of permanently closed investigations, of which those that had been prescribed *(prescrito)* were determined to belong under the category of "no court proceeding initiated." Ernesto Zedillo Ponce de León, *Anexo Estadístico del Segundo Informe de Gobierno*, September 1, 1996 (Mexico City: Presidencia de la República, 1996), 9. The cited source in the *Anexo* is the Procuraduría General de Justicia, Federal District.

17. The states with the highest proportion of permanently filed inquiries are Morelos (38.5 percent), Nuevo León (37.9 percent), Baja California Sur (24.4 percent), and Zacatecas (21.7 percent).

18. Interview with José Elías Romero Apis, Suprocurador "A" in the Procuraduría General de Justicia, Federal District, in "Desarticulada y corrompida, la procuraduría de justicia es un mero apéndice de gobernación y el DDF: Romero Apis," Raúl Monge, *Proceso* 1096 (November 2, 1997).

19. As noted earlier, not all complaints necessarily involve crimes, and not every complaint should result in bringing someone to trial. For any single inquiry, it is possible that several suspects may be tried. On average, there are two suspects per offense. The trend in the number of complaints has little to do with the authorities' ability to respond.

20. Julio Acero, *Procedimiento penal*, 6th ed. (Puebla: José María Cajica, Jr., S.A., 1968).

21. This possibility was not regulated by implementing legislation. Nevertheless, in 1997 the jurisprudence of federal courts established that the failure to send a case to trial could be challenged by means of a *juicio de amparo*.

22. This average comes from the fourteen states that report disaggregated data under the label of *"dilación de la procuración de justicia"* (delay in the administration of justice). The percentage varies greatly among the states, with the highest being Chiapas (17 percent) and Coahuila (12 percent), and the lowest, Campeche (1.33 percent) and Quintana Roo (4.2 percent).

23. Most reports issued by the executive branch at the local level have referred to the district attorney's offices' inexorable pursuit of arrest warrants, arraignments, and sentences.

24. Marco Antonio Díaz de León, *Código de Procedimientos Penales para el District Federal Comentado* (Mexico City: Porrúa, 1990), 490.

25. One of the subdirectors of investigation in the Procuraduría de Justicia in the Federal District was convicted of kidnapping. In addition to the damage this did to the institution's reputation, it later came to light that he served his fourteen-year sentence in only four and a half years. *Crónica,* October 14, 1998.

26. For example, legislators in the Federal District have opposed certain nominations made by the Party of the Democratic Revolution (PRD), which was the majority party in the assembly and the mayor's party as well.

27. This rule has been in effect since the constitutional reforms were published in the *Diario Oficial* on March 8, 1999. The data presented here are from 1997, when prosecutors still had to prove all evidence *de tipo penal.*

28. For example, the courts in Coahuila granted 94 percent (3,844 of 4,087) of the warrant requests it received. *V Informe de Gobierno de Gobernador Constitucional de Coahuila,* 1998. In Chihuahua, 70 percent (4,739 of 6,783) of warrant requests were granted, according to a document issued by the Procuraduría General de Justicia del Estado de Chihuahua, 1998, 58.

29. This article of the Mexican Constitution was modified in March 1999. Because this change is so recent, the data presented here correspond to judicial decrees made under the earlier requirements, which, as was the case with arrest warrants, call for proof of the existence of all evidence of a criminal nature, as well as probable cause.

30. If the difficulties of the process continue and it becomes apparent during trial that the evidence was insufficient to prosecute or sentence, this indicates a miscarriage of justice: the trial of an innocent person, surpassed in gravity only by the sentencing of someone who is innocent.

31. This proportion is estimated by subtracting the number of arrest warrants that resulted in detentions from the number of writs of constitutional limitations.

32. The Federal District has the highest percentage (94.8 percent), followed by Puebla (94.7 percent) and Nuevo León (94.1 percent). The states with the lowest levels are San Luis Potosí (82 percent) and Veracruz (82.1 percent).

33. It seems that a large number of sentenced prisoners are "represented" by overworked and undermotivated public defenders. Although there is no field research confirming this perception, the data compiled here seem to corroborate this impression. For example, in the governor's report for the state of Coahuila, in reference to the question of criminal justice it was noted that in this area, "2,580 trials were set, 1,708 cases were appealed, and 1,964 cases were in process." The total number of suspects in this jurisdiction was 4,831, of whom

2,067 were sentenced. In Querétaro "the public defender handled 3,688 files," and the state reported that 3,384 suspects were sentenced.

34. The prosecutors' goal is not to obtain a sentence but to clarify the facts and deliver justice. Nevertheless, if their evidence has shown that a suspect should be arrested and charged and evidence of guilt has been presented during the trial, then at the very least the prosecutors should be expected to prove their case. Failure to win a "guilty" judgment is a miscarriage of justice on the part of both the prosecutors and the judges, because it means that they have tried an innocent person and deprived him or her of liberty for up to two years.

35. The remaining 12.5 percent received prison sentences of between three and four years in length. The 72.5 percent sentenced for minor crimes plus the 12.5 percent sentenced for three to four years and the 15 percent sentenced to more than five year gives us the total of those found guilty. *Cuaderno de Estadísticas Judiciales* 6 (1998): 302, 334.

36. Robbery accounts for 40 percent of the crimes reported in Mexico.

37. This is the proportional average found in the twelve states that report in two separate categories: *robos simples* (theft) and *robos calificados* (aggravated theft).

38. Sentences and averages were drawn from thirty Mexican penal codes. At the time the table was compiled, the penal codes for Puebla and Yucatán were not available.

39. The same pattern can be observed in crimes such as homicide and fraud.

40. Art. 9, *Código de Procedimientos Penales para el District Federal.*

41. In the wake of a rash of student vandalism, Mexico City's minister for public security was questioned about his subordinates' failure to take action. He responded that no complaint had been filed upon which they could act, and, moreover, the constitution empowers any citizen to make an arrest when someone is caught in the act of committing a crime.

42. *Anuario Estadístico del Estado de Baja California,* 1998, 186–87.

43. "En Baja California avanza la *procuración* de justicia," *Reforma,* August 28, 1998.

44. Guillermo Colín Sánchez, *Derecho mexicano de procedimientos penales,* 17th ed. (Mexico City: Porrúa, 1998), 338. Marco Antonio Díaz de León, *Código federal de procedimientos penales comentado,* 3d ed. (Mexico City: Porrúa, 1991), 92.

45. Procedural forms in the Procuracy of the Federal District make specific reference to ratification of the complaint, although none of the articles invoked as a basis for it make mention of ratification. In an interesting case in the México State, an alleged criminal about to be lynched was rescued. He was set free within hours when no one showed up to ratify a complaint against him.

46. For example, a professional soccer player was unable to accompany his team to an international competition because he had to wait six hours to identify a suspect who had assaulted him months before.

47. Document, National Chamber of Commerce, Mexico City, 1998 (with information relating to 1997 from the Procuraduría General de Justicia, Federal District).

48. For example, the police recommended that a businessman who was receiving telephone threats tape the calls, at his own expense, in order to discover their origin. He complied, but the information could not be used in a criminal action because there was no court order for obtaining the evidence. Worse, the police never bothered to apprehend the culprit or investigate the public telephone used to make the calls. *Reforma*, February 8, 1999.

49. The statistics on complaints received in Baja California Sur, Jalisco, Nuevo León, San Luis Potosí, and Tamaulipas were either incomplete or missing from the *Anuarios Estadísticos*, published by INEGI.

50. This figure includes 17,520 complaints still in process from prior years, as well as 25,999 new complaints made during 1997.

51. It should be noted that some local human rights commissions are significantly backlogged in their review of complaints.

52. In the Federal District, 45 percent of the complaints were lodged against the Procuracy. See *Quinto Informe Anual de la Comisión de Derechos Humanos del Districto Federal* (Mexico City, 1998), 23–55.

53. The majority of the complaints to the Federal District's Human Rights Commission cite delays and failure to investigate a case thoroughly (*Quinto Informe Anual*, ibid., 13). This may be due to the excessive workload of the Federal District Procuracy and the more demanding attitude characteristic of urban residents.

54. Human rights commissions have documented some of these complaints and issued recommendations. *Abuso y desamparo: tortura, desaparición forzada y ejecución extrajudicial en México* (Human Rights Watch, 1999). "Documentan tortura policiaca," *Reforma*, September 13, 1999.

55. Stojkovic, Kalinich, and Klofas, *Criminal Justice Organizations*, chaps. 8, 13, and 14, especially "Broken Windows, Damaged Gutters, and Police Supervision," 205–208. In Mexico, some officials routinely alter official records to keep someone under arrest longer than the period allowed under the Constitution. "Choca teoría con realidad," *Reforma*, February 25, 1999.

56. See *Abuso y desamparo*, 9–19, 37–60.

57. Ibid., 10.

58. A presidential decree for constitutional reforms to reduce requirements for the issuance of arrest warrants and holding of arraignments was issued in December 1997 and passed in November 1998. It states, "it is observed that an equilibrium has not been achieved between the action of prosecuting crime and a citizen's right to freedom."

59. Interview with subprocurador "A" from the Procuraduría de Justicia in the Federal District, in Romero Apis, "Desarticulada y corrompida."

60. For example, because both are state-level organizations, one rarely encounters instances in which the Procuracy denounces inefficiency or corruption on the part of the preventive police (*policía preventiva*) (unless it happens that political differences exist between the two agencies). It is much more common to see municipal-level police and state-level judicial and preventive police forces casting blame on each other.

61. In Mexico, this perception, based on an erroneous diagnosis of the public security problem, has led the federal Congress to pass laws that lower the bur-

den of proof that the procuracies are required to produce and that create exceptions to, and a reduction in, procedural guarantees. This perception is pervasive in many sectors of society. Recently, a politician used as a successful propaganda slogan, "human rights are for humans, not rats."

62. In 1997 and 1998, well-known jurists such as Dr. Ignacio Burgoa and groups like the Barra Nacional de Abogados (National Bar Association) came out in favor of "tightening the law."

63. *Quinto Informe Anual*, appendix of tables and figures.

64. Opposition lawmakers in the legislative assembly of the Federal District asked the public attorney for Mexico City to report on the legal status of more than a dozen preliminary investigations against judges. Compare the three newspapers: *El Economista, Crónica,* and *Reforma,* September 20 and 21, 1999.

65. The effectiveness of the procuracies varies from state to state. This chapter has concentrated on statistics aggregated at the national level and average trends. Currently, the Centro de Investigación y Docencia Económicas is preparing a study that compares regions and states.

66. There are arguments both for and against the notion that offenses are reported more often in rural areas, even though the cost of reporting crime may be lower in the city. Social cohesion is greater in smaller towns, which is an inducement for reporting. It is also claimed that the crisis over public security and credibility is gravest in Mexico City, for which reason the proportion of crimes reported there would be lower than in other cities in Mexico.

67. Michael Rand, *Criminal Victimization 1997: Changes 1996–97 with Trends* 1993–97 [sic] (Bureau of Justice Statistics, U.S. National Crime Victimization Survey, 1998).

68. Gavin S. Dingwall and Alan Davenport, "The Evolution of Criminal Justice Policy in the UK," in *Criminal Justice in Europe: A Comparative Study*, edited by Phil Fennell et al. (Oxford: Clarendon, 1995.

69. Fundación Paz Ciudadana, Chile, April 1999.

70. See, for example, "The Evolution of Criminal Justice Policy in the UK," 21.

71. *Reforma*, October 20, 1997. This daily newspaper has published quarterly surveys since 1995. In 1996, 36 percent of respondents cited this reason for not filing a crime report. In the September 14, 1999, issue, 39 percent answered that they had not filed a report because it would not solve anything, and 19 percent said they mistrusted the authorities. Between 1997 and 1999, 5 to 7 percent of those surveyed indicated that they did not file a complaint because they were afraid.

4

The Police in Mexico: Political Functions and Needed Reforms

Ernesto López Portillo Vargas

INTRODUCTION

The police as an institution forms part of a social project shaped by specific historical circumstances. It is appropriate, therefore, that studies of this institution take into account the particular context that molded it. The police form part of the social organization principles that support the paradigm of a modern state. However, every society has assigned its police specific attributes, both formal and real, and these attributes respond to the cultural, social, political, and economic demands that emerge from society's core.

This chapter encompasses three levels of analysis. The first approaches the police as an abstract paradigm that contains its original conceptual proposal. The second refers to the formal construction through which the police are justified legally and politically. And the third comprises the empirical reality through which the police evolves as an institution.

This examination of police in Mexico seeks answers to the following questions: Why and for what ends are the police created? What goals should they meet according to the official perspective? What goals do they achieve in practical terms? If we find contradictions—that is, if we find that the police are not what they should be—it means that the police do not respond to the demands that formal discourse sets for them, but to other demands of an informal nature.

The distinction can be better understood by taking the following into consideration. Although the Mexican Constitution states that legality must be the guiding principle in police actions, there is sufficient evidence to demonstrate that law enforcement has been guided historically by other, arbitrary criteria. But if the law serves only as a malleable reference point for the police (viewed as a social product), this means that a social context exists in Mexico that permits arbitrariness. However, the generalized public perception of the police in Mexico fails to heed this fact. Collectively, Mexicans share a Manichean image of the police, who are viewed as a "deviation" from society—that is, as something foreign to generally accepted "good values."

This perception appears unsustainable. When the police are viewed as detached from society's generally accepted values, the circumstances that condition police behavior can be ignored. Perhaps this is the simplest approach because it avoids coupling the questioning of the model of the police with the social circumstances surrounding it. But it is not a rigorous approach. For example, if there is a basis for claiming that Mexico City's preventive police (*policía preventiva*) are corrupt, then the role that the city government and society play in that situation should be studied as well. We should consider the features of the relationship that each community establishes with its police agencies.

The police do not represent values or interests that are foreign to society. On the contrary, social values and interests acquire a concrete meaning through the police.[1] I suggest two hypotheses in regard to this perspective. First, the informal code that guides the exercise of power in the Mexican political system repeats its schema within the police. And second, illegal acts by police in their daily operations express a function assigned to illegality by society as a whole. In other words, if it can be shown that police abuse power and resort to illegality, the same thing very likely happens in other public or private spaces, with other nuances.

It is not my intention to excuse police institutions of the responsibility they bear in the current situation. On the contrary, I seek to clarify the situation by utilizing a methodological approach that comprises both an external and an internal analytical perspective. The former views the police as a social product conditioned by specific values and interests accepted by the broader community; the latter is concerned with an examination of police institutions.

THE POLICE, THE POLITICAL REGIME (EXTERNAL PERSPECTIVE)

Following the paradigm of a police created in the origins of the modern state, the police were assigned specific attributes that correspond to cultural, social, political, and economic demands that emanate from society's core.[2] It is the political demands, derived from the character of the Mexican regime, that play a lead role in the construction of the police. In other words, it is primarily (though not solely) from the regime perspective that the features of the police paradigm are reinterpreted for the benefit of those who hold power.

My central hypothesis is that the absence of effective limits on the exercise of political power in Mexico has caused the regime itself to undertake such a reinterpretation, assigning to the police a support role of political loyalty. Such loyalty is guaranteed through negotiated mutual commitments and benefits between those who represent the police and those who represent the regime. This complicity, surrounded by a wide margin of impunity, constitutes the main bond that simultaneously unites and benefits both parties.

Likewise, such impunity assures the police a relative degree of autonomy through which it informally establishes internal arrangements that allow for the distribution of a variety of privileges.[3] For some, this autonomy is the fundamental characteristic of the Mexican police, who "through both legal and illegal recourses, evade all effective external supervision and control." It permits the "predominance of personal loyalties and informal internal networks, corporate or clientelist protection and concealment, and subordination of institutional demands to the particular interests of the commands."[4] Thus loyalty, complicity, impunity, and autonomy form the main components of a complex mechanism that has constituted the historical basis for the behavior of police institutions in Mexico.

A detailed history of the police in Mexico is beyond the scope of this chapter. Nevertheless, some attributes assigned to the police shortly after Mexico's independence deserve note because of their significant influence on the historical construction of the police throughout the twentieth century.

All evidence indicates that the legal institutionalization of public safety principles in Mexico's liberal project, which made safety an instrument of citizen protection, belongs to a tradition "that proved unsuccessful in Mexico given that neither the Constitution of Cádiz nor any other legal text or subsequent constitution refers to this citizens' right." It is only in the Provisional Regulatory Statute of the Mexican Republic of 1856 (Estatuto Orgánico Provisional de la República Mexicana de 1856) that safety as an individual right or guarantee is incorporated into a constitutional text. Article 30 stipulates that "the nation guarantees freedom, safety, property and equality to its citizens."[5]

This text had little impact, however. Mexican law was imbued with a model of security as authority exercised by the individual in power, and this model was assimilated into the notion of public safety.[6] The Mexican legal system, with its boundaries obscured, remained closely linked to state security rather than developing as a system strictly governed by the rule of law.[7]

The defeat of the liberal concept of public safety must be viewed, however, in light of the highly conflictive context in which various elements converged toward a repressive expression of public safety and, consequently, of the police. Three of these elements are particularly noteworthy: the political instability that resulted from armed confrontations between diverse forces within Mexico, the presence of banditry as an important social influence, and the weak separation between army functions and police functions that stemmed from a European model imported to Mexico.[8] These elements blocked the construction of a democratic police force during the first years of Mexico's independence from Spain.

A historical example that supports this hypothesis is the police force known as the *rurales*. In the mid-nineteenth century, President Benito Juárez's efforts to centralize power included as a core component the establishment of a police force dedicated to fighting crime and repressing political opposition. Consequently, political loyalty was fundamental in the originating concept of the police.

Furthermore, the state's profound weakness led it to pursue these goals through a complex process of negotiation in which law enforcement was subordinated to political convenience. On the one hand, it was common for the government to tolerate guerrillas and bandits if this accorded with its own interests.[9] On the other hand, it was also common for entire companies of *rurales* to switch factional loyalties, or for them to enforce public order while simultaneously engaging in criminal activities.

The priority was not compliance with the law, but rather the ability to collaborate in ensuring the government's centralization of political control at any cost. Judging by the evidence, it was not necessary to ensure the professional quality of the *rurales*. "A genuine selection of recruits did not take place because the police had to be content with the men it could get." In addition, the *rurales* were an unstable force in which only about half of its members fulfilled the standard tour of four or five years. Desertion became a common recourse for more than a third of the personnel, and near the end of the nineteenth century "the government had to recruit over 20,000 *rurales* ... merely to maintain the 2,400 positions budgeted for the police."[10]

Internal corruption was the norm. "The government tried to provide this police force with the most modern weapons.... However, supply officers often sold the new equipment to the locals and left the members of the organization to fend for themselves.... In 1910 an inspector reported that chronic alcoholism affected much of the organization. Almost half of all officers committed crimes that were serious enough to be entered in their service record."[11]

The lack of a professional service and the tolerance of impunity became consolidated as "necessary costs" of a police model transformed into a political resource. In this regard, we should recall that a primary concern of Porfirio Díaz upon his return to power in 1884 was to ensure the loyalty of the rural police. To this end he appointed Colonel Pedro A. González to shape the rural police in a "Porfirian mold."[12]

The Mexican state made a deal—impunity and a certain degree of autonomy in exchange for political loyalty—and Mexico is still paying the price. As a consequence of this compact, political control prevailed over legal control. The notion of legality was reworked into a circumstantial tool, to be applied only when politically necessary.

The Mexican Constitution of 1917, a watershed in the national project of the twentieth century, also failed to frame public safety as a civil right. Until 1994 public safety appeared only under the powers of the municipality (Article 115), and public safety was not incorporated into the democratic system of guarantees. The same is true of the police; it was not until 1994 that constitutional limits (legality, efficiency, professionalism, and honesty) were specified for the police.

The fact that Article 115 failed to identify public safety and the police as part of the foundations of democratic guarantees meant that the regime had chosen to blur the boundaries between state protection and citizen protection. This continued the privileging of a political interpretation and the preeminence of political controls over the police in postrevolutionary Mexico. Although the onset of the twenty-first century brought radical transformation, the police were trapped by the rules imposed by an authoritarian political model that ensured the structural weakness of the legal system.[13] The police did not operate under democratic controls because the Mexican state did not.

The regime revolved around a political party that constituted itself into "a powerful adhesion of loyalties that extolled unity as supreme power and operated as a portentous machine of electoral legitimization." This hegemonic party established "a long and complex process of presidential dominance" that ensured "the subordination of the legislature, the irrelevance of the judiciary, and local politics' dependence upon the dictates of the center." The centralization of power made the system unassailable and enabled it to undermine civil society and take control of its spaces.[14]

The correlate to this history is the crowning of illegality. "The political underdevelopment of the nation is synthesized in the unlikely subjection of power to law. The pretense of legality under which Mexico has lived for decades constitutes the distinguishing feature of its nondemocratic nature: a political order incapable of complying with its own law."[15] If the law is not the reference point, informal codes are. These codes are based on vertical lines of power from the top to the bottom; these lines are reproduced in reverse verticals of loyalty moving from the bottom up. This perspective reveals the state to be a patrimonial space colonized by "a vast political family linked by ties of kinship, friendship, fictive kinship, regional allegiance, and other factors of a personal nature. Patrimonialism constitutes private life encrusted into public life."[16]

"Corruption is a principle that occupied the core of the regime because it was the key to the government's preservation. The majority of authoritarian states have confronted dissent with brutal repression, but in Mexico dissent has been met with bribes, co-optation, agreements, and privileges." Illegality is the norm because it blocked transparency in "an opaque system that cultivated impunity."[17]

Historical examples that predate this regime show a utilization of the police in periods marked by political instability and state weakness. However, the hegemonic party system strengthened the state and did away with instability. Centralization of power allowed for the institutionalization of conflict and ensured a solid framework of clientelism. This framework shaped the performance of the entire bureaucratic apparatus, including police institutions.

Nonetheless, the pretense of legality placed the police in a growing dynamic of conflict, both internally and externally. Law enforcement did not become a regime priority, nor did its instruments. As in the nineteenth century, the police (and, to a degree, the entire justice system) were excluded from the modernization policies of the Mexican state.

With respect to police institutions themselves, the state failed to allocate sufficient resources to ensure their professional character. A clear example of this is that it was not until the 1990s that educational programs (special courses, master's degrees, and doctorates) were developed for the study of the police. As for their contacts with the rest of society, the police institutions were not—and are not—capable of comprehending the changing needs of society, creating a widening gap between the police and the public.[18]

Today the Mexican government and civil society are united in their criticism of the nation's police. Discrediting the police institutions has become commonplace, and the police have been designated as a priority problem. The issue has become sensationalized thanks to its extraordinary coverage in the media, where "the news continuously builds and re-builds social problems, crises, and enemies."[19] In other words, in addition to the real problems regarding the police, the issue has become an ideological tool that generates adherents and detractors. Political connotations are attached to the police issue and are then used to promote consensus and dissent.

Public exposure of the controversies surrounding the police institutions increases the perception of public insecurity, which, paradoxically, then builds a consensus for more police intervention and a toughening of the criminal justice and penal systems. The growing sense of insecurity—both objective and subjective—legitimizes official discourse that calls for an emergency response. According to officials, the only way to combat crime is immediately and exponentially to increase the resources assigned to the police and to the justice system.[20]

Such assertions should prompt the following questions. Are sufficient controls over the police in place to oversee a program of strengthening? And can the Mexican state demonstrate that it exercises reasonable levels of risk management over the police? Another element directly related to the link between the regime and the police suggests that the answer to both questions is negative; I am referring here to organized crime.

In 1994, I participated in a study that identified specific processes that link Mexican police institutions with organized crime.[21] The hypotheses of that study have been amply supported by a recent body of research by Alejandra Gómez Céspedes.[22] Gómez Céspedes's main finding is that political and economic changes up to 2000 did not alter the corporate and authoritarian character of the Mexican political system, which was dominated by a one-party bureaucratic apparatus crosscut by extensive relationships of a clientelistic nature between the political and financial elites.

Widespread (and tolerated) corruption made illegality the rule rather than the exception, and imbedded Mexico's security, intelligence, and law enforcement elites as part of the problem. Clearly, they were not reliable instruments in the battle against organized crime and corruption. Gómez Céspedes also found that, even in the absence of a rationale maintaining that Mexico cannot accomplish vital reforms, only an important counterweight of national and international forces in the political and criminal justice contexts could significantly affect the manner in which organized crime operates in politics and in economics.

Gómez Céspedes makes the following important observations. The single-party political system that held power in Mexico for almost seventy years benefited from a monopoly over a system of corruption, illegal transactions, and powerful interests. The absence of legality reached scandalous dimensions. Drug trafficking became a major organized crime activity, closely followed by fraud, kidnapping, and vehicle theft. And extortion within police forces, unions, and public administration exacerbated the problem. Unwritten, deep-rooted rules protected corrupt politicians, businessmen, and commanders of the police and the army, who as a rule were primary actors in the nucleus of criminal organizations in Mexico.

Gómez Céspedes's research recognizes that—notwithstanding the difficulty in obtaining data on the subject, which must then be viewed with caution—it is possible to characterize the structures of crime prevention, criminal justice, and politics and economics as elements in the explanation of organized crime. Mexico's situation is seen as a consequence of a process of concentrating resources and power that has been under way since the colonial period, with plentiful evidence for the state's involvement in organized crime activities. In regard to the police, her research shows that this long process led to the present situation in which the highest levels of official corruption, as well as a complete loss of regard for the general welfare, occurred within the security forces.

Gómez Céspedes asserts that, practically speaking, the police were created not to protect the population but to control it, and that it was allowed to repress, extort, and bribe as long as its loyalty to authority held firm. In her search for the origins of this situation, Gómez Céspedes reviewed the history of the Mexican federal police and uncovered evidence of a long continuum of links between crime and the police. This continuum developed as a result of official policies, especially the informal practice of compensating the police for services rendered.[23]

Gómez Céspedes's historical reconstruction, which includes the contemporary problems of the police, is helpful for understanding the experience of Mexico's Federal Security Directorate (DFS), created in the early 1940s. Gómez's research shows that the security forces' behavior was an essential element for understanding organized crime as a monopoly of the Mexican state.

The DFS operated at the international level with the U.S. Central Intelligence Agency (CIA) through a strategy intended to fight communism. Gómez Céspedes shows that collaboration between the CIA and the DFS exceeded all legal boundaries. Furthermore, she presents grounds for arguing that the DFS played an important role in the history of the U.S. government's tolerance toward large-scale drug trafficking.[24]

Turning to the Mexico City police, Gómez Céspedes presented the Division of Investigations for Crime Prevention (DIPD), created in the 1970s, as an example of how corruption in police departments is organized in a hierarchical form and according to an authoritarian model. It is most common for this type of corruption to extend upward from the police to higher levels of responsibility in the state, including federal law enforcement and political authorities.[25]

The fundamental point of these examples, commonly recognized as extreme cases, is that they denote behavior that serves illegal interests and that is promoted from within the organization itself. This hypothesis leads me to suggest a distinction between corruption that is aimed at personal benefit and corruption that appears linked to organizational objectives.[26] In other words, corruption in these cases is not so much a deviation from the structure, a result of a conscious choice of the individuals involved, as it is a result of the way in which police work is an extension of the broader sociopolitical context.

To summarize, the police in Mexico have operated on the basis of a historical mechanism that traded political loyalty for impunity and relative autonomy. The basis of police behavior—and of the regime as a whole—has been political, not legal. The police were excluded from the modernization policies of the state and were consolidated as a privileged resource of repression and corruption.

The official response to the growing influence of crime in Mexico has been to increase resources for punishment, including those assigned to the police, despite the controversies surrounding police institutions. Historical evidence attests to the police forces' involvement in crime from their very origins. And the nature of the present relationship between the state and organized crime has made the police a privileged connecting instrument between them.

POLICE INSTITUTIONS' PERFORMANCE (INTERNAL PERSPECTIVE)

Before describing the present state of police institutions in Mexico, I would suggest that it is not appropriate to bolster public investment in the police. Given their present condition, it would first be necessary to create instruments to ensure control over resources already allocated, along with any additional resources. Whether it is necessary to increase the power of the police rests on another question: Is the state able to meet its responsibility for controlling police institutions and guaranteeing their professional quality?

Ensuring a minimal level of effectiveness regarding the four constitutional principles of police performance (legality, efficiency, professionalism, and honesty) should take precedence over conferring more power on the police. It is ill conceived to reinforce an institution that has not earned the trust of the citizens unless concrete and sufficient measures are put in place to guarantee such trust.

Expanding the police is nothing new.[27] However, the skew in the federal government's current strategy exceeds a gradual, sustained rise in the number of police officers and has driven an exponential increase in resources allocated to the National Public Security System (SNSP). In fiscal year 1998, the federal budget included an allocation of 2.72 billion pesos to the SNSP, twelve times more than the 226.5 million pesos allocated in 1996.[28] The resources that the states and federal government together allocated in 1999 were in the neighborhood of 9 billion pesos, which means that the SNSP's resources increased almost forty-fold in three years.[29]

Yet despite the substantial increase in resources allocated to public security from 1996 to 1998, only marginal increases were reported in the eradication of marijuana and poppy fields; in seizures of cocaine, opium, heroin, and vehicles and weapons used by drug traffickers; or in the destruction of clandestine drug laboratories.[30] These data are highly suggestive of inconsistencies between official discourse and achievements in areas that the government has identified as priorities.

Before examining Mexico's police institutions, we should widen the scope of the analysis to include some indicators relevant to the context surrounding this issue, including rising crime rates, an ineffective and inefficient judicial system, and problems in crime prevention policies.[31]

At the national level, the number of alleged criminals grew by an average 14 percent per year between 1980 and 1996, compared with an overall population growth rate of just over 2 percent. In other words, reported crime increased about seven times faster than the population.

According to the 1995–2000 National Public Security Program (PNSP), between 1980 and 1994 crime rates increased 102 percent in state and local jurisdictions (*fuero común*) and 286 percent in the federal jurisdiction (*fuero federal*). If we calculate crime rates by the number of sentences imposed, state and local crime increased by 112 percent, and federal crime by 209 percent.

The data on impunity are eloquent. Mexico's Interior Ministry (Secretaría de Gobernación) stated in 1996 that approximately 1,400,000 crimes had been reported throughout the nation, 90 percent of which corresponded to state and local jurisdictions. Yet, according to the National Institute of Statistics, Geography, and Informatics (INEGI), only 181,743 persons were charged with crimes in 1996.[32] This means that charges were brought in fewer than 13 percent of the crimes reported at the national level. In April 1998 the Interior Ministry admitted that only 10 of every 100 individuals who commit a crime are charged.

The PNSP identified several "institutional" problems regarding crime prevention that are of particular importance. These include impunity, a failure to educate about crime prevention, a weak civic culture, disregard for the dictums of good government, loose administrative standards, a dysfunctional police, and poorly developed measures for communication and community relations. Additional problems include abuse of citizens' freedoms and rights; noncompliance with traffic laws; a lack of professional standards in crime prevention and in preventive police work; little assistance and counseling for victims, minors, and the elderly; flawed rehabilitation programs for minors and adults; and limited institutional promotion of citizen participation in crime prevention programs.[33]

The main problems confronted by police forces to one or another degree throughout the country, as indicated in the National Public Security Program, include: lack of planning criteria to guide the organization and operation of police services, inadequate budgets, resource allocation not based on specific criteria, lack of adequate criteria in determining salaries, low pay, high rates of personnel turnover which, in turn, complicate efficient resource allocation over the medium and long term, and a lack of standard merit policies on promotions or dismissals.

Police forces also suffer the constant shuffling of personnel between one or another agency across the country. Some former police officers leave public service to enter the "criminal labor market." There are considerable disparities across communities in terms of police presence in proportion to population. Coordination among police forces is inadequate. Educational backgrounds, pay and training, and working conditions for the police are below minimum professional and constitutional standards for the society.

The PNSP's review of the training of the preventive police found that academic and professional training is a recent policy. Of the fifty-eight police academies in Mexico, twenty-five began their programs within the past two decades. Nationwide, basic training lasts an average of 4.5 months, compared to 21 months in Europe. Only seventeen academies enforce a minimum educational requirement. In other words, prior to 1995 two-thirds of Mexico's police academies did not even require trainees to meet minimal scholastic requirements.

The PNSP also made note of the absence of any organization in Mexico dedicated to developing personnel who would then train police officers. In addition, the majority of Mexico's police officers (223,533, or 55.6 percent) have no education, some elementary school, or have completed elementary school. Nearly a quarter (99,450, or 24.7 percent) fall into the categories of "some middle school" and "completed middle school"; 55,342 (13.7 percent) have some high school or have completed high school; and 788 (0.19 percent) have partially completed or completed normal (teacher training) school. The Interior Ministry noted in 1998 that 80 percent of police training institutions in Mexico had obsolete programs.

A long history of no minimum quality standards and no controls in the allocation of resources contributed to the internal structural decay of Mexico's police institutions. Evidence of that decay include a lack of guidelines for the performance of police duties, arbitrariness and spreading corruption at all levels, insufficient training, and little specialized expertise to support an effective division of labor. Additional problems include a lack of technically appropriate, systematic, and reliable tools for evaluating job performance; minimal ethical standards; no respect for human rights; obsolete oversight and information systems; few opportunities for showing initiative; insufficient technical support; a lack of guidelines to direct decision making; a predominance of fragmented interest groups; a lack of group solidarity and cohesion; little attention to community relations; low group recognition of professional merit; and a lack of institutional resources for protecting police officer.

This structural decay means that problems in police performance do not derive from isolated behaviors. Rather, they are the product of a policy that systematically postponed the overall modernization of police institutions and turned them into reactive instruments for political purposes. These institutions' systematic involvement in problems of violence is perhaps the most dramatic consequence of neglect and decay.

International organizations share this interpretation. In *Mexico: The Shadow of Impunity* (1999), Amnesty International reports a serious deterioration in human rights in Mexico, noting that torture, extrajudicial executions, disappearances, and arbitrary arrests are common. This document identifies the police and military as the unpunished authors of such practices. It also quotes the May 1998 annual report of the National Commission on Human Rights (CNDH) citing the rise in complaints of torture from forty-six in 1997 to fifty-eight in 1998. Amnesty International states that the majority of the reported disappearances and extrajudicial executions took place in the context of operations targeted against common crime, insurgency, and narcotics.

The Inter-American Commission on Human Rights of the Organization of American States published a report on Mexico in September 1998 in which it reported that it had found indiscriminate repression of civic organizations by security forces. This document also reports that several states are being militarized in the battle against drug trafficking and crime, and the military presence has caused an increase in complaints of human rights violations, including civilian deaths.[34]

The chapter on Mexico in the 1998 Human Rights Watch world report documents that serious violations against human rights and impunity are the norm, adding that some of these violations are the result of a campaign that, although necessary, is poorly designed for fighting both ordinary crime and organized crime. Human Rights Watch also points out that Mexico's police and judicial system are implicated in the violations.[35]

At the national level, the CNDH issued more that two hundred recommendations in cases in which the reported violation involved the police, leading the Commission to conclude that "police abuse and irregularities are routine."[36]

One final indicator of the current status of the Mexican police comes from the citizenry. A rigorous opinion poll on public security conducted in Mexico City in March 1999 found that some 70 percent of citizens do not think that the Mexico City police can solve the public security problem. The same proportion do not trust the police, think they are weak on crime, and believe that the police are linked to crime.[37] The study's author finds further that "more than expressing their fear about crime, people are stating their dissatisfaction with the level of protection they receive."[38]

The author hypothesizes that people are evaluating their lack of security as "a lack of protection against being victimized."[39] The study points to a complex aspect that merits exploration: the population's feelings of insecurity may be directly related to their negative perception of the police. "The population is evaluating the parameters of freedom, for which it assigns responsibility to those who have the duty of guaranteeing it, such as the police."[40] On this basis, it is reasonable to formulate a related hypothesis: it is probable that the police themselves are generating insecurity. In other words, the outcome they are generating is exactly opposite to the purposes for which they were created.

DEMOCRACY AND PUBLIC SECURITY (FREEDOM AND POLICE)

My theoretical premise is that freedom is the primary value of the democratic project of the modern state. Security is one of the instruments the state creates to guarantee the exercise of freedom, and it constitutes the underlying meaning of the police. Consequently, the police are an instrument in support of freedom.

According to Norberto Bobbio, the minimal definition of democracy refers to respect for rights "based upon which the liberal state was born and upon which the doctrine of the rule of law was built. In other words, the state not only exercises power subject to the law but also within the limits derived from the constitutional recognition of the individual's so-called inalienable rights.... The assumption of rights is required for the proper functioning of the same mechanisms ... that characterize a democratic regime. The constitutional norms that confer these rights are not the rules of the game; they are preliminary tenets that permit the development of the game."[41]

This definition suggests that democracy is a liberal project of the state in which the exercise of power, in addition to being subject to the law, is based on the recognition of the individual's basic rights, which are the core assumption of democracy itself. In other words, in this kind of state, inalienable rights do more than serve as the limits of power; they are the foundation that gives meaning to power.

The political philosophy that inspired the establishment of the modern liberal state instilled freedom and security precisely as limits to, and as the basis of meaning for, the exercise of power. This is why freedom and security appear as inalienable rights in Article 3 of the Declaration of Human Rights and Citizen Rights of 1789. This also explains why Article 12 of this declaration assigns the mission of protecting freedom to the security forces, given that such forces are created for the purpose of guaranteeing those rights and "are instituted for the benefit of all and not for the personal gain of those to whom [power] is entrusted." The French Constitution of 1793 and the Declaration of the Rights of Man and of Citizens also assign the protection of persons, their rights, and their property to the security forces.

The historical formula that makes freedom the preeminent value is the following: individuals are free to establish themselves in a society, and they accept the limits on freedom imposed by life in society. This hypothetical collective negotiation of freedom inspired the two fundamental principles that have justified the modern state since its origins—the social contract and popular sovereignty. This is why the state assumes the adjective of "liberal," precisely because it is created by the will of all for ensuring freedom.[42] Freedom is the foundation of democracy, and its transgression means the fracturing of a democratic state. Security is essentially a principle that serves the interests of freedom; and the police, as an instrument of security, must necessarily be considered as a resource for the protection of freedom.

These observations are not merely theoretical. On the contrary, they relate directly to the constitutional foundations that define Mexico's political regime. National sovereignty resides in the people (Article 39), who constitute themselves in a representative, democratic, federal republic (Article 40). The state must strengthen such sovereignty and its democratic regime and create conditions that will allow the full exercise of freedom (Article 25) and the political, social, and cultural democratization of the nation (Article 26). In other words, democracy is the result of the popular will that guarantees it and that ensures the exercise of freedom through representation in the state. Democracy is a national project with explicit concepts, not "a catalog of wishes that inspire but do not obligate."[43]

As noted previously, seventy-seven years passed before the Mexican Constitution explicitly linked public security and police with the project of a democratic state of law. Public security was incorporated into Article 21 in 1994 as a "function entrusted to the Federation, the Federal District, the states, and the municipalities." The same article contains the constitutional guarantee that "the performance of the police institutions will be ruled by the principles of legality, efficiency, professionalism, and honesty." Put another way, public security and police compliance with said principles are simultaneously the functions of the state and the right of every individual.

However, the Constitution defines no specific requirements regarding either public security or the police, and this ambiguity prevents citizens from demanding the enforcement of their clearly defined right.[44] The democratic function is incomplete because there are no set goals that explicitly link public security and the police to the full exercise of freedom prescribed by Article 25.[45]

There are sufficient theoretical foundations that legitimize the democratization of the police based on the principle of freedom. Far from constituting a theoretical scenario, this framework can lead to the reformulation of conceptual, legislative, administrative, and operational practices.

A FORMAL DESCRIPTION OF THE POLICE

By the most general definition, the police comprises public security forces entrusted with the prevention and investigation of crimes and misdemeanors, in support of the Public Ministry (Ministerio Público) and the courts.[46] There are two general criteria for the organization of police institutions in Mexico: by function and by jurisdiction.

In terms of functions, Mexico's police are divided into preventive (the uniformed *policía preventiva*) and judicial (the plain-clothes *policía judicial*).[47] The former are empowered to apply administrative norms (called governmental and police regulations in constitutional article 21). They have the role of "maintaining public security in cities and towns" and assisting the Public Ministry at its request. The judicial police (so named in constitutional article 21; the word "judicial" was deleted under a recent reform) is an auxiliary to the Public Ministry and acts under its authority and immediate command.

Jurisdictional criteria follow the federal pattern for the distribution of powers. Each of the three levels of government (municipal, state, and federal) manages its own police institutions. The municipal level has only preventive police; the states (and the Federal District) and the federal government maintain both preventive and judicial police. In the states and the Federal District, the judicial police enforce state and local law (*fuero común*). The federal Public Ministry employs its own judicial police in the investigation and prosecution of federal crimes.

Mexico contains 2,395 *municipios* (akin to U.S. counties), which demonstrate a wide range of social, cultural, demographic, economic, and political characteristics. These differences are reflected in the development of their respective police institutions. The 1995–2000 National Social Security Program's analysis found that 335 *municipios* have no police officers at all, while eighty-seven of them account for 68.7 percent of the 280,000 preventive police at the three levels of government nationwide. The organization of municipal police institutions can be very simple (as in the 2,000 *municipios* with fewer than 100 officers) or extremely complex (as in the Federal District, where there are some 100,000 uniformed officers).

Several features stand out concerning the federal police. The judicial police were established under the Constitution of 1917 to serve as an investigative agency. This work, previously done by judges, was assigned to a "special body of judicial police, for the federation and Federal District and [federal] territories, but under the authority and command of the Public Ministry."[48]

Under the current Organic Law of the Attorney General's Office (Ley Orgánica de la Procuraduría General de la República Mexicana), the Federal Judicial Police is an adjunct of the Public Ministry,[49] which is headed by the attorney general (Article 19).[50] The General Law provided for the creation of the General Office of Planning and Operations of the Federal Judicial Police, whose director pledges that the Federal Judicial Police will act under the authority of the Public Ministry, oversees the agency's strategic planning and investigations, and evaluates the results (Article 23).[51] The PNSP reported in 1995 that there were 4,400 federal judicial police officers (and 7,000 federal preventive police officers) and 21,000 state-level judicial police officers.

The Law of the Federal Preventive Police (LPFP)[52] establishes the guidelines for combining and reorganizing the administrative police agencies of Migration, Treasury, and Highways, which traditionally have pertained, respectively, to the Ministries of the Interior, Finance, and Communications and Transportation. The LPFP outlines the authority and the general organizational and operational bases of the Federal Preventive

Police. The hierarchical relationships, normative and operational structures, territorial organization, and jurisdictions of command and discipline are set by internal regulations issued by the federal executive.

The LPFP was the most important police-related initiative of the administration of Ernesto Zedillo (1994–2000). The Federal Preventive Police was created to become a key instrument in the development of operational coordination within the framework of the SNSP. It is autonomous technically and operationally, even though it is subordinate to the Interior Ministry. It is headed by a commissioner appointed (and able to be removed) by the president (LPFP, Article 2). The Federal Preventive Police (PFP) will operate throughout Mexico and will collaborate with the police forces of the *municipios*, the states, and the Federal District.

The importance of the PFP is clearly visible in the broad authority accorded it under Article 4 of the LPFP. The PFP is charged with preventing criminal and administrative violations of federal law; safeguarding public security, in collaboration with appropriate authorities; and guaranteeing, maintaining, or reestablishing public order in international border zones, coastlines, Mexican sections of border connectors and bridges, customs offices, entry and inspection points, immigration centers, treasury precincts, federal highways, railways, airports, maritime ports authorized for international traffic, and modes of transport operating in general routes, as well as all auxiliary services.[53] The PFP is also authorized to assist requesting authorities in investigating and prosecuting crimes and making arrests and recovering objects related to crimes, to make arrests in flagrante delicto cases, to collaborate with state and municipal authorities in protecting persons and their property in dangerous situations, and to participate in joint operations with other police agencies under the SNSP framework.

The following also fall under the PFP's jurisdiction: collecting and analyzing information related to public security, implementing crime-prevention measures, protecting general communications routes and traffic on them, levying fines for land use violations along communication routes, cooperating with civilian emergency services in times of calamity or natural disaster, protecting federal public servants and foreign visitors conducting official business in Mexico, and collaborating with civilian protection services when requested.[54]

To join the PFP, an applicant must be a Mexican citizen by birth and hold no other citizenship, be of sound mind, have a high school diploma or equivalent, not abuse illegal drugs or alcohol, and have no criminal record. Applicants must pass an entrance exam and basic courses, and they must pledge to abide by the basic principles of conduct specified by the LPFP. Article 13 of the LPFP further specifies that all members of the PFP must also be members of Mexico's civil service. And all must be cleared through the National Public Security Personnel Registry (Registro

Nacional de Personal de Seguridad Pública). Tenure in the PFP depends upon successfully completing personnel development and continuing education programs. A special appointed body evaluates personnel and recommends promotions.[55]

The PFP will assume its authority in stages over time. Police agencies currently in operation will be combined and will continue to carry out their duties for a period not to exceed twenty-four months from the effective date of the LPFP. Responsibility for coordinating these various forces was given to the PFP commissioner, with the instruction that officers of currently operating police forces can enter the PFP only if they meet its entrance and tenure requirements.

The first PFP commissioner took office in March 1999, published the recruitment announcement for the first generation of officers in June, and then left office in July. The second commissioner identified four "essential" working strategies: vigilance in maintaining public security and deterring crime, the investigation and prevention of conditions that permit crime, efficient and rapid response to situations of "grave danger," and the establishment of the analytical capacity to produce "select police intelligence."[56]

In addition to its Office of the Commissioner, the PFP includes offices for: internal administration; intelligence (civilian command); federal support forces (military command, including strategic installations, special operations, reaction and immediate support); regional security (federal highways, airports, seaports, and international borders); a police academy, learning center, and center of advanced studies; citizen relations; and internal affairs.[57] The functions and organization of the PFP make it the first police institution whose structure and goals combine preventive policing and crime investigation, transcending the traditional division between these tasks.

On July 8, 1999, the Interior Ministry and the Ministry of National Defense (SEDENA) signed an agreement transferring the following resources to the PFP: 4,899 military police personnel; 352 multiple-use vehicles; 99 search-and-rescue and drug- and bomb-sniffing dogs; communications equipment; and 1,862 firearms.[58] The military personnel form the Reaction and Immediate Support Forces, which "will under no circumstances be used in missions other than those directed toward reestablishing public safety." The PFP commissioner specified that these military personnel would be billeted in barracks and be charged with fighting organized crime in remote areas.[59]

As of mid–2000 the PFP numbered more than 11,000 personnel: 4,000 from the Federal Highway Police; 5,000 from the military; 700 from the Interior Ministry's Center for Research and National Security (CISEN); and 1,500 enrolled in the Federal Preventive Police Academy.[60] In other words, the entire current personnel of this "new" police institution has previous experience in police work.

This discussion leads one to ask whether the PFP represents the first stage in unifying crime prevention and investigation. If so, have the policy's advantages and disadvantages—and the constitutional and legal issues it entails—been analyzed? Will policymakers take account of public opinion? Will the PFP's functions and any increase in its jurisdiction be open to congressional review? As yet, there are no answers to these questions, which involve fundamental definitions of democracy versus authoritarianism. I advocate that the PFP should be submitted to oversight, with the Mexican Congress establishing permanent mechanisms to undertake such oversight activities. Furthermore, information about the PFP must be made available to the public. These democratic controls are necessary to prevent placing a police institution above the law.

Were the PFP to carry out criminal investigations and prosecutions on its own, it would be in violation of constitutional article 21, which authorizes the Public Ministry, assisted by the police under its command, to carry out these activities. The PFP would be in a situation similar to that of the Special Organized Crime Unit (UEDO) of the federal Attorney General's Office (PGR), which received exclusive investigative authority that demanded constitutional reforms and that continues to generate controversy. In addition to questions of constitutionality, giving the PFP autonomy in investigative matters would create a potentially dangerous and conflictive situation between the PFP and the Attorney General's Office. And it could pose a serious risk of violating citizens' rights in penal matters because any criminal investigation conducted outside of the Public Ministry would bypass constitutional and legal controls.

Furthermore, incorporating the PFP into the Interior Ministry puts at risk the technical and operational autonomy provided by law. Recent police experiences do not offer sufficient evidence to believe otherwise. In addition, the team that heads the PFP was transferred from CISEN, which is an instrument of the executive branch, is subordinate to the Interior Ministry, and is dedicated to the political control of national security. The risk of political contamination in police activities is clear.

The need to reestablish the judicial order that had been violated by the creation of extra-constitutional police institutions was one of the arguments the legislature used to justify creation of the PFP. It also offered the advantage of avoiding modifying the functions of the army and the Federal Judicial Police. The military's inclusion in the PFP goes against the legislature's intent, and it also violates a fundamental characteristic of democratic models of the police, which is precisely its civilian character.

The issue of whether the character of the PFP is civilian or military has to do not only with the nature of its officers but also with its ideological foundations. I noted earlier that Mexico's military model of the police was imported from Europe, and various internal circumstances strengthened this model of conceptualizing and regulating police and police operations. The adoption of a police of military-style organization and behavior has been a constant in Mexican history.

A recent study, which reviews the distinction that John Lea and Jock Young made between the consensual model of police and the military-inspired model,[61] provides some useful observations on the disjunction between the civilian and military models. These authors characterize the consensual model as follows:

> Social support for the police derives from the community's perception of the benefits it gains from protection against crime. There is an important flow of information from the community to the police regarding criminal behavior; the population is motivated to give this information and await the results. As a consequence of the close ties and communications between the community and the police, the police achieve higher success rates in their investigations, which increases the certainty that the police will detain only those who merit detention. The concept of the police apprehending persons indiscriminately in their search for a guilty party simply does not fit within this framework. When a closer relationship is established between the police and the community, the meaning of stereotypes changes as well. Police action as reaction to stereotypes gives way to actions directed toward individuals suspected of legal violations based on information obtained with the community's help.[62]

Other features of the consensual model of police include the absence of any unnecessary political interference in police activities, demilitarizing all aspects of police service, full respect for basic rights, transparency of behavior, and executive and legislative branch control over police activities.[63]

> At the opposite end of the spectrum from the consensual model of police is the military-inspired model, which entails a very different relationship with the community. In this case, the community does not support the police, nor does it provide it with information. The community is actively or passively hostile toward the police, who are perceived as an oppressive political force. The distancing that occurs under this model—between a distrustful population and a police force under social and political pressure in the fight against crime—makes it necessary for the police to resort to other sources of information, such as clandestine informants, undercover agents (who are frequently linked to criminal activities), and forced collabora-

> tion of citizens arrested arbitrarily based on subjective and often contradictory criteria. There is a saying in Mexico: "the police arrest in order to investigate; they do not investigate in order to arrest."[64]

Lea and Young emphasize that "a spiral of violence and insecurity develops, creating a situation that worsens with the participation of elite or special groups who, in fact, have had military training and operate in a strictly military manner, inasmuch as they consider that they have in front of them not citizens but enemies."[65]

A series of articles published in the Mexico City daily *Reforma* in January 2000 reveals the predominance of the military model in the personnel training and development of the PFP.[66] According to the series, the main element of cohesiveness among cadets is not the PFP's mission and goals, but rather the image of a crewcut, uniformed officer and the "rush" from intense physical exercise. "The discipline is like faith," the journalist wrote, quoting the institute's director as saying: "in order to get our message across, this has to be like a monastery." The cadets immediately become familiar with military lingo. They are organized into companies, there is a marching band, and sergeants and corporals head the groups. Daily activities, including marching, emphasize military discipline as an essential ingredient in police training and development. The most important value instilled in the aspiring police officers is discipline.

Moreover, the military's participation in the PFP disregards international recommendations, such as the "Report on the Human Rights Situation in Mexico" issued by the Inter-American Commission on Human Rights of the Organization of American States in September 1998. The report exhorts Mexico "to revise the contents of the General Law of the National Public Security System in order to restrict the armed forces to their proper role, in accordance with the precepts of the international assembly on the matter, especially Article 27 of the American Convention."[67] Nevertheless, out of the approximately 10,000 members of the PFP, not a single one has come from a training and development background that accords with the parameters set in the LPFP for a new, professional force subject to effective controls. As noted above, of its active personnel, approximately 1,000 came from the CISEN, 4,000 from the Federal Highway Police, and 5,000 from the military.

Both the abstract meaning and the concrete behavior of police institutions must be subjected to open and systematic public scrutiny. Only in this way can Mexico work rigorously and systematically toward the construction of an alternative police model.[68] Clearly it is not possible to transform the police without a concomitant change in the demands the police have historically satisfied. In other words, police reform is not feasible until there are changes in the police's relationship with political power.

It is too early to foresee the fate of Mexico's political transition, but much is known about successful transitions:

> A political outcome such as a change of regime in favor of democracy and its consolidation is not determined by economic, social, or cultural structures. A society with given structures and even with relatively stable citizen preferences can choose political alternatives, such as democracy, dictatorship, or revolution.... Different results can be obtained according to the diverse political actors' initiatives, strategies, and luck.[69]

What is needed in Mexico is a police reform that does not respond to the politics of the moment or the interests of a single group. On the contrary, political neutrality is essential for guaranteeing a rigorous police reform—and for serious research into the problems of the Mexican police and possible alternative models.

When writing this chapter, I came across a book of stories narrated by children who have lived on the streets.[70] For these children, the police officer is not a figure to emulate. He is someone to fear and is always associated with violence. This is not a question of political discourse or interpretation. Nor is it an issue of the government's programs, intentions, or justifications. The violence the police inflict on penniless minors forms part of the reality of daily life, a reality that very few are willing to talk about.

This is perhaps the most dramatic expression of the ethical, social, and legal schism that characterizes the relationship between the police and citizenry in Mexico. At an ethical level, it assumes the police's total abandonment of their supposed responsibility. On the social level, it implies a lack of trust in the police. And on a legal level, it means the annulment of all formal limits on police action.

Absent responsibility, trust, and legal efficiency, the police circulate in a sphere created by their own rules. And these rules have not yet been adequately analyzed. We already know that most people distrust or fear the police. The next step is to rigorously study the values, attitudes, and opinions that unite and divide police and society. There are many unanswered questions. For example, why and under what circumstances does a police officer resort to violence? Is it in response to concrete social expectations? How does public opinion influence police behavior? What values determine police behavior in urban and rural areas of Mexico, and how does police behavior vary between the city and the countryside? How does society make value judgments and form opinions about the police?

The institution of the police is a social product, and it is essential to understand it in that perspective. The historical social attributes assigned to the police in Mexico can offer better explanations than can a legal framework or official discourse. Police behavior—seemingly inefficient, corrupt, and violent—is in reality part of the set of values that characterizes Mexican society.

Notes

Translated by H. Campbell.

1. Interpretations of police behavior should incorporate sociological studies, based on empirical research, that can place the police's expressed understanding of the moral universe in a defined social context. The lack of such studies clouds interpretations of the real perceptions that police agents have of their work. For example, no one has analyzed the value that the police themselves assign to corruption, even though one study states that "the starting point for any serious work aimed at controlling corruption should take into account the personal perspectives of the people whose conduct is intended to be regulated." See Juan Lozano and Valeria Merino Dinari, *La hora de la transparencia en América Latina: el manual de la anticorrupción en América Latina* (Argentina: Granica/CIEDLA, 1998), 47.

2. An interesting approach to the police as a response to a society's concrete historical demands can be found in Amadeu Recasens I Brunet, *Los efectos de los cambios políticos, sociales y económicos en la criminalidad y en la justicia penal* (Strasbourg: XXI Conference on Criminological Investigations, November 19–22, 1996).

3. This perspective echoes similar approaches in research on other police institutions in Latin America. Such is the case in Argentina, where analyses have shown that the police are strongly subordinated to the interests of government ministries at both the federal and local levels, but "with a strong dose of autonomous institutional power." See Alicia Oliveira and Sofía Tiscornia, "Estructura y prácticas de las policías en la Argentina: las redes de la ilegalidad," in *Control democrático en el mantenimiento de la seguridad interior*, edited by Hugo Frülig (Santiago, Chile: Centro de Estudios del Desarrollo, 1998), 158.

4. See Beatriz Martínez de Murguía, *La policía en México: ¿orden social o criminalidad?* (Mexico City: Planeta, 1999). In that work, this statement is supported through research conducted by the human rights commissions. I agree in essence; however, I believe it is necessary to place that autonomy in the double perspective that approaches it as a benefit that is exchanged for political loyalty.

5. José Arturo Yáñez Romero, "La policía en la modernización cultural de la Ciudad de México, 1821–1876: arbitrariedad y cultura de gobierno" (Ph.D. dissertation, Universidad Autónoma Metropolitana–Xochimilco, 1997), 54. This text covers historical reconstruction with special depth and rigor.

Editors' note: The "liberal project" refers to a nineteenth-century political movement that stressed individual rights and liberties and saw the state as the protector of those rights.

6. That notion, in turn, possesses a long tradition that has made it synonymous with the police. Public security has been understood in a collective manner as the

substance of police activity, but also as "a means of intervention in the realm of the freedom of individuals." See José Luis Carro Fernández-Valmayor, *Policía y sociedad* (Santander, Spain, 1989).

7. The way in which public safety is understood in Spain provides important explanatory elements regarding the concept in Mexico and its application to the police. Consider, for example, the following: "Public safety, defined as the responsibility of the police and other authorities more generally, has long been used to limit rights and to justify authorities' seizure of vast sanctioning powers in order to cover up infractions of legal principle and of the foundations underlying the power that authorities hold on behalf of society.... The concept of public safety ... has been invoked in an encompassing range of actions, none of which would be legitimate in a democratic state of law." Javier Barcelona Llop, *Policía y constitución* (Madrid: Tecnos, 1997), 26.

8. Article 1 of the 1826 legislation provides an eloquent example of the symbiosis between the army and the police in tasks of public safety. This article, "which refers to thieves operating in gangs, is extended to all thieves apprehended in the Federal District and the territories by political authorities, permanent troops, and active or local militia, even though they may not be intended for the pursuance of thieves. Should the local militia be lacking in officers, it may supply itself from other forces." Jesús Martínez Garnelo, *Policía nacional investigadora del delito* (Mexico City: Porrúa, 1999), 98.

9. In the words of Benito Juárez: "I regret the excesses of guerrillas such as Rojas, Carbajal, González Ortega, and Pueblita, but it is necessary to tolerate them because otherwise they would abandon us, and I have made it understood to our allies [the Yankees] that said guerrillas proceed in that manner under our instructions and for the purpose of removing all kinds of resources from the enemy." Nicole Girón, *Heraclio Bernal: bandolero, cacique o precursor de la revolución* (Mexico City: Instituto Nacional de Antropología e Historia, 1976), 35. Quoted in Martínez Garnelo, *Policía nacional*, 136.

10. Harry E. Cross, "The Mining Economy of Zacatecas: Mexico in the 19th Century" (Ph.D. dissertation, University of California, Berkeley, 1976). Quoted in Martínez Garnelo, *Policía nacional*, 146.

11. Martínez Garnelo, *Policía nacional*, 147.

12. José C. Valdés, *El Porfirismo: historia de un régimen* (Mexico City: Antigua Librería Robledo de J. Porrúa e Hijos, 1941), 316. *Mexico Herald*, January 15, 1911, 5; quoted in Martínez Garnelo, *Policía nacional*, 151.

13. I am referring to Juan Linz's concept of an authoritarian regime, which is characterized by a limited and nonresponsible ideological pluralism, with no elaborated ideology, without an intensive political mobilization, and in which a chief or a small group exercises power within limits that are formally ill defined. The first aspect refers to selection and co-opting mechanisms from the top; the second to the poor degree of organization and conceptual elaboration of theories that justify power; the third to the moderate participation of the population; and the fourth to the power of the chief or of the elite being exercised within limits that are well understood, though not formally established. Taken from Norberto

Bobbio, Nicola Mateucci, and Gianfranco Pasquino, *Diccionario de política* (Mexico City: Siglo Veintiuno, 1997), 133.

14. These ideas are drawn from one of the most accurate recent critiques of the "old regime." See Jesús Silva-Herzog Márquez, *El antiguo régimen y la transición en México* (Mexico City: Planeta/Joaquín Mortiz, 1999), 17–46.

15. Ibid., 35.

16. Octavio Paz, *El ogro filantrópico* (Mexico City: Joaquín Mortiz, 1979), 91. Quoted in Silva-Herzog Márquez, *El antiguo régimen y la transición en México*, 44.

17. Silva-Herzog Márquez, *El antiguo régimen y la transición en México*, 44–45.

18. For some thoughts that might broaden these comments, see Ernesto López Portillo Vargas, "No más sino mejores policías," *Etcétera* (Mexico City) 284 (July 9, 1998).

19. See Murray Edelman, *La reconstrucción del espectáculo político* (Buenos Aires: Manantial, 1991), 8.

20. A sharp critique of the state's urgency to strengthen its instruments of punitive intervention can be found in the first part of Luis Armando González Plascencia, *Hacia un modelo democrático de seguridad ciudadana: entre la justicia cívica y el sistema penal*, Working Paper No. 15 (Mexico City: Fundación Rafael Preciado Hernández, November 1998).

21. These processes fell within the framework of a broader analysis. See Samuel González Ruiz, Ernesto López Portillo Vargas, and José Arturo Yáñez Romero, *Seguridad pública: problemas, perspectivas y propuestas* (Mexico City: Coordinación de Humanidades, Universidad Nacional Autónoma de México, 1994).

22. Alejandra Gómez Céspedes, "The Dynamics of Organized Crime in Mexico" (Ph.D. dissertation, Cardiff University, 1998). The project, completed in England, was based on fieldwork conducted in Mexico.

23. Ibid., 200.

24. Ibid., 235.

25. Ibid., 242.

26. Oliveira and Tiscornia, *Estructura y prácticas de las policías en la Argentina*, 157.

27. In 1994 Mexico had 41 police officers for every 10,000 citizens. This number has since risen to 68 officers for every 10,000 citizens fourteen years of age or older. In 1994, Mexico had more police officers per capita than Belgium, Canada, Denmark, Germany, Great Britain, Holland, Spain, Switzerland, and the United States. The ratio of 68 officers per 10,000 citizens exceeds the comparable figures in ten of the twelve nations in the European Union. See González Ruiz et al., *Seguridad pública*, 103–107.

In 1994 Mexico City had 54,000 police officers, or 65 officers for every 10,000 citizens, compared to 37 in Washington, D.C., 53 in Rome, 56 in Paris, 44 in Madrid, and 40 in Rio de Janeiro. For every 100 officers in Mexico City, there are 86 in Paris, 68 in Madrid, 53 in New York, and 39 in London. When correlating the number of crime reports and of officers, Mexico City has 6.6 more officers than the international average. One officer in any of these other cities does the work of 55 in Mexico City. Mexico City has more police officers than comparable large cities worldwide, more officers assigned to investigate reported crimes, and more officers in relation to the number of citizens. See Rafael Ruiz Harrel, *Criminalidad y mal gobierno* (Mexico City: Sansores-Aljure, 1998).

28. *Plan Nacional de Desarrollo: informe de ejecución 1998* (Mexico City: Secretaría de Hacienda y Crédito Público, 1999), 27.

29. *Quinto Informe de Gobierno,* Ernesto Zedillo Ponce de León, 1999.

30. Ibid., 45. Another example that merits attention is the reported decrease in "criminals apprehended on highways" between 1997 (2,900) and 1998 (2,042). The federal government considers this criminal activity to be one of the fundamental problems created by organized crime. Compare the *Informes de Ejecución* of 1997 and 1998.

31. The absence or incompleteness of statistical information on public safety and criminal justice, as well as the enormous difficulty in accessing current information, force me to present indicators based on scattered data or my own constructions. For this reason, I indicate the source only when all of the information on an indicator has been collected directly.

32. The alleged criminals are identified as such by constitutional judicial decree emitted by the appropriate agency. See *Cuaderno de estadísticas judiciales* (Aguascalientes), No. 5, 7.

33. The same document summarizes other problems in crime prevention, defined as "social factors." They are unemployment and underemployment, illness, extreme poverty, marginality, conflict of cultural values, rising addiction rates, increased family violence, violent and accidental deaths, and illegal trafficking in drugs, firearms, and stolen vehicles and auto parts.

34. Organización de los Estados Americanos, Comisión Interamericana de Derechos Humanos, *Informe sobre la situación de los derechos humanos en México* (September 24, 1998), chap. 11, 2.

35. Ibid.

36. Martínez de Murguía, *La policía en México,* 170.

37. Luis González Placencia, *Estudio exploratorio acerca de la actitud de los capitalinos frente a la seguridad pública en el Distrito Federal* (Mexico City: Rafael Preciado Hernández, 1999), 14. It is probable that these findings are representative of the situation at the national level, but I do not have reliable information that confirms this.

38. Ibid., 17.

39. Ibid., 19.

40. Ibid.

41. Norberto Bobbio, *El futuro de la democracia* (Mexico City: Fondo de Cultura Económica, 1993), 15.

42. It is worth recalling the argument of Baruch Spinoza, for whom the true purpose of the state was to "liberate everyone from fear so they can live in safety in as much a measure as possible, and this is so they can maintain the natural right to existence without any damage to themselves or others. The true purpose of the state, therefore, is freedom." Quoted in Yáñez Romero, "La policía en la modernización cultural de la Ciudad de México," 26.

43. "In Mexico, the setbacks constitutionalism has suffered come from long ago.... The origin of all vices is a conceptual confusion.... It is the conviction that

the Constitution cannot be considered as a simple law. Thus it must be read as a catalog of wishes that inspire but do not necessarily obligate.... Understood in this manner, as a decision, the Mexican Constitution has been analyzed as an act of will of the sovereign, as a political determination, and not as a normative principle that clearly delimits what is lawfully possible." Silva-Herzog Márquez, *El antiguo régimen y la transición en México*, 36.

44. It is useful to compare this with the fact that the first element defined in the reform of the Colombian police was determining the constitutional basis of the National Police. Rosso José Serrano Cadena, *Policía Nacional: una nueva era* (Bogota: Prolibros, 1994), 3.

45. In Spain the constitutional design of the police revolves around freedom. Article 104.1 of the Spanish Constitution states that the mission of the security forces is to "protect the free exercise of rights and freedoms and guarantee public security." This text is the result of a historical battle that specifically assigned to these forces a task linked to democratic roles. Preamble of the reorganization law of the branch of vigilance and security, March 8, 1941. Quoted in Barcelona Llop, *Policía y constitución*, 194.

46. Instituto de Investigaciones Jurídicas, *Diccionario Jurídico Mexicano* (Mexico City: Porrúa/Universidad Nacional Autónoma de México, 1998), 2454.

47. There is also the Military Judicial Police, regulated by Article 47 of the *Código de Justicia Militar* of August 1933 and by the institution's own internal code of May 1941.

48. Instituto de Investigaciones Jurídicas, *Diccionario Jurídico Mexicano*, 2454.

49. The job category of "Federal Judicial Police agent" appears in the civil service manual of this ministry.

50. Article 23 specifies the requirements for becoming and remaining an officer of the Federal Judicial Police. Article 26 lists the officers' functions. Article 27 establishes two technical councils: Operations Planning and Coordination, and Administration, created "for greater efficiency and control in the planning, coordination, and administration of the services of the judicial police." *Diario Oficial*, May 10, 1996.

51. *Diario Oficial*, August 27, 1996.

52. The LFPF was published in the *Diario Oficial* on January 4, 1999.

53. It will also carry out its functions in national parks, water treatment facilities and dams, reservoirs and riverbeds, urban spaces defined as federal land, real estate, installations, and services subject to the federation, and all spaces subject to federal jurisdiction.

54. According to Article 12 of the LPFP, PFP officers must act according to the basic constitutional principles of legality, efficiency, professionalism, and honesty. It is necessary to review the complete article in order to grasp the basic principles of performance that should guarantee the effectiveness of those four constitutional limits.

55. The internal regulations of the federal executive branch establish criteria for promotion, which include, at minimum, the results achieved in personnel development and continuing education programs, effective job performance, and leadership abilities. The regulations also contain a set of perquisites and benefits,

as well as sanctions (warnings, suspension, removal, and termination) to be decided by an appointed body that includes representatives of the PFP. The sanction procedure includes the right to appeal in all cases. The regulations also contain additional requirements and procedures for personnel selection, enrollment, training, and tenure and promotion.

56. *Reforma*, July 5, 1999, 8A.

57. *Reforma*, September 13, 1999, 4A.

58. SEDENA "will maintain a steady stream of trained replacements to fill vacancies that occur, and the necessary measures will be taken so that said personnel fulfill the requirements for entering the PFP, including the minimum academic level required" (SEDENA Web site, September 10, 1999). The brief argument with which the SEDENA justifies its intervention in matters of public safety, through its presence in the PFP, can also be found at this Web site.

59. *Reforma*, September 13, 1999, 4A.

60. Ibid.

61. See John Lea and Jock Young, *What Is to Be Done about Law and Order* (Harmondsworth: Penguin, 1984).

62. Antonio López Ugalde, Carlos Ríos Espinosa, and Miguel Sarre, *Bases ideológicas de la función policial en México*, Working Paper No. 36 (Mexico City: Fundación Rafael Preciado Hernández, December 1999), 6–7.

63. Ibid., 7–8.

64. Ibid., 8–9.

65. Ibid., 9.

66. "From Reporter to Cadet," *Reforma*, January 12, 13, and 14, 2000.

67. Organización de los Estados Americanos, *Informe sobre la situación de los derechos humanos en México*, 7.

68. I have conducted interviews with representatives of the police forces of Argentina, Brazil, Chile, Colombia, Cuba, El Salvador, England, France, Germany, Guatemala, Holland, Honduras, Italy, Panama, Peru, Spain, and the United States. During June 1999 I was in residence at the Police School of Cataluña, Spain. In July 1999 I paid a working visit to the National Police Training Center in Bramshill, England. I also joined a delegation of the Catalonian police, which paid working visits to several cities in Holland in order to learn about the recently implemented national police reform.

69. Josep M. Colomer, *La transición a la democracia* (Barcelona: Anagrama, 1988), 12.

70. *Cuentos de la Calle*, C.O.D.I. Literary Workshop (San Luis Potosí: Consejo Nacional para la Cultura y las Artes, Coordinación General de Cultura Infantil, and Instituto de Cultura, 1996).

5

Combating Organized Crime in Mexico: Mission [Im]possible?

Sigrid Arzt

Formerly, criminal activities that developed within a country were seen as a problem of police security and, hence, as a local issue. The prosecution of organized crime was seen in this light as well, and it was from this perspective that the tools and techniques to combat this phenomenon were developed. Nevertheless, as the globalization process has gained momentum—as reflected in a sharp increase in commerce, communications, finance, and information in a vast majority of countries—we see how this new context facilitates criminal groups' trafficking in illegal goods.

Today organized crime is the engine driving illicit markets and informal economies, gaining additional strength from two factors. First, organized crime has adapted easily to the international context and has taken advantage of porous borders, transforming organized crime into a transnational phenomenon. Second, the convergence between globalization and the rise of transnational crime benefits from the institutional weaknesses of Mexican law enforcement, which lacks the human and material resources to make the necessary adjustments to combat new forms of criminality. That is, given the clandestine and illegal nature of organized crime, we learn more about it when an investigation is made public, usually by a successful police action.[1] Unfortunately, police successes against organized crime are not a daily occurrence in Mexico.

This essay reviews various institutional and legislative initiatives that the Mexican government has undertaken to forge effective tools with which to combat organized crime. The discussion of organized crime focuses especially on drug trafficking, even though Mexico's federal law against organized crime identifies eleven additional offenses for prosecution.

If the goal is to attack organized crime, the government must develop a three-pronged strategy that targets its three lifelines. The first strategic approach is to identify and attempt to eradicate the criminal group's operations. The second is to sabotage its financial base (money laundering). The third is to undermine its political-institutional protection.[2] In order to succeed against organized crime, these three actions must be executed in a coordinated, systematic manner. The most difficult of the three is to undermine political-institutional protection, but unless this is accomplished it will be very difficult to achieve any real success in the fight against organized crime.

Today, there are states in Mexico where someone dies every day as a result of their ties to organized crime.[3] Nevertheless, the core problem is the impunity and corruption that characterize the institutions responsible for prosecuting these criminals. It has been seven years since passage of the law that established the National Public Security Council (CNSP)[4] and more than four years since passage of the Federal Organized Crime Law (LFCDO),[5] yet Mexico is hard pressed to demonstrate substantial results.[6]

The following discussion covers the innumerable reforms introduced in Mexico's constitutional, institutional, and penal arenas, but its primary focus is on the Federal Organized Crime Law. Clearly we need a fuller understanding of the connection between public power and organized crime in Mexico. Unfortunately, reliable public sources crucial to conducting such a study are hard to come by.[7] This study will attempt to show that organized crime's strength originates within and is reinforced by the same police institutions that are charged with pursuing criminals. And the legislation discussed below has been unable to dismantle this "virtuous circle."[8]

This essay undertakes a historical and analytical review, divided into three sections, of the Mexican government's strategy to combat organized crime. The first section examines legislative changes aimed at organized crime. These include the Federal Organized Crime Law and other laws, constitutional amendments and regulations, and the institutional reforms implemented within the Attorney General's Office (PGR). Also falling within the federal anticrime strategy are the passage or reform of the Federal Chemical Precursors Law,[9] the Federal Law for Administering Seized Property,[10] and the Federal Firearms and Explosives Law, among others.[11] These laws are all designed to support a more effective battle against organized crime in Mexico and to strengthen the LFCDO.

The second section includes guidelines for determining what types of data should be considered when evaluating efforts against organized crime. Information does exist, but it is not presented systematically and it is not available to the public. Nevertheless, the PGR publishes annual statistics on the number of preliminary investigations initiated with respect to drug trafficking. It is worth noting that although nearly four hundred federal offenses fall within the jurisdiction of the Attorney General's Office, three-fourths of the data in this office's annual reports pertain to only four crimes (property crimes, crimes against health, firearms violations, and contraband).

The third section evaluates the achievements of the LFCDO by examining two of the tools contained in this legislation: the witness protection program and wiretaps. Ever since the law's passage, both tools have been questioned on the grounds of their legality and effectiveness.

INSTITUTIONALIZING THE FIGHT AGAINST ORGANIZED CRIME

In 1993 a series of reforms were introduced to modernize Mexico's penal legislation. The proposals came out of national debates convened in 1992 by the Judicial Committee of the federal Chamber of Deputies to discuss both federal and state-level criminal and procedural codes. These efforts, dubbed the "Gómez Mont reforms,"[12] trace their roots to studies in 1984 by jurists in the National Institute for Criminal Science (INACIPE).

The legislative changes—to constitutional articles 16, 21, and 119—were passed in 1993 with the support of President Carlos Salinas de Gortari (1988–1994).[13] Discussions in Congress revolved around three fundamental points: (1) inclusion of the human rights issue in the Constitution, especially in reference to criminal procedures; (2) establishment of clear action guidelines for authorities in criminal investigations to counter prosecutors' extensive abuses and excesses; and (3) the establishment of a National Public Security System to control and professionalize police forces and related institutions.[14] The administration of President Ernesto Zedillo (1994–2000) saw passage of the General Law of the National Public Security System (LG–SNSP),[15] which was designed to set the bases for coordination among law enforcement agencies at all levels of government—municipal, state, and federal.[16]

The reforms passed by the Salinas administration went into effect in February 1994. They affected the federal criminal code and that of the Federal District, as well as the Federal Code of Criminal Procedures (CFPP), in which the first reference to "organized crime" appears. From this point forward, organized crime was defined as cases in which three or more people organized under rules of discipline and hierarchy to commit in a violent and persisting way, or for mainly lucrative purposes, any legally proscribed act. It is important to note that, at the time, the CFPP served to extend the detention period if a case involved organized crime. Even after the reform, a pattern of criminal behavior was not a crime in itself, so it was not possible to prosecute someone solely for belonging to a "criminal organization" as defined by law. Rather, someone had to commit one of a set of specific crimes, including drug trafficking, highway robbery, arms trafficking, kidnapping, or armed robbery, among others. This limitation disappeared after passage of the LFCDO.

One antecedent is the reform to Article 16 of the Law of the Federal Preventive Police (LFPP), which indicates that the Public Ministry (Ministerio Público) can double the length of time a suspect can be detained depending on the seriousness of the crime—in this case, organized crime. The special importance of Article 16 came with the introduction of the "organized crime" concept. Even so, this provision offered little concrete advantage in practice.

During the 1993 congressional debate, legislators considered the possibility of drafting a law against drug trafficking, but they ultimately decided it would be inappropriate to create a special law to combat a particular form of organized crime. They reasoned that this would beget a fragmented legal code and do little to improve effectiveness against criminals.[17] However, three years later, the government needed a political response to the public security emergency. The arguments of 1993 were brushed aside, and Congress passed the Federal Organized Crime Law.

The LFCDO is unique. As Francisco Molina, former commissioner of the National Institute to Combat Drugs (INCD), noted: "it is a special law that utilizes unprecedented procedural mechanisms, criteria, and remedies that are not offered by any other law. The LFCDO does not penalize criminal conduct; rather, it penalizes conduct leading up to the crime, but without its actual commission. That is to say, it is a law targeted against a special type of criminal."[18]

The notion of organized crime was adopted in the reforms of CFPP sanctions dealing with crimes against public health. Chapter 1, Title 7 of the CFPP included organized crime and bans on chemical precursors, identifying drug trafficking as a crime against health. Nevertheless, reform of the judicial code has not produced the institutional infrastructure needed to professionalize the fight against drug trafficking. In the last ten years, a multitude of proposals were advanced for fighting drugs. Most were responses to two types of precipitating events—public scandals (when public authorities were unveiled as participants in drug trafficking or when a cartel committed a murder), and an escalation in demands emanating from the U.S. government.

An early step in the drug war was the creation in 1990 of the National Drug Control Center (CENDRO). According to Francisco Molina, CENDRO was "fashioned in the mold of U.S. intelligence centers, but its operational style was *a la mexicana*—obsolete equipment, unreliable information, influence peddling, ubiquitous leaks, inefficiency, and general disorder. What CENDRO manages is information to create power centers, with the groups within CENDRO competing to barter information."[19] Initially, the information generated by CENDRO went directly to the Federal Judicial Police (PJF) to guide police operations. The judicial police made no real effort to professionalize its intelligence and anticrime capacity. It was not until the murder of Archbishop Juan Jesús Posadas

Ocampo in March 1993 that the government announced the creation of the National Institute to Combat Drugs, with retired General Jorge Carrillo Olea directing both CENDRO and INCD.[20] Carrillo Olea later went on to head the Center for Research and National Security (CISEN) and then held the governorship of Morelos. In 1998 Carrillo Olea was forced to take a leave of absence following allegations that he and several colleagues from the aforementioned institutions were involved in kidnapping and drug trafficking. Ultimately, personnel of the state's security forces and employees of the state attorney general's office were arrested and jailed on charges of kidnapping, homicide, and drug trafficking.

The numerous changes in leadership of the INCD, combined with institutional evolution and internal adjustments within the PGR,[21] have injected chronic discontinuity into the plans, programs, and bilateral agreements related to the fight against organized crime. Between 1988 and 2000, Mexico had seven attorneys general. About an equal number headed the fight against drug traffickers during roughly the same period—from the Assistant Attorney General's Office against Health Crimes to the Office of the Special Prosecutor for Crimes against Health (FEADS).[22]

Tracing the construction of anti-trafficking institutions is very useful when trying to outline the way in which the fight against organized crime has evolved in Mexico. This fight has traditionally focused narrowly on combating drugs, without a full understanding of the transnational dynamic of this phenomenon and the possibilities this implies for the commission of other crimes. Until mid–2000 the only known investigative effort to adopt a global perspective was the "*maxi-proceso*" that examined the activities of the various cells of the Juárez cartel.[23] The focus on illegal drugs derives from two circumstances: first, from their status as an issue of national security and, second, from U.S. government pressure on Mexico to create a prosecutorial framework to address the nation's criminal reality.

The Federal Organized Crime Law, passed in November 1996, contains tools specifically designed to fight drug trafficking,[24] although the law also covers other crimes, including money laundering and kidnapping.[25] Passage of the LFCDO faced important obstacles. For example, President Zedillo, in a political gesture to give greater autonomy to the PGR, named a member of the opposition National Action Party (PAN) as attorney general. This act, although applauded domestically and internationally, motivated members of the ruling Institutional Revolutionary Party (PRI) to block any effort to pass a special law against organized crime. Indeed, a year went by between the bill's introduction and the final vote. During the intervening months, Zedillo sent legislators and other public officials of various parties on trips to countries that had legislation similar to his proposal so that they could directly observe the utility of this kind of legal tool.

The extreme severity of organized crime and its transnational character are recognized in the preamble to the law. The law also notes that this type of crime overwhelms institutions, which justifies the adoption of a modernized juridical norm,[26] and it stresses the link between organized crime and drug trafficking. Further, as previously noted, it conceptualizes organized crime as a society that seeks to operate beyond the control of the people and government. It involves thousands of criminals that work in complex, organized, and disciplined structures like those of any corporation that operates with fixed rules.

Paraphrasing the law, the state recognizes the danger of the organized crime phenomenon and the way in which government structures are defeated by criminal groups' specialized skills, such as their use of high technology and their capacity to launder money and recruit specialized talent. It characterizes organized crime as having the following identifying characteristics:

- Vertical hierarchy with ranked authority.
- Limits on membership and strict selection of the individuals involved in the criminal enterprise.
- Continuing operation.
- Use of violence and corruption to achieve objectives.
- Territorial and geographic domination of an enterprise, be it legitimate or illegitimate.
- Operation through compartmentalized cells.

Article 2 of the LFCDO states that "when three or more individuals agree to organize to carry out, in a permanent or ongoing form, activities that by themselves or combined with others result in committing ... crimes, [they] will be sanctioned for that sole fact, as members of organized crime."[27]

The first draft of the LFCDO, released in October 1995, was amended in forty-eight of its fifty-two articles prior to the first reading in the Senate.[28] The legislators rewrote about 95 percent of the executive proposal and decreased the number of articles from fifty-two to forty-four. Specialists in criminal law, representatives of nongovernmental organizations, and public officials participated in the amendment process. During the presentation of the law, Senator Amador Rodríguez Lozano, president of the Legislative Studies Committee, emphasized that one of its key points is the priority role for judges in authorizing searches, ordering home detention, safeguarding seized property, and approving wiretaps.[29] The judges' central role grew out of the recognized excesses committed in the past by both the Public Ministry and the Federal Judicial Police.

The LFCDO also highlighted the need to professionalize the police and the public prosecutor, and to create an elite anticrime unit. Article 8 states that "the PGR should have a specialized unit for the investigation and prosecution of crimes committed by members of organized crime. This unit should be established by the Public Ministry and buttressed by Federal Judicial Police and experts."[30] This provision—the creation of the Special Organized Crime Unit (UEDO)—is one more facet of the institutionalization of law enforcement.

In November 1996, after a year in congressional committees, the LFCDO was approved. The Senate vote was 111 in favor and 1 abstention out of a total of 128 members. When voting on the particulars of the bill, 92 voted in favor, with members of the PAN and the Party of the Democratic Revolution (PRD) opposing specific provisions. The PAN objected to the flexibility the law would give the Attorney General's Office to request Treasury audits on suspect persons or entities. The PRD opposed the dispensation that gives one-time pardons to persons who cooperate with the authorities against organized crime. On the other hand, the bill incorporated a PRD proposal that doubled the penalty for law enforcement officials found to be involved in organized crime. In the Chamber of Deputies, the final vote was 326 in favor, out of a total of 500 deputies. Only the PRD voted against.

The fact that the bill was held up in committee for one year reflects the powerful interests that would be affected by its passage into law. This fact was recognized by former assistant attorney general Moisés Moreno, who noted: "we find opposite reactions; some applaud the law and others fiercely oppose it, which is consistent with the veiled attacks financed by criminal organizations who sought to undermine the strength of the law. These attacks give an idea of how deeply rooted organized crime is in national politics and the resistance to measures that jeopardize these criminals' particular interests."[31]

The impact of rising crime rates and the violence and impunity with which criminal organizations operate is alarming.[32] In 1998 alone, the PGR reported that drug-trafficking organizations had executed over two thousand people in Baja California, Chihuahua, Jalisco, Sinaloa, Sonora, Tamaulipas, and the Federal District.[33] In Sinaloa, over four hundred murders associated with drug trafficking were committed in 1999. Even more alarming, less than half of these cases have been solved, which leaves ample space for impunity.

In a second phase of institution building to combat crime—and in response to public outrage when INCD Commissioner Jesús Gutiérrez Rebollo was accused in January 1997 of collaborating with the Juárez cartel—Attorney General Jorge Madrazo Cuéllar decided to move ahead with the following efforts:

- Institutional reorganization within the Attorney General's Office to transform the INCD into the Office of the Special Prosecutor for Crimes against Health.
- Reforms of various constitutional and criminal codes to classify crimes and increase flexibility in prosecutors' range of actions against organized crime.
- Stiffer sentences, particularly in cases of organized crime.

This essay emphasizes the first two of these points. When the INCD reformed as the FEADS in April 1997, the name change did not signify a major reformulation of operations. Almost three months passed between the removal of General Gutiérrez Rebollo and the appointment of Mariano Herrán Salvatti as the FEADS special prosecutor. In the interim, the army took control of the INCD and gave the FEADS its current shape. According to former INCD commissioner Francisco Molina, "the archives and dossiers, sacked by the UEDO and the police, along with the intelligence gathered up to that time, were integrated operationally into the Ministry of Defense." Molina further noted that Herrán Salvatti lacked key attributes for his FEADS position, and this undercut the agency's efforts against organized crime.[34]

Broadly, the FEADS is organized in four directorates (*coordinaciones*). The Investigations Directorate concentrates efforts to investigate crimes against health. The Administration and Information Directorate was charged with coordinating the special Border Task Forces from 1996 to 2000. The Operations Directorate, which coordinates the Federal Judicial Police in combating drug trafficking, contains at least two subdivisions: the office that implements drug eradication strategies and the office that coordinates land, sea, and air interdiction operations. The final unit is the Advisory Directorate, which includes experts and advisers.

The Special Organized Crime Unit has its own elite structure. Until February 2001, UEDO Commissioner José Trinidad Larrieta reported directly to Attorney General Jorge Madrazo, and thereafter to Attorney General Rafael Macedo de la Concha.[35] In general terms the UEDO, through its Operations Division, controls the general directorate of the Federal Judicial Police, technical experts, intelligence, and wiretaps. There is also a coordinator for each of the crimes that the LFCDO covers, as well as coordinators to monitor each drug cartel and to head related investigations. That is, there is one coordinator for the Juárez cartel, another for the Arellano Félix brothers, and so forth. These coordinators have teams who carry out the activities required to move the investigations ahead. The UEDO will eventually include a body of wiretap experts, who will need to be trained and evaluated for their competence in their specialized tasks. It is not clear who currently performs such evaluations of these technical personnel, but it is known that the first team completed two years of training in the United States.[36]

By law, UEDO officials are the only persons authorized to use the special tools provided by the LFCDO, including: a witness protection program (articles 14 and 34),[37] wiretaps (articles 15–28),[38] seizure of assets (articles 29–32), legal relief and benefits in exchange for cooperation in investigations (articles 35–37, 42–44),[39] use of undercover agents, secrecy in preliminary investigations, home detention,[40] and searches.[41] It is important to underscore that the evidence that UEDO officers gather with these tools in the course of their investigations can be legally used to prosecute organized crime groups.

Table 5.1 illustrates the relatively small size of the UEDO staff of commissioners and support personnel, such as the Federal Judicial Police and technical experts. Clearly this is an elite group, but its small size also means that the number of cases that can be managed at one time is limited. In deciding which cases receive attention, it sometimes seems that political interests take precedence over a coordinated operation. Up to mid–2000, UEDO efforts seemed to be concentrated primarily against the Juárez cartel through the *maxi-proceso*.[42]

Table 5.1 **UEDO Personnel by Category, 1998 and 2000**

Area	1998	2000
Administrative personnel	62	80
Public Ministry agents	16	46
Functionaries	11	27
Federal Judicial Police agents	73	38
Total	162	191

Source: *Anuarios Estadísticos* of the Procuraduría General de la República.

Keeping the UEDO small in size facilitates outside oversight, but it must be remembered that these officials are expected to be highly professionalized and resistant to corruption. (Even though one of the reasons for creating such an elite group was to prevent its penetration by organized crime syndicates, the UEDO has not been free of scandals.) The small number of UEDO officers also allows for building a close relationship with U.S. counterparts, and exchanges of information can be better controlled.

For the most part, cases handled by the UEDO were selected by the attorney general and the heads of the UEDO and FEADS. One might speculate that the concentrated efforts against the Juárez cartel reflected at least three coinciding factors: the lack of an overall criminal policy, pressure from the United States to give priority to one cartel or another, and the links one or another cartel had with the administration.

It is still somewhat difficult to assess the LFCDO's impacts on organized crime, especially on drug trafficking. On the contrary, an assessment of advances made during President Zedillo's term in office raises more questions concerning, for example, the flight of ex-governor of Quintana Roo Mario Villanueva in March 1999, and the murder of the head of the Tijuana police in February 2000, just days after Zedillo's warning that he would not yield to criminality. At the end of the day, it appears that the institutional protection of criminal groups and their illegal activities has not been affected.[43]

It is important to emphasize that the UEDO's first commissioner, Samuel González Ruiz (January 1997–December 1998), was the person primarily responsible for gains made in the *maxi-proceso,* and he also established the basic criteria for the LFCDO's operation. The fact that his resignation coincided with progress in the investigation of Governor Mario Villanueva begs scrutiny. With González's resignation, the UEDO's investigation of the Quintana Roo organization hit an impasse. And this case, which was not reopened until just before the U.S. Congress's 1999 certification of Mexico, held implications for other ongoing UEDO investigations.[44]

Following the resignation of González Ruiz, Attorney General Madrazo named José Trinidad Larrieta to head the UEDO. From this point forward, every line of investigation had to be cleared and approved by the attorney general. This change proved to be a major obstacle; it led to delays in decision making on investigative strategies and in achieving results that would lead to the apprehension of important drug kingpins. It even slowed the mechanisms of information exchange with foreign authorities, hindering efforts to combat transnational organized crime.

Another major institution-building initiative in the fight against organized crime was the creation of the Special Anti–Money Laundering Unit (UECLD) in January 1998. Prior to the UECLD's establishment, money-laundering cases were investigated by units of the PGR, FEADS, and UEDO, an institutional fragmentation that produced inconsistency, overlap, and poor coordination—and little by way of accomplishments against organized crime syndicates.

Without doubt, this particular type of crime calls for a specialized structure with technical experts who can manage money-laundering investigations, conduct fiscal and financial inquiries to identify the techniques used by criminals, and compile and analyze data to track the means by which money is laundered. When undertaking a money-laundering investigation, the Treasury Ministry must initiate the inquiry, after which the PGR is brought into the investigation. Because of the sensitivity of these various activities, applicants to the UECLD—and to the

FEADS and UEDO—must pass a battery of exams to demonstrate their suitability for such a position.[45] (See table 5.2 for a breakdown of UECLD personnel.)

Table 5.2 **UECLD Personnel by Category, 1998 and 2000**

Area	1998	2000
Administrative personnel	20	19
Experts	—	—
Public Ministry agents	11	9
Functionaries	7	9
Federal Judicial Police agents	—	—
Total	38	37

Source: *Anuarios Estadísticos* of the Procuraduría General de la República.

The UECLD must work in close coordination with the Treasury Ministry (SHCP), which has the support, in turn, of the Financial Crimes Enforcement Network (FINCEN) of the U.S. Department of the Treasury. Currently, Mexico's federal Taxation Division (Procuraduría Fiscal de la Federación) houses economic data, including suspicious operations and cash deposits. Despite Treasury personnel's access to such sensitive information, they are not submitted to the same sort of rigorous control as are officials of the Attorney General's Office, on the assumption that Treasury personnel are above private or political interests and are not subject to corruption.[46]

In March 1999, the head of the Taxation Division, Ismael Gómez Gordillo, indicated that his division was still in the process of constructing the infrastructure needed to detect proceeds from illegal sources[47] and that techniques for accurately assessing suspect operations were being evaluated.[48] Gómez Gordillo indicated three factors that make the fight against money laundering such a complex undertaking. First, the illegal aspect of money laundering is not found in the transactions made or the activities generated, but the origin of the resources. Second, the primary product of money laundering is cash, which can serve equally in legal and illegal transactions. And third, it is very difficult to detect illegal operations by financial intermediaries that are, by profession, engaged in the exchange of money, and even more difficult when dealing with nonprofessional channels.

Money laundering was first categorized as a crime in Mexico in 1990 (Article 15 of the Federal Fiscal Code).[49] In May 1996, Article 400 outlawed financial operations involving illegal resources, although for practical purposes this regulation did not take effect until 1998 and was limited to banks, stock funds, limited partnerships, and exchange houses.[50]

Banks are required to report binational cash transactions of US$20,000 or more in national or foreign currency. As of mid–2000, Treasury officials acknowledged that, three years after amending the money-laundering statute and a year after implementing the new regulations, the financial system was not capable of regulating or controlling currency transactions in the banking system. (Tables 5.3 and 5.4 present data on cash transactions and regulatory responses.)

Table 5.3 **Reports on Cash Transactions by Financial Entities (as of March 31, 2000)**

Type of Activity	Number of Reports
Reports of suspicious or unusual operations	2,866
Reports of operations over US$20,000	14,322,783
Other unusual operations	107

Source: *Anuarios Estadísticos* of the Procuraduría General de la República.

Table 5.4 **Regulatory Responses by the Treasury Ministry (as of March 31, 2000)**

Basis of Governmental Response	Number of Responses
Article 115 of the Federal Tax Code	64
Article 400 of the Federal Penal Code	32

Source: *Anuarios Estadísticos* of the Procuraduría General de la República.

The head of the Taxation Division indicated that the intense attention, particularly U.S. attention, accorded to the recommendations for new anti–money laundering mechanisms led to literal translations of concepts such as "suspicious transactions" (as "*transacciones sospechosas*"), even though they have a different meaning in Spanish. According to Gómez Gordillo, a more accurate term might have been *operaciones atípicas* ("atypical operations"). Unfortunately, given the lack of comparative references and the short time span that the UECLD has been operating, we cannot as yet draw firm conclusions about its performance.

It is important to note that in June 2000 Mexico became a member of the Financial Action Group (GAFI), the international mechanism for combating money laundering. Membership indicates that Mexico has the necessary legal framework and procedures to investigate and combat money laundering. What remains to be done is to recruit qualified and experienced personnel.

Roughly paralleling the implementation of the LFCDO are new or amended federal laws concerning related crimes, such as the Chemical

Precursors Law [51] and the Law for Administering Seized Property.[52] Before passage of the new law on seized property, this responsibility fell to the Public Ministry and judicial authorities, but the administration and use of secured property is now subject to judicial norms.[53] There are procedures for the allocation of seized property among state and municipal authorities and foreign authorities collaborating in investigations leading to seizures. Some of the laws developed to combat organized crime in Mexico have been in force for more than three years. Nevertheless, little is known about their impact due to a lack of public information in a format that lends itself to analysis.

ASSESSING MEXICO'S SUCCESS AGAINST ORGANIZED CRIME

Given public perceptions of organized crime's stranglehold on Mexico and the huge investments of human and financial resources made to combat this evil, it is essential to identify criteria by which to determine if these resources are being used effectively. For example, table 5.5 shows the number of preliminary investigations opened in 1994–1998 in the various field offices of the Attorney General's Office for various kinds of crime. Highest among them are cases involving crimes against health, which, as noted earlier, is another way of referring to drug-related crime. Table 5.6 shows the rank order of the top five field offices in initiating preliminary investigations for health crimes. A problem with these data, drawn from statistical yearbooks of the Attorney General's Office, is that they show only the number of preliminary investigations initiated. We do not know how many of these investigations resulted in convictions or over what period of time. Therefore, the data are of use only to illustrate the pattern of increases in the commission of health crimes.

Table 5.5 **Preliminary Investigations of Activities Involving Organized Crime, 1994–1998**

Year	Health Crimes	Robbery	Fire Arms	Contraband
1994	12,384	2,581	6,950	302
1995	12,773	2,989	8,592	266
1996	23,992	10,030	12,827	905
1997	21,071	6,235	13,852	—
1998	19,629	9,491	14,761	—

Source: *Anuarios Estadísticos* of the Procuraduría General de la República.

Table 5.6 **Preliminary Investigations of Health Crimes: Rank Order of PGR Field Offices, 1994–1998**

1994	1995	1996	1997	1998
Metro-politan	Metro-politan	Metro-politan	Metro-politan	Federal District
Baja California	Jalisco	Jalisco	Jalisco	México State
Sinaloa	Baja California	Baja California	Sinaloa	Oaxaca
Jalisco	Sinaloa	Sinaloa	Baja California	Jalisco
Nuevo León	Mexico	Sonora	Chihuahua	Baja California
Sonora	Sonora	Chihuahua	Sonora	Tamaulipas

Source: *Anuarios Estadísticos* of the Procuraduría General de la República,

Evaluating how effectively resources are being used in the government's fight against organized crime is made extremely difficult by the restrictions placed on access to information. As Jorge Chabat noted, "the problem with the information coming from the Mexican government is that any information that is generated internally is considered confidential unless proven otherwise."[54] In the best of cases, information comes to light through leaks to journalists.

Nevertheless, a review of federal budget allocations to the ministries in charge of fighting drug trafficking (Defense, Navy, and Interior, in addition to the Attorney General's Office) allows a first approximation to such an evaluation of effectiveness. The data in table 5.7 reveal two important facts. First, the Attorney General's Office has the smallest budget for combating drug trafficking, even though it is supposed to be the lead agency. Second, the budget allocated to the Defense Ministry has grown steadily, in large part due to its role in internal security issues. One could speculate that this pattern of rising financial appropriations is a result of the militarization of the fight against drug trafficking, which, in turn, is due to the failure to clean up and professionalize Mexico's police forces.

Some questions remain. Do these data offer a clue to the success or failure of Mexico's organized crime efforts? And what key information is missing, and how can it be obtained? These questions reflect the challenge posed by limited access to information.

In February 1999, Interior Minister Francisco Labastida announced the "New Antidrug Strategy" and projected allocating nearly US$500 million to it over the following three years.[55] If such sums were actually expended, it is very difficult to see any correlation between bigger budgets and better results. Moreover, it apparently takes extreme events to evoke a response. For example, only after the gruesome murders of police officers in Baja California did federal authorities announce special expenditures for training and equipping police in Chihuahua and Baja California to confront organized crime.[56] We can find no visible results from the millions of dollars allocated via the legislation that set up the National Public Security Council. Nor is there any evidence of specific standards for police training and for purchasing technology and weapons. What have the states that received federal monies done regarding public security? What has happened with the resources injected into federal police forces? The federal government recently announced that it had invested twelve billion pesos (more than US$1 billion at the 1999 exchange rate) in public security matters for all three levels of government, the largest sum in recent history and triple the amount designated in 1997.[57]

Table 5.7 **Federal Budget Allocations to Ministries Involved in Combating Drug Trafficking (billions of current pesos)**

Year	Attorney General's Office	Defense	Navy	Interior
1996	1,727.6	9,903.5	3,430.8	2,329.3
1997	2,538.9	12,110.6	4,419.4	2,324.6
1998	3,485.9	14,220.8	5,883.5	6,627.9
1999	3,970.9	16,593.4	6,607.0	7,057.8

Source: *Diario Oficial de Egresos de la Federación*.

Another obstacle to evaluating the effective use of resources is the inconsistency in the presentation of information. Some information relates to programs that operate year to year, while other data come from six-year initiatives that correspond to the term of presidential administrations. Typically, each new administration creates and funds new offices, but rarely are there any follow-up institutional evaluations of performance and effectiveness. And each new administration develops its own form of presenting program information. Of course, the difficulty of finding useful, consistent, and accessible data for evaluating programs is not unique to Mexico. Systematizing information on organized crime is a problem in itself,[58] one recognized by the United Nations Office for Drug Control and Crime Prevention.[59]

Despite the problems of access to and systematization of information, there are some categories that would prove useful in establishing a framework for evaluating the efficiency and effectiveness of efforts against organized crime in Mexico. In order to establish a general context for organized crime and its impact on society, one could examine the number of criminal investigations related to violent homicides,[60] criminal conspiracy, drug and people trafficking, car theft, kidnapping, smuggling, crimes against health, and armed robbery. And in order to determine the level of implementation of the LFCDO, one could examine: (1) the allocation of human resources (number of personnel involved, under what criteria, and for how long) and (2) normal and exceptional allocations to enforcement activities of the Ministries of Defense, the Navy, and the Interior, as well as the Attorney General's Office.

It is imperative to establish criteria for evaluating the use of resources. For example, one key question is, what gets done in implementation? Answers would include information such as (1) the number of preliminary investigations involving crimes covered under the LFCDO, particularly investigations initiated by the UEDO; (2) the number of apprehensions by the UEDO; and (3) the number and length of sentences for organized crimes and related offenses. A second key question is, what is the overall impact of the LFCDO's implementation on (1) the dismantling of cartels through, for example, arrests of their leadership; (2) the seizure of assets; and (3) prices for illegal drugs and chemical precursors, firearms, and trafficked migrants and human organs?

This is an ambitious goal, one that will not be accomplished overnight. Nevertheless, other countries have taken steps to assess the impacts of measures directed against organized crime, suggesting that this goal is not unachievable. For example, since 1990 Europol's Drug Unit has been compiling and systematizing information on organized crime in the European Union, which is then released in annual reports.[61]

The difficulty in assessing progress against organized crime reflects at least two challenges. First, the field is not clearly defined, either by police authorities or by scholars. Second, law enforcement has long been carried out largely in secret, with occasional leaks of important information to the media. Important arrests, typically proclaimed with great fanfare, do not necessarily come as the result of an effective policy against organized crime but often as the result of a new direction taken in the investigation. Evaluating the "effectiveness" or "efficiency" of the implementation of the law solely by looking at the number of arrests is an enterprise that should be undertaken with great care.

For example, Attorney General Jorge Madrazo told a plenary session of the federal Chamber of Deputies in 1998 that the indictment of an entire drug-trafficking gang and the dismantling of the Amezcua brothers' organization was one of the most important accomplishment of the year.[62] We now know that these "Kings of Methamphetamines" were detained in Mexican prisons not for charges brought in Mexico (they had been arrested on charges of organized crime and money laundering, but the Mexican prosecutor could not prove the allegations) but because the U.S.

government had asked for their extradition. This leads one to question why the Mexican prosecutor lost the case. Was the prosecutor incompetent? Did the Amezcuas bribe the judge? Or was it both?

The fight against organized crime in Mexico has long pursued a repressive and militarized strategy, a fact that follows from those agencies that headed the campaign. There is no evidence that the four leaders of the anticrime effort (Defense, Navy, Interior, and the Attorney General's Office) implemented the preventive strategy prescribed in the 1995–2000 National Antidrug Program, which called for collaboration with at least seven other ministries. The "preventive" strategy was simply rhetoric. Also, given the institutional crisis that developed within the Attorney General's Office, the Defense Ministry has clearly strengthened its presence in the country's antidrug activities.

This leads to one further question: who is supervising the fight against organized crime? There are very good reasons for posing this question. In 1998 the Interior Ministry announced the creation of the new Federal Preventive Police (PFP). That same year additional appropriations were announced for anti–drug trafficking tasks that involved special efforts by the Ministries of Defense, the Navy, and the Interior, along with the Attorney General's Office. Also, it is clear that the armed forces have increased their prerogatives along with their increased participation in and strategic control over the fight against organized crime, especially against drug trafficking.[63]

Impunity and Corruption

It is public knowledge that there has been criminal penetration into the ranks of the Attorney General's Office. Both attorneys general who served during the Zedillo administration acknowledged the severity of this problem, which was dramatically revealed by the Gutiérrez Rebollo scandal in February 1997.

In response, a series of internal strategies were adopted under Zedillo that were designed to combat criminal infiltration of government agencies. These included a campaign to clean up the police following the unmasking of Gutiérrez Rebollo's links with the Juárez cartel[64] and the announcement in April 1997 of Mexico's intention to institute an Ethics Center (Centro de Control de Confianza).[65]

The Ethics Center, formally instituted in July 1999 within the Attorney General's Office, was founded to verify the trustworthiness of officials working directly in the antidrug effort (including employees of the FEADS, UEDO, and UECLD).[66] It is responsible for the continuous vetting of PGR officials to ensure that they uphold principles of legality, efficiency, professionalism, honesty, loyalty, and impartiality, as required by the Constitution. Although the Ethics Center is charged with vetting all personnel, priority attention is given to prosecutors, technical experts, and members of the Federal Judicial Police.

In Senate testimony in September 1999, Attorney General Madrazo indicated that the Center had examined 6,268 individuals, of whom 919 did not meet set standards and had been terminated or were in the process of being terminated. Meanwhile, the External Review Board and the Internal Affairs Unit dismissed 598 employees, and criminal charges were brought against 351, or nearly 60 percent. Taken together, these figures suggest that nearly a quarter of the employees failed to meet minimum standards of integrity and honesty. According to the 1999 annual report of the Attorney General's Office, 93.4 percent of the employees in five of its most critical areas failed to meet at least one of the employee evaluation criteria.[67]

On the other hand, FEADS and UEDO employees are carefully monitored, something that U.S. agencies have required as a way to build the trust necessary for information sharing among cooperating agencies. Yet even with strict monitoring, the UEDO was not free from scandal. In November 1999, Commander Mario Silva Calderón, also known as "The Animal" or "The Coyote," was arrested for allegedly supplying information on operations that the UEDO and the armed forces conducted in Quintana Roo. He sold this information to a Quintana Roo cell headed by Alcides Ramón Magaña, alias "El Metro," for hundreds of thousands of dollars. Silva Calderón was the right-hand man to Commander Cuauhtémoc Herrera, technical coordinator of the UEDO, who in 1998 failed a polygraph test and was transferred to the PGR office in Madrid. This same Commander Herrera subsequently returned from Spain with an assignment to Mexico's Presidential Guard.

Clearly the penetration by drug traffickers reached into the most elite bodies within the Attorney General's Office and other institutions charged with Mexico's public security.[68] Without a doubt, this level of infiltration reinforced public distrust in authorities and planted doubts about the effectiveness of the measures announced by the Zedillo administration. Although Zedillo's policies may have been well intended, his strategy ignored the core problem: the ties between the networks in Mexico's political system and organized crime.

LEGAL TOOLS FOR COMBATING ORGANIZED CRIME

This discussion will focus on two of the tools employed against organized crime in Mexico. Both have generated controversy or evoked outright opposition to their application. The tools are wiretaps and the witness protection program (PPT).

Wiretaps

It is very difficult to assess the usefulness of wiretaps. The only publicly available information comes from Attorney General Jorge Madrazo's testimony before the Mexican Senate on September 29, 1998: "judicially approved wiretaps are presently operating on ten members of organized crime." (There is no information on how many wiretaps are currently in place.) This tool is important precisely because it is the provision that generated the most controls and involves judges in a key role. The reasons for caution and controls lies in the federal intelligence agencies' past abuse of wiretaps, particularly the state's abuse of wiretaps against members of the political opposition.[69]

Of all the tools granted by the LFCDO, wiretaps are the most strictly regulated. Eighteen articles govern their use, and there are specified procedures for requesting judicial authorization for a wiretap, placing a tap, and using the evidence collected. Broadly, the law specifies that authorization for use is based on gathering evidence for the prosecution of some member of an organized crime network.

Concern over the supervision and control of wiretapping has not abated, even though agencies other than the UEDO use wiretaps (illegally) without supervision.[70] Virtually any government agency, and even public or private political groups, can use wiretaps for their own purposes. The federal government itself, through agencies other than the Attorney General's Office (including the Ministries of Defense and the Interior), makes use of unauthorized wiretaps to gather information, but no questions have been raised regarding the abuse that this use of wiretaps implies.

Witness Protection Program

The second tool is the Witness Protection Program. The PPT is covered in Article 35 of the LFCDO, which grants various benefits to a member of a criminal organization who supplies useful information for the investigation and prosecution of criminals.

The head of UEDO, José Trinidad Larrieta, affirmed in January 2000:

> This legal tool has helped us optimize and make more efficient the enforcement of the law against criminal organizations.... The PPT has accomplished the function of neutralizing intimidation, which is one of the main operating tools of organized crime,... guaranteeing that investigations are not truncated due to people's fear and insecurity.... It also has allowed us to be more efficient in the prosecution, indictment, and punishment of members of organized crime by strengthening our preliminary inquiries with materials that produce convictions.... Its ef-

> fectiveness is clearly demonstrated by the results.... Currently, ninety-three witnesses have given statements under the terms of the new law, and sixty-nine have entered the PPT. Of the remaining twenty-four witnesses, some left the program voluntarily, and three witnesses died.[71]

Although cooperation between Mexican authorities, the U.S. Drug Enforcement Administration (DEA), and the U.S. Federal Bureau of Investigation (FBI) is presumed in the fight against organized crime, it is nonetheless noteworthy that the head of the UEDO freely acknowledged that these agencies offer protection and share witnesses in investigations undertaken on either side of the border. This statement is surprising because it contradicts two directives. First, according to the regulatory framework governing DEA operations in Mexico, this agency has no authority to extend protection.[72] Second, there is no regulatory basis for authorization of exchanges of protected witnesses. In fact, the LFCDO still lacks guidelines regulating the program's operation. Yet another problem is the broad discretion that officials have to grant protection to witnesses. To date, the Attorney General's Office has not been transparent in its management of the PPT.

Several cases raise questions about operations within the PPT. For example, when Samuel González Ruiz headed the UEDO, he sent a former commander of the Federal Judicial Police (Adrián Carrera, who had been charged with money laundering) to Houston, Texas, to testify against former assistant attorney general Mario Ruiz Massieu, all without the knowledge of the appropriate Mexican authorities. In another instance, four witnesses received joint protection from Mexico and the United States, which again raises the question: what is the framework under which witness protection—now "binational"—is regulated?

Two types of witnesses can receive protection under Mexico's witness protection program. According to Article 34 of the LFCDO, "the Attorney General's Office will provide adequate support and protection to judges, experts, witnesses, victims, and others when their participation is needed in a criminal proceeding on crimes pertinent to this law." The second type is the "protected witness" who seeks protection under the law to avoid incrimination. That is, when no incriminating evidence is presented against an individual in a preliminary inquiry and that person decides to cooperate, the information that the witness provides in a formal statement cannot be used against him or her by the prosecutor.[73]

An important feature of the PPT is to safeguard the identity of a person implicating another member of organized crime until the preliminary inquiry phase has been completed. Thereafter, the accused has the right to confront the accuser. If the witness does not feel sufficiently well protected by the government, that witness may contradict prior statements when testifying before the judge, thus undermining the proceedings. In fact, the two first witnesses who received protection under the PPT (they were collaborating in an investigation of the Juárez cartel) were murdered during the preliminary inquiry. José Trinidad Larrieta, head of the UEDO, indicated that the agency assumed they were murdered for having given testimony.[74]

In order to gain a better understanding of the results of the witness protection program, we must ask what purpose it serves if protected witnesses are not really being protected. Commissioner Larrieta indicated that the witnesses who had been murdered had waived PFP protection of their own free will. If so, the question becomes, what does the witness protection program do? Why would witnesses choose not to be protected when they are giving testimony that could topple the large cartels?

Such questions reveal the public's ignorance regarding the internal workings of the PPT when negotiating with a witness who can provide valuable testimony or offer solid evidence in a trial. The murders of witnesses speak volumes about the danger of offering information to prosecutors of Mexican drug kingpins. As of April 2000, a total of ninety-three persons had testified under the umbrella of the law, and sixty-nine of them were continuing to cooperate. But we know nothing of the content of their testimony or about sentences handed down against organized crime figures. We know only that two witnesses died.

CONCLUSION

The short answer to the question posed at the outset—can the Mexican government combat organized crime?—must be "no." However, it is essential that President Vicente Fox (2000–2006) and his administration know in detail the ties between drug trafficking and the political powers that have governed Mexico in recent decades. This link extends to states governed by the PAN, including Baja California and Jalisco.

Second, it is imperative that the Fox government introduce democratic mechanisms to oversee the policies and resources that are invested in strategies against organized crime, and particularly against drug trafficking.

Third, although a restructuring of the institutions charged with security and justice would certainly be welcomed, if the fight against organized crime is to succeed, it needs an energetic and coordinated attack on three key fronts: political power, illegal proceeds, and illegal drugs, arms, or other material.

Fourth, the Fox government should adopt a different approach to the fight against organized crime. Taking a fresh tack, the government can limit and define how the armed forces will be used against drug trafficking and in public security more generally. These ought to be priority decisions.

And fifth, organized crime by its very nature creates complexities that call for resources, trained personnel, and effective institutions to combat the crime phenomenon, but it also requires that the officials in charge of this task take a global, transnational view. If organized crime continues to be viewed as something that happens within national boundaries, little will be accomplished to eradicate it or prevent its continued spread throughout Mexico's territory.

Notes

1. Phillip Williams, "Emerging Issues: Transnational Crime and Its Control," in *Global Report on Crime and Justice* (New York: United Nations, 1999), 221.

2. Tonatiuh García, "Análisis de la Ley Federal Contra la Delincuencia Organizada en México," seminar presentation at the Instituto Nacional de Ciencias Penales, Mexico City, July 2000.

3. The daily average of persons murdered in Sinaloa because of their ties to organized crime is 1.2. Sixty-five percent of the homicides in Baja California in 1999 were linked to drugs. In Jalisco there were 344 violent homicides, 17 percent of them drug related. Seventy-four percent of all arrest orders for federal offenses were not implemented. Claudia Guerrero, "Admiten corrupción policiaca," *Reforma,* March 5, 1998.

4. *Diario Oficial,* December 4, 1995.

5. *Diario Oficial,* November 16, 1996.

6. Rosa Elvira Vargas and Gustavo Castillo, "Zedillo, inacabada la depuración de la PGR," *La Jornada,* September 5, 2000.

7. Some examples suffice to make the point: the murder of presidential candidate Luis Donaldo Colosio in March 1994; the murder of José Francisco Ruiz Massieu in September 1994; the murder of numerous state attorneys in the last decade; the imprisonment of General Jesús Gutiérrez Rebollo; and the imprisonment of Adrián Carrera Fuentes (former commander of the Federal Judicial Police and close ally of former assistant attorney general Mario Ruiz Massieu) for money laundering.

8. The objective here is not to probe into this theme in depth; this is another line of research in progress. But see Instituto Mexicano de Estudios de la Criminalidad Organizada, *Todo lo que ud. debería saber sobre el crimen organizado en México* (Mexico City: Océano, 1998).

9. *Diario Oficial,* December 26, 1997.

10. The law originated in 1997, but it was not approved by the legislature until September 24, 1999. It took effect on December 31, 1999.

11. The Senate Commission finalized the law on April 28, 1998. See www.senado.gob.mx/comunicacion/dictamenes/doc/dictproy5.html.

12. The reforms were dubbed "Gómez Mont" because Fernando Gómez Mont headed the Judicial Committee in the Chamber of Deputies.

13. For more details on the academic exchanges with official authorities, see PGR, "La procuración de justicia, problemas, retos, y perspectivas" (Mexico City, mimeo, 1993), especially pp. 383–413, which deal with criminal policy toward organized crime.

14. Important in this context was the need for the government to appear to react against criminality, especially the murder of the PRI's general secretary in September 1994. In November 1994, President Salinas created the National Public Security Council, headed by Arsenio Farell Cubillas.

15. *Diario Oficial*, December 4, 1995.

16. When first established, the council was within the Interior Ministry, along with the armed forces. Today it is part of the Ministry of Public Security.

17. René González de la Vega, *Política criminológica mexicana* (Mexico City: Porrúa, 1993), 213.

18. Interview with former commissioner of the INCD Francisco Molina, July 1998.

19. Ibid.

20. During the Salinas administration, before the creation of the INCD, the Attorney General's Office contained a subdivision against drug trafficking, headed by Javier Coello Trejo, "the Iron Prosecutor," a nickname awarded by his North American counterparts in the fight against drug trafficking. Coello's ties to numerous criminal groups came to light later.

21. For more on the impact of these changes, see Sigrid Arzt, "Scope and Limits of an Act of Good Faith: The PAN's Experience at the Head of the Office of the Attorney General of the Republic," in *Organized Crime and Democratic Governability: Mexico and the U.S.–Mexican Borderlands*, edited by John Bailey and Roy Godson (Pittsburgh, Penn.: University of Pittsburgh Press, 2000).

22. As of July 2001, the FEADS was headed by Estuardo Bermúdez, former assistant attorney for electoral crimes during the administration of Attorney General Lozano (1994–1996).

23. "*Maxi-proceso*" refers to the preliminary investigation initiated following the arrest of General Jesús Gutiérrez Rebollo, which coordinated investigations against the various cells of the Juárez cartel. These cells ranged from money laundering through the Anahuac Bank to ties to the ex-governor of Quintana Roo, Mario Villanueva. The *maxi-proceso* is still considered the biggest investigation of drug trafficking in Mexico; its documentation runs to 205 volumes and 12 appendices.

24. For clarity, I include in drug trafficking everything from production, possession, and trafficking to membership in a criminal organization.

25. Other crimes covered include things like theft of autoparts; trafficking in undocumented migrants, arms, organs, and infants; and terrorism. See Article 2 of the LFCDO for the complete list.

26. PGR, Document CRIORG.DOC, October 18, 1995, 1.

27. *Federal Law against Organized Crime*, Commentary (Mexico City: Sista, 1998) presents a commentary on the implementation of each article.

28. "El Presidente Zedillo…," *Proceso*, October 30, 1995.

29. Ismael Romero, "Formar bandas criminales será delito federal," *La Jornada*, October 15, 1996.

30. *Diario Oficial*, November 7, 1996.

31. Moisés Moreno Hernández, *Política criminal y reforma penal, algunas bases para su democratización en México* (Mexico City, 1999), 351.

32. To illustrate I offer some press reactions three years after passage of the General Law Establishing the Bases of Public Security, two years after passage of the Federal Organized Crime Law, and one year after the creation of UEDO. "Hemos fallado en combate a la delincuencia, Ernesto Zedillo," *El Financiero*, August 27, 1998; "Dulces planes, realidades amargas," *Reforma*, November 17, 1998; "Señalan errores y demagogia, en el Programa Nacional de Seguridad Pública," *Reforma*, August 28, 1998; "Piden gobernadores superar el discurso," *Reforma*, August 27, 1998; "Gobiernos priístas, panistas y perredistas rebasados por la seguridad," *Proceso*, August 27, 2000.

33. *Excélsior*, July 31, 1998.

34. Interview with former INCD commissioner Francisco Molina, July 1998.

35. Attorney General Macedo de la Concha was appointed in December 2000.

36. PGR, *La lucha de México contra el narcotráfico (reducción de la oferta)*, August 2000, at www.pgr.gob.mx.

37. The identity of a witness is protected only during the preliminary investigation. According to legislators, to keep the identity secret after the preliminary investigation violates the Constitution, which gives the accused the right to know the identify of his or her accuser.

38. Wiretaps are not permitted in electoral, fiscal, trade, civil, labor, or administrative matters, or in the case of communications between lawyer and client. Public officials placing unauthorized wiretaps are subject to five to ten years in prison, with fines equal to between 500 and 1,000 days of work at minimum wage. Anyone who reveals or abuses any information or images obtained through a wiretap will also be penalized.

39. The law contemplates that a member of organized crime that lends useful assistance in the investigation and prosecution of said organization can receive special treatment depending on the stage at which the help is offered. The earlier the assistance, the more generous the advantages. The law gives broad discretionary power to the head of the UCDO and the attorney general, which might lead to abuses.

40. Under the terms of the law, a judge should approve arrest warrants within twelve hours of their request by the UEDO.

41. Prior to passage of this legislation, the PGR used informal methods to protect witnesses. This was true for witnesses in the trial of Raúl Salinas de Gortari (brother of President Salinas) for the murder of José Francisco Ruiz Massieu.

42. See note 23 on the *maxi-proceso*. This investigation led to the arrest of two generals in September 2000, Francisco Quirós Hermosillo and Arturo Acosta Chaparro, both associates of the defense minister at the time of their arrest.

43. José Galán, "El narcotráfico, negocio de la élite en el poder: Astorga," *La Jornada*, August, 31, 2000.

44. Confidential author interview, May 1999.

45. The Ethics Center administers toxicological, psychological, social, financial, medical, physical, and polygraph tests. See Arzt, "Scope and Limits."

46. Author interview with a PGR official, May 1999. This type of situation makes the exchange of information, and even the spirit of cooperation, between government agencies involved in money-laundering investigations very difficult.

47. The meaning of illegal origin is covered in Article 400 of the Federal Penal Code.

48. Presentation in the seminar "Narcotráfico: un análisis interdisciplinario," at the Centro de Investigación y Docencia Económicas, Mexico City, March 5, 2000.

49. PGR, *La lucha de México contra el narcotráfico (Reducción de la oferta).*

50. Ibid.

51. *Diario Oficial,* December 26, 1997.

52. The law was introduced in 1997, published in May 1999, and implemented in August 1999.

53. *Diario Oficial,* February 23, 2000.

54. Interview with Jorge Chabat, Mexico City, July 1999.

55. Press conference by the ministers of the interior, defense, and the navy, and the attorney general, Mexico City, February 4, 1999.

56. *Reforma,* March 1, 2000, reports the murder of the director of the Baja California state police.

57. Interior Ministry, press bulletin 659/2000, October 7, 2000.

58. Michael D. Maltz, *Measuring the Effectiveness of Organized Crime Control* (Chicago: Office of International Criminal Justice, University of Illinois at Chicago, 1990).

59. *Global Report on Crime and Justice* (New York: United Nations, 1999).

60. According to experts, executions or drug-related murders are registered as violent homicides. The profile includes execution-style murder, signs of torture, strangulation, mutilation of body parts, and setting one person free and executing a second on the spot. See *Reforma,* January 31, 2000.

61. *Global Report on Crime and Justice,* 61.

62. Testimony by Attorney General Jorge Madrazo Cuéllar before the federal Chamber of Deputies.

63. Sigrid Arzt, "A Challenge to Mexico's Democracy: The Military in Public Security" (manuscript, 2000).

64. It appears that this discovery was just the tip of the iceberg.

65. Appointments of new attorneys general in the administrations of Presidents Salinas and Zedillo were usually accompanied by an effort to clean up the police. Unfortunately, a frequent result was to add government-trained officers to the ranks of organized crime. For a more detailed study, see Miguel Sarre, "Citizen Security and Penal Justice: Federalism and the Separation of Powers," in *Seguridad policiaca, federalismo, y consolidación a la democracia en México,* edited by Arturo Alvarado and Sigrid Arzt (Mexico City: El Colegio de México, forthcoming).

66. PGR, *La lucha de México contra el narcotráfico (reducción de la oferta),* August 2000, www.pgr.gob.mx.

67. Vargas and Castillo, "Zedillo, inacabada la depuración de la PGR."

68. Miguel Badillo, "Soborno narco a tres jefes de la PGR, revelan," *El Universal*, January 12, 2000.

69. Among the numerous articles on this subject, see, for example, *Proceso* 949 (1995).

70. A review of the last three appearances by the attorney general before the federal Chamber of Deputies shows that legislators do not seem bothered by the fact that such activities continue.

71. Press conference by the UEDO director, January 17, 2000, at www.pgr.gob.mx/news/170100.html. Two of the three cases received press coverage that referred to "settling the score" because the witnesses allegedly linked prominent political figures with the Juárez cartel.

In January 2000, General Capelliti, General Gutiérrez Rebollo's driver, was murdered while in the witness protection program. Although the Attorney General's Office claims that this is an unrelated homicide and that Capelliti had refused formal protection, at the time of his murder he was carrying the credential of an UEDO technician, an anomaly that lends itself to abuse of authority.

Another case of apparent abuse concerns permits to carry a concealed weapon that the Interior Ministry gave to comedian-actor Paco Stanley and others. Such a permit and an Interior Ministry identification card were found on Stanley the day of his murder.

72. *Diario Oficial*, July 3, 1992.

73. For more details, see Articles 35–38 of the Federal Organized Crime Law.

74. Press conference on the witness protection program, January 17, 2000.

6

The Evolution of Intelligence Services in Mexico

Leonardo Curzio

INTRODUCTION

The main objective of this chapter is to examine the changing role of Mexico's intelligence services in recent years. The analysis focuses on civilian intelligence, leaving aside military intelligence and intelligence agencies specialized in combating narcotics trafficking.

The discussion is divided into two broad sections. The first analyzes the role that intelligence services have played in Mexico's political life. Specifically, the analysis considers three basic issues. The first is the way in which society perceives the term "intelligence." Recognizing the concept's negative connotations will help explain why it has been difficult to conduct a constructive debate on the role and nature of intelligence activities in Mexico, in which a notable deterioration in the state's security institutions paralleled the shift from an authoritarian regime to incipient pluralism. The second issue is the manner in which the role of intelligence services depends on a country's institutional and political culture at a given time, which means that changes in intelligence activities are directly related to transformations in the country as a whole. And the third is the determinism that the national and international contexts imprint upon the structuring and prioritization of an intelligence agency. An intelligence agency's structure, capacities, and objectives clearly respond to the perceived threat that dominates a given moment. For example, the end of the Cold War marked a clear displacement of priorities from ideological struggles to combating organized crime.

The second section of the discussion examines Mexico's principal civilian intelligence agency, the Center for Research and National Security, known as CISEN, and analyzes its scope of action and its priorities. It also reviews the creation of CISEN's operational arm, the Federal Preventive Police (PFP), with which the Mexican government purports to counter the country's serious public safety problems.

INTELLIGENCE, A WORRISOME CONCEPT

The word "intelligence" stirs up suspicion among most sectors of public opinion. For example, some periodicals treat all subjects that deal with intelligence as grist for scandal or cause for concern.[1] Why does an activity that dates from the very beginning of political organization generate such animosity? One answer lies in the charged semantics associated with the concept of "intelligence" in Mexico today. People associate different semantics with certain concepts at different moments in their history. For example, the socialists adopted their name in a context in which the word democracy and its derivatives were perceived as suspicious and subversive to the established order. In another example, for some countries, including the United States, the term "liberal" takes on a series of connotations associated with radicalism, a perception that in other countries seem incomprehensible. In Mexico there is a glorification of concepts that evoke insurrection against the established order—as in the broad urban avenues named "Insurgents" and "Revolution"—that in other countries would seem ludicrous.

The word intelligence is particularly unacceptable in Mexico for three key reasons. The first and foremost is that of the four components that generally constitute intelligence activity (information gathering, analysis, counterintelligence, and special operations), the most widespread conception of intelligence activity concerns the latter, which is also the most polemic.[2] Contributing greatly to this impression is the mass dissemination of three types of material—movies about spies and secret agents, televised documentaries about the special operations of the CIA, and books about spies and deserters[3] and the prowess of both.[4] These recountings of action and adventure tend to overlook the fact that intelligence services spend most of their time processing information from open sources.

As Abraham Shulsky, the renowned theorist on intelligence, noted:

> In popular fiction and for the public, intelligence frequently has been seen as synonymous with espionage and intrigue, like the sexual blackmail of a Mata Hari and the feats of a James Bond. Although activities of this type have their own place in the intelligence world, the total concept is much more complex. We begin by observing the phenomenon that is dubbed "intelligence"; this includes certain types of information-gathering activities and organizations. "Intelligence" refers to the information deemed important for the formulation of policies and governmental strategy to promote national security interests and to face threats coming from potential adversaries. Intelligence activity, in fact, entails the collection and analysis of intelligence information. It also includes measures taken to

> counter the intelligence activities of adversaries, whether by denying them access to information or by misleading them about certain events and their importance.[5]

In short, intelligence comprises a wide gamut of activities, not just covert operations. It is evident, however, that the task of the intelligence services is not limited to gathering and processing information from open sources. Although the basic duties of intelligence services involve processing public information readily available through newspapers, magazines, radio, television, and the Internet, this does not rule out the fact that the fundamental and distinctive component of intelligence activity is the element of secrecy.

All intelligence capacities base their value-added in meeting the information needs of decision makers. Their information must be relevant, timely, and trustworthy. If it is not timely, relevant, or accurate, it is worthless, as presumably occurred when the uprising by the Zapatista Army of National Liberation (EZLN) in the southern Mexican state of Chiapas in January 1994 took Mexican authorities by surprise. Intelligence is not simply information. In order to be elevated to the rank of intelligence, the information flow must include the element of secrecy, which makes it qualitatively different than the rest of governmental information. The secrecy component could be some minor detail, a name, a photograph.

The methods used to discover "secrets," or information that some group deliberately wants to hide, generate a natural suspicion in a democratic regime governed by the rule of law. The debate over intelligence capacities is waged from two extreme positions: that of compatibility and that of incompatibility with a democratic regime. Theodore Draper, for example, frames the problem of an absolute incompatibility between democracy and the activity of intelligence services in these terms:

> Apart from particular questions about the CIA, there is the problem of the place of a secret agency in a democracy. Secret agencies, especially those which can conceal their secrets more or less permanently, necessarily operate outside the democratic process. They are the most difficult to control and even scrutinize. They tempt presidents to use them to escape from ordinary political oversight. They offer a quick panacea instead of patient long-term policies. Without a war, hot or cold, they can do more harm than good.[6]

At the root of this predicament are three significant dilemmas that a democracy faces:

- Deciding whether to authorize a government agency to obtain information clandestinely that could actually or hypothetically affect the social fabric, democratic institutions, and, ultimately, national security.
- Defining the targets of an intelligence capacity. Against which actors in national life should intelligence services be able to licitly but clandestinely extract information about their organization, structures, and objectives?
- Determining the limits of "state interest" in legitimating intelligence work, so that the rule of law, which intelligence serves, is not undermined.

The dilemma between secrecy and transparency in an open society is not linear,[7] and reducing the problem to a dichotomy of official secrets/transparency leads to a dead end. The binary "transparency/secrecy" relationship cannot be equated with that between democracy and authoritarianism. Transparency is both democracy's underpinning and its claim, while secrecy is the standard mode of operation for authoritarianism. But that does not automatically imply that a democracy cannot have secrets. Modern democracies cannot be based entirely on transparency, as not all actors respect all laws all the time. There will always be agents, actors, and organizations that deliberately intend to undermine the harmony and peace of a country. Thus a democratic government should have secrets and guarantee that its information be as reliable and factual as possible.

As Ann Florini explains,[8] universal transparency presents certain problems. In the absence of universally shared or at least mutually compatible norms, transparency will aggravate conflict. Some secrets are legitimately worth protecting. Information can easily be misused or misinterpreted. And even if all the conditions are right, transparency does not always work.

Therefore, in order for intelligence services to function with a reasonable degree of social acceptance and institutional legitimacy, two circumstances rarely seen in contemporary Mexico must come about simultaneously. The first is an understanding of the nature of intelligence activity; the second is confidence in the government intelligence apparatus and, especially, its services.

Public perceptions of intelligence services in Mexico have alternated between fear and derision. In a society like Mexico's that purports to create institutions and organizations rooted in democracy, intelligence services should provoke neither fear nor laughter. As Sergio Aguayo pointed out at the beginning of the 1990s:

> One knows little, almost nothing, about Mexican intelligence services. This ignorance is absurd and almost dangerous, because what they do or don't do is of tremendous importance. If we don't want to have unpleasant surprises, the Congress, the executive branch, and society must incorporate them into the agenda as issues of priority.... In other words, to guarantee our safety, intelligence services and security agencies must be democratized. Mexico is changing and the speed with which we reach our democracy and the very strength and solidity of this Mexican democracy depends in part on the interrelationships between our society in transition and our intelligence and security capacities.[9]

THE INSTITUTIONALIZATION OF INTELLIGENCE

A country that is building its democracy must, in effect, legitimize and legalize the work of its intelligence agencies, pointing them toward priorities that serve national security and steering them away from political temptations and the interests of the regime in power. Confidence in the governmental apparatus, and especially in its intelligence services, will only come about as these services attain three major objectives. They must be de-politicized. They must be professionalized. And there must be oversight mechanisms that are duly regulated and that can reduce possible deviations and improve the social prestige of intelligence activity.

We will look first at the problem of the politicization of intelligence. The distance between Mexico's intelligence services and its decision makers has varied over time. In his pioneering book, Sherman Kent proposed distancing intelligence services, especially those doing analysis, from politicians in order to guarantee the autonomy of their reasoning.[10] Many authors feel this type of "political quarantine" is impossible because intelligence services are motivated by an agenda sanctioned by the government. Their specific task is to help the government achieve its objectives and safeguard its interests. The bulk of an intelligence service's activities respond to specific requirements identified by the government itself. Thus, as Stack affirms: "If intelligence exists to serve policy, then intelligence products provided to decision makers must contain hard-hitting, focused analysis relevant to current policy issues."[11]

This question continues to divide theorists, but it does not generate friction in consolidated democracies, where the public, the government, and its officials share fundamental principles and values. In contrast, the issue is especially relevant in countries like South Africa or the Russian Federation which are in the process of radically altering their basic philosophies and tenets for governance. It is easy to envision the many problems that might ensue during this shift in national security doctrines—which by definition oversee intelligence activities—when the enemy (black communities in South Africa or anti-Communists in Russia) are no longer the enemy and instead become an integral and fundamental part of the government. In the so-called *White Book* of South Africa, we find a clear reflection of this:

> Reforming and transforming intelligence in South Africa is not only a question of organizational restructuring; it must begin by clarifying its philosophy and redefining the mission, focus and priorities of intelligence and, in this way, establish a new culture of intelligence. Before the advent of democracy, security policy was determined by a minority government; thus its capacity to define the national interest was inherently impeded.[12]

Similar circumstances must have arisen in Russia, especially when it came time to transform or recycle KGB agents assigned to the office that had formerly been charged with suppressing ideological dissent.

In countries like Mexico that do not experience a radical shift in fundamental values but do change the nature of their regime and political system, the problem is similar but less intense. It might be posed as follows: how to ensure that intelligence services traditionally politicized in favor of the regime in power will be converted into an organ at the service of the state that will loyally and efficiently serve all those political forces traditionally considered as enemies, and therefore as targets of espionage?

In an ideal world, intelligence services should offer information in the most objective and politically neutral way possible. Reality proves that intelligence capacities have always been narrowly linked to the ideology and political preferences of the regime they serve and the values prevailing in the international arena. Mexico's dilemma in recent years has been to transition from an intelligence service that is highly intertwined with and protected by a one-party hegemonic regime and that often operates against a democratic opposition, to an intelligence service that is politically neutral and operates as a system for information gathering and information processing governed by law.

The professionalization of the service is a prerequisite to reducing political bias. The degree to which public administration is politicized depends on three factors: the mechanisms of recruiting and hiring, the regulation of promotions and tenure of public officials, and the autonomy of these public officials.

It is evident that, absent a statute that guarantees the three aforementioned factors, the politicization of intelligence will be unavoidable. The 1994 crisis in Chiapas demonstrated that it is bad business, even for a nondemocratic government, to rely on an intelligence service that is politicized and amateur. The main threats to stability that a country faces do not stem from institutional political competitors, but rather from domestic destructive forces that oppose not only the regime but the incipient democracy as well.

The reform of the Mexican state should lead to administrative reform to remedy these weaknesses and to avoid perpetuating the "spoils system" that privileges the interests of a group or political party over the quality of public services and impartiality in public administration.[13] Unfortunately, the political reform and the advent of democracy in recent years have not been sufficient to resolve these problems of the professionalization and neutrality of public administration, although they have provided the necessary framework. Any government fully legitimized through the ballot box, regardless of its political persuasion, can still misuse its administrative apparatus and intelligence services if it lacks a professional career service.

A professional intelligence service should, in principle, display three fundamental features. It must have a well-defined mission. It must have its own autonomous identity. And it must understand its social responsibility.

The tasks of an intelligence service—identifying groups and factors that threaten the established order—should be legitimated by the principal democratic forces of the country. A clear self-identity is crucial to persuade those involved to play by the rules. When an institution is morally degraded and corrupt, as has occurred with many police forces in Mexico, its capacity for reform is reduced. Repeated failed efforts to purge the judicial police are the best examples. If an organization's members lack the sense of pride that distinguishes them socially as a corporate body, their corruption is more probable. In these circumstances, they lack the ethical profile that gives meaning to their belonging, which is the fundamental basis of self-control. Ultimately, their responsibilities before Congress or to society must be defined by laws. President Ernesto Zedillo (1994–2000) made the following point as he established the priorities for Mexico's 1995–2000 National Development Plan:

> We should update the legal framework governing intelligence capacities, with the end goal of typifying and regulating the work carried out on this subject. The objective should be to ensure, at every moment, the efficiency and adherence to the law of the national intelligence services and to take full advantage of international cooperation in the interchange of information pertaining to drug trafficking, criminals, and terrorism.[14]

It now remains for the administration of Vicente Fox (2000–2006) to pursue debate of an intelligence framework law that addresses the issues discussed above.

THE SPIRIT OF THE TIMES

The internal changes that a country undergoes do not alone shape the anatomy and functioning of that nation's intelligence services. Dominant ideas in the international arena also have significant, often decisive weight in defining intelligence services' organization and mission. During the Cold War, intelligence services governed by a strong anticommunist doctrine proliferated in Latin America. The persecution of the "internal enemy" within the East/West logic offered an umbrella identity to the different intelligence units at a time when a hemispheric mission was giving them purpose.

The end of the Cold War marked a shift toward the de-ideologization of intelligence services. The question being posed from various quarters concerned the utility of maintaining intelligence structures that had been built specifically within the context of the Cold War. At its root, the question derives from the following logic: if intelligence services were created with a specific political purpose, once this goal is achieved, the intelligence organizations should disappear. There were other voices, however, such as that of noted historian Walter Laqueur, that disagreed with this position and proposed retaining a reformed intelligence service dedicated to new functions responding to new threats.

> With the collapse of communism the Cold War has ended, but the prospects of world peace have not notably improved. While a nuclear war seemed virtually impossible even at the height of the Cold War, it has become more probable in the age of proliferation—to mention but one of the major dangers facing mankind at this time. Perhaps the most outstanding factor in international politics during the Cold War was the straightforward character of the confrontation; at present and in the foreseeable future the world will be an infinitely more complex place. While some of the old dangers have disappeared, new ones have surfaced, and to know about them has become infinitely more difficult. But why worry if anarchy prevails in certain parts of the world and two (or more) minor, far away countries decide to make war against each other? This king of argument had much to recommend itself two hundred years ago and perhaps even a hundred, but it is no longer very helpful at the end of the twentieth century, in the age of weapons of mass destruction. Someone ought to worry, and it is in this context that intelligence is, and will be, needed.[15]

The new missions of the state's security elements are being deduced from the new security agenda, each time more firmly anchored in issues such as preventing and combating organized crime, especially drug trafficking. Mexico will not be an exception to this rule. The changes on the national and international stage imply a series of transformations that intelligence capacities will need to undergo in order to adapt to their new context. These transformations, analyzed in greater detail in following sections, are of both an organizational and a philosophical nature.

THE MEXICAN INTELLIGENCE SERVICE

The Center for Research and National Security (CISEN) is Mexico's civilian intelligence service. The fact that the word "intelligence" does not figure into this agency's official name is revealing of the limited understanding of the term "intelligence" in Mexico, as noted previously.

Background

The history of Mexico's intelligence agency, which dates at least to the 1920s, lies within the Interior Ministry (Secretaría de Gobernación). Toward the end of the 1920s, the ministry's Confidential Department (Departamento Confidencial), whose functions were guarded, began operations. By the end of the 1930s an Office of Political Information (Oficina de Información Política) appeared, later to become the Department of Political Research (Departamento de Investigación Política).

In 1947, the Federal Security Directorate (DFS) appeared on the institutional map, coinciding approximately with the beginnings of the Cold War. Its initial focus was control of foreigners and foreign influences (the storied contacts between DFS director Fernando Gutiérrez Barrios and Fidel Castro date from this period). As years passed, the DFS was gradually corrupted, to the point of being unsalvageable, and it was dissolved in 1985.

In the mid–1960s a new General Directorate of Political Research (Dirección General de Investigaciones Políticas) emerged within the Interior Ministry. Its mission—internal affairs—was basically to cover the analytical aspects of intelligence that the DFS had failed to carry out. The crisis of the DFS had generated a veritable earthquake in Mexico's institutional architecture. On the one hand, drug trafficking had begun to devour the entrails of the security apparatus. On the other, some sectors were seriously reconsidering the role of intelligence services and even their very existence. During this same period, national security became a prominent issue on both the academic and the political stage. Parallel to these developments, many observers posited the need to purge and purify the security forces, removing some of their operational responsibilities and emphasizing their analytical role.

A compromise solution between the diametrically opposed visions of "operations" versus "analysis" as the proper mission of the intelligence services was attempted in 1985 with the creation of the General Directorate of Research and National Security (DISEN), the predecessor of the present-day CISEN. The DISEN model was based on the separation of the operational arm from departments responsible for intelligence processing. DISEN was fated to be short-lived. In 1989, incoming president Carlos Salinas de Gortari (1988–1994) restructured the entire national security system by creating a specialized cabinet post and transforming DISEN into the Center for Research and National Security.

In 1992, the expanding drug trade and its corrupting influence prompted Salinas to appoint part of the CISEN team to head a new National Institute to Combat Drugs (INCD) and its intelligence arm, the National Drug Control Center (CENDRO). This decision stemmed from the need to establish a kind of "firewall." By concentrating all antidrug activities in one agency, the government could limit corruption. If drug traffickers corrupted one government agency, the reasoning went, the impact could be contained within that single agency.

Not everyone shared this vision. Some government sectors felt that isolating the lead agency in the nation's fight against drugs would actually facilitate its corruption. They held that the best strategy was to have several agencies coordinate their efforts in the battle against drug trafficking, fomenting a kind of Foucaultian "generalized vigilance." This chapter does not propose to analyze the strategies employed in the fight against drugs. Rather, the point to be made is that, according to this perspective, it would be necessary to deliberately marginalize the civilian intelligence agency from the drug war in order to preserve the agency and consolidate it.

The storm that broke in Mexico on January 1, 1994, radically changed the panorama for intelligence. The emergence of guerrilla groups presented new challenges. In fact, the EZLN uprising brought to light all the weaknesses of an intelligence agency that was both highly politicized and highly ineffective. Ten days into 1994, President Salinas restructured his cabinet, vowing that he would change "everything that didn't work."

Jorge Carpizo accepted the Interior Ministry portfolio and announced a policy of dialogue and strict enforcement of the law. Under Carpizo, the task of restructuring the intelligence services began. The CISEN would not change its name or structure, but it would attempt to modernize and adapt to the new realities facing the country. Jorge Tello Peón left his post at INCD, where he had led the war against drug trafficking, to return to the leadership of the CISEN and initiate a new phase in its operations. The job of restructuring national security and the intelligence apparatus during 1994 consisted of the following, according to an Interior Ministry report:

> Task agendas were established in the areas responsible for national security information systems, defining priorities and directing the research topics and analysis toward more prospective and policy-oriented work, abandoning a strictly reactive and descriptive posture. Information distribution systems were revised and adjusted to ensure their availability in time and form for the different levels of decision making, permitting good use of data and conclusions, and allowing for wiser allocation of resources. Coordination with state authorities was strengthened, and permanent links were established for the exchange of information related to national security. Similarly, prototypes of security systems were developed for strategic installations, and their implementation was coordinated and supervised with the agencies and enterprises responsible for their operation and safekeeping. Specialists were trained for these subjects; many of them expanded their knowledge of intelligence in foreign academic institutions. Moreover, we worked with several state governments in the technical reinforcement and improvement of their personnel in security matters. CISEN established and strengthened linkages and relationships with foreign counterpart institutions. There was good coordination with other federal government agencies whose functions had a bearing on national security, holding meetings at least once a week.[16]

These measures laid the groundwork for a new understanding of intelligence services in Mexico. The work that began in 1994 continued throughout the Zedillo administration, and the team that initiated the reform process has continued into the Fox administration. Jorge Tello continued as director of CISEN until 1999, when he was appointed undersecretary for public security in the Interior Ministry. His replacement as director of CISEN was Alejandro Alegre, who had previously served there as secretary general.[17]

Roles and Responsibilities

According to the regulations of the Interior Ministry, CISEN's official duties are to coordinate actions concerning national security. According to Article 33 of the regulations:

> The Center for Research and National Security is a deconcentrated administrative organ with technical and operational autonomy, assigned directly to the Secretary, that will have the following duties:

1. To establish and operate a system of investigation, research, and information for the security of the country.
2. To collect and process the information generated by the system referred to in the previous section, determine its tendency, value, significance, and exact interpretation, and to formulate conclusions that are derived from the corresponding evaluations.
3. To conduct studies of a political, economic, and social nature that are related to its duties.
4. To conduct public opinion surveys about issues of national interest.

Article 34 stipulates that:

> The Center's budget and the principal guidelines for its execution will be subject to the norms established by the Treasury Ministry [SHCP] for units with autonomous expenditure. The authorized budget cannot be subject to transfer to other administrative units or deconcentrated administrative units of the Interior Ministry.
>
> For this purpose, the head of the Center will send the budget proposal as authorized by the Treasury, to the Interior Ministry, in order that it be integrated into the overall budget for that agency.

Article 32 establishes the generic functions of the heads of the decentralized bodies, highlighting those relative to legal and juridical representation, labor relations, and the resolution of legal issues in general. And, finally, the regulations stipulate that CISEN is charged with collecting, processing, and disseminating information related to national security, as well as conducting opinion polls. It also performs a supplemental role, discussed below.

THE NATIONAL SECURITY CABINET

The director of CISEN also serves as the technical secretary of the National Security Cabinet, created by President Salinas in December 1988. The cabinet originally comprised the ministers of the interior, foreign relations, defense, and the navy, as well as the attorney general and Salinas's adviser, José Córdoba Montoya. In early 1994 Salinas broadened the composition of the cabinet in order to include the issues of crime and public safety, with the launching of an initiative (headed by former labor minister Arsenio Farell) on National Public Security Coordination (Coordinación de Seguridad Pública de la Nación). The primary role of this unit, assigned to the President's Office, was to coordinate all efforts addressing issues of public safety. This precursor to the Zedillo administration's Council on Public Safety (Consejo de Seguridad Pública) acted as a liaison among the federal Attorney General's Office (PGR), the state-level attorneys general, and the various ministries represented in the National Security Cabinet.

The public security initiative did not appear on the institutional landscape by chance. It was created at a moment when Mexico was undergoing a period of chaos following the assassination of PRI presidential candidate Luis Donaldo Colosio in April 1994. Public safety concerns were putting unrelenting pressure on the government, and in many ways these security threats—closely linked to concerns of national security—were far more serious than the common crime the local police were used to, and able to, deal with. The fact that authority for coordination of public security was placed within the National Security Cabinet only underscored the interdependence of public security and national security as these two concepts were merged in the coordination machinery of the higher levels of government.

The methodology and institutions that the Zedillo government forged to tackle the problem of public safety once again traced a line dividing public safety and national security—at least in principle. Nevertheless, toward the end of Zedillo's term, these boundaries blurred once again with the creation of the Federal Preventive Police, a direct descendant of the operational arm of CISEN. Public safety and national security, concepts that are totally different in theory, continue to coexist in symbiosis in contemporary Mexico.

The National Security Cabinet underwent another modification halfway through the Zedillo administration, when the special cabinets were restructured.[18] Within the President's Office, cabinets (including National Security) were to propose, and trace the progress of, executive branch policies. According to newly passed resolutions, these agencies would be presided over by the president and would include the interior minister and the heads of the other agencies, dependencies, and federal administrative entities as designated by the president. Presumably, the coordinator of advisers for domestic and foreign policy issues would assume responsibility for the cabinets on Domestic Policy, Foreign Policy, and National Security, among others, and track the decisions and agreements reached in these cabinets.

Internal Structure

CISEN's structure was designed around the "cycle of intelligence." The president appoints CISEN's director general, whose duties and rank make this position equivalent to that of an undersecretary. The second-ranked position is the secretary general, whose main task is the functional integration of the organization. The secretary general oversees five units charged, respectively, with planning, the dissemination of information, international relations, issues involving the courts, and internal affairs.

CISEN's Research Department includes a director who controls the field offices for information gathering (thirty-two state delegations and a metropolitan section). The field offices are responsible for feeding raw data (much of it collected by law enforcement agencies) into the system. Heads of field offices fulfill a delicate task as integrators of the intelligence communities in the states and also as the technical secretaries to the state-level public security cabinets.

The Analysis Directorate integrates intelligence projects and determines the agenda of national security risks. The Technical Services Directorate provides logistical support for the operation of the overall system and for CISEN's technological development.

The Center for Human Resources Development provides support to the various offices, and it recruits and trains personnel who are transferred to other federal agencies and even to some state governments. Recruitment is a pillar of CISEN's success. A battery of tests—ranging from conventional psychological profiles to polygraphs—is employed to select personnel for the security apparatus. CISEN's recruitment system has shown positive results; its officers have remained free from charges of illegal behaviors, something that had been common in security forces in contemporary Mexico. Indeed, the CISEN model has been exported to other federal and state agencies. The "trustworthiness units" (*unidades de control de confianza*) implemented in the federal Attorney General's Office and various other agencies were created with CISEN's advice and technical support. Another important support program for federal agencies and state governments is the training for polygraph operators that helps recruit "clean" personnel for sensitive positions in the prosecutorial and administrative branches of the courts.

The Protection Directorate, recently renamed the Counter-Intelligence Directorate, is in charge of counter-terrorist and anti-subversion operations. Pressure from the many threats to public security, such as high-profile kidnappings, began to force public safety issues into this directorate's sphere, but these were later redirected to the newly created Federal Preventive Police.

THE EVOLUTION OF THE INTELLIGENCE AGENDA

The evolutionary trajectory of risks to Mexican national security is marked primarily by the increase and spread of public insecurity as an issue of national security, and this confluence has shaped the subsequent development of intelligence services as they have confronted these risks. Two stages are identifiable in this process: one of coordination, the other of transformation.

The data on insecurity are alarming. In 1995 there were 548 kidnappings reported in Mexico. The situation was particularly severe in certain areas; there were 93 kidnappings in Guerrero, 70 in Chiapas, 56 in the Federal District, 33 in Michoacán, and 32 in Morelos. Auto theft statistics are equally alarming; from January to August 1997, 38,584 cars were stolen in the Federal District alone, and two-thirds of these thefts involved violence.[19]

President Zedillo characterized this growing lawlessness as follows:

> With great sadness I recognize that the State has not met the demand for the public safety of Mexicans. And I speak of the State in its broadest interpretation, because on matters of public safety we are clearly co-responsible, all three powers of the union [federal, state, municipal] and all three branches of the government. In fact, more than 90 percent of crimes committed fall within the jurisdiction of state law, and their prosecution is the responsibility of state governments. We have had to confront multiple problems such as weak laws; obsolete institutions, many of which have been infiltrated by corruption; lack of resources and good programs. Faced with the gravity of these problems, the federal government has not stood idly by, unresponsive.
>
> During the past five years, there have been five reforms of codes and ordinances, and over eleven new laws dealing with public safety and justice have been put on the books. This year, the federal and state governments are investing 9 billion pesos[20] in public safety measures. This sum is over twice the amount, in real terms, that was invested last year and over triple the amount from 1997. Moreover, almost 70 percent of these funds are being used by states and municipalities in exchange for implementing specific programs to purge their district attorney's and attorney general's offices and police forces of corruption, for the training and development of their agents, and for the modernization of their equipment.
>
> For its part, the federal government is also buttressing its security forces. The Federal Preventive Police has been created with new mechanisms to enhance selectivity, training, and control to prevent its infiltration by tainted elements.
>
> Very soon we will begin winning the battle against crime. Before long, we will start to reverse the trends toward criminality and insecurity that we have been enduring in recent years.[21]

CISEN's achievements in two key areas—forming interinstitutional groups and developing a recruitment system to prevent the criminal infiltration of security forces—stand as the pillars of Zedillo's efforts in the realm of public safety. They represent a blending, once again, of the two levels of security—public safety and national security—leaving the intelligence agency again facing the dilemma of refashioning itself following the transfer of its operational duties to the Federal Preventive Police.

FROM COORDINATION TO SEPARATION

Interinstitutional coordination among the army, navy, Attorney General's Office, and Federal Highway Police originated in coordinating committees that included members from different agencies working at the operational level (the Anti-Terrorist Group [GAT], the special group for strategic installations, and a group to deter kidnappings). The growing autonomy in this area of responsibility is a natural development of the work of these coordinating committees and of the exponential escalation of the threats that rising levels of criminality pose for national security. Thus the part of CISEN dedicated to protection and crime prevention constituted the embryo for a new force, the PFP.

Strategic coordination in the fight against organized crime was CISEN's first big success. Given that organized crime was the top item on the national security agenda, the intelligence agency could not remain on the sidelines. But the challenge CISEN faced was the same one faced in previous years—the greater its operational level, the greater the risk of contamination, infiltration, and corruption. The great paradox was that, in reality, CISEN was fulfilling a maternal role: structuring, nurturing, and then yielding forth its new crime-fighting creation. The fact that operational duties have been transferred to these new police forces has given greater impact to police actions such as the arrest of the leaders of the Insurgent People's Revolutionary Army (ERPI) in October 1999.

Although CISEN is poised yet again to consolidate itself as a true strategic intelligence agency, certain issues will continue to threaten the country in upcoming years. For example, the drug trade, international terrorism, and other forms of organized crime remain serious threats to national security—even though they may appear to be problems better suited to the realm of law enforcement and its police forces. Mexico's intelligence services frequently participate in the battle against such threats. And, given the gravity and magnitude of the problem, it is probably inevitable that this will occur, for a number of reasons. First, these threats imply activities in which national police forces lack jurisdiction and in which local forces may be unable and/or unwilling to collaborate effectively. More importantly, the focus of police work generally implies waiting to intervene until a crime has taken place or is about to take place. Intelligence services approach crime from a more anticipatory and preventive stance.

The PFP contains an intelligence unit and specialized cadres developed within CISEN that will enable it to develop into a intelligence system able to meet challenges that combine public safety and national security. Assuming the PFP succeeds in this regard, CISEN can devote itself once again to consolidating a modern, professional intelligence capability that can help Mexico's policymakers remove or neutralize threats to national security, a necessary precondition for reconstituting the role of intelligence services in a democratic society.

In any case, CISEN cannot separate itself from the destructive effects of organized crime because these will remain a major national security issue. Like the Sicilian proverb a colorful member of the Italian Mafia once quoted in regard to countries that, for political or organizational reasons, lack continuity and cooperation in the fight against organized crime: "*calati juncu, ca passa la china*,"[22] which translates loosely as "hunker down and ride it out; this wave of persecution will not last." Organized crime thrives by simply waiting for police efforts to fail.

Mexico is at a perilous point in its history. President Zedillo's term in office, which ended in 2000, was characterized by the creation of new structures and new laws. The results should soon be visible. If these efforts do not bear fruit, public insecurity will become the worst threat to the stability of Mexico's young democracy and the primary engine of political involvement.

Notes

Translated by Janelle Garret.

1. See, for example, Raúl Monge, "2 de octubre: espionaje estilo 1999," *Proceso* 1197 (October 10, 1999): 16–17.

2. There is extensive discussion of this issue in countries like the United States. See, for example, Michael Reisman and James Baker, *Regulating Covert Action* (New Haven, Conn.: Yale University Press, 1992).

3. There is an abundance of literature on this theme. See, especially, Philip Agee, *Acoso y fuga* (Barcelona: Plaza y Janes, 1988); Peter Wright and Paul Greengrass, *Cazadores de Espías* (Barcelona: Círculo de Lectores, 1988).

4. The most impressive is perhaps W. Jordan Prange, *Le reseau Sorge* (Paris: Pygmalion, 1987).

5. Abraham N. Shulsky, *Silent Warfare: Understanding the World of Intelligence* (Washington, D.C.: Brassey's, 1993).

6. Theodore Draper, "Is the CIA Necessary?" *New York Review of Books* 44:13 (August 14, 1997): 22.

7. See Pat Holt, *Secret Intelligence and Public Policy: A Dilemma of Democracy* (Washington, D.C.: Congressional Quarterly, 1995).

8. Ann Florini, "The End of Secrecy," *Foreign Policy*, Summer 1998, 60–61.

9. Sergio Aguayo, "El espionaje ante la cultura cívica," *La Jornada Semanal.*

10. Sherman Kent, *Inteligencia estratégica para la política mundial norteamericana* (Buenos Aires: Pleamar, 1987).

11. This negative view of competitive analysis is found in Kevin P. Stack, "The Non Use of Intelligence," *International Journal of Intelligence and Counterintelligence* 10 (4): 456.

12. Government of South Africa, *White Book*. Notebooks of the CISEN (translated from Spanish).

13. The issue of the professionalization of government was again placed on the agenda for discussion given the political situation in 2000. See Esteban Moctezuma and Andrés Roemer, *Por un gobierno con resulatados* (Mexico City: Fondo de Cultura Económica, 1999).

14. Ernesto Zedillo, *Plan Nacional de Desarrollo 1995–2000*, 10.

15. Walter Laqueur, *The Uses and Limits of Intelligence* (New Brunswick, N.J.: Transaction, 1995), 8.

16. Jorge Carpizo, "Informe de Labores 1994" (Mexico City: Secretaría de Gobernación, November 1994), 62–63.

17. *Editors' note*: Tello and Alegre were replaced by Fox appointees in March 2001).

18. Resolution through which the specialized agencies of the federal government that respond directly to the president were restructured and the executive branch was restructured, creating the President's Office.

19. Dirección General de Supervisión de los Servicios de Protección Ciudadana, in *Carpeta Informativa del Sistema Nacional de Seguridad Pública*, no. 1 (October 1997), 34.

20. *Editors' note*: This is approximately US$1 billion.

21. Dirección General de Supervisión, *Carpeta*, 34.

22. Cited in Giovanni Falcone, *La lucha contra el erimen organizado* (Mexico City: INACIPF, 1992), 45.

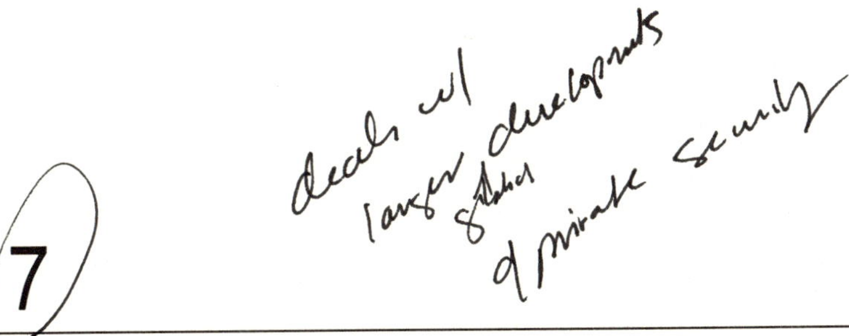

7

Public Security versus Private Security?

Jorge Regalado Santillán

INTRODUCTION

As Mexico entered the twenty-first century, it was experiencing a public security crisis. Never before had crime achieved such high levels of efficiency and enjoyed such impunity. The Mexican government and its public security forces had never before been so completely penetrated and corrupted by organized crime and drug-trafficking networks. Corruption, a low level of professionalization of the police, and the deterioration of the law enforcement and judicial system explain much of the government's inability to fight crime. The public security crisis took root within a greater crisis, that of the Mexican political system. The regime established by the Institutional Revolutionary Party (PRI), which had lasted for more than seventy years, was toppled by the free and democratic election of Vicente Fox of the National Action Party (PAN) as president of Mexico in July 2000, greatly raising expectations regarding the future of public security in Mexico.

Fox's victory also ushered in changes in the composition of the Mexican Congress, where the PRI lost its nearly six-decade majority, although no other party obtained a majority. This situation has forced each legislative party bloc to hone its negotiating skills so that the Congress can begin to function as an autonomous power and counterweight to the metaconstitutional powers traditionally enjoyed by the Mexican president.

Following the Mexican Revolution of 1910–1917, the country went through a complex sociopolitical process that laid the groundwork for Mexico's pacification and reconstruction, as well as the creation of new laws and institutions to regulate social life and postrevolutionary politics. A defining moment in this process was the elaboration, debate, and legitimization of the Constitution of 1917. From that time until the year 2000, all presidents came from the ruling party, as did the overwhelming majority of congressional representatives and officials at the state and municipal levels throughout the country. Only in 1988 did democratization begin to emerge in Mexico; the corporatist system of social control began to lose efficiency at the same rate that newly articulate citizens began to discover the power of the vote and to demand the extension of their rights.

Political debate and civic action were significantly enriched during the 1990s. Nevertheless, unlike democratic transition and the liberalization of the political system, the issue of public security has not received the same level of attention in fact as it has in speeches by governmental and societal actors. Despite all the programs proposed, all the economic resources invested, all the changes in police commands, and the militarization of these forces, government and society have not addressed the public security problem with concrete political actions. In effect, society and government have not yet realized that this problem should take priority above all others, at least for the short term.

The state of public insecurity in Mexico is such that all the "force of the state" should be used to combat it, as President Ernesto Zedillo (1994–2000) observed. Bearing in mind that the rule of law should always prevail, the state should still employ the intensive use of intelligence and public information in the fight against crime. The force of the state is none other than the rule of law; it should be employed not only to combat organized and professional crime but also to fight against abuses committed by public officials, especially law enforcement and judicial officials responsible for the failures of the system.

It is no exaggeration to assert that law enforcement in Mexico is class based and responds to the highest bidder. This is a public truth, abundantly obvious to the majority of low-income Mexicans who have been victims of crime or who have needed to seek law enforcement and justice services. If one reads, for example, the State of the Nation addresses delivered by the last three presidents of Mexico (Miguel de la Madrid, Carlos Salinas de Gortari, and Ernesto Zedillo Ponce de León) as well as those given by governors and many of the nation's nearly 2,400 mayors, one finds multiple references to the problem of insecurity—regardless of whether the district is urban or rural, or densely or meagerly populated. Traditional hypotheses regarding the variables that define "insecure environments" have been thrown out the window. In addition, police paradigms to fight crime by hardening penalties have been demonstrated to be inadequate. The overwhelming proof of this is found in the prodigious development and diversification of organized and professional crime.

In his fifth and penultimate State of the Nation address, President Zedillo said, "with great sadness I recognize that the State has not met the demand for the public safety of Mexicans." He added, however, that "the federal government has not stood idly by," and he listed a number of constitutional reforms, codes, orders, and new laws to strengthen public security and justice. Zedillo acknowledged that "the citizens are within their rights to complain, to be dissatisfied and angry with authorities for the amount of crime in Mexico."[1]

As in previous administrations, Zedillo promised that "very soon we will begin winning the battle against crime. Before long, we will start to reverse the trends toward criminality and insecurity that we have been enduring in recent years."[2] A few days later Zedillo acknowledged that police forces and justice officials in Mexico found themselves "in some measure, afflicted by corruption and crime," and he noted that "to have the enemy living in your house increases the state's vulnerability to carry out its avowed mission to uphold public security."[3] Soon after delivering these remarks, Zedillo visited Mexicali, Baja California, where he warned, "we have to make criminals understand that Baja California is not their home; the only place these criminals deserve is jail.... Next week, we will meet to discuss this and then we will tell the people of Baja California how we are going to fight this crime wave." Forty-eight hours later, the president received a graphic response when Tijuana police chief Alfredo de la Torre Márquez was gunned down in a hail of bullets.[4] Evidently, drug traffickers and criminal gangs do not fear the government or its attempts to strengthen the law and apply stricter penalties.

THE POLITICS OF PUBLIC SECURITY IN MEXICO

It is difficult to give credence to past presidents' statements that a proper public security policy—that is, one defined and structured as a public policy—has been developed in Mexico over the course of recent administrations. Rather, what has generally prevailed has been a reactive policy designed to fight crime. Preventive policies have only served as a rhetorical device. While the typical police viewpoint has dominated, the problem is by nature essentially social.

If we accept that the Zedillo administration developed a public security policy, we should note that it was developed precisely within the boundaries of traditional policy-making strategies. What does this mean? The Mexican state, through its government institutions and particularly through its police and military forces, continues to do the same thing it has done for decades, with proven inefficiency. The routine consists of increasing spending on personnel, weapons, vehicles, and the like, and passing a multitude of laws with harsher penalties, all in the hope that the theoretical utilitarian model of rational expectations will hold true: "to root out crime by increasing the accompanying risks ... so that the individual will, out of fear, abstain from committing a crime."[5]

In his fifth State of the Nation address, President Zedillo stated:

> We now have adequate laws to prosecute and punish organized crime; those who possess and traffic in proscribed firearms or use them to commit crimes; those who commit violent crimes such as armed robbery, rape, kidnapping, and homicide; those who illegally profit from the savings and property belonging to Mexicans; and those who abuse their probation sentences to commit crimes again. Now the federal judicial branch is authentically independent and enjoys the means to act with strict impartiality, honor, and growing professionalism among its judges and magistrates. A Federal Preventive Police has been created according to new methods of selection, training, and supervision to detect and prevent the infiltration of criminal elements.[6]

Despite these initiatives, one must ask whether these laws can have any impact if the people who are supposed to enforce them do not do their job correctly. What end is served if augmenting the police merely serves to swell the ranks of a force cursed by corruption, arrogance, and the abuse of power that can come with a badge and a gun?

In light of current crime levels in Mexico, the government must reflect on its policing efforts over the last three decades and admit that these efforts have failed. Then it must take action. This fact has already been acknowledged, at least in public rhetoric, but it remains to move forward to solve the problem. It is not an easy undertaking to make innovative decisions in this sensitive area, but it makes no sense to remain on the current path, which in broad strokes has led to a profoundly serious situation that poses risks to social stability.

PUBLIC VERSUS PRIVATE SECURITY FORCES

Even though the Mexican state has not renounced its responsibility to provide security for its people, a new trend, encouraged by the exponential increase in common crime and the government's inability to begin to contain organized crime, is a permissiveness that has allowed private security services to proliferate. The problem with the private security industry is that, although it began providing services in the 1970s, it only recently became subject to oversight and regulation. Moreover, the government does not have sufficient resources to effectively police this industry. Although there are regulations on the books to regulate private security firms,[7] the problems alluded to earlier have yet to be solved. We still lack precise data about the number of private police services in operation; how many vehicles and arms they have, and what type of weapons they employ; and what type of training these forces receive before entering service. For this reason, private security forces exist in a kind of "gray zone." The government knows little (and society, even less) about these forces that play such an important role in social stability and governability.

The concept of public security will surely remain in Mexican law, even though it may appear incongruous to speak of and legislate on *private* services for *public* security. According to this line of thinking, public security forces will continue to be a government responsibility. However, there is no way to ensure that the quality of such services will improve significantly, despite the great quantity of economic and human resources and infrastructure begin invested in them.[8] The paradox is that even though more resources are being employed, we are not seeing clear signs of improved security conditions in the near future. On the contrary, all indications point in the opposite direction, toward an unimaginable burgeoning of insecurity.

During the Fox administration (2000–2006) we will surely continue to see two coexisting types of security services, each meeting the demands of one of two social groups. Both of these groups demand security, but they differ radically from one another. One group comprises the social minority that has sufficient wealth to hire private security services and to purchase high-technology devices to ensure personal and family security. The second is composed of the majority of the population; this group cannot afford private services and must make do with the services provided by the various public security forces run by federal, state, and municipal governments.

Notably, it is difficult to demonstrate which of the two types of security services is superior. One cannot assume that private services are, by definition, better than public services. No studies have been conducted that would enable us to confirm that private police forces are more professional, less corrupt, and less abusive of their power than public forces. Concerning public security forces, one can argue that they are flawed, but this is not because they are public. Rather, their defects are due to the profound disintegration of police forces in Mexico. In any case, given that crime rates continue to rise and that insecurity has become a generalized and multi-class phenomenon in Mexico, we can affirm that public and private security services have not been sufficiently effective to reduce the widespread social perception of inadequate security protections. Society realizes that the government, overwhelmed by the crime problem, is not able to offer better security conditions, even though the government continues to view security as a public responsibility.

We can suppose that society's recognition of the constraints limiting the government response is the driving force behind the public's search for alternatives to public security. Within this context, one can better understand the private security industry as an alternative way to improve security conditions, even if for only a minority of the population. There are two noteworthy elements in the trend toward privatization of security services. The first involves a series of measures that support what could be termed a "bunker city" mentality. The second is the unchecked development of the private security industry itself.

TOWARD THE "BUNKER CITY"

The tendency toward privatization is discernable in decisions by neighborhoods and governments to "privatize" public spaces, alleging problems of crime and insecurity. A variant of this trend is reflected in changes in housing construction and in urban planning. These include closed streets, speed bumps, road barriers, and security booths; gated communities whose high walls block the public's view of homes within; and the installation of sophisticated electronic security systems and totally fenced yards.

For example, in Guadalajara,

> after suffering two robberies and four robbery attempts, Federico installed an electric entry to his office, which he reinforced with multiple locks. He installed bars on the windows, closed off doors, roofed the patio, bought a handgun, and embedded bars in the top edges of the exterior walls. His last additions were an infrared alarm connected to the police station and the hiring of a permanent security guard.[9]

Many Mexican citizens view closing off access to their neighborhoods as a way to protect themselves. Closed neighborhoods with controlled entrance gates are becoming increasingly common. The municipality of Zapopan, Jalisco, has approved seventy-five of these closed neighborhoods, and new applications are arriving daily. The inhabitants of Cerro del Tesoro are seeking ways to close off the streets in their neighborhood because, according to a neighborhood committee,

> We are left with no other option. We can't take any more insecurity. Since there isn't any police supervision, we have to protect ourselves. Last year, some houses were robbed six times....
>
> Backyards, large windows, and patios are slowly disappearing from Guadalajara houses, replaced by high walls and exterior bars. Houses are becoming fortresses, with a stark construction style that reflects a sense of fear. Building security has become an important element of building plans. The prototype of a secure house has many elements of a jail:

> high walls, electric fences, automatic doors, and a rear entrance. The family room is built with reinforced doors and vandal-proof windowpanes, and comes complete with a monitoring and alarm system connected to the police station.[10]

Obviously, we are talking about upper-class homes and social classes with substantial disposable income. According to some urban planners, these types of security reinforcements:

> tend to lead toward the disintegration of society because they create a lack of communication between people who live in "fortified compounds" and those who live outside them, which alters the perception of living in the same city. The spirit of the city as a meeting place for its inhabitants is lost; to live an isolated life behind bars changes the perception of space, making people feel like they live in a cage.[11]

To the above-mentioned factors that feed into the concept of "bunker cities," we can add the security forces' abandonment of "dangerous" areas, in effect, turning increasingly broad swathes of the city over to control by criminals. To rectify this situation, some governors have suggested that at certain hours, only police and criminals should be on the streets, and citizens would leave their homes at their own risk. César Coll Carabias, mayor of Guadalajara from 1995 to 1997, suggested a 10 PM "curfew," on the assumption that people had no reason to leave their homes after this hour. Obviously this idea, which never went beyond a media furor, was resolutely opposed by Guadalajara residents. Its primary effect was to demonstrate the mayor's profound ignorance of the multiple activities that occurred around the clock in the city he governed.

Security also figures as an important priority for businesses. "Businesses must protect the delivery of merchandise and their distribution sites. First, there were the security boxes welded to a vehicle's floor. Now, as if this were an outpost of the Wild West, armed police escort deliverymen, even those who are transporting only cigarettes or eggs."[12]

THE PRIVATE SECURITY "BOOM"

The type of entrepreneurial activity that private security services represent is also known as the "industry of fear." The fear of becoming a victim of crime drives the rapid expansion of these businesses' services and technologies. The boom in this industry dates from the 1990s. In

1970, there were only forty private security firms in Mexico. In 2000, these numbered more than 1,400 firms, according to the National Council of Public Security Companies (CNESP).[13] These private security firms charge more than US$200 million annually for their services, and Mexico is the third largest purchaser of private security technologies in the world. The cities that register the highest demand for and consumption of residential, commercial, and industrial security services are Guadalajara, Monterrey, Puebla, and Cuernavaca.[14]

According to Carlos Mortera Solano, committee coordinator for Expo Seguridad, there are three hundred firms in Guadalajara dedicated to the production and sale of security products and services and the provision of security personnel. Expo Seguridad is a product fair for security systems, products, and services which has been held annually in Guadalajara since 1995. In terms of fair sales, the lead product category is car alarms; the second is closed-circuit video cameras and access control systems; and the third includes private security guard services, contracted principally by banks, factories, and commercial establishments.[15]

There is also strong demand for armored cars, "super protected" housing units, closed-circuit television and infrared security systems for businesses, offices with magnetic doors and electronic openers, commercial sites with specialized police forces, and trained dogs. And added to this is a complete menu of personal accessories, ranging from bulletproof vests to devices that shoot "T-waves," which immobilize an assailant by paralyzing the nervous system.[16] Ninety-eight percent of these products are imported. The remainder, such as steel, special glass, bars, and some fabrics, are produced locally.

Distributors and installers of car alarms are flourishing in Mexico. There are approximately two thousand such establishments in Mexico City, each of which installs three to four alarms a day on average. The variety of alarms is also significant. They range from systems activated by panic buttons to alarms that are tracked by satellite systems. There are alarms that cut off a car's ignition system, block gasoline flow to the engine, and act as panic buttons able to be activated from a remote location. Mexico City residents have reportedly spent some 150 million pesos on the purchase and installation of car alarms since 1997.[17]

The largest security investment has been in armored cars, which cost a minimum of US$40,000. There are approximately two thousand armored cars in Mexico City and five thousand in the country as a whole. The clients for such vehicles are industrialists, national and Mexico-based foreign businessmen, celebrities, military figures, and, of course, politicians. For example, former governor of Jalisco Alberto Cárdenas Jiménez and his close advisers opted for armored vehicles. The catalyst for the increasing demand for this product is the rising number of high-profile kidnappings. Kidnappings occur at the rate of one every twenty-four hours in Mexico City and one per week in Jalisco, according to the state attorney general's office.[18]

In metropolitan Guadalajara, "private security firms, weapons sales, security equipment, and guard dogs have proliferated. Military sources estimate that handguns can be found in more than 80 percent of Guadalajara homes."[19] It has also been estimated that more than one thousand security guards in forty-eight private security agencies work without any regulation. These and other irregularities were noted by the State Council of Public Security in its analysis of the functions of private security companies. This lack of oversight is explained both by the rapid proliferation of these firms and by the failure of the relevant public security agencies to provide minimal supervision.[20]

Advertisements in the Guadalajara telephone directory provide one measure of this industry's growth; listings for private security companies filled two pages of the Yellow Pages in 1994, seven pages in 1997, and sixteen pages in the year 2000. A parallel phenomenon is discernible in the number of newspaper columns devoted to crime stories. In the 1980s, crime stories filled only one page of the leading newspaper; by the 1990s, all newspapers dedicated at least two pages to crime stories, and some began special reports on crime, giving a new twist to traditional media coverage.

CONCLUSION

As Mexico continues its process of political transition, the government should reflect on the proper roles of the state, the government, its security forces, and society in a sociopolitical context in which criminal forces are clearly outstripping government's and society's efforts to combat the causes of public insecurity.

The grim truth is that insecurity has become an ingrained characteristic of the nation, and insecurity is outstripping the endeavors of the government and its security forces. It does not matter whether civilians or the military direct these forces; nor does it matter which party is in government. Political alternation at the state and municipal levels has not improved public security.[21] In some cases, like Jalisco, political transitions have actually increased crime in all its forms, because these processes have led to the breakdown of the equilibria established between authorities and criminals.

Insecurity and crime affect all social classes. Crime and violence in Mexico, just like social exclusion and polarization, have become defining elements that contribute to the profound disintegration of the country's social fabric. Despite their promises and pledges, Presidents Salinas and Zedillo, both of the PRI, did not make major progress on this front. On the contrary, crime increased during their administrations, due in part to a stubborn insistence on employing the same strategies against organized crime that had already proven ineffective. President Fox faces this same challenge; to meet it, he must change the form and substance of the fight against crime in Mexico. During his campaign, Fox proposed anticrime measures, and shortly after his inauguration the federal government presented various proposals in this regard (see appendix) that merit careful analysis followed by implementation.

The rich continue to be criminals' preferred targets, but we can begin to speak of "the democratization of criminal targets." In Mexico, for example, the list of kidnapping targets now includes people other than rich and powerful businessmen. It extends to any person with the capacity to pay even small ransoms, which have the benefit for the criminal of not involving drawn-out, complex, and risky negotiations.

In summary, Mexico has experienced the profound deterioration of its law enforcement and judicial system over the last thirty years. Organized crime, meanwhile, has grown in inverse proportion. These two overlapping and intersecting trajectories form the backdrop to a generalized feeling of insecurity and defenselessness among Mexican society. And this sense of insecurity has not been overcome by either public or private security services.

Notes

Translated by Ruth Urry.

1. *Quinto Informe de Gobierno*, Ernesto Zedillo Ponce de León, September 1, 1999. See the section on public security in Mexico, at www.presidencia.gob.mx.

2. *La Jornada*, September 2, 1999, 3.

3. *La Jornada*, September 8, 1999, 23.

4. *Mural* [Mexico City], February 28, 2000.

5. Richard Quinney, *Classes, State, and Delinquency* (Mexico City: Fondo de Cultura Económica, 1985), 34.

6. *La Jornada*, September 2, 1999, 3.

7. In the case of Jalisco, it took until July 1999 for the state congress to pass the "Regulation of Private Services of Public Security," which regulates the authorization and registration of security personnel, their duties, uniforms, emblems, and ranks, the types of vehicles and arms to be used, as well as their training, oversight, and so on.

8. In 2000, the National Public Security System (SNSP) boasted a budget of more than 12.7 billion pesos (roughly US$1.3 billion).

9. *Siglo 21*, March 2, 1997, 6.

10. Ibid., 6–7.

11. Ibid.

12. Ibid.

13. Reportedly, fewer than 10 percent of these companies were providing high-quality services

14. Fernando del Collado, "Protección privada: en defensa propia," Suplemento Enfoque, *Reforma* 227 (May 24, 1998).

15. Ibid.

16. Ibid.

17. Ibid.

18. Ibid.

19. *Siglo 21*, March 2, 1997, 6.

20. Jorge Regalado Santillán and Marcos Pablo Moloeznik Gruer, "Privatization of Public Security," in *Mexico and Jalisco in a Joint Context, Avances*, Cuadernos de Investigación y Análisis del ITESO, no. 8 (1998), 116–19. A good part of this section was based on this article.

21. The processes of political alternation at the state and municipal levels have not proven effective to date in the fight against crime. In fact, some new governors are criticized for repeating many of the same public security policies. Moreover, these governments continue to apply a police vision to the problem of the lack of public security.

PART 2

Challenges to the United States

8

Building Bridges and Barricades: Trade Facilitation versus Drug Enforcement in U.S.–Mexico Relations

Peter Andreas

INTRODUCTION

During the past decade, U.S. policy toward Mexico has been largely driven by two sharply contrasting objectives: on the one hand, the facilitation of legal trade and, on the other, the enforcement of controls against the illegal drug trade. An estimated 60 percent of the cocaine and 29 percent of the heroin sold in the United States in 1998 came across the U.S.–Mexico border, and Mexico is also a major supplier of marijuana and methamphetamines.[1] Thus, although not reflected in official trade statistics, illegal drugs are clearly a leading U.S. import from Mexico.[2] At the same time, the cross-border flow of legitimate commerce more than doubled in the 1990s, making Mexico the United States' second largest trading partner.[3] Indeed, the border is the busiest land crossing in the world: in 1998, 278 million people, 86 million cars, and 4 million trucks and railcars entered the United States from Mexico.[4]

Although generally analyzed as separate policy spheres, trade facilitation and drug enforcement issues overlap a great deal, both in the policy debate and in policy implementation. This chapter focuses on the practice and politics of managing the awkward and uneasy relationship between these economic and law enforcement objectives. In the first section I provide some pre–1990s historical context for understanding more recent developments. I then focus on the early 1990s, when officials in both countries went to great lengths to keep the drug issue from derailing the making of the North American Free Trade Agreement (NAFTA). I then move on to explain how managing the drug issue became much more cumbersome once the trade accord was passed. The politics of trade, I emphasize, has increasingly become entangled in the politics of drug control. Reconciling unrealistic expectations for effective drug interdiction and the practical realities of economic integration has become an ever more challenging and frustrating task. In the final section I outline various scenarios for the future of U.S.–Mexico drug control on the border.

THE TRANSFORMATION OF CROSS-BORDER DRUG SMUGGLING

Smuggling has been a core component of economic exchange across the nearly 2,000–mile U.S.–Mexico border ever since the borderline was drawn a century and a half ago. In other words, there never has been a time when the border was truly controlled. As Peter Reuter and David Ronfeldt have noted, "Mexicans have always been available to supply whatever Americans want but cannot obtain legally in their own country—just as Americans have always been ready to provide whatever Mexicans want and cannot acquire readily in Mexico."[5] Illegal drugs became integrated into the smuggling economy early in the twentieth century. However, the nature and organization of such smuggling has undergone a metamorphosis since the 1980s.

Mexico's traditional role in the drug trade has primarily been as a local producer and exporter of marijuana and heroin for the U.S. market. This began to change in the mid–1980s as Mexico became an increasingly popular transshipment point for Colombian cocaine. Although the amount of cocaine smuggled through Mexico was negligible in the early 1980s, by the early 1990s Mexico had become the transshipment point for a majority of the cocaine bound for the U.S. market. It should be emphasized that the new prominence of Mexican traffickers in the cocaine business was an unintended side effect of U.S. law enforcement. Intensified drug interdiction in the Caribbean/South Florida forced Colombian smugglers to find alternative methods and routes of entry to the U.S. market. The most logical choice was to shift to land routes across the United States' southwest border. To do so required hiring the transportation services (off-loading, storing, smuggling) of Mexican trafficking organizations. This dramatically elevated Mexico's role and status in the international drug trade—with profound consequences for Mexico, the border region, and U.S.–Mexico relations.

An early sign that the Mexican drug smuggling business was becoming a more violent enterprise was the 1985 murder of U.S. Drug Enforcement Administration (DEA) agent Enrique Camarena in Guadalajara. The DEA claims that Camarena's murder was in retaliation for the agency's Operation Padrino, a crackdown on a new cocaine-trafficking network. The Camarena affair deeply scarred U.S.–Mexico relations, and even resulted in a partial closing of the border through Operation Intercept II in February 1985. The diplomatic crisis continued into 1986, when on March 8 most of the U.S. Customs Service houses on the border were temporarily closed (the official reason was to search for weapons and drugs being smuggled into the United States by Libyan terrorists). In subsequent years, U.S. and Mexican officials would expend considerable energy trying to repair the damage inflicted by the Camarena affair.

As the cocaine flow shifted from the southeastern to the southwestern United States, so too did the focus of U.S. enforcement efforts. Operation Alliance was launched in June 1986 to coordinate interdiction efforts along the U.S.–Mexico border, and the military's Joint Task Force Six was established in the fall of 1989 at Fort Bliss, Texas, to provide assistance to law enforcement agencies on the border. In 1990 the border was formally designated a "High Intensity Drug Trafficking Area," which brought with it more federal attention and antidrug resources.

Importantly, U.S. interdiction efforts propelled a shift not only in the location of drug smuggling but also in the methods of such smuggling. The building of a "Maginot Line" of radar across the southern border in the 1980s significantly curbed air smuggling.[6] Although this did not translate into a reduced drug flow, it did push the flow from the air to the ground. This enforcement "success," however, would create significant complications for the U.S.–Mexico trade relationship. The ground transportation routes for the drug trade were the same as those being used to move the growing volume of legal trade across the border. Equally significant, grounding the cocaine trade made Colombian traffickers more reliant on their Mexican counterparts, who controlled the road smuggling networks across the border.[7]

Years before NAFTA was even proposed, the border trade community was already becoming increasingly concerned that drug checks at the official ports of entry were slowing the rise in cross-border commerce (vividly reflected in severe traffic jams at the ports of entry). Thus both law enforcement advocates and the private sector pushed for more federal funding to upgrade the official border crossings with more personnel and improved infrastructure. As the president of one brokerage firm told a congressional committee: "The significant increases in commercial and civilian traffic coupled with the need to address the drug problem are creating a disastrous situation for manufacturers, importers, and border city retailers." He warned, "If Customs is going to service the needs of the commercial sector and civilian sectors and at the same time increase their surveillance and interdiction program for drugs, international trade and relations are going to suffer irreparable harm unless the appropriations for improved facilities and manpower are provided."[8]

These concerns reflected the bind that U.S. law enforcement officials had partly created for themselves: they had pushed much of the cocaine flow from the southeast to the southwest, but the push to seal the border ran up against the policy goal of facilitating legal trade. In an effort to reconcile this dilemma, in February 1987 the Customs Service initiated the Southwest Border Strategy, "a seven point action plan designed to improve our ability to facilitate cargo at the border while at the same time increasing our ability to prohibit the use of commercial cargo, trucks and rail cars from being used to conceal narcotics." The most important part of the plan was the implementation of a "line release" system that allows the processing of "routine, repetitive shipments in a minute or two."[9] While drawing little public attention at the time, this system would in later years attract intense media scrutiny and political attacks that interdiction was being sacrificed to promote trade.

THE POLITICS OF DRUG CONTROL DURING THE MAKING OF NAFTA

Carlos Salinas de Gortari took office as president of Mexico in late 1988 with an ambitious economic agenda of massive market-based reforms at home and increased market integration with the United States. Antidrug initiatives during this period must be evaluated and understood within this context. Although not formally part of the NAFTA negotiations, an improved Mexican antidrug effort was a political precondition for the trade accord's success. For Salinas, demonstrating a greater will to combat drugs, even if this did not translate into a reduced drug flow, would help cement the new economic relationship.

The Salinas government initiated an aggressive antidrug campaign, declaring drugs to be the number one security threat facing the country.[10] Indicating a greater willingness to cooperate with U.S. antidrug objectives, Mexico signed a bilateral cooperation agreement with the United States that facilitated the creation of a variety of bilateral interagency working groups to coordinate antidrug operations. Bolstering the country's international image, Mexico also signed the 1988 United Nations Convention Against Trafficking in Illicit Narcotics and Dangerous Drugs. The Salinas government increased drug control spending and antidrug personnel threefold between 1989 and 1993, revamped the antidrug apparatus, and expanded the military's role in drug interdiction. These initiatives were especially impressive because they were taking place in an era otherwise characterized by major cutbacks in government spending and a shrinking of the state apparatus.

Mexico's antidrug efforts helped sustain the upbeat mood in U.S.–Mexican relations on the eve of the NAFTA vote. Salinas certainly understood that a positive antidrug image was important for the smooth passage of the trade accord. In reviewing Mexico's expanded sage of the trade accord. In reviewing Mexico's expanded antidrug effort, an internal 1992 U.S. Defense Intelligence Agency memorandum observed that "perhaps the most important of all of Salinas' motivations is his perception that a better image of Mexico will figure prominently and favorably in the outcome of ongoing free trade negotiations."[11]

Salinas's U.S. counterparts collaborated in crafting Mexico's new and improved antidrug image.[12] U.S. law enforcement agents who worked in Mexico during the Salinas years were reportedly warned by their superiors not to let the drug issue undermine progress toward a new economic relationship.[13] A former top drug policy official in the George Bush administration (1988–1992) noted that "People desperately wanted drugs not to become a complicating factor for NAFTA." Another official explained that "once Bush and Salinas decided to go with NAFTA as the No. 1 goal, then everything else had to be made manageable."[14] One U.S. State Department employee acknowledged that his job was to make the Mexican government look good so that Congress would be more willing to pass the trade agreement.[15]

Pushing NAFTA through the U.S. Congress also required deflecting any worries that facilitating trade would benefit the illegal drug trade. In May 1993, two members of Congress—Maryland Republican Representative Helen Bentley and Ohio Democratic Representative Marcy Kaptur—wrote a bipartisan "Dear Colleague" letter insisting that "Congress should not approve the NAFTA deal unless it and our borders are locked tight from drug runners."[16] Their concern had been provoked by a front-page story in the *New York Times* reporting that traffickers were preparing to take advantage of NAFTA as a cover for drug smuggling.[17]

For the time being, officials in the Clinton administration (1992–2000) were able to calm such worries by pointing to the apparent progress made by the U.S. and Mexican interdiction campaigns, and they argued that the free trade agreement would further encourage cross-border antidrug collaboration. They stressed that the border was being made not only more business-friendly but also more secure: "While the increase in legitimate trade across the U.S./Mexican border could offer ... opportunities for increased drug smuggling, the U.S. is increasing the number of Customs inspectors at the border, enhancing inspection technology, increasing coordination with other U.S. law enforcement agencies, as well as developing cooperative relationships with Mexican law enforcement agencies and with legitimate Mexican exporters."[18] Agencies were instructed in how to handle questions about NAFTA's impact on the drug trade.[19] Law enforcement agents who worried that NAFTA would facilitate the drug trade were reportedly told to keep quiet.[20]

At the same time as U.S. and Mexican officials repeatedly praised their joint progress on the antidrug front and pointed to rising seizure, arrest, and eradication statistics, the drug trade was in fact not only surviving but thriving. As the *Economist* reported, "During Mr. Salinas's tenure, drug bosses consolidated their fiefs.... American anti-drug agents knew of the spreading rot.... But other American officials, keen to cement Mr. Salinas's economic reforms with the North American Free Trade Agreement, turned a blind eye, often issuing statements praising his anti-drug efforts, despite evidence to the contrary."[21] According to one senior State Department official, staff at the U.S. Embassy in Mexico City glossed over problems of drug-related corruption in their reports in an effort to push NAFTA forward.[22] But although the U.S. and Mexican effort to project a positive drug control image was successfully sustained long enough for the free trade agreement to be ratified, managing bilateral relations over the drug issue became far more difficult in the post-Salinas, post–NAFTA era.

BORDER DRUG INTERDICTION IN THE AGE OF FREE TRADE

Although NAFTA has helped turn the border into a more expansive bridge for legal trade, some of its unintended consequences have helped to reinforce domestic calls to barricade the border against the illegal drug trade. The predicament facing U.S. law enforcement strategists is that NAFTA has made the task of border interdiction more difficult and at the same time has drawn heightened political and media attention to the border and the deficiencies of the interdiction effort.

As discussed earlier, the problem has been partly self-created. Past law enforcement initiatives not only pushed cocaine smuggling to the southwestern border of the United States, but they also pushed it from the air to the ground. Smugglers quickly adapted to the heightened law enforcement pressure by increasingly hiding their drug shipments within the rising volume of legitimate cross-border trade. Worries that smugglers might benefit from NAFTA were deliberately not discussed during the negotiations over the free trade accord. "This was in the 'too hot to handle' category," noted Gary Huffbauer of the Institute for International Economics.[23] Although they did not voice their concerns publicly at the time, some officials apparently were well aware of the problem. An internal report written by an intelligence officer at the U.S. Embassy in Mexico City noted that cocaine traffickers were establishing factories, warehouses, and trucking companies as fronts in anticipation of the boom in cross-border commerce expected under NAFTA. The traffickers, the report said, "intend to maximize their legitimate business enterprises within the auspices of the new U.S.–Mexico free trade agreement."[24] Some traffickers reportedly even hired trade consultants to determine what products move most swiftly through border inspection under NAFTA guidelines.[25]

Mexico has deregulated its trucking industry (meaning licensed trucks can travel anywhere within the country without inspections), and under NAFTA guidelines, Mexican truckers will eventually be able to travel throughout the United States and Canada. According to an October 1992 internal DEA report, the lifting of trucking restrictions will "prove to be a definite boon to both the legitimate food industry, and to drug smugglers who conceal their illegal shipments in trucks transporting fruits and vegetables from Mexico to U.S. markets." The report also noted that "the projected overhaul of the Mexican road system will expedite the exportation of both legitimate and illegitimate crops."[26]

The sheer volume of border crossings has provided an ideal environment for drug smuggling. The DEA has estimated that most cocaine enters the United States through regular ports of entry along the border in commercial trucks and passenger vehicles.[27] On any given day, 220,000 vehicles flow across the border into the United States from Mexico. It takes only nine large tractor-trailers loaded with cocaine to satisfy the United States' drug demand for one year.[28] Thus the enforcement challenge is the equivalent of finding a needle in a haystack—and the haystack keeps getting bigger and the needle keeps getting better at hiding. U.S. border officials searched more than a million commercial trucks and railway cars crossing from Mexico in 1997 and found cocaine in only six of the searches.[29]

Trade between the United States and Mexico increased from US$75.8 billion in 1992 to $157.3 billion in 1997, and approximately three-fourths of that trade crossed the border via commercial trucking. In fiscal year 1998, some 3.9 million trucks entered the United States from Mexico—a 30 percent rise from fiscal year 1996. At some of the busiest ports of entry, up to 2,500 commercial vehicles enter the United States daily.[30] In Laredo, Texas (the busiest truck crossing point on the border), nearly one million trucks entered from Mexico in 1997—up from 185,000 a decade earlier.[31] And the number of trucks is expected to double by 2010.

Given the magnitude of border traffic, Customs agents cannot realistically inspect most of the vehicles entering from Mexico without causing massive delays and traffic jams. Customs, of course, must claim that "Narcotics enforcement ... comes first, even if trade facilitation suffers when counter-narcotics operations slow the flow of commerce."[32] Domestic political sensitivities over the drug issue lead officials to declare their allegiance to border drug interdiction, even though economic realities dictate that the border must remain highly porous. Prioritizing enforcement over facilitation is simply not viable under current border conditions. As one senior Customs official has pointed out:

> If we examined every truck for narcotics arriving into the United States along the southwest border ... Customs would back up the truck traffic bumper-to-bumper into Mexico City in just two weeks—15.8 days. In 15.8 days, there would be 95,608 trucks backed up into Mexico. That's 1,177 miles of trucks, end to end, or the distance from Mexico City to the city of Laredo in the United States.[33]

Heightened political concern that free trade unintentionally aids the drug trade has made border officials increasingly wary of giving the impression that they are facilitating commerce at the expense of enforcement. Some officials have even eliminated the word "facilitation" from their vocabulary, opting instead to talk in terms of "traffic management." As one senior Customs official put it, facilitation has become the "F" word. Using the language of facilitation, he says, sends the "wrong message" to Congress, the public, and the trade community.[34] Similarly, any evidence that the border has become easier to cross legally is handled with reassurances that the border is also being made more difficult to cross illegally. For example, the release of a study that showed that traffic was moving more quickly through the San Ysidro port of entry south of San Diego (the busiest border crossing in the world) was delayed until it could also be shown that enforcement had been tightened.[35]

Despite these efforts to project an image of enhanced border controls, the boom in cross-border trade has provided an opening for some political critics to attack the administration as "soft" on border control. Particularly outspoken has been California Senator Dianne Feinstein, who latched onto the border interdiction issue in the mid–1990s after the *Los Angeles Times* reported that Customs was being lax on truck inspections at the border in order to promote trade. In a February 5, 1996, letter to President Clinton, Feinstein blamed the Customs' "customer-friendly" policies for the influx of cocaine, and she asked the president to fire George Weise, commissioner of the Customs Service.[36]

What provoked Feinstein's attacks was the Customs Service's Line Release program, which allowed Customs agents to wave pre-approved trucks through the border port of entry without inspection. Criticizing Line Release for failing to run background checks on trucking companies and drivers, Feinstein called the program "a superhighway for smugglers."[37] Although Line Release began in 1987, it did not attract much media and political attention until after the 1994 implementation of NAFTA. In 1994, NAFTA's first year, 2.7 million Line Release vehicles crossed the border—a 44 percent increase over 1993.[38]

The free trade accord has also provided an opportunity for some voices in the law enforcement community to deflect blame for policy failure, promote more intensive inspections, and generally draw greater attention to the border. For example, Operation Alliance, which helps coordinate federal law enforcement efforts along the border, produced a May 1997 internal report on NAFTA's negative repercussions for drug control. The report was subsequently leaked to the press, generating widespread media coverage (including articles in the *Wall Street Journal, Dallas Morning News,* and *San Diego Union-Tribune*). This, in turn, provided further ammunition for those in Congress pushing for beefed-up border controls.[39] Some prominent law enforcement voices have generated media attention with provocative comments about the NAFTA–drug connection. Former DEA agent Phil Jordan, for example, has called NAFTA a "deal made in narco-heaven,"[40] and former Customs commissioner William von Raab has claimed that some officials in the government refer to NAFTA as the "North American Free Drug Agreement."[41] Similarly, Texas Attorney General Dan Morales has argued that "Without thorough inspections of Mexican trucks, these Mexican cartels will feel like NAFTA means the North American Free Trafficking Agreement."[42] "NAFTA is doing what it is supposed to do, dramatically increase trade," says Morales. "But it is clearly doing what it was not intended to do—give the Mexican [drug] cartels what has become a virtually open border in which to move drugs into the United States."[43]

NAFTA critics from across the political spectrum have also opportunistically used the drug issue to bolster their position. Patrick Buchanan, for example, has attacked both Republicans and Democrats for supporting NAFTA, which, he argues, has made the border "wide open" to drug trafficking.[44] Three days before the November 1997 congressional vote on whether to grant President Clinton fast-track authority to negotiate trade agreements, Representative Maxine Waters (D–CA) held a press conference to release a report titled "Drug Trafficking on the Fast Track."[45] Waters asserted that there had been a "post–NAFTA surge in drug trafficking," suggesting a causal connection to the free trade accord. She was joined at the press conference by Richard Gephardt, who added: "We must insist on a NADFA, a North American Drug Free Agreement, within our NAFTA." Gephardt said further that giving the president fast-track authority "dooms anti-drug efforts."

The report from Waters's office demanded that Customs inspect 75 percent of all trucks and commercial maritime vessels at points of entry into the United States. Such a dramatic increase in the level of inspection is technically possible but realistically unthinkable. In practice, it would virtually shut down the border, translating into a form of drug control–driven protectionism. The Nixon administration, it should be remembered, tried such intensive inspections for a few weeks during Operation Intercept in 1969. Today, as one Customs official acknowledged, it couldn't even be done for a few days because of the damage to trade.[46]

But even as increased cross-border economic exchange has placed severe practical limits on border controls, domestic political imperatives have required that the administration devote ever more resources to enhance such controls. The administration has attempted to reply to political charges that it is "facilitating too much and enforcing too little" by increasing cargo inspections at ports of entry.[47] Thus in February 1995 the Customs Service announced Operation Hard Line, an intensified effort to target drug smuggling in commercial cargo. Customs received 657 new positions through Hard Line in fiscal year 1997—roughly a 25 percent increase in personnel on the border.[48] Operation Hard Line provided a major boost to the San Diego sector in particular, which had been the focus of Senator Feinstein's attacks. Staffing for the San Diego office of Customs Investigations, for example, almost doubled between 1994 and 1996. Many staff were also moved to the San Diego sector from the interior.[49]

A year after Operation Hard Line was launched, the Customs Service issued a press release praising the program's "record-breaking success." Hard Line produced 24 percent more seizures of cocaine, heroin, and marijuana than in the previous year. Another press release highlighted a 76 percent increase in the number of drug seizures along the California-Mexico border over the same period the year before. The fine print, however, revealed that while the overall number of seizures was up, the actual amount of drugs seized had fallen, suggesting that smugglers had adapted to increased enforcement by breaking their loads down into smaller packages to reduce their risks.[50] The smuggling trend has been toward more but smaller drug shipments—creating more and harder work for Customs.[51] Inspectors spend most of their time making small-scale marijuana busts. Indeed, some officials believe smugglers use these small marijuana shipments as decoys to distract inspectors while they move larger and better-hidden shipments through the ports of entry.

Seizures have never represented more than a small percentage of the overall quantity of drugs crossing the border.[52] Moreover, some officials have suggested that traffickers assume that a certain percentage of their product will be seized, and they calculate this into their profit projections.[53] Seizure statistics, however, are the most important measure used by Customs to justify its mission, fend off political attacks, and assure continued funding. In other words, there is a powerful bureaucratic imperative to generate seizures to project a positive impression of enforcement effort—despite the ambiguity regarding what these seizures actually indicate.[54] Thus, when Customs Commissioner George Weise appeared on *Nightline* to respond to charges of being lax on border truck inspections, he pointed to the increase in drugs that had been seized in commercial cargo since the initiation of Operation Hard Line—even though the increase could simply indicate that use of commercial cargo had become a more popular smuggling method.[55]

Falling cocaine seizures in 1997 predictably set off alarm bells within the Customs Service. A November 28, 1997, National Treasury Employees Union memo noted that Congress had provided millions in new funding for enforcement positions for Operation Hard Line and warned that, "no doubt Congress will be highly upset with these 1997 [seizure] figures.... [B]order drug interdiction is becoming a major political issue in Washington." A second memo, dated December 22, affirmed that new enforcement efforts were necessary: "the objective being to increase our seizures so Customs and the union don't get their heads handed to them by the politicians in Washington when the budget meetings start in March."[56]

The fall in seizures did indeed generate political grumbling. "Congress has directed almost every possible resource toward drug interdiction efforts, including more agents, better technology and several hundred million dollars in additional funding," said Representative Ron Packard (R–CA). "These are not the results we expected. If interdiction is down, the American people deserve some answers." In response, Customs launched Operation Brass Ring in early 1998, which the commissioner of Customs promised would "dramatically increase drug seizures" along the southwest border.[57]

Thus Customs has been trapped by its own measures of effectiveness. To assure funding it has continued to overstate the viability of interdiction, but it then faces a political backlash when interdiction seizure levels fail to impress. Rather than stressing the inherent inefficiencies and deficiencies of interdiction, Customs follows its own bureaucratic incentives by promising bigger and better results if more resources are forthcoming from Congress. When the promised results fail to materialize and seizure levels drop, the political heat predictably intensifies.

Meanwhile, more intensive inspections at the ports of entry have provoked loud protests from the trade community. "Things aren't working too smoothly right now for commerce," according to Bill Summers, director of a business group called the Rio Grande Valley Partnership. "We feel that, sure, they have a job to do on drug interdiction, but they also have a commitment to honest people to get the trucks through as fast as they can because some are carrying perishable goods." He further pointed out: "They have to remember it was trade that built these bridges." Contributing to the growing frustrations at the border, businesses are upset that Customs officials often drill holes in their vehicles looking for drugs. "they're drilling all up and down the border," complains William Cain, who operates Cain Customs Brokers in Progreso. "There isn't as much drilling going on in the oil fields." He says that "the authorities have gone overboard, and are hurting legitimate business in their efforts to stop the flow of illegal narcotics." In trying to explain the difficult situation to merchants, Customs officials say they are "under incredible pressure to put drugs on the table."[58]

It is perhaps no surprise that the debate over the connection between NAFTA and drug trafficking has become polarized, distorted, and highly politicized. On the one hand, free trade supporters have largely ignored or downplayed the intermingling of drugs with the rising volume of commercial cargo across the border. On the other hand, some NAFTA opponents and frustrated law enforcement voices have simplistically blamed the free trade accord for the influx of drugs. Unfortunately, neither position—denial or denouncement—has been very helpful in understanding the problem.

As discussed earlier, the boom in cross-border trade has certainly facilitated drug trafficking by making smuggling via commercial cargo more difficult to detect. And the magnitude of cross-border trade has added pressure on the Customs Service to minimize delays at border crossings. However, it should be remembered that the poor results of border drug interdiction predate NAFTA, and there is no reason to believe that interdiction would be significantly more successful in the absence of NAFTA. Moreover, with or without a formal free trade agreement, cross-border commercial flows between Mexico and the United States were expected to increase significantly, making the interdiction of drugs at ports of entry more difficult. NAFTA may provide an easy political target for some critics, but the fact is that the border has never been (and is unlikely to become) a particularly effective barrier against drug flows.

FUTURE TRENDS IN U.S.–MEXICO BORDER DRUG INTERDICTION

The degree of harmony or conflict in U.S.–Mexico relations will continue to depend heavily on how the drug issue is managed politically, even if it is not resolved. The three following scenarios can be envisioned in this regard.

Further Militarization

In the "further militarization" scenario, the military is increasingly called in to the front lines of the antidrug campaign. On the U.S. side of the border, this option is most forcefully articulated by conservative isolationists like Patrick Buchanan. It has also become a popular option for some members of the U.S. Congress. Indeed, for three consecutive years the U.S. House of Representatives approved a resolution sponsored by Ohio Representative James Traficant (a NAFTA critic) to deploy thousands of U.S. troops to help secure the border. These initiatives have died in the Senate and have been opposed by the Pentagon and the administration. Plans to further militarize the border often emerge during election season, when the border can become a political stage. For example, during the 1996 presidential race, Bob Dole pledged to significantly expand the National Guard's drug interdiction role along the U.S.–Mexico border, and he promised that if his measures proved inadequate he would turn to the military as the lead antidrug agency on the border.[59]

Although the military already plays a substantial border support role (in road and fence maintenance, training, and surveillance), some key factors inhibit their deeper involvement. A more expansive and direct military role is opposed by the law enforcement community, mainstream political elites, and the military itself. Indeed, after U.S. soldiers on a patrol mission along the Texas border shot a teenage goatherd in May 1997, the military suspended such operations indefinitely and indicated an interest in scaling back some of its border duties. The shooting prompted outcries from border communities in Texas and from human rights advocates. At the diplomatic level, an expanded and more visible U.S. military role on the border could have disastrous consequences for cross-border ties (in terms of both Washington–Mexico City relations and relations between local communities along the border). Full militarization would also impede the cross-border travel and commerce that both countries have enthusiastically encouraged.

It is important to emphasize, however, that there has already been a substantial militarization of drug control on the Mexican side of the border in recent years. And this will probably continue, despite problems of corruption within the military and concerns about human rights abuses and lack of public accountability. The militarization of Mexican drug control has also involved more intimate cross-border military relations. In reaction to the pervasive corruption within Mexico's federal police forces—brought into the spotlight by international scrutiny—the government of Ernesto Zedillo (1994–2000) placed the military in charge of drug control operations in many Mexican states, especially those in the northern border region.

One concern is that the militarization on the Mexican side of the border may provide political ammunition and legitimacy for advocates of militarization on the U.S. side: "the Mexicans are deploying their military on the border and Washington is supporting it, so why can't we do the same on our side?" So far, administration officials and key congressional voices on border enforcement issues (such as Texas Democratic Representative Silvestre Reyes) have fended off calls for an expanded military role, partly by promoting more law enforcement. Enhanced law enforcement thus provides a substitute for (and a response to calls for) further militarization of the border.

De-escalation

De-escalation could take a variety of forms, all of which remain unlikely in the current political context. First, any measure that could be remotely characterized as leading down the path toward legalization or decriminalization of drugs will no doubt meet stiff political opposition in Washington, and few policymakers have an incentive to swim against the current. However, it is also difficult to envision widespread political support for even a more moderate turn toward a domestic-focused public health approach to the nation's drug problems.[60] Despite shifts in official discourse (most notably by Barry McCaffrey, who prefers the metaphor of fighting a cancer, rather than a war, to describe the antidrug effort), efforts to address the domestic demand for drugs continue to take a backseat to supply-focused law enforcement, and there is little indication that the prioritization of enforcement will diminish. While the federal antidrug budget has mushroomed since the 1980s, one thing has remained the same: roughly 70 percent of spending is devoted to law enforcement, and only 30 percent goes to demand-side measures such as treatment, education, and prevention.

Even if Mexico's role in the drug trade is reduced and/or U.S. consumption of imported drugs sharply declines, the southwest border will likely remain a major smuggling corridor.[61] Continued U.S. media and congressional scrutiny of Mexico and the border region, as well as bureaucratic incentives within the drug control apparatus, inhibit a significant policy re-evaluation and change in course. Regardless of the fact that the current policy continues to fail as a significant deterrent against the influx of drugs, any appearance of retreat risks projecting an image of being "soft" on drugs. With the political rewards of a major policy shift uncertain and the potential political risks of such a move extremely high, most policymakers are unwilling to publicly promote a de-escalation of border enforcement (even while privately admitting its inherent deficiencies).

High-Tech Escalation as a Form of "Muddling Through"

Based on current trends, high-tech escalation is the most likely policy path in the near and medium term. In this scenario, bureaucratic and political incentives continue to propel a steady expansion of the anti-drug campaign on both sides of the border—regardless of its actual effectiveness. This involves an increased reliance on high-tech interdiction techniques designed to filter out drug shipments, but without significantly impeding the rapidly rising cross-border flow of legal commerce. The White House Office of National Drug Control Policy (ONDCP) and the National Institute of Justice (NIJ) are especially enthusiastic promoters of new interdiction technologies. A Border Research and Technology Development Center funded by NIJ and ONDCP was opened in San Diego in 1995. The purpose of the center is to test new technologies, many of which are provided by the military and intelligence agencies, for border control tasks.

Innovative border management methods are creating both a superhighway for business and a more intensive border surveillance system. For example, a voice-recognition system is being tested at the Otay Mesa border crossing south of San Diego that allows entry to the United States by speaking into a hand-held computer inside the car. At the Otay Mesa and San Ysidro ports of entry, commuter lanes have been opened for low-risk frequent business travelers who pay a user fee, are fingerprinted, undergo background checks, and have a transponder installed in their cars. Similar commuter lanes are being planned for other border ports of entry. License plate readers have also being installed to monitor both northbound and southbound traffic. "What we see now is just the beginning of the trend," says Raymond Mintz, director of applied technology at the Customs Service. "In another year or two, the whole face of the way things are done at the border is going to change."[62]

Rather than manually unloading and inspecting cargo containers (a labor- and time-intensive process), there is a growing turn toward the use of nonintrusive inspection technologies.[63] For example, Customs is installing giant X-ray machines—which resemble a car-wash and can scan entire truck cargoes—at each of the thirty-nine official ports of entry by the year 2003.[64] Currently, these machines, which cost US$3.5 million each, are in place at only a handful of border ports.[65] Mobile truck X-ray machines are also being tested and evaluated; these can be moved from port to port, making the inspection process less predictable for smugglers.[66] Customs is also using devices that can peer into gas tanks for hidden stashes of drugs, and it is testing hand-held sniffing machines and other devices that can detect cocaine vapors.[67] Railcars are also being targeted. In Laredo, Texas, for example, Customs is installing a gamma-ray inspection system to scan railcars entering from Mexico.[68] These changes in interdiction technologies, in turn, will likely prompt further changes in the methods of drug smuggling. One result is that the least skilled smugglers are the most likely to be weeded out, increasing the market share of the most sophisticated smuggling groups.

The trade community, of course, enthusiastically favors the use of nonintrusive inspection technologies. "We're all for the high-tech X-ray machines versus drilling holes and damaging our equipment," says Charles Griffin, who heads border operations in Laredo for Landstar Rangers. "X-ray the heck out of them!"[69] For years, trucking associations in the United States and Mexico have complained about the delays and damage caused by drilling holes in equipment (especially refrigerated units). Backing their objections has been a recent appellate court ruling limiting drug searches involving drilling without reasonable suspicion.[70] Although the ultimate outcome of such court decisions is uncertain, potential legal complications have certainly given the Customs Service an added incentive to develop new nonintrusive interdiction technologies.

The reliance on state-of-the-art high-tech equipment is also increasingly evident between ports of entry, such as more night-vision goggles, motion sensors, and low-light TV cameras. Reflecting this trend, there has been a fivefold increase since 1995 in the number of heat-detecting infrared scopes along the border, and the number of seismic ground sensors has nearly doubled since 1994.[71] Much of this enhanced enforcement has been directed at curbing illegal immigration, but it overlaps with the drug control mission as well.

The high-tech escalation option is evident on the Mexican side of the border as well. In February 1999, Mexican officials announced a US$400 million, three-year antidrug plan. Much of the funding will be used for new equipment such as infrared cameras for airplane surveillance, X-ray machines at border ports of entry, and encrypted satellite-communications gear. New helicopters, airplanes, and speedboats will also be bought.[72] The February announcement followed an announcement in October 1998 that new resources and technologies would be channeled to cut off drug-trafficking routes across Mexico's border with Guatemala and Belize and along the Atlantic and Pacific coasts.

CONCLUSION

Drug control efforts along and across the U.S.–Mexico border during the past decade have done little to diminish the overall flow of drugs. Importantly, however, these efforts have helped U.S. and Mexican leaders fend off political attacks, and they have kept the drug issue from derailing the creation and maintenance of a closer trade relationship. In other words, a policy that has largely failed in its stated instrumental goal (reducing the drug supply) has nevertheless helped to promote other key policy objectives. This has been especially evident in the political struggle to create NAFTA. In the post–NAFTA era, however, drug interdiction has further exposed, sharpened, and politicized the inherent policy tensions between enforcing laws against illegal flows and facilitating legal flows. Trying to reconcile inflated political desires for control and the practical realities along the border has been an increasingly frustrating task.

Thanks to NAFTA and the politics of drug control, cross-border relations have become both more intimate and more strained during the past decade. Indeed, the border is arguably more blurred *and* more sharply demarcated than ever before—reflecting how close the countries have become and how very far apart they remain. The enduring political challenge is to reduce expectations regarding the deterrent effect of border interdiction. At best, the border can provide a limited antidrug "shock absorber."[73] Stepped-up border enforcement can influence the methods, organization, and location of smuggling, but it has (and will most likely continue to have) only a minimal impact on the drug supply. Border interdiction is an inherently inefficient policy instrument.[74] Ultimately, the border is neither the underlying source of the drug problem nor the most cost-effective location for a policy solution. Recognizing this fact, rather than denying it, would help minimize the role of the border as a source of tension and conflict in the U.S.–Mexico relationship.

Notes

1. General Accounting Office, *U.S.–Mexico Border: Issues and Challenges Confronting the United States and Mexico* (July 1999), 2.

2. A 1993 Congressional Research Service report notes that, "if one takes higher estimates of U.S. illicit drug expenditures, it is possible that the dollar amount received by Mexican based traffickers from illicit drug shipments to the United States could begin to approach the amount spent by Americans on all legal imports from Mexico, i.e. $35 billion." Raphael F. Perl, "NAFTA: Implications for Illicit Drug Supply to the United States" (Washington D.C.: Congressional Research Service, November 11, 1993), 2.

3. Total U.S.–Mexico trade increased from $75.8 billion in 1992 to $157.3 in 1997. Approximately 75 percent of this trade crosses the southwest border by truck. General Accounting Office, *U.S.–Mexico Border*, 29.

4. Office of National Drug Control Policy, *National Drug Control Strategy* (Washington D.C.: 1999), 69.

5. Peter Reuter and David Ronfeldt, *Quest for Integrity* (Santa Monica: RAND, 1991), 10.

6. Congressional Research Service, *Drug Interdiction: U.S. Programs, Policy and Options for Congress*, report prepared by the Senate Caucus on International Narcotics Control, September 1996; Proceedings of a Seminar held by the Congressional Research Service, December 12, 1995, 19–20.

7. As the then-head of the DEA testified in 1993, U.S. enforcement initiatives "have forced the Colombian cartels to do something they'd just as soon not do, and that is enter into an arrangement with Mexican traffickers rather than directly fly these loads in themselves." See testimony of Robert Bonner before the Subcommittee of the Committee on Appropriations, February 24, 1993.

8. Statement of Russell L. Jones, president of Richard L. Jones Customhouse Brokers, before the Subcommittee on Appropriations, United States Senate, August 19, 1987, 143–44.

9. Testimony of James C. Piatt, U.S. Customs Service, before the Subcommittee on Appropriations, United States Senate, August 19, 1987, 306–308.

10. In Mexico's National Development Plan (PND–89) of May 1989, drug trafficking is defined as the leading security threat facing Mexico. Sergio Aguayo Quezada, "The Uses, Abuses, and Challenges of Mexican National Security, 1946–1990," in *Mexico: In Search of Security*, edited by Bruce M. Bagley and Sergio Aguayo Quezada (Coral Gables, Fl.: North-South Center, University of Miami, 1993).

11. Defense Intelligence Agency, *Defense Intelligence Assessment. Mexican Counterdrug Security Forces: Problems and Prospects* (Washington, D.C.: Defense Intelligence Agency, June 1992), iv. (Obtained through the Freedom of Information Act by the National Security Archive.)

12. For a summary of State Department statements, see Larry K. Storrs, "Mexico's Counternarcotics Efforts, 1985–1995," *CRS Reports for Congress* (Washington D.C.: Congressional Research Service, March 14, 1996).

13. *New York Times*, July 11, 1997.

14. *New York Times*, July 31, 1995.

15. National Public Radio, *Morning Edition*, May 23, 1995.

16. *Christian Science Monitor*, June 4, 1993.

17. Congress, *Congressional Record-House*, May 25, 1993, H2776.

18. U.S. Department of State, *Administration Position Paper: NAFTA and the War on Drugs* (Washington, D.C., October 1993).

19. For example, a Customs Service memorandum dated August 17, 1993, listed a number of talking points that could be used in handling public inquiries. Customs Service, "United States Customs Service Memorandum from the Deputy Commissioner to the Commissioner" (Washington, D.C., August 17, 1993).

20. According to one former DEA official who had been the head of the El Paso Intelligence Center, "we were prohibited from discussing the effects of NAFTA as it related to narcotics trafficking, yes. I mean, it was a subject that we could not discuss." ABC News interview with Phil Jordan on *Nightline*, May 6, 1997.

21. *Economist*, December 16, 1995, 38–39.

22. Author interview, Washington D.C., August 2, 1996.

23. Quoted in the *New York Times*, May 24, 1993.

24. Ibid.

25. *New York Times*, July 30, 1995.

26. Drug Enforcement Administration, *The New Agricultural Reform Program and Illicit Cultivations in Mexico* (October 14, 1992). (Obtained by the National Security Archive through the Freedom of Information Act.)

27. *Los Angeles Times*, February 12, 1995.

28. Testimony of Alan D. Bersin, U.S. Attorney for the Southern District of California, before the Subcommittee on Immigration and Claims, Committee on the Judiciary, U.S. House of Representatives, April 23, 1997.

29. *New York Times*, September 20, 1998.

30. General Accounting Office, *U.S.–Mexico Border*, 29.

31. *New York Times*, March 20, 1998.

32. U.S. Customs Service, *Enhanced Truck Inspection*, 5.

33. See remarks of Harvey G. Pothier, Deputy Assistant Commissioner, Office of Air Interdiction, U.S. Customs Service, in the Congressional Research Service, *Drug Interdiction*, 22.

34. Author interview, U.S. Customs Service, San Diego, April 4, 1997.

35. Author interview, San Diego Dialogue, La Jolla, Calif., May 12, 1997.

36. *Washington Post*, February 20, 1996.

37. Mike Allen, "Importers' Ire Up Over Border Inspection Rise," *San Diego Business Journal*, July 31, 1995.

38. *Narcotics Enforcement and Prevention Digest* 1:10 (March 9, 1995).

39. *Drug Trafficking, Commercial Trade, and NAFTA on the Southwest Border* (Operation Alliance, May 1997).

40. Quoted in *Dallas Morning News*, May 10, 1998.

41. William von Raab and F. Andy Messing, Jr., "Will NAFTA Free the Drug Trade?" *Washington Post*, August 15, 1993.

42. Quoted in *Houston Chronicle*, January 4, 1998.

43. Quoted in *Houston Chronicle*, March 1, 1998.

44. *Reuters*, June 22, 1999.

45. Congress, House, Office of Representative Maxine Waters, *Drug Trafficking on the Fast Track: Executive Summary* (Washington, D.C., November 4, 1997).

46. Author interview, U.S. Customs Service, San Diego, March 21, 1997.

47. Sam Banks, the U.S. Customs commissioner, has claimed that "Over the last four years, we've gone from inspecting 5 percent of the trucks to 25 percent of the trucks" crossing the border. Quoted in the *Journal of Commerce*, March 16, 1998.

48. Author interview, U.S. Customs Service, Washington D.C., June 4, 1997.

49. Author interview, U.S. Customs Service, San Diego, March 21, 1997.

50. Customs Service, press releases, February 26 and 28, 1996.

51. This has been a problem for other agencies as well. While the number of cocaine seizures by the DEA in the southwest border area was constant between FY 1995 and FY 1996, the amount seized actually dropped by 70 percent.

52. The Congressional Research Service notes that the 5 to 15 percent seizure rate at the border is lower than the percentage of goods lost to shoplifting by some retail stores. Perl, *NAFTA: Implications for Illicit Drug Supply*, 3.

53. Author interview, U.S. Customs Service, San Diego, April 7, 1997.

54. What the Office of Technology Assessment concluded over a decade ago is still true today: "Measures of effectiveness for interdiction are difficult, if not impossible, to quantify. One commonly stated interdiction measurement has been total drug seizures or seizure rates. While seizure quantities can be easily collected, they are difficult to interpret. No seizures may indicate great success that drugs are no longer being smuggled through a particular location. Or a lack of seizures may indicate that smugglers are circumventing interdiction efforts. In fact, the limited seizure and trafficking data available indicate seizures increasing as smuggling increases." See Office of Technology Assessment, *The Border War on Drugs* (Washington, D.C., March 1987), 51.

55. ABC News, *Nightline*, May 6, 1997.

56. *Los Angeles Times*, February 4, 1998.

57. Ibid.

58. *Houston Chronicle*, January 4, 1998.

59. *Los Angeles Times*, September 2, 1996.

60. On the obstacles to such an approach, see Eva Bertram et al., *Drug War Politics: The Price of Denial* (Berkeley: University of California Press, 1996).

61. While casual drug use has declined significantly since the 1980s, hardcore abuse and addiction have not—and this user group consumes the bulk of the imported cocaine and heroin supply.

62. Quoted in *Los Angeles Times*, December 25, 1998.

63. Office of National Drug Control Policy, *Ten Year Counterdrug Technology Plan and Development Roadmap*, February 1999.

64. *San Francisco Examiner*, August 31, 1998.

65. Along the Texas-Mexico border, for example, four of these machines were in place as of January 1999. *San Antonio Express News*, January 22, 1999.

66. Testimony of Raymond Kelly, U.S. Commissioner of Customs, House Trade Subcommittee, Committee on Ways and Means, April 13, 1999.

67. *Los Angeles Times*, December 25, 1998; *New York Times*, March 20, 1998.

68. *Journal of Commerce*, July 16, 1999.

69. *Journal of Commerce*, March 16, 1998.

70. *Journal of Commerce*, March 3, 1999.

71. *Washington Post*, February 19, 1999.

72. *Washington Post*, February 5, 1999.

73. See testimony of Alan D. Bersin before the Committee on the Judiciary, U.S. House of Representatives, April 23, 1997.

---

74. For example, a 1994 RAND study concluded that $34 million invested in treatment reduces cocaine use as much as $366 million invested in interdiction. Cited in Council on Foreign Relations, *Task Force Report: Rethinking International Drug Control* (Washington D.C., 1997), 55.

9

Drug Demand Reduction Policy and Practice in the United States: A Preliminary Review

W. Carsten Andresen and Graham Farrell

MEXICO–U.S. COOPERATION ON DRUGS

Mexico, like many other countries, believes that the United States does little to curb domestic demand for illicit drugs, while placing the burden on non–U.S. "producer" countries to halt the production and trafficking of illicit drugs. This chapter examines the measures taken to reduce demand for illicit drugs in the United States and evaluates their effectiveness.

The chapter represents an effort to chart and document the nature and scope of U.S. demand-side drug policy and practice—a necessary precursor to the development of a critique. Policy and practice must be reviewed separately because they may differ. Moreover, policy and expenditure at the federal level are reasonably transparent, but those within individual states are largely uncharted territory. Since the aggregate picture of U.S. efforts on the demand side is imperfect, a more formal survey of state- and local-level demand-side activities related to illegal drug use could provide information to enhance policy development and practice in the future.

The *U.S./Mexico Bi-National Drug Threat Assessment*[1] was the first published joint effort between the two countries to assess "the common drug threat." It stimulated a political commitment by both sides: the Declaration of Alliance Against Drugs, announced by the U.S. and Mexican presidents in May 1997. In February 1998, the *U.S./Mexico Bi-National Drug Strategy*[2] identified action that both countries would take.

The subsequent *Bi-National Drug Control Strategy: Performance Measures of Effectiveness: Implementation and Findings*[3] became the primary tool regarding the implementation and assessment of these efforts. As such, it warrants brief discussion. The "Bi-National Performance Measures of Effectiveness" (PME) lists sixteen "alliance points," the first of which relates to efforts to reduce the demand for illicit drugs. Most of the action points address the manner in which the two countries will exchange information regarding their respective efforts. The potential exists that the alliance points could serve as a justification to develop mechanisms whereby each country could monitor, and thereby influence, the activity of the other.

The Office of National Drug Control Policy publishes the key federal document relating to U.S. domestic drug policy—the annual "U.S. National Drug Control Strategy"—which includes demand reduction. According to its 1999 incarnation, the National Drug Control Strategy "is a ten-year plan for reducing drug use in America." Its stated goal is "to cut today's drug use in half—to 3.1 percent of the population—by the year 2007."[4] This policy document sets a broad agenda, in which "education, prevention, and treatment are the components of demand reduction." In addition to covering prevention, treatment, and rehabilitation, the policy agenda also focuses on illicit drug use in the criminal justice system. US$5.9 billion, or over a third of the overall federal drug control budget, is targeted to such demand reduction programs.

Federal government spending on programs to counter illicit drug use is typically presented in nominal terms in White House publications. This long-accepted fiscal sleight of hand gives the impression that spending on drug control policy has rocketed. Although it is true that spending has increased substantially, much of the gain disappears when one controls for inflation (see figure 9.1). The drug control budget request for the year 2000 incorporated a 3 percent reduction in real terms.

DEMAND AND DEMAND REDUCTION

Some context might prove useful at this point. The vast majority of drugs consumed in the United States are legal. Psychoactive substances are legally consumed for medical and recreational purposes. Both pharmaceutical and recreational drugs (the latter comprise primarily alcohol, nicotine, and caffeine) are multi-billion-dollar industries. There is a historical connection between the legal and illegal drug businesses. Many of the more famous illicit drugs in the United States—including heroin, cocaine, LSD, and amphetamine-type stimulants—were developed and initially used for medicinal purposes and hence were legal at one time. The connection between licit and illicit drugs continues; in November 1998 five U.S. states legalized cannabis for medical purposes.[5]

This preamble is intended to demonstrate that, in the overall picture of drug use, illicit use is a marginal activity. When one takes the overall

Figure 9.1. **Federal Government Spending on Drug Control Policy (controlled for inflation)**

Annual Real Change in National Drug Control Budget 1991-2000

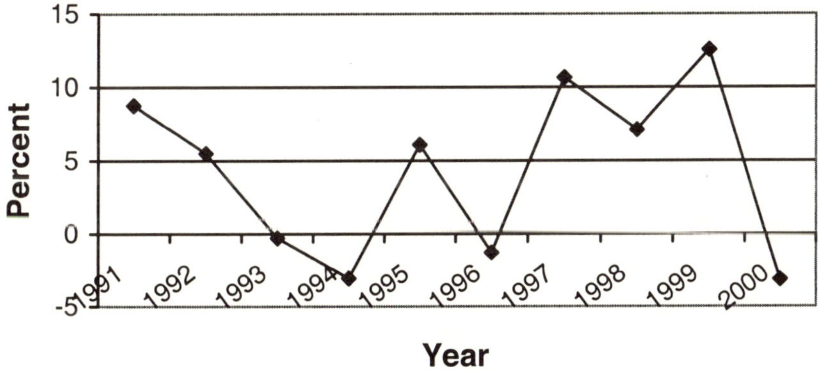

Sources: U.S. Department of Labor, Bureau of Labor Statistics (inflation for 2000 was estimated); White House National Drug Control Policy (various years up to 1999).

population into consideration, frequent use of "hard" drugs is a statistical rarity. In contrast, use of illicit drugs has a seemingly disproportionate draw as a focus of attention among the public, the media, and policymakers. This is probably more marked in the United States than elsewhere, perhaps because of the coincidence of and interaction between illegal drug dealing and relatively unrestrictive gun laws, a strong economy that produces an attractive market for illicit drug retailing, and localized urban social problems in which illicit drugs are often cited as cause or consequence.

So how should the illicit demand for drugs be defined? In its broadest sense, the list of factors potentially influencing drug demand could cover almost anything. There is a range of factors that are wholly independent of the illicit drug market but that influence it nevertheless. Such exogenous factors include geography and economic, political, social, and technological change. The mechanism by which these factors influence demand can be complex: drug traffickers target profitable markets, which in recent history have disproportionately been the United States and Western Europe. As transport and communications have become faster and cheaper, and as developing economies and economies in transition have become more economically attractive, market forces have driven up the size of the illicit drug market.[6]

The implication of this simple story is that consumption—or realized demand—is, and by inference will continue to be, significantly influenced by supply-side factors relating to opportunity. Expanding opportunities for trafficking produces increased supply, which in turn produces increased opportunity for illicit consumption. Hence, although demand is undoubtedly influenced by other factors, it is foolish to believe that supply does not play a significant role, at least when we consider realized rather than potential demand. Despite this recognition, the emphasis in what follows falls on the demand side rather than the supply side. Although the two are necessarily related, it is a convenient distinction for analytic purposes.

Some of the other factors influencing illicit demand for drugs are hard to fathom. What causes attitudes and behavior to change in a population? Fashions and fads in clothing and accessories come and go without anyone being able to offer a clear explanation. Given that illicit drug use is often related to social interaction, it may be influenced by factors similar to those that sway fashions and fashion accessories. This thinking is reflected in recent demand reduction efforts that portray illegal drug use as unfashionable, including advertisements using famous sports and media stars to promote an antidrug message.

The term "demand" is used here to mean actual consumption—realized demand—rather than potential or unrealized demand, which is probably very large. People want more illicit drugs than they can get their hands on, dare get their hands on because of their reluctance to transgress the law, or can afford. Hereinafter, "demand" is used as synonymous with actual consumption, rather than the more intangible notion of potential demand. This distinction is important for policy analysis. That there may be a significant difference between potential and actual demand is important in relation to policies that influence the *motivation* to take drugs rather than policies that influence the *opportunity* to take drugs. For example, whether or not some aspects of individual consumer motivation can be influenced may be a somewhat different question than whether or not aggregate realized demand can be influenced.

This chapter concentrates on consumption-reduction efforts that fall into the categories of primary and secondary demand reduction as defined below. However, it recognizes from the outset that exogenous and indirect factors influencing demand may well be more influential than the strategies and tactics described as primary or secondary demand reduction efforts. Hence the forest of influences upon demand should be kept in sight when examining the trees of demand reduction policy. This, in turn, presents an insight of relevance to the analysis of policy; it may be that, all things considered, the demand reduction policy trees are but a thicket in the overall demand-side influences upon illicit consumption.

Demand reduction is one aspect of demand-side drug policy. The broader demand-side framework typically includes efforts to reduce risks to, and improve the health of, users of illicit drugs. This includes efforts to reduce the risks of infection by disease and to encourage safe (or the least dangerous) practices in relation to drug use. The United States is one of the few democratic industrial nations that appears not to overtly integrate many aspects of a public health perspective into its overall demand-side drug policy. Although many grassroots efforts exist to reduce risks to the health of illicit drug users, these are typically not receiving federal funding, and such efforts are conspicuous by their absence from federal policy.

The definition of demand reduction used here equates with primary and secondary prevention as defined by the World Health Organization (WHO), which also includes tertiary prevention efforts in its definition:

- Primary prevention is aimed at ensuring that a disorder, process, or problem will not occur.
- Secondary prevention is aimed at identifying and terminating or modifying for the better a disorder, process, or problem at the earliest possible moment.
- Tertiary prevention is aimed at stopping or retarding the progress of a disorder, process, or problem and its sequelae, even though the basic condition persists.[7]

The national drug policies of most industrialized nations contain varying but typically far stronger elements of tertiary prevention than U.S. drug policy. Particularly at the federal level, U.S. demand-side policy and efforts focus mainly upon primary and secondary prevention. While cross-national comparison is not a focus of this chapter, the demand-side policies of other industrialized countries may provide information useful for the development of U.S. policy in terms of both the good and the bad lessons to be learned.

EXPENDITURE ON DEMAND REDUCTION

Funding for demand reduction programs comes from different sources—namely, federal government, state governments, municipal governments, and private sources (see figure 9.2). These different funding sources make it difficult to discern exactly how much is being spent on demand reduction programs.

Figure 9.2 **Federal Funding for Demand Reduction Programs**

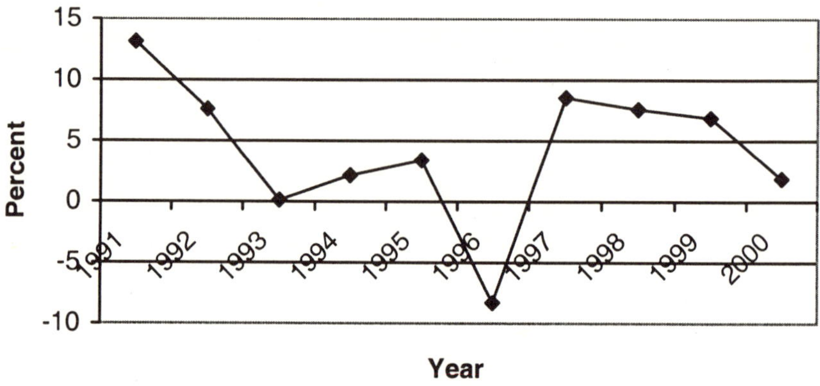

Sources: U.S. Department of Labor, Bureau of Labor Statistics (inflation for year 2000 was estimated); White House National Drug Control Policy (various years).

Federal Funding

U.S. federal government spending on demand reduction programs is about one-tenth the estimated amount that U.S. citizens spend annually to buy illicit drugs. In 1999, federal spending on demand reduction was US$5.9 billion, while "What America's Users Spend on Illegal Drugs 1988–1995" estimated 1995 citizen spending at $57 billion—or about $212 each, assuming a population estimate of 269 million.[8] The amount spent buying drugs illicitly has been declining in recent years, but this drop is seemingly due primarily to falling street prices rather than to contracting demand.

Specific demand reduction programs are earmarked for federal funding. These include $50 million for school drug prevention coordinators for approximately 6,500 middle schools nationwide; $51 million for drug and underage alcohol research; $146 million for initiatives that discourage tobacco use among youths; and $200 million to "mobilize resources to increase substance abuse treatment services nationwide."[9]

Federal funds are distributed via a grant process. Grant funds come in two varieties: formula grants and discretionary/demonstration grants. Formula grants use a formula prescribed by the U.S. Congress to award money whereby "in many cases, the formula is population- or need-based." Discretionary/demonstration grants are awarded "on the merit of competitive applications submitted by eligible agencies or activities.... Applications are ranked in order of merit, and the highest ranking applications are awarded funds."[10]

Federal funds can provide grant money to state and then local governments for demand reduction programs. This means that activities at the local project level may receive federal funding indirectly, in addition to state or local government funding.

State and Local Funds

It is difficult to determine the amount that each state gives to demand reduction. States are not required to publish expenditure figures for demand reduction programs. (Arizona is exceptional in that it does publish a report.) However, there are two available indicators from which to gauge expenditures at the state level, one from the U.S. Department of Health and Human Services and the other from ONDCP.

The U.S. Department of Health and Human Services provides information on state appropriations to state rehabilitation services. In particular, this provides documentation of state government expenditures for state-supported alcohol and other drug abuse services.[11]

ONDCP has also published information on drug control activities by state. "State and Local Spending on Drug Control Activities: Report from the National Survey of State and Local Governments"[12] documents drug control expenditure by state and categorizes state and local spending on drug control according to whether it was for police protection, corrections, health and hospitals, or education. But because the report appears not to have been updated (the 1999 version seems to present information on 1991), charting current state and local expenditure is a complicated task.

Types of Programs and Projects

Demand reduction efforts are delivered by different mechanisms as part of different programs. The key types of programs to be covered here (outlined in table 9.1) may not be an exhaustive listing of potential types of primary and secondary demand reduction efforts. Classifications entail some subjectivity regarding their orientation and decisions on what to include and what to exclude. For example, a classification could include something like "community building" if it is believed that efforts to build communities could indirectly reduce the illicit demand for drugs. But because the mechanism by which demand would be reduced is unclear, and at best very indirect, such activities are excluded.

Table 9.1 **Types of Primary and Secondary Demand Reduction Efforts**

Primary Prevention
- Media campaigns
- In-school education
- Drug testing

Secondary Prevention
- Drug-free treatments
- Rehabilitation
- Substitute or alternative drugs (opioids, methadone; LAAM, buprenorphine, substitution pharmacotherapies)

Alternative orientations may also prove fruitful for guiding future research efforts in this area. For example, a classification that divided projects and programs according to the mechanism by which they were intended to reduce demand (for example, an opportunity reduction mechanism, compared to a motivation reduction mechanism) might prove informative. A step in this direction is suggested in the concluding section.

The most notable exclusions from the present classification are the demand-reducing effects of law and law enforcement. Although law and law enforcement are typically not classified as demand reduction (and domestic enforcement is classified separately in the national drug control budget), they clearly can have a demand-reducing effect. Consequently, as with exogenous factors influencing demand, they are excluded here only for reasons of space and to allow a greater focus on the "core" demand reduction programs.

THE EVALUATION FRAMEWORK

Assessing Theory and Implementation

How should programs and projects be assessed? It is important to recognize the difficulties in assessing what works and what does not. Projects and programs typically fail at one of three stages: theory (the approach was ill founded); tactics development (the specific tactic was ill founded); or implementation (the program is not implemented correctly). An example will illustrate the difference between theory failure and tactic failure; the theory might be that drug testing can reduce demand in a target population, but the specific tactic might be breath testing which is only useful to test for alcohol in a short-term context.

There are various permutations on these patterns. Some demand reduction programs could be poorly conceived and poorly implemented, some poorly conceived but well implemented, some well conceived but poorly implemented, and others well conceived and well implemented. The three stages or factors outlined above yield eight permutations of outcome, only one of which results in a successful program or project. Note that this does not mean that seven out of eight projects are doomed to failure, but it does highlight the fact that a project must have success at each stage to be successful. In contrast, a project need have failure at only one stage to be unsuccessful. Determining which permutation has occurred is a tricky task of evaluation.

Assessing Evaluations

A significant share of demand reduction projects or programs have never been evaluated. Those evaluations that do exist vary greatly in scope, methodology, and competence. Evaluations can fail if they wrongly conclude something worked or if they wrongly conclude something failed to work (evaluation failure Types I and II, respectively). For example, it has been suggested that many of the early evaluations of in-school drug education programs made a Type I error in (wrongly) concluding that the programs produced a reduction in illicit drug use.[13]

Even the difficulty of defining what constitutes a successful program and what parameters and criteria define "success" or "failure" blur the evaluation picture somewhat. Indicators of program success are often unclear. Has a publicity program succeeded if it reaches a large audience? If it reaches a specific target audience? Or only if it is understood by those it reaches? These indicators, although often necessary, are not sufficient to indicate success in terms of outcome. What if the same publicity program is understood and results in a change in behavior? What level of change is required? Is a minor shift a success? And for what proportion of the target audience? Would a change in behavior indicate success whether it is short term or long term? Recent applications of cost-benefit analysis in the field of criminal justice would suggest that a program succeeds if its overall benefits are greater than its overall costs. Yet even here there can be a range of issues to address in categorizing and measuring costs and benefits. Such issues cloud many evaluations of drug demand reduction efforts.

One of the more significant recent contributions to the field of evaluation is Pawson and Tilley's formulation of mechanism, context, and outcome as part of a realist evaluation perspective.[14] It is in essence a formal statement of a straightforward notion: evaluation should incorporate an understanding of precisely how an intervention works. That is, we must analyze how a particular preventive mechanism is applied in a particular context in order to produce a specific outcome. This formulation can be used in a variety of ways, and the effort is made here to apply it where possible to the analysis of demand-side drug policy.

An example might illustrate the uses of Pawson and Tilley's formulation. The *mechanism* by which education is intended to reduce demand for drugs is indirect. The target audience needs to be reached, which can be difficult, and it will vary with *context* (for example, which age groups, where, in what environment?). If the target audience is reached, education may or may not influence attitudes and understanding of the issues, again with variation according to *context.* Depending upon the nature and level of change in attitudes and understanding, the intervention may or may not influence behavior. Behavior may be influenced so as to reduce or increase illicit drug use. The impact of education will vary in different places, at different times, in different circumstances, for different target audiences, for different types of education, for different types of messages, for different types of drugs, and depending upon the different types and qualities of educators (or other mediums) that present the educational initiatives. The potential permutations of context are limitless. What works here may not work there, but if the underlying preventive mechanism can be identified, then there is a greater possibility that it can be replicated.

In what follows, we attempt to apply this type of analysis to very broad areas of drug policy. In so doing, we acknowledge that some of the micro-level specificity advocated by Pawson and Tilley may be lost.

Primary Prevention

The first two types of primary prevention to be addressed are media campaigns and in-school education. The mechanism by which each aims to influence illicit demand for drugs is two-step and indirect. The aim is to directly influence attitudes by exposing people to an antidrugs viewpoint of varying specific character. The specific viewpoint and medium of delivery can vary. The weakness of the mechanism lies in the fact that the core target audience (those with the greatest predicted "risk" factors relating to illicit drug use) is difficult to reach, and influencing attitudes is different from influencing behavior. Even if the audience is reached and attitudes are influenced, they may not be influenced in such a way as to produce a change in illicit drug–related behavior.

Most general education campaigns largely preach to the converted, given that most people do not use most types of drugs illicitly, and of those who do, most use them infrequently. But the intention is that the "scattergun approach" also reach those in the audience who may already use, or have a greater statistical likelihood of using, drugs illicitly.

A second important aspect of information campaigns relates to whether it is proper to disseminate information that may deliberately mislead or be factually incorrect in order to drive home an antidrugs message. Drug issues have become so polarized and polemical that it is sometimes hard to differentiate truth from fiction. A recent United Nations publication argued, in relation to demand reduction programs, that:

> Effectiveness need not necessarily be based upon the provision of a rational argument or correct information. The bulk of evidence in relation to political history and the advertising industry suggests that programme effectiveness is determined by five criteria: the credibility of the message; the credibility of the message giver; the means of message delivery; the absence of a strong countervailing message; and the absence of alternative sources of information that might contradict the propagated message.

This is a sobering thought: the implication that evidence and truth need not necessarily be major determinants of outcome.

Media Campaigns

Advertising works. There are countless examples of television, radio, magazine, newspaper, Internet, and other advertising increasing market share and market size. So it seems logical to put forward the notion that antidrug advertising, if done correctly, should reduce demand. This seems to represents a sound theory base for such strategies.

Public awareness campaigns seek to reduce or eliminate drug use by broadcasting antidrug messages. Media campaigns attempt to reach people, change their attitudes, and ultimately change their behavior. The assumption is that if attitude can be changed, then behavior can be changed. Yet media campaigns are not necessarily the same as education campaigns if their aim is to reduce illicit drug use rather than to educate. History is replete with examples of successful publicity and propaganda campaigns that do not necessarily educate—and in some instances deliberately mislead. We know, sometimes to our cost, that people—even whole nations—can be indoctrinated and coerced into believing things that are patently false, and then change their behavior accordingly.

It has been suggested that some antidrugs messages, particularly those relating to cannabis, are explicitly and/or implicitly misleading in their content. The question of whether the end justifies the means in a democratic society is rarely posed. Yet it would be difficult to draw up strict lines to denote truth and fiction in relation to illicit drugs. Specifically, although some demand reduction advertising clearly and deliberately displays an overtly negative image that may, in its specifics, misrepresent the aggregate truth, it is unclear whether this constitutes a breach of public trust. Paradoxically, it may be that more extreme, and factually less correct, messages may be more effective in reducing the illicit demand for drugs.

The National Drug Control Strategy includes a range of public awareness campaigns to be transmitted via different media: television, radio, newspapers, and magazines. The aim is to ensure that everybody sees four antidrug messages each week.[15] Two campaigns dominate at the national level: the Partnership for a Drug-Free America and the National Youth Media Campaign, each of which will be described below.

Partnership for a Drug-Free America

The Partnership for a Drug-Free America (PDFA) is a private organization whose mission is to reduce the demand for illicit drugs in America. It began its media campaign in 1986. The PDFA, which bills itself as "ONDCP's primary creative partner," created five hundred antidrug ads between 1987 and 1998, and by mid–1999 it had fifty-four state- and city-based locations.[16]

Much of what follows draws upon the very comprehensive analysis that Buchanan and Wallack (1998) conducted of PDFA efforts. These authors sum up the goals of the PDFA as: "(1) to reduce demand for drugs by changing attitudes or 'denormalizing' drug use through media communications, (2) to track changes in attitudes toward illegal drugs, and (3) to evaluate the impact of PDFA messages on attitude changes."[17]

Buchanan and Wallack claim that the PDFA has put out mixed messages about demand reduction. Although the PDFA no longer accepts funding from the alcohol and cigarette industry, this was a key source of its income only a few years ago. In 1994 the PFDA, "after receiving a large $7.5 million grant from RWJ Foundation," stopped soliciting donations from the alcohol and tobacco industry.[18] Currently, the PDFA is funded in part by pharmaceutical companies.

Although the PDFA has clearly stated goals, its research and evaluations are more opaque. Because it is a private organization, it is under no public disclosure requirement. Consequently, there seems to be no real accountability or means of checking the validity of PDFA claims. Buchanan and Wallack suggest that some of the PDFA's demand reduction messages have been extremely misleading, designed around a principle of propaganda and indoctrination rather than information or education. The PDFA has claimed "success" based on research by the Department of Pediatrics at the Johns Hopkins School of Medicine and the Stern School of Business at New York University. The PDFA Web site quotes the *New York Times* as saying that the PDFA is "one of the most effective drug education groups in the U.S." Yet, at the time of writing, the www.pdfa.org Web site did not provide citations to, or any sections of, the evaluation results from the original sources.

Buchanan and Wallack are scathing in their assessment of PDFA evaluation efforts:

> First, many researchers have questioned the validity of the sampling technique. Clearly, it is not a random sample, but more closely represents a convenience sample, with all the attendant problems of skewing and bias. Second, comparisons of people who recall ads with those who do not raise the issue of selective attention. People with personal concerns about the topic are more likely to pay attention to the ads, thus introducing another form of bias and confounding into group comparisons. Third, it is difficult to draw any conclusions from these data because they are selectively reported. With a few notable exceptions, the results made available in reports by the Gordon Black Corporation show only those data that support the appearance of an effect. A complete accounting has not been made publicly available. Finally, any inferences from the data are questionable due to an incomplete labeling of charts and figures. There are only sporadic indications of whether or not any apparent differences are statistically significant and the types of statistical tests used are never stated.

In essence, Buchanan and Wallack suggest that the PDFA may, deliberately or otherwise, bias their research results in order to appear more successful than is truly the case. The absence of public accountability means that a formal assessment of the program's success is unlikely. However, in light of the PDFA's prominence and importance in current U.S. demand reduction programs, an independent evaluation would seem appropriate. This could be conducted with the cooperation of the PDFA, perhaps initiated as an open tender via ONDCP, and as such could be a good investment. Such an evaluation could examine the questions that Buchanan and Wallack pose and provide some important lessons for U.S. demand reduction policy. It would also inform existing and prospective funders regarding the use to which money is being put.

The National Youth Anti-Drug Media Campaign

The National Youth Anti-Drug Media Campaign (NYADMC), overseen by ONDCP, seeks to attract an audience comprising both children and their parents. The campaign began in January 1998 as a three-phased program to "reduce drug use through a nationwide integrated communications program to educate and enable America's youth to reject illegal drugs." Two reports purport to evaluate the progress of Phase I, a 26–week pilot run in twelve cities. The NYADMC's report states that they "achieved significant increases in awareness of specific ads among the target audiences."[19] While this suggests that some people were aware of the advertisements, it does not mean that the ads necessarily produced a change in behavior.

Phase II of NYADMC sought to reach a larger audience of youth and parents. Its evaluation, based on a nationwide school survey (of 4th through 12th graders) and a national telephone survey of 8,500 parents, concluded:

- The Campaign met the goal of reaching 90 percent of the target audiences (youths, teens, and parents) on a national level with 4 to 7 antidrug messages a week, through paid ads.
- Awareness of specific Campaign ads increased up to 14 percentage points.
- The percentage of youths who agreed that the ads "made them stay away from drugs" increased from 61 percent to 69 percent.
- The percentage of youths reporting they "learned a lot about the dangers of drugs from TV commercials" also increased, from 44 to 52 percent.[20]

These measurements mean that many people were aware of the advertisements. However, because there are no measures of illicit drug use, these Phase II numbers cannot be taken as demonstrating that the advertisements produced a change in behavior.

The third phase of the NYADMC was intended to expand the target audience and increase antidrug sentiment among youths and parents.

To increase the audience, the campaign is to incorporate additional Internet components and to attract "corporate participation."

While these measures document the implementation or process of the NYADMC media campaign, there are no measures of impact upon the key variable—the use of illicit drugs. A quasi-experimental evaluation using control groups would have been relatively simple to develop from the outset in the twelve cities. Such an evaluation would compare illicit drug–taking behaviors in matched geographical areas and samples subjected to and not subjected to the media campaign. Given the large investment in this demand reduction campaign, it seems unlikely that such an obvious evaluation possibility was overlooked. This seems to leave two possible explanations. The first is that NYADMC evaluators lacked knowledge about basic evaluation methods, but given the campaign's funding level and the emphasis on the evaluation, it stretches credibility to accept that this is the case. A second possibility is that the full results of the evaluation have not been released to the public because they are not the desired results. If this second possibility is true, the logical conclusion is that the NYADMC advertisements did not reduce illicit drug use.

Commentary on Media Campaigns

If we know that advertising campaigns can work, there is a reasonable logic or theory behind using this approach to reduce demand for illicit drugs. This is true irrespective of ethical questions relating to the extent to which advertisements may be misleading. However, there is little hard evidence to date of any substantial impact upon illicit drug use due to negative advertising. This seems to suggest three broad possibilities: (1) that there are flaws in advertising theory when it is applied specifically to illicit drug consumption, including the fact that this advertising is negative rather than positive; (2) that there are flaws in implementation (perhaps the campaigns are not reaching their target audience) or that the advertising is inappropriate or of insufficient quality; or (3) that there are flaws in the evaluations conducted to date since, for example, it is almost impossible to account for the countervailing effect of pro-drug media messages without at least a quasi-experimental design.

In-School Education

School-based education programs ensure a largely captive audience, supposedly at a receptive and malleable age. This is the policy of "nipping it in the bud": reaching children before they use drugs or when they have just began to use drugs. The mechanism is to reduce demand by influencing the attitudes, and subsequently the behavior, of schoolchildren in a manner that turns them away from illicit drug use.

D.A.R.E.

Drug Abuse Resistance Education (D.A.R.E.) is probably the most extensive and best-known in-school education program designed to reduce illicit drug taking. It began in 1983 in Los Angeles, with police officers educating elementary school students as part of the school curriculum, for one hour per week for seventeen weeks. DARE now receives considerable federal funding and has grown into a national, even international, program.

A 1998 follow-up evaluation of DARE presents one of the most scientifically compelling assessments to date among the range of school-based programs. The evaluation used a randomized, longitudinal field experiment to assess DARE's impact among sixth- to twelfth-grade schoolchildren from urban, suburban, and rural areas. It concluded that:

> The results indicate that DARE had no long-term effects on a wide range of drug use measures, nor did it show a lasting impact on hypothesized mediating variables, with one exception. Previously documented short-term effects had dissipated by the conclusion of the study. Some DARE-by-community interactions were observed: Urban and rural students showed some benefits, whereas suburban students experienced small but significant increases in drug use after participation in DARE.[21]

These are not particularly surprising findings. What is new is the scientific strength of the evaluation. The findings add weight to similar findings from a 1994 evaluation that found generally similar outcomes: "The effectiveness of the programme has yet to be demonstrated.... DARE had no statistically significant main effects on drug use behaviors and had few effects on attitudes or beliefs about drugs."[22]

It is important to stress the scientific quality of these evaluations. DARE has been presented in a positive light by so many less scientific evaluations that it has become far larger, more popular, and more important than may be warranted. The bulk of the more sophisticated evaluations are not positive. Lyman and colleagues tracked one thousand DARE students over ten years, beginning with their entrance into the program.[23] They found that DARE did not affect whether children use drugs, alcohol, and cigarettes. A randomized, longitudinal five-year study of twenty-three elementary schools in Lexington, Kentucky, produced similar findings. Other evaluations that concluded that

DARE does not reduce illicit drug use include a six-year follow-up in Colorado Springs, Colorado; a longitudinal study in rural Tennessee; a three-year follow-up in Colorado Springs; a review of "8 methodologically rigorous DARE" programs; a review of four schools in a New Jersey town in 1989; an assessment in Kokomo, Indiana; and a quasi-experimental design with a pretest/posttest comparison design in South Carolina.[24] An evaluation conducted by Coggans et al., which was based on over one hundred schools in Scotland, found results similar to those cited for the United States.[25] Most of these evaluations were done in the mid– or late 1990s, when the DARE bandwagon was moving at full steam, and substantial money, time, and personal commitment had gone into it.

There are also evaluations that find DARE effective, and these may explain the program's early and rapid growth. However, none is as rigorous as the studies by Rosenbaum and his colleagues, and none uses a randomized design. Further, it was primarily the earlier studies that indicated success, and they tend to use poor outcome measures, such as attitude. These studies found that DARE significantly changed attitudes, but they rarely measured illicit drug use. The more recent among them measured attitudes toward substance use, positive peer association, association with drug-using peers, and alcohol use during the past year.[26] Sigler and Talley found that DARE students in Los Alamos had more of an "attitude favorable to avoidance of drug use than students who did not complete the program." They also found "stronger anti-drug attitudes"[27] However, they also determined that "no significant improvement was found in self-reported drug use when DARE students were compared with 2 control groups."

Other favorable reviews of DARE concentrate on public and police support for the program. AH–Training and Development Systems Inc. evaluated the Illinois State Police's DARE program. They surveyed participants and found "very high levels of acceptance among school personnel, community representatives and law enforcement officers, but much less acceptance among alcohol and drug abuse service providers." A full 92 percent of children "demonstrated full refusal skills." Whether they used these skills and what became of the other 8 percent are unknown, and the evaluation did not seem to include the critical outcome measure of whether there was any real impact (that is, a measure of delay or reduction in the onset of illicit drug use).[28]

DARE spread very rapidly because it presented the politically acceptable approach of appearing to do something positive to work with children. It supposedly tackled the problem in a very vulnerable group—schoolchildren—and presented a practical method of program delivery (police officers visiting schools). The continued spread of DARE is more difficult to explain, other than that it may help people think something is being done to address their concerns. As a political palliative, therefore, it is probably attractive. Furthermore, pressure groups supporting DARE can be quite vehement, and any politician suggesting that DARE is not successful will likely come under fire as "soft on drugs." Regardless of the validity of such claims, politicians will tend to avoid the risk that this mud will stick, and this may mean that DARE will continue for years to come, even though it is seemingly ineffective at everything except wasting education time and money.

There are other types of school-based programs as well. Clyde Dent and colleagues examined a program in a "continuation school" in California, an alternative high school for students unable to continue in "traditional" high schools. The study randomly assigned twenty-one continuation high schools to the following categories: "(1) classroom-based program component only, (2) classroom program plus the school-as-community program component, or (3) a "'standard care' (no program) control."[29] The Dent et al. evaluation, which measured attitude rather than behavior, lacked strong indicators of program success. The study included a process evaluation that measured "quality," although the concept of quality was operationalized as "reports of generally liking the material and finding it interesting, informative, appropriate, and helpful."[30] No measures of impact upon behavior were developed.

Drug Testing

Drug testing has been used increasingly in the United States in recent years. It aims to reduce demand for illicit drugs via a combination of detection and deterrence; its primary mechanism is deterrence due to the threat of detection. If detection results in reduced illicit drug use via another mechanism (for example, if it serves as a feeder to treatment), then detection may also reduce demand. Increasing numbers of criminal justice and private agencies have adopted drug testing since the mid–1980s. The number of companies relying on drug testing reputedly rose from 21.5 percent in 1987 to 87.3 percent in 1994, and the American Civil Liberties Union reported an increase in workplace testing of "277 percent from 1987." However, some sources suggest that drug testing leveled off in the early 1990s.[31]

Drug testing varies in its method of administration. Tests can be conducted upon individuals who are under suspicion. In other instances, tests are conducted upon entire groups (all employees, for example). The third technique is random testing, designed to maximize deterrence due to uncertainty while minimizing the costs of conducting the tests. At the time of writing there appear to be no studies that assess the relative effectiveness of the different administration methods using the same or different techniques.[32] Such studies pose an interesting research prospect in terms of measuring the relative detection and deterrence effects under different modes of administration.

The most common application of drug testing in the private sector is to test all employees. Critics have challenged such widespread drug testing by citing the Fourth Amendment, which prohibits unreasonable search and seizure. In contrast, some proponents of drug testing suggest that mandatory testing from an early age would be an efficient means of stopping the onset of illicit drug use during adolescence, and hence of preventing or delaying extended illicit drug use. De la Salle High School and five other Catholic schools in New Orleans have started mandatory hair drug tests for their students, something that at present can only be undertaken in private schools. Wren argues that "the federal government, which has set strict standards for urine testing, has not done so for hair tests because it has yet to be convinced of their accuracy."[33]

The effectiveness of these strategies is a potentially important area for drug-related evaluation research, given that drug testing seemingly has one of the most direct preventive and deterrent mechanisms due to the threat of detection. Testing addresses the individual and the specifics of his or her illicit drug use, and—despite anecdotal evidence to the contrary—there is little chance of cheating on a properly administered test.

An emerging important application of drug testing is in support of secondary prevention efforts to deter relapse among known illicit drug users receiving treatment. Some methadone programs, for example, make the provision of methadone conditional upon passing frequent drug tests. It is controversial, however; it has been suggested that such stringent conditions can simply deter illicit users from entering secondary prevention programs, and it can increase the rate at which they drop out. These empirical questions remain to be definitively resolved.

Even though it may make intuitive sense that mandatory testing will reduce illicit drug use among those subjected to it, few sound evaluations have been conducted. Importantly, however, the key location for such testing is the workplace, but a primary target group—frequent illicit drug users—are likely to be elsewhere. Hence the main focus of drug testing may fall on a minority of infrequent users. This does not weaken the preventive mechanism; it simply means that it is only applicable in a certain context. Given that stated U.S. policy is to reduce the prevalence of use (number of people involved) rather than the overall amount or frequency of use (the tiny fraction of users who are frequent users account for most illicit drug consumption), drug testing could also be deemed acceptable from this perspective. However, the possibility exists that workplace tests will not effectively capture the most frequent users who account for the bulk of illicit drug consumption.

Urine tests and hair assay tests are the two current drug-testing techniques. Though private agencies often employ urine tests to determine illicit drug use, the literature concentrates mainly on offenders in the criminal justice system. Illicit drug use within the criminal justice system is sometimes used as an indicator of the likelihood of future offending (illicit use indicating greater likelihood of recidivism). Consequently, key uses of urine testing are to inform whether offenders should be released on their own recognizance and to monitor parolees and probationers. It is debatable whether illicit drug use is a good predictor of future offending for persons who have committed non-drug crimes. Nevertheless, it is by definition an indicator of current illicit use of drugs.[34]

The accuracy of immunoassay urine tests has historically been questioned.[35] Certainly the level of accuracy is important; inaccuracies mean that people may be denied jobs or unfairly treated based upon inaccurate test results. This said, the accuracy of tests is likely to continue to increase, and the costs of administering the tests are likely to decline.

Although there are anecdotal accounts of employees shaving themselves *in toto*, such behavior is rare, making hair testing more difficult to avoid than urine testing (where sample switching can occur). Hair testing is also generally more accurate than urine testing and detects use further back in time. People also tend to object less to hair tests, perhaps because it appears to be less invasive.[36] A seven-month evaluation of the New Orleans Diversionary Program, a pretrial program for nonviolent offenders, found that hair tests (in combination with counseling and close supervision) "can have a major impact on increasing detection sensitivity, bolstering therapist morale, discouraging or defeating evasion by clients, and creating higher degrees of compliance in the target populations."[37]

Drug testing appears to be one of the stronger preventive mechanisms for deterring and detecting illicit drug use among the populations upon whom it can be imposed. Drug-testing technology continues to become less expensive, more widely available, and easier to administer, making this mechanism potentially the most significant extant tool to reduce demand for illicit drugs. Drug testing is used in a range of contexts to complement other types of demand-reduction measures. In those contexts (for example, if an education program is enforced by testing), the testing may well play a stronger role than the other elements employed. The degree of drug testing's effectiveness in the future seems likely to be limited only by the arguments relating to civil liberties which seek to restrict testing's wholesale application in public and private life. Absent the civil liberties questions, or perhaps despite them, testing for illicit drug use seems likely to prove the most significant tool in the portfolio of antidrug techniques.

Secondary Prevention

Secondary prevention programs seek to reduce demand among individuals who are already using illicit drugs. Three types of secondary demand reduction programs will be discussed here: drug-free treatments, rehabilitation, and legal alternative drugs. A recent United Nations review concluded that:

> There is growing evidence that it is fitting the programme to the needs of the individual, and the quality of service delivery, rather than the type of service, which brings about effectiveness. Thus the flexibility of the programme, the quality of the staff and the morale of patients and staff may have a greater influence on outcome than the actual nature of the service delivered.[38]

Determining program effectiveness can be difficult at the level of secondary prevention, just as at the level of primary prevention. It is often difficult to keep patients in voluntary secondary prevention for the duration of treatment. Reasonable completion rates are a necessary condition for, but not necessarily a measure of, successful treatment. For example, of those who complete treatment, how long does a patient have to be drug free to constitute a "success"? Should the absence of illicit drug taking be measured on the day they leave the program? A month later? Six months later? At the end of their life?

Drug-Free Treatment

Drug-free treatment, as its name suggests, is treatment without drugs. Its specific nature varies from regimes that essentially confine addicts and make them go "cold-turkey" (a technique that has been criticized on humanitarian grounds) to regimes adopting a range of different treatments. Drug-free treatment's preventive mechanism is relatively weak. First, by definition, it applies primarily to the more addictive drugs. Second, unless the treatment is coercive, many people will fail to complete it and will return to illicit drugs. Third, of those who do complete treatment, many will nevertheless obtain illicit drugs later. Consequently, drug-free treatment seems to have a weak preventive mechanism unless it is conducted in conditions where the user is monitored both during and after becoming drug free. If monitoring involves drug testing, then the primary preventive mechanism may be the testing and its application rather than the drug-free treatment itself.

Rehabilitation

Rehabilitation can be voluntary or coerced. Coerced treatment, as an alternative to prosecution or a heavier sentence, gained usage as law enforcement increasingly focused on drug offenders and drug offenses in the 1990s. Lipton specified three types of diversionary treatment programs:

- Probation, with a mix of counseling, support, and surveillance (the most typical).
- Surveillance, components of which includes house arrest, electronic monitoring, and urinalysis.
- Diversion, which is represented by the TASC (Treatment Alternatives to Street Crime) program.[39]

Consequently, rehabilitation is a means of delivering specific mechanisms of demand reduction rather than a mechanism in itself. Nevertheless, because delivery of mechanisms in different contexts can produce different outcomes, this approach deserves consideration. Specific rehabilitation programs will be discussed in turn.

Do Drugs, Do Time

Do Drugs, Do Time (DDDT) is a demand reduction program in Maricopa County, Arizona. It began in 1989 as an alternative to prosecution in non-felony drug arrests. Refusals and felonies are prosecuted. The DDDT program is a partnership among municipal, county, state, and federal law enforcement agencies that undertake buy-and-bust and reverse-sting operations to catch drug offenders.

An evaluation by John Hepburn and colleagues found that the program achieved its two goals:

- Creating community-wide awareness of the severity of the drug problem and the need to hold all users accountable.
- Increasing and coordinating law enforcement activities in combination with increased prosecutions or participation in drug treatment programs.[40]

Four techniques are used as part of DDDT to implement demand reduction: (1) an education program, (2) high-profile arrest operations, (3) retention within the criminal justice system in drug cases that might otherwise have been dismissed, and (4) diversion of a large number of drug-use offenders into treatment, most at the pre-filing stage.[41]

The evaluation by Hepburn et al. included over 7,000 cases in 1989 and 1990. These authors concluded that DDDT "worked" in four respects. First, the program reached offenders who might have had their cases dismissed in court. Second, the program diverted cases at the pre-filing stage, thus theoretically freeing up the courts. Third, it created revenue through charging program participants for drug treatment. Fourth, participants that completed the TASC (Treatment Assessment Screening Center) program "had the lowest rates of rearrest for a new charge of any offender category." The evaluators list these four reasons as "hard facts" that support the program's success.[42]

It is possible that the evaluation design contained limitations. Offenders were not necessarily selected because of their specific drug dependence problem; they may have self-selected, perhaps because the program was seen as an easy alternative to prosecution. The most frequent charge (41 percent of cases) was "attempt to possess an illicit drug," and 32 percent of the cases were arrests for possession of cannabis, which together suggest that this was a stream of minor offenders who would not want to be prosecuted officially. However, because the offenders were not serious offenders (non-felony cases only), then it was probably a sample of low-risk recidivists relative to any available control group. The resulting rates of recidivism (prior to May 1991) were 26 percent of those who did not respond to the offer of treatment, 18 percent of those who refused treatment, and 11 percent of those who entered treatment.[43] As the authors acknowledge, however, there is a strong possibility that a significant self-selection process took place that biased the results in favor of a finding of reduced recidivism. In an evaluation such as this, it is not unreasonable to suspect that the use of non-equivalent comparison groups that are strongly suspected to incorporate selection biases could significantly influence the results.

The Drug Treatment Alternative-to-Prison Program

The Drug Treatment Alternative-to-Prison Program (DTAP), begun in 1990 in New York City, allows offenders to chose long-term drug rehabilitation over incarceration. As of 1996, there were four district attorneys responsible for admitting participants and thirty-nine community-based treatment providers (an increase from two in 1990). Unlike DDDT, the DTAP program is open to felony offenders in the category of "drug-addicted, nonviolent, prison-bound defendants."[44] It is aimed at "repeat felony offenders" who could face substantial mandatory prison sentences (three to six years) under New York State's Rockefeller

Drug Laws.[45] If a participant successfully completes DTAP, criminal charges are dismissed.

Most treatment takes less than a year, but DTAP can last longer. Though the final five-year evaluation of DTAP is not available at the time of writing, Trone and Young suggest the program shows high retention and low recidivism rates:

> Overall, 63 percent of those admitted to the program have graduated or remain in treatment. Of all the participants, 89 percent were still in treatment at least 3 months after admission, 75 percent stayed at least 6 months, and 63 percent stayed at least 1 year. These rates are 1½ to 4 times those reported by comparable treatment programs.
>
> Based on a review of official arrest records, researchers at the Brooklyn DTAP office have found that for 2 years after completing the program, their graduates are half as likely to be rearrested as offenders with similar records.[46]

With a follow-up from official records, Trone and Young found that DTAP graduates "are half as likely to be arrested as offenders with similar criminal records who were paroled from prison."[47]

Bodega de la Familia: A Neighborhood Drug Crisis Center

The Bodega de La Familia Neighborhood Drug Crisis Center began in 1996 in New York City. It provides outpatient drug treatment services to a caseload averaging forty-five families, both in their homes and in the community. The program uses the family case management approach (FCM) which includes the drug user's family in the treatment to help avoid isolating participants from the community. An evaluation by Siegal et al. concluded that the Bodega de la Familia has been shown to have "a positive effect on a range of outcomes, including reducing recidivism, increasing retention in treatment, reducing HIV–related risk behaviors, and reducing employment problems."[48]

Drug Courts

The first drug courts opened in New York in 1987 and in Dade County, Florida, in 1989. By 1998–99, there were almost 600 drug courts in forty-eight U.S. states, and over 90,000 people had undergone drug treatment through them.[49] The number of drug courts continues to rise.

There are two main types of drug court: Speedy Trial and Differentiated Case Management courts (DCM) and Dedicated Drug Treatment courts (DDT). The DCM drug court separates drug and non-drug cases in order to speed up the processing of cases within the court system.

The goal of the DDT, on the other hand, is to offer specialized treatment to the drug offender. In other words, the DDT court separates drug and non-drug cases to reduce future criminality among drug users. The DDT court offers the offender rehabilitative services in an attempt to curtail future criminal behavior. The treatment is offered as a diversion for deferred prosecution or a deferred prison sentence. Drug courts seek participants that are long-term drug users, among whom they attempt to deter future illicit drug use via a multifaceted program. In addition to emphasizing sobriety, many drug courts require participants to pursue a high school diploma or high school equivalency diploma (GED), to maintain employment, and to comply with financial responsibilities (including child support).

Recent evaluations have yielded mixed results. Adele Harrell evaluated a drug court in which participants were assigned to three felony dockets: day treatment, sanctions, and control. Day treatment used the most intensive (daily) supervision and involved daily drug testing. The sanctions group was tested weekly and punished with a graduated series of sanctions when testing positive on drug tests. The control group received two drug tests a week. The treatment success rate was poor, with only 41 percent participating and 19 percent graduating. The sanctions group was found to be more likely, at a statistically significant level, to be drug free than the control group; the latter averaged 4 drug test failures versus 5.3 for the former group. After one year, fewer members of the sanctions group had been arrested compared to the control group.[50]

Shaw and Robinson evaluated juvenile courts. Shaw examined a drug court in Santa Clara, California, and concluded that drug court graduates stayed sober longer, had higher levels of motivation, and were more likely to disclose any illicit drug use. Robinson evaluated a drug court in Wilmington, Delaware, and concluded that program participants were less likely to recidivate (23 percent) than both those who terminated the program (75 percent recidivism) and a control group (51 percent recidivism).[51]

Belenko reviewed thirty evaluations of twenty-four drug courts in the United States, reporting that "offender drug use and criminal behavior were substantially reduced while offenders participated in drug courts."[52] Gottfredson, Coblentz, and Harmon conducted a short-term evaluation of a Baltimore drug court, finding that "participation in the drug court was associated with a 50 percent reduction in the odds of an arrest resulting from a new offense during follow up" after 180 days.[53]

Some studies did not find drug courts to be effective. Granfield, Eby, and Brewster conducted a retrospective study of three hundred offenders who went through the Denver Drug Court. They used a control group of offenders from two years before the drug court began.

Although the Denver Drug Court reduced case processing time and "slightly reduced" pre-sentence confinement for offenders, "there was no significant difference in revocation of rearrest rates."[54] Benedict, Huff, and Corzine studied court-ordered drug treatment in 183 male property offenders who attended treatment as part of their probation. Although there was no control group, the researchers concluded that recidivism rates differed among program graduates along racial lines. According to Benedict et al., the recidivism of Caucasians was unaffected, while African American and Hispanic men were significantly less likely to recidivate (as measured by arrest rates). The lack of a control group could impose a limit upon the strength of the conclusions that can be based upon this study.[55]

Boot Camps

Boot camps have been used to deliver drug treatment programs. A National Institute of Justice study analyzed forty-five programs and found that drug treatment programs in boot camps did not reduce recidivism for drug offenses. The evaluation found that boot camp drug programs lacked a "therapeutic community approach" and "individualized treatment approaches were rare,"[56] so that drug treatment services were not adapted to the unique needs of each participant. The boot camp treatments also did not offer aftercare services. The evaluation found that, after release, criminality was high for the first three months among substance users, and then declined. This was a finding also noted by Wexler and Williams, suggesting that aftercare services may be important for at least the first three months after release, when the risk of re-offending is particularly high.[57]

Corrections-based Treatment

Treatment for illicit drug use is often delivered as part of corrections. In terms of implementation, the key advantage of corrections is that it provides a captive treatment group. Although drug treatment as part of corrections began in the late 1930s, prison budgetary measures suggest it is not widespread in the United States. The number of rigorous evaluations of impact is limited. Lipton notes that corrections offers five options: (1) no specialized services (the most typical); (2) drug education and/or drug abuse counseling; (3) residential units dedicated to drug abuse treatment; (4) client-initiated and/or client-maintained services (self-help groups); and (5) specialized services for drug abusers that are not directly targeted at the drug problems.[58]

Tunis and colleagues evaluated five corrections-based drug treatment programs:

> All programs addressed recovery from a physical, psychological, emotional, and social perspective. They offered "traditional" drug treatment services including counseling and self-help groups. Two programs (DEUCE and REACH) were primarily curriculum based, while the others relied more heavily on counseling. Only one program (SAID) did not continue drug testing as part of the treatment. Although individuals had not been randomly allocated to treatment, the evaluation matched individuals by "race, age, primary offense, and sentence length."[59]

Upon release, "17 percent of the treatment group and 23 percent of the comparison group were reconvicted at least during the 1–year follow-up period, most for property or drug crimes."[60] Persons were less likely to recidivate if they were known to use one rather than multiple drugs and if they did not prematurely leave the programs. Tunis and colleagues concluded that there was insufficient evidence to state that the treatment program was effective in reducing illicit drug use. However, inmates in the treatment programs were found to have fewer instances of behavioral problems than other inmates, although the researchers were unsure whether some self-selection bias had occurred. The primary methodological concern was that the better-behaved inmates might have chosen to undergo treatment.

Many assessments of treatment focus upon rearrest rather than on illicit drug use. Two corrections-based programs using the Therapeutic Community Model (TC) reduced recidivism among participants although levels of illicit drug use were not reported. Graduates of the two programs—New York's "Stay'n Out Program" and California's "Amity Prison TC"—had lower reincarceration rates than non-graduates. However, both evaluations measured recidivism using measures of arrest and reincarceration rates rather than illicit drug use. Hence inferences regarding the effectiveness of the therapeutic community model are limited.[61]

Wexler and Lipton stressed the importance of aftercare when presenting a summary of the Key program, a corrections-based drug treatment program in Delaware. Key also offers aftercare treatment for offenders who are released. Once released, the offender enrolls in the Crest Outreach Center for six months, living at the aftercare center for the first three months. The initial research results were:

> Although after 6 months the Crest group's progress was almost as good as the Key-Crest group's, after another year its progress had declined in comparison with that of offenders who had received the longer continuum of treatment.

> Members of the comparison and Key groups were less likely to be drug- and arrest-free at 6 and 18 months after release than the groups of offenders who received longer periods of treatment.
>
> At 18 months after release, there was no statistically significant difference between the comparison group and the Key group.[62]

In short, corrections presents a picture of mixed results. In some instances, the lower rates of recidivism may imply reductions in demand for illicit drugs. However, the dearth of methodologically sound evaluations means that conclusive evidence, particularly for specific forms of treatment and different applications, seems to be lacking.

Case Management

Treatment by case management seeks to reduce the harm associated with drug use, including both health risks and criminality. Case management differs from most other rehabilitation programs in that it is not intended to be coercive. It is directed mainly at HIV prevention and other kinds of health risks.[63]

Rhodes and Gross evaluated case management of intravenous drug users (IVUs). IVUs were selected as the target group because of their high rates of HIV infection. The evaluation was a six-month controlled experiment with nearly 1,400 arrestees from Washington D.C. and Portland, Oregon.[64] Two interventions were implemented that aimed at changing participants' behaviors: "(a) social support, including perceptions of peer norms favoring risk reduction and encouragement from others to change behavior; and (b) removal of practical barriers that might discourage behavioral change."[65] Even though the authors acknowledged the possible limitations of self-reported offending as the key outcome measure, the evaluation found that participants who received case management reported lower rates of criminal activity.

Methadone Programs

Methadone is a synthetic narcotic analgesic that is used primarily as a legal substitute for heroin. It was created in the United States in the 1960s by physicians Vincent Dole and Marie Nyswander. The treatment goal of methadone programs is to eliminate heroin use through "stabilizing" an addict on methadone. Methadone maintenance is generally intended as a long-term treatment, not a short-term detoxification procedure. As a long-term program, it involves daily dosages of a synthetic drug, leading some observers to conclude that methadone does not reduce drug dependence or use but simply replaces illegal heroin with a "legal" drug. There appears to be no clear consensus regarding the optimal duration of methadone treatment, but it is not uncommon to hear of methadone patients that have been in treatment for over ten years.[66]

Methadone programs were implemented on a large scale beginning in the 1970s. There were approximately 25,000 methadone patients in 1971.[67] By the mid–1990s it was estimated that there were 115,000 patients nationwide, 40,000 of them residing in New York State.[68]

Methadone programs have received several favorable evaluations. Methadone maintenance has been found to be an effective method of reducing heroin use, drug-related harm, and drug-related criminality. Several studies report reduced heroin use among methadone participants. The Treatment Outcome Prospective Study (TOPS) found that, after three months of treatment, fewer than 10 percent of methadone patients used heroin on a weekly basis.[69] A further study found that after two to three years on methadone, only 15 percent of participants used heroin.[70] In addition, methadone participants reported engaging in fewer crimes, because they no longer had to support a costly heroin habit.[71]

Other Maintenance Programs

One treatment that has received widespread publicity outside of the United States comprises the heroin maintenance programs adopted in Switzerland. Arguably, evaluations of these programs are some of the more sophisticated reviews of medical prescription treatment programs. They have found that, when adopted along with treatment and social support (such as assistance in finding employment), prescribing heroin may be a valuable tool in reducing many of the severe negative aspects of illicit drug use, particularly health problems and criminality.[72] Such programs could be considered to reduce illicit demand for drugs if prescribing heroin is categorized as medical treatment; medical treatment falls within the permitted legal uses of heroin as defined by the various drug control treaties of the United Nations.[73]

While heroin prescription programs may fall within the category of reducing illicit demand for drugs, they have not been adopted in the United States and will not be addressed here at length. The existence of such programs is noted primarily to draw attention to the fact that the portfolio of demand reduction programs and activities may continue to develop, adapt, and change as progress is made in research and understanding of the issues.

CONCLUSION

But what of Mexico? Clearly, drug policy and practice is and will continue to be a political minefield that lies between Mexico and the United States. Because a range of activities and expenditures take place in the United States under the general rubric of reducing illicit demand for drugs, it would be difficult for Mexico to claim that the United States is doing nothing. However, it may not be too inaccurate to say that there is little firm evidence that any of the current demand reduction efforts discussed above have had a substantial impact. In some instances, such as media campaigns which are rarely properly evaluated, the mechanism by which demand might be expected to be reduced is indirect and therefore likely to be diluted in it's impact. Some evidence is fairly clear: the available evidence suggests that some of the most prominent primary reduction efforts—notably, DARE and its derivatives—do not reduce the illicit use of drugs.

In response to criticism, the United States can claim a few instances in which the mechanism for reducing demand is clear and would be expected to be strong. Mandatory drug testing is probably the best example, and it is one that will get cheaper and easier to implement as time goes by. Legal issues relating to coercion and the freedom of the individual currently slow wider implementation of drug testing. If there were a useful and properly funded evaluation of the impact of drug testing in schools, this option could present a significant landmark in demand reduction. As of 2000, however, the United States could claim that it was at least making some effort—more than previously—to reduce demand. As a political bargaining chip, the United States could probably claim that, in relation to reducing illicit demand, it is making as much effort, or more, than Mexico has made in relation to reducing the illicit supply of drugs.

Further, the United States could claim that the demand for illicit drugs, when measured in terms of prevalence, has been reduced over the long term within the U.S. population. This same claim could not be made in relation to frequent users or, more importantly, in relation to the overall instances of illicit drug use or the volume of drugs consumed.[74] Yet such aggregate changes appear to be largely independent of the types of demand reduction efforts discussed in this chapter. The clearest evidence is that most of the demand reduction efforts discussed here are relatively new and, hence, cannot yet have produced long-term impacts. That the prevalence of illicit drug taking in the United States may have declined due to changes in law, law enforcement, sentencing, and other criminal justice practices is a question that remains to be answered definitively. However, it is possible that it will never be answered, because of weaknesses in the relevant data sets and because correlations do not prove causality.

A range of activities undertaken in the United States purport to reduce the demand for illicit drugs. Whether this is "enough" depends on how "enough" is defined and on whether magnitudes of effort and expenditure are really the relevant variables. Pushing against an immovable object is futile. Much better to go around or over to reach the objective. For drug policy, the aim should be the aim of all public policy—to maximize the overall welfare of the population efficiently and without unduly reducing the welfare of any particular group.[75] This objective is particularly important in the larger context in which drug policy takes place. It serves to remind us that efforts to reduce drug use should be developed only within the context of overall policy goals of maximizing social well-being.

Assuming that reducing drug use is an intermediate objective within the aim of maximizing overall public welfare, what does this mean in practice? It means that there may be other roads to the overall goal. There may be different intermediate objectives to pursue. Given that our analysis has suggested that demand reduction efforts are costly and of uncertain success, it may be preferable to look for more efficient intermediate goals and the strategies to achieve them.

We are left with the unenviable, though not unexpected, conclusion that the United States can claim it is making an effort to reduce the illicit demand for drugs, even if much of that effort is not particularly effective. The gas pedal is pressed to the metal and the wheels are spinning, but the car isn't moving. We would be satisfied, however, if this essay provides sufficient information as to warrant the term "preliminary review," perhaps even providing a platform for future work.

A summary of the main conclusions, given below, incorporates a mix of elements relating to different aspects of the present research.

- There is strong evidence that the United States spends substantial amounts of money, via various public and private channels, on reducing the illicit demand for drugs. The proportion of public drug control spending that is linked to demand reduction has increased over the last decade.
- There is little evidence that the bulk of money for drug demand reduction is well spent.
- In some instances—notably the in-school DARE education program and its derivatives—there is strong evidence that substantial time and money have been, and continue to be, wasted.
- Drug testing appears to be the demand reduction tactic with the strongest preventive mechanism. Drug testing, adapted for context

and application method, can produce a strong deterrence mechanism supported by a real threat of detection. Those demand reduction efforts that show indications of reduced demand often seem to be those that incorporate drug testing. As testing technologies improve and costs decline, the effectiveness of drug testing is likely to be limited only by the extent to which it can be applied in the public and private arenas.

- Evaluation research on the effectiveness of drug policy is likely to be enhanced by an emphasis on the identification and analysis of preventive mechanisms.
- Within the spectrum of demand-side drug policy in the United States, the focus on primary and secondary prevention (demand reduction)—at an implicit cost to tertiary prevention (health risk reduction)—may be to the detriment of the health and lives of the citizenry.

Notes

1. Office of National Drug Control Policy, "Reducing Drug Abuse in America," October 1997.

2. Bi-National Demand Reduction Conference, United States and Mexico High Level Contact Group: Proceedings of the United States and Mexico, Office of National Drug Control Policy, March 1998. At www.whitehousedrugpolicy.gov.

3. Bi-National Performance Measures of Effectiveness 1999, United States/Mexico, ONDCP, 1999. At http://www.whitehousedrugpolicy.gov.

4. Office of National Drug Control Policy, "1999 National Drug Control Strategy." At www.whitehousedrugpolicy.gov.

5. James Broke, "5 States Vote Medical Use of Marijuana," *New York Times*, November 5, 1998.

6. See Douglas Keh and Graham Farrell, "Trafficking Drugs in the Global Village," *Transnational Organized Crime* 3:2 (1997) for a fuller version.

7. World Health Organization, "WHO Expert Committee on Drug Dependence: Twenty-eighth Report," WHO Technical Report Series, 836 (Geneva: WHO, 1993). In relation to the decision to use this WHO definition and other aspects of the paper, Graham Farrell acknowledges a debt to work previously undertaken with Dr. Cindy Fazey.

8. William Rhodes, Raymond Hyatt, and Paul Scheiman, "Predicting Pretrial Misconduct with Drug Tests of Arrestees: Evidence from Eight Settings," *Journal of Quantitative Criminology* 12:3 (1996): 315–48.

9. ONDCP, *1999 National Drug Control Strategy* (Washington, D.C.: ONDCP, 1999).

10. Department of Justice, *Edward Byrne Memorial State and Local Law Enforcement Assistance Program*, 1999. At www.whitehousedrugpolicy.gov.

11. See U.S. Department of Health and Human Services, Substance Abuse and Mental Health Services Administration.

12. Office of National Drug Control Policy, "State and Local Spending on Drug Control Activities." Report from the National Survey of State and Local Governments, October 1993.

13. Dennis P. Rosenbaum and Gordon S. Hanson, "Assessing the Effects of School-Based Drug Education: A Six-Year Multilevel Analysis of Project D.A.R.E.," *Journal of Research in Crime and Delinquency* 35 (1998): 381–412.

14. Ray Pawson and Nick Tilley, *Realistic Evaluation* (Thousand Oaks, Calif.: Sage, 1997). A learned colleague described Pawson and Tilley's book as "Monty Python Do Cook and Campbell." His compliment captured the tone and quality but may have understated the contribution of the context-mechanism-outcome formulation.

15. ONDCP, *1999 National Drug Control Strategy*, 43.

16. Partnership for a Drug Free America Web site, www.pdfa.org.

17. David R. Buchanan and Lawrence Wallack, "This is the Partnership for a Drug-Free America: Any Questions?" *Journal of Drug Issues* 28 (1998): 329–56.

18. Ibid., 350.

19. "The National Youth Anti-Drug Media Campaign. Testing the Anti-Drug Message in 12 American Cities, Phase 1" (Report No. 1), September 1998; "Testing the Anti-Drug Message in 12 American Cities, Phase 1" (Report No. 2), March 1999. At www.mediacampaign.org/publications/index.html. Web site accessed on October 10, 1999.

20. "Investing in Our Nation's Youth: National Youth Anti-Drug Media Campaign Phase II, Final Report." At www.mediacampaign.org. Web site accessed on October 10, 1999.

21. Rosenbaum and Hanson, "Assessing the Effects of School-Based Drug Education," 381.

22. Dennis P. Rosenbaum, Robert L. Flewelling, Susan L. Bailey, Chris L. Ringwalt, and Deanna Wilkinson, "Cops in the Classroom: A Longitudinal Evaluation of Drug Abuse Education (DARE)," *Journal of Research in Crime and Delinquency* 31:3 (1994): 10.

23. Donald R. Lyman, Richard Milich, Rick Zimmerman, et al., "Project DARE: No Effects at 10–Year Follow-Up," *Journal of Consulting and Clinical Psychology* 67:4 (1999): 590–93.

24. R.R. Clayton, A.M. Cattarello, and B.M. Johnstone, "The Effectiveness of Drug Abuse Resistance Education (Project D.A.R.E.): Five-Year Follow-up Results," *Preventive Medicine* 25 (1996): 307–18; R. Dukes, J. Stein, and J. Ullman, "The Long Term Effects of Dare," *Evaluation Review* 20 (1996): 20:49–66, R. Dukes, J. Stein, and J. Ullman, "The Long Term Effects of DARE," *Evaluation Review* 21 (1997): 473–500; Matthew J. Zagumny and Michael K. Thompson, "Does D.A.R.E Work? An Evaluation in Rural Tennessee," *Journal of Alcohol and Drug Education* 42:2 (1997): 32–41; S.T. Ennett, N.S. Tobler, C.L. Ringwalt, and R.L. Flewelling, "How Effective is Drug Abuse Resistance Education? A Meta-Analysis of Project D.A.R.E. Outcome Evaluations," *American Journal of Public Health* 84 (1994):1394–1401; Donna S. Kochis, "The Effectiveness of Project DARE: Does It Work?" *Journal of Alcohol and Drug Education* 40:2 (1995): 40–

47; F. Wysong, R. Aniskiewicz, and R. Wright, "Truth in DARE," *Social Problems* 41 (1994): 448–72; and M.A. Harmon, "Reducing the Risk of Drug Involvement among Early Adolescents: An Evaluation of Drug Abuse Resistance Education (DARE)," *Evaluation Review* 17 (1993): 221–39.

25. N. Coggans and J. Watson, "Drug Education: Approaches, Effectiveness, and Delivery," *Drugs Education Prevention Policy:* 2:3 (1995): 211–24.

26. Harmon, "Reducing the Risk of Drug Involvement."

27. Robert T. Sigler and Gregory B. Talley, "Drug Abuse Resistance Education Program Effectiveness," *American Journal of Police* 14:3/4 (1995): 111–21; quote, 111.

28. Evaluation of the Illinois State Police Pilot DARE Program. AH Training and Development Systems Inc., 1987.

29. Clyde W. Dent, Steve Sussman, Michael Hennesy, Elisha R. Galaif, Alan W. Stacy, MaryAnn Moss, and Sande Craig, "Implementation and Process Evaluation of a School-Based Drug Abuse Prevention Program: Project Towards No Drug Abuse," *Journal of Drug Education* 28 (1998): 361–375; quote, 362.

30. Ibid., 363.

31. Debra R. Comer, "An Evaluation of Fitness-for-Duty Testing," presented at the Convention of the American Psychological Association, New York, August 15, 1995; E.R. Greenberg, C. Canzoneri, and T. Straker, *1994 AMA Survey on Workplace Drug Testing and Drug Abuse Policies* (New York: American Management Association, 1994); ACLU, "Drug Testing: A Bad Investment," ACLU Briefing Paper, September 1999; American Management Association, "Drug Abuse: The Workplace Issues," 1987, 13.

32. However, note that such an evaluation potentially would be open to the use of a randomized experimental design.

33. Christopher Wren, "Hair Testing by Schools Intensifies Drug Debate," *New York Times*, June 14, 1999.

34. See, for example, Rhodes, Hyatt, and Scheiman, "Predicting Pretrial Misconduct with Drug Tests of Arrestees"; Christy Visher, "Using Drug Testing to Identify High-Risk Defendants on Release: A Study in the District of Columbia," *Journal of Criminal Justice* 18:4 (1990): 321–32; Susan Turner, Joan Petersilia, and Elizabeth Piper Deschenes, "The Implementation and Effectiveness of Drug Testing in Community Supervision: Results of an Experimental Evaluation," in *Drugs and Crime: Evaluating Public Policy Initiatives*, edited by D.L. MacKenzie and C.D. Uchida (London: Sage, 1994); Steven Belenko, Drita Iona Mara, and Jerome E. McElroy, "Pre-arraignment Drug Tests in the Pretrial Release Decision: Predicting Defendant Failure to Appear," Brief Report Series (New York: New York City Criminal Justice Agency, 1992); and John S. Goldkamp and Peter R. Jones, "Pretrial Drug-Testing Experiments in Milwaukee and Prince George's County: The Context of Implementation," *Journal of Research in Crime and Delinquency* 29:4 (1992): 430–65.

35. Christy Visher and Karen McFadden, "A Comparison of Urinalysis Technologies for Drug Testing in Criminal Justice" (Washington, D.C.: National Institute of Justice, U.S. Department of Justice, 1991).

36. Thomas Mieczowski, Harvey J. Landress, and Richard Newel, "Testing Hair for Illicit Drug Use," *National Institute of Justice In Brief* (Washington, D.C.: U.S. National Institute of Justice, 1993).

37. Thomas Mieczkowski, Rosemary Mumm, and Harry F. Connick, "The Use of Hair Analysis in a Pretrial Diversion Program in New Orleans," *International Journal of Offender Therapy and Comparative Criminology* 39:3 (1995): 222–41.

38. United Nations (ECOSOC), "Principles and Practice of Primary and Secondary Prevention in Demand Reduction Programs: State of Knowledge in Primary and Secondary Prevention," Report of the Secretariat to the Commission on Narcotic Drugs at Its 39th Session, Document E/CN.7/1996/6 (UNDCP: Vienna, April 1996), 12.

39. Douglas S. Lipton, *The Effectiveness of Treatment for Drug Abusers under Criminal Justice Supervision* (Washington, D.C.: National Institute of Justice, U.S. Department of Justice, 1995), 1–65, quote, 19.

40. John Hepburn, Wayne Johnston, and Scott Rogers, *Do Drugs. Do Time: An Evaluation of the Maricopa County Demand Reduction Program* (Washington, D.C.: National Institute of Justice, U.S. Department of Justice, 1994), 19.

41. Ibid.

42. Ibid.

43. Ibid., 8.

44. Jennifer Trone and Douglas Young, *Bridging Drug Treatment and Criminal Justice* (Vera Institute of Justice, 1996), 3.

45. Ibid., 6.

46. Ibid., 43–44.

47. Ibid., 14.

48. Harvey A. Siegal, Jichuan Wang, Robert G. Carlson, et al., "Ohio's Prison-based Therapeutic Community Treatment Programs for Substance Abusers: Preliminary Analysis of Re-arrest Data," *Journal of Offender Rehabilitation* 28:3/4 (1999): 33–48; Bureau of Justice Assistance, "La Bodega de la Familia: Reaching Out to the Forgotten Victims of Substance Abuse," Bulletin citing National Center on Addiction and Substance Abuse, April 1998; La Bodega de la Familia: A Neighborhood Drug Crisis Center. At www.vera.org.

49. Timothy Egan, "Crack's Legacy: A Special Report in States' Anti-Drug Fight, A Renewal for Treatment," *New York Times*, June 10, 1999. Drug Court Clearinghouse and Technical Assistance.

50. Adele Harrell, "Drug Courts and the Role of Graduated Sanctions" (Washington, D.C.: National Institute of Justice, U.S. Department of Justice, 1998), 1–2.

51. Michelle Shaw and Kenneth Robinson, "Summary and Analysis of the First Juvenile Drug Court Evaluations: The Santa Clara County Drug Treat-

ment Court and the Delaware Juvenile Drug Court Diversion Program," *National Drug Court Institute Review* 1:1 (1998): 73–85.

52. Belenko et al., "Pre-arraignment Drug Tests in the Pretrial Release Decision."

53. Denise C. Gottfredson, Kris Coblentz, and Michele A. Harmon, "A Short-term Outcome Evaluation of the Baltimore City Drug Treatment Court Program," 1996.

54. Robert Granfield, Cynthia Eby, and Thomas Brewster, "An Examination of the Denver Drug Court: The Impact of a Treatment-oriented Drug-Offender System," *Law and Policy* 20:2 (1998): 183–202.

55. Benedict W. Reed, Lin Huff, and Jay Corzine, "'Clean Up and Go Straight': Effects of Drug Treatment on Recidivism among Felony Probationers," *American Journal of Criminal Justice* 22:2 (1998): 169–87.

56. Ernest L. Cowles, Thomas C. Castellano, and Laura A. Gransky, *"Boot Camp" Drug Treatment and Aftercare Interventions: An Evaluation Review*, 1-13. Document NCJ 155062 (Washington, D.C.: National Institute of Justice, Research in Brief, July 1995), 9.

57. Harry K. Wexler and Ronald Williams, "The Stay 'N Out Therapeutic Community: Prison Treatment for Substance Abusers," *Journal of Psychoactive Drugs* 18:3 (1986): 221–30.

58. Lipton, *The Effectiveness of Treatment for Drug Abusers under Criminal Justice Supervision."*

59. Sandra Tunis, James Austin, Mark Morris, Patricia Hardyman, and D. Bolyard, *Evaluation of Drug Treatment in Local Corrections*, 1–2 (New York: National Institute of Justice, U.S. Department of Justice), 1.

60. Ibid.

61. Lipton, *The Effectiveness of Treatment for Drug Abusers under Criminal Justice Supervision.*

62. Harry K. Wexler and Douglas S. Lipton, "From Reform to Recovery: Advances in Prison Drug Treatment," in *Sage Criminal Justice System Annuals*, edited by James A. Inciardi, vol. 27 (Newbury Park, Calif.: Sage, 1993).

63. William Rhodes and Michael Gross, "Case Management Reduces Drug Use and Criminality among Drug-involved Arrestees: An Experimental Study of an HIV Prevention Intervention," NIJ Research Report (Washington, D.C.: U.S. National Institute of Justice, 1997).

64. Ibid., 1.

65. Ibid., 2.

66. Phil Coffin, *Methadone Maintenance Treatment*, 1997. At www.lindesmith.org/library/methadone_index.html.

67. Edward M. Brecher, "The Overdose Explanation Is a Myth So Why Do Heroin Addicts Drop Dead?" *New York Times Magazine*, November 19, 1972.

68. Institute of Medicine, *Federal Regulation of Methadone Treatment* (Washington, D.C.: National Academy Press, 1995).

69. R.L. Hubbard, J.V. Rachal, S.G. Craddock, and E.R. Cavanaugh, "Treatment Outcome Prospective Study (TOPS): Client Characteristics and Behaviors Before, During, and After Treatment," in *Drug Abuse Treatment Evaluation, Strategies, Progress, and Prospects,* edited by F.M. Tims and J.P. Ludford. NIDA Research Monograph (Rockville, Md.: U.S. Department of Health and Human Services, 1984).

70. Institute of Medicine, *Federal Regulation of Methadone Treatment.*

71. Hubbard et al., "Treatment Outcome Prospective Study (TOPS)."

72. See, for example, Martin Killias and Ambros Uchtenhagen, "Does Medical Heroin Prescription Reduce Delinquency among Drug Addicts? On the Evaluation of the Swiss Heroin Prescription Project and Its Methodology," *Studies on Crime and Crime Prevention* 5:2 (1996): 245–55; Martin Killias and Juan Rabasa, "Less Crime in the Cities through Heroin Prescription?" paper presented to the International Seminar on Environmental Criminology and Crime Analysis, Oslo, Norway, June 1996; Ambros Uchtenhagen, "Summary of the Synthesis Report," in *Programme for a Medical Prescription of Narcotics: Final Report of Research Representatives,* edited by A. Uchtenhagen, F. Gutzwiller, and A. Dobler-Mikola (Zurich: Institute for Social and Preventive Medicine, University of Zurich, 1997).

73. The three key conventions are: (1) the Single Convention on Narcotic Drugs, 1961 (as amended by the 1972 Protocol amending the Single Convention on Narcotic Drugs, 1961) (New York: United Nations); (2) Convention on Psychotropic Substances 1971 (New York: United Nations); (3) United Nations Convention against Illicit Traffic in Narcotic Drugs and Psychotropic Substances, 1988 (New York: United Nations).

74. Peter Reuter, "Foreign Demand for Latin American Drugs: The USA and Europe," in *Latin America and the Multinational Drug Trade,* edited by Elizabeth Joyce and Carlos Malamud (New York: St. Martin's, 1998).

75. Moreover, of course, with due recognition of rights and preferably without making some people worse off (the move should, if possible, meet the Kaldor-Hicks criterion). The specifics of these constraints can be found in any basic public policy text. For a more extensive discussion of this argument in relation to the specifics of drug policy, see Jonathan P. Caulkins and Peter Reuter, "Setting Goals for Drug Policy: Harm Reduction or Use Reduction?" *Addiction* 92:9 (1997): 1143–50.

10

Changing Security Challenges and Mexico–U.S. Military Interaction

Graham H. Turbiville, Jr.

INTRODUCTION

As the twenty-first century begins, many military establishments around the world remain focused on redefining their missions and roles in light of post–Cold War changes in the security environment. In particular, for a number of states and regions, the increased prominence of nontraditional challenges to national security and public safety have blurred the distinction between military and law enforcement problems, complicated the process of identifying and countering threats, and raised complex questions about the proper relationships and interaction among state institutions charged with executing internal and external security responsibilities.[1] In addition, the transnational nature of many enduring and emerging threats places a premium on bilateral, regional, and international cooperation.

For the Mexican military—and for the U.S. armed forces as well—all of these factors are engendering national debates about basic military structure, roles, and relationships in multiple ways. In the United States, discussions have centered on the need for creating lighter, more readily deployable forces better able to respond to contingencies like those in the Balkans and elsewhere, while also remaining prepared to fight major regional conflicts and perform additional "operations other than war." U.S. planners have also focused increasingly on the role of the military in "Homeland Defense," which under still-developing concepts could encompass modified military roles in counter-terrorism, drug interdiction, border security, and other internal security functions supporting civil authorities.[2]

South of the U.S.–Mexico border, in a far different institutional context, the Mexican military establishment is challenged by internal security concerns that began to intensify with the January 1994 appearance of the Zapatista Army of National Liberation (EZLN) in the southern state of Chiapas. These concerns have accelerated since that time as a consequence of severe economic problems, political turbulence and assassinations, and the appearance in several southern states of new guerrilla groups—particularly the far more lethal Popular Revolutionary Army (EPR) and Insurgent People's Revolutionary Army (ERPI), which continued to inflict casualties on army and police units in Guerrero, Oaxaca, and several other states. These developments (specifically identified by the Mexican government as threats to the nation's security) have been accompanied by rising levels of street crime and criminal violence, unending revelations of endemic institutional corruption, and the increasingly effective operations of drug traffickers and other organized crime groups. In some respects, a number of these issues have become common problems for the United States and Mexico, and they have fostered closer interaction, new tensions, and an uncertain future. This chapter focuses on three of the interrelated issues that are particularly acute for the Mexican military and that echo on both sides of the border:

- The Mexican military's increased (and sustained) role in countering burgeoning organized and street crime of all types at federal, state, and local levels.
- The simultaneous restructuring and modernization of the Mexican military with U.S. and other foreign military assistance.
- U.S.–Mexico military and law enforcement interaction along the border, where enforcement organizations are coming into closer proximity than in the past.

Indeed, as the twentieth century ended, these three areas signaled key arenas of concern for the century ahead. As regards the first issue, for example, the widely heralded creation of a new Mexican Federal Preventive Police (PFP) in 1999 was overshadowed by the announcement some months later that the national police force would be assigned thousands of military police personnel from the army. This move (following four years of increased military involvement in civil law enforcement) elicited controversy, criticism, and concern from political opposition figures in Mexico, as well as other official and unofficial commentators.

Regarding the second issue, Mexico's military modernization efforts and U.S. military assistance efforts took a step backward in October 1999 when Mexico decided to return more than seventy Viet Nam–era UH–I helicopters that the United States had provided three years earlier to aid Mexican military counter-drug efforts. The helicopters, delivered with fanfare in 1996, were returned unceremoniously by truck to

U.S. territory because of their high maintenance costs and continuing mechanical problems—as well as the Mexican army's obvious disdain for this old equipment. The occasional charges that the helicopters had been used in counterinsurgency roles had also irked the Mexican military. The helicopters' return underscored the uncertainties and complexities of U.S.–Mexico military relations and cooperation, however carefully pursued.

Finally, as regards the third issue, the continuing intensity of border security problems was exacerbated in multiple ways by the hyperbole of the U.S. presidential election season. Examples include the 1999 passage of a House of Representatives bill designed to move thousands of U.S. troops to the Mexican border to help halt smuggling, illegal immigration, and terrorists; increasing vigilantism along some border areas where local ranchers and residents on the U.S. side perceived threats to life and property from increased illegal border crossers; and a call from a major U.S. presidential candidate for nearly tripling the size of the Border Patrol, making greater use of the military, and promptly decertifying Mexico and other countries if they didn't cooperate in halting drug trafficking and illegal immigration. All of these developments are illustrative of broader trends that have profound implications for the U.S.–Mexico relationship, particularly its military, law enforcement, and overall security dimensions. This chapter focuses particularly on the first two of the issues; border-related police and military topics are treated at length by José García in his chapter in this volume.

THE MEXICAN MILITARY AND LAW ENFORCEMENT

Most countries have first had to answer, and then periodically revisit, the question of what is the "proper" relationship between military forces and the civil sector. For nations with newly democratic governments—or for states whose governments and societies are threatened by external, internal, or transnational threats of one kind or another—the issue is an essential one. The fundamental questions center on the roles and relative authority of military and civilian leaders, the extent to which military forces should be involved in civil activities and how they should best undertake these responsibilities, how military forces should be trained and organized for internal roles, and to what extent military establishments could or should contribute to building political, economic, and social institutions. The answers to these questions have varied substantially from country to country, depending on the nature of the given government, society, and culture, as well as historical development factors, resource availability issues, and the internal and external security situation.

One of the most perplexing issues for affected states around the world has been the extent to which military establishments (often the most organized, resourced, and capable institutions in a country) should be used to deal with criminal activities and armed violence that have exceeded law enforcement capacities and threaten national stability. For these states, there is a sharp clash between the pressing need to act quickly and effectively, versus the multiple dangers that engaging soldiers for policing presents to society and to the military institution itself. Yet, when criminality has reached critical proportions, there are often few other available options.

The issue of using regular military forces in police roles has met with some success and, very often, with long-term failure. Within the last ten years, new states in Eastern Europe and Central Eurasia, for example, undertook a range of experiments to deal with skyrocketing crime rates. Joint army and police patrols, various forms of logistical support to law enforcement, riot control, and assistance in arms and drug interdiction have been the most common roles assigned to the military. For the most part, these efforts were not successful; for better or worse, most states in the region (including Russia) have come to focus instead on establishing a whole array of special police and paramilitary units.

There are many similar examples in the Americas. The Guatemalan army stages periodic anticrime deployments in major urban areas. El Salvador has army-police patrols (Plan Guardián) and provides military logistical support to the new and still ineffective civil police establishment. In Honduras, the army transferred its internal security functions and public security forces to civil control in late 1997 and now has a diminished direct policing role. Brazil undertook large-scale combined arms deployments in 1993 against an acute drug-trafficking and crime problem in a successful joint military and police effort called Operation Rio. And in Ecuador, the army took control of the corrupt customs establishment in an effort to reform it in 1996, although the program continues to have major corruption problems.

To generalize, then, despite some successes, the extensive use of regular military forces for what are essentially police tasks does not usually produce a highly positive outcome. Assigning policing duties to the military holds the potential for human rights abuses by poorly instructed military forces—or at least the perception of responsibility for abuses. For the civilian population, all people in uniform are considered soldiers, any armored vehicle is a tank, and any militarized presence is the army. There is a risk of spreading corruption, particularly in counter-drug operations. There may be a reduction in combat effectiveness through training disruptions. Policing duties divert military resources needed for more traditional security requirements. Tensions among military, law enforcement, and civil bodies are exacerbated. And, finally, long-term reductions in criminality levels are rarely evident; indeed, the contrary outcome is sometimes the case.

The preceding discussion frames the Mexican armed forces'—the Defense Ministry (including the army and air force) and the Ministry of the Navy (the navy and amphibious elements)—assumption of an increasingly prominent role in internal security and law enforcement. Mexico's public safety environment began to deteriorate markedly in the mid–1990s, due largely to the confluence of economic, political, and insurgency problems. Mexicans saw the rising crime rates—common crime and more serious federal offenses—as a national security problem that further threatened stability. According to the Interior Ministry, by 1996 the rate of serious crimes recorded in Mexico was about twice that in the United States. In 1997 crime rose 6.8 percent above 1996 levels. Crime rates continued to rise in 1998, with some 1.5 million crimes reported (though only 6 percent of these actually resulted in arrest warrants).[3]

Police corruption has been evident at every administrative level and in every state in Mexico. There is scarcely a single criminal enterprise—major or minor, commonplace or bizarre—in which police complicity has not been charged.[4] Police corruption takes place against the backdrop of an international perception of generalized institutional corruption. For example, the 1998 annual Transparency International survey of perceived business corruption ranked Mexico 55th out of 85 (85 being the most corrupt), and in 1997 Mexico ranked 47th out of 52 countries.[5]

Low pay and other under-resourcing, meanwhile, have hindered efforts to professionalize Mexico's police. According to Mexican statistics, less than 10 percent of reported crimes are solved. Moreover, the country's 586 general jurisdiction courts are overwhelmed by unmanageable caseloads, with the result that only 28 percent of preliminary case investigations ever come to trial.[6]

Given this situation, Mexican authorities needed to take action, but they had only limited options and resources to draw upon. In the mid–1990s, the government turned to the most readily available option to deal with out-of-control crime: the increased use of the most effective state security institution, the armed forces. This strategy took two basic forms: replacing police personnel with military officers and soldiers, and increasing the use of military units to support counter-drug and anticrime missions. The following discussion addresses the genesis of this increased military involvement and then reviews the results and examines ongoing programs.

ASSUMING POLICE LEADERSHIP

By the mid–1990s, observers asserted that six of every ten crimes in Mexico City involved policemen.[7] Although such assertions are difficult to verify, reports from Mexican citizens, foreign travelers, and active and former police officials suggest endemic police criminality—from shakedowns for minor traffic violations to participation in the most serious kinds of crime.[8] Collusion in drug trafficking, extortion, bribery, robberies, assaults, and kidnappings are among the crimes alleged—and often proved—against members of the Mexican police. In addition to eroding public confidence in a key institution, escalating police corruption and criminality raised profound questions about the ability of law enforcement in Mexico City and nationwide to meet increasing threats from criminals—ranging from pickpockets, to well-armed and internationally linked criminal groups, to insurgents.

Responding to these collective concerns, authorities began a dramatic restructuring of Mexico's Public Security Ministry (SSP) in 1996. Before restructuring, the SSP was responsible for ensuring the safety of Mexico City residents through police deployment, operational actions, and joint actions with other organizations.[9] During its restructuring, virtually every major SSP official was replaced by a military officer. Division General Enrique Tomás Salgado Cordero was appointed in June 1996 to head the restructured agency. Salgado was a highly respected army officer with extensive command experience in Guerrero and Puebla, among Mexico's poorest and most violence-ridden states. He was well versed in complex security problems and perceived to be a disciplined, capable organizer and leader.[10] General Salgado framed the early SSP changes by invoking the positive aspects of military values and seeking to allay worries about the militarization of law enforcement in the capital city.[11] His ambitious 21–point program for reforming the Federal District police called for a full review of SSP structure and personnel selection policies, training and professionalization, citizen support in the battle against crime, increased economic resources, integrity among police personnel, and adherence to legal and human rights norms.[12]

Within months, General Salgado claimed that his cleanup campaign was showing results, including disciplinary actions taken against fifteen police officers per week. He also stressed that the SSP was working closely with the Federal District's Human Rights Commission to ensure respect for human rights while the police pursued the "100 criminal bands" in the Federal District.[13] Nevertheless, crime in Mexico City climbed to historic highs in 1996, with an average of 686 crimes reported daily.[14]

Even before the assignment of military personnel to the SSP, military officers had been moved into police leadership positions around the country to counter continuing allegations of police corruption, misconduct, and criminality within the Federal Judicial Police (PJF) and the State Judicial Police (PJE).[15] For example, former navy captain Américo Javier Flores Nava was named national head of the Federal Judicial Police, and in the state of Tabasco a former army general ran the State Judicial Police.[16] By 1996, the Defense Ministry controlled judicial commands and agents in Chihuahua through military prosecutors targeted against the Juárez cartel and had substituted soldiers for law enforcement personnel in Baja California.[17] The police had been increasingly "militarized" in Tamaulipas as well with the appointment of army officers as Federal Judicial Police commanders and soldiers "on leave" as police agents.[18] In fact, police forces were actively seeking to recruit former Mexican soldiers.[19]

Simultaneous with this militarization of police forces, the Attorney General's Office (PGR) purged 737 agents from PJF organizations.[20] The mass firings in August 1996 were undertaken when many officers (including Flores Nava, the new head of the PJF) failed to meet the required "ethical profile" because of the heavy penetration of PJF ranks by drug traffickers and other criminals.[21] One PGR official indicated that about 70 percent of the PJF groups working in collusion with drug traffickers were dismantled as a result of these dismissals.[22]

Overall, by the end of 1996 there was some form of military involvement in law enforcement in most of Mexico's thirty-one states and the Federal District.[23] Nevertheless, it was far from clear that the military presence had generated permanent, positive change.[24] Moreover, the extent of the militarization of law enforcement worried many Mexican and foreign observers concerned with the potential abuse of state power, even though the corruption and inefficiency that plagued the PJF, PJE, and other police bodies pointed to the possibility of continued military support to Mexican law enforcement.

In late 1996, Jorge Madrazo Cuéllar, chairman of Mexico's National Human Rights Commission, was named as Mexico's new attorney general.[25] Pledging to clean up corruption, Madrazo signaled his intention to use military leadership in counter-drug and other law enforcement roles, and he appointed General Jesús Gutiérrez Rebollo as head of the National Institute to Combat Drugs (INCD).[26] As commander of Military Region V, Gutiérrez Rebollo, who was reputed to be a tough officer with strong personal integrity, had had extensive experience running army operations against drug traffickers in the Guadalajara area.[27] Gutiérrez had also come head to head with corrupt federal counter-drug agents in the performance of his duties in the Guadalajara area, and he appeared to have well-developed views on the problems of police corruption.[28] Regrettably, within weeks of his appointment, Gutiérrez Rebollo's reputation as a tough, honest commander was shattered when Mexican authorities arrested him in February 1997 for collaborating with Amado Carrillo Fuentes, notorious head of the Juárez cartel.[29]

In hindsight, it appears that General Gutiérrez Rebollo earned his reputation as tough on narco-traffickers from his efforts against drug traffickers—such as the Arellano Félix brothers—who were rivals of Carrillo Fuentes. His criminal involvement gave rise to immediate concern that he had compromised sensitive intelligence, including information on U.S. drug agents, and reports linked him with a wave of kidnappings and disappearances of suspected drug traffickers.[30]

The Gutiérrez Rebollo affair and other developments that reflected badly on Mexico's antidrug efforts threatened to scuttle the United States' "certification" of Mexico as a reliable partner in the war on drugs. Although certification ultimately was granted, the scandal had lasting impacts, especially within the Mexican military establishment. Even though Gutiérrez's successor as INCD chief, Mariano Federico Herrán Salvatti, passed a rigorous background check,[31] endemic corruption and inefficiencies at INCD prompted its dissolution in April 1997 and its replacement by the Office of the Special Prosecutor for Crimes against Health (FEADS), whose staff is to be better paid, trained, and vetted.[32]

Ironically, Gutiérrez Rebollo's arrest did not curtail military participation in law enforcement. Quite the contrary; soldiers continued to substitute for PJF and INCD agents in Chihuahua and Baja California. By February 1997, at least ninety-five military personnel were assigned to law enforcement duties in these two states. Clearly, the major casualty of the Gutiérrez Rebollo debacle was the belief that Mexico's military establishment was somehow protected from the drug corruption that has undermined military and police establishments throughout the world.

THE ARMED FORCES VERSUS DRUGS AND CRIME

The involvement of Mexican military units in counter-drug operations (both interdiction and eradication) is not new. Army and police collaboration against narco-trafficking gained momentum during the administration of José López Portillo (1976-1982), developed into a "systematic campaign" during the terms of Miguel de la Madrid (1982-1988) and Carlos Salinas de Gortari (1988–1994), and intensified further under Ernesto Zedillo (1994–2000).[33] Mexican and U.S. commentators assert that the increasing involvement of Mexican military units in counter-drug operations was a direct consequence of U.S. pressure to "confront drug trafficking as if it were a foreign invasion."[34] Clearly, though, Mexican law enforcement's futile efforts to counter the country's increasingly powerful and violent drug-trafficking organizations have also provoked domestic demand for more support for the nation's police. President Zedillo's October 1996 statement that the drug trade had become the biggest threat to Mexican national security underscored this concern.[35]

Responding, then, to both external and internal pressures, Mexico's military forces became more directly active and visible in counter-drug and other anticrime activities. Despite legislative challenges to the assignment of military forces to these roles, the Mexican Supreme Court determined in March 1996 that "the army, air force, and navy may intervene in public security matters as long as civilian authorities, including the government itself, request it."[36] Because there is often no clear distinction between drug traffickers, arms traffickers, other heavily armed criminal groups, and insurgents, military support to law enforcement has been directed against a variety of targets. This has prompted human rights advocates and political activists to allege that these counter-drug missions have been used to cover crackdowns in Chiapas, Guerrero, Oaxaca, and other areas.

With this background, then, there are numerous illustrations of the military's increased role in combating drugs and crime in the mid–1990s:

- Elite U.S.–trained GAFE elements—intended primarily for counter-drug operations in the field—were assigned to provide general security at Mexico City's Benito Juárez International Airport in spring 1997.[37]
- The Mexican army supported PGR raids in Tijuana in March 1996 aimed at arresting members of the Arellano Félix brothers' drug-trafficking organization. In one phase, some 500 armor-mounted army troops wearing ski masks established roadblocks and checkpoints, searched vehicles, and aided PGR agents in searching residential areas.[38]
- A Mexican navy helicopter, after being fired upon by two drug-trafficking vessels off Carmen Island, Baja California Sur, in March 1996, sank one boat with return fire and captured four drug traffickers.[39]
- In January 1997, two army brigadiers general were assigned to take over the administration of airports in Toluca and Cuernavaca, following the discovery that, under the previous airport directors, these airports had been used by Juárez drug cartel chief Amado Carrillo Fuentes.[40]

The military's growing role in law enforcement was accompanied by increasing evidence of extensive corruption within the military establishment. By August 1997, thirty-four military officers had been arrested for collaborating with drug criminals. The publication of Mexican military intelligence documents in the weekly news magazine *Proceso* suggested that military corruption went even deeper.[41] Following the *Proceso* report and other revelations, the defense minister forbade military contacts with the press, and officers accused of leaking documents were arrested.[42]

TOWARD THE NEW CENTURY

Even though programs to involve the military in a range of law enforcement roles had produced equivocal results by the end of the 1990s, it was decided that some of these efforts would continue. After removing many corrupt police officers from the SSP, General Salgado instituted a community-wide bicycle police program that won some citizen support. But his policy of conducting large police raids in poor, crime-ridden neighborhoods was strongly criticized, as was the use of 2,600 army troops to supplement the SSP's 36,000 preventive police.

Specifically, beginning in March 1997, the first of what eventually totaled over 2,500 Mexican soldiers were deployed as street patrols in Iztapalapa, an area of Mexico City with approximately 1.4 million residents. Troops were to rotate every few months across all neighborhoods of Mexico City. SSP chief Salgado felt that this measure would allow regular police to participate in broad professionalization programs without compromising the security of the city's residents.[43] Yet crime continued to rise in the Federal District. The murder of three youths by police in late 1997 in a Mexico City neighborhood tarnished both the military's role and Salgado's leadership.

When Cuauhtémoc Cárdenas became mayor of Mexico City in December 1997, he replaced Salgado with a civilian (former army officer Rodolfo Debernardi) and pledged to remove the military from the SSP.[44] However well intentioned Salgado may have been, his deployment of the military failed to reduce corruption or crime in the city and ended in scandal. When Debernardi resigned under fire in the summer of 1998, Cárdenas appointed former prosecutor and law professor Alejandro Gertz Manero, whose last law enforcement experience was in the 1970s. By February 1999, Gertz was expressing his frustration in bringing "order" to the SSP, his disappointment that some 650 crimes were reported daily, and his dismay that the SSP had the "lowest productivity rate in the world."[45]

Despite revelations of military corruption and enduring charges of militarization, the military's participation in counter-drug and anticrime operations has produced some positive results. Nevertheless, some within the military itself remain critical of increasing military support to law enforcement. For example, army, air force, and navy spokesmen have pointed to the perils of direct military engagement with drug traffickers, including the well-founded danger of corruption if soldiers involved in front-line police work are exposed to the corrosive effects of drug money.[46] Evidence of endemic police corruption stands as a daily reminder to military personnel of how easily drug corruption can penetrate the highest institutional levels, undermining institutional legitimacy. The military has, nevertheless, moved forward to carry out their broader range of tasks, even as they remain cognizant of the dangers they face. Military involvement in drug interdiction, eradication of marijuana and poppy crops, patrols and sweeps, and intelligence gathering seems likely to continue.

In December 1998 the Mexican Senate passed legislation that called for the creation of the Federal Preventive Police (PFP), a national law-enforcement body that combines the Federal Highway Police (Policía Federal de Caminos), the Federal Fiscal Police (Policía Fiscal Federal), and the Federal Immigration Police (Policía Migratoria Federal).[47] Initial criticism of the legislative proposal (mostly from the Party of the Democratic Revolution, PRD) focused on fears that such a politically motivated national police could be used to intimidate the political opposition and to collect political intelligence. This worry soon gave way to a new concern, however, when it was announced that the PFP would be reinforced by the 4,899 soldiers, 1,862 weapons, 352 vehicles, and 99 dogs of the Third Military Police Brigade—the same unit that General Salgado had used to carry out patrols in Mexico City neighborhoods.[48]

These developments elicited the expected criticisms and denunciations, but none had any impact on the PFP's implementation. Of continuing interest, however, are the suggestions that Mexico needs a force to bridge the gap between its police and military forces. As early as September 1996, a group of National Action Party (PAN) senators proposed that a "national guard" be raised to deal with instability and violence.[49] In September 1999, the PAN president of the Senate Defense Commission, Norberto Corella Gil Samaniego, indicated that the PAN would present an initiative to remove the armed forces from that spectrum of missions that were not strictly military, including "health projects, education, municipal patrolling, and antidrug efforts, among others." Rather, responsibility in these areas would rest with the appropriate agencies and organizations, and law enforcement duties would fall to a national guard.[50] This proposal went nowhere, however, and President Vicente Fox (2000–2006), a member of the PAN, has continued to rely on military forces in police roles in the early months of his presidency.

Beyond the PFP initiative, a look at the overall level of Mexican military involvement in law enforcement is instructive. One laudable effort to quantify the military's involvement was made by *La Jornada* in mid–1999. According to the author of the *La Jornada* article, the Mexican military was involved in major ways in at least twenty-eight states and the Federal District.[51]

These developments regarding the Mexican military affected the United States in two major ways. On the one hand, the United States (and other foreign militaries) began to play a more active role in providing military assistance to Mexico in the form of equipment and training for counter-drug activities. Second, Mexican military activity against drug traffickers and other criminals began to be far more visible along the U.S. border with Mexico. This added a new dimension to border security as military establishments on both sides undertook roles that generated controversy and raised questions about future border security approaches.

MEXICAN MILITARY MODERNIZATION AND U.S. SECURITY ASSISTANCE

The few distinguished U.S. scholars who have studied the history and recent development of the Mexican military have all remarked on the difficulty of assessing an organization that so strongly protects itself from outside scrutiny.[52] John Cope has provided an excellent history of U.S.–Mexico military relations, especially U.S. efforts from the late 1980s to 1995 that were intended to build a stronger relationship through various liaison venues and carefully instituted military assistance programs.[53] Cope pointed out that by 1995 the efforts of Army Chief of Staff General Gordon Sullivan and others had resulted in warmer, but still cautious, military ties in several areas, and far more robust projections for International Military Education and Training (IMET) fund grants and limited military sales.[54]

U.S. Secretary of Defense William Perry's visit to Mexico in October 1995 signaled an uptick in U.S. security assistance programs. His visit was widely publicized in Mexico, including through re-broadcasts of a speech in which he thanked the Mexican military for its counter-drug successes, noted ongoing military education and training efforts, and pointed to U.S.–sponsored military modernization plans that would help Mexico protect its air and sea sovereignty. Perry met with Mexican Defense Secretary General Enrique Cervantes and with President

Zedillo to discuss disaster relief, drug trafficking, naval sovereignty, and the "implementation of an equipment-updating program."[55]

Equipment and training provided by the U.S. military following the Perry meeting were strongly supportive of the Defense Ministry's "Mexican Army and Air Force Development Plan,"[56] which included territorial and command reorganizations and training improvements, and especially emphasized special forces, mobility, communications, and intelligence.[57] Mexico's goals were to meet multiple military challenges, including the insurgencies in southern Mexico as well as counter-drug efforts, disaster relief, and humanitarian assistance. Although the number of Mexican soldiers trained and the amount of equipment provided is not precisely known, a few examples illustrate the nature and scale of the programs and the continuing bumps in the path of U.S.–Mexico military relations.

U.S. military sales to Mexico have included equipment ranging from night vision devices to body armor to Humvees. One of the most publicized U.S. military assistance efforts was the 1996 decision, discussed earlier, to send seventy-three Viet Nam–era UH–1 helicopters to Mexico for counter-drug operations. Although public spokespersons on both sides of the border lauded the effort, Mexican generals privately expressed disdain for the outdated equipment. The equipment transfer also encountered opposition in the U.S. Congress because of the potential to use these aircraft in counter-insurgency operations.[58] Although these political obstacles were overcome and the transfer was completed, the refurbished aircraft had continual maintenance problems and proved to be of limited usefulness.[59] In early October 1999, all but one (one had crashed) were returned unceremoniously to the United States.[60]

At the same time, Mexico's armed forces were expanding in response to domestic insurgencies and the military's growing counter-drug and law enforcement roles. According to Mexican sources, by late 1996 Defense Ministry forces had increased by 34 percent to 237,500 troops.[61] Training in the United States for Mexican military personnel grew substantially; about 2,100 personnel from all Mexican services reportedly trained at seventeen different U.S. military installations between 1996 and1998.[62] Mexico was the top Latin American beneficiary of US IMET programs during 1996 (US$1,000,000), 1997 ($1,008,000), and 1998 ($921,000). (Totals for 1999 and 2000 are estimated at about $1,000,000.)[63] The U.S. Department of State's Congressional Presentation for Foreign Operations offered the following goals for the fiscal year 1999 program:

> FY 1999 IMET funding for Mexico will provide professional and military training in areas of mutual concern, including

> strengthening military command, professionalizing the Mexican military, increasing technical capabilities, teaching English language and resource management skills, and providing instruction in the protection of human rights. Education and training provided by the U.S. will foster a greater sense of common purpose and interests with the U.S. among Mexican trainees. This training and education should also promote a greater willingness to cooperate with U.S. counterparts and establish more common operational assumptions and procedures. An important element of strategy will be to encourage U.S.–Mexico high-level civilian defense and military-to-military contacts, as well as greater Mexican defense cooperation within the hemisphere.[64]

As part of its military expansion, Mexico began to form a number of special operations forces, including the company-size GAFE units reportedly deployed in most Mexican states (there were four in Chiapas, three in Guerrero, and two each in Oaxaca, Puebla, Tabasco, and Veracruz).[65] According to U.S. and Mexican reports, personnel for these units received U.S. training in both the United States and Mexico. Between 1996 and 1998, more than 430 GAFE personnel received training in the United States in air assault, drug interdiction, and human rights.[66] In a further expansion of special forces–type units, the Defense Ministry announced in summer 1999 that it was forming thirty-six Special Forces Amphibious Groups (GANFES) for counter-drug operations. These marine counterparts to the GAFES will presumably carry out riverine and coastal operations.[67]

The performance of GAFE and other units has been disappointing. GAFE personnel have been implicated in torture and illegal detentions, and reportedly they have been allocated for roles other than those for which they were trained. This was the case for the above-mentioned assignment of GAFE elements to Mexico City's International Airport, a group subsequently charged with smuggling illegal drugs and undocumented immigrants.[68] In any event, despite training and careful vetting of candidates for elite units like GAFE and other forces, corruption continues, frustrating both Mexican and U.S. officials.

Continuing U.S.–Mexico military cooperation will remain a delicate undertaking. Since the mid–1990s, several incidents have added tension to the relationship. One was the (erroneous) March 1996 announcement by then secretary of defense William Perry that U.S.–Mexican ground and naval exercises were planned for the near future. Perry's remarks evoked quick denials from the Mexican minister of foreign relations and heated words from many Mexican commentators. Mexico's Ministry of Foreign Relations made it clear that U.S.–Mexico military cooperation was confined to "the modernization of equipment, training courses, and the academic exchange of officers," as well as cooperation in "the fight against drug trafficking and assistance in facing natural disasters."[69] This defined in sharp terms Mexico's view of the limits of the bilateral military relationship.

Similarly, Mexico holds enduring memories of past U.S. violations of its sovereignty. Former defense secretary Caspar Weinberger's *The Next War*, published in 1996, envisioned the impending election of a narco-government in Mexico, mass flows of refugees into the United States, and acts of terror in major cities of the U.S. Southwest—followed by a U.S. ground and amphibious invasion of Mexico in 2003. This and the other scenarios contained in the book were presented as based on actual "Pentagon war games," further raising concerns among long-suspicious Mexicans.[70]

The United States' certification of states cooperating in the struggle against drug trafficking has been a yearly trial for the Mexican government, which views the process as an insulting and unjustified intrusion into Mexico's internal affairs. Nevertheless, given certification's importance for bilateral relations, it is not uncommon for Mexico to make new counter-drug and enforcement initiatives just prior to the certification decision. But the impact of such initiatives is often undercut by continuing revelations of high-level corruption in Mexico. One such case that outraged the Mexican government was the recent Operation Casablanca, a money-laundering scheme aimed at Mexican banks and bankers that resulted in widely published (though unproven) allegations of corruption against General Cervantes himself.[71] Such developments remain a constant threat to the bilateral relationship.[72]

CONCLUSION

By all indications, the Mexican military is continuing to grow and modernize. The changing nature of Mexican military training, deployment, and operations is evident in the country's interior as well as along the U.S.–Mexico border, where a complex mix of military and law enforcement issues portends an important time for decision making. The Mexican military's continuing role in law enforcement, the evolving scope and pace of U.S.–Mexico military interaction, and the associated border security developments will all have profound impacts on U.S.–Mexican relations overall and also on important national security and public safety issues for both countries.

The stepped-up use of military forces to augment Mexico's police has not generated a record that inspires confidence—and in many respects seems doomed to fail regardless of the military's level of dedication. Overall crime rates remain high, and some kinds of crime are rising substantially. The military's more visible involvement in law enforcement has damaged its reputation and distracted it from its central duties and professionalization efforts. Corruption has not diminished; it is institutionalized in the police and has become far more evident in the military, where dozens of officers have been arrested in recent years for criminal acts and criminal collusion. Whether corruption is actually increasing in the military or has just become more visible is not yet clear.

The only good option at this point would seem to be a serious, sustained police reform. According to a former army officer, "If military officers are bad and lawyers are worse, the police are members of the Brotherhood [of institutionalized corruption]."[73] Many well-conceived and innovative plans have been advanced for dealing with police and judicial reform in Mexico. Yet the question remains whether the country has the political will, resources, and capability to implement them.

Vicente Fox's July 2000 election as president of Mexico offered potential new ground for profound change in Mexico's military and law enforcement establishments as new leaders formulate programs to deal with enduring and evolving security problems. Early on, Fox stated his intention to reduce the militarization of law enforcement by withdrawing institutional armed forces from policing duties and removing thousands of officers and men from temporary assignment to law enforcement duties, especially with federal and state police forces. Yet even before taking office he acknowledged that, because Mexico's public safety and national security requirements greatly exceeded the capabilities of corrupt and inefficient law enforcement agencies, this was not a prospect for early execution. Instead, Fox has adopted a gradual approach in which the Mexican military continues to play a major law enforcement role while police forces are being professionalized.

In the meantime, Fox is fostering close cooperation among the military, the Attorney General's Office, and the newly created Public Security Ministry. The new ministry has nationwide responsibilities and is headed by Alejandro Gertz Manero, previously Mexico City's chief law enforcement officer. Within this new organization—also designated SSP, like Gertz Manero's earlier command—Gertz controls a formally institutionalized PFP that will target major drug-trafficking and organized crime areas along the U.S.–Mexico border and other key areas of Mexico, working in tandem with the PGR, the military, and other security and law enforcement organizations. Fox and his military and law enforcement teams appear to be addressing Mexican and U.S. security problems with energy and realism and stressing Mexican solutions, recognizing that approaches may have to change fundamentally in order to be effective.

U.S.–Mexico military interaction and border security are influenced by widely differing perspectives within and between countries. Deciding on the proper approaches and balance in unilateral and bilateral cooperative efforts is challenging, but even more difficult is the task of translating good intentions into real, positive results. As the United States and Mexico address issues of future military cooperation and joint security, it is evident that their efforts will benefit from closer communications and measured, realistic cooperation among law enforcement and the military. Existing venues of exchange range from the government's highest policy-making levels to informal, periodic coordination between counterparts in the field.[74] High Level Contact Group meetings, for example, deal with bilateral policy issues such as drug control and arms trafficking.[75] Annual U.S.–Mexico military border commanders' conferences bring together the senior leadership of both militaries to address major issues that affect their respective military establishments, although there seems to be only limited interaction at the level of field operations.[76] International Military Education and Training programs offer a valuable opportunity to bring Mexican officers into U.S. military-educational academic venues. And the attendance of U.S. military personnel at Mexican military institutions has been instructive and useful as well.

High levels of corruption in Mexican law enforcement continue to hinder the further strengthening of U.S.–Mexican working relationships. Nevertheless, the various bilateral border task forces in principal border cities (which bring together federal antidrug judicial police, agents of the Public Ministry, and personnel from the Drug Enforcement Administration [DEA], Federal Bureau of Investigation [FBI], and U.S. Customs) represent a point of departure.[77] Some law enforcement training and information exchanges are contributing to Mexican police professionalism as well, and informal cross-border coordination efforts are also valuable points of interaction.

Overall, the U.S.–Mexico security relationship will remain an important (and perhaps crucial) focus of U.S. strategic planning, unilateral law enforcement–military actions, and cross-border law enforcement and military cooperation. For the present, the many complex issues associated with U.S.–Mexico security relations raise a special challenge to law enforcement and supporting military resources on both sides of the border, whose successes or failures will play a central role in Mexican and regional stability.

Notes

1. Notably, challenges that transcend national and regional borders (and typically center on non-state participants and causes) include: international

organized crime in its many dimensions, particularly the drug trade; black-market and gray-market weapons trafficking; unprecedented legal, illegal, and conflict-associated population shifts, including organized alien smuggling; evolving terrorist organizations and agendas; ongoing and potential ethnic and religious conflict; epidemic health problems, famine, and serious environmental degradation; and the trade in materials and technologies associated with weapons of mass destruction. Some of these issues have obvious military content, while in others the role of the armed forces is less clear.

2. See, for example, Roberto Suro and Bradley Graham, "Army Plans Lighter, More Mobile Forces," *Washington Post*, October 8, 1999; Lt. Col. Joseph L. Robinson, LCDR Carl R. Graham, and Maj. Jeffery R. Oeser, "Homeland Defense: The American Challenge for the 21st Century," *A Common Perspective: USACOM Joint Warfighting Center's Newsletter*, April 1999, 6–11; Richard J. Rinaldo, "Saving Citizen Ryan: U.S. Military Support to Homeland Defense," *A Common Perspective: USACOM Joint Warfighting Center's Newsletter*, April 1999, 6–11; and U.S. Army Training and Doctrine Command (Joint and Army Doctrine Directorate), *White Paper: Supporting Homeland Defense* (Ft. Monroe, Virginia, April 22, 1999).

3. "A Broader and More Efficient Fight against Impunity, Insecurity and Drug Trafficking" (Mexican Embassy, Washington, D.C., Fall 1999). At www.world.presidencia.gob.mx/pages/library/english_wp/drugs.html; and paper by Interior Minister Francisco Labastida Ochoa at the Economist Panel Discussion on Mexico, Mexico City, March 31, 1998, received via Internet.

4. Among unusual charges are allegations that federal and/or state police personnel in Oaxaca protect poachers who have stolen hundreds of thousands of endangered Olive Ridley sea turtle eggs from the state's ecologically sensitive Pacific beaches. The eggs are sold on the black market for their presumed aphrodisiac qualities. "Mexico Police Charged with Turtle Poaching," United Press International report, October 18, 1996, received via Internet.

5. In 1998 Mexico was tied for 55th place with Ghana, the Philippines, and Senegal. By 2001, the annual Transparency International survey ranked Mexico 51 out of 91 countries (tied with Panama and the Slovak Republic), for at least a perceived marginal improvement. The 2000 rating for Mexico was 59 out of 90 states, and the 1999 ranking was 58 out of 99. See the Internet Center for Corruption Research at www.gwdg.de/~uwvw/icr.htm, for ratings that reflect the perceptions of businesspeople, risk analysts, and the general public. Mexico's score in 2001 was 3.7; the highest score for the least corrupt was 9.9 (Finland) and the lowest 0.4 (Bangladesh). The United States—in the 16th ranking—scored a none-too-lustrous 7.6.

6. Labastida Ochoa presentation at the Economist Panel Discussion on Mexico.

7. "Human Rights Atrocities in Mexico," *MEXPAZ Bulletin: Human Rights* 96 (October 22–29, 1996), received via Internet.

8. See Sam Dillon, "Line between Police and Criminals Continues to Blur," New York Times News Service, September 3, 1996, received via Internet.

9. Alfredo Joyner, "Military Officials to Head Security Secretariat," *Reforma,* June 14, 1996, as translated in FBIS-LAT-96-117, 15; and Raúl Monge, "Duros, pero igualmente ineficientes, los militares jefes de policía capitalina," *Proceso* 1024 (June 17, 1996).

10. Other army officers replaced police as directors of Operational Control, Groups, Preventive Actions, the Grenadiers, Task Force "Zorro" (a counter-terrorist unit), the Banking and Industrial Police (the "Jaguares"), Women's Group, Mounted Patrols, Motorcycle Patrolmen, the Special Unit, the Auxiliary Police, and so on. Joyner, "Military Officials to Head Security Secretariat," and Raúl Monge, "En 12 años la policía capitalina ha creado casi una decena de grupos élites," *Proceso* 1000 (January 1, 1996): 10–11.

11. Salgado noted: "We intend to work so Mexico City residents will trust their police once again. We intend to do this by transforming the police into a more professional body, strengthening its ethical values, which does not mean it is going to be militarized. We intend to buttress the force based on the same principles that have shaped us as military men." See Miriam Posada García, "Niega la SSP que haya una militarización del cuerpo policiaco," *La Jornada,* June 10, 1996.

12. "24 Hours newscast," XEW Television Network, 0300 GMT, July 12, 1996, as translated in FBIS-LAT-96-135, 10.

13. Miriam Posada García, "La SSP no puede violentar su quehacer," *La Jornada,* September 25, 1996, received via Internet.

14. *El Financiero,* August 5, 1997, as reported in *Mexico Update* 134 (August 6, 1997).

15. Alejandro Gutiérrez, "Ex-Military Replace PGR Antidrug Forces," *Proceso* 1001 (January 8, 1996): 18–19, as translated in FBIS-TDD-96-009-L.

16. "New Police Officials Taken from the Army," *Mexico Report* 5:12 (June 24, 1996), received via Internet; and Dudley Althaus, "Greater Military Presence Crosses Political Lines," *Houston Chronicle,* July 29, 1996, received via Internet.

17. Concha, "Militarización," and, for subsequent developments, Jorge Alberto Cornejo, Alejandro Romero, and Martín Sánchez, "Más relevos militares a la PJF y al INCD en BC y Chihuahua," *La Jornada,* February 21, 1997.

18. Concha, "Militarización," and Melitón García and Miguel Domínguez, "Soldiers Replace Police in Tamaulipas," *Reforma,* March 5, 1997, as translated in FBIS-LAT-97-048.

19. See William V. Wilkenson and Enrique Malagón, "Mexico: Structure, Training, and Education in Policing," *CJ (Criminal Justice): The Americas Online,* 1994, 5–6, received via Internet.

20. The PGR itself has long been accused of corruption. The most notorious recent example is that of former Mexican deputy attorney general Mario Ruiz Massieu, who allegedly smuggled millions of drug dollars to U.S. banks before fleeing Mexico. U.S. officials froze his U.S. deposits and sought permanent possession of them. Mexico sought Massieu's extradition. See Sam Dillon, "Concerning Mexican Aide's Millions, U.S. Charges Drug Link," New York Times News Service, November 12, 1996.

21. Norma Jiménez and Xochitl Maldonado, "Mexico: Attorney General Lozano Views Complete Revamping of PJF," *Reforma*, August 20, 1996, as translated in FBIS-LAT-96-165; "Mexico Attorney General Fires More than 700 Police," Reuter, August 16, 1996, received via Internet; and "Mexico: Attorney General Reports Federal Judicial Agents Dismissals," NOTIMEX, 2353 GMT, August 16, 1996, as translated in FBIS-TDD-96-026-L, received via Internet.

22. Jiménez and Maldonado, "Mexico: Attorney General Lozano."

23. Gregory Gross, "Mexican Army Takes Command of War on Crime," *San Diego Union-Tribune*, December 5, 1996, received via Internet. One estimate asserted that twenty-nine of thirty-one Mexican states had military involvement in some type of law enforcement.

24. For example, in Chihuahua (Mexico's largest state and a major staging area for drugs entering the United States), a pilot program to replace PJF officers with ex-military personnel or soldiers placed "on leave" was begun in late 1995. The program was conducted under the joint auspices of Mexico's Attorney General's Office and Defense Ministry. A former lieutenant colonel and head of the Military Judicial Police took over as deputy commissioner of the Chihuahua field office of the PJF, while 120 former soldiers moved into PJF ranks. It was hoped that the "integrity and discipline" of the former soldiers could reshape the PJF, break the alleged links between police and drug traffickers, and generally clean up PJF operations. The pilot program was accompanied by a number of announced army redeployments in the state aimed at interdicting drug and arms traffickers. Although the army has conducted counter-drug operations for many years, their role in Chihuahua became much more prominent. The program was halted temporarily in September 1996, when military members were withdrawn and reassigned to deal with the EPR. At that time, participating personnel pointed to successes in drug and weapons seizures, substantial numbers of arrests, ten months of strong pressure applied to the Juárez drug cartel, and momentum for continued military-police cooperation. Nevertheless, the Juárez cartel remained intact and effective. See Alejandro Gutiérrez, "La militarización en Chihuahua no dio resultados: el grupo conjunto de la Defensa y la PGR se disolvió poder desinteger al Cártel de Juárez," *Proceso* 1038 (September 22, 1996): 26–27.

25. Lozano was removed from his post by President Zedillo on December 2, 1996, presumably because of his office's failure to solve the murders of two leading political figures (presidential candidate Luis Donaldo Colosio and PRI secretary general José Francisco Ruiz Massieu).

26. "Mexico's New Top Lawman Promises to Clean House," Associated Press Report, December 4, 1996, received via Internet.

27. Retired General Barry McCaffrey, former commander-in-chief of U.S. Southern Command and at the time the director of the Office of National Drug Control Policy (ONDCP), described General Gutiérrez Rebollo as "an extremely forceful and focused commander." Carolyn Skorneck, Associated Press Report, December 6, 1996, received via Internet.

28. When Gutiérrez Rebollo's troops participated in the 1994 arrest of drug trafficker Luis Héctor Palma Salazar, the drug traffickers' reportedly had seven federal drug agents serving as his bodyguards. Ibid.

29. For a good review that appeared among the many articles that followed in the wake of the general's arrest, see Agustín Ambriz, "Informe militar sobre el general Gutiérrez Rebollo: otros oficiales del Ejército, agentes y comandantes del INCD y de la PGR, cómplices de Amado Carrillo," *Proceso* 1060 (February 23, 1997): 7, 11–12. Also see other associated pieces appearing in the same issue.

The investigation of Gutiérrez Rebollo ultimately led to new allegations against the former INCD chief and the arrest in March 1997 of Brigadiers General Alfredo Navarro Lara and Arturo Cardona Pérez for their involvement with Gutiérrez and Carrillo Fuentes. Mark Fineman, "2nd Mexican General Arrested on Drug Charges," *Washington Post,* March 19, 1997; Gerardo Rico and Antonio González Vázquez, "House Arrest Ordered for General Cardona," *La Jornada,* March 22, 1997, as translated in FBIS-LAT-97-057.

30. Steve Fainaru, "Drug War in Mexico Put at Risk: Trafficker May Have Seen Files," *Boston Globe,* February 23, 1997, received via Internet; Julia Preston, "Drug Connection Links Mexican Military to Spate of Abductions," *New York Times,* March 9, 1997.

31. Mark Stevenson, "Mexico Names New Head of Drug Control Institute," Associated Press report, 10 March 1997. Received via Internet.

32. Tracey Eaton, "Mexico's Attorney General Replaces Old Drug Agency," *Dallas Morning News,* April 31, 1997.

33. For a good treatment of Mexico's counter-drug efforts, see María Celia Toro, *Mexico's "War" on Drugs: Causes and Consequences, Studies on the Impact of the Illegal Drug Trade* (Boulder, Colo.: Lynne Rienner, 1995).

34. Eduardo R. Huchim, "Narcotráfico: la corrupción militar," *La Jornada,* April 8, 1996.

35. Molly Moore and John Ward Anderson, "Drug Trade Called Greatest Threat to Mexico," *Washington Post,* October 23, 1996.

36. Edgar Muñoz, "Night Monitor" program, Mexico City *Radio Red,* 0000 GMT, March 20, 1996, as translated in FBIS-LAT-96-058, received via Internet. It was reported also that one of the articles of the Constitution would be revised to better reflect what the military was legally permitted to undertake in supporting civil authorities.

37. Douglas Farah and Molly Moore, "Elite Anti-Drug Troops Investigated in Mexico," *Washington Post,* September 9, 1999.

38. Rocío Galván, "Army, PGR Raid Tijuana Cartel Properties," *Excélsior,* March 2, 1996, as translated in FBIS-TDD-96-012-L, received via Internet; Martín Espinosa, "Night Monitor" newscast, Mexico City *Radio Red,* March 6, 1996, as translated in FBIS-LAT-96-047.

39. Mexico City XEW Television Network, 0400 GMT, March 20, 1996.

40. "Mexican General Named to Head Two Airports," Reuter Report, January 25, 1997, received via Internet.

41. Carlos Marín, "Documentos de inteligencia militar involucran en el narcotráfico a altos jefes, oficiales y tropas del Ejército," *Proceso* 1082 (June 27, 1997): 6–15.

42. "Military Bans Contact with Press," Associated Press, August 21, 1997.

43. Miriam Posada García, "Propone la SSP remplazar con soldados a 2 mil 598 policías para vigilar las calles," *La Jornada*, February 28, 1997; Raúl Llanos Samaniego, "Confusión entre los militares-policías," *La Jornada*, March 2, 1997; Paige Bierma, "Shape Up and Stop Taking Bribes! Mexican Police Get Some Basic Training," Associated Press report, March 8, 1997, received via Internet.

44. Gerardo Jiménez, "Comienzan a verse resultados en seguridad," *Reforma*, March 13, 1998.

45. *Reforma*, February 26, 1999, translated in FBIS FTS 19990226001575, received via Internet.

Other instances of military personnel assigned to police have also proved disappointing. In May 1998, for example, members of the attorney general's supposedly elite anti-kidnapping unit in Ciudad Juárez were arrested and charged with participating in a kidnapping.

46. For the navy's view, see Jesús Aranda, "Sería desleal no usar a la Marina contra el narco: Lorenzo Franco," *La Jornada*, March 18, 1996.

47. Jorge Camargo, "Senate Approves PFP Legislation," *Reforma*, December 12, 1998, as translated in FBIS FTS 19981215001392. The PFP is discussed at length by Ernesto López Portillo Vargas in this volume.

48. "Riesgos de militarizar las policías," *La Jornada*, July 9, 1999. In addition, a "special forces group" of unspecified origin was added to the PFP. Jesús Aranda, "La Sedena apoyará a la Policía Federal Preventiva," *La Jornada*, July 8, 1999.

The soldiers of the Third Brigade were to be on a leave of absence during their tenure with the PFP, with no timeline given for the duration of these duties. "Terms of Sedena, PFP Transfer Cited," *Reforma*, July 16, 1999, as translated in FBIS 19990716001702.

49. Ismael Romero, "Guardia Nacional, propone el PAN," *La Jornada*, September 18, 1996.

50. Olga Valenzuela, "The PAN Suggests that Federal Departments Should Fulfill Their Responsibilities," *La Jornada*, September 4, 1999, as translated by Leslie López (Chiapas-L message, September 4, 1999).

51. Alberto Nájar, "De soldados a policías, el mapa nacional," *La Jornada*, August 15, 1999.

52. Most notably, Roderic Ai Camp, "Militarizing Mexico: Where Is the Officer Corps Going?" Policy Paper on the Americas, CSIS Americas Program, January 15, 1999, received via Internet; Camp's *Generals in the Palacio: The Military in Modern Mexico* (New York: Oxford University Press, 1992); Stephan J. Wager, "The Mexican Military Approaches the 21ST Century: Coping with a New World Order," Strategic Studies Institute Special Report, U.S. Army War College, Carlisle, Penn., February 21, 1994.

53. Colonel John A. Cope, "In Search of Convergence: U.S.–Mexican Military Relations into the Twenty-first Century," in *Strategy and Security in U.S.–Mexi-*

can Relations: Beyond the Cold War, edited by John Bailey and Sergio Aguayo Quezada (La Jolla: Center for U.S.–Mexican Studies, University of California, San Diego, 1996).

54. Ibid., 194–95. For a broader discussion of IMET, see also John A. Cope, Jr. "International Military Education and Training: An Assessment," McNair Paper No. 44 (Institute for National Strategic Studies, October 1995).

55. "Perry Meets Mexican Counterpart," Mexico City *Radio Red,* 0000 GMT, October 24, 1995; "Perry Speaks to Mexican Commanders," Mexico City XEW Television Network, 0400 GMT, October 24, 1995; "Perry Meets with Zedillo," 0000 GMT, October 25, 1995, as translated in FBIS-LAT-95-206.

56. See Camp, "Militarizing Mexico."

57. In the first of the three-part series "The Enemy Is Also Within: The Army of Rangers and Green Berets" (*El Financiero,* September 25, 1995, as translated in FBIS FTS 19950925000048), Ignacio Rodríguez Reyna summarized principal elements as calling for: (1) the organization of the army into smaller, highly qualified commando units that would have great mobility, precision, and effectiveness; (2) the shaping of a true military intelligence system; the laying of the foundations for the creation of a future unified body that will coordinate the actions of the air force, the marines, and the army; (3) the carrying out of joint operations with the Mexican navy (the last joint operations were carried out in 1964); (4) the development of the air force by furnishing it with new equipment; (5) the purchase of sophisticated equipment and weapons; (6) the technological and computer "revolution" within the armed forces; (7) the creation of "special forces" squadrons in each military region, particularly Chiapas and Guerrero, equipped with sophisticated equipment and weapons; (8) the incorporation of civilians onto the army roster; and (9) the radical redefinition of the national security concept the military hierarchy has had.

58. This opposition led the Mexican government to approach Russia regarding the possible purchase of MI–8 and MI–17 Russian helicopters. Dolia Estévez, "Government Takes Steps to Purchase Russian Helicopters," *El Financiero,* September 3, 1996, as translated in FBIS-LAT-96-176.

59. David Aponte, "Investiga EU si se usan helicópteros Huey contra el EPR," *La Jornada,* June 3, 1997.

60. Molly Moore, "Mexico Sends 'Junk' Choppers Back to US: Aircraft Donated To Aid Drug War," *Washington Post,* October 6, 1999.

61. Jesús Aranda, "La Paz en Chiapas pasa por la desmilitarización," *La Jornada,* May 28, 1999. Carlos Fazio Salvador Corro ("The Third Link," December 1, 1996, as translated and excerpted by Nuevo Amanecer Press, received via Internet) placed the size of the Defense Ministry (minus the navy) at 236,000. By 1998, Camp ("Militarizing Mexico") put the number at 239,000.

62. David Aponte, "Instrucción antidrogas del Pentágono a más de 2 mil militares mexicanos," *La Jornada,* July 10, 1999; Pascal Beltrán del Río, "In Just Two Years, Some 3,000 Mexican Soldiers Will Have Been Trained at 17 US Military Bases," *Proceso* 1122 (May 3, 1998), as translated by Nuevo Amanecer Press.

63. See the extensive Latin America IMET data compiled since 1996 (including estimates for 1999) at www.ciponline.org/facts/imet.htm.

64. Ibid. An extensive list of courses and past Mexican unit recipients is included as well.

65. Aranda, "La Paz en Chiapas."

66. Aponte, "Instrucción antidrogas del Pentágono."

67. Jesús Aranda, "Participan 26 mil militares en la actividad; de 95 a la fecha han muerto 65," *La Jornada,* August 1999.

68. Nájar, "De soldados a policías," and Farah and Moore, "Elite Anti-Drug Troops Investigated in Mexico."

69. "Denial of Joint Military Exercises with U.S.," *La Jornada,* March 18, 1996, as translated in FBIS-LAT-96-053.

70. Caspar Weinberger and Pete Schweizer, *The Next War* (Washington, D.C.: Regnery, 1996).

71. Nick Anderson, "Mexican Drug Certification Faces Attack," *Los Angeles Times,* March 25, 1999; Tim Golden, "Top Mexican Off-Limits to U.S. Drug Agents," *New York Times,* March 24, 1999.

72. "A Broader and More Efficient Fight against Impunity, Insecurity and Drug Trafficking."

73. Bertha Teresa Ramírez, "Tomará de 10 a 15 años formar mandos de primer nivel en la SSP," quote from Luis Alamillo Gutiérrez, director of the Technical Police Training Institute, *La Jornada,* February 2, 1998.

74. A number of these are addressed most instructively in Cope, "In Search of Convergence," 189–96.

75. See the increasingly useful Mexican Embassy Web site under the "Mexico–US Relationship" section, at www.embassyofmexico.org/english/4/mexico_US.htm.

The May 1997 "US/Mexico Bi-National Drug Threat Assessment" was one early result of the High Level Contact Group program, as are some of the newly formulated Mexican counter-drug efforts and the acquisition of new technologies. See "US–Mexico Drug Cooperation Detailed," *La Jornada,* February 18, 1999, as translated by FBIS, received via Internet. A letter to the editor (*Washington Post,* September 24, 1996) from the Mexican ambassador to the United States discussed the March 1996 establishment of a High Level Contact Group for Drug Control, which consisted of various working groups addressing issues like money laundering, essential chemical control, and arms trafficking, as well as specialized border task forces. Group meetings began in December 1996. See also Gross, "Mexican Soldiers Increase Presence," for other kinds of cross-border interaction at the tactical level.

76. A recent remark addressing military cooperation was attributed to former U.S. principal deputy under secretary of defense Jan Lodal, in *La Jornada,* February 10, 1999, as translated in FBIS, received via Internet. Lodal reportedly said that "while neither Mexico nor any other nation can by itself solve the problem of drug trafficking, many U.S. officials find it difficult to coordinate efforts with the Mexican military because 'there is no one in charge … especially someone inside the Mexican armed forces who is responsible for coordinating the antinarcotics fight.'"

77. "US–Mexico Drug Cooperation Detailed."

11

U.S. Foreign Intelligence and Mexico: The Evolving Relationship

Brian Latell

For approximately three decades following the 1954 covert intervention by the Eisenhower administration in Guatemala, few issues in bilateral relations were as certain to provoke widespread public outrage in Mexico as the real and imagined activities of the Central Intelligence Agency. During most of those years of intense Cold War in Latin America, little imagination was required for Mexicans, or other Latin Americans, to identify the CIA as the shrouded instrument used by a succession of U.S. presidents to intervene—often violently—in the internal affairs of their countries. Many Mexicans essentially equated the CIA's Cold War missions in the region with the nineteenth- and early twentieth-century indignities and defeats their country suffered in its agonized relations with the United States. Mexico's historical vulnerabilities, proximity to the United States, and the unquestioned primacy in its foreign policy of the need to protect national sovereignty helped promote a hostile view of the CIA among Mexican nationalists, leftists, and intellectuals that endured until the 1980s.[1]

Mexican governments objected to U.S. interventions in Guatemala in 1954, Cuba in 1961, and the Dominican Republic in 1965, and stood alone in the region in 1964 by refusing to honor the diplomatic and trade sanctions voted by the Organization of American States (OAS) against Cuba. Mexico was soon the only OAS member country to maintain diplomatic relations with Cuba and to permit a Cuban embassy in its capital. Mexican leaders routinely insisted that Cold War U.S. concepts of regional security requirements violated the most cherished principles of their foreign policy. Beginning with the Mexican Revolution early in the century through the late 1980s, Mexicans did not question their country's commitment to the principles of self-determination and non-intervention, nor the extension of those ideals to abhor U.S. intrusions, covert or overt, in other Latin American countries.

This insistence on demonstrating independence of the United States was supported by critical domestic political imperatives. In November 1964, for example, president-elect Gustavo Díaz Ordaz (1964–1970) resisted pressures from President Lyndon Johnson for the adoption of tougher Mexican policies against Fidel Castro's Cuba. He told Johnson that "[a] Mexican government policy not supported by the Mexican people would not endure."[2] In fact, he and other Mexican leaders during the 1960s and 1970s were not exaggerating the domestic political difficulties they faced in trying to assuage and deflect extreme left-wing and Marxist pressures on them. Sympathy for Fidel Castro's regime was particularly strong, and widespread vilification of the CIA was largely a reaction to the numerous covert actions it mounted against Castro.

TENSIONS CAUSED BY U.S. COVERT ACTION IN LATIN AMERICA

On a larger scale, the long and tortuous record of CIA Cold War covert actions in Latin America provided some of the most inciting evidence of U.S. interventionist impulses. It was almost impossible for Mexicans to develop a positive view of the Agency in the 1960s and 1970s. There was no informed literature about U.S. or other foreign intelligence by Latin American authors, and works published in English were generally tendentious. Therefore, the Agency's multiple overseas missions and activities were easily misunderstood, and its most conspicuous and controversial function—covert action—dominated discussions of its activities.[3]

Distinct from espionage, covert action was defined by Richard Bissell, the CIA deputy director for plans at the time of the Bay of Pigs, as "influencing people, organizations, and events in other countries secretly, using a variety of inducements and pressures while attempting to conceal sponsorship."[4] Known in the Soviet Union as "active measures" and in other countries as "special operations," covert action was neither a Cold War invention nor a policy instrument wielded only by the major powers.[5]

The mythology of a monolithic, interventionist CIA operating at will throughout Latin America took shape during the 1960s and 1970s largely as a result of revelations about covert actions in the region. It began forming after the downfall of the Arbenz government in Guatemala as a result of the CIA's "Operation PBSUCCESS," and then coalesced after the Bay of Pigs fewer than seven years later. Large, covert paramilitary incursions in which the hand of the U.S. government was not supposed to be evident were a wholly new form of intervention, and one that might be applied again anywhere in Latin America. Somehow, however, the ineptitude evident in every critical aspect of planning and execution at the Bay of Pigs was largely overlooked by Latin Americans, who were inclined instead to be preoccupied with the large size, audacity, and intended deniability of the plan.

Soon, growing Latin American fears and misperceptions of the CIA were also goaded by Soviet and Cuban propaganda and disinformation campaigns that portrayed the Agency as a primitive and virulent force operating out of the darkest fringes of American society. But even without those intentional distortions, credible reports of CIA covert actions in Latin America accumulated during the 1960s, and by the middle of the next decade substantial and incontrovertible evidence was on the record. In 1975, the Senate Select Committee on Intelligence Activities (known as the Church Committee, after its Chairman, Senator Frank Church of Idaho) held open hearings and later published a lengthy report describing many other covert actions proposed and conducted by the CIA in the region.[6] The Church Committee confirmed that the Agency's reach in Latin America indeed was continental, that it was willing to consider bizarre and murderous plots against Latin American leaders, and that even democratically elected governments were susceptible.

The Kennedy administration's "Operation MONGOOSE" was bared. Intended to inflict maximum pain on Fidel Castro's regime through sabotage and other clandestine assaults, it may also have been intended to provoke a military retaliation by Castro that could have provided a pretext for a definitive U.S. military intervention in Cuba. A number of working-level CIA proposals for Castro's assassination were revealed by the committee, along with more serious plots involving Mafia hitmen. It was confirmed that during the Kennedy administration, the CIA had also supported the assassins of Rafael Trujillo, the dictator of the Dominican Republic.[7] In Chile alone, the committee found that thirty-three covert action projects had been mounted between 1963 and 1974.[8] These included lavish financing of the presidential campaign of the 1964 Christian Democratic candidate, Eduardo Frei and the so-called Track Two operations to undermine the Socialist-Communist government of Salvador Allende. It was clear that the covert actions exposed by the Church Committee affected Latin America more than any other region of the world. And when Senator Church, in an open hearing, falsely described the CIA as "a rogue elephant," the worst fears of Mexicans, along with many others throughout the hemisphere, were confirmed.

COVERT ACTION AND PROMOTION OF DEMOCRACY

The use of covert action in Latin America appeared to diminish between 1977 and 1980 as the Carter administration emphasized the centrality of human rights and democratic development in its regional policies. Former CIA director Robert Gates has revealed, however, that "contrary to the conventional wisdom," Carter "turned almost from the outset to CIA to carry out covert actions."[9] Gates cited actual operations in El Salvador and Nicaragua, as well as another aimed at Grenada that was authorized by the administration but blocked by Congress. Unacknowledged until the publication in 1996 of Gates's memoirs, these covert actions were of course not issues in the public debate about U.S. policies in Latin America in the late 1970s. It appears in retrospect that Carter's covert actions in Latin America were in fact the most truly clandestine of those of all Cold War U.S. presidents. But his earnest emphasis on promoting human rights and democracy also seems to have marked a turning point in the way that Mexicans and other Latin Americans viewed the United States.

Covert action in the region reached a new intensity with the Reagan administration's commitment to stemming, even reversing, the gains of Marxist revolutionaries in Central America. Support for the Nicaraguan Contras raised the visibility of CIA operations to unprecedented heights, and for the first time the U.S. Congress became publicly embroiled in debates over whether to fund covert action. Thus, when the Contras were overtly funded, their insurgency was transformed into something entirely new for the CIA, a *semi*-covert action. As a result, the Contras at various times were overtly funded through congressional appropriations and managed by the CIA in a fashion that preserved a high degree of operational clandestineness.

Extreme incidents—such as the CIA–sponsored mining of a Nicaraguan harbor and discovery of a guerrilla assassination manual the Agency published for the Contras—provoked furious criticism in the United States and echoes of the "rogue elephant" charges of 1976. But in Latin America, with the exception of the Cuban and Sandinista governments and groups allied with them, criticism of the Reagan administration and the CIA was surprisingly muted and limited in scope. And although the Contra war was a vastly larger paramilitary enterprise than anything the CIA had sponsored in Latin America before, it generated considerably less outrage in the region.

In Mexico, in particular, the conflicts in Nicaragua and El Salvador and the CIA role there had little resonance after the mid–1980s.[10] The reasons for this evolution in Mexican attitudes about these once-volatile issues suggest that the old consensus among Mexican leaders and leftist circles about a predatory, interventionist CIA was breaking down. It was giving way to an entirely new awareness in Mexico of new and more destabilizing challenges to internal security coming from different sources and directions. At the same time, the Mexican public was beginning to recognize that there was a broad and widening correlation of security and intelligence needs they shared with the United States. The long preoccupation with interventionist CIA covert actions was expiring.

CHANGING RELATIONS AND EVOLVING MEXICAN ATTITUDES

Ironically, these shifting Mexican attitudes about security and the role of U.S. intelligence roughly coincided with the development of the Reagan Doctrine in the Caribbean Basin.[11] But they also coincided with the sweeping transformation from authoritarian to democratic governments that was occurring in Latin America. There was no contradiction between these two phenomena. The Reagan Doctrine emphasized not only paramilitary operations to roll back Marxist regimes in the Third World but also an idealistic commitment to promoting democracy.

It was the latter objective that helped in the mid–1980s to dispel fears that had been powerful in the region during the twenty years between the CIA's anti-Arbenz and anti-Allende covert actions. It had seemed clear then—with only a few exceptions (notably, covert support for Chilean Christian Democratic presidential candidate Eduardo Frei in 1964)—that the CIA was promoting repressive, right-wing governments while destabilizing or toppling progressive reformers. But by the beginning of Reagan's second term in 1985, this no longer appeared to be true. In El Salvador, for example, it was the progressive Christian Democrat José Napoleon Duarte who may have received covert American support, rather than Roberto D'Aubuisson, his violent, extreme right wing opponent for the presidency. And in Nicaragua, as the Contra forces grew large and attracted broad support from the civilian populace, once-credible allegations that they were dominated by henchmen of former dictator Anastasio Somoza lost validity.

During Reagan's second term, moreover, he and Soviet leader Mikhail Gorbachev began negotiating the end of the Cold War. And as a result, the East-West security issues and ideological tensions that had motivated so much U.S. policy in Latin America were disappearing. The regional Communist parties and Marxist activists were in broad retreat, reconsidering absolutely their own ideological commitments and precepts. Marxist guerrillas were laying down their arms, or negotiating how to do so. The most vociferous critics of U.S. policies—and of the CIA—were gradually falling silent during the late 1980s.

Perhaps most importantly, a new array of security challenges emerged in Mexico during the administration of Miguel de la Madrid (1982–1988). Mexican opinion began shifting from fears of U.S. covert intervention to concerns about these new challenges. Among them was the dangerous growth of narcotics trafficking and related crime, and unprecedented instability along Mexico's southern border. Hundreds of thousands of refugees were fleeing violence in Guatemala to settle in already depressed and politically sensitive regions of southernmost Mexico. And most alarming, during de la Madrid's entire administration, Mexican leaders had to deal with multiple economic and political crises in the aftermath of the devastating financial crisis of 1982.

Simultaneously, the ability and will of Mexico's semi-authoritarian, one-party political system was eroding. Mexicans in greatly increasing numbers were demanding democratic and accountable government, and opposition parties to the left and right of the ruling Institutional Revolutionary Party (PRI) were gaining support throughout the country. The egregious official corruption that was so blatant by the mid–1980s was a galvanizing issue for opposition elements, in particular because of the depressed economic conditions most Mexicans had to endure. De la Madrid made some limited concessions to these demands and grievances, but it was his successor, Carlos Salinas de Gortari (1988–1994) who implemented numerous reforms that have resulted in the gradual dissolution of the old authoritarian order. And as the political system has decentralized since the late 1980s, popular fears of the state's coercive powers have declined.

Finally, it is important to note that as Mexicans reassessed the relationship between the CIA's missions and their country, it may have become evident to many that the record of revealed U.S. covert actions during the entire Cold War included none ever reported to have been conducted against domestic political targets in Mexico.

The Special Strategic Relationship

Even during the years when Mexican fears of U.S. covert action were greatest, the official bilateral relationship was considerably more complex than it appeared to most. In fact, between 1941 and 1989, a special strategic relationship continued, perhaps without serious interruptions, as successions of Mexican and U.S. administrations quietly collaborated on security issues. Over the course of about five decades, bilateral tensions provoked by U.S. interventions in the hemisphere, and other East-West tensions, were nearly always manageable for both countries in the context of the special relationship.

There were few agreements, treaties, or covenants that described or regulated the special strategic relationship, and it operated with scarcely any public acknowledgment or attention on either side of the border. Instead, it evolved almost entirely behind the scenes, informally guiding decision making on critical Cold War issues, particularly those involving U.S. and Soviet tensions. Because it was never institutionalized in any formal sense, its validity and continuity depended in large part on the readiness of successive administrations in both countries to depend on career bureaucrats in the foreign secretariats and elsewhere in the two governments who appreciated the hidden complexities of the bilateral relationship.

In Mexico, this special strategic relationship was bounded by an elaborate code of restrictions, masking, and deniability. Fearing political backlash, Mexican presidents and leaders were loath publicly to acknowledge collaboration with U.S. intelligence, military, or law enforcement agencies. Nonetheless, U.S. leaders were assured of Mexican cooperation in a variety of spheres, first against the Axis powers during World War II, and later on critical East-West issues during the Cold War. Eventually the special strategic relationship provided the bases and useful precedents for a new, more open, and formal array of security collaboration and agreements that have developed since the administration of Carlos Salinas.

Mexican leaders through those five decades faced enormous challenges in managing their side of the strategic relationship. Most notably, they had to balance the contradictions between the demands of Mexico's nationalist foreign policy principles against pressures from the United States that they more frequently and unequivocally support U.S. positions in the East-West conflict. During the Kennedy administration, for example, Mexican leaders resisted strong pressures to acknowledge the special relationship and to collaborate openly with the United States to contain Cuban subversion in the hemisphere. They placed a high priority on concealing the special strategic relationship, fearing they would be humiliated and seen as hypocrites by Mexican nationalists if it were revealed.

It appears that strong U.S. leverage for a strategic relationship was first exerted on Mexican leaders before and during World War II. Under pressure from the Roosevelt administration, President Manuel Ávila Camacho (1940–1946) agreed to limited military cooperation before Pearl Harbor, while prohibiting the presence of uniformed U.S. military personnel on Mexican territory. After the Japanese attack, Ávila Camacho yielded to intensifying U.S. concerns about safeguarding its southern border by consenting to the creation of a Joint Mexican-American Defense Committee.[12] Mexico remained a reluctant ally, however, and when, in May 1942, it finally declared a "state of war" (rather than actual belligerence) against the Axis powers, it was only after Nazi U–boats had sunk two Mexican freighters.[13]

During the war years, Mexico City emerged as a major center of Nazi espionage activities directed at the United States, just as it would be one of the most important covert intelligence collection centers for the Soviet Union and other communist countries during the Cold War. The FBI, which had foreign intelligence responsibilities in Latin America before the creation of the CIA in September 1947, shared counterintelligence information with the five Mexican services then engaged in counterintelligence.[14] This FBI action may have marked the beginning of official security cooperation between the United States and Mexico.[15]

Only fragmentary information about U.S. intelligence and counterintelligence cooperation with other countries, both in theory and in practice, is available to researchers. Probably the most comprehensive generic description is included in the 1996 report of the Aspin-Brown Commission that examined the U.S. intelligence community. It indicates that "bilateral cooperation almost always involves sharing of intelligence information and analysis on topics of mutual interest. Beyond this, cooperative arrangements may take any of several forms."[16] These include sharing of intelligence collection and analysis, joint collection operations, exchanges of intelligence personnel, and training.[17] It should be emphasized, however, that this report did not mention Mexico, or any other country, in its discussion of such relationships.

At least one author has written explicitly about a U.S. intelligence liaison relationship with Mexico. He asserts that "during the 1960s and 1970s Mexico cooperated extensively with US intelligence agencies in monitoring, among other things, Cuban diplomatic activity in Mexico."[18] Arguing that Mexico maintained a "high degree of flexibility and independence," he also asserts that "the absence of a written agreement for this cooperation permitted Mexican leaders to restrict these intelligence sharing operations when it suited Mexican interests."[19]

A few declassified documents from the Kennedy administration State Department appear to provide primary information on intelligence liaison with Mexico. They suggest that Kennedy himself took a keen interest in expanding intelligence cooperation and strongly pressured his counterpart, President Adolfo López Mateos (1958–1964), to agree. In June 1962 when the two met in Mexico City, Kennedy "returned again and again to what President López Mateos thought was the best way to deal with the obvious danger of an expansion of Communist influence in Latin America."[20] But López Mateos was unwilling to admit that any new security measures were justified, repeating "his view that rapid economic development and social programs was the answer." Kennedy persisted. He was eager "to deal with the problem of Communist penetration in the hemisphere in cooperation with other Latin American states like Mexico" and wanted to keep in close touch on this point and to reach agreement on practical measures that could be taken.[21] The declassified State Department memorandum of conversation noted that "in the end" President López Mateos "said he would give the matter more thought."[22]

That September Secretary of State Dean Rusk revived—and intensified—Kennedy's démarche during a meeting with the Mexican ambassador in Washington. Rusk expressed the concerns of other Latin American governments that were, he said, preoccupied by the large numbers of their citizens passing through Mexico en route to Cuba. At that time, the Castro regime was stepping up its training of young Latin Americans in guerrilla warfare techniques and energetically supporting Marxist subversion in a number of countries. Rusk pressed the ambassador for a "stricter watch by Mexico" on Cuban activities and less secrecy in doing so. He said, "he knew that Mexico maintained some surveillance against possible movements to and from Cuba ... and expressed the hope that this could be increased and that Mexico could announce publicly its action." Rusk complained of subversive activities carried out at the Cuban Embassy in Mexico City, and he urged Mexico to reduce the number of Cuban diplomatic personnel accredited there.[23]

The extent of Mexico's willingness to cooperate with the United States on critical security issues became evident during the 1962 Cuban Missile Crisis. On October 22, President Kennedy revealed the presence of Soviet strategic missiles in Cuba and announced that he would impose a "strict quarantine on all offensive military equipment" deliveries to the island. He called on the Latin American nations to support that action by invoking the Rio Treaty "in support of all necessary action" by the United States. The OAS met throughout the following day in Washington before voting unanimously to support Kennedy's demand that all offensive Soviet weapons be withdrawn from Cuba. Mexico did not stand alone in Latin America during this nuclear American confrontation with the Soviet Union, as it would following the July 1964 OAS vote to isolate Cuba diplomatically.

Thus, despite López Mateos's nationalistic and independent foreign policies and his apparent refusal to bow to Kennedy's desire for closer intelligence collaboration against Cuba, he supported the United States without hesitation. In his memoirs, Dean Rusk revealed that he and the State Department "didn't have to twist arms or bludgeon anyone" in lobbying OAS members before the October 23 vote.[24] Nonetheless, Assistant Secretary of State for American Republic Affairs Edwin Martin has revealed that "we were especially anxious to get the votes of Mexico and Brazil, both lukewarm enemies of Castro."[25] This was complicated by the fact that López Mateos and his foreign secretary were traveling in the Pacific when Kennedy delivered his speech, and it was difficult for them to get a copy of the full text.

López Mateos's support for Kennedy's demand that the Soviets remove their offensive weapons from Cuba did not result in any dilution in Mexico's long-vaunted nationalistic foreign policy principles. Although Mexico voted for the OAS resolution as a whole, according to Martin, it abstained on the critical second paragraph that approved the use of "all measures, individually and collectively, including the use of force."[26] Yet, in the aftermath of the Missile Crisis, López Mateos appears to have provided less qualified assurances to the Kennedy administration. Meeting with Martin in March 1963, he "made quite clear that Mexico would give its public support to any action against Cuba necessary to prevent a serious direct threat to the security of the United States or the hemisphere."[27]

López Mateos's successor, Gustavo Díaz Ordaz, is also known to have provided similar assurances. In November 1964, when President Johnson met privately with him, Díaz Ordaz recalled Mexico's OAS vote during the Missile Crisis and confided that "the United States could be absolutely sure that when the chips were really down, Mexico would be unequivocally by its side."[28] But he also took the opportunity to emphasize a key provision of Mexico's interpretation of the special strategic relationship. He said, "there was considerable advantage when the issues at stake were not great if Mexico could continue to demonstrate its political independence and divergence on relatively minor issues." In return for the assurance of Mexican support on any truly critical East-West issue, its leaders expected considerable freedom of action in articulating nationalistic foreign policies on a range of lesser issues.

Key Characteristics of the Special Strategic Relationship

The special strategic relationship was an unusual arrangement that worked to the advantage of both countries for most of the five decades following Pearl Harbor. Mexico pursued nationalistic policies—sometimes in sharp conflict with U.S. positions—that appealed to important domestic constituencies, while invariably supporting the United States on important East-West issues. Mexican administrations distinguished between the requirements of strictly bilateral relations and the more nationalistic positions that could be aired in international organizations and forums. Thus it was in the OAS, the United Nations, the nonaligned movement, and other Third World arenas during the Cold War that Mexico was most likely to challenge and criticize the United States, though never with the stridency of, say, Castro's Cuba. With rare exceptions—as, for example, intermittently during the administration of José López Portillo (1976–1982)—bilateral issues were handled constructively by Mexico and without intent to humiliate or hurt.

Meanwhile, the United States, interested above all in Mexico's continued political and social stability, rarely disputed this exquisite balancing act. Henry Kissinger has written admiringly of it, noting that "whatever their rhetoric, Mexican leaders knew that the destinies of our two countries were intertwined."[29] President Luis Echeverría's (1970–1976) vote at the United Nations in 1975 in favor of the resolution declaring Zionism a form of racism—and other assertive Third World initiatives—were certainly vexing, but Kissinger notes that "bilateral relations during the Nixon and Ford administrations were remarkably constructive."[30]

Other Cold War U.S. administrations may have understood less well or simply cared less about indulging Mexican artifices. The Kennedy administration, for example, unavailingly applied strong pressures in an effort to get López Mateos to perform as a more traditional ally. The Carter administration, as will be explained briefly below, often fared poorly in bilateral relations, but probably more because of the extravagances of López Portillo than misunderstandings by Carter or others in his administration of Mexican sensibilities. And finally, it was during the Reagan administration when the special strategic relationship began to break down. That was because of the many new pressures for change in Mexico, nationalistic outbursts by the López Portillo administration that put severe strains on the special relationship, and the desire of some Reagan advisers fundamentally to alter the relationship by promoting a more demanding and conditioned relationship with Mexico.

Yet, on balance, it appears that during nearly all of the Cold War there was broad understanding among foreign policy–making elites in both countries about the unique characteristics of the special relationship. It seems to have evolved over time as the boundaries were tested and confirmed by satisfactory experience. Its contours remained flexible and shifted over time depending on specific Cold War dynamics. The relationship was always informal and appears to have been conveyed from one administration to another on both sides of the border while generating scarcely any public debate. It apparently never wavered in exempting strategic Mexican commodities, such as petroleum. Most importantly, the special strategic relationship reflected the overriding importance that each side placed on the maintenance of smoothly working relations.

The management of the strategic relationship during World War II and through most of the Cold War testifies to the skill and sophistication of foreign-policy decision makers in the two countries. The advantages of the ingenious arrangement were numerous. Most critically for Mexico, it was able effectively to immunize itself from virtually all of the stresses and conflicts of the Cold War. No other Latin American country so successfully avoided internal social and political strife from Marxist and extreme leftist groups. Unlike a number of its neighbors, Mexico never had to accept U.S. military tutelage in developing counterinsurgency skills, enter into agreements for the basing of U.S. troops on its soil, enhance the role of its military in critical national decision making, or ratify explicit Cold War alliances. Mexico steered a benign Cold War course that allowed it to invest instead in economic and social development without the need to make large expenditures on defense and national security.

And from the U.S. perspective, the benefits of the special relationship were just as significant. There was never a time during the Cold War when U.S. officials really had to worry about chaos or challenges on its southern border.[31] Administrations did not have to seek large military appropriations from Congress to better secure the southern border, and the Department of Defense was able almost entirely to ignore Mexico in its strategic planning.

Mexican governments seem to have made only one absolutely unequivocal concession: that they would support the United States in any extreme East-West crisis. But in practice their cooperation extended to a variety of other lesser threats, including Soviet intelligence and counterintelligence capabilities in Mexico. Through the entire Cold War, the Soviet Embassy in Mexico City provided cover for one of the largest intelligence collection centers in the world. Soviet operatives successfully recruited and debriefed Americans in Mexico, while enjoying a high degree of immunity from U.S. surveillance. And they were known to have achieved some major espionage successes there.[32]

Yet it appears that consecutive Mexican governments felt compelled under the informal guidelines of the special strategic relationship to place limits on Soviet espionage. Despite Soviet interest, for instance, in opening one or more consulates (in addition to the one they maintained in Veracruz), they never were permitted to establish consular covers for additional intelligence collection centers in other Mexican cities. It would have been especially confrontational from the U.S. perspective, for example, if Moscow had been allowed to open consulates in Mexican cities along the U.S. border (in Ciudad Juárez or Tijuana, for example), where their intelligence capabilities would have been enormously enhanced.[33]

Mexico's willingness to collaborate with the United States in security or intelligence relationships against Castro's Cuba appear, in contrast, to have been especially ambiguous. It is possible that one or more Mexican presidents were more willing than López Mateos in the early 1960s to collaborate with U.S. agencies. However, because only a few relevant declassified documents are available, it is only possible to speculate about how the special strategic relationship may have evolved over the years as the attitudes of Mexican presidents toward Cuba fluctuated.

During the López Portillo administration, such collaboration may well have been more constrained than at other times. Furthermore, the application of the special strategic relationship to Cuba was also inhibited by the reality that Mexican governments apparently maintained a similar unacknowledged and informal understanding with Havana. During the era of determined Cuban efforts to support Marxist insurgents in many Latin American countries, Mexican leaders had little to fear from Cuba. No violent pro-Castro groups appeared there, and Cuba's militant, pro-revolutionary propaganda always exempted Mexico. Some authors have suggested that this reflected a Cuban quid pro quo in response to Mexico's refusal to terminate diplomatic and commercial ties with Havana after the imposition of the 1964 OAS sanctions.

Relations between the Mexican and U.S. military establishments do appear to have reflected to a considerable degree the parameters of the special strategic relationship. During the Cold War, Mexican political and military leaders looked exclusively to Western countries for military supplies and other defense requirements. More Mexican military personnel received training in the United States during the latter years of the Cold War than in any other country. And no Mexican military officers are reported to have received training in the Soviet Union.[34]

Finally, it seems reasonable to speculate that the special strategic relationship was more severely strained—if not actually suspended in part—during much of the administration of José López Portillo. With increased leverage and exuberance following the confirmation of large new petroleum reserves, his government became more assertive and impatient in relations with the United States, even to the point of conducting its own version of covert actions in the hemisphere. López Portillo helped the Sandinistas win power, confronted U.S. policy in El Salvador, collaborated more intimately with Fidel Castro than any Mexican president before or since, and saw to a broadening and intensification of relations with the Soviet Union.[35] One Mexican scholar, writing about that era, commented on the steadily diminishing willingness of Mexico to "collaborate with the United States on problems relating to the East-West conflict."[36] However, the nationalistic initiatives launched by López Portillo lost virtually all their momentum following Mexico's 1982 financial crisis, just as he was preparing to leave office.

POST–COLD WAR INTELLIGENCE AND SECURITY COOPERATION

Since the mid–1980s, Mexico's security needs have changed and greatly multiplied as it has confronted an array of new challenges, including massive narcotics trafficking and related crime and political corruption. These problems, the end of the Cold War, and the advent of multiparty democracy seem to provide ample justification for Mexico to continue restructuring and redefining its security relations with the United States in a manner that will enjoy similar legitimacy and longevity on both sides of the border. Ironically, all of the positive developments since the end of the Cold War have produced more rather than fewer social and security problems in Mexico.

For five decades, the special strategic relationship provided the foundations and understandings that will facilitate and legitimize more concerted security collaboration between the two countries. Meanwhile, a number of developments within Mexico appear to make such cooperation more attractive to large segments of the population. Most importantly, as the power of the old one-party political order has dissolved, public fears of its coercive powers have faded. In an increasingly more open and democratic environment, Mexicans are more likely to trust and depend on state security and law enforcement agencies. Fears of the CIA and its ability to mount intrusive covert actions have apparently all but disappeared since the end of the Cold War, and discussions and revelations of covert action have evanesced. The CIA is no longer viewed as harshly as it was, and greater collaboration should therefore be possible.

The inauguration of new presidents in Mexico and the United States in December 2000 and January 2001, respectively, amid intensifying exchanges of all types and greater mutual respect and understanding, provides unprecedented opportunities in bilateral relations. It would be logical, therefore, for the new administrations to expand and modify the special strategic relationship that prospered from the mid-1940s through the 1980s into an enhanced special security relationship. Security issues and threats of common concern for Mexico and the United States are numerous. At the national level they include: (1) the monitoring of international terrorist and criminal organizations, (2) counternarcotics collaboration, (3) joint programs in deterrence of the proliferation of weapons of mass destruction, (4) counterintelligence, and (5) general law enforcement cooperation. Moreover, at the state and local levels, the need for greater and better-organized security coordination will also become progressively more urgent.

The new presidents will have the opportunity to perfect an expanded special security relationship based on the lessons learned in the earlier arrangements that, to a substantial extent, became obsolete with the end of the Cold War. Most importantly, perhaps, evolving security relations should—as the Kennedy administration preferred in the 1960s—be acknowledged and confirmed through open political discourse on both sides of the border. As the transparency and vitality of democratic processes continue advancing in Mexico, security issues and cooperation with the United States will necessarily be debated in the Mexican Congress and by the electorate. In a democracy, the masking and deniability of security collaboration with the United States that Mexican administrations insisted on for decades would serve no legitimate purposes.

However, this is not to argue that the articulation and exercise of expanded special security relations will be politically easy in either country. U.S. policymakers will need to be especially sensitive to Mexican internal security priorities that are unique or may conflict with dominant U.S. approaches and policies. Gun and small arms control, for example, is likely to persist as a vexing bilateral issue as long as the purchase and trafficking of such weapons are not rigorously controlled in the United States. The illegal flow of weapons across the border is a legitimate Mexican concern that will be difficult to accommodate. Extradition of alleged narcotics offenders from Mexico to the United States will also remain a highly divisive issue. However, on balance, the likelihood is great that a special security relationship similar in many key respects to the Cold War special strategic relationship will endure indefinitely and prevail despite bilateral differences on specific issues.

Notes

1. See, for example, Manuel Buendía, *La CIA en México* (Mexico City: Rayuela, 1996). This popular collection of Mexican newspaper commentaries and speculations about the CIA was first published in 1984 and enjoyed wide circulation.

2. "Mexican-Cuban Relations," Department of State, Memorandum of Conversation, November 12, 1964. Available at the National Security Archive, Washington, D.C.

3. Traditionally, the four principal overseas missions of the CIA have been: (1) covert action, (2) espionage (the clandestine collection of information through the use of agents or spies), (3) counterintelligence, and (4) security liaison.

4. Richard Bissell, *Reflections of a Cold Warrior: From Yalta to the Bay of Pigs* (New Haven, Conn.: Yale University Press, 1996), 207.

5. In Latin America, the Castro regime and other governments have employed their own forms of covert action, sometimes audaciously and on a large scale. For example, the covert provision of over a million pounds of arms and ammunition to the Sandinista guerrillas in Nicaragua during the first half of 1979 was orchestrated by Cuba, with the assistance of other countries, especially Costa Rica and Panama. See Robert Kagan, *A Twilight Struggle: American Power and Nicaragua, 1977–1990* (New York: Free Press, 1996), chap. 10.

6. United States Senate, Final Report of the Select Committee to Study Governmental Operations with Respect to Intelligence Activities, April 26, 1976.

7. Ibid., Book I, 25.

8. Ibid., 150.

9. Robert M. Gates, *From the Shadows: The Ultimate Insider's Story of Five Presidents and How They Won the Cold War* (New York: Simon and Schuster, 1996), 141–52.

10. In 1983 President Miguel de la Madrid took a key leadership role in the Contadora regional peace process that sought to broker peaceful settlements to the civil wars in Nicaragua and El Salvador, and the following year he hosted a series of negotiations between the United States and the Sandinistas in the Mexican port of Manzanillo. These initiatives had no enduring results, however, and soon the Mexican leadership pulled back.

11. The October 1983 U.S. invasion of Grenada and the resulting termination of the Marxist New Jewel government there evoked little opposition in Latin America, much to the surprise of many U.S. observers at the time.

12. María Emilia Paz, *Strategy, Security, and Spies: Mexico and the United States as Allies in World War II* (University Park: Pennsylvania State University Press, 1997), 61–64.

13. Ibid., 135–38.

14. Ibid., 170–71.

15. In its published report, the Church Committee noted that: "throughout the entire period of the CIA's history, the Agency has entered into liaison arrangements with the intelligence services of foreign powers. Such arrangements are an extremely important and delicate source of intelligence and operational support." Final Report of the Select Committee to Study Governmental Operations with Respect to Intelligence Activities, Book II, April 26, 1976, 459.

16. *Preparing for the 21st Century: An Appraisal of U.S. Intelligence.* Report of the Commission on the Roles and Capabilities of the United States Intelligence Community, March 1, 1996, 127.

17. Ibid.

18. Wesley A. Fryer, *Mexican Security*: March 1, 1996, 127, at http://wtvi.com/wesley/mexicansecurity.html.

19. Ibid.

20. Memorandum from Acting Secretary of State Ball to President Kennedy, *Foreign Relations of the United States*, 1961–63, Vol. XII, 313.

21. Ibid.

22. Edwin Martin, the assistant secretary of state for Latin America at the time, has written that López Mateos promised Kennedy in the June 1962 meeting that "in a real pinch Mexico would support the United States." The declassified Memorandum of Conversation of the meeting does not include such an observation, however. See Edwin M. Martin, *Kennedy and Latin America* (Landham, Md.: University Press of America, 1994), 420.

23. *Foreign Relations of the United States*, 319.

24. Dean Rusk, *As I Saw It* (New York: W.W. Norton, 1990), 236. Rusk also commented that "OAS members believed Soviet missiles in Cuba were dangerous to the hemisphere and something had to be done about it."

25. Martin, *Kennedy and Latin America*, 419.

26. Ibid., 420.

27. *Foreign Relations of the United States*, 346.

28. Memorandum of Conversation, Part II of II, *Mexican Cuban Relations*, November 12, 1964. Available at the National Security Archive, Washington, D.C.

29. Henry A. Kissinger, *Years of Renewal* (New York: Simon and Schuster, 1999), 719.

30. Ibid.

31. Several prominent officials of the Reagan administration were associated with more alarmist views. CIA Director William Casey, for example, reportedly told another senior CIA official that "destabilizing Mexico is a fundamental objective of the Soviet Union." And Casey appointee, National Intelligence Officer for Latin America Constantine Menges, feared that "if the Communists took over Central America, Mexico would fall next," and he referred to Mexico as "the Iran next door." See Joseph Persico, *Casey: The Lives and Secrets of William J. Casey from the OSS to the CIA* (New York: Viking, 1990), respectively, 318, 386.

32. See for example, Robert Lindsey, *The Falcon and the Snowman* (New York: Pocket Books, 1980).

33. See Brian Latell, "The USSR and Mexico," in *The USSR and Latin America*, edited by Eusebio Mujal-León (Boston: Unwin Hyman, 1989), 315.

34. Ibid., 297.

35. See Brian Latell, "Continuity and Change in Mexican Foreign Policy," *California Western International Law Journal* 18:1 (1987–88), for an examination from a U.S. security perspective of López Portillo's assertive foreign policy during the last few years of his administration.

36. Humberto Garza Elizondo, "Mexican-Soviet Relations," in *Soviet-Latin American Relations in the 1980s*, edited by A. Varas (Boulder, Colo.: Westview, 1987), 206.

PART 3

Challenges in the Border Region

12

Security Regimes on the U.S.–Mexico Border

José Z. García

INTRODUCTION

Prominent in the U.S.–Mexico security milieu is the rapid expansion of two parallel sets of law enforcement agencies with roughly similar functions operating near each other along the 2,000–mile frontier. Among these are military units; drug enforcement agencies; customs and immigration authorities; federal investigative and prosecutorial agencies; state, county, and municipal police departments; and a host of interagency task forces. Although it may seem obvious, it warrants emphasis at the outset that these were *not* designed to counter potential threats stemming from the actions of cross-border governments. Rather, they monitor, regulate, deter, and sometimes punish the behavior of individuals and groups—often but not always—engaged in cross-border activities. A "security community" is sometimes said to characterize the relations between the two nations,[1] meaning that bellicose conflict between the national governments is so highly remote that it is not contemplated in the national plans of either country.

Although the concept of security community suggests a convergence of security goals sufficient to elicit significant mutual cooperation in security issues, empirical observation reveals this is not the case between the United States and Mexico in their border security operations. Interaction, although growing, is infrequent, and little cross-border operational cooperation or coordination is evident between law enforcement agencies at any level within the border region. National and local interagency cooperative mechanisms have recently been instituted, but these are clearly in their infancy. Thus far they seem aimed at reducing cross-border interagency irritants and misunderstandings rather than inspiring coordinated operational efforts. At local levels, cooperative mechanisms have longer and sometimes more successful histories, but there is a great deal of variation from place to place and from time to time. Thus, although hostility in U.S.–Mexico relations is absent, a security community between the two countries cannot be said to exist, although long-term trends in that direction can be detected.[2]

This chapter provides a broad characterization of the contemporary border security milieu on both sides under conditions of changing priorities, escalating law enforcement activity, and cross-border constraints preventing significant cooperation at the operational level. Although the entire border region is the subject, special emphasis is given to the El Paso–Ciudad Juárez region. What follows is a brief review of historical practices, the evolution of the border security regime, recent trends, and an evaluation of the overall border security milieu.

HISTORICAL BACKGROUND

Historians Harris and Sadler's work suggests that a border security regime, now being eclipsed, emerged out of the Mexican Revolution.[3] That is, security priorities, institutional configurations, and practices lasting several decades were established to deter and control border scenarios encountered during the revolution. Until the revolution, there were fewer than 150 U.S. law enforcement officers for the entire Texas–New Mexico border and fewer still on the Mexican side.[4] Border security consisted largely of half-hearted efforts to monitor smuggling or physically to mark the border.[5] The revolution would change this. One action that had an impact on both sides was the raid by Pancho Villa's troops on Columbus, New Mexico, in 1916 and its aftermath. While the specific motivations for the raid are still obscure, it was one in a series of movements undertaken by Villa in his quest to overthrow the Mexican government. Eighteen U.S. citizens were killed, and U.S. territory had been penetrated. In response, the U.S. government sent out several thousand troops to capture Villa in what was called the Punitive Expedition. When members of the expedition conferred on May 25, 1916, with General Calles, the Mexican commander, they expressed the view that General Carranza, leader of revolutionary forces in the north, was to blame for the expedition because he had refused to cooperate in capturing Villa.[6] They informed Calles that they would withdraw from Mexican territory when Villa was captured. Villa was not captured; the Punitive Expedition returned to the United States without him.

Other border areas were affected by the revolution as well. In South Texas in the first decade of the twentieth century, tensions between Anglo Americans and Mexican Americans increased as rapid growth caused property values to soar and Anglo in-migration changed the ethnic and political composition of the region. Armed conflict broke out between 1915 and 1917 when the Plan de San Diego was uncovered. The Plan called for an uprising against the U.S. government in February 1915. South Texas would become an independent republic and then incorporate itself into Mexico. One of the authors of the plan, Basilio Ramos, fled to Mexico, but others began raids from Mexico into the United States, attacking irrigation works, bridges, and trains. These were countered with severe repression, including lynchings, shootings, and generalized violence against Mexican Americans. Especially brutal were the Texas Rangers. Historians suspect Carranza, major leader of the revolution, may have instigated some of the violence as a means of gaining recognition for his government. When he received de facto recognition in December 1915, the raids stopped.

Even though these spectacular conflicts received much attention, they made little difference to the outcome of the revolution. Strategically, northern revolutionaries such as Madero and Villa were more advantaged than their southern counterparts because they were closer to the U.S. border, where they could purchase weapons and find sanctuary when needed. Since domestic ammunition supplies were far short of demand, success or failure depended on access to foreign arms. When U.S. authorities banned the export of arms and munitions to Pascual Orozco in 1912, for example, his defeat in the battle of Juárez was assured.[7]

The revolution provided different security lessons to Washington and Mexico City. For Washington, political instability *within* Mexico became a key concern. Following World War I, the only two divisions in the U.S. army maintained at full strength were located on the U.S.–Mexico border, at Ft. Sam Houston and Ft. Bliss. The primary motivation for maintaining a border military presence appears to have been precaution against the likelihood that insurgent movements might spill over to the U.S. side of the border.[8] U.S. officials provided support to both the Obregón and Calles governments when armed movements rose against them. Growing migration rates from Mexico to the United States, arising from the dislocations of the revolution, were also a concern. The U.S. Border Patrol, initially placed under the Department of Labor, was created in 1924. More agents of the Federal Bureau of Investigation (FBI) were stationed on the border. U.S. Customs offices were expanded, and stronger immigration controls were instituted. Nor was the border's importance lost on the Mexican side. Arms smuggling from the United States became a border priority in Mexico City, customs laws and practices were strengthened, and regional policies tacitly acknowledged lessons learned from experiences with northern Mexico and the border during the revolution.

Although the revolution pointed out a need for stronger border vigilance, however, interest groups on both sides had benefited by the laxness of border controls. When the shooting stopped, interest groups remained, and their power helped shape the emerging border security regime. Sadler identifies several "rules of the game" that characterized these new relations.[9] Problems were to be handled locally. If at all possible, local conflicts—within agencies, between agencies, between agencies and the public, or between agencies and binational counterparts—should not be referred to Washington or Mexico City. Local power structures, relevant political leaders, and regional or district administrators handled local conflict. They were also consulted in the selection of federal border personnel and policy. An informal, pragmatic, and tolerant understanding developed in the protocol between cross-border counterparts. Personal relationships with local elites on both sides were understood to be useful. In turn, agents exercising their authority in ways compatible with the needs of local elites, as well as their own mandates, easily became part of the local power structure itself. On the U.S. side, Customs enjoyed the greatest prestige, followed by the Immigration and Naturalization Service (INS), the Border Patrol, and state and local law officials. On the Mexican side, Aduana (Customs) officials were dominant but subject to the influence of state governors and party leaders. Lower in status were the Federal Judicial Police (PFJ) and local security officials.

Veteran border law enforcement officials confirm Sadler's findings. Interviews with old-timers suggest that local elites understood the implications of the low official priority of the border. In cases of conflict, local elites, when pressed, could often get local decisions reversed in Washington. As late as 1989 in El Paso, for example, a joint U.S. Customs–El Paso Police Department operation went into effect when a rash of auto thefts was linked to cross-border activities. All vehicles heading south were stopped and visually inspected, an extremely unusual measure which congested the bridges. When two-hour periods of operation were extended to twenty-four, a large number of complaints, articulated through the mayor's office, were registered from local elites concerned about the adverse impact of the slowdown on commerce. In response, the operation was shut down on the third day and was not resumed for several years.[10]

Today operations that halt traffic on the bridges are commonplace. Security priorities now trump all but the strongest protests from local elites. In less than two decades, from the early 1980s to the end of the century, this relatively relaxed border regime was "hardened" in various ways, especially on the U.S. side. Border enforcement rose as a national priority. Budgets were increased. Priorities shifted. New strategies and tactics were employed. New relationships developed between the growing security apparatus and the border public. Local elites were forced to adjust.

THE NEW BORDER SECURITY REGIME: THE U.S. SIDE

One of the earliest indicators of heightened priority was a reinterpretation of the *posse comitatus* statutes in the United States in December 1981, as part of the Defense Appropriations Act of 1982.[11] The prohibition against the participation of military personnel in the search, seizure, or arrest of individuals in domestic law enforcement activities was maintained. But the armed forces would now be allowed to share intelligence information with domestic law enforcement officers, and to loan equipment to agencies involved in monitoring "the movement of air and sea traffic." An interface developed between the extensive military installations along the U.S.–Mexico border (and elsewhere) and federal law enforcement agencies. In 1983 President Reagan created the National Narcotics Border Interdiction System, a coordinated effort among various federal agencies apparently aimed at improving surveillance systems against aircraft and, possibly, illegal immigrants. A more comprehensive effort to coordinate antinarcotics efforts began in 1986 with the creation of the Southwest Border Drug Task Force, later designated Operation Alliance, comprising federal, state, and local agency representatives.

Another milestone occurred in 1986 when President Reagan signed a secret directive that formally designated drug trafficking as a "significant threat to national security." Heightened prestige is conferred to officials falling under the cone of the national security clearance apparatus and culture. Moreover, agency heads can justify strong funding increases for new assets relevant to national security threats. Over the next few years, drug enforcement took on great momentum in Washington. In 1991 the armed forces began antidrug training programs for civilian police. In 1987 Border Patrol agents were cross-designated to permit them, for the first time, to enforce customs and drug enforcement codes. And in 1991 the Office of National Drug Control Policy (ONDCP) officially recognized the Border Patrol as the lead agency in the interdiction of drug traffic between ports of entry on the borders.

The same year that drug trafficking was elevated to the status of a national security priority, the U.S. Congress passed the 1986 Immigration Reform and Control Act (IRCA), raising the profile of migration control as a border-intensive project. Illegal migration and drug abuse had been viewed until then largely as complex issues related to domestic labor markets, labor surpluses in Mexico, domestic social disorder, media-driven glamorization of drug use, and complex international drug and labor markets. After 1986 there was a much greater tendency to view drugs and migration as "supply side" issues that could be attacked through stronger, parallel, and sometimes coordinated border interdiction policies. While the Bush and Clinton administrations varied from time to time in their approaches to migration and antidrug issues at home and abroad, border-specific, supply-driven policies and practices have only expanded upon the overall strategic logic in place by the late 1980s. In 1996 the Illegal Immigrant Reform and Immigrant Responsibility Act was passed, facilitating removal of undocumented migrants, increasing the size of the Border Patrol, and creating pilot employer sanction programs and other measures designed to make illegal migration control more comprehensive and efficient, but still strongly border intensive.

THE NEW BORDER REGIME: THE MEXICAN SIDE

On the Mexican side, of course, migration to the United States is not a national security priority; migration has long been viewed as an inevitable function of the proximity of lucrative wage markets to the north. Moreover, Mexican drug addiction rates, although climbing, are still below U.S. rates.[12] Nevertheless, after some reluctance and under pressure from the United States, President Miguel de la Madrid (1982–1988) declared drug trafficking a national security threat in 1987, a status it has enjoyed since then. According to one source, by 1988 one-third of Mexico's defense budget and 25,000 soldiers were engaged in antidrug programs.[13] President Carlos Salinas de Gortari (1988–1994) deepened military involvement in counter-drug activities, created antidrug units for the Federal Judicial Police, and strengthened the attorney general's ability to enforce drug laws. When he became president in 1994, Ernesto Zedillo stated that "narco-trafficking is the primary threat to national security, the greatest risk to social health, and the most pitiless source of violence."[14] By 1999 the Mexican military was spending about US$450 million, about 25 percent of its total annual budget, on counter-narcotics activities, and using 26,000 troops.[15]

Rhetorical elevation of the drug priority has been accompanied by strong increases in federal budgets and personnel, which tripled in the late 1980s and then tripled again in the 1990s.[16] President Zedillo appointed a member of the opposition National Action Party (PAN) to head up the Attorney General's Office (PGR), which restructured federal police forces, called for better training, redefined missions, and fired more than 1,200 federal police agents, hoping to reduce official corruption.[17] In addition, the Mexican Congress adopted an organized crime bill authorizing electronic surveillance, witness protection programs, and prosecutions on the basis of conspiracy.[18]

In Mexico, counter-drug activities have not been strongly border intensive, and they have involved the armed forces much more centrally than is the case in the United States. Mexican drug strategy has focused on domestic drug-crop eradication, interdiction of drug transportation throughout the nation, and disruption of criminal organizations. Only the latter is border intensive. The most visible actor in Mexican counter-drug activities is the armed forces; military personnel have patrolled rural areas, burned marijuana and poppy fields, and replaced officers of the Federal Judicial Police in efforts to curb corruption. Thus, while not as border intensive as the United States in their approach, but with stronger military involvement, Mexican strategists adopted a supply-side approach to drug enforcement.

Although migration is not a high priority in Mexico, several steps have been taken to protect the sizable and growing population of Mexican emigrants—whether living in the United States or transiting through the border region. Mexican consulates began in the 1990s to monitor Mexican populations in the United States—legally and illegally—to try to better understand that population. Various legislative proposals have been discussed, but not approved, that would allow Mexican migrants living in the United States to vote in Mexican elections. Mexican consular services have also instituted improved monitoring of citizens apprehended by the Border Patrol, INS, and other security agencies to assure their dignified treatment, a move that has been met with cooperation from INS officials. Finally, the National Migration Institute has shown increased concern for the safety of migrant citizens near the border, and devoted resources to these efforts through the creation of Grupo Beta, a law enforcement agency discussed below and in the chapter by McDonald in this volume. In short, as the United States hardened its border regime against drugs and undocumented persons coming from the south, Mexico adjusted its policies toward drug trafficking and migration too, although in a less border intensive way.

LAW ENFORCEMENT STRATEGY AND TACTICS ON THE BORDER: THE U.S. SIDE

The dramatic growth in U.S. federal agencies on the border is summarized in tables 12.1 and 12.2. The strongest growth occurred in Immigration and Naturalization Service personnel, which nearly tripled in less than a decade, and in the Border Patrol, which more than doubled. The FBI southwest border component grew faster than it did elsewhere, increasing from around 6 percent of the national total in 1990 to almost 9 percent in 1998, while growing absolutely on the border by over 36 percent. The Drug Enforcement Administration's (DEA) border increases were similar. By 1998 there were almost 13,000 federal law enforcement officers in the Southwest, 70 percent more than in 1993.

Federal law enforcement budgets (table 12.2) for the southwest border increased at about the same rate, nearly doubling from US$1 billion in 1993 to about $1.7 billion in 1998. Drug enforcement activities consumed nearly 40 percent ($652 million out of $1,715 million) of the total federal southwest law enforcement budget in 1998. Most of the rest went to immigration enforcement. By any criteria, the growth of federal law enforcement is striking.

Table 12.1 **Security Personnel on the United States' Southwestern Border**

Year	FEDERAL								LOCAL		
	FBI/ U.S.	FBI/ SWB	Border Patrol	Customs	Customs Inspector	DEA	INS	Total SW	EPPD	EPSO	Grand Total
1990	9,506	568	3,160	437		587	523				
1991	9,780	572	3,072	460		710	530				
1992	9,743	614	3,503	416		725	596				
1993	9,649	737	3,389	410	1,590	721	640	7,487	950	230	8,667
1994	9,493	822	3,670	401	1,703	723	660	7,979	954	230	9,163
1995	9,761	757	4,337	415	1,715	733	702	8,659	990	230	9,879
1996	9,892	837	5,281	457	1,736	737	1,162	10,210	969	230	11,409
1997	10,360	804	6,213	489	1,822	806	1,413	11,547	972	230	12,749
1998	10,524	894	6,698	489	2,342	902	1,413	12,738	992	233	13,963
El Paso 1998		100	1,125	70	750	150	540	2,655	992	233	3,890

Sources: Compiled from ONDCP, Annual Budget Reports, 1998, 1999, and ONDCP's Southwest Border document, 1997. See www.whitehousedrugpolicy.gov/ for these documents.

Note: EPPD refers to the El Paso Police Department; EPSO refers to the El Paso Sheriff's Department.

Table 12.2 **Law Enforcement Budgets for the U.S. Southwest Border (millions of U.S. dollars)**

	FEDERAL									LOCAL		
Year	FBI	FBI Drug	INS	INS Drug	Customs	DEA	High-Intensity Drug Trafficking Area	Total	Drug Total	EPPD	EPSO	Grand Total
1993	320	56	410	61	134	98	38	1,000	387	54	35 (est)	1,089
1994	343	75	412	65	144	104	38	1,041	425	57	36	1,134
1995	334	84	525	72	196	115	38	1,208	504	62	37	1,307
1996	376	99	612	88	207	116	36	1,347	545	69	38	1,454
1997	387	107	805	102	231	127	37	1,587	604	73	39	1,699
1998	405	111	878	119	238	157	37	1,715	652	76	40	1,831

Sources: Compiled from ONDCP, Annual Budget Reports, 1998, 1999, and ONDCP's Southwest Border document, 1997. See www.whitehousedrugpolicy.gov/ for these documents.

Note: EPPD refers to the El Paso Police Department; EPSO refers to the El Paso Sheriff's Department.

Part of the buildup reflects a fascination with technology. In 1991 the U.S. Congress established a Counterdrug Technology Assessment Center (CTAC) within the Office of National Drug Control Policy to serve as the major counter-drug research and development organization.[19] Peter Andreas found that experimental technologies developed for the army and CIA were being made available to the INS in the mid–1990s, including "ion scanners" used to detect illegal drugs, computer software to identify voice prints, AWACS planes, helicopters, and so on.[20] By the late 1990s CTAC was funding the development of "immunassay field test kits" to detect narcotics residue on hands and surfaces, concealed "audio transceiver surveillance systems," body-worn transmitters to produce "low probability of intercept and low probability of Detection Systems," miniature "gamma ray backscatter machines" to be mounted on a Custom's inspector belt for examining hard-to-inspect areas, and other equipment.[21] Surveillance technology deployed on the border before CTAC included infrared nightscopes, low-light television cameras, ground sensors to detect movement of persons, fences, encrypted radio communications systems, and electronic identification schemes to record and track the migration of persons across the border.

Even more impressive than technology, however, are improvements in the organization of strategy, tactics, and operational coordination among law enforcement agencies along the border. Law enforcement doctrine is moving away from the static, function-oriented view of the border in which separate agencies handle separate categories of illicit activity. The emphasis is toward a more fluid, proactive, and threat-specific orientation in which security targets are attacked by interagency task forces that draw on the combined resources and jurisdictional authority of several agencies. Some of these changes required congressional approval, such as the addition of drug enforcement authority to Border Patrol agents, and the change in *posse comitatus* to permit U.S. military assistance in the drug effort. Some required administrative policy changes or voluntary interagency cooperation. All of them, to succeed, required changes in the parochial, turf-jealous, and notoriously uncooperative attitudes of law enforcement agencies toward each other.

By the late 1990s there were several federal coordinating mechanisms dealing with drugs alone: the Interdiction Committee, organized by ONDCP in 1987, brings together leaders of customs, INS, DEA, the Department of State, and the U.S. armed forces to coordinate interdiction efforts. The Attorney General's Executive Committee brings together Justice Department officials to coordinate border crime efforts. Operation Alliance coordinates and prioritizes law enforcement requests for military counter-drug assistance provided through Joint Task Force Six (JTF–6), which, in turn, solicits military assistance for law enforcement officers requesting it. On the border this is often in the form of road and fence building from volunteer National Guard units supporting the Border Patrol between ports of entry. The Southwest Border Council, created in 1994, also a Justice Department coordinating group, supports the Southwest Border Initiative, which provides incentives for state and local law enforcement authorities to cooperate with federal agencies in attacking organized Mexican traffickers. Added to this are joint task forces created at all levels to deal with specific targets of opportunity, especially in drug interdiction missions. At any given time on the border there are dozens of mixed groups working on specific targets, often using code-word levels of secrecy. Because most drug smuggling runs in south-north corridors through ports of entry, these are heavily targeted. For migration interdiction, occasional border-length exercises are initiated, requiring the close coordination of East-West administrative sectors.

The design and configuration of these systems required years of effort. Although they are still evolving, rough divisions of labor are emerging. The first line of defense is the creation of a shield against entry of contraband goods or persons. The U.S. Customs Service is the lead agency for drug interdiction at the ports of entry, where most illegal drugs are said to enter. Customs is supported by INS, DEA, JTF–6 and/or FBI agents, or other agencies acting alone or in interagency groups. Illegal migrants are the responsibility of the INS and their law enforcement arm, the Border Patrol. Between ports of entry the Border Patrol, often supported by JTF–6 and other agencies, is the lead agency for drug interdiction as well as undocumented migrants.

Once illegal goods or undocumented persons penetrate the border, a host of federal, state, and local law enforcement agencies, often with overlapping authority, intervene in a second border-intensive line of defense. The object is to disrupt the chain of activities that begins after goods and persons have crossed illegally, preventing their distribution throughout the country. Warehousing, money laundering, transportation, sales of drugs, and other activities are targeted. While disruption activities can occur anywhere, the border is a target-rich opportunity zone. Two related but distinct border-intense security processes are thus in evidence: interdiction to prevent border crossing, and disruption of organizations dealing in people or goods already smuggled in. At a third level of activity are efforts to disrupt the distribution of illicit goods to local markets in and outside the border region, tasks relegated largely to local law enforcement officials and lower in the hierarchy of federal priorities.

The relatively low priority given to enforcement of local drug violations highlights a dilemma affecting relationships between federal and local security officials. Federal agents are tasked with national-scale law enforcement responsibilities, and they receive budgets commensurate with national goals. The rapid buildup of federal forces on the border, however, was not matched by equivalent municipal or state security increases. This is readily seen in the personnel and budget figures in tables 12.1 and 12.2. While federal jobs in the Southwest rose 70 percent from 1993 to 1998 (from 7,487 to 12,738), El Paso municipal police officer positions increased less than 5 percent, from 950 to 992. Moreover, the prestige and pay grades of federal law enforcement officers are significantly higher. These factors have tended to create a caste-like differentiation between federal officers and state and local officers. As federal antidrug activities expanded, state and local officers were not often fully engaged in the effort. Local law officers, however, are often better situated than federal officers to deal with some aspects of border-intensive law enforcement activities. They are more familiar with the region, have closer contact with relevant publics, and, if mobilized, can make the difference between success and failure in investigative and operational activities. How to find ways to engage this potentially powerful resource in drug enforcement activities has been a major concern of federal agents for some time.

One of the more ingenious efforts to address this concern is the High Intensity Drug Trafficking Area (HIDTA) program, funded by the ONDCP since 1988. An executive committee is created consisting of top federal, state, and local drug enforcement actors within a designated region. The board determines priorities. State, federal, and local law enforcement officers are then combined into teams that may engage in investigative work, intelligence gathering, operations, prosecutions, and so on. To motivate city, county, and state police agencies to permit their officers to participate, salaries are reimbursed, equipment may be paid for, and other costs may be borne by the HIDTA program. Forfeited assets are also distributed to local agencies in proportion to the effort invested. In El Paso, recent HIDTA priorities include dismantling drug-smuggling transportation cells, location and apprehension of fugitives, improving intelligence dissemination, and investigation of major international drug traffickers. In California, an HIDTA–organized Border Alliance Group of about forty state, federal, and local agencies pool intelligence resources, target major Mexican drug traffickers, investigate border corruption, counter maritime smuggling, develop strategies, focus on violent crime, experiment with technology, coordinate methamphetamine efforts, and so on in various task forces. In South Texas, an HIDTA–sponsored partnership coordinates activities in fourteen counties along similar lines.[22] Overall, the proportion of HIDTA funds spent on state and local agencies has increased from about 40 percent to over 60 percent in the past six years. Although by no means the only interagency program, HIDTA is perhaps the single most effective mechanism for motivating interagency cooperation down to the municipal level, even though it consumes only about 5 percent of the border drug enforcement budget.

The rapid buildup of U.S. security forces in the new border regime, then, is aimed at interdicting the passage of unwanted persons and goods entering from Mexico. Failing that, the goal is to foil the transportation of illicit cargo to other regions through seizures or disruption of organizations engaged in these activities near the border. As these systems fail and contraband leaves the border region or is consumed locally, other law enforcement systems attempt to disrupt distribution and sales organizations aimed at targeted markets.

LAW ENFORCEMENT STRATEGY AND TACTICS ON THE BORDER: THE MEXICAN SIDE

The Mexican approach to border security is different primarily because drugs and persons do not tend to move in a southerly direction across the border. Efforts to reduce contraband from the United States are not drug driven, nor do they rely on technological innovation. They remain labor intensive, they are centered on ports of entry, and they focus on enforcing limitations on legal imports. Moreover, since U.S. citizens do not in great numbers migrate illegally to Mexico, there is no Mexican equivalent of the Border Patrol. Thus the shielding and filtering logic that propelled much of the U.S. buildup on the border in recent years—doubling the Border Patrol, constructing technology-intense fencing and sensor and surveillance systems, and directing coordinated interagency operations toward border interdiction—is missing in the Mexico–U.S. border security problematic, although it is present on Mexico's southern borders. This asymmetry explains some of the difference in the border security approaches of the two countries. Other asymmetries can be traced to different mixtures of jurisdictional authority and resource allocations between local, state, and national police forces in each country, and to the sheer differences in absolute resources devoted to security matters.

Although border information on federal security budgets for the Mexican border are not available, a rough estimate of the comparative expenditures of funds can be gleaned from estimates of overall expenditures per capita in select border twin cities, as shown in table 12.3. Overall, the ratio of absolute per capita government expenditures varies from about five to about seven times more on the U.S. side than on the Mexican side. The ratios for security expenditures appear to be reasonably equivalent. The Ciudad Juárez Municipal Police Department, for example, after receiving a very strong increase in 1999 (nearly 100 percent), was budgeted at about US$23 million, while the El Paso Municipal Police and El Paso Sheriff's Office were budgeted at nearly $120 million. Since Ciudad Juárez has about twice the population of El Paso County, per capita ratios are on the order of ten times higher in absolute terms on the U.S. side for local police forces. Comparing force structures (perhaps a better measurement of capability than dollar expenditures), Ciudad Juárez had 1,200 municipal police officers in 1999, about 250 state police, and 40 federal law enforcement officers. El Paso, with a population size about half that of Ciudad Juárez, had about 1,200 police officers, 330 state police, and 445 federal law enforcement officers.

Table 12.3 **Per Capita Government Expenditures for Border Twin Cities (current U.S. dollars)**

City	Municipal (1995)	State (1993)	Federal (1995)	Total
Tijuana, Baja California/	49	430	1033	1511
San Diego, California	1069	3350	5936	10355
Nogales, Sonora/	43	271	1033	1347
Santa Cruz, Arizona	663	2845	3250	6758
Cd. Juárez, Chihuahua/	44	129	1033	1206
El Paso, Texas	576	2168	4134	6878

Source: Andrés Suárez, *Profile of the US–Mexico Border* (Ciudad Juárez: FEMAP, Secretaría de Educación Pública, 1996).

In comparison with the United States, Mexico has a sharper division of labor between local, state, and federal enforcement authorities. Consistent with José María Ramos's discussion in his chapter in this volume, in Mexico the federal government is the sole enforcer of drug laws. State and local law enforcement officials who, in the course of their duties encounter drug violations, may detain suspects, but they must immediately relinquish them to federal authorities for investigation, indictment, and prosecution. Municipal police are solely preventive bodies; except for minor offenses, they have no authority to investigate, indict, or prosecute. When municipal authorities are called to a homicide, for example, they must relinquish the case to state authorities, which have investigative and prosecutorial jurisdiction in most homicide cases. Municipal authorities encountering an illegal drug sale must call federal agents. On the U.S. side, many jurisdictions overlap. Customs agents seizing a packet of cocaine in a vehicle attempting to enter the United States, for example, will typically turn the case over to a state or local law enforcement officer if the cargo falls below a standard threshold of weight—even though Customs has full jurisdictional authority to prosecute the case. This is not possible under Mexican law.

Even though these jurisdictional rigidities may have advantages (they prevent the kinds of turf battles frequently observed in U.S. law enforcement practice), a primary disadvantage is that they discourage resource sharing between agencies of differing levels. This is particularly troublesome where resource scarcities are acute. In 1999, for example, there were only forty agents assigned by the national attorney general to enforce federal law in Ciudad Juárez, the operational base of one of the largest drug cartels in the world. Moreover, most of these are rotated frequently and are relatively unfamiliar with Ciudad Juárez. On the other hand, although overworked, there was a force of about 250 state police officers and 1,200 municipal police officers, many of them with a strong working knowledge of the city crime landscape. The state government controls one of the best forensics laboratories in Mexico. The paradox is that the agencies with the greatest effective capability to resolve drug violations have the least jurisdictional capacity to do so. As the power of drug cartels has grown and as crime rates have risen, various experiments in interagency operational cooperation have been undertaken, although these are not nearly as comprehensive as those in the United States.

One such effort was the formation of Grupos Orión in Chihuahua and other states. In 1995 a *convenio* (accord) was approved between the federal attorney general's field office in Chihuahua State (similar to the U.S. Attorney's Office) and the state attorney general. It established an interagency operational entity known as Grupo Orión, composed of a small group of federal judicial and state police officers. These operate as a single unit and are cross-designated to investigate, exchange information, and prosecute federal criminal violations—mainly drug infractions, drug-related homicides, and arms and other contraband.

In 1996 the Ciudad Juárez municipality created an accord with the state government that permitted a small cadre of city police to be cross-designated into a Grupo Orión unit which established a base of operations there. This permitted municipal, state, and federal agents assigned to the unit to conduct joint investigations, operations, indictments, and prosecutions. In 1997, the Chihuahua, Cuauhtémoc, and Parral municipalities added groups (called "bases") as well, for a total of four in the state. Each base has approximately ten to fifteen cross-designated police officers combining city, state, and federal forces. Each sets its own priorities; in southern Chihuahua the priority has been marijuana crop eradication, while in Ciudad Juárez and Chihuahua the priority is to stem the proliferation of "*picaderos*" (places where drugs are sold and consumed). A statewide coordinator supervises activities in each base. In turn, Grupo Orión activities are overseen by committees that include the municipal president (mayor), the state attorney general's office, and the federal delegate.

Grupo Orión permits a flexible, target-specific, and efficient combination of all law enforcement assets in a locale. Federal agents have the legal mechanisms to enforce national law, but not the personnel or investigative resources. State agents have strong investigative and operational capacities, but not enough manpower or authority. And municipalities have strong manpower and intimate knowledge of the local scene, but no jurisdiction to investigate or pursue serious crimes. Grupo Orión combines all of these resources. Base members also have operational access to the databases of all three levels of law enforcement—something rare even on the U.S. side. Moreover, crimes that violate any combination of federal, state, or local statutes can be pursued seamlessly rather than through the cumbersome referral protocols normally used in cases of ambiguous jurisdiction. A drug-related homicide, for example, can be investigated through Grupo Orión simultaneously for both drug-related and homicide-related violations.

Grupo Orión is the first intergovernmental agency capable of investigating, indicting, and prosecuting a single crime from beginning to end. This was impossible for municipal police and possible for state police only in a narrow range of crimes, and it has stimulated the introduction of police undercover work, something unheard of just a few years ago. Over 50 percent of the federal indictments in Chihuahua now derive from Grupo Orión investigations, and so far extensive or systemic cases of corruption have not surfaced. Grupo Orión accords have not yet been signed in other border states. In Tijuana, interagency units are formed on an ad hoc basis, without formal agreement; and in Sinaloa, state and federal authorities discussed forming a counterpart to Grupo Orión but failed to conclude an agreement.

Another effort to combine federal, state, and local law enforcement agencies into operational units was the creation of *células mixtas* ("combined cells") through interagency accords similar to those creating Grupos Orión. One was signed in Ciudad Juárez in late 1997 with state governor Francisco Barrio. *Células mixtas* are municipal-level police groups incorporating state and federal officers on loan to permit investigations—but not prosecutions—of municipal, state, and federal violations. Unlike Grupo Orión bases, which are permanently formed and into which officers are rotated, combined cells are formed on an ad hoc basis. When an investigation has concluded, the cell is disbanded and loaned personnel return to their original units. In late 1999 there were six such cells in operation in Ciudad Juárez. Rather than conducting undercover investigations, their work consisted of setting up random roadblocks to check for contraband. Accords in the other border states also permit the use of combined cells.

Grupo Beta

Mexico's Interior Ministry created Grupo Beta in response to pressure from U.S. officials concerned about growing violence against migrants in the Tijuana area of the border. Accords were drawn up between the Interior Ministry, Baja California governor Ernesto Ruffo (the first member of the PAN party to become governor of a Mexican state), and Tijuana municipal police to provide protection to Mexican citizens on the border. The group began operating in 1990 with thirty-six municipal, state, and federal migration officers, who were given salary increases and provided with weapons, radios, safety vests, and training by the U.S. Border Patrol, the sheriff's department in San Diego, and the California Highway Patrol. Unlike any other law enforcement agency on either side of the border, Beta could communicate with cross-border law enforcement officers, facilitating the capture of persons fleeing to the other side. The first Beta team's success at halting robberies, beatings, and drug deals, and at uncovering corrupt police officers became legendary.[23] Beta groups now exist in seven northern border towns and in Chiapas. In Nogales, for example, a Beta group was formed in 1994, with a force of twenty-one officers and six vehicles. During 1996, the first full year of operation, Beta records show that more than 85,000 migrants were "assisted" and 207 suspects were turned over to state and local agents for investigation and prosecution. The next year the latter figure was 697.[24] A Beta group was formed in Agua Prieta in 1996.

Since 1997, however, the Nogales Beta group has focused less on criminal apprehension and more on services to migrants. Moreover, the force was cut to fewer than ten agents. In the summer of 1999, the force was only eight officers, split about evenly between federal migration agents and local municipal police officers (with no participation of state police), each of whom earned about US$500 per month. These agents spent a good deal of time searching tunnels frequented by migrants hoping to cross into the United States, passing out a "Migrants' Guide to Human Rights" jointly sponsored by the National Commission for Human Rights and the National Migration Institute, and supporting programs to deal with repatriated minors and indigent deportees. In this latter program, migrants are given work to perform in Nogales until they are able to save enough money to return to their homes.

FEADS and Bilateral Task Forces

The Office of the Special Prosecutor for Crimes against Health (FEADS) was created in 1997 after the arrest of General Gutiérrez Rebollo, head of the Mexican National Institute to Combat Drugs (INCD), on charges stemming from his close association with leaders of the Juárez cartel. The

INCD was dismantled and replaced by the FEADS, now the counterpart to the DEA in the United States. The DEA provided assistance to the Organized Crime Unit of the Mexican Attorney General's Office, operating in the FEADS headquarters in Mexico City, for training and to improve the vetting system for antidrug agents. In 1999, sixty-four FEAD agents had been assigned to vetted units. In February 1998, a FEADS agent in Ciudad Juárez was removed from his position after it was discovered he was associated with Rafael Muñoz Talavera, leader of one of the drug organizations he was investigating. Two FEADS agents in Tijuana were arrested in September 1998 on kidnapping charges, and three were arrested in Monterrey in March 1999 on extortion charges.[25] In Ciudad Juárez in 1999 the FEADS presence consisted of a force of three persons. They lived in hotels and were rotated every few months.

As part of the U.S.–Mexico Binational Drug Strategy process initiated in 1996, Bilateral Task Forces were established in Tijuana, Ciudad Juárez, and Monterrey to investigate major Mexican criminal organizations. Initially the groups were formed to promote exchange of information and greater operational cooperation between U.S. and Mexican federal authorities. But they were dismantled after the INCD was found to be corrupted at all levels. In 1998 and 1999, they were reconstituted and expanded to eight cities, but there have been no joint operations with U.S. counterparts, and they have only begun to conduct investigations. Contact with U.S. law enforcement agents appears to be minimal.

The Armed Forces on the Border

Northern Mexico is split into three military regions, each of which is subdivided into zones. Headquarters along the border zone are located in Baja California, Chihuahua (recently divided into two zones), Coahuila, Nuevo León, and Tamaulipas. Military garrisons, cross-designated with customs and drug control responsibilities, are located in all of the border cities. As part of the border buildup, garrison troop strengths were increased during the late 1990s and have shifted from static assignments to active patrolling between ports of entry. Moreover, light cavalry units without armor or artillery have been placed in border regions to assist in patrol activities. The air force in northern Mexico was also upgraded during the late 1990s in response to antidrug operations.

The border mission of the armed forces has recently been restructured to permit stronger focus on illegal activities. There are no *posse comitatus* statutes prohibiting Mexican military forces from engaging in law enforcement activities. Article 29, section 24 of the Constitution permits the armed forces to search persons for weapons, a legal instrument that has made it possible for armed forces personnel to engage in a number of drug interdiction activities. Moreover, under Mexican law, military forces may be deployed in support of civilian law enforcement activities if requests come from agency heads and follow a formal protocol. Thus federal law enforcement heads may supplement their very scarce personnel resources with significant operational assets drawn from nearby military detachments. In the fall of 1999 the armed forces used agreements with several state prosecutor's offices within which joint state-military operations could be conducted under military leadership. The program is known as Base of Mixed Operations (B.O.M.). BOM activities included burning illegal crops, patrolling, setting up roadblocks, and confiscating illegally obtained assets. The program is run from Mexico City by the armed forces in multi-state operations including Chihuahua, Durango, Sinaloa, and Sonora. State police agents accompany BOM forces and cooperate in the investigation and prosecution of violations of state law encountered in these activities.

By the end of the 1990s, then, Mexico had created new administrative and operational configurations to deal with security issues. On the border, antidrug components were initiated, drug-related crime was targeted in the larger border cities through increases in municipal budgets, and efforts were made to strengthen protections for migrants increasingly vulnerable to predatory criminals. Interagency operational units like Grupo Orión and the *células mixtas* addressed relatively low-level drug trafficking activities at the local level. The armed forces focused on interdiction of drug transportation and crop eradication at regional, largely rural levels. And the FEADS and some elements of the Federal Judicial Police, both under control of the PGR, investigated national crime syndicates such as the Arellano Félix and Juárez cartels. Unlike the U.S. border buildup, Mexican law enforcement has no parallel border interdiction machinery, and Mexico has much more readily deployed the armed forces in a number of law enforcement activities. Like their U.S. counterparts, Mexican security officials have experimented with a more integrated approach, combining local, state, and federal officers into flexible operational units.

CROSS-BORDER COOPERATION

Since 1996, increasing attention has been devoted to strengthening bilateral security cooperation. A cabinet-level High Level Contact Group was established in 1996, among other reasons to develop a bilateral counterdrug strategy. By 1998 binational drug control strategy was summarized in sixteen "alliance points," each with specific targets and performance measures.[26] Most of these involve making available non-sensitive information regarding each other's antidrug activities, improving educational outreach and professional training, and putting into place infrastructure through which more cooperation between security agencies on both sides and at all levels is enabled through the articulation of goals that imply closer cooperation. Some—such as the goals of improving extradition procedures, cooperation in illegal firearms traffic, and making efforts to reduce drug-related corruption (points 5, 6, 7, and 9)—are designed to reduce strong traditional irritants in the relationship, normalizing bilateral relations that have been highly strained rather than significantly enhancing operational cooperation.

The most border-relevant portion of the strategy is point No. 10, enhancing border cooperation to increase security. In 1993 the United States and Mexico created the Border Liaison Mechanism (BLM) to improve cross-border official communication. Consulates in twin cities along the border are tasked with organizing quarterly meetings with law enforcement officials and civic leaders to discuss problems of mutual concern. In the El Paso–Ciudad Juárez area, the BLM was able to get the Texas Transportation Department to fund lane modifications at the border to permit U.S. cars to turn around before reaching Mexico, and to help pay for warning signs to U.S. citizens that transporting firearms into Mexico is a federal offense.

These measures were precipitated when a U.S. citizen—a tourist from outside the border region—with a handgun in his glove compartment got onto the wrong freeway lane, found himself in Mexico, and explained to authorities there what had happened. He was arrested for a felony violation. Mexican authorities took the case as seriously as U.S. authorities might take the case of a person trying to explain the presence of illegal drugs in his glove compartment. Public opinion on the U.S. side was aroused, the U.S. consul got involved, and Mexican authorities eventually released the man after a thorough investigation. In fall 1999 a similar case was resolved after a U.S. Marine Corps soldier with several weapons in his automobile accidentally drove into Tijuana.

The Arizona Highway Department installed a dedicated phone line in the office of the chief of police in Nogales, Mexico. This phone line is connected to a database that will permit Mexican officials to trace license plates of vehicles thought to be stolen. Perhaps the most significant result so far of BLM activity is in the San Diego–Tijuana area. Through the BLM, a working interface was created between cross-border law enforcement to permit officials rapid response to emergency situations, facilitate cross-border crime scene investigations by local or federal agents, and assist in prosecution of minor cross-border drug transporters. Most of these advances are due in part to personal relationships that have been established between cross-border officials. But the BLM mechanism encourages such relations to develop, and over time highly innovative interfaces at the local level are likely to develop, as long as the overall relationship between the two countries and within the border environment is positive.

Law enforcement officers from both sides of the border who attend BLM–coordinated meetings in the El Paso–Ciudad Juárez and Nogales regions generally believe the BLMs are useful. They establish an agenda to prevent or resolve cross-border conflict between security agents on both sides. They encourage law enforcement officials to become acquainted with their cross-border counterparts. But they have not yet resulted in exchanges of intelligence or other sensitive information, nor in long-term operational interfacing.

EVALUATION OF THE BORDER BUILDUP

Perhaps the most striking feature in the contemporary border security milieu is the sharp asymmetry in overall goals of, strategies for, and resources devoted to security on each side of the border. The overall U.S. goal is to prevent the passage of unwelcome *persons* and illegal *substances* into the United States from Mexico. Major strategies revolve around efforts to intercept unwanted persons and goods as they attempt to enter, to disrupt organizations conspiring to distribute illegal drugs inside the United States, to ferret out near the border people and goods who/that have crossed illegally, and to encourage enforcement of migration and drug laws where supply meets demand outside the border region. Significant resources to accomplish these goals have been made available to federal government agencies, but local agencies have sometimes benefited from federal expenditures as well through asset forfeiture laws and interagency task forces such as HIDTA and the Organized Crime Drug Enforcement Task Forces (OCDETF). The security of persons living on or near the border is of peripheral interest to the federal government and is largely left to local agencies.

On the Mexican side, the major federal goal appears to be to increase the *security* of persons living near the border. The dominant border strategy is to improve local-federal police capabilities to combat growing crime rates through agreements that permit combined federal-state-local police operations. Antidrug operations seem aimed primarily against the lower end of the organizational hierarchy—that is, against local transportation and sales of drugs, rather than against the international operations of cartels. Relatively few resources are devoted at the border itself to targeting criminal organizations through the FEADS and attorney general's offices—even though major cartel operations are headquartered in Tijuana and Ciudad Juárez. Another security strategy is extensive crop eradication and disruption of transportation of illegal drugs in rural areas. Finally, significant efforts have been made to protect potential migrants against the actions of predators through Grupo Beta and, where abuse occurs on the U.S. side, through stronger consular activity.[27] The passage of persons or illegal substances to the United States is not a strong priority. Differences in resource allocations are suggested by manpower figures between El Paso and Ciudad Juárez. In El Paso, the federal presence, calculated on a per capita basis, is more than twenty times greater than it is in Ciudad Juárez. The per capita municipal police force in El Paso, however, is only twice as great as the one across the river in Ciudad Juárez.

For more than two decades the U.S. government has sought greater cooperation from Mexico in attacking Mexico-based organizations that transport and sell drugs across the border. The modest effort in Mexico to target cartel activity on the border suggests these efforts have largely failed. And although drug-related corruption within police institutions is a serious concern to most Mexicans, law enforcement racket-protection schemes have a long history predating drug cartel activity. Police kidnapping rings, police extortion, and other forms of corruption require attention too. Mexico's acceptance of U.S. advice on institution-building measures for security forces thus reflects an overall understanding of public dissatisfaction with law enforcement institutions in general, not just those engaged in antidrug activity. Similarly, Mexican government actions toward illegal migration to the United States focus on abuse of migrants on either side of the border, not on dissuasion of migration itself.[28] Given these differences in goals, strategies, and resource allocations, it is not surprising that cooperation between the two countries is restricted largely to the use of diplomatic channels and other mechanisms to manage tensions that arise when the priorities of security agencies do not coincide with those of cross-border counterparts.

If there has not been much goal convergence on major border security issues, however, the U.S. government has had a stronger influence in Mexico's selection of tactical security instruments, largely by providing technical assistance. Vetting of security agents, emphasis on stronger training, experimenting with interagency operational teams, fascination with technology, creation of rapid-response mobile teams, greater coordination among federal agencies—all of these reflect strong U.S. influence and suggest a genuine improvement in the tactical capabilities of Mexican security agencies. Most of this assistance was provided by drug-budget funds. That Mexican security agencies have adopted some of the tactics and institutional configurations of their U.S. counterparts, however, does not imply that strategic goals are more convergent. And given the strong differences in the countries' approaches to border security, it is not surprising that a functional security interface has failed to materialize at the border between parallel agencies. Nor, perhaps, is it surprising that the border security regimes of each country have failed. Drug trafficking, drug-related crime rates, and migration between the United States and Mexico are simply too bilaterally interconnected. Addressing these issues independently on each side of the border, with different goals and priorities, limited by "supply-side" ideologies, and with virtually no operational interfacing—these are formulas for failure.

There is little evidence that border drug interdiction efforts have reduced the supply of drugs entering the United States. Approximately 60 percent of the cocaine available in the United States in 1998 (about 300 metric tons) is believed to have entered the United States across the U.S.–Mexico border, most of it through official ports of entry.[29] Up to 80 percent of the foreign-grown marijuana and 29 percent of the heroin used in the United States is smuggled through Mexico.[30] Even with vastly improved technology, the task of interdicting drugs at the border is daunting, with 4 million trucks, more than 450 million persons, and 75 million cars crossing into the United States from Mexico each year. For each technological improvement, counter-strategies are possible. In 1999, for example, the General Accounting Office (GAO) reported that a new chemical process has been discovered that permits the creation of "black cocaine," a product that can evade detection by drug-sniffing dogs and chemical tests.[31] It seems likely that in a $38–billion-dollar industry in cocaine alone, traffickers are likely to find inventive ways to smuggle illegal substances into the United States. Whatever else may be said about U.S. drug policy in other arenas, border interdiction has thus far failed.

Drug enforcement officials themselves are not highly optimistic about interdiction strategies. Pressed by Congress through the GAO to set performance measures for effectiveness, border-relevant interdiction goals are to reduce the rate at which illegal drugs enter the United States by only 10 percent by 2002 and 20 percent by 2007, compared to a base year of 1996.[32] Current seizures are said to represent about 30 percent of U.S. consumption of cocaine and between 10 and 15 percent of heroin. It has been estimated that at least 75 percent of international drug shipments would need to be intercepted to substantially reduce the profitability of drug trafficking.[33] A 20 percent reduction in the flow of cocaine under present conditions would represent only about 53 percent of shipments destined for the United States, substantially short of that threshold.[34] The statistics of supply and demand projections aside, demand reduction, rather than supply control, appears to be gaining support as a major strategic component in U.S. drug policy: the percentage of antidrug funds available for demand reduction has doubled in recent years, after falling to about 17 percent of the drug policy budget.[35]

On the Mexican side, drug cartel activities appear to be as strong or stronger than ever at the U.S.–Mexico border, and collateral problems deriving from cartel activities—corruption of law enforcement officials, rising crime and drug addiction rates—appear to be continuing or growing more severe. Two of the largest drug cartels in the world—the Arellano Félix organization in Tijuana and the Juárez cartel—continue to operate with impunity in the two largest cities on the Mexican side of the border. The death of Amado Carrillo Fuentes, leader of the Juárez cartel, in 1997 apparently did not interrupt the ability of the cartel to export drugs into the United States. Drug seizures in El Paso, an indicator of the volume of overall traffic, remained about the same during a bloody war between rival factions struggling to gain control of the cartel in the weeks and months following Carrillo Fuentes's death. There have been no major cartels dismantled by the Mexican government, and Mexico continues to be the route for most cocaine shipped into the United States.

Drug-trafficking activities on the Mexican side of the border, moreover, have produced significant violence in large cities over the past few years. In the first seven months after the death of Amado Carrillo Fuentes, Ciudad Juárez was shaken by several dozen murders (some in public places) thought to be related to a power struggle within the Juárez cartel. In Tamaulipas the homicide rate reached a record of 156 in 1998; the rate was 216 in Sinaloa, where drug-related violence is rampant.[36] In September 1998 a suspected marijuana drug trafficker and eighteen relatives were killed in a small town near Tijuana. A month later six people were killed by young men with AK–47 assault rifles. These are only the most dramatic and publicized events. According to the DEA, at one point 90 percent of police officers, prosecutors, and judges in Tijuana and the state of Baja California were reportedly on the Arellano Félix payroll.[37] Witnesses have said the cartel pays up to US$1 million a week in bribes to law enforcement officials.

Moreover, drug-related social problems in the large cities appear to be getting worse. Drug traffickers have for several years now paid some of their workers near the border in kind, rather than in cash. This has meant that a certain percentage of illegal drugs has remained on the Mexican side of the border, creating a growing secondary market for drugs, especially in the large cities. In Ciudad Juárez in 1999, police were investigating 900 "*picaderos*," where drugs are sold, although there are estimates that as many as 2,000 *picaderos* service a population of nearly two million. In Tijuana there were an estimated 500 *picaderos* in 2000. While statistics are difficult to obtain, it appears there is a sharply growing heroin addiction problem in Ciudad Juárez and Tijuana, and cocaine addiction is the leading problem associated with troubled youth. Recent crime rates are also difficult to calculate with precision, but it appears that during the mid–1990s crime rates were growing faster on the Mexican border than in the interior. Burgues, Cortez, and Fuentes[38] found that the northern border states experienced a 9 percent annual average increase in criminal prosecutions from 1990 to 1995, compared with a 2.3 percent growth rate in the rest of Mexico. Arrest records in Ciudad Juárez suggest a rapidly growing crime problem, although rates have apparently stabilized in some categories (homicides and auto thefts). In Tijuana, crime rates appear to have doubled during the first half of the 1990s. In Matamoros, crime rates declined rather sharply after the collapse of the Gulf cartel (see table 12.4).

In contrast to what appears to be rapidly escalating crime rates on the Mexican side of the border, on the U.S. side crime rates appear to be dropping relative to the rest of the country. In 1997, crime rates in all border cities except Laredo were lower than they were in 1992 (see table 12.5). Moreover, in San Diego, Yuma, San Luis, El Paso, Presidio, and Roma, the 1997 rates were lower than those of non-border U.S. cities of similar size. In the other cities they were higher. In relation to the rest of the country, however, crime rates had improved in all cities except Laredo (compare columns 1 and 5 in table 12.5). In 1992, for example, the crime rate in Nogales was 66 percent higher than the average crime rate in cities of similar size. Although the crime rate was still higher in 1997 than average (at 42 percent), it had nevertheless cut the gap by one-third. In McAllen and Brownsville, Texas, the relative drops were even more dramatic. Of the eight border cities for which data are available, only Laredo experienced a relative increase in crime rates. Beginning in 1992, its rates were slightly lower than expected, but by 1997 they were 16 percent higher than expected—even though in absolute terms the crime rate was only 2 percent higher than it had been in 1992.

Illegal migration interdiction is more difficult to evaluate. About 1.5 million illegal immigrants were apprehended annually in 1997–1999 while attempting to enter the United States; they were immediately turned back. Most such cases occur at the United States' southwest border. Removals of persons—a more formal process than apprehension—were up 50 percent in 1998 over 1997, and up again 3 percent in 1999, to a record of 176,990. Of these, 83 percent were Mexican citizens. A growing proportion of persons removed (over one-third) are criminal aliens, deported upon completion of their sentence, and identified through an improved communications system with prison administrators. Of the 114,631 noncriminal removals in 1999, 89,000 were expelled under the "expedited removal" process, by which persons attempting to enter the United States with forged travel papers or without travel documents are removed. Another 72,000 aliens departed voluntarily after being charged with immigration law violations. Clearly the INS has its hands full.

It is not entirely clear, however, that INS enforcement efforts have significantly changed the overall patterns of migration from Mexico to the United States. Despite the enormous budgetary increases of the past few years, the INS estimates that 275,000 illegal migrants are absorbed into U.S. society each year, representing a 5 percent increase over the approximately 5.5 million already believed to be in the United States at any given time. Moreover, to the extent that security agents have succeeded in reducing the supply of undocumented migrants in, for example, agri-

Table 12.4 **Crime Rates on Mexico's Northern Border by City, 1990–1998**

	1990	1991	1992	1993	1994	1995	1996	1997	1998
TIJUANA									
Federal: Persons	174	445	388	313	491	556			
Federal: Property	30	60	39	32	54	3			
Federal: Arms	20	133	151	187	349	0			
Local: Persons	396	526	568	569	525	431			
Local: Property	698	905	939	1,165	1,208	203			
TOTAL	1,318	2,069	2,085	2,266	2,627	1,193			
CIUDAD JUAREZ									
Federal: Persons	198	247	273	230	200	319			
Federal: Property	11	24	15	45	61	1			
Federal: Arms	23	51	130	140	166	0			
Local: Persons	508	604	465	466	570	556			
Local: Property	557	630	655	643	653	695			
Total Arrests (1,000s)[1]					111.5	150.8	176.2	176.4	
Stolen Auto Reports[2]				5,513	4908	4623	5,088	5,344	5,280
Homicides[2]					213	250	213	188	189

Table 12.4 continued

	1990	1991	1992	1993	1994	1995	1996	1997	1998
MATAMOROS									
Federal: Persons	211	319	244	258	232	209			
Federal: Property	50	36	22	49	34	8			
Federal: Arms	175	132	173	121	0	0			
Local: Persons	307	254	198	136	221	183			
Local: Property	254	254	226	223	234	0			
TOTAL	997	995	863	787	721	400			

Sources: All but the Ciudad Juárez data on total arrests, stolen auto reports, and homicides was adapted from Vicente Sánchez Munguía, "Delincuencia en la frontera norte," *Ciudades* 40 (October–December 1998): 46–51. Data on total arrests, stolen auto reports, and homicides were provided by the Ciudad Juárez municipal police department.

[1] Statistics from state police.

[2] Statistics from municipal police.

cultural labor markets, political action appears to be under way to simply legalize migrant agricultural laborers.[39] If enacted, this policy change would highlight the cyclical and somewhat disingenuous nature of U.S. attitudes toward migration from Mexico. These tend to vary according to economic conditions within the United States, but they are often justified by the evocation of somewhat more abstract principles such as welfare reform, crime reduction, or outright chauvinism.

Table 12.5 **Absolute and Relative Crime Rates on the U.S. Side of the Border by City, 1992 and 1997**

City	Difference between Actual and Expected Crime Rate, 1992 (%)	Crime Rate per 100,000 Inhabitants, 1997	Average Expected Crime Rate for Non-border Cities of Similar Size, 1997	Difference between Actual and Expected Crime Rate, 1997 (%)	Trend in Crime Rate, 1992–1997
San Diego	-12	4,986	6,743	-26	-24
Yuma		1,810	5,664	-67	
San Luis		4,008	4,388	-09	
Nogales	+66	6,050	4,269	+42	-26
Douglas		6,685	4,269	+57	
El Paso	-10	6,997	7,817	-11	-17
Presidio		537	4,388	-88	
Del Rio	+20	5,624	4,808	+17	-20
Eagle Pass	+134	6,228	4,808	+29	-46
Laredo	-5	7,975	6,875	+16	+2
Roma		3,071	4,388	-30	
Rio Grande City		7,086	4,269	+66	
McAllen	+107	9,199	6,879	+34	-32
Brownsville	+61	7,746	6,879	+13	-26

Sources: Adapted from Uniform Crime Reports, 1992 and 1997.

Meanwhile, the costs of current supply-side migration policies are beginning to be felt. In the past few years the INS has become, among other things, a huge prison administrator, with neither the personnel nor experience to handle the load.[40] In San Diego in 1998 the INS ran out of beds and local jail space, forcing it to release detainees not accused of crimes. Overcrowding throughout the INS prison system is common. Complaints of human rights abuse are up; officials are sometimes prone to bully persons entering with false documents in order to get them to admit to violations and thus avoid having to process them. Compounding these issues, the very success of INS enforcement policies in one region sometimes creates severe hardship in other regions. In 1999, as migration policy in El Paso and San Diego made it relatively difficult to cross illegally at these two points, thousands of undocumented migrants tried to enter the United States from Arizona. This, in turn, created something of a crisis; Nogales and Douglas were overwhelmed, and frustration levels increased.

On the Mexican side the introduction of Grupo Beta constituted a major step—not only in addressing the exploitation of migrants but also in designing operational interfaces with U.S. law enforcement officers. Nevertheless, Grupo Beta was always underfunded and overwhelmed, and its fate is now uncertain. The Federal Preventive Police (PFP), a new federal law enforcement agency, may absorb it or replace it. Although it is perhaps too early for a thorough evaluation of Grupo Beta, it appears that it assisted a significant proportion of migrants in need, but the force faced many administrative obstacles and has had trouble integrating itself into the larger law enforcement milieu on the Mexican side of the border.

After many years of massive buildup, enormous amounts of illegal drugs now enter the United States each year from Mexico, and drug supplies more than meet demand. Drug cartel activity in Mexico continues with impunity. The collateral effects of cartel activity—high rates of homicide, corruption of officials, money-laundering operations, and so on—have overwhelmed the capacity of law enforcement officials on the Mexican side. Costs are beginning to mount on the U.S. side as well. Drug arrests have tripled since 1980, disproportionately affecting African American and Hispanic populations. Corruption of U.S. officials is a growing problem. Public officials and the U.S. private sector are voicing stronger dissent against drug policies. Migration labor supplies to the United States also meet what appears to be a reasonably stable demand, despite huge budget increases for migration control. Moreover, migration policies have created a host of collateral problems affecting the border. These include administrative bottlenecks associated with increased incarceration rates for migrants, uneven enforcement of employer sanctions, increased crime on the Mexican side, criminal activity against migrants, and the more generalized decline in public confidence in law enforcement institutions that accompanies public awareness of policy failure.

SECURITY AND CIVIL SOCIETY

Prior to the recent border buildup, local elites on both sides, often working together informally, helped shape the local articulation of security policy. In recent years, as budgets and personnel increased dramatically and national priority status was invoked, federal agencies have achieved greater autonomy in their local activities. As a result, relationships between security agents and civil society have become more complex. A watershed event was the initiation of Operation Blockade in 1993, a bold and unprecedented move to seal parts of the border in El Paso through forward deployment of agents at the borderline itself. This move greatly inconvenienced large numbers of El Paso employers who hired day-time workers as domestic servants, hurt some retail businesses in downtown El Paso, and served notice that the relatively lax enforcement regime of the past was coming to an end. The tactics later became part of official Border Patrol policy in urban areas on the border.

Astonishingly, Silvestre Reyes, the Border Patrol chief who implemented Operation Blockade, consulted with virtually no sector of the population beforehand. He briefed local security officials, the county judge, the mayor, and the Mexican consul about the operation two days before it began; he was met with "great skepticism."[41] He implemented the operation anyway and maintained it in the face of diplomatic protests from Mexico, protests from merchants in El Paso, criticism from Roman Catholic Church leaders in the region, and protests from some Mexican American leaders. Even more astonishing, Reyes apparently had little support from Washington prior to implementing the program. But it worked. Within a few days Operation Blockade became highly popular among overwhelming sectors (up to 92 percent) of the El Paso population, including the Hispano Chamber of Commerce and a large proportion (up to 78 percent) of the Hispanic population.[42]

According to Tim Dunn, author of a detailed study of the operation, Reyes succeeded largely because he cast the operation as an "anticrime" measure in a town in which crime rates were rising.[43] His success was also due to his skillful efforts with various sectors of the population after the operation began. Moreover, it is widely believed that, as a Spanish-speaking Hispanic born near the border, Reyes's very presence removed the potential trump card of charges of ethnic bias against affected populations. Thus, although there appears to be a strong element of luck in Reyes's gamble, it also appears that he understood and trusted the society within which he was operating. He justified his actions—not in terms of the abstractions of "orderly borders," or the economics and politics of labor markets under NAFTA, or the dangers of illegal drug use—but rather in the concrete language of persons—poor and rich, Hispanic and Anglo, newcomer or old-timer—who experienced the border on a daily basis. Indeed, the fact that Reyes bothered to consult at all in the days following his move was a powerful statement in a community that had grown accustomed to a "colonial arrogance" on the part of law enforcement agencies and their leaders, who tended to invoke the sacred mantra of "national security" when challenged, blithely unmoved by the security concerns of the people living on the border. The meta-message was more about the proper relationship between federal law enforcement agencies and civil society than about border patrol tactics, and that Reyes's career itself was on the line may well have contributed to his popularity: he too resented Washington's insensitivity, and he too might suffer from it.

CONCLUSION

Just as the contemporary border security regime on the U.S. side began with a rhetorical elevation of drug and migration issues to the status of national security priorities, a first step toward a more sound border strategy might well be to lower the status of drugs, migration, and border management back to the level of "ordinary" politics and policy. Such a move might encourage a reexamination, through healthy debate, of the premises and costs and benefits of U.S. border policy. In fact, during most of 1999 such a debate was already taking place on the U.S.–Mexico border through the public statements of public officials, such as Governor Jane Hull (R) in Arizona, who called for a return of the "Bracero" program to permit farm laborers entry visas to the United States, and Governor Gary Johnson (R) of New Mexico, who characterized the antidrug effort as a "miserable failure" and called for decriminalization of drug usage. These border governors' challenges to existing policy strongly suggest the effort to "securitize" drug and migration policy above and beyond the fray of partisan debate has failed. To continue these policies as though there were still a national consensus about placing them on the security agenda is an invitation for trouble.

On the Mexican side there is strong debate over the relationship between citizens and law enforcement institutions, given the alarming increase in crime in Mexico City and on the U.S.–Mexico border, as well as the overwhelming evidence that law enforcement institutions have often participated in many of the very crimes they were created to suppress. This debate is intimately connected to a larger ongoing debate over the transition in Mexico away from the clientelistic politics of one-party rule. Within this context, "desecuritizing" drug policy seems less useful, since much of the public does not believe drug trafficking is a national priority anyway, except at a rhetorical level. What the Mexican government needs to prove to the public is that when an issue has been securitized rhetorically, it will be followed by actions that indicate its high priority. Making the construction of healthy law enforcement agencies a high national security priority might be a more useful exercise than making security promises about drug trafficking that are unlikely to be kept.

Second, although drug and migration strategies may not have succeeded, clearly the capabilities of security actors on each side of the border are greatly improved. This is especially true of the U.S. side. Interagency cooperation, coordination, intelligence sharing, and combined operations, while still far from seamless, are infinitely better than they were even a decade ago. Particularly impressive is the creative combination of local, state, and federal assets made possible through such programs as HIDTA, which have proven they could move different agencies in common cause toward specific targets. While important elements in civil society have properly voiced concern over the potential abuse of authority inherent in these enhanced organizational configurations, if directed against threats over which strong public consensus existed and with strong mechanisms of accountability, they could be formidable.

The trick in designing future interagency security alignments is to create strong mechanisms of local, state, and national accountability with strong public transparency and strong public support. The HIDTA program has been successful precisely because there is interagency participation in definitions, goal setting, and tactical selection. Likewise, in the future it would seem wise for public officials to seek full public participation in the *definition* of security threats and priorities. This would avoid the narrow, relatively unstable national political coalitions that at times decisively affected border security policy toward drugs or migration, but which had little solid support among affected populations along the border itself or in specific labor or drug markets.

On the Mexican side, where resources are scarcer, it is even more important to design interagency configurations that can maximize resource allocations. The use of flexible mobile units deployable to various sites, the creative use of state governments as liaisons between federal and municipal police forces, cross-designation of jurisdictions—all of these tactical improvements seem likely to continue. The trick in Mexico is to avoid the rampant criminalization of these agencies. One way to prevent this would be to assign security agents against relatively easy targets, such as burglary, where success is likely, rather than against difficult targets such as drug trafficking, where temptations are extraordinarily high. As in the United States, it is also important for Mexican law enforcement agencies to seek strong public input in the initial definition of security threats and security priorities, and to have clear-cut lines of accountability.

Third, while the bilateral mechanisms for cooperation in security issues should remain in place, greater attention should be focused on achieving *mutual definitions* of security threats, *mutual goals* to reduce them, and *mutual strategies and tactics* to counter them. Moreover, there should be *binational public support* for public security goals and priorities. If there is a single most important cause of the failure of recent U.S.–Mexico security relations, it is the hegemonic, unilateral pressure of the United States to get the Mexican government to cooperate toward resolving U.S. supply-side drug priorities. Even though the Mexican government formally cooperated, largely for reasons unrelated to its security priorities, the results were disastrous. The congressionally mandated "certification" procedure displaced bureaucratic energy once a year on both sides to engage in drug activity rather than action. Cooperation, at least on the border, did not materialize. The publics on both sides became frustrated. Relations between the two countries were strained. Drug trafficking through Mexico continued unabated.

Finally, if a security community does not now exist on the U.S.–Mexico border, there are strategic ways of getting there.

Notes

1. Paul Ganster and Alan Sweedler, "U.S.–Mexico Border Region," in *United States–Mexico Border Statistics since 1900*, edited by David E. Lorey (Los Angeles: Latin American Center, University of California, Los Angeles, 1990), chap. 10. The authors explicitly state they believe a security community exists between the two nations, and they devote several pages to this argument. They do not, however, rely on evidence of operational cooperation in the border security regime, but rather on evidence that the United States and Mexico have respected each other's national security concerns.

2. For a fuller treatment of the concept of "security community," see Emanuel Adler and Michael Barnett, eds., *Security Communities* (Cambridge: Cambridge University Press, 1999). In that volume, after a review of various periods of U.S.–Mexico relations, and using a broader definition of the term, Guadalupe González and Stephan Haggard conclude that the United States and Mexico "are still a long way from a deep or tightly coupled Deutschian security community." Haggard and González, "The United States and Mexico: A Pluralistic Security Community?" 326. For this paper I define "security community" as the presence of binational operational cooperation in defining and containing a mutual security threat.

3. Charles Harris and Louis R. Sadler, *The Border and Revolution* (Las Cruces: Center for Latin American Studies, New Mexico State University, 1988); Harris and Sadler, *Bastion on the Border: Ft. Bliss 1854–1943*, Historic and Natural Resources Report No. 6 (El Paso: U.S. Army Air Defense Center, 1993).

4. Harris and Sadler, *Bastion on the Border*.

5. See Books One and Two, Leon Metz, *Border: The U.S.–Mexico Line* (El Paso: Mangan, 1989).

6. Sadler and Harris, *The Border and Revolution*, 14.

7. Ibid., 53, 67.

8. See footnote 21 in Harris and Sadler, "Bastion on the Border," which cites Russel S. Weigley, "The Military and American Society," published by the George C. Marshall ROTC Award Conference Report, Lexington, Virginia, Marshall Foundation, no date given, 39–41.

9. Louis Ray Sadler, "The Historical Dynamics of Smuggling in the United States–Mexico Border Region, 1550–1998: Reflections on Markets, Culture, and Bureaucracies," in *Organized Crime and Democratic Governability in Mexico and the U.S.–Mexican Borderlands*, edited by John Bailey and Roy Godson (Pittsburgh, Penn.: University of Pittsburgh Press, 2000).

10. This anecdote was told to the author by a retired El Paso municipal law enforcement officer currently working for a federal agency. He participated in the operation. Interview, June 1999.

11. The best study on the early buildup of the current border security regime is Timothy Dunn, *The Militarization of the U.S.–Mexico Border: 1978–1992* (Austin: Center for Mexican American Studies, University of Texas at Austin, 1996).

12. As Mexican authorities began to respond to U.S. pressure to counter drug trafficking, there was little evidence of a drug abuse problem. A 1989 study of the national health department showed only 2.5 percent of the population had used marijuana at least once. Only 0.28 percent had tried cocaine, and 0.09 percent had used heroin. María Celia Toro, "Drug Trafficking from a National Security Perspective," in *Mexico in Search of Security*, edited by Bruce Bagley and Sergio Aguayo (Somerset, N.J.: Transaction, 1993), 320.

13. Gregory Treverton, "Narcotics in US–Mexico Relations," in *Mexico and the United States: Managing the Relationship*, edited by Riordan Roett (Boulder, Colo.: Westview, 1988), 215.

14. "Esfuerzo y dedicación," *Revista del Ejército y Fuerza Aérea Mexicanos*, July 1996, 12.

15. "Sedena destina 25 por ciento de su presupuesto a la lucha antidrogas," *La Jornada*, August 30, 1999.

16. Peter Andreas, "The Political Economy of Narco-Corruption in Mexico," *Current History*, April 1998, 161.

17. Sigrid Arzt, "Scope and Limits of an Act of Good Faith: The PAN's Experience at the Head of the Office of the Attorney General of the Republic," in *Organized Crime and Democratic Governability*, edited by Bailey and Godson.

18. "Mexico: International Narcotics Control Strategy Report" (Bureau for International Narcotics and Law Enforcement Affairs, U.S. Department of State), at www.usis.usemb.se/drugs/Canmex/mexico.htm, March 1997, 1.

19. U.S. General Accounting Office, *Drug Control: Planned Actions Should Clarify Counterdrug Technology Assessment Center's Impact*, GGD-98-28 (Washington, D.C., 1998).

20. Peter Andreas, "US–Mexico: Open Markets, Closed Border," *Foreign Policy*, Summer 1996. Other writings dealing with the rise of technology for U.S.–Mexico border security include Peter Andreas, "The Rise of the American Crimefare State," *World Policy Journal*, Fall 1997; Dunn, *The Militarization of the U.S.–Mexico Border*; and Peter Andreas, "The Escalation of US Immigration Control in the Post–NAFTA Era," *Political Science Quarterly*, Winter 1998–1999.

21. U.S. General Accounting Office, *Drug Control.*

22. ONDCP HIDTA home page, www.whitehousedrugpolicy.gov/enforce/hidta/ca-fs.html.

23. Sebastian Rotella, *Twilight on the Line* (New York: W.W. Norton, 1998), 90–102.

24. Secretaría de Gobernación, Instituto Nacional de Migración, "Informe del Grupo de Protección a Migrantes Beta Nogales" (Mexico City: Secretaría de Gobernación, February 1999).

25. Congressional testimony by Richard A. Fiano, Chief of Operations, DEA, September 21, 1999, at www.usdoj.gov/dea/pubs/congrtest/ctO92499.htm.

26. These are: (1) reduce demand through information, education, and rehabilitation; (2) reduce production and distribution of drugs; (3) focus law enforcement efforts against criminal organizations; (4) strengthen law enforcement cooperation and policy coordination, and assure the safety of law enforcement officers; (5) bring fugitives to justice, negotiate protocol to extradition treaty; (6) identify sources of and deter illegal trafficking in firearms; (7) hemispheric agreement to outlaw illegal firearms traffic; (8) work for success of the UN Special Session on Illicit Drugs in 1998; (9) increase abilities to attack and root out corruption; (10) enhance border cooperation to increase security; (11) control precursor chemicals; (12) make more effective laws penalizing money laundering in both countries; (13) seize and forfeit proceeds of drug trafficking and money laundering; (14) interrupt air, land, and sea shipment of drugs to Mexico and the United States; (15) training and technical cooperation; (16) enhance exchange of information and ensure the security of information provided. ONDCP, *National Drug Control Strategy*, 1999.

27. In 1999 the INS decided to provide an office, on some of the busiest border bridges, for a Mexican consular official who can register complaints of abuse by U.S. authorities, assist with minors being removed from the United States, and generally act as a guarantor for humane treatment of Mexican citizens caught in the web of U.S. migration or security policy.

28. Beta officers interviewed by the author in June 1999 in Nogales were quite clear on this point.

29. Congressional testimony by Richard A. Fiano, September 21, 1999.

30. In March 1996 the Department of State indicated that up to 80 percent of the foreign-grown marijuana came from Mexico. In 1999 Richard A. Fiano, Chief of Operations, DEA, testified that "most" of the foreign-grown marijuana was from Mexico. Congressional testimony, September 24, 1999.

31. U.S. General Accounting Office, *Drug Control: Narcotics Threat from Colombia Continues to Grow* (Washington, D.C.: U.S. Government Printing Office, 1999), 5.

32. ONDCP, "Goals, Objectives, Targets, and Performance Measures of Effectiveness," 1999, at www.whitehousedrugpolicy.gov/policy/99ndcs/iii-g.html.

33. Associated Press, "UN Estimates Drug Business Equal to 8 Percent of World Trade," June 26, 1997.

34. Calculated as follows: Approximately 300 metric tons of cocaine are consumed in the United States each year. Current interception rates are about 100 metric tons, from production to retail sales. A 20 percent reduction in the total flow of drugs would add another 60 metric tons to the 100 intercepted, representing about 53.3 percent of total consumption. This scenario is extremely optimistic. The U.S.–Mexico border seizure rate is much lower, estimated by U.S. Customs at 10 to 20 percent of the flow across the border. Some officials privately put the figure as low as 2 to 3 percent. See, for example, *Christian Science Monitor*, August 27, 1998, 3. Assuming 60 percent of the 300 tons (180 metric tons) of cocaine consumed in the United States crosses the U.S.–Mexico border, a 20 percent reduction in this flow would raise the total interception rate to only 45

percent (136/300). Should the real border interdiction rate be significantly lower than 10 percent, it would require a mammoth effort to be able to reduce the amount flowing across the border by 20 percent.

35. See ONDCP, *National Drug Strategy 1999.*

36. Michelle Ray Ortiz, *La Prensa* [San Diego], December 11, 1998.

37. Ibid.

38. Alejandro Burgues, Willy W. Cortez, and Noé Arón Fuentes, "Inseguridad pública en la frontera norte," *Ciudades* 40 (October–December 1998).

39. In 1999 a number of U.S. legislators began discussing the need to reinstitute the so-called Bracero program which ended in 1964. Silvestre Reyes (D–Texas), who initiated Operation Blockade in 1993 when he was with the Border Patrol, supported this initiative.

40. Demetrios Papademetriou, Carnegie Endowment for International Peace; senior associate and co-director international migration policy program, Carnegie Endowment for International Peace speaker, Tuesday, November 24, 1998, at www.ceip.org/programs/migrat/Old/BBDP.htm.

41. Timothy Dunn, "Immigration Enforcement in the U.S.–Mexico Border Region, the El Paso Case: Bureaucratic Power, Human Rights, and Civic Activism" (Ph.D. dissertation, University of Texas at Austin, May 1999), 181.

42. Ibid., 220.

43. Frank Bean, Roland Chanove, Robert G. Cushing, et al., *Illegal Mexican Migration and the United States/Mexico Border: The Effects of Operation Hold the Line on El Paso–Juárez* (Austin: Population Research Center, University of Texas at Austin, 1994).

13

Cooperation on Narco-Trafficking and Public Security on the U.S.–Mexico Border

José M. Ramos

INTRODUCTION

This chapter analyzes cooperation in the U.S.–Mexico border region on matters relating to narco-trafficking and public security. The topic of cooperation is important because it reveals the history, problems, and challenges that exist in an environment of increasing drug smuggling and deteriorating public security along the border. Estimates indicate that in 1998 Mexico supplied approximately 60 percent of the cocaine and 20 percent of the heroin sold in the United States.[1] Notably, almost 70 percent of the narcotics and chemical drugs destined for the United States cross the border between Baja California and California.[2]

The central argument presented is that the creation of bilateral antidrug cooperative agreements is not precluded by the jurisdictional, administrative, and political limitations that currently exist for Mexican state- and local-level law enforcement agencies. Specific, informal, and ad hoc accords across the U.S.–Mexico border are viable.[3]

This hypothesis is proposed in a context in which municipal and state law enforcement agencies lack the constitutional authority to forge agreements with their U.S. counterparts, because drug trafficking is defined as a federal crime. Mexican federal entities, such as the Attorney General's Office (PGR) and the Interior Ministry (Gobernación) are the agencies with jurisdiction for creating such accords. Nevertheless, state and local entities along the border have a history of participating in cooperative initiatives, especially in cities where public security and drug smuggling are serious issues. By associating public security issues, which fall within the purview of state and local governments, with narco-trafficking, it becomes possible for Mexican actors to propose collaborations with U.S. antidrug agencies. It is assumed that the U.S. authorities would want to work with their local-level Mexican counterparts because the U.S. actors view the municipality as the closest jurisdiction within a governmental frame of reference and because border-related problems are a shared concern.

In the near future, Mexico's model of federalism must be revised, both politically and juridically, because federal issues—such as narco-trafficking—also affect municipalities, threatening their legitimacy and social well-being. In light of the deleterious impacts that drug smuggling entails for society and the threat it poses to public security, there is a tremendous need to upgrade the coordination and planning of collaborative efforts at the three levels of government.[4] The challenge is to create more effective public administration in intergovernmental terms.

Bilateral agreements between the United States and Mexico at the federal level face limitations when implemented in different regions along the border. This is particularly true because of the decentralization of authority in U.S. federal, state, and local agencies. Additionally, federal-level bilateral agreements—although justifiable from a juridical perspective—tend to marginalize Mexican state and municipal governments, the very entities that have some informal experience in collaborating with U.S. agencies operating along the border. The shortcomings of a solely federal perspective are visible in the impacts of the 1998 U.S.–Mexico Binational Antidrug Strategy. This antidrug strategy, based on the viewpoint from Washington and from Mexico City, ignores the vision of narco-trafficking that exists along the border. A blending of central and local viewpoints is necessary to develop an efficient and effective antidrug policy and strategy.

The chapter is divided into five major sections. The first examines the context for and recent history of narco-trafficking. The next considers U.S. federal perspectives on narco-trafficking, including some characteristics of federal antidrug policy and its importance for the border region. The third analyzes regional viewpoints and examines the effects of narco-trafficking in the U.S. Customs Districts of San Diego, Nogales, El Paso, and Laredo. The fourth reviews the principal strategies and measures available in the pursuit of bilateral antidrug cooperation. And the final section analyzes the main political, juridical, administrative, and social impediments to cross-border antidrug cooperation.

CONTEXT OF DRUG TRAFFICKING ON THE U.S.–MEXICO BORDER

Since 1993, the Baja California cities of Tijuana and, more recently, Mexicali have become recognized as important distribution centers for illegal drugs destined for the United States. The assassination of Cardinal Jesús Posadas Ocampo in Guadalajara, Jalisco, in May 1993 highlighted the influence of the Baja California–based Tijuana cartel, led by the Arellano Félix brothers,[5] which controls the production of methamphetamines all along the border.

The flow of drugs from Baja California to the United States, and particularly to California, gained additional relevance with the onset of Mexico's 1994 financial crisis. The crisis produced economic impacts in all facets of narco-trafficking, and these impacts, in turn, affected public security in Mexico, not only because of the increase in antidrug activities but also because of rising corruption in law enforcement agencies.

A massacre of drug traffickers just south of Tijuana in September 1998[6] and the generally high murder rates in Ciudad Juárez, Mexicali, and Tijuana of individuals involved in organized crime reveal the magnitude of the problems facing border cities.[7] Narco-trafficking continues to expand, due both to the rising level of drug consumption in the United States and to the ready supply of cocaine, marijuana, and heroin from Mexico, along with Mexico's recent entry into the production and distribution of synthetic drugs. Drug consumption has also increased substantially in Mexico's major border cities. Another factor underlying the challenges confronting border towns is the corruption of Mexican law enforcement officers,[8] along with agents of the U.S. Customs Service and the Immigration and Naturalization Service (INS) who work the major border crossings.[9] These various factors reflect the failure of the governments in both countries to control trafficking and consumption.[10]

The taint of corruption has sullied Mexico's reputation in the international arena. U.S. media on the border—such as the *Los Angeles Times* and the *San Diego Union-Tribune*, as well as San Diego television stations—have reported drug-related corruption and money laundering within Mexico's border law enforcement agencies.[11] "Operation Casablanca," made public in May 1998, revealed the magnitude of the money-laundering problem and helps explain the unilateral action of the United States in that undercover sting operation.[12]

Also worth noting is the fact that U.S. government agencies—the Federal Bureau of Investigation (FBI) and the Drug Enforcement Administration (DEA)—have confidential information tying certain Mexican federal and state officials to drug-related and other criminal activities. It is possible that these agencies have used this information to exert political pressure on Mexico[13]—that is, to encourage Mexico's cooperation based on priorities set by the United States and outside formal, interagency agreements. The level of bilateral cooperation outside the formal agreements made at the federal level is also influenced by the fact that, at the border, the United States and Mexico confront shared problems. An example of border-area cooperation is the Special Group on Border Issues (Grupo Especial de Asuntos Fronterizos), which attempts to coordinate the activities of law enforcement agencies on both sides of the Baja California–California border.[14]

The Special Group on Border Issues can be viewed as the California state government's effort to overcome limitations encountered in previous attempts at coordination, including the Bilateral Border Task Force, comprising agents from the DEA and Mexico's Office of the Special Prosecutor for Crimes against Health (FEADS) within the PGR. The Special Group attempted to investigate criminal organizations along the border, especially in Tijuana, San Luis Río Colorado, Nogales, Ciudad Juárez, and Monterrey, and including linkages to Reynosa and Matamoros.[15] Several cross-border regions—Tijuana and Mexicali with California; San Luis Río Colorado and Nogales, Sonora, with Arizona; Ciudad Juárez, Nuevo Laredo, and Matamoros with Texas—share an economic dynamism. But these areas share another characteristic as well; all are linked to the flow of drugs from Mexico to the United States and with growing local drug consumption.

U.S. FEDERAL PERSPECTIVES ON NARCO-TRAFFICKING

The Clinton administration was inconsistent in the importance it accorded counter-narcotics efforts. Until late 1995, antidrug policy was not high on the domestic agenda. In fact, the budget for the Office of National Drug Control Policy (ONDCP) had been substantially reduced from its level during the previous administration. However, in 1996, the agency's visibility rose significantly with the appointment of General Barry McCaffrey as director. The change was especially noteworthy in regard to foreign policy and the growing interest in the U.S.–Mexico border.[16]

U.S. foreign policy on narco-trafficking has been rooted in the assumption that the threat is external. Consequently, the focus has been to seek closer collaboration with the governments of countries that are the principal producers of drugs or through which drugs flow. Although the United States has gradually moved away from its former aggressively unilateral posture, it nevertheless tries to pressure principal producer countries by taking advantage of their economic vulnerability and government corruption.[17]

A second issue is the ONDCP's inability to articulate an effective drug interdiction policy or a policy to substantially reduce the level of drug consumption in the United States. Despite advances, none of the efforts made to date has succeeded in reducing the growing U.S. demand for drugs from Mexico.[18] U.S. pressure on Mexico to increase its efforts and, basically, its cooperation in regard to combating drug traffic appears in that context.

The U.S. Congress has begun allocating more money and personnel to federal agencies involved in border drug control, such as U.S. Customs and the Border Patrol.[19] This support reflects not only growing recognition of the gravity of the problem but also these agencies' successful lobbying of U.S. legislators and interest groups for more resources for police intervention. Nevertheless, because narco-trafficking encompasses many social, economic, and political issues, there is no automatic relationship between additional resources and success in drug interdiction. Indeed, despite the increase in antidrug resources, drug traffic from Mexico to the United States has increased substantially since 1994, underscoring the structural limitations of the border drug-interdiction policy.[20]

Drug interdiction policy cannot achieve a substantial reduction in the flow of drugs unless it is combined with efficient and effective actions to reduce drug consumption in the United States. Nevertheless, one can predict that the policy will go unchanged because of the complex bureaucratic and political issues that would surround an attempt to redirect priorities.

Drug interdiction efforts have created another issue: an increase in human rights violations against migrants and unwarranted inspections of Mexicans wishing to cross the border legally. Human rights violations occur because the U.S. Border Patrol has powers both to intercept drugs and to detain undocumented migrants.

The structural factors affecting narco-trafficking—supply, demand, corruption, and the sums of money involved—make it difficult for law enforcement agencies to resolve the problem. Thus the goal of the United States is to avoid political impacts serious enough to call the governmental structure into question. An effective policy to reduce both consumption and distribution of drugs would require more effective law enforcement interdiction, a reduction in corruption, and decreased demand for illegal drugs. Nevertheless, there are barriers to implementing supply and demand policies. One indication of this is the level of funding to prevention programs in the United States. These programs typically receive between 5 and 10 percent of the budgetary support provided to police surveillance programs, with the latter accounting for almost 80 percent of the federal antidrug budget.[21]

Despite the increasing number of arrests of drug traffickers and the seizure and confiscation of goods on both sides of the border, narco-trafficking, in its various forms, has expanded and become more specialized. Neither the U.S. nor the Mexican government has successfully adapted to changes in drug traffickers' contraband strategies and mechanisms. Mexico's efforts, in particular, have been hindered by a shortage of economic resources and a lack of professionalism among law enforcement personnel. The rising toll that narco-trafficking has taken in the country's social, political, financial, economic, and cultural arenas has made it a national security issue and ultimately prompted Mexico to involve its army as a participant in the drug war.[22]

BINATIONAL REGIONS ON THE U.S.–MEXICO BORDER

This analysis looks at the options for bilateral cooperation regarding drug trafficking and public security in a number of cross-border subregions: (1) San Diego, California–Baja California; (2) Nogales, Arizona–Nogales, Sonora; (3) El Paso, Texas–Ciudad Juárez, Chihuahua; and (4) Laredo, Texas–Nuevo Laredo, Tamaulipas. These corridors were selected because they are the major gateways for imports and exports between Mexico and the United States, and all confront a narco-trafficking problem.[23]

A binational regional analysis can overcome the flaws inherent in generalized observations about U.S.–Mexico border issues, which lead to superficial diagnoses and limit the possibilities for finding solutions. A study of these cities can help us assess the impacts of U.S. antidrug policy at the border and evaluate whether the U.S. Customs Service has developed border-related policies that—while not corresponding exactly to policy priorities set by Washington—do respond to the economic and sociopolitical context of the corridors in which they are implemented. This affects the scope of bilateral cooperation efforts against drug trafficking.

"Regional perspective" is understood here as encompassing the attitudes, politics, and actions of governmental and nongovernmental actors in regard to narco-trafficking and public security. Regional or local actors' point of view is subject to the economic, political, and social context that characterizes each subregion in its binational interaction. Thus the environment influences the roles of actors and the kinds of responses they make to the border and cross-border issues they face. And because government agencies determine local- and state-level capacity to deal with public safety, it is of the utmost importance that these agencies propose local, regional, and binational public policies.

The roles of context, environment, and institutional power differ across border states and border cities. Although there are similarities—to the degree that common factors affect the impact of narco-trafficking and public security threats—there are key differences in the importance that these two issues claim across regions. Moreover, responses vary across regions depending on the political party in power, the character of the administration, and the type or intensity of its relationship with the Mexican federal government and with U.S. actors. For example, although Tijuana and Ciudad Juárez have similar concerns regarding public security and narco-trafficking, they differ in terms of the influence that these problems exert. They also differ in terms of the strategies that their respective local and state actors have followed in regard to public policies and the means to promote cooperation with their U.S. counterparts and with the Mexican federal government.

Governmental and nongovernmental actors along the border shape the regional perspective in important ways. Among nongovernmental actors, the business community holds special importance because it is able to exercise some influence over public policies affecting security and narco-trafficking.[24] The business community's involvement stems from the fact that drug trafficking has negative social consequences that threaten investments, especially in the *maquiladora* and tourism sectors.[25] Although nongovernmental actors' interest in public security and narco-trafficking may lead to more attention being given to these areas of concern, nongovernmental actors' involvement varies from city to city and region to region along the border, depending on their socioeconomic importance. Their influence also has repercussions for the role of government agencies working in drug control.[26]

Mexicans need to be aware of U.S. nongovernmental actors' influence on antidrug policy making in Mexico. A better understanding of these actors' role and their targeted strategies to influence governmental actors involved in antidrug policy (and border issues more generally) could ease bilateral tensions and conflicts, which could lead, in turn, to agreements for cross-border cooperation.[27]

Despite the recent tightening of links between Mexico and the United States, especially along the border, no effective agreements and strategies to reduce narco-trafficking have yet been developed. One reason for this lack of success is the poor understanding of regional political dynamics in the United States. Moreover, Mexican government officials with border-level authority are prohibited from establishing agreements for cross-border cooperation with their U.S. counterparts at the federal, regional, and local levels. This situation exists because neither drug trafficking nor public safety is perceived in public policy terms from a binational or cross-border perspective.

Also affecting the regional perspective are the roles of the various U.S. government agencies. For example, although the duties of the U.S. Customs Service, the INS, and the DEA are formally defined, these organizations nevertheless exercise some discretion in their actions (for example, increasing the number of commercial vehicles inspected or detaining presumed criminals). This means that these agencies play an important part in the execution of antidrug policy along the border. How each performs its role is tied into the decentralization of power and authority that characterizes the U.S. political system, and this explains why federal-level policies are not necessarily implemented in a consistent manner all along the border. This creates a gap between federal policy and the practices that agencies actually carry out on the frontier with Mexico.[28]

Also relevant to the regional perspective are the conflicts that exist between some U.S. agencies. Interagency conflict is driven by each agency's interest in increasing its influence in decision making regarding border antidrug policies, and this conflict often undercuts the foundation for coordinated implementation of antidrug and commercial policies.[29] The nature and degree of such conflicts vary from one border crossing to another, depending on the different actors' role and the particular socioeconomic and political context.[30]

In conclusion, a regional-level analysis reveals that the factors that affect public security and narco-trafficking do not exert the same influence across all border cities. The effects also differ across U.S. customs districts. The socioeconomic and political context and the role and influence of governmental actors involved in antidrug policies combine to determine regional specificity. Differentiating among regional contexts is an important step toward designing policies for bilateral antidrug cooperation that respond to regional determinants of public-security and narco-trafficking issues on the U.S.–Mexico border.[31]

San Diego, California–Baja California

The U.S. Customs District for San Diego covers the border crossings at Andrade–Los Algodones; Calexico–Mexicali; Tecate, California–Tecate, Baja California; Otay Mesa–Mesa de Otay; San Ysidro–Tijuana; and Virginia Street–Chaparral. This region is especially important because of the commercial checkpoints between Mexico and the state of California through which all manufactures from the border *maquiladora* industry pass.

From a sociopolitical point of view, the region is also important because of narco-trafficking—both by air and by land.[32] According to the San Diego Customs District, during fiscal year 1999–2000 California's international border checkpoints registered more than 176 seizures of cocaine (a total of approximately 4 tons), up from 138 seizures (about 2 tons) in fiscal year 1998–1999. This increase is due to the fact that the various drug-trafficking groups operating in the Baja California–California region have taken advantage of the proximity of Los Angeles and San Francisco, important centers for illegal drug consumption. According to the DEA, since the end of 1997, the major drug cartels have been able to forge alliances to operate in Tijuana, San Ysidro, and San Diego, and to extend their routes to Arizona, Texas, and Nevada.

Illegal migration also influences regional politics surrounding drug trafficking because of the growing use of migrants to transport drugs into the United States.[33] The Border Patrol and the INS now point to a relationship between undocumented migration and narco-trafficking, one result of which was the construction of a steel barrier at the Tijuana–San Ysidro border begun in 1992.[34] Construction began on a similar wall between the two Tecates in 1993, when improved interdiction on the western end of the border shifted smuggling to the eastern portion of the San Diego County border, where areas are less well patrolled by law enforcement agencies.[35] The same logic has led some drug cartels to relocate to the Mexicali–Calexico border in Imperial County, increasing the U.S.–bound drug flow through the port of San Felipe and through San Luis Río Colorado in Sonora.

Narco-trafficking has brought a significant increase in organized crime in the Tijuana–Mexicali border area. Some 400 deaths resulted from drug-related crimes between the end of 1998 and August 1999, prompting Baja California Governor Alejandro González to call for the creation of a special prosecutor to investigate murders linked to organized crime in the state.[36] In an article on the public security threats associated with drug trafficking, governmental corruption, and the ineffectiveness of Baja California authorities, *New York Times* correspondent Tim Golden made the following point: although alternation between political parties in Baja California may have increased administrative efficiency in certain respects, this was not the case for public security and judicial processes.[37]

At the National Conference on Public Security Policies in Mexico's Major Cities (Seminario Nacional de Políticas de Seguridad Pública en las Grandes Ciudades de México) in Chapala, Jalisco, in September 1999, academics and public security specialists presented research documenting that public security problems had worsened under PAN administrations.[38] Structural antecedents—institutionalized corruption and inefficacy, and inefficiencies in preventing public security problems and in the justice-delivery system—were cited as basic causes. By early 2000, growing public security concerns associated with narco-trafficking had prompted some observers to suggest that Baja California suffered from a lack of governability.[39] As evidence, they offered the assassination of Tijuana's chief of police in February 2000.[40]

The extent of the public security problem gave rise to several cross-border collaborations. For example, Baja California authorities requested assistance from the FBI in training state investigative police in criminal investigation in hopes that this training would help reduce the backlog of murder investigations, some 50 percent of which remain unsolved.[41] The Tijuana and San Diego police exercised another bilateral option when they signed an agreement in June 1999 to establish a joint databank on cross-border crime that would include members of gangs and organized crime families.[42] And, according to a press report, DEA agents were training members of Mexico's special forces stationed in Baja California.[43] Along with these various initiatives, state-level authorities announced that Israeli police would come to Tijuana to train the judicial police (*policía ministerial)* in riot control and in handling public disorders.[44] In the wake of the assassination of the Tijuana's police chief, authorities in the State Secretariat of Public Security (Secretaría de Seguridad Pública) requested information from the San Diego Police Department to help in the investigation.[45] In response, Congressman Brian Bilbray (49th Congressional District) asked Congress to take the necessary steps to combat drug trafficking in border cities, particularly in San Diego.[46]

Despite these several regional-level initiatives for international and bilateral collaboration to improve public security along the border,[47] it remains unclear what role cooperation should play. Cooperation has been advanced both as the optimal means to promote a public security plan and as a complement to government policies on public security and narco-trafficking. Moreover, in neither case has consideration been given to the effect of collaboration on greater law enforcement efficacy among local, state, and federal agencies—and on the possible costs in terms of national sovereignty. Nor has consideration been given to whether police corruption is an obstacle to cooperation and to the goals sought.[48]

Cooperation should be viewed most appropriately as a complement to measures that address public security and narco-trafficking at the three levels of government. The challenge is to achieve greater success through effective action at each level of government and through intergovernmental law enforcement cooperation and coordination. Such cooperation has been lacking or limited in the San Diego–Tijuana case because of corruption, the vested interests of law enforcement agencies, a lack of institutional leadership, the absence of mechanisms for citizen participation, and the weak history of intergovernmental cooperation on public security and narco-trafficking issues. In sum, what is needed are effective public policies guided by greater institutional capacity.

Nogales, Arizona–Nogales, Sonora

The U.S. Customs District for Nogales comprises the border crossings at Douglas–Agua Prieta, the two Nacos, the two Nogaleses, the two Sasabes, Lukeville-Sonoita, and San Luis–San Luis Río Colorado. The major crossings are those at Nogales, Douglas, and San Luis, where agricultural exports and *maquiladora* activity are significant.[49]

Nogales, Sonora, is important from a sociopolitical perspective as a key crossing point for marijuana and cocaine destined for the United States. Law enforcement in this desertic region is inadequate, making it possible for most of the illegal drug traffic to go by land.[50] In January 1999, the *Today Show* reported that two tunnels had been discovered in Nogales, Arizona, heightening recognition of the importance of this illegal crossing for drugs coming into the United States.

Because of the relative prevalence of contraband in Nogales, Sonora, most INS and Customs agents believe that the residents of this border city—and other border cities generally—have ties to crime or to narco-trafficking.[51] The laundering of drug money is also thought to be a primary criminal activity in Nogales, Sonora, creating an "underground economy" in car dealerships, hotels, and currency exchanges.

El Paso, Texas–Ciudad Juárez, Chihuahua

The U.S. Customs District for El Paso comprises crossings at Presidio-Ojinaga; Fort Hancock–El Porvenir; Fabens-Guadalupe; Ysleta–Zaragoza II; Ysleta–Zaragoza I; the International Bridge of the Americas (Cordova); and Stanton Street (from the United States to Mexico)–Paso del Norte (from Mexico to the United States) in Santa Fe. The crossings between Ciudad Juárez and El Paso are the most important in this customs district—because of the region's sizable *maquiladora* industry but also because of the social and political effects of organized crime. Public officials and nongovernmental entities from both cities meet frequently to address shared concerns about the border[52] and to promote the economic integration that is vital to the region's success.

Drug trafficking (measured by the number of seizures) was not a serious problem at El Paso's commercial border checkpoints in 1994–1995[53]—primarily because drug smugglers were using other routes. But between 1994 and 1998, the Juárez cartel consolidated its control in the region and took advantage of the area's inadequately patrolled desert to smuggle drugs by both land and air.[54] The region's strategic importance as a primary crossing point for illegal drugs coming into the United States has not abated since the implementation of the North American Free Trade Agreement (NAFTA). Cross-border flows of both trade goods and illegal drugs have increased since the trade pact came into effect, but infrastructure, personnel, antidrug technology, and bureaucratic coordination have become increasingly inadequate.[55] The fact that antidrug efforts have failed to keep pace with the severe drug-trafficking problems in the El Paso–Juárez corridor justified beefing up the El Paso Intelligence Center (EPIC) at Fort Bliss, Texas, in December 1999. At this DEA–managed center, officers from fifteen federal agencies involved in antidrug efforts share intelligence information and equipment.

The regional importance of narco-trafficking was underscored in November 1999 when Mexico's Federal Judicial Police (PJF) undertook a joint operation, with support from the army and technical assistance from sixty-five FBI agents, to investigate four Mexican ranches believed to contain the hidden graves of some one hundred victims of the drug trade.[56] In effect, bilateral cooperation in this joint operation took the form of technical assistance to compensate for limitations in the different Mexican law enforcement agencies.[57] Technically, the FBI agents were not police; because formal agreements exist for binational cooperation on drug trafficking, their involvement did not pose a problem from a diplomatic perspective (even though Mexico's Foreign Relations Ministry, SRE, was never consulted and did not participate in the operation). Moreover, the participation of FBI personnel in Ciudad Juárez reflects the tendency for police and the military to promote cooperation outside of diplomatic and legal channels. Nevertheless, among the Mexican citizenry, the presence of FBI personnel on Mexican soil was perceived as a violation of their nation's sovereignty.[58] From the public's perspective, the involvement of the United States was interventionist. The sociopolitical and criminal significance of narco-trafficking in Ciudad Juárez led Mexico's secretary of the interior and attorney general to attend meetings on the border in February 2000 that aimed to institutionalize the means to reduce violence associated with narco-trafficking on the border and its impact on public security.[59]

Laredo–Nuevo Laredo

The U.S. Customs District for Laredo encompasses fifteen border crossings. The most important of these are Brownsville-Matamoros; McAllen-Hidalgo-Reynosa; Laredo–Nuevo Laredo II (Lincoln-Juárez); Laredo–Nuevo Laredo I; Eagle Pass–Piedras Negras I; and Del Rio–Ciudad Acuña. This district—the most important of the four U.S. Customs Districts on the United States' southern border—accounts for half of all commercial traffic between Mexico and the United States.[60]

The sociopolitical significance of the Laredo–Nuevo Laredo border crossings is related to the history of the two cities' integrated urban development, the role of local authorities (most of Hispanic origin) on the U.S. side, and the importance of drug smuggling. Seventy percent of the illegal drugs flowing into the United States are believed to enter along the southeastern portion of the U.S.–Mexico border on a journey up from the Gulf of Mexico. Smuggling along this route led to the consolidation of the Gulf cartel between 1988 and 1994.

The prevalence of trafficking in the Laredo–Nuevo Laredo region led to a meeting between Governors Tomás Yarrington of Tamaulipas and George W. Bush of Texas in April 1999 to discuss possible mechanisms to improve anticrime cooperation. One of the problems the governors discussed was the need for more effective strategies by border governments to reduce narco-trafficking and other threats to public security.

In this binational region, as in those discussed previously, formal and informal agreements coexist among the area's various law enforcement agencies in the area of counter-narcotics activities and public security concerns. DEA agents are among those who play a significant role in the region. According to regulations established in 1992, when DEA agents are in Mexico they are required to work in tandem with Mexican personnel at all times and to avoid any involvement in possible armed confrontations. However, DEA agents who foiled a kidnapping attempt by supposed Mexican police officers in Matamoros in mid–November 1999 appear to have been armed. This incident holds the potential to undermine regional cooperation. On one hand, it calls into question the role of antidrug law enforcement officials and, on the other, it could lead to accusations that U.S. agents' activities violate a binational accord. Moreover, the history of corruption among Mexican police officers can subvert U.S. law enforcement officers' trust of their Mexican counterparts, further eroding the prospects for binational cooperation.[61]

The foregoing analysis demonstrates that the same set of structural factors—supply and demand of illegal drugs, corruption, lack of professionalism, ineffective policy evaluation, and so forth—underlies narco-trafficking and threats to public security all along the border, yet each border region exhibits specific traits as it addresses these issues. These traits are shaped by each region's unique pattern of cross-border interaction. Consequently, it is impossible to make general diagnoses or to design general public policies that could obstruct narco-trafficking and improve public security for the border region as a whole.

U.S. Customs officials in the various border districts are aware of the extent of narco-trafficking in each area. They also take care to ensure that efforts to intercept illegal drugs do not hinder the flow of commerce. This recognition of the primary importance of economic ties reflects the position of the two governments as well as that of nongovernmental actors in each locale. Thus, even through drug dealers presumably bring narcotics through Laredo's commercial border crossings, the U.S. Customs Service agents there have sufficient flexibility so that drug interdiction is not their only objective. This situation holds at other crossing points as well, albeit with different nuances at each one.

OPTIONS FOR COOPERATION AGAINST NARCO-TRAFFICKING

Mechanisms have long been in place for informal cooperation between state and municipal law enforcement agencies in addressing narco-trafficking on the U.S.–Mexico border. This informality has prevailed because law enforcement agencies involved in day-to-day duties on the border sometimes prefer actions, attitudes, or policies that diverge from diplomatic and legal directives based in Washington, D.C., and Mexico

City. Lately, however, attempts have been made to formalize those contacts.

For example, police departments in Mexico's major border cities have established international affairs offices or liaison offices. These offices' goal is to work closely with U.S. counterparts at the local or state level to exchange information and provide assistance across a range of law enforcement targets, including narco-trafficking, car theft, weapons smuggling, the transport of precursor chemicals used in synthetic drugs, kidnappings, and trafficking in minors.[62] On several of these issues—such as narco-trafficking and gun smuggling—officials must follow norms set by the Mexican federal government in its interactions with the United States. In most cases, however, municipal and state authorities operate without taking the federal government into consideration.

Different criteria prevail when cooperation is informal. Decision making can be more effective within an informal framework, especially when U.S. law enforcement agencies have significant autonomy. Informal cooperation also foments interest in achieving mutual support and its beneficial side effect—increased decision-making authority and influence.[63] Such is the violent environment of narco-trafficking and threats to public security in states like Baja California that local governments have even proposed inviting Israeli antiterrorism special agents as consultants for enhancing law enforcement efficiency.[64]

Alongside informal law enforcement relationships, there is an institutionalized bilateral strategy for a war on drugs. The Declaration of the U.S.–Mexico Alliance Against Drugs was signed by the presidents of Mexico and the United States in May 1997 and received the support of the High Level Contact Group on Drug Control (HLCG) in June. The U.S.–Mexico Binational Antidrug Strategy took effect in January 1998. As is to be expected, several measures contained in the Binational Antidrug Strategy involve actors and activities along the U.S.–Mexico border. The following are some of its principal border-related strategies and measures:

- *Reduce the demand for illegal drugs through enhanced education and public information.* Because of the rising tide of drugs flowing through principal border cities, places like Tijuana, Mexicali, Ciudad Juárez, and Laredo have experienced rising levels of illegal drug consumption, and the problem is worsening. Reducing consumption is the top priority and should involve all three levels of government. If prevention policies are not put in place, drug demand will increase, especially among young people in border cities. The possibilities for cooperation in this area are enormous. The school districts of San Diego, Los Angeles, El Paso, and Laredo already have extensive experience with drug prevention programs. However, to implement such programs more broadly will involve adapting available information to the cultural idiosyncrasies of Mexican border communities and forming adequate numbers of trained personnel.

A priority strategy to drive down the demand for illegal drugs is to raise communities' capacity to involve civil society in developing measures appropriate to each community. The situation is more challenging in developing societies, where there is little tradition of active community involvement and especially where local governments have not encouraged participation.

- *Reduce the production and distribution of illegal drugs—particularly marijuana, methamphetamines, cocaine, and heroin—in both countries.* This fundamental step, which has been present in most bilateral antidrug initiatives, implies the participation of federal officials in border cities. State-level government officials have also participated by providing support to federal law enforcement efforts.

  The substantial increase in drug trafficking through major border crossings suggests that effective bilateral cooperation to reduce the flow of drugs has been nonexistent, or at best insufficient. It also reveals the political and bureaucratic difficulties inherent in generating cooperation among Mexico's three levels of government, each of which has its own institutional priorities, politics, and bureaucracy. To the extent that law enforcement agencies at the three levels fail to promote effective cooperation to reduce narco-trafficking, the problem will continue to grow.

- *Direct the criminal justice system's efforts to counter organized crime.* Strengthening its criminal justice system is not a new goal for the Mexican government. But the fact that this issue remains on the agenda indicates that past efforts have been unsuccessful, and the situation may actually be worsening. A weak or flawed justice system cannot effectively or uniformly pursue the leaders of the major drug cartels, such as the one in Tijuana. Instead, such a system provides impunity to many criminals.

  Cooperation in this area is hindered by differences in the two countries' antidrug laws. Nevertheless, certain mechanisms, such as extradition treaties, represent an option for indicting alleged criminals in either country. Some of these mechanisms, especially those that can involve U.S. police actions in Mexico, hold implications for Mexican sovereignty. Operation Casablanca provides one example of the way in which the United States can carry out successful unilateral actions that are not particularly adapted to antidrug procedures as they currently exist in Mexico.

- *Strengthen bilateral cooperation and law enforcement policy coordination, and ensure the protection of law enforcement officials.* In light of the myriad administrative and bureaucratic limitations hindering police and judicial cooperative efforts (in addition to the entire issue of corrupt police), it remains questionable whether U.S. law enforcement officials can feel confident about the feasibility of joint operations. And further, if such efforts are feasible, can U.S. law enforcement officers trust their Mexican counterparts enough to share with them confidential information on antidrug activities? The purported connections of some members of the Mexican police to narco-trafficking make it likely that U.S. authorities will not be inclined to share such information.[65]

  Both the Mexican and U.S. governments have increased the resources allocated to antidrug and public security programs. Nevertheless, these investments have not necessarily produced a substantial reduction in drug trafficking across the U.S.–Mexico border. This suggests that the solution to the drug problem lies less in the amount of resources available than in the effectiveness with which funds are used to improve performance and institutional efficiency and effect a change in police administration at its different levels.

  As is the case with several other issues on which recommendations are offered, policy coordination and protection of officials are concerns that have appeared in other antidrug proposals. Inadequate coordination appears at the level of both federal and state government. The autonomy and decentralization of power that characterize the U.S. political system affect the potential scope of initiatives for intergovernmental cooperation and coordination on antidrug policy. Thus the recommendation on this point is that Mexico modernize its antidrug policy making to mesh more easily, from an intergovernmental standpoint, with the character of the U.S. political system.

- *Identify sources of illegal firearms and repress arms trafficking.* Illegal trade in firearms has formed part of the border's "smuggling culture" for years. The Mexican cartels have accumulated stockpiles of sophisticated weaponry, and trafficking continues, demonstrating the inability of border customs officials to control both gun trafficking and police corruption.

  Curtailing arms trafficking is difficult when the administrative culture tolerates corruption. Cooperative initiatives cannot succeed as long as such tolerance persists, even though it may be part of law enforcement agencies' modus vivendi. Furthermore, arms trafficking will not diminish until strict gun control exists in the United States. The United States' relatively lax controls have favored the flow of illegal weapons into Mexico. And finally, authorities in both countries have failed to improve public security substantially, giving citizens cause to acquire arms—legally or otherwise—in order to protect themselves from criminals.

- *Combat corruption.* Information exchanges must be fostered regarding programs, regulations, procedures, and the skills needed to prevent, identify, and combat cases of corruption in government institutions involved in antidrug efforts. This recommendation is the first institutional recognition that corruption has an impact on bilateral and national success in combating drugs.

  The question now is whether there is sufficient governmental will to stamp out corruption. The growing number of cases of law enforcement corruption in agencies on both sides of the border shows the difficulty of addressing this issue. And the perception of widespread corruption on the Mexican side creates a lack of institutional trust, exacerbated by cultural stereotypes, that leads back to the issue of whether U.S. government agents will be open to exchanges of confidential law enforcement information with Mexican authorities.

- *Strengthen cooperation on both sides of the border to promote security.* This recommendation focuses squarely on the border. Authorities in both countries are aware of the principal elements that affect border security. Nevertheless, a lack of political will, the vested interests of the various government entities, and the character of bureaucratic culture have shaped a situation in which narcotrafficking has been able to expand significantly.

  The role of government actors is especially relevant along the border, where the municipal, state, and federal governments interact according to distinct sets of norms and bureaucratic logic. The resulting diversity and heterogeneity of policies complicates bureaucratic coordination in the war on drugs. Consulates, for example, seem limited in their ability to contribute to this endeavor. Traditionally, Mexico's consulates in U.S. border cities have not been formally involved in the coordination of border-related issues such as drug smuggling. And U.S. consulates in Mexico's border cities tend to focus their efforts on administrative tasks—expediting passports, cultural events, and trade-related matters.

- *Control chemical precursors to prevent illegal uses.* Bilateral cooperation is needed to reduce the burgeoning contraband in precursor chemicals. On the Mexican side, inadequate training on the ways in which these materials are being smuggled may be a factor in the increasing rate at which the substances are passing through border crossings. Better training can redress this shortcoming.[66]

- *Detect and punish money laundering in both countries and strengthen bilateral and multilateral exchanges of information.* Money laundering has grown on par with increased drug trafficking along the border.[67] Both governments, but especially Mexico, have had only limited success in addressing this problem, stymied in part by corrupt officials at all levels of government.

  Operation Casablanca, conducted by U.S. authorities in May 1998, revealed the limited level of cooperation that can be expected from Mexico in undercover operations, especially those involving money. By failing aggressively to pursue money launderers, Mexican law enforcement agencies are effectively allowing them to continue their activities. In sum, there is a need for increased political will to reduce money laundering, as well as a need for training to improve institutional performance.

  To date, academic and government analysts have given little attention to the "underground economy" that results from laundering monies derived from the illegal drug trade. Ironically, given that a sizable portion of commercial investment in the border region is linked to the need to hide profits deriving from illicit activities, narco-trafficking could be portrayed as a stimulus to investment and employment.[68]

- *Strengthen the capacity to interrupt the flow of drugs by land, air, or sea.* One of the principal methods for bringing drugs into the United States is via maritime routes—by way of the Gulf of Mexico, the Gulf of California, and the Pacific Ocean. Although Mexico has increased its efforts to intercept these flows, the vast size of the ocean expanses under Mexico's jurisdiction and the limited size of the government's resources have undermined Mexico's law enforcement efforts. Additionally, there is the risk that involving the Mexican navy in the war on drugs could cause that service to become tainted by drug-related corruption.

- *Develop training and technical cooperation programs for antinarcotics agents.* Most cooperative strategies to combat the drug trade imply some form of training for Mexican law enforcement agencies. Such training is basic to any attempt to improve the efficiency and effectiveness of antidrug policies. Nevertheless, the history of similar technical training programs suggests that they have not reduced the level of corruption among Mexican law enforcement officials, underscoring the need to address bureaucratic culture as part of any initiative to combat narco-trafficking more effectively.

STRUCTURAL IMPEDIMENTS TO ANTIDRUG COOPERATION

Despite our hypothesis that jurisdictional and political limitations on Mexican government officials do not preclude state- or local-level agencies on the border from entering into informal, ad hoc agreements, Mexico's centralist political system does prevent state and local governments from developing initiatives to mitigate the negative impacts of U.S. policies. In Mexico, the executive branch is considered to be the sole representative of the national interest abroad and the only entity that can establish international accords. However, globalization makes this framework obsolete. The federal government's border policies have failed to promote an effective working relationship with the United States to address narco-trafficking, environmental pollution, labor migration, and infrastructure needs.[69] Moreover, given NAFTA's effects on the border, it is clear that state governments must assume certain tasks in order reduce the deleterious impacts of border policies developed at the different levels of government in both the United States and Mexico.[70]

Within the current model of intergovernmental relations, state governments' involvement in border issues would not be problematic if there were cooperation, coordination, and efficient joint planning among all levels of government. However, bilateral interaction has focused mainly on legal issues, which are only a fraction of governmental relations at the state and local levels. This ineffective relationship among the three levels of government has allowed border problems to mushroom over the course of many years. For example, the Border Governors Conference, which has met annually for almost two decades, provides the governors of border states an opportunity to discuss shared problems and opportunities. However, most of the agreements reached in these conferences have not been implemented in Mexico because of that country's centralist government—and also because of a lack of vision on the part of actors in the border region regarding political strategies that might help reduce the deficiencies of the centralist model.[71]

One challenge facing Mexico is to reformulate the border governments' role in international affairs. Failure to meet this challenge will mean worsening problems on the border. Even though civil society is gaining a stronger voice on border issues, it will not be able to help significantly in the redesign of intergovernmental relations.[72]

The following are the principal limitations that have shaped or influenced cooperation on antidrug initiatives along the U.S.–Mexico border.

Power Asymmetry

The differences between the United States and Mexico in terms of economic development give predominance to U.S. policies. This is visible, for example, in U.S. Border Patrol agents' violations of the human rights of Mexican migrants and in the United States' insistence that Mexico demonstrate greater commitment in its antidrug efforts.

The fact that U.S. agencies have information linking certain Mexican officials to drug smuggling has also allowed the United States to put additional pressure on Mexico. Thus, even though a certain level of cooperation prevails in the informal bilateral working relationships in the border region, it is easier for U.S. officials to request assistance from their Mexican counterparts than vice versa, especially when the U.S. actors can offer material or monetary compensation.

In addition to differences in economic development, a lack of competence and vision on the part of Mexican government actors in their relations with the United States also contributes to shaping the bilateral negotiation of power. Taking steps to remedy these problems could reduce asymmetry in bilateral negotiations.[73]

The presence of a growing Mexico-origin population in the United States is a factor that Mexico could use in negotiations. Asian nations have formed pressure groups among the members of their national communities residing in the United States. Rather than promoting cultural rapprochement, however, the Mexican government until recently distanced itself from its U.S. residents. The rejection of this population's right to vote in Mexico's 2000 presidential election reflected the former Institutional Revolutionary Party (PRI) government's lack of interest in Mexicans living in the United States.[74]

In its dealings with the United States, Mexico has also displayed a very limited vision, in a social sense, of bilateral negotiations. For example, one might contrast Mexico's motto of "no aid, just trade" with the Spanish government's initiative to win financing to promote the growth of Spain's underdeveloped areas. The Spanish government proved proficient in negotiating European Community funding for its poorer regions, arguing that the long-term advantages of such growth would make Spain more competitive in world markets.

Corruption

Corruption within Mexican law enforcement has already been mentioned as an obstacle to controlling narco-trafficking, crime more generally, and, most recently, human rights violations. It is unlikely that corruption can be rooted out in the short term because the Mexican government lacks the necessary political will and because organized crime has vast economic resources with which to subvert law enforcement officials. At some border crossings, corruption has likely extended into the U.S. Customs Service and the INS.

Sovereignty

From the perspective of the Mexican federal government, cooperative agreements made by law enforcement agencies in the border region might be construed as a violation of national sovereignty because state and local governments lack jurisdiction to enter into accords or joint actions with their U.S. counterparts. The federal viewpoint is justified, given the constitutional powers of the executive branch in international relations. However, as noted above, globalization, changes in international relations, and particularly the effects of NAFTA have circumscribed executive power. Perhaps most important, narco-trafficking, though international in character, is local in its impacts. Although the central government has proposed cooperation, it is local- and state-level actors who promote and implement cooperative initiatives along the border.

Within the new context of globalization, national sovereignty is no longer absolute. Mexico's traditional rhetoric about defending national sovereignty has been superceded by the current framework of globalization, and the country's international relationships need to evolve to a more mature level. In this framework, law enforcement officials from both the United States and Mexico have established certain routines that respond to shared interests and problems relating to the border. In these dealings, sovereignty is not necessarily a pressing concern for the actors. At the same time, the DEA's presence in undercover operations in Mexican border cities reflects the degree of public unawareness about practices that might well be considered a threat to Mexico's national sovereignty.

Deficient Police Culture

Professional culture is a set of ethical values that serve as a foundation on which to achieve a high level of performance and to improve productivity. It is a way of conceptualizing the role of law enforcement—the purpose that officers of the law serve—within society. It is through e purpose that officers of the law serve—within society. It is through its professional culture that law enforcement—and the act of governing—is legitimated in the eyes of society. From this perspective, a disconnect arises between the values that shape police culture and the professional training that police officers receive. Even if Mexican police officers received the best possible training in the finest military schools in the United States, they would, upon returning to Mexico, be enveloped once again in an environment of corruption and inefficiency.[75] Moreover, Mexican law enforcement agencies are full of officers who are simply under-trained, especially in technical areas such as investigative techniques. What little preparation these individuals receive is not imbued with a notion of professionalism, and performance suffers as a result.

Thanks to geographic proximity, U.S. local and state police have trained Mexican police officers at all levels of government. Nevertheless, this training has not sufficed to reduce the high levels of police corruption in Mexico, which continues to undermine antidrug efforts along the border. Because narco-trafficking and public security threats along the border will increase in the future, it is crucial to inculcate a culture of law enforcement. If this is not done, the electoral legitimacy of the parties in power will be weakened.[76]

Two Legal Systems

Differences between the Mexican and U.S. legal systems have impeded the promotion of more effective antidrug efforts. In Mexico, narco-trafficking falls within the purview of the federal Attorney General's Office. The PGR's authority in this area has justified the official position that state and municipal governments have no jurisdiction in this regard, even though narco-trafficking has become a local-level public security issue. Unfortunately, the PGR has also succumbed to corruption and has not performed its duty. Hence the need for local-level enforcement initiatives.

Intergovernmental coordination in the war on drugs has failed because of police officers' vested interests, ineffective techniques, and—above all—distrust among forces. Thus border state governments must alter the model of intergovernmental management in the area of law enforcement if they truly want to confront narco-trafficking.

Stereotyping and Racism

A lack of understanding of Mexican culture, high levels of corruption among Mexican officers, and inefficiency in police administration in

Mexico have led U.S. law enforcement officials to adopt certain stereotypes and racist attitudes with respect to the Mexican police. Absent such attitudes, the cooperation among border law enforcement agencies might well increase. The negative impressions left by a few corrupt police officers in Mexico damage the trust required for open exchanges of information. Without such exchanges, bilateral antidrug activities suffer. Thus one goal should be to reduce the stereotyping of Mexican law enforcement agencies, which presumes, in turn, a primary challenge for Mexican authorities—eradicating police corruption.

Language

One social and cultural contradiction for Mexican society in the border region is that most border residents do not speak, read, or understand English.[77] Lack of English language skills extends to law enforcement agencies along the border, although so-called bilingual police officers have worked in Tijuana and other border cities in the past. Without more bilingual law enforcement officers, Mexican agencies' ability to cooperate with or influence their U.S. counterparts is diminished.

A first step must be to develop special English courses for the personnel of law enforcement agencies involved in cross-border cooperative activities. Similarly, U.S. authorities should offer Spanish language courses, although the substantial number of Mexico-origin U.S. police makes consulting and cooperation with their Mexican counterparts easier.

In summary, the various limitations outlined above have not entirely blocked bilateral cooperation in policing the U.S.–Mexico border. A common factor shaping the different options for cross-border law enforcement cooperation, both informal and formal, is the existence of a narrow law enforcement perspective on reducing narco-trafficking that differs from diplomatic, military, political, and social perspectives on the problem. A "police mentality" has both defined and limited bilateral antidrug cooperation. Thus one challenge for cross-border public policy is to incorporate broader perspectives into shared and integrated strategies to address the drug problem.

Another key challenge is to design more effective cross-border policies. This will require, among other things, promoting greater efficiency on the part of Mexican law enforcement officers, so that cooperative initiatives can better respond to regional and national priorities. This challenge implies a redefinition of Mexico's national law enforcement culture.

CONCLUSION

The foregoing analysis attempts to clarify the history, obstacles, and challenges to bilateral cooperation on the border in a context of increasing narco-trafficking, public security threats, and violence. Although jurisdictional, administrative, and political limits may appear to impede state and local law enforcement agencies' cross-border, bilateral cooperation, there is a history of state- and local-level cooperation on the part of law enforcement agencies. The key point is that by associating public security issues (which fall within the purview of state- and local-level governments) with narco-trafficking (seen in Mexico as a federal crime), it becomes possible for Mexican actors to propose collaborations with their U.S. counterparts.

At the same time, the 1998 U.S.–Mexico Binational Antidrug Strategy has enabled federal entities in Mexico and the United States to carry out cooperative operations, exchanges, consultations, and training in counter-narcotics work along the border. However, federal-level bilateral agreements between the United States and Mexico have encountered limitations when implemented in the different border corridors, especially because of the impact of decentralized decision making and authority in U.S. federal agencies.[78] These agreements, although justifiable from a jurisdictional viewpoint, tend to marginalize state and municipal governments, which are the very entities that have gained experience in collaborating with U.S. border agencies.

In coming years, the model of Mexican federalism will have to be revised politically and legally because local communities face problems, such as drug trafficking, that call into question their very legitimacy and social well-being. Given the social and administrative impacts of narco-trafficking and public security issues, the coordination, cooperation, and planning of joint actions by the three levels of government must be redesigned to deal with those issues. The challenge is to create an intergovernmental public administration that is more effective and efficient.

The analysis offered of the possible impacts of the 1998 U.S.–Mexico Binational Antidrug Strategy recognizes the scope of that initiative. The strategy arose from a federal perspective—from Washington, D.C., and Mexico City—that takes into account one part of the problem but overlooks the perspectives on narco-trafficking that exist in different regions along the U.S.–Mexico border. Integrating both perspectives into a single whole is a prerequisite to developing the political will and effective policies and strategies that are needed to combat narco-trafficking.

Notes

Translated by Patricia Rosas.

1. Mexico continues to be a principal supplier of the marijuana sold in the United States. The U.S. Drug Enforcement Administration estimates that most of the methamphetamine distributed in the United States also comes from Mexico. General Accounting Office, *U.S.–Mexico Border: Issues and Challenges Confronting the United States and Mexico* (Washington, D.C.: GAO, July 1999).

2. The Baja California–California border represents 7 percent of the length of the U.S.–Mexico border, but it holds 60 percent of the border's population. Its ports, beaches, deserts, and forested mountains, plus its geographic proximity to one of world's largest cities, facilitate drug smuggling.

3. The institutional mechanism for formalizing such agreements is letters of intent rather than treaties or binational accords, which state-level governments in Mexico are banned from signing.

4. See Macías and Castillo, this volume. Mexico's national public security system is a policy framework that establishes intergovernmental coordination and cooperation among local, state, and federal agencies. Nevertheless, in the case of Baja California, it has not been effective in reducing public security and narco-trafficking threats. Differences in politics and ideologies, and perhaps conflicts of interest among federal and state-level actors, have been blamed. Baja California's importance in regard to Mexico's public security and narco-trafficking is so great that Interior Minister Diódoro Carrasco and Attorney General Jorge Madrazo met in Tijuana in February 2000 as part of the State Council on Public Security. President Ernesto Zedillo visited Baja California just prior to their meeting, and Tijuana's chief of police was assassinated later in the same month.

5. The Tijuana cartel is so important that the FBI listed Benjamín and Ramón Arellano Félix among its "Ten Most Wanted" (*El País* [Madrid], September 28, 1997). See "Mexican Gang Is Still on Loose Despite Search," *New York Times*, January 10, 2000. It is also rumored that the cartel, whose activities earn an estimated US$230 million annually, has become so powerful that its members have had to "sell" control over their area of influence to lessen their presence in the two Californias. See "Un 'cartel' de narcotraficantes mexicanos 'vende' su zona para dedicarse a cobrar peajes," *El País* [Madrid], February 22, 2000.

6. In that incident in the town of El Sauzal, nineteen members of a family involved in narco-trafficking were murdered in a dispute over a drug shipment. San Felipe, a Baja California port, has been important in the maritime and air delivery of drugs since 1995. These events justified the policy of "sealing the border" between the Gulf of California and the Pacific Ocean, for which state-of-the-art technology would be required. San Luis Río Colorado, Sonora, located in the desert between Arizona and Sonora, is also involved in aerial drug smuggling to the United States.

7. There were 616 murders in Baja California during 1999 and 70 more in the first two months of 2000, giving Baja California a murder rate (one per 3,500 inhabitants) higher even than that of Mexico City (one per 6,000). It is believed that most of the Baja California murders were drug related.

8. The case of former deputy attorney general Mario Ruiz Massieu is evidence of the importance of drug trafficking in Mexico. See "The Owl Doesn't Blink When he Calls Mexico a Narco-Democracy," *Los Angeles Times,* October 1, 1994; "Mexico Hints at Cover-Up by Ex-Official," *Los Angeles Times,* March 6, 1995. Other incidents include the detention of General Jesús Gutiérrez Rebollo, then director of the INCD (Mexico's version of the DEA) and the former governor of Quintana Roo, Mario Villanueva, for suspected ties to narco-traffickers. See Arzt, this volume.

9. This calls to mind the corruption cases related to narco-trafficking against INS agents at Calexico, California, and the investigation of the former regional commissioner of the U.S. Customs Service, San Diego District. "Two Inspectors at Border Charged in Drug Probe," *Los Angeles Times,* February 14, 1995; "U.S. Agents' Drug Trade Ties Probed," *Los Angeles Times,* June 16, 1995. The GAO has also acknowledged that an obstacle to U.S. antidrug policy has been police corruption in both countries. GAO, *U.S.–Mexico Border.* On the corruption in the INS and the Customs Service, see GAO, *Drug Control: INS and Customs Can Do More to Prevent Drug Related Employee Corruption* (Washington, D.C.: GAO, March 30, 1999).

10. Concerns over narco-trafficking and the record of police corruption in Mexico led the U.S. Congress to decertify Mexico's antidrug war in March 1997. President Clinton eventually vetoed that decision.

11. "DEA Touts Sting of Drug Millions," *San Diego Union-Tribune,* April 4, 1995; "Drugs: Web of 'Narco-Politics' Entangles Mexico," *Los Angeles Times,* June 15, 1995; "Mexico: Cartels Spread War," *Los Angeles Times,* June 16, 1995. The *New York Times* has closely followed drug trafficking in Mexico and along the border.

12. "U.S. Arrests in Bank Probe a Black Eye for Mexico," *Los Angeles Times,* May 20, 1998; "Small Town Is Focus of Drug Launder Probe," *Los Angeles Times,* May 22, 1998; "Mexico to Prosecute U.S. Agents Who Ran an Antidrug Sting," *New York Times,* June 4, 1998.

13. See "U.S. Calls Mexico's Drug War Corrupt," *San Diego Union-Tribune,* April 6, 1994. The GAO also analyzed police corruption among Mexican agents in *Drug Control: Update on U.S.-Mexican Counter-narcotics Activities* (Washington, D.C.: GAO, March 4, 1999).

14. Information provided by California Attorney General Bill Lockyer during the Second Binational Conference on Security (San Diego, April 1999). This Special Commission will focus its work on narcotics contraband, trafficking in minors, and stolen vehicles. These agreements were ratified during the visit between Baja California Attorney General Juan Manuel Salazar and Lockyer in Los Angeles, September 17, 1999.

15. International Narcotics Control Strategy Report, March 1998.

16. It is worth noting that General McCaffrey visited the Tijuana–San Diego border once and the Ciudad Juárez–El Paso border twice during 1998–1999. This reflects the government's concerns about border narco-trafficking. According to the ONDCP, during the first eight months of 1999, more drugs were confiscated at border crossings in the Ciudad Juárez–El Paso area than along

the whole remainder of the border. Additionally, in mid–September 1999, DEA agents confiscated almost two tons of cocaine in El Paso.

17. One principal strategy is the annual "antidrug certification" that the U.S. government applies to nations that are primary producers and distributors of drugs internationally. In contrast to previous years, the certification of Mexico's antidrug program for the year 2000 had little political impact bilaterally. One reason is that a bilateral consensus exists that this mechanism has not been effective in substantially reducing narco-trafficking, nor has it helped in the detention of the major criminal groups.

18. Consumption of drugs such as marijuana and cocaine increased in the United States in 1998, especially among individuals between the ages of 18 and 25. Approximately 13.6 million people in the United States used some kind of drug during 1998—despite government expenditures of US$18 billion in 1998 to combat narco-trafficking and drug addiction. For more information on the estimates of drug use in the United States by social class, see Office of National Drug Control Policy, *1998 National Household Survey on Drugs* (Washington, D.C., 1999).

19. For an evaluation of these agencies' effectiveness in combating drug smuggling along the United States' southern border, see José María Ramos, *Las políticas antidrogas y comercial de Estados Unidos en la frontera con México* (Tijuana: CONACYT–COLEF, 1995).

20. In light of the increase in narco-trafficking along the border and the inability of national policies to reduce the problem, New Mexico Governor Gary E. Johnson proposed studying the possibility of legalizing drug consumption. He explained his position: "The supposed goal of antidrug policy is to reduce the use of drugs, yet we are spending more and more money on the war on drugs, and, at the same time, more and more people are using drugs. Are we winning the war?" (speech at the closing ceremonies of the Annual Border Governors Conference, Tijuana, September 10, 1999.

21. Officials and specialists from both countries discussed the advances in, and limitations on, policies for drug-addiction prevention and treatment during the second U.S.–Mexico Binational Conference on Drug-Demand Reduction (Tijuana, June 1999). During that meeting, the "Binational Collaboration on Border Initiatives" workshop focused on border-region issues.

22. The recent case of corruption on the part of a high-level Mexican antidrug official showed the limits to greater Mexican government participation in antidrug policy. Moreover, the experience of the United States shows that its participation does not guarantee a significant reduction in narco-trafficking. For more information on the role of the army in the war on drugs, see Roderic Camp, "Militarizing Mexico: Where Is the Officer Corps Going," Policy Papers on the Americas (Washington, D.C.: Center for Strategic and International Studies, 1999). Also see Turbiville, this volume.

23. See Andreas, this volume.

24. In the case of Baja California, members of the business community are active in the Citizens' Councils for Public Security (Consejos Ciudadanos de Seguridad Pública) at the state and municipal levels. Nevertheless, their rec-

ommendations have not weighed heavily in the government's creation and implementation of public security policy.

25. Interestingly, increased public security threats in major border cities like Tijuana do not appear to have reduced the level of tourism from San Diego or Los Angeles. This may be the case because only specific places and individuals are targets of violence, and the normal ambit of criminal activity does not include traditional tourist spots. All the same, risk does exist to the degree that violence can occur in public places.

In the case of the *maquiladora* industry, the attraction of an abundant unskilled labor force to Tijuana and Ciudad Juárez has lessened concerns over public security. Moreover, the kidnappings and murders of Japanese businessmen in Tijuana in 1999 have not reduced the level of investment—both general and Japanese—in the *maquiladora* industry. Japanese investment is estimated at US$11 billion in Baja California. Sixty-seven companies are members of the Japanese Maquiladora Industry Association (Asociación de la Industria Maquiladora Japonesa). In October 1999, in response to these crimes, the association proposed to the Baja California government that Japanese law enforcement experts provide training to the state-level ministerial police (information provided by Masafumi Matsunaga, association representative). Also see "Alarma a japoneses la ola de violencia," *La Voz de la Frontera*, Mexicali, March 3, 2000.

26. The variation in influence occurs because of the diversity among business organizations, the political importance of some of their members through ties to regional or federal government officials, and skillful negotiation strategies.

27. According to Luis F. Aguilar Villanueva, "public administration of border states, municipalities, and regions improves its strategic vision and the effect of its actions if it incorporates—substantively and permanently—the potentialities of cross-border communication and cooperation in its conceptualization and initiatives" (in José María Ramos, *Desarrollo regional y relación transfronteriza: el caso de México–California* [Mexico City: Instituto Nacional de Administración Pública, 1996]), xvi.

28. This has been an obstacle to understanding the regional functioning of agencies such as the U.S. Customs Service and the U.S. Border Patrol. For further discussion on this topic, see Ramos, *Las políticas antidrogas*.

29. The issue arises at three levels. The first is coordination with the INS, in regard to assignment of personnel at border crossings and inspection methods. The second is coordination with the other agencies involved in infrastructure and services, roads, and bridges, such as the U.S. Department of Transportation, the General Accounting Office, and the Committee on Bridges and International Border Crossings. Finally, there is the issue of coordination with Mexican authorities. For more on the coordination issue, see GAO, *U.S. Customs Service: Concerns about the Adequacy of Border Infrastructure*, Report to the Chairman, Committee on Finance, United States Senate, May 1991.

30. This occurs because, at certain border crossings, the Border Patrol may acquire influence as a result, for example, of having information on contra-

band, which might potentially block the work of Customs or the DEA. From this, one can assume that the Border Patrol's influence on antidrug policies along the border is not the same at the San Diego border crossing—where its influence is relatively minor—as at the Laredo or El Paso border crossings—where its influence is significant.

31. A characteristic of most proposals for developing Mexico's northern border region is that they fail to incorporate U.S. influence, locally and regionally, on Mexican border development. This may be the case because the individuals charged with directing or coordinating such programs may not know how to gauge the level of U.S. influence in Mexico's regional development. See Ramos, *Desarrollo regional y relación transfronteriza.*

32. In 1988 the San Diego Customs District seized 3,661 lbs. of cocaine; seizures rose to 15,535 lbs. in 1992. This substantial increase—as well as other irregularities—led to the investigation of former Customs District Director Allan J. Rappoport for allegedly having ties to narco-traffickers and of abetting their activities during his tenure. "Corruption Probe Focuses on Ex-Customs Official," in *Los Angeles Times,* March 20, 1993.

33. See Larry Storrs, *Drug Certification of Mexico in 1999: Arguments For and Against,* RS20127 (Washington, D.C.: Congressional Research Service, 1999).

34. A sense of the ideological context leading to the construction of these projects can be gained from "Border Crossings Near Old Record" and "U.S. to Crack Down," *New York Times,* February 9, 1992; and "Seymour Proposes Battle on Crime by Illegal Immigrants," *Los Angeles Times,* August 4, 1992. The wall, completed in 1997, is located in El Cajon, home to the author of the initiative, Republican congressman Duncan Hunter. The INS predicts that construction on a second, 21–kilometer metal wall will be completed in 2002.

35. There have been incidents at the Tecate border crossing in which trucks have smuggled both illegal drugs *and* undocumented immigrants. "Border Fence Will Go Up at Tecate," *Los Angeles Times,* November 25, 1992; "Bust Puts Much-Traveled Trailer out of Business," *Los Angeles Times,* December 5, 1992.

36. Notably, as of December 1999 the three agencies of Mexico's Combined Public Ministry (Ministerios Públicos Mixtos) comprising officials from the state and federal prosecutor's offices were still not in operation.

37. Tim Golden, "Mexican Tale of Absolute Drug Corruption," *New York Times,* January 9, 2000. Golden later reported on the role and influence of the Arellano brothers in the distribution of drugs to the United States. "Mexican Gang Is Still on Loose Despite Search," *New York Times,* January 10, 2000. The government's inability to catch this group was evident in the statements of former DEA director Thomas Constantine. "DEA Chief Warns Senate on Traffickers in Mexico," *New York Times,* February 25, 2000. In this way, the problems of public security and narco-trafficking continued to receive coverage in a premier daily, the *New York Times,* which in turn had some influence on the antidrug policies of the United States in regard to Mexico.

38. See José María Ramos, "Políticas de seguridad pública en la frontera México–Estados Unidos: contexto y alternativas"; V. Sánchez, "Políticas de seguridad pública en Tijuana: la reiteración de un diagnóstico"; J. Regalado,

"Estado de derecho, seguridad pública y participación ciudadana"; M. Moloeznik, "La seguridad pública en transición, Jalisco antes y después del proceso de alternancia política"; B. Romero, "Análisis de las políticas del gobierno del estado de Querétaro en materia de seguridad pública"; and M.A. Ordaz, "La seguridad pública en la ciudad de Torreón: la visión y acción de un gobierno, 1997–1999."

39. For a juridical and social analysis, see Jorge A. Bustamante, "Seguridad pública y gobernabilidad," *Frontera*, January 12, 2000, and "Gobierno y seguridad pública," *Frontera*, January 19, 2000. For a political science perspective, see Víctor Espinoza, "Baja California ¿Crisis de gobernabilidad?" *Frontera*, February 10 and 17, 2000. For its part, the PRI had its party leader in the state congress, Jaime Martínez Veloz, inform the national media that Baja California suffered from ungovernability. "Baja California en la ruta de la ingobernabilidad," *Frontera*, January 24, 2000.

40. "Tijuana Police Chief Fatally Shot," *New York Times*, February 28, 2000.

41. The increase in violence related to drug trafficking has led some state officials to distance themselves from the problem by declaring that it falls outside the states' or municipalities' jurisdiction.

42. This proposal emerged from a binational meeting of law enforcement agencies from Tijuana and San Diego. From the outset, both sides recognized the technological challenges to creating such a databank.

43. *New York Times*, February 25, 2000.

44. According to Rommel Moreño Manjarrez, who has served as director of analysis and strategy planning and as deputy attorney general in the Baja California state attorney general's office: "given the proposals for exchanges with the United States, Japan, and Israel, the state is in the vanguard on public security." "Capacitarán a PME contra terrorismo," *Frontera*, December 8, 1999. It was also thought that these exchanges, especially the one with Israeli law enforcement officials, would help to achieve a reorganized and effective program to combat criminal activity in the state. In Moreño's words, "The idea is to work on a new vision of public security." "Capacitarán policía de Israel a mexicanos," *Frontera*, February 26, 2000.

45. From an academic perspective, public security in Baja California is binational in character, and thus it should be addressed in terms of binational policies. Jorge Santibáñez, "Los costos de vecindad mal administrada," *Frontera*, March 3, 2000.

46. Congressman Bilbray posed the need to solidify efforts to combat drug traffic and to cooperate with the Mexican government in breaking up the drug networks, especially in the border region. Senator Dianne Feinstein (D–California), commenting on the assassination of the Tijuana chief of police, said that if Mexico were to request it, she would ask the FBI to appoint investigators to help solve the crime. "Piden intervención de Washington," *Frontera*, March 3, 2000.

47. Along with these initiatives and in preparation for the millennium celebrations, U.S. Customs Service agents proposed a special operation, "Millennium Border Security." Its primary goal was to respond to any contingency,

such as riots or demonstrations, that might occur on New Year's Eve 1999. This was an attempt to provide immediate medical assistance as needed, to avoid civil disturbances, and to resolve traffic congestion. Mexican Customs agents agreed to work with their U.S. counterparts.

48. According to DEA agents who trained law enforcement officials in Baja California, an atmosphere of mistrust prevailed because of Mexican police officers' presumed links to narco-traffickers; *New York Times*, February 25, 2000. It was revealed in February 2000 that Mexicali state police were protecting drug smugglers. It is also believed that police assassinated the director of the guard detail for Baja California's attorney general in June 1999, also in Mexicali. It is noteworthy that the police investigation into the assassination of Tijuana's police chief found that a former member of the Special Forces was among those responsible, along with two other active-duty officers in the Tijuana Police Department.

49. Of all traffic entering Arizona from Mexico, almost 40 percent of private vehicles and 66 percent of commercial vehicles cross at Nogales. Arizona Economic Council, *Arizona-Sonora Complementarity: A Gateway between the United States and Mexico* (Phoenix, July 1992).

50. The openness of the Arizona-Sonora border has been a factor in shifting narco-trafficking routes from the Gulf of Mexico to this border region.

51. In Nogales, Sonora, drug-related violence may have predisposed border agents to take particular note of the style of clothing worn by the middle and lower-middle classes, as well as the vehicles these groups drive (such as Suburbans and Grand Cherokees, usually with tinted windows).

52. A basic problem is how to promote agreement among the different actors on proposals to facilitate the flow of commerce at the border. Among those involved are the El Paso Foreign Trade Association, the Greater El Paso Chamber of Commerce, El Paso's Industrial Development Council, the Economic Development for El Paso County, and the El Paso Customs Brokers Association.

53. In the El Paso district, marijuana was the primary drug confiscated in the early 1990s. In fiscal 1990, 418 seizures yielded 19,399 pounds of marijuana; 449 seizures yielded 20,490 pounds in 1991; 415 seizures intercepted 20,464 pounds in fiscal 1992. By contrast, in 1992 there were 37 cocaine seizures, yielding 1,275 pounds, and in the previous year, only 40.6 pounds were confiscated. U.S. Customs Service, Office of Enforcement Systems, El Paso, 1992.

54. "Soldiers Bolster Patrol Near Border," *El Paso Herald Post*, May 16, 1991; "More Drug Fighters to Be Sent to El Paso," *El Paso Herald Post*, November 8, 1992.

At that time, one of the key leaders was Amado Carrillo Fuentes. His death in June 1997 led to battles for control of the group. During 1997 and 1998, 206 people disappeared, most presumably linked to narco-trafficking.

55. This hypothesis is based on the conceptual position presented in Ramos, *Políticas antidrogas*. Leslie Fraser examines the relationship between commercial opening and drug flows ("Wilsonian Policy Prescriptions and National Secu-

rity in U.S. Mexican Relations: The Cold War, the War on Drugs and NAFTA," Ph.D. dissertation, La Trobe University, 1999).

56. "Five Bodies Found at Border Ranches," *New York Times*, December 1, 1999. The investigation ultimately found nine victims.

57. It is not generally known that several Mexican state-level law enforcement agencies have agreements to have FBI agents train police personnel. These agreements are seen as a means to promote police efficiency. They also give implicit recognition to the fact that the proximity of the United States can constitute an opportunity to work together on shared problems.

58. The possibility that U.S. police personnel were among the victims was used to justify the immediate involvement of the FBI. "Excavation of Suspected Drug Cartel Graves Begins," *New York Times*, December 1, 1999.

59. Ciudad Juárez mayor Gustavo Elizondo called the meeting in response to increased violence linked to narco-trafficking. He stressed the need to implement the actions that participants had agreed to pursue, including greater coordination, enhanced law enforcement efficiency, and the channeling of financial resources. In concrete terms, the goal was to counter the influence of regional groups involved in narco-trafficking. "Juárez Probe Is Sign of Drug Cartels' Tenacity," *New York Times*, December 3, 1999.

60. In 1990, the value approached US$25.5 billion. In 1997, according to U.S. Customs, the southern district of Texas, where Laredo is located, processed US$38.8 billion (of a total of US$75.5 billion) in commercial transactions crossing the border from Mexico. GAO, *U.S.–Mexico Border. Issues*, 29. Similarly, an estimated 2,500 trucks from Mexico enter the United States at Laredo every day. Of these, only 20 to 30 percent undergo secondary inspection.

61. "Acuerdo de las Secretarías de Gobernación, de Relaciones Exteriores y de la Procuraduría General de la República que regulan la estancia temporal de los agentes representantes de entidades de gobiernos extranjeros que, en su país, tienen a su cargo funciones de policía, de inspección o vigilancia de la aplicación de leyes y reglamentos, así como técnicos especializados," *Diario Oficial*, July 3, 1992.

62. With the eastward shift in illegal migrant flows, U.S. Border Patrol agents in towns like Mexicali, Nogales, and Agua Prieta frequently request help from municipal police officers on the Mexican side of the border, who can arrest people who attempt to smuggle undocumented migrants into the United States. This collaboration is one instance of the informal cross-border agreements that already exist. The increased involvement of Mexican police officers has, however, sometimes led to cases of extortion of migrants.

63. A growing practice on the part of some U.S. companies and citizens is to hire Mexican police or former police officers to capture—on Mexican soil—presumed criminals fleeing the United States. Two events significant for the bilateral relationship were the kidnappings of Humberto Álvarez Macháin and René Verdugo, both of whom had been involved in the 1985 murder of DEA agent Enrique Camarena.

64. A problem with these types of consultation is that they may lack thorough evaluation, especially in regard to their impact on possible human rights violations or differences in the code of conduct for law enforcement officers.

65. It is worth noting that joint operations were terminated after only one year. It seems that the Mexican government denied FBI, DEA, and Customs agents permits to carry arms while on Mexican soil. For its part, Mexico unilaterally established ground intelligence units (*inteligencia de base*) in nine border locations. The main problem with the units was lack of resources, in response to which the DEA contributed almost US$460,000 to support their activities. Another limitation was that some members of the Special Unit against Organized Crime failed polygraph tests administered by DEA and FBI agents.

66. See GAO, *U.S.–Mexico Border.*

67. For more detail on these illegal activities, see Subcommittee on General Oversight and Investigations, Committee on Banking and Financial Services, U.S. House of Representatives, *Money Laundering Activity Associated with the Mexican Narco-Crime Syndicate* (Washington, D.C.: U.S. Government Printing Office, 1996).

68. U.S. authorities estimate that Mexican drug smugglers earned US$30 billion from drug trafficking in 1995. See the testimony of Jonathan Winer, Deputy Assistant Secretary of State, Money Laundering Activity, Hearing, ibid., 120. Also see the testimony of Thomas Constantine to the Committee on Foreign Relations, U.S. Senate, *The Drug Trade in Mexico and Implications for U.S.–Mexican Relations* (Washington, D.C.: U.S. Government Printing Office, 1995), and Peter Andreas, "U.S.–Mexico: Open Markets, Closed Border," *Foreign Policy* 103 (Summer 1996): 51–69.

69. See Ramos, *Desarrollo regional,* for additional detail.

70. An analysis of this topic appears in José María Ramos, "Gobiernos y administraciones públicas con una perspectiva transfronteriza," presented at the "Primer Congreso Regional de Ciencias Sociales y Humanidades," Ciudad Juárez, November 18–19, 1999. See also, Michelle Saint-Germain, "Similarities and Differences in Perceptions of Public Service among Public Administrators on the U.S.–Mexico Border," *Public Administration Review* 55:6 (November/December 1995).

71. The administration of Baja California governor Alejandro González displayed better follow-through on initiatives and accords forged in the framework of meetings in the Californias and the border governors' conferences. There was an effort to professionalize the role of public administration at the state level on border issues with California and on international issues more generally. Interview with Yolanda Jiménez, director of international affairs, Secretaría de Gobierno, Mexicali, March 6, 2000.

72. Jorge A. Bustamante ("Una vecindad inescapable," *El Financiero,* September 11, 1999) argues for greater flexibility and decentralization to permit border governments to operate more effectively in today's global and binational context.

73. On the importance of governmental competence in the U.S.–Mexico relationship, see José María Ramos, "Estados Unidos y la gobernabilidad en México," *Espiral* 6:18 (May–August 2000): 155–81.

74. *Editors' note:* The policy of relative neglect of the Mexico-origin population in the United States has been reversed by the Vicente Fox administration.

75. See Arzt, this volume.

76. For an analysis of options for antidrug public policy in the border region, see José María Ramos, "Narcotráfico: algunas opciones de política pública fronteriza," in *Baja California: economía, política y cultura: escenarios del nuevo milenio escenarios al final del siglo*, edited by Tonatiuh Guillén (Mexico City: Universidad Nacional Autónoma de México).

77. This may result from a rejection of the English language on cultural and ideological grounds, or simply from a general rejection of all things American.

78. Two initiatives in the U.S. Congress could call bilateral cooperation into question. One is a proposal, introduced in June 1999, to have the U.S. military support the INS and Customs in combating drug smuggling. Interestingly, General Barry McCaffrey has opposed that initiative. The second is an amendment approved by the U.S. Senate on July 22, 1999, that would legalize and expand a 1995 executive order by President Bill Clinton and permit the confiscation of U.S. property belonging to alleged drug smugglers. The amendment was based on the International Emergency Economic Powers Act, designed to block economic activity with nations considered to be security threats to the United States.

14

U.S.–Mexico Subnational Cooperation in Public Security and Law Enforcement: The Arizona/Sonora Judicial Relations Project

Bruce Zagaris

INTRODUCTION

The United States and Mexico engage in broad cooperation in the area of international law enforcement. One area in which such cooperation is particularly fruitful is subnational enforcement cooperation. Subnational cooperation is especially effective when the collaborating subnational units meet in a border relationship and when their respective countries both have federal systems in which subnational units play important roles—as is the case, for example, with Sonora and Arizona.[1] When state and municipal law enforcement entities from two nations come into daily contact, as they do in the Sonora-Arizona region—and, for that matter, along the entire length of the 2,000–mile border between Mexico and the United States—officials gain knowledge of each other's laws, culture, criminals, and criminal problems, as well as personal acquaintance with each other's law enforcement personnel. This knowledge, in turn, enables these entities to cooperate informally to resolve problems, rather than adhering to the more formal, time-consuming procedures outlined in agreements between Washington, D.C. and Mexico City.

The Arizona/Sonora Judicial Relations Project, in operation from mid–1993 through 1997, offers a positive example of cross-border cooperation in legal matters. Two of its task forces addressed areas of substantive enforcement: criminal law and juvenile justice. Others dealt with areas that interact with criminal justice and/or international criminal/enforcement law—judicial/training, environmental, bankruptcy, and civil law. This chapter outlines the background and goals of the Arizona/Sonora Project and then discusses the project groups that were concerned with international and comparative law enforcement—the Juvenile Justice Procedure Task Force and the Criminal Law Task Force. The policy significance of the Arizona/Sonora Project for other subnational enforcement efforts is also considered.

CONTEXT

Sonora and Arizona share a sociopolitical past. Prior to 1848, both were part of Mexico, and Arizona still bears the marks of this shared history. Following the Treaty of Guadalupe Hidalgo (1848), however, Sonora and Arizona diverged into distinct geopolitical entities. Yet, even though communication barriers rose and eventually became the norm, cross-border family ties held fast, providing a source of continuity. The strongest cross-border links developed at border towns, where interdependent but asymmetric economic infrastructures converged even as distinct ideological frameworks came to define Arizona's and Sonora's legal and judicial cultural patterns and ministrations.

Recent sociodemographic and economic trends in the region have affected local entities' search for effective, collaborative approaches to regional problems, as well as their expectations for future interaction. For example, there has been a marked rise in illegal activities, which argues strongly for collaboration on the law enforcement front. The North American Free Trade Agreement (NAFTA), meanwhile, is expected to transform social and historical realities and bridge the structural space between the two states' respective legal and judicial systems.[2]

Responding to the need for enhanced cross-border collaboration, the National Law Center for Inter-American Free Trade in Tucson, Arizona, provided the impetus for the Arizona/Sonora Project at a June 1992 meeting of the Arizona and Sonora Supreme Courts.[3] The concept was developed further in follow-up meetings in Sonora, which involved people from the Law Center and members of Sonora's Supreme Court. The participants applied to the State Justice Institute for funding to facilitate improved judicial understanding between the states. The Arizona Supreme Court filed a concept paper in August 1992, and the Arizona Supreme Court submitted the full application in March 1993 and revised it in May 1993.

The stated purpose of the project was to identify areas of judicial procedure in the United States and Mexico in which harmonization of dispute resolution mechanisms would increase efficiency and decrease the costs of resolving cross-border commercial and other disputes. The formal proposal of the Arizona Supreme Court's Administrative Office specified three major goals: (1) to enhance understanding of the differences between cross-border judicial systems, (2) to foment cross-border judicial cooperation, and (3) to educate the judicial and legal community on both sides of the border.[4]

STATES' POWER TO ENGAGE IN INTERNATIONAL COOPERATION

A legal issue that arises when one subnational unit (such as Arizona) makes an agreement for international cooperation with another (for example, Sonora) is whether subnational units have the authority to enter into such accords. Individual states do manage their internal affairs, even in the international arena. Indeed, private legal rules regarding tort or contract principles—including state choice of law principles that determine whose substantive legal rules will govern the resolution of a particular private conflict—generally originate under state law.[5] Moreover, NAFTA encourages development of procedures for the resolution of private disputes consistent with the treaty. Hence state-level judicial programs may be consistent with federal policy as set forth in NAFTA.[6]

Absent either a federal attempt to occupy the field by treaty or a clear federal policy that conflicts with state rules, border states' efforts to implement international judicial cooperation should be permissible, and even promoted. A state can regulate the conduct and business of foreign nationals whose actions affect the legitimate interests of that state, if two conditions are fulfilled. First, this regulation must not have as its goal the furtherance of the state's own view of proper foreign policy objectives. Second, no federal foreign policy, statute, treaty, executive agreement, executive order, or regulation should conflict with the state's own laws or be intended to replace state regulation.

Although the Compact Clause of the U.S. Constitution forbids states to make any agreement or compact with another state or with a foreign power without the consent of Congress,[7] the courts have construed this clause to preclude only those agreements that are designed or tend to increase "political power in the States, which may encroach upon or interfere with the just supremacy of the United States."[8] Efforts by states to devise ways to minimize cross-border disputes and gaps and to strengthen cross-border cooperation between courts, prosecutors, and legal professionals would not seem to contravene the Compact Clause.[9]

The Mexican Constitution also contains a "compacts clause," similar to that found in the U.S. Constitution, which forbids individual Mexican states to enter into compacts or agreements with sister states or foreign powers.[10] However, in January 1992 Mexico enacted a law that provides blanket authorization to state and local governments to make agreements with foreign governmental entities or with international organizations. The objectives of this legislation, the Law Regarding the

Making of Treaties,[11] are to preserve and strengthen Mexican national sovereignty, protect Mexicans' rights and interests in foreign affairs, and support international cooperation.[12] The law does not seem to place any restrictions on the subject matter of an interinstitutional agreement, and whatever the intended scope of the new law may be, the decree clearly contemplates state and local government accords covering cross-border dispute resolutions. Article 8 of the law identifies only three prerequisites for a local or state initiative directed at the resolution of cross-border disputes to be valid: (1) Mexicans and foreign adversaries who are parties to a controversy covered by interinstitutional agreement must receive equal treatment, in conformity with principles of international reciprocity, (2) the parties must be guaranteed an opportunity for hearing of their claims and defenses, and (3) the ultimate decision maker must be impartial.[13]

THE JUVENILE JUSTICE PROCEDURE TASK FORCE

The Juvenile Justice Procedure Task Force of the Arizona/Sonora Project met in Rio Rico, Arizona, in March 1994 to discuss appropriate remedies to problems with juvenile Mexican nationals in Arizona's border counties. All parties agreed that some type of formal agreement was needed on this issue. One suggestion was that Arizona would place problem Mexican youths under some kind of protective custody while necessary legal, medical, and social paperwork could be prepared. If possible, Arizona would identify each youth's place of origin in Mexico, and immigration services could help transfer the child to the custody of the proper Sonora agency and/or individuals, from whence the youths would be returned to their home states for proper processing.

At a meeting of the full Arizona/Sonora Project in Rio Rico in April 1994, the Juvenile Justice Procedure Task Force resolved to develop all necessary agreements for the transfer of juveniles between the two states. And the task force determined to examine the possibility of international cooperative funding arrangements to support programs of mutual interest along the border.[14]

These steps led to the signing of an agreement of understanding on the transfer of Mexican juveniles from Arizona to Sonora in Hermosillo, Sonora, in July 1994. Essentially, the agreement provided that Mexican juveniles arrested for minor offenses in Arizona would have their prosecution suspended prior to any type of final adjudication, and they would be turned over to the proper authorities in Sonora for subsequent processing. The state of Arizona would provide funding to Sonora, along with vans for transportation. Before signing a final agreement, however, the parties resolved to undertake a pilot project, initiated in August 1994.[15]

Initial Diagnosis and Recommendations

At its first meeting, in November 1993, the Juvenile Justice Procedure Task Force identified the following problems regarding juvenile Mexican nationals detained in Arizona:

- No dispositional alternatives exist for dealing with young Mexican nationals detained in Arizona for delinquent acts. Arizona can only release them, detain them, or send them to the Department of Youth Treatment and Rehabilitations (DYTR).
- Mexican youths can be detained for up to thirty days to ensure their appearance at an upcoming hearing. This rule effectively subjects them to more punitive treatment than any U.S. counterpart.
- A lack of communication between Arizona and Sonora precludes locating a Mexican youth's family.
- Many Mexican nationals have no parents and are "street kids."
- There is little accountability within the system. Each part mistakenly assumes that someone else will solve the problem.
- The problem of Mexican youths' delinquent behavior has been costly to the Arizona judicial system.
- The system for tracing Mexican youths is insufficient and would benefit from automation.
- The safety/welfare issue must be addressed. On the one hand, Mexican youths are exploited by adults on both sides of the border; on the other, local communities must be protected from Mexican youths who present real crime threats.
- No meaningful cooperation exists between the state of Arizona and the U.S. government.
- The problem of Mexican youths has a negative economic impact on local communities.
- A general bias exists against Mexican nationals.
- U.S. federal and state juvenile legislation assumes that a Mexican youth has a legal status in the United States and in local society, but it does not directly address the problem of Mexican or other foreign nationals.
- Sonora's juvenile justice system, begun in 1984, has a comparatively short (and unstable) history. Although the system is complex

and offers a full array of services, there is broad variation from community to community.

- The "reciprocity" issue implies consideration of the way in which U.S. youths are treated in Mexico.
- Certain educational needs must be met. Mexican nationals need educational opportunities, and the general population needs education about the Mexican national problem in general.
- Communication problems exist with the Mexican consulates, and these must be resolved.
- Insufficient attention has been devoted to intercultural problems.
- Problems with Mexican nationals, and the Arizona cases involving them, have increased.
- There is no long-term plan or commitment for resolving the Mexican youth problem.

The task force based its recommendations for addressing these shortcomings on two important premises. The first is that no solution can be achieved by focusing solely on the Mexican youth in Arizona; attention must be extended to include rehabilitating the youth's family in Mexico. Second, juvenile legislation in Arizona, both federal and state, assumes that Mexican youths have legal status in Arizona, whereas, in fact, they do not; this legislation requires amendment.[16] The task force's recommendations were as follows:

- Legal mechanisms must be devised to help Sonora treat its own young people in Sonora, which would be a more economic alternative for Arizona.
- Permanent state and local commissions must be established, with all interested parties participating.
- Juvenile legislation at the federal and state levels must be amended to deal with the issue of Mexican nationals.
- Arizona and Sonora need an agreement to deal with the transfer of juveniles to Sonora, along with funding to cover such transfers.
- An economic forecast must be developed for the problem and the strategies to address it.
- There is need for appropriate statistics on Mexican juveniles, including an adequate system for tracking Mexican youths.
- A broad-based education program is needed to inform the general public about the problem of Mexican nationals.
- The Administrative Office of the Courts (AOC), Arizona Supreme Court, must develop a program to educate state legislators about

the problem of Mexican nationals, including on-site visits to affected locales, especially on the border.

- A statewide agreement should be developed for all juvenile probation officers regarding how Mexican nationals are to be handled.
- The Administrative Office of the Court, Arizona Supreme Court, must create a state support staff position in Nogales, Arizona, to serve as a general resource and clearinghouse for all problems connected with Mexican nationals.
- Once disposition alternatives are identified and developed, the task force must explore "summary procedures" to handle Mexican youths in a manner that protects their rights and contains due process protections.
- The task force should explore alternatives in the handling of Mexican youths that distinguish between the more serious and less serious offender, allowing the latter to be diverted into some type of alternative program (such as community service) and the former to be processed through the regular system.
- The task force must explore the availability of funding from private and international sources.
- The task force must respond to the "gang problem" developing among Mexican youths.
- The task force must be continued under the auspices of the Arizona/Sonora Project, with an expanded membership.[17]

Juvenile Service Programs in Sonora

Sonora's Juvenile Service Agency has been in existence since the mid–1980s, providing social assistance and juvenile probation services for youths between the ages of eleven and eighteen. The agency does not render investigative or enforcement services. Rather, it verifies the accuracy of a police investigative report after police issue the complaint and turn the youth over to the organization.

Sonora has five centers for the internment of juveniles, three of them in Hermosillo and all regulated by the federal government. Depending on a youth's age and the nature of the crime, he or she is sent to one of these centers, all of which have counselors (much like the U.S. system) and use a team of experts to determine what steps will follow. A youth can be put in "provisional placement" within seventy-two hours of arrest and detained for thirty days. A "final resolution" decision must be reached within this thirty-day span. Proof or evidence is then entered into the record, at which point the youth has the right to a public defender and can appeal the results of the administrative hearing to the

Family Court in Sonora. The Juvenile Service Agency must, of course, be able to document that its personnel have followed the law in all placement decisions.

A Mexican youth remanded to prison receives occupational therapy to learn a trade, and each of the five youth centers also provides educational classes (high school equivalence). The Sonora Juvenile Service Agency employs a "point system" in which the length of confinement is based partly on time but also on "good time served"; that is, credits for good behavior, up to a maximum number, can reduce the length of sentence.

The Sonora system responds to age, not to the kind of crime. Minors can remain in prison for up to one year, at which point they earn their liberty without regard to any rehabilitation. However, Sonora has experienced a rise in serious juvenile crimes, similar to what is occurring in the United States, which has prompted the state to consider changing its system to take into account the severity of the crime in sentencing.

Drug addiction is the most serious problem among Mexican youths. Each juvenile center in Sonora has a detoxication clinic, where youths spend up to two months. Detained youths' families are involved in the drug treatment process in the hope they will constitute positive reinforcement.

Sonora's Juvenile Service Agency handled about 6,000 cases in 1994, or just over 1 percent of the state's population of 450,000 minors. Of these 6,000 youths, approximately 1,500 were remanded to prison and 4,500 were provided alternative placement (a type of probation). Juveniles may also receive "conditional liberty," such as community service, which is usually conducted under supervision.[18]

Achievements

In July 1994, the Arizona Administrative Office of the Courts and the Juvenile Justice Procedure Task Force signed a memorandum of understanding (MOU) that provided for a 90–day pilot (subsequently extended to 180 days) to transfer Mexican national youths to Sonora.[19] The MOU provided for Sonora's Juvenile Service Agency to assume certain responsibilities. It must accept into its custody all Mexican national juvenile offenders who have violated the law in Arizona and who may be turned over to the agency through a process established by the Arizona court. The agency must provide to the juvenile offenders transferred from Arizona sequential interdisciplinary treatment, as well as the educational and vocational training necessary to permit their reintegration into society. Through its duly authorized agent in Nogales, Sonora, the Juvenile Service Agency must take custody of returning minors and ensure that those Mexican national juvenile offenders who have no established residence in Sonora are relocated to their respective states of origin in Mexico. Moreover, it must provide the maximum economic and human resources available to transport these Mexican national juvenile offenders to their respective homes. Further, the agency pledges to exchange all information necessary to achieve the goals of the MOU.[20]

Under the MOU, the Arizona Supreme Court agreed to transfer to the Juvenile Service Agency's duly authorized agent in Nogales all Mexican national juvenile offenders (following a process established by the court). It also pledged to provide all available documentation regarding each offender's nationality and the specific violation of the law committed in Arizona.

Young Mexican nationals spend significant periods of time in Arizona juvenile detention and correction facilities, at significant financial and emotional cost to themselves, their families, and Arizona taxpayers. Moreover, the people and governments on both sides of the border suffer when juveniles mark time in foreign detention centers instead of receiving the treatment and attention that juvenile programs are designed to provide.[21] Many of these young people ultimately become gang members, causing incalculable harm on both sides of the international frontier. At the time when the pilot project was being developed to reduce costs and to promote Mexican youths' integration into their home society, two-thirds of the juveniles detained in the Santa Cruz Detention Center were from Mexico.

Implementation of the Project: Judicial Roadblock

According to the MOU between Sonora and the Juvenile Justice Procedure Task Force, the main objective was to return to their families Sonoran youths who were brought to the attention of the Arizona Juvenile Court Services Division (AJCSD). When the AJCSD deemed it appropriate and in the best interests of the juvenile and the community, it pursued the standard transfer-of-custody procedure.[22]

The following is the process that applied to Mexican juveniles in Arizona under the terms of the MOU. Upon arrival at the AJCSD, Sonoran juveniles underwent a medical examination, the results of which accompanied the youths upon transfer to Mexican officials. The AJCSD collected as much personal information as possible on each juvenile, including full name, birth date, family's location, parents' names, addresses of family and relatives, and so on. The "fact sheet" prepared during juvenile intake in Arizona and the police report, both of which were translated into Spanish, also accompanied the juvenile. At a designated time, the Santa Cruz County Juvenile Probation Department delivered the Sonoran juvenile to the proper Mexican officials for return to his or her family or for care and custody by Sonora's Juvenile Justice Agency.[23] The Santa Cruz Juvenile Probation Department kept signed copies of all custodial/detention release forms as well as statistical information relating to the number of juveniles involved in the transfer project, information to which the Administrative Office of the Courts (AOC) and any other parties would have access.[24]

One setback to the transfer program was a court decision that held the program in violation of Arizona law. The Superior Court in Cochise County, Court of Appeals Division Two, overturned an order directing the transfer of a Mexican juvenile national to Sonora.[25] The court ruled that the Arizona constitution (article VI, '15) gives the superior court "exclusive original jurisdiction in all proceedings and matters affecting dependent, neglected, incorrigible or delinquent children, or children accused of crime under the age of eighteen years.... The powers of the judges to control such children shall be as provided by law." The court's authorities in handling such children are limited to those expressly granted to the legislation. Maricopa County Juvenile Action N. J-74275, 117 Ariz. 317, 572 P.2d 451, 452 (App. 1977). A.R.S. '8-241 sets forth the court's disposition and commitment alternatives for children who have been adjudicated dependent, delinquent, or incorrigible. Subsection 2 provides in relevant part that the court may award a delinquent child: (1) to a probation department, subject to such conditions as the court may impose, and (2) to a reputable citizen of good moral character, subject to the supervision of a probation department.

The Court of Appeals reasoned that the transfer of a minor determined delinquent by the juvenile authorities to another country over which the courts of Arizona have no control does not come within either of these dispositional alternatives. Hence the court explained that the statutes do not grant Arizona courts the authority to conclude an agreement supplementing the designated alternatives for handling juveniles under A.R.S. '8-241. The decision posed a serious obstacle to the transfer program, compelling the task force to reexamine the transfer program and determine ways of complying with the court's directive. The Appeals Court did not issue a permanent injunction against the transfer process; rather, it directed its decision at the way in which the process was handled and whether the case before it for adjudication complied with existing statutes. Thereafter, the transfer program continued to process juveniles without objection.[26]

To respond to the court decision, the task force organized an educational workshop at Rio Rico in August 1996 to improve Arizona prosecutors', the defense bar's, juvenile service agencies', and the court's understanding of the juvenile transfer program. Officials and academics discussed the Arizona and Sonora juvenile programs, as well as transfer programs that San Diego and El Paso were conducting with their respective Mexican counterparts. And legislative language was developed to ensure that in the future the transfer program would comply with statutes. This was followed in November 1996 with a trip to Hermosillo so that all parties could observe the workings of the juvenile system in Mexico.[27]

CRIMINAL LAW TASK FORCE

The fact that Sonora and Arizona are geographically close but very distant in their economic circumstances has presented opportunities for individuals and organizations interested in perpetrating crimes, and, indeed, cross-border crime has increased dramatically in recent years. In this context, the Arizona/Sonora Project decided to examine procedures that reduce crime—or at minimum accelerate the production of evidence in criminal prosecutions—while simultaneously ensuring that such evidence satisfies the litigants' concerns for due process and that the judicial process remains free from influence and corruption. Both Arizona and Sonora have an urgent need to cooperate in the areas of criminal investigations and evidence sharing.

Limitations

In both Sonora and Arizona, treaties, evidentiary rules, and constitutional provisions limit the process of collecting and exchanging evidence. These states must, therefore, develop an evidentiary-sharing agreement that has the force of law and avoids existing vehicles approved by the United States and Mexico, such as the Letters Rogatory or the Mutual Legal Assistance Treaty (MLAT).

The Criminal Law Task Force concluded that the states could make such agreements as long as these are recognized as informal and are not considered enforceable. Further, such agreements must not violate the terms of existing treaties and laws; it is not clear whether such agreements could extend beyond cooperative law enforcement exchanges of information into the private sector to obtain evidence. The ultimate limiting factor is that all courts must follow their own respective rules and procedures. Courts cannot admit evidence that is not properly authenticated. The production of evidence must be subject to the due process protection of each country, especially given the fact that an individual's liberty is often at stake.[28]

Specific Issues and Problems

Absent Witness in a Foreign Country

It is sometimes the case that someone in one country has evidence that appears to be relevant in a criminal prosecution in a second country, but that person may, for fear of arrest, refuse to enter the first country to give testimony. The court and litigants must determine how to obtain the evidence in a way that will make it admissible while accommodating the due process concerns of all parties.

Oath

Witnesses' statements must be taken under oath. Although various procedures exist for administering the oath when taking statements from witnesses who reside abroad,[29] problems arise when the oath is administered under penalty of perjury according to U.S. laws but is administered in a country that will not extradite citizens to the United States. And if the oath is administered in a country that will not extradite its citizens, the statement may not be "under oath." In effect, the oath may be a nullity, and the witness is unsworn if there is no consequence for false testimony. Hence the testimony would not be admissible.

Letters Rogatory and MLATs respond to evidence-gathering problems by seeking the assistance of the witness's host country. A legal representative obtains an affidavit under penalty of perjury or its equivalent. Theoretically, if the requesting state establishes that the statement is false, it can seek to prosecute for perjury. Little opportunity exists to develop an alternative state-to-state evidence-sharing procedure in this context that would not violate federal law.[30]

Cross-Examination

The task force also considered problems of cross-examination. In general, the party against whom the evidence is sought for admission has a right to examine the witness. U.S. law permits cross-examination by counsel for the opposing party. Mexican law gives the magistrate the right to examine witnesses who may consider interrogatories submitted by both counsels. Hence in Mexico there is no cross-examination as it is known in the United States. Unless a party can examine the witness, evidence is generally not admissible unless other indicia of reliability are present, such as the death-bed statement.

Pursuant to MLATs and Letters Rogatory, a representative of the requesting state or court—usually an investigator and potentially an attorney—acts as an information resource for the representative of the requested state to assist in the examination. However, as U.S. litigators know, it is very difficult, and often impossible, to prepare a complete set of written interrogatories for every potential development or possible alternative response to examination questions. If a formal deposition attended by representatives of both litigants cannot be taken, the next best alternative is to rely on the professionalism of the legal representative of the host country. This representative can be provided with a detailed outline of the problem, issues, and evidence expected to be produced, as well as information on the witness's relationship to the parties. Armed with this information and material provided by a foreign investigator, the legal representative of the requested state then continues the investigation as a commissioner of the foreign court.

In such circumstances, special agents or representatives of a foreign court operate within the parameters of the host country and may only serve with the agreement of the host country's government.[31] A party who perceives that the evidence collected by such a procedure has been harmful to his case would likely challenge the development of such procedures on a due process basis as a violation of constitutional rights. In this context, disparities between the Mexican and U.S. criminal justice and legal systems provide limited opportunities to develop an alternative state-to-state evidence-sharing procedure that would not violate federal law in either or both countries.[32]

Official Records and Documentation

In general, official documents are admissible if they are properly validated. A party or court can obtain documents by treaty request or Letter Rogatory. However, official records, including bank records, can be presented based on generally accepted conventions.[33]

Prosecution versus Extradition

The Criminal Law Task Force considered issues linked to the need—and international obligation—to prosecute or extradite offenders from one country who are charged with committing crimes in the other country. Mexico's extradition treaty with the United States is not the "Supreme Law of the Land," as it is in the United States. Rather, its provisions are overridden by the Mexican Constitution and by a statute prohibiting the extradition of a Mexican citizen to a foreign country, including the United States. In recent years, Mexico has begun to implement a policy to extradite Mexican citizens in exceptional circumstances. The Mexican government is still refining the definition of "exceptional circumstances." At this time, it is limited to crimes of violence, such as murder and rape, or to organized crime figures, such as persons with long-standing convictions and/or multiple charges for high-level trafficking crimes. It has not yet been extended to include extradition for perjury.

However, Mexico has established a unique alternative mechanism under Article 4 of the Mexican Federal Penal Code to apply in instances when it is unable to extradite its citizens. This mechanism permits the prosecution of an individual for a crime committed outside Mexico, upon the request of a foreign state, if the crime was committed either by or upon a Mexican citizen. The circumstances under which Mexico will prosecute a defendant in Mexico with evidence developed and presented by U.S. law enforcement agencies are the following: (1) the defendant must be in Mexico, (2) the defendant must not have been tried in the country where the crime occurred, and (3) the act for which the defendant is charged must be a crime in both countries. With international law enforcement cooperation, such cases can be litigated effectively.

To ensure successful prosecution of such cases in Mexico, the Mexican Attorney General's Office (PGR) has developed a memorandum on domestic prosecution and evidentiary rules[34] which guides U.S. prosecutors regarding the requirements to convict a person in Mexico. The memorandum outlines the type and kind of evidence required in cases of homicide, rape, drug-related crimes, fraud and breaches of trust, tax crimes, firearms and explosive crimes, and criminal association, thereby helping U.S. prosecutors provide the types of evidence that the Mexican prosecutor needs to prosecute the crime.[35]

The Mexican Attorney General's Office also acts as a clearinghouse and monitor for Article 4 prosecutions. It receives and assigns the evidence for Article 4 cases to prosecutors in the field. It identifies and helps resolve difficulties in problem cases. And it responds to political questions that often flow from the handling of these cases.

In cases involving the extradition of persons from the United States to Mexico, U.S. courts routinely extradite the suspect if Mexico can demonstrate fulfillment of due process requirements with respect to the identity of the defendant and probable cause that the suspect committed the crime(s) for which extradition is sought. Several aspects of this process are problematic. Mexico typically submits summary statements of a public prosecutor, often without reference to the underlying facts. Such statements, basically findings of fact by an officer of the court, are sufficient for an arrest in Mexico. But to U.S. courts, these lengthy recitations appear to be little more than detailed police reports.

A Mexican national can block extradition from the United States through resort to *amparo*. Like a habeas corpus petition in the United States, an *amparo* suit often takes months to resolve, well beyond the period required by the extradition statute. A suspect wanted in Mexico can often defeat extradition merely by filing repeated *amparo* actions and seeking delay until after the United States' extradition procedure is dismissed.[36] The filing of an *amparo* is akin to an appeal in Mexico.

From a law enforcement perspective, the *amparo* is a frequently abused *ex parte* procedure. A defendant can file an *amparo* in any court, regardless of the court's jurisdiction, venue, or any investigation pending in the court. An individual seeking the *amparo* is not required to provide a copy of the filing to the government, and it need not be produced or delivered until a government representative attempts to serve an arrest warrant or other process. Hence the *amparo* can be kept secretly in reserve as a mechanism to secure one's release and liberty.

Recommendations about Cooperation

Following its initial analysis, the Criminal Law Task Force made several recommendations to improve coordination of criminal cases between Arizona and Sonora. Although these suggestions will probably not result in the development of new procedures for the exchange of evidence, they may provide a substantial resource for explaining the process to judges and practitioners alike.

- The existing procedures to obtain evidence from a party/witness in a country other than the country in which criminal litigation is proceeding should be identified, summarized, and explained.
- The existing procedures to obtain documentary evidence and other official records without resorting to treaty requests should be identified, summarized, and explained.
- The time constraints facing U.S. prosecutors generally, and especially the requirements of extradition of suspects to Mexico, should be explained.
- The *amparo* procedure should be explained, especially within the context of an extradition procedure. The task force should explore whether a basis can be established to complete the extradition process subject to the *amparo* process. Hence, in such a case, the filing of an *amparo* in Mexico could be considered as an admission of jurisdiction for the Mexican court to consider the issues raised therein, thereby confessing extradition to Mexico in the United States courts.
- Procedures under Article 4 of the Mexican Federal Penal Code should be described.

EVALUATING THE CRIMINAL LAW AND JUVENILE JUSTICE PROCEDURE TASK FORCES

The Arizona/Sonora Judicial Relations Project holds implications for judicial and legal cooperation far beyond these states' shared border. The same cross-national problems exist along the whole length of the Mexico–U.S. border, as well as on the borders of most countries in the hemisphere in which significant subnational units exist. The project's successes have demonstrated that cooperation is possible when neighboring states enjoy good relations based on personal contacts between their judicial and other governmental branches and when both work at fostering that cooperation in an organized way.[37]

The Arizona/Sonora Project officially ended when its funding expired in June 1997. Although it continues to receive requests for information on its operation and to participate in other initiatives,[38] as of September 2000 there were no prospects for the project's renewal, primarily because of a lack of financial resources. Moreover, the large number of Sonoran juveniles in Arizona who were the project's chief target has been significantly reduced due to a substantial increase in the number of border patrol agents assigned to deny entry to illegal migrants from Mexico, including these Sonoran juveniles.[39]

It may well be that the Arizona/Sonora Judicial Relations Project was ahead of its time. Although the Juvenile Justice Procedure Task Force achieved some success, other task forces in the project never extended beyond information exchange. Undeniably, the educational process was useful, but participants, especially U.S. participants, were frustrated by the lack of concrete results. This failure may have been due in part to a lack of experience with international disputes on the part of the Arizona judiciary. Another contributing factor may have been the two groups' differing approaches to the collaboration. While U.S. participants were anxious to define issues and fashion solutions, Mexican participants were more interested in first becoming acquainted with their U.S. counterparts, primarily through social meetings, and this difference may have created some misunderstanding.[40]

The project clearly achieved its first goal—to enhance understanding of the differences and similarities between the two judicial systems, even though some gaps of understanding remain and incompatibilities between trial procedures in the two countries will continue to exist. It is still too early to judge whether the project achieved its second goal—judicial cooperation. Both domestic and international law regulating procedural aspects continue to constitute structural barriers. The remedy is to circumvent the bureaucratic inefficiency at the federal levels, which hinders the execution of legal matters across the U.S.–Mexico border. Cooperation in juvenile matters did achieve some success in this regard,[41] but the project was not in operation long enough for some recommendations to undergo proper development.

The project went some way toward meeting its third goal—to educate and train the judiciary and legal communities. Extending this kind of training to a wider audience could significantly improve understanding of the respective legal-judicial systems and help develop a confident social environment for judicial cooperation.[42] And efforts should be made to disseminate project results to other border states, federal court administrators, legislators, policymakers, and academicians. One project shortcoming in this regard was the comparative lack of participation by the Arizona judiciary and lack of teamwork among Arizona participants.

Subnational enforcement cooperation has many potential applications to border problems in the Americas: on the U.S.–Canada, Colombia-Panama, and Mexico-Belize borders, as well as among the members of Mercosur, the Central American Common Market, and the Andean Pact. A worthwhile exercise would be to study the variables under which subnational enforcement cooperation occurs in the Americas in order to identify the environment and laws that facilitate and hinder successful subnational enforcement cooperation.

CONCLUSION

Cross-border enforcement cooperation between Sonora and Arizona exemplifies the positive spin-off that has occurred as a result of the NAFTA process. But globalization and trade liberalization have encouraged more than the growth of commerce. They have also stimulated an expansion in transnational crime, which increases the pressure on national governments and international organizations to explore ways to facilitate subnational enforcement initiatives. However, the limited accomplishments and teething problems of the Arizona/Sonora Judicial Relations Project reflect the difficulties of trying to conceptualize and operate such new enforcement mechanisms without proper funding, broad encouragement, and a national framework.

One way that international organizations, governments (national, state, and local), academic institutions,[43] nongovernmental organizations (including bar associations and police and criminal justice associations),[44] think tanks,[45] and others can strengthen confidence-building measures is to conduct studies on subnational enforcement initiatives—both formal and informal—on the Mexico–U.S. border and in the hemisphere.[46] The studies should analyze the components that enabled these initiatives to emerge and succeed—or fail. For instance, the fact that the offices of U.S. state attorneys general and other state law enforcement agencies on the border have prepared their own memoranda and guidelines for prosecuting cases in Mexico indicates that many U.S. subnational law enforcement agencies are replicating the response to Mexico's Article 4 prosecution procedures. Similarly, U.S. subnational agencies have developed specialized responses to the execution of penal sanctions conventions on the transfer of prisoners, and they have evolved specialized responses to the recovery and return of stolen and embezzled aircraft and vehicles—as have Mexican subnational agencies.

There are a number of issues that must be addressed in any analysis of subnational enforcement initiatives. These include the role of interest groups, the degree to which the three branches of government participate, and comparisons to subnational regimes and initiatives in other parts of the world. Interestingly, the Arizona/Sonora Project did not involve non-judicial officials. In the real world, cross-border crime, and the solutions to it, require the involvement of a broad range of governmental agencies. Parliaments must make decisions on laws and appropriate money, and executives must promulgate and apply regulations and accord priorities to various activities of their agencies. Hence cross-border enforcement cooperation projects that involve only one branch of government may rest on a political base that is too narrow to provide sufficient support to flourish.

Any discussion of subnational enforcement regimes and initiatives should also review carefully the role of national governments and the role of specific agencies. While some policy and implementation on border enforcement issues comes directly from national capitols, some emanates from agencies and persons outside the capital cities, and it is important to achieve a proper balance between the two. Persons interested in creating and developing effective enforcement regimes should try to build prototypes and incubate them in academic[47] and think tank scenarios or in pilot projects such as the Arizona/Sonora Project.

The cross-border programs of the National Center for State Courts (NCSC) are worth reviewing for the lessons they may hold regarding the impacts on subnational enforcement at the judicial level. The NCSC has a cooperative agreement with the U.S. Agency for International Development (USAID) to bring judges from the United States and Mexico together to exchange ideas and experiences. The NCSC also conducts a U.S.–Mexico Judicial Exchange Program, which facilitates informal exchanges when a judge from one country visits the other country. Another NCSC activity involves assisting the National Autonomous University of Mexico (UNAM) with its master's program in judicial education, and the NCSC is currently assessing cross-border judicial cooperation, particularly the extent to which there is mutual enforcement of judicial opinions on the border.[48]

Although the Arizona/Sonora Judicial Relations Project will require additional investment and experimentation before it can ripen and realize its true potential, programs like this must be pursued. The trend toward globalization and increasing cross-border U.S.–Mexico (and Arizona-Sonora) transactions will require bold experimentation and cooperation on subnational levels.

Notes

1. So frequent is the interaction between bordering states on the U.S.–Mexico frontier that the two national governments hold twice-yearly meetings of the states' attorneys general to discuss law enforcement trends and strategies. Various other state and local agencies meet over sectoral issues, such as the environment and migration.

2. *Balancing the Future, Appendix, Project Evaluation* 4, 1996. On file with author.

3. This meeting, in Phoenix, Arizona, was held in connection with the semiannual plenary meeting of the Arizona-Mexico Commission and the Commission on Arizona/Sonora.

4. Arizona Supreme Court, Administrative Office of the Courts, *Arizona/Sonora Project*, 1.

5. See Wendelken vs. Superior Court, 137 Ariz. 455, 671 P.2d 896, 1983, in which the Arizona Supreme Court decided that Arizona's personal injury law, not Sonora's, applied to an action arising out of an accident at a vacation home owned by the defendant in Puerto Peñasco, Sonora. Both the plaintiff and the defendant were U.S. citizens and Arizona residents. The court dismissed sovereignty concerns in holding that the law of Arizona governed the liability of the property owner to the plaintiff/invitee.

6. See D. Michael Mandig, "The Role for Border State Judicial Cooperation," *Toward Seamless Borders: Making Free Trade Work in the Americas* 716 (1993): 726–27.

7. U.S. Constitution, art. I, '10, cl. 3.

8. Northeast Bancorp. Inc. vs. Board of Governors of the Federal Reserve System, 472 U.S. 159, 175, 105 S.Ct. 2545, 2554, 86 L.Ed.2d 112, 1985.

9. Mandig, "The Role for Border State Judicial Cooperation," 733.

10. *La Constitución de los Estados Unidos Mexicanos*, Tit. IV, Art. 117.

11. "Ley Sobre la Celebración de Tratados," *Diario Oficial*, January 2, 1992.

12. This decree is based on the concept of an "*acuerdo interinstitucional*" (interinstitutional agreement), defined as an accord between any state or local governmental entity in Mexico and any foreign governmental entity. Ibid., art. 2, 1.II.

13. Mandig, "The Role for Border State Judicial Cooperation," 734–35.

14. Ibid., 123–26.

15. Ibid., 128–29.

16. Ibid., 47–48.

17. Ibid., 49–50.

18. Ibid., 50–52.

19. Financial support for the project came from a Juvenile Crime Reduction Fund Grant to Santa Cruz County, Arizona, which then provided funding to Sonoran officials to implement the project.

20. Ibid., 54–55.

21. Mandig, "The Role for Border State Judicial Cooperation."

22. Arizona Supreme Court, Administrative Office of the Courts, *Arizona/Sonora Project*.

23. The Santa Cruz County Juvenile Probation Department is the agency that coordinated with the Mexican consulate and with Sonoran government officials. Juveniles detained in other Arizona counties were first transferred to Santa Cruz (with proper notice given to Santa Cruz prior to transfer).

24. Arizona Supreme Court, Administrative Office of the Courts, *Arizona/Sonora Project*, 43–44.

25. The case was JV-95000306.

26. Arizona Supreme Court, Administrative Office of the Courts, *Arizona/Sonora Project*, 44–45.

27. Ibid.

28. Ibid., 46–47.

29. See 28 U.S.C. '1746.

30. Arizona Supreme Court, Administrative Office of the Courts, *Arizona/Sonora Project*, 47–48.

31. The development of less formal procedures would probably conflict with the federal mandate in this area.

32. Arizona Supreme Court, Administrative Office of the Courts, *Arizona/Sonora Project*, 48–49.

33. Ibid., 49–50.

34. Miguel A. Méndez, "Domestic Prosecution and Evidence Required in Mexican Criminal Cases," Embassy of Mexico to the United States, November 1995, unpublished. On file with author.

35. The Mexican Attorney General's Office has also prepared an English translation of the Mexican rules of evidence from its Federal Criminal Prosecutorial Law of Evidence. See Chapter of Evidence, *Código Federal de Procedimientos Penales*, 1993, at www.cddhcu.gob.mx/leyinfo/9/.

36. See United States vs. Fowlie, 24 F.3d 1049, 1064 (9th Cir.), 1994.

37. Ibid., 1–2.

38. For example, Dennis Metrick, the project coordinator, participated in the 1999 San Diego conference on international cooperation sponsored by the National Center for State Courts and other organizations. Letter from Metrick, dated June 17, 1999, to the author.

39. Telephone interview with Dennis L. Metrick, Project Coordinator, Arizona Supreme Court, April 21, 1999.

40. Letter from Metrick.

41. Ibid., 14.

42. Ibid., 17.

43. Especially important are universities with existing programs on U.S.–Mexico relations. The University of New Mexico has an affiliation with the United States–Mexico Law Institute, which holds an annual institute on U.S.–Mexico legal issues. Similarly, Georgetown University has a Mexico project that has produced a series of studies on national security issues between Mexico and the United States. The North-South Center, at the University of Miami, and the University of Arizona Law School have extensive programs on border and/or hemispheric cooperation that have included enforcement issues.

44. In the United States the Section of International Law and Practice, American Bar Association, is a cooperating sponsor of the annual United States–Mexico Law Institute. The American Society of International Law has organized a seminar with the National Autonomous University of Mexico (UNAM) on international law and border issues of common interest.

45. The Center for Strategic and International Studies, in Washington, D.C., has produced several publications on U.S.–Mexico relations. See, for example, José Antonio Crespo, "Raising the Bar: The Next Generation of Electoral Reforms in Mexico" (2000); Sidney Weintraub, "NAFTA at Three: A Progress Report" (1997); and Joyce Hoebing, Sidney Weintraub, and M. Delal Baer, eds., *NAFTA and Sovereignty Trade-offs for Canada, Mexico, and the United States* (1996). The Inter-American Dialogue and the Institute for International Economics, both in Washington, also have relevant publications series and have sponsored briefings on cross-border issues and on NAFTA.

46. For instance, in 1975 the California attorney general established a Mexican Liaison Program in the Bureau of Investigation of the California Department of Justice. The attorney general authorized special agents of the California Department of Justice to travel to Mexico to confer with Mexican authorities and establish guidelines and procedures in accordance with the laws of Mexico to facilitate locating and prosecuting fugitives in Mexico. When a suspect of Mexican nationality is located in Mexico, the concerned law enforcement agency in California can contact the Mexican Liaison Unit and request assistance in filing a foreign prosecution. See Bruce Zagaris and Julia Padierna Peralta, "Mexico–United States Extradition and Alternatives: From Fugitive Slaves to Drug Traffickers—150 Years and Beyond the Rio Grande's Winding Course," *American University Journal of International Law and Policy* 12:519 (1997). The Mexican Liaison Unit helps to coordinate many conferences and meetings between Mexican and U.S. officials.

47. Courses on international relations, political science, international law, international organizations, environmental policy, and the like, especially in border states, may want to support research and other projects that have as hypothetical the continuing cross-border crime issue, and encourage research on proposed solutions, some of which may be ongoing or experimental.

48. Phone conference with Cathy Gill, NASCA, September 8, 2000.

15

Mexico, the United States, and the Migration–Crime Nexus

William F. McDonald

INTRODUCTION

A full assessment of the threat of criminality to public security and governability, particularly along the border between the United States and Mexico, must include an examination of the nexus between migration and crime. Both legal and illegal migration are continuing sources of corruption, violence, and disorder in the borderland and the interiors. Neither country has been able to stem the flow of illegal immigrants entering their respective territories. In this respect they are like many governments grappling unsuccessfully with illegal immigration.[1] Nor have they been able to administer a fair and efficient guest worker program that might contain the problem.[2] These failures have resulted in policy responses affecting crime control as well as introducing new levels of binational cooperation. Some responses suggest the promise of viable Mexican institutions and mutually beneficial cooperation. Others illustrate the unintended costs of single-minded policies.

Mexico created law enforcement units (such as the Beta groups, discussed below) that for several years appeared to be able to maintain integrity, effectively perform their mission, and win the respect not only of U.S. law enforcement agents but also of the more skeptical Mexican public. On the other hand, American frustration with the failures of U.S. immigration control policies has resulted in political backlashes and a shift in policy to focus on the criminal dimension of migration. Consequently, Mexican border towns have been forced to absorb destabilizing busloads of young, unattached male criminals, and Mexicans are angered by what they interpret as a racist policy directed against them.[3]

With regard to the migration–crime nexus, there have been several positive developments. Mexico continues to emphasize the constitutional right of its citizens to emigrate. Since the early 1990s, however, Mexico has tempered this absolute principle in ways intended to increase public security along the border. For its part, the United States has increased the U.S. Border Patrol's search and rescue capabilities, including special joint efforts with Grupo Beta; cooperated in the production and broadcasting of public safety campaigns directed at migrants; permitted Mexican consuls to be located at U.S. ports of entry; notified Mexican officials of shipments of deportees to the border; returned some deportees to other ports of entry to avoid swamping border towns; and stepped up efforts to prosecute violence or abuse against migrants by officials or others.[4]

A paradigm shift—driven by demographic, economic, and cultural changes—is now occurring with respect to the U.S.–Mexico relationship. Today's leaders are repudiating the traditional antagonisms and tensions that often have distorted relations between the two countries. Increasingly they regard binational cooperation as a requirement for meeting new social and economic realities. Crime in the borderlands—just as air and water pollution, health hazards, and economic development—is believed to require a regional solution.[5] Yet the new binationalism is as fragile as it is hopeful. Some faction of the public greets cooperative successes with suspicion and hostility. Others wedded to the old ways or to personal agendas can escalate blunders and honest differences into major setbacks. In the long term, however, there is reason to be cautiously optimistic.

This chapter assesses the migration–crime nexus and Mexico's and the United States' responses to it. It focuses primarily on the role of organized crime and illegal migration in the borderland region, making reference to the interiors when relevant. It places the developments in larger historical and comparative contexts. The approach is informed by Jerome Hall's analysis of the Carrier's Case in fifteenth-century England,[6] in which the high court dramatically expanded theft laws to protect burgeoning international commercial interests through the criminal justice system. Hall's analysis remains relevant today. The integration of national economies into regional blocs, such as NAFTA, and into the new global economy has implications for the administration of criminal justice within and among participating states. It is not just the law merchant that will have to be predictable for a state to compete successfully in today's globally integrated market. The institutions of criminal justice will be expected to provide a secure environment and cooperation with their counterpart institutions across borders to achieve a global level of public security and legal predictability. This will not happen quickly or automatically, but it is happening. The United Nations has opened for signing the first convention against transnational organized crime. President Clinton issued the United States' first international crime control strategy in 1998.[7] The Mexican Attorney General's Office (PGR) stationed legal attachés in the United States in the 1990s and created a branch to assist foreign law enforcement officials prosecuting criminals who flee to Mexico.[8] Mexico's president established an elite law enforcement unit (Grupo Beta Sur) to protect migrants illegally transiting through Mexico from Central America.

THE BORDERLAND AND CRIME

International boundaries constitute criminogenic structural conditions when they divide a market by restricting the exchange of goods and people, creating differentials in the costs and consequences of goods and transactions.[9] These opportunities are often capitalized upon by criminal enterprises that span the border. The examples of auto theft, baby trafficking, and white-collar fraud illustrate the variety of crime.

While examining the effects of peso devaluations on crime in Texas border towns, Miller was intrigued by an unexpected finding.[10] Regardless of economic conditions, these communities had lower violent and property crime rates than cities elsewhere in Texas. A striking exception was auto theft, which increased sharply over ten years. In 1980 an estimated 20,000 stolen units entered Mexico from the United States. By the mid–1980s auto theft had become a greater problem in border towns than in interior cities of similar size.

Although auto theft rates had been stable for the United States as a whole over a decade, rates for Texas generally, and border towns particularly, had doubled by 1986 (from 346 to 714 per 100,000 population). In McAllen and Laredo, they tripled. In Brownsville, they quadrupled. Miller concluded that cross-border auto theft was primarily the work of professional rings based in *frontera* communities such as Ciudad Juárez, Nuevo Laredo, Reynosa, and Matamoros. From there, they easily staged their thefts and were able to operate largely with impunity due to the "permissive, if not supportive law enforcement environment in Mexico."

Miller learned that *frontera*-based rings used several strategies. They themselves did not usually steal vehicles in the interior communities. Cars were stolen from these areas by local professionals, then driven south to the border by aliens returning to Mexico. At the border they were either "chopped" and the parts sold, or they were taken across the border by the *frontera* rings. Alternatively, some vehicles were used to transport drugs and undocumented workers to San Antonio or Houston, where other units would be obtained from local thieves and driven back to the border. Most frequently, vehicles taken for the illicit Mexican market were stolen from border communities, typically from downtown streets and shopping malls during business hours. Vehicles were easily entered and started, and then moved quickly across the border without interference, given that U.S. authorities generally ignored outbound lanes at international bridges. Once in Mexico, the cars were often altered so they could not be identified as stolen and could be sold on the black market.

A follow-up study in 1991–1992 concluded that no auto theft rings organized in the way that Miller described existed in the Brownsville area. Instead, auto theft at the border was characterized by "the temporary association of chauffeurs, mounters, and specialists. Quasi-groups are created for the purpose of stealing, but these affiliations are temporary. The property offenders [who were interviewed] do not believe themselves to belong to an organized group."[11]

In contrast to auto theft, baby trafficking is a highly sensitive crime. Unscrupulous adoptive parents obtain infants at baby markets run by smugglers and lawyers. These individuals do an estimated US$125 million a year supplying infertile couples and others with Mexican children, along with forged adoption papers and other documentation.[12] When caught, they frequently strike the pose of compassionate humanitarians.

Attorneys for Mario Reyes, a lawyer charged with smuggling twenty-three Mexican babies into the United States, for example, claimed that their client was trying to help "unwanted children of prostitutes and impoverished people who could not afford another child," and that he was a devout Catholic who "loathes abortion." But it was also alleged that Mr. Reyes earned $20,000 for each adoption he arranged. This prompted Eunicia Soto, who runs an orphanage in Mexico, to ask, "If he a humanitarian who wanted to help poor children, why did he charge so much money?"[13]

White-collar fraud is another prominent concern. In the mid–1990s the Federal Bureau of Investigation (FBI) received numerous complaints from private insurance carriers in California and elsewhere regarding fraudulent billing practices by foreign physicians. An investigation determined that U.S. billing agencies used by physicians in towns along the southwest border encouraged foreign based doctors to utilize their services to defraud insurers.[14]

Private insurers generally use their own investigators to determine the validity of claims. However, hospitals and clinics have been constructed outside the United States to thwart investigations and prevent the rejection of claims. Over time, foreign physicians and U.S. billing agencies had begun coaching their staffs and patients on what to tell investigators. Most U.S. insurers complained that foreign clinics and hospitals lacked the facilities and equipment necessary for the procedures for which they were billing. Insurers also complained that patients never received the treatment for which claims were being submitted.

In one case a Mexican physician, Dr. Joaquín Merlos, and a U.S. billing service owner, LeRoy Alexander, worked together to defraud an insurance company of more than $300,000 per month. They were suspected of simultaneously billing more than forty-eight other insurance companies as well, generating losses in the millions of dollars. The investigation resulted in the indictment of seventeen Mexican physicians and an assistant, two U.S. bankers, one U.S. billing service owner, and two U.S. durable medical equipment suppliers.[15]

Migration-Related Crime

There are various types of migrants who cross the U.S.–Mexico border. One is "sojourners," who maintain their principal residence in Mexico and enter the United States, legally or illegally, for brief periods. Another is "settlers," including both resident settlers (legal or illegal, who habitually reside in the United States) and naturalized settlers, who have met the five-year legal residence and other requirements and have become U.S. citizens.[16]

The estimated resident Mexico-born population in the United States in 1996 was about 4.8 million legal residents plus 2.3 to 2.4 million illegal residents.[17] Mexico-born individuals constitute about 54 percent of the total number of persons who were in the United States illegally as of October 1996.[18] The illegal alien resident population was estimated to be growing by about 275,000 per year in 1996.[19] On the other side of the border, there were an estimated 200,000 Americans living in Mexico illegally in 1994, plus 150,000 living there as legal permanent residents.[20]

The number of legal temporary visits between Mexico and the United States is substantial. In fiscal year 1998 an estimated 278 million to 351 million people crossed the border legally from Mexico to the United States.[21] The San Ysidro Port of Entry, fifteen miles south of downtown San Diego, is reputedly the busiest land border crossing in the world. It inspects more than 40 million persons and 15 million vehicles annually.[22] In 1992 at the San Diego–Tijuana border there were 1,400,000 border crossings per month for the purpose of shopping in the United States. These crossings were made by somewhere between 45,000 and 60,000 individuals, who spent an estimated US$2.8 billion (annualized) in the United States. Nearly 40,000 people a day cross the San Diego–Tijuana border to work legally in the United States.[23]

The number of unauthorized entries into the United States from Mexico is unknown. In fiscal year 1998, more than 1,516,000 persons were apprehended attempting to enter without inspection along the Mexico–U.S. border, and more than 1,484,000 were allowed "voluntary return," whereby the arrestee returns to Mexico without being formally deported.[24] During fiscal year 1999, more than 29,000 apprehensions along the United States' southwest border were of Central Americans, an increase of almost 40 percent over the previous year.[25]

Discussing the criminal dimensions of migration raises ideological as well as theoretical issues. The notion that illegal migration could be treated as a crime vexes people sympathetic to migrants. A bumper sticker seen in a Washington, D.C., suburb read: "A human being cannot be illegal."[26] In 1997 Mexico's Foreign Ministry declared: "Mexico affirms categorically that the migratory phenomenon ... should not be confused with criminality."[27] In his discussion of "criminal aliens," Daniel Wolf stresses that while unlawful entry into the United States is legally defined as a crime, it is not a "real" crime like theft or assault.[28]

Rhetorical arguments notwithstanding, entering the United States without inspection has been defined by law as a crime since 1924.[29] Unlawful reentry after deportation is also a crime. The penalties for these offenses have been stiffened as part of the reaction to massive illegal immigration over the past two decades. Reentry after formal deportation is now punishable by twenty years imprisonment. Current policy is to deter reentry by diligent application of these new provisions.[30]

For purposes of assessing lawfulness along the U.S.–Mexico border, the decision to include or exclude acts of unlawful entry and reentry obviously makes a big difference. Even if one would like to avoid over-demonizing the illegal immigrant as a serious criminal, there is no escaping the fact that illegal entry constitutes an act of contempt for the rule of law and for democratic governance. One and a half million attempts per year to violate a democratically established public policy represent a serious assault on law and democracy. Such acts of defiance reinforce a culture of lawlessness and impose real costs. In addition to the enormous public expense of securing the border, there are the individual costs borne by ranchers and borderland communities who must endure thousands of illegal immigrants trespassing through their backyards, degrading their natural environments, and exposing them to contagious diseases.[31]

THE MIGRATION-CRIME NEXUS: A GLOBAL PHENOMENON

With accelerating globalization and the openness of national borders to trade, travel, and tourism, the illegal movement of people across borders has emerged as one of the most problematic items on the policy agendas of states and the international community. The problem is predicted to get worse.[32] An estimated 2 percent of the world's population are migrants living outside their homelands. An unknown fraction of them are illegal. The rest are legal immigrants, refugees, or seekers of political asylum (many of the latter are making fraudulent claims). The smuggling of migrants has become a growth business for transnational organized crime networks. In 1996 it was estimated to have grown into an activity generating between US$5 and $7 billion per year.[33] In March 2000, the estimate was $17 billion.[34]

A related matter is the trafficking in women and children. As of 1998 the United Nations High Commissioner for Human Rights estimated that some 4 million people a year are being "trafficked" for diverse purposes, including "forcing women and children into sexually or economically ...

exploitative situations ... as well as other illegal activities."[35] A November 1999 Central Intelligence Agency (CIA) report put the estimate between 700,000 and 2 million women and children being trafficked per year worldwide. Mexico is now listed as a primary source for traffickers, along with Russia, China, Vietnam, and the Czech Republic.[36] Mexico also has joined the ranks of transit and/or destination countries for trafficked persons. To protect security as well as suppress human rights abuses, criminality, and other costs associated with illegal immigration and alien smuggling, many states and the international community are seeking policies and cooperation to control the problem.[37] The United States and Mexico have joined together with Central American states and Canada to address the problem in their region.[38] Originating at a meeting of high-level officials in Puebla in 1996, the joint discussions have continued under the Puebla Process (discussed below).[39]

Migrant Trafficking in the U.S.–Mexico Case

The United States and Mexico share a common interest in preventing the smuggling of illegal immigrants from Mexico into the United States and in not allowing Mexico to be a country of transit for thousands of illegal immigrants from Latin America, Asia, and elsewhere who are seeking to reach the United States via Central America. A substantial illegal immigrant population has already settled in southern Mexico, aggravating unemployment, burdening the government, and increasing the potential for revolutionary instability.[40] Illegal immigrants and the international criminal networks that smuggle them add to the problems of corruption and lawlessness. Smuggling of humans is a criminal violation in both Mexico and the United States.

Immigrants who are smuggled are subjected to horrendous crimes and violations of human rights during transit and/or at their destinations. The tightening of the U.S. border has raised the cost of smuggling and also the risks for immigrants who enter either by themselves or with smugglers. Migrants are carrying larger amounts of cash than previously, and hence have become even more lucrative targets for bandits.[41] About 330 migrants die per year attempting to enter the United States illegally, and at least half are never identified.[42] Many more are rescued from near death. A substantial proportion of these tragedies has been attributed to the ruthless and reckless activity of smugglers. Immigrants have been abandoned in the desert, locked in railroad cars in searing heat or freezing cold, forced to lie on rags used to clean up chemical waste, and killed in crashes of overloaded cars and trucks.[43] At their destinations, smuggled immigrants are often exploited, degraded, and enslaved. The true extent of such treatment is unknown and can only be guessed at from anecdotal evidence.

By the early 1970s illegal immigration was rising rapidly. The "Bracero" guest worker program that had imported thousands of Mexican workers to the United States was abolished in 1964. The U.S. Border Patrol was making 400,000 apprehensions a year, up from 86,000 in 1964.[44] People smuggling had become a thriving racket, yielding some $125 million a year.[45] In 1977 the borderlands were described as "a free-fire zone where living bodies become the goods in a kind of slave trade."[46] In addition to many amateur smugglers, dozens (perhaps hundreds) of large operations developed. On the West Coast the best known was that of a Tijuana businessman called "El Indio," whose operation was estimated to employ 150 people. Observers on both sides of the border claimed that alien smuggling had become the leading industry in some border cities.

Mexican attitudes and policies toward illegal immigration and alien smuggling changed in this period. During the last half of 1976, Mexican officers had stepped up enforcement of Mexican laws against human smuggling. Between September 1976 and late February 1977, Mexican immigration officers arrested 277 smugglers in Tijuana; many of them were sentenced to six years or more in prison. Additionally, the immigration office in Tijuana was deporting 100 foreign nationals a week who were working there illegally. Mexico had become alarmed by the large number of non-Mexican nationals traversing their country illegally and by alien smuggling. Mexico City newspapers called it a scandal.[47] In the mid–1990s, López Castro found that *coyotes* (professional smugglers) who had been around since the 1970s claimed there had been comparatively little demand for their services back then.[48] Entering the United States illegally was easy, and there were too many *coyotes*. That changed with the Immigration Reform and Control Act (IRCA)[49] of 1986, and again in 1993 when the U.S. government clamped down on the border. The latter action drove smuggling fees up and may have changed the risks and nature of smuggling, possibly bringing about an unintended consolidation of previously distinct smuggling operations in drugs and humans (although the evidence for this consolidation is imprecise and less than compelling).[50] Nevertheless, with its amnesty guarantees for illegal migrants who could prove they had resided in the country since January 1, 1982, IRCA stimulated demand for false documents and for *coyotes*. The unlawful moving of illegal immigrants became enormously profitable. After the tightening of the border in 1994, *coyotes* with experience and a network of safe houses and vehicles quickly capitalized on the new conditions, charging migrants fees of between US$500 and $1,500.[51]

Human Smuggling and Organized Crime

By the early 1990s the problem of human smuggling across the U.S.–Mexico border was being constructed in a new frame. It was depicted as part of an emerging worldwide problem in the trafficking of illegal aliens, an emerging worldwide problem in the trafficking of illegal aliens, which in turn was described as part of the burgeoning new threat of international criminal syndicates. The Cold War was over, but former intelligence officers and analysts had discovered an even more ominous threat: global organized crime.[52]

The global smuggling of humans was described as rivaling drug trafficking for profitability. Intelligence reports claimed that international criminal syndicates of varying sizes and degrees of sophistication were moving tens of thousands of people from poorer countries to richer ones. Thousands of smuggled Asians were reportedly showing up in Moscow, the Netherlands, France, South Africa, and Central America. Traditional "mom and pop" operations that smuggled just a few people were believed to have been replaced by major operations moving hundreds of people at a time, seaborne in large freighters and airborne in commercial jumbo jets.[53] The worst scenario was that traditional organized crime groups (the Italian Mafia, the Chinese Triads, and the Cali cartel) were forming alliances with or replacing transnational human smugglers. The extent to which this happened, however, is open to question because of the ambiguity of the concept of "organized crime," as well as its political uses.

In 1994 the International Organization for Migration (IOM), an intergovernmental body, convened a global seminar on the issue of migrant trafficking. One of the outcomes was the establishment of three "regional dialogues" among sending, receiving, and transit countries.[54] Central America had become a major conduit for smuggling people from outside the region. In 1990, the Comisión Centroamericana de Directores de Migración, an intergovernmental body, was established to reinforce migration structures and assist in regional development. By 1995 the flow of third-country nationals through Central America was growing rapidly. The commission asked the IOM to organize a seminar on trafficking of human beings in Central America. The seminar, held in Panama in October 1995, was attended by governmental representatives from Costa Rica, the Dominican Republic, El Salvador, Guatemala, Honduras, Mexico, Nicaragua, Panama, and the United States. The Panama seminar led to the Regional Conference on Migration, hosted by the Mexican government in March 1996,[55] which created the Puebla Process, a mechanism for ongoing consultation and cooperation.

According to Willard Myers, in the 1970s the smuggling of Chinese through Central America was controlled by Cantonese families. It was small scale and went through Mexico City and on to the U.S.–Mexico border, with one exception: Lin Tao Bao, a Fujianese smuggler, operated from Bolivia. At the time there were few *shetous* ("snakeheads," or alien smugglers) and smuggling was not an integrated enterprise. Tao Bao was among the first. He flew his clients to Miami with forged passports, but complaints about long waits in Peru forced him to contract with smugglers using the land route through Mexico.[56]

Things changed in the early 1980s. After the United States cut off assistance to Guatemala, that country accepted aid from Taiwan, supported Taiwan's readmission to the United Nations, and permitted Taiwanese smugglers to operate with impunity. By 1991 a Taiwanese group held functional control of smuggling operations in Central America.

With the passage of IRCA in 1986, the modern era of transcontinental smuggling of humans to the United States had begun. IRCA's amnesty provisions removed the last constraint on the attractiveness of large-scale smuggling operations. With readily forged documents, job opportunities were easily had. By the fall of 1988 more than 20,000 Fujianese were supposedly being smuggled in by air for fees that had risen to $22,000 (compared to the $1,800 that Lin Tao Bao had charged in the 1970s).

On June 5, 1989, in the aftermath of the massacre at Tiananmen Square, President George Bush signed an executive order allowing all Chinese nationals who had entered the United States by legal or illegal means on or before June 4, 1989, to remain. They could be employed simply by proving nationality and date of entry. Subsequent presidential orders gave the Chinese reason to hope they would be able to remain permanently.[57] By December 1989, *shetou* fees were up to between $32,000 and $50,000, and Fujianese were paying them. If official reports are to be believed, in each of the next four years more than 100,000 Fujianese paid for these services, generating a smuggling trade worth $9 million a day.[58] Some Fujianese were flown to Central America and trucked through Mexico. Others were given stolen or "rented" Taiwanese passports containing valid U.S. visas, disguised as tour groups, and flown to major U.S. airports. INS detention facilities quickly became overcrowded as forgeries were detected, and migrants had to be released without bond pending an immigration hearing. Many disappeared, not to be found again.

According to Myers, by May 1990 airborne smuggling had reached capacity. A group of Taiwanese smugglers led by the two men who controlled all routes leading to and from Central America, plus some Taiwanese shipowners, decided to develop a seaborne alternative by refitting cargo ships to hold between one hundred and five hundred migrants. In January 1991 they met with *shetous* in New York's Chinatown and offered blocks of fifty spaces at $300,000, payable in advance. The first ships were on their way in July 1991.[59]

In the 1990s the U.S. Coast Guard began interdicting an increasing number of alien-smuggling ships from the People's Republic of China. For the entire period FY1982 through FY1990, a total of only 28 ships had been interdicted. The number jumped to 138 in FY1991 alone, 181 in FY1992, and 2,511 in FY1993.[60] By February 1993 U.S. officials were sounding the alarm that China was the fastest-growing source of illegal immigrants to the United States. They continued to cite the estimate of 100,000 illegal Chinese immigrants a year entering the country.[61]

Central America and Mexico became popular destinations for Chinese smuggling ships. Asian smuggling networks began contracting with Mexican smugglers.[62] In the spring of 1993 the Mexican navy was turning back Chinese smuggling ships, and Mexico was repatriating hundreds of Chinese migrants and prosecuting smugglers.[63] By June 1993 the U.S. Border Patrol had arrested 500 Chinese illegal aliens; 400 were in San Diego, up from 34 the previous year.[64]

U.S. concern about the smuggling of Chinese into the United States peaked in June 1993 when the Golden Venture ran aground off New York City with three hundred illegal immigrants aboard. Six immigrants perished in the surf, and many others staggered ashore under the full glare of live television news coverage. President Clinton convened an interagency working group which in November 1995 reported that the smuggling of humans was an "enormous" and "growing" problem that "earns smugglers billions of dollars in annual profits."[65] The group estimated that annual smuggling traffic from Central America included 100,000 people from outside the region plus 200,000 to 300,000 Central Americans. It claimed that Chinese smuggling gangs were moving about 50,000 aliens a year to the United States. There is reason, however, to suspect that estimates of the numbers of third-country smuggled immigrants were exaggerated. As recently as June 1998 an INS spokesperson was quoted in a news article that implied that a large number of Asians were being smuggled through Mexico. It read:

> In the last five years, Border Patrol agents have reported about 1.5 million arrests at the country's Southwest border. The vast majority involve Mexicans and Central Americans, but immigration officials have seen a gradual increase there in the number of Chinese, Indians and Pakistanis—"nationalities whom we would not typically see at the Southwest border."[66]

To be more precise, in FY1997 there were only 13,877 apprehensions of Central Americans on the United States' southwest border.[67] As for Chinese and Indians, the numbers of apprehensions at the southwest border have been as follows—FY1997, 49 Chinese, 61 Indians; FY1998, 196 Chinese, 63 Indians; FY1999, 206 Chinese, 39 Indians.[68] For the years 1991 through 1997, the Border Patrol "located" the following numbers of alien smugglers: 18,826, 17,237, 15,266, 14,143, 12,796, 13,458 and 12,523, respectively. During the same years, the INS investigative unit "arrested" the following numbers of alien smugglers: 13,944, 13,454, 11,244, 8,787, 8,580, 4,699, and 3,381.[69]

Regardless of these reality checks, government agents continue to give high estimates of the problem. An "exhaustive" CIA report completed in November 1999 estimated that, in each of the previous two years, 50,000 women had been brought into the United States under false pretenses and forced to work as prostitutes, servants, or abused laborers.[70]

Migration-Related Corruption

Corruption associated with migration is a perennial threat at all official levels in virtually all countries. Migration offers multiple opportunities for corruption, from bribing officials at the border to the sale or improper issuance of migration documents such as visas, passports, and work permits. At the U.S.–Mexico border, migration-related corruption has a long history.[71] In the past decade, as the United States and other countries tried to tighten borders at the same time that the illegal movement of immigrants from poor to rich countries was increasing, the profit in migration-related corruption reached unprecedented levels. High officials as well as petty bureaucrats exploited the situation. According to President Clinton's working group on alien smuggling, this billion-dollar industry is "made possible by staggering levels of official corruption."[72]

At the border, some venality among U.S. Border Patrol and U.S. Customs Service officers has occurred.[73] Officials say that the problem is not systemic; it reflects, rather, individual dishonesty and inadequate training.[74] A General Accounting Office report criticized the agencies for laxness in the use of procedures to prevent corruption.[75] On the Mexican side, low-level migration-related corruption was endemic prior to the institution of the Beta Groups, whose mission has been to suppress the exploitation of migrants—which often took the form of extortion by Mexican officials. This practice was part of systemic corruption. Combating this tradition has placed the Beta Groups in direct conflict with other Mexican officials. It has resulted in the harassment of Beta officers, and it appears to have provoked the assassination of one Beta commander.[76]

Corruption at the higher levels of migration control has occurred in both countries. In July 1994 the directors of Mexico's National Immigration Institute were accused of receiving payoffs from smugglers who were bringing Asians and Central Americans into the United States. Mexican investigators determined that the smugglers had five safe houses and twenty hotels in Tijuana from which migrants were smuggled into the United States.[77] In May 1996, U.S. officials broke up a smuggling ring that they described as a "classic" example of the new trend in the international trafficking of illegals through Mexico. The organization was believed to have smuggled hundreds of Asians into the United States via Russia, Cuba, and Central America over at least seven years. The alleged leader, Gladys Perdomo Board (alias Gladys Garza Cantú), a Honduran-born naturalized U.S. citizen, and fourteen others were indicted. Included among them was a Mexican Federal Judicial Police officer to whom Ms. Garza paid $9,200 to move seven Indian immigrants through the border town of Reynosa.[78] Ms. Garza, who had connections in Moscow and recruiters in several Asian countries, was earning more than US$1 million a year.

An even larger human smuggling ring, considered the biggest in Latin America at the time, was broken up in December 1995 with the arrest of a Costa Rican mother of five, Gloria Canales, and her co-conspirators. The Canales organization is believed to have moved more than 10,000 aliens of various nationalities through Central America and Mexico. The ring's "take" was estimated to be between $60 and $80 million over eight years.[79]

Border Bandits and Their Suppression

Immigrants attempting to enter the United States illegally from Mexico make easy targets for local bandits. They are in unfamiliar, isolated circumstances at night, and they carry cash. From Brownsville to San Ysidro, U.S. Border Patrol officers can point out the spots where many an immigrant was waylaid.[80]

In 1976, to suppress the banditry against illegal immigrants, a U.S. Border Patrol officer persuaded the San Diego Police Department to field a special police unit in the hills adjacent to the border at Tijuana. In the previous year there had been over one hundred robberies, three rapes, and three known homicides in that small patch of no-man's-land. Many other crimes were believed to have gone unrecorded.[81] The unit's members, known as the Border Alien Robbery Force (BARF), disguised themselves as *pollos* (literally "chickens," a derisive name for illegal immigrants) and at considerable personal risk lurked around the canyons and mesas at night, inviting bandits to rob them. Eighteen months and more than one hundred arrests and seven shootings later, the unit was terminated. Border banditry had been reduced, but the solution was causing tensions with Mexico.[82]

In the mid–1980s the San Diego Police Department reestablished a similar unit called the Border Crime Prevention Unit (BCPU). During its first incarnation between 1984 and 1989, the BCPU shot forty-four suspects, killing eighteen of them. It was disbanded after the shooting of two Mexican suspects who witnesses said were in handcuffs.[83] The unit was subsequently reinstituted in mid–1989 and continues to operate as the Border Crime Intervention Unit (BCIU). The current unit does not operate in plain clothes; rather, uniformed officers walk the same canyons and mesas at night, looking for immigrants trying to sneak into the country. They do not force the immigrants to return to Mexico, nor do they turn them over to the Border Patrol. They only check to make sure the immigrants are not being victimized.[84]

Mexico had a border law enforcement unit (the Border Inspection Group), which was dissolved in 1989 because of corruption, and for a while the stretch of no-man's-land north of the border reverted back to a kind of primeval jungle. In 1990 bandit violence and depredations escalated to unprecedented levels, accounting for hundreds of beatings, robberies, and rapes. There were ten murders on the U.S. side.[85] The Binational Center for Human Rights in Tijuana claimed that 65 percent of immigrants had been robbed, raped, beaten, or extorted (or killed) by the time they crossed the border. This usually happened at the hands of bandits or Mexican police, but Americans inflicted some of the carnage as well.[86]

San Diego Chief of Police Robert Burgreen and the new chief of the Border Patrol called for a crackdown on the bandits. With help from the Tijuana municipal police, Burgreen conducted a coordinated operation with the Border Patrol, netting eighty-six arrests for robbery and assault on migrants.[87] In Mexico, psychologist Javier Valenzuela Malagón, together with a group of Mexican police officers, responded with an experimental law enforcement unit that evolved into both a showpiece and a welcome ally for the United States.[88] The chaos at the border was jeopardizing the NAFTA negotiations, and both President Carlos Salinas de Gortari and Baja California's Governor Ernesto Ruffo Appel were promoting reforms. So Valenzuela, an administrator for immigration services in Tijuana, was able to get federal, state, and local officials to agree to establish a new law enforcement unit, Grupo Beta, whose purpose was to protect immigrants and suppress violence at the border.[89]

Grupo Beta was lauded by both U.S. and Mexican officials. It is credited with helping to reduce murders at the border from ten in 1990 to zero in 1991.[90] It helped to increase drug seizures by the Border Patrol in 1991.[91] It developed good working relations with the San Diego Police Department's BCIU. Officers from the two units practice shooting together, hold monthly training sessions, maintain radio contact, and share criminal intelligence. The BCIU donated bullet-proof vests and hand radios to their Mexican counterparts. Officers from the two units often visit with each other in Grupo Beta's office just inside the Tijuana port of entry.[92]

Mexican leaders have also been effusive about Grupo Beta. Gabriel Székely, a professor at El Colegio de México, wrote in the Mexican magazine *Nexos*, "Beta represents a model of what it is possible to achieve. It's not easy to establish a group of police officers who work with enthusiasm and are incorruptible."[93] Víctor Clark Alfaro, a Tijuana human rights advocate, said, "Grupo Beta is demonstrating how, with political will, there can be a police force free of corruption. It is an example for other Mexican police agencies."[94] The Beta officers themselves were pleased with their work. One experienced officer said, "The custom of police in Mexico was, the first thing after you arrested someone, to slap him around. What I learned in Beta was respect for human rights, whether of migrants or criminals. Beta was based on respect for the law. It was a policeman's dream."[95]

In 1991 Grupo Beta was assigned to help crack down on "port running" at the San Ysidro Port of Entry. This represented a delicate policy shift for Mexico given its traditional defense of the right of citizens to emigrate. The construction of a new fence along the border by the United States had forced immigrants and their smugglers to find new routes. Professional smugglers began staging mass runs of groups of immigrants through the port of entry into oncoming traffic in southbound lanes of Interstate Highway 5.[96] Mexican officials have no authority to stop migrants from entering the United States illegally. They could not arrest the port runners on those grounds. But they could act to enforce public safety, and they could arrest migrant smugglers.[97] With the NAFTA negotiations in progress, Mexican officials worried about anarchic images being broadcast from the border of families sprinting headlong into waves of speeding cars. After a high-level consultation between the two countries, the Mexican Immigration Service announced that it was posting agents around Puerta Mexico to prevent people from gathering and, further, that Grupo Beta would be pointing out smugglers to immigration agents. This led to the arrest of forty people in one weekend.[98]

Grupo Beta has not been without controversy. In Mexico it encountered resistance, threats, and ostracism. Beta members arrested fellow Mexican police officers for robbing and abusing migrants, thereby cutting off a traditional source of illicit income for corrupt officers. Some Mexican police responded by issuing threats, refusing to provide backup when Grupo Beta called for it, and ridiculing Beta members as traitors. Grupo Beta upset Mexicans who worry about being too helpful to the United States. It has also caused tensions with U.S. immigration officials (who otherwise are favorably impressed) by providing eyewitness accounts of alleged excessive force by the Border Patrol.[99]

In February 1993, Grupo Beta's future seemed in jeopardy. Mexican observers suspected that smugglers had succeeded in corrupting it.[100] But Grupo Beta survived and became a model for policing in the rest of the country. In 1995 the Tijuana Beta Group was cited by Mexico's National Human Rights Commission as the most honest and efficient police organization in the country.[101] Encouraged by Beta's success, the Mexican government has established nine similar Beta units at other border areas.

Yet whether Mexico could sustain the performance of the Beta Groups beyond their initial successes remained to be seen. In November 1998 U.S. police were still favorably impressed with Grupo Beta, but in one location they were beginning to suspect incipient corruption. Beta officers, who once carried old weapons and ammunition that was green with age, began sporting expensive new weapons.[102] Nevertheless, a report released in February 2000 by Alejandro Carrillo Castro, commissioner of the National Migration Institute, states that Mexico's Groups for Migrant Protection have produced excellent results. They gave assistance to 280,000 migrants in 1998, 21 percent more than in 1997.[103]

Grupo Beta's record of successes, however, ended ignominiously in July 2001 when the government stripped it of its police powers because of allegations of corruption. A wide-ranging investigation by the newly installed Vicente Fox administration and another by the *Washington Post* revealed a remarkably well organized underground highway to the United States. It was operated by Mexican officials who exacted bribes from an estimated thirty to sixty third-country immigrants a day (11,000 to 22,000 a year) in exchange for allowing safe passage through Mexico to the U.S. border. They deported those who did not pay.[104]

Grupo Beta will continue as a civilian agency whose mission is to rescue injured migrants and to warn them of the dangers that lie ahead. Beta's law enforcement role will probably be assumed by the even newer Federal Preventive Police (PFP), in which reformers have high hopes. Meanwhile, Grupo Beta serves as a reminder of the difficulties involved in achieving integrity in law enforcement even when special precautions are taken.

CONCLUSION

As with many neighboring countries worldwide, Mexico and the United States are attempting to cope with the threats to public security and governance associated with international migration and with international borders. For decades the coping was left largely to local officials who sometimes relied upon irregular methods but increasingly have devised more progressive solutions.

In earlier times migration and border issues were regarded as the private troubles of the neighboring states. In the post–Cold War, global environment, with economic integration running apace and the international community alarmed at the threat of global organized crime and massive smuggling of humans, migration and border issues are seen in a new light. Bilateral and multilateral solutions are becoming more common, as are policies and institutions that uphold a respect for the rule of law.

Beginning in the late 1970s, the United States and Mexico have inched toward greater law enforcement cooperation at federal, state, and local levels. NAFTA accelerated those efforts, which now include multilateral efforts to control human smuggling as well as bilateral efforts to protect illegal immigrants and to enforce criminal law and reduce impunity sought by criminals who try to exploit the protection formerly afforded by the international border. These efforts, however, are unevenly distributed along the border and are unlikely to have a systemic effect until Mexican law enforcement agencies are provided the resources to rise to a certain minimum level of professionalism. Yet, as the fate of Grupo Betas reveals, even extra resources and training are no guarantee. Maintaining integrity in police institutions is a challenge in any environment. It is all the greater in one with a tradition of corruption and where the rewards for integrity are low and dangerous.

The border continues to exert a powerful criminogenic influence by virtue of the differentials it creates in the labor and commodity markets, as well as in the different attitudes between Mexico and the United States regarding whether the border should be open to Mexicans. The tightening of border controls against illegal immigration has not only raised the profitability of smuggling and the lure of corruption, but it has also increased the conviction among common people that the law need not be respected. The first act of Mexicans entering the United States illegally is an act of civil disobedience, a violation of immigration laws with which they disagree. Moreover, the U.S. policy of deporting criminal aliens (most of whom are Mexicans delivered to the border) adds to the instability of the border communities.

The world is changing. The relationship between Mexico and the United States is changing. There is reason to be hopeful—but also reason to be patient.

Notes

Research for this report was supported by grant #95-IJ-CX-0110 from the National Institute of Justice, Office of Justice Programs, U.S. Department of Justice, and by Georgetown University. Special thanks go to Roberto San Miguel, without whose assistance much of this chapter could not have been written. Points of view and opinions in this document are solely those of the author and do not necessarily represent the official position or policies of the U.S. Department of Justice, Georgetown University, or Mr. San Miguel. The author dedicates this chapter to the people of Tacámbaro, Michoacán, in gratitude for their warm hospitality.

1. Wayne A. Cornelius, Philip L. Martin, and James F. Hollifield, eds., *Controlling Immigration: A Global Perspective* (Stanford, Calif.: Stanford University Press, 1994).

2. Arthur F. Corwin, "Mexican Policy and Ambivalence toward Labor Emigration to the United States," in *Immigrants-and Immigrants: Perspectives on Mexican Labor Migration to the United States*, edited by Arthur F. Corwin (Westport, Conn.: Greenwood Press, 1978); Richard B. Craig, *The Bracero Program: Interest Groups and Foreign Policy* (Austin: University of Texas Press, 1971); Kevin Galvin, "Report: Farm Program Ineffective," *Associated Press*, April 2, 1998.

3. But reading the response as racism risks misunderstanding the larger complexity involved. The Poles have similarly interpreted the hardening of the border between Poland and Germany. But the underlying problem is not simply racist or xenophobic attitudes. Many legitimate concerns—including the cost and control of labor, the environment, population, and pollution, as well as issues of culture and law—are at stake. Rick Atkinson, "Europe's Two Worlds Divided by More Than a River," *Washington Post*, August 2, 1995.

4. Ignacio Ibarra, "Agua Prieta Wins Attention of U.S. on Its Migrant Woes," *Arizona Daily Star*, April 18, 2000; Alan D. Bersin, "A Joint Response to Border Violence," *San Diego Union-Tribune*, June 25, 1997.

5. Alan D. Bersin, "Threshold Order: Bilateral Law Enforcement and Regional Public Safety on the U.S./Mexico Border," *San Diego Law Review* 35 (Summer 1998): 715.

6. Jerome Hall, *Theft, Law and Society* (Boston, Mass.: Little, Brown, 1935).

7. William J. Clinton, U.S. President, "International Crime Control Act of 1998," at www.pub.whitehouse.gov/ uri-res/I2R?urn:pdi:// oma.eop.gov.us/ 1998/ 5/13/18.text.1, May 12 1998.

8. Juan José Briones, "Foreign Prosecutions," documentation prepared for the International Liaison Unit of the San Diego District Attorney's Office (San Diego, July 1996).

9. William F. McDonald, "Globalizing Criminology: The New Frontier Is the Frontier," *Transnational Organized Crime* 1 (Spring 1995): 1–22.

10. Michael V. Miller, "Vehicle Theft along the Texas-Mexico Border," *Journal of Borderlands Studies* 2:2 (Fall 1987): 12–32.

11. Rosalva Reséndiz and David M. Neal, "International Auto Theft: The Illegal Export of American Vehicles to Mexico," in *International Criminal Justice: Issues in a Global Perspective*, edited by Delbert Rounds (Boston, Mass.: Allyn and Bacon, 1999), 16.

12. Pilar Franco, "Children–Mexico: Illegal Adoption Trade Flourishing," *Inter Press Service*, June 6, 1999; Marina Jiménez, "Mexican Group Accuses B.C. Couple of Smuggling Children to Canada," *National Post*, February 3, 2000; Associated Press, "Bail Denied for Man Charged in Adoptions," *New York Times*, June 3, 1999; United Press International, "INS: Children Will Remain with Parents," *New York Times*, May 28, 1999.

13. Ginger Thompson, "Defense Cites Compassion, Not Greed," *New York Times*, June 1, 1999; Frank Eltman, "U.S. Trio Sentenced for Smuggling Mexican Babies," *Mexico City News*, April 18, 2000.

14. Jan Caldwell and Edward P. Allard III, "News Release," Federal Bureau of Investigation, San Diego (San Diego, Calif., October 15, 1997).

15. Ibid.

16. Mexico–United States Binational Commission, *Mexico–U.S. Binational Study on Migration* (Mexico: Author, 1997), iv.

17. Ibid.

18. About 41 percent of the total illegal population in the United States in 1996 were non-immigrant overstays—that is, they entered legally but failed to depart. The proportion of overstays varies considerably by country of origin. Non-immigrant overstays represented about 16 percent of the total Mexican illegal

population, compared to 26 percent of the Central American illegal population and 91 percent of illegals from all other countries. U.S. Immigration and Naturalization Service, *Statistical Yearbook of the Immigration and Naturalization Service, 1997* (Washington, D.C.: U.S. Government Printing Office, 1999).

19. Ibid.

20. Andres Oppenheimer, "U.S. Citizens Live Illegally in Mexico: Drybacks Seeking Jobs," *Dallas Morning News*, July 17, 1994.

21. General Accounting Office, *U.S.–Mexico Border: Issues and Challenges Confronting the United States and Mexico*, 10.

22. Alan D. Bersin, "El Tercer País: Reinventing the U.S./Mexico Border," *Stanford Law Review* 48:5 (May 1996): 1417.

23. San Diego Dialogue, *The San Diego / Tijuana Binational Region, 1996: A Briefing Book for Media Covering the Republican National Convention* (La Jolla: Division of Extended Studies and Public Service, University of California, San Diego, 1996), 59.

24. U.S. Department of Justice, Immigration and Naturalization Service, *Monthly Statistical Report: September FY 1999 Year End Report*, Office of Policy and Planning, 11/03/99 Southwest Border Apprehensions. From the Internet, (Web site: Author, 1999). These statistics are counts of events, not of individuals.

25. U.S. Department of Justice, 1999.

26. Author's personal observation, January 25, 2000.

27. Associated Press, msk@us.net, "Mexico Holds Meeting About U.S," 199708271658.MAA27105@us.net, CISNEWS@cis.org (August 27, 1997).

28. Daniel Wolf, *Undocumented Aliens and Crime: The Case of San Diego County* (La Jolla: Center for U.S.–Mexican Studies, University of California, San Diego, 1988). We use the terms "illegal immigrants" and "aliens" because of their succinct accuracy and common use in the literature. We disavow any demonizing or negative connotations associated with these terms.

29. 43 Statutes-at-Large 153.

30. In 1992 the average sentence for all immigration offenses was six months. By 1999 it was nineteen months. The toughest sentences were for ex-convicts who reentered after deportation. Almost half of all INS prosecutions are for illegal reentry. In the past few years the number of criminal prosecutions for immigration offenses has increased fivefold. See Marc Robbins, "Immigration Crimes Get Stiffer Terms," *San Antonio ExpressNews*, July 26, 1999, at www.expressnews.com/pantheon/news-bus /metro/ 2601amaa.shtml.

31. See, for example, Gale Holland, "Border Jumpers Trample Nature, California Crackdown Leads to Paths of Destruction," *USA Today [ATLANTA FINAL Edition]*, July 21, 1996; Daniel B. Wood, "The Path of 'Fire': Rural Counties on Border Struggle with Surge of Dangerous Crossings: Locals Pay Millions in Police and Heath-Care Costs, While Illegals Face Dangers of Desert," *Christian Science Monitor*, May 4, 1999.

32. Paul Kennedy, *Preparing for the Twenty-First Century* (New York: Random House, 1993); Paul J. Smith, "Introduction," in *Human Smuggling*, edited by Paul J. Smith (Washington, D.C.: Center for Strategic and International Studies, 1997), ix.

33. Alex P. Schmid, ed., *Migration and Crime* (Milan: International Scientific and Professional Advisory Council of the United Nations Crime Prevention and Criminal Justice Programme, 1996), 17ff.

34. Joel Brinkley, "Vast Trade in Forced Labor Portrayed in CIA Report: Traffickers Prey on Women and Children," *New York Times*, April 2, 2000.

35. United Nations Office of the High Commissioner for Human Rights, "Trafficking in Peoples: The Human Rights Dimension," International Conference on Responding to the Challenges of Transnational Crime (Courmayeur, Italy, September 24–27, 1998).

36. Brinkley, "Vast Trade."

37. In 1993 the United Nations General Assembly adopted Resolution 48/102 on the Prevention of Alien Smuggling. It urged states to: amend laws to criminalize or increase penalties for trafficking; improve procedures for detecting forged documents; prevent traffickers from using transit points; strengthen existing international conventions; and more aggressively monitor their air and sea ports as well as ships and aircraft of their registry. At the 1997 session of the General Assembly, the Austrian government proposed a draft International Convention Against Smuggling of Illegal Migrants which was to be considered by the UN Commission on Crime Prevention and Criminal Justice. International Organization for Migration, "Austria Proposes Convention against Trafficking," *Trafficking in Migrants* 17 (December 1997/January 1998).

38. United States Embassy in Mexico, "Joint Communiqué on Regional Conference on Migration," *U. S. Newswire*, February 3, 1999.

39. In 1995 President Ernesto Zedillo affirmed his commitment to improved bilateral cooperation with the United States on illegal immigration and alien smuggling. To enhance mutual efforts to reduce the use of Mexican territory by third-country nationals as a springboard for entry into the United States, the Mexican government created a special police group to patrol its southern border and also increased the number of interior checkpoints. The U.S. Immigration and Naturalization Service and its Mexican counterparts have begun sharing sensitive information on alien smugglers. Mexico is now making arrests based on that information. In 1995, Mexico deported over 110,000 third-country migrants and assisted with the repatriation of Chinese migrants planning to enter illegally into the United States but interdicted off the west coast of Mexico. U.S. Department of State, "Fact Sheet: Cooperation with Mexico: In Our National Interest," in Office of Mexican Affairs, at www.state.gov/ www/regions/ wha/ mexico_index.html, June 5, 1996.

40. Louis Freedberg, "Mexico Slowly Getting Tougher On Illegals," *San Francisco Chronicle*, August 12, 1994.

41. Mark Shaffer, "Immigrants Get Caught in Web of Crime, Drugs: Illegals Often Targets Due to Status," *Arizona Republic*, December 24, 1998.

42. The University of Houston's comprehensive study, "Death at the Border," concluded that the border blockades had not raised the overall number of deaths but did increase the number of deaths due to exposure in remote areas. From 1993 through 1996 there were at least 1,200 deaths, the majority of which were in the San Diego region. Drowning was the most common cause, accounting for 851 in total and 800 in the Rio Grande/Río Bravo. Anne-Marie O'Connor, "Study Finds

Changes in Causes of Border Deaths: Immigration Researchers Say Crackdown Hasn't Raised Total, But More Result from Exposure in Remote Areas," *Los Angeles Times*, August 12, 1997.

43. Reuters, msk@cis.org, "U.S. Warns Mexicans about Ruthless Alien Smugglers," at www.cis.org/cis, April 29, 1998.

44. U.S. Immigration and Naturalization Service, *Statistical Yearbook of the Immigration and Naturalization Service, 1994* (Washington, D.C.: U.S. Government Printing Office, 1996), 160.

45. One Los Angeles smuggling operation was making $120,000 a trip, packing up to forty-five illegal immigrants per panel truck. Jack Webb, "Flesh Peddlers I: People-Smuggling Racket Is $125 Million Business," *Austin Statesman*, May 29, 1973; Jack Webb, "Flesh Peddlers III: Sometimes Death Waits along Live Cargo Route," *Austin Statesman*, May 31, 1973.

46. Evan Maxwell, "U.S.-Mexico Smuggling: The Buying and Selling of Humans: Borderlands Are a Free-Fire Zone Where Living Bodies Become the Goods in a Kind of Slave Trade," *Los Angeles Times*, February 22, 1977.

47. Ibid.

48. Gustavo López Castro, "Factors That Influence Migration: Coyotes and Alien Smuggling," in *Migration between Mexico and the United States: Research Reports and Background Materials*, Mexico–United States Binational Migration Study (Washington, D.C.: Mexican Ministry of Foreign Affairs/U.S. Commission on Immigration Reform, 1998).

49. 100 Statutes-at-Large 3359.

50. Dianne Solis, "Smugglers Thrive with Crackdown on Mexican Border," *Wall Street Journal*, March 22, 1996; Gale Holland, "A Higher Price for Illegals and Their Smugglers," *USA Today*, May 28, 1996.

51. Solis, "Smugglers Thrive"; López Castro, "Factors that Influence."

52. McDonald, "Globalizing Criminology."

53. See Smith, *Human Smuggling*, especially chapters by Willard H. Myers III, "Of Qinqing, Qinshy, Guanxi, and Shetou: The Dynamic Elements of Chinese Irregular Population Movement," and Paul J. Smith, "Chinese Migrant Trafficking: A Global Challenge." See also, Jonathan M. Winer, *Alien Smuggling: Elements of the Problem and the U.S. Response*, U.S. Working Group on Organized Crime (Washington, D.C.: National Strategy Information Center, 1997); Alex P. Schmid, "Migration and Crime: A Framework for Discussion," in Schmid, *Migration and Crime*.

54. International Organization for Migration, hq@iom.int, "Trafficking in Migrants: IOM Policy and Responses," in Migration Web, www.iom.int/defaultmigrationweb.asp, March 1999.

55. International Organization for Migration, hq@iom.int, "Central America: Anti-Trafficking Initiatives, No.13," in Migration Web, www.iom.int/defaultmigrationweb.asp, December 1996.

56. Myers, "Qinqing, Qinshy, Guanxi, and Shetou."

57. Ibid., 113. President Bush directed that "enhanced consideration under the immigration laws be given to persons expressing fear of persecution related to forced abortion or coerced sterilization." See also Malcolm Gladwell and Rachel

E. Stassen-Berger, "U.S. Policy Seen Encouraging Wave of Chinese Immigration," *Washington Post*, June 13, 1993.

58. Myers, "Qinqing, Qinshy, Guanxi, and Shetou." By these estimates there should have been about 400,000 illegal Chinese immigrants on their way to the United States by 1993. Even if 75 percent of them failed to make it, one would have expected that by 1996 there would be about 100,000 Chinese illegal aliens resident in the United States. However, according to INS statistics, by 1996 there were fewer than 30,000. U.S. Immigration and Naturalization Service, "Illegal Alien Resident Population," in Immigration and Naturalization Statistics, at www.ins.usdoj.gov/ stats/illegalalien/index.html, 1998.

59. Myers, "Qinqing, Qinshy, Guanxi, and Shetou."

60. For U.S. Coast Guard's statistics and history regarding alien interdiction, go to its website: www.uscg.mil/hq/go/gopl/mle/amiostats1.htm#fy.

61. Robert Benjamin, "Illegal Immigration from China Surges," *Chicago Sun Times*, February 28, 1993. In fact, the Chinese were not the fastest-growing group of illegal immigrants. According to INS statistics, they were not even among the top ten groups.

62. Pamela Burdman, "7 Ships May Have Set Out: INS Thinks All Were Headed for Mexico until One Was Intercepted," *San Francisco Chronicle*, June 3, 1993; David Clark Scott, "Chinese Seek Illegal Entry to U.S. on Well-Worn Paths," *Christian Science Monitor*, May 17, 1993; Myers, "Qinqing, Qinshy, Guanxi, and Shetou."

63. In April Mexican officials arrested 306 undocumented Chinese migrants discovered near Ensenada. In May the Mexican navy turned back a shipload of 200 undocumented Chinese intercepted off the Baja California coast. Five Mexican nationals were arrested for involvement in the smuggling of the Chinese. Gregory Gross, "Mexico Boards, Turns Away Vessel Carrying 200 Chinese off Baja," *San Diego Union-Tribune*, May 12, 1993.

64. Sebastian Rotella and Lee Romney, "Smugglers Use Mexico as Gateway for Chinese," *Los Angeles Times*, June 21, 1993.

65. Branigin, "Report to Clinton."

66. Somini Sengupta, "Traffic in Illegal Immigrants Is Being Slowed, Officials Believe," *New York Times*, June 1, 1998.

67. U.S. Department of Justice, *September FY 1999 Year End Report*. In 1994 Mexico's National Institute of Migration reported that Mexico had deported 3,651 illegal aliens between January and November. Most were from Guatemala; others came from Egypt and India. Tod Robberson, "Mexico Denounced as Anti-Migrant: U.S.–Bound Itinerants Complain of Beatings, Rape while in Jail," *Washington Post*, December 20, 1994.

68. Special analysis provided by the INS.

69. U.S. Immigration and Naturalization Service, *1997 Statistical Yearbook*, T 59, T60.

70. Brinkley, "Vast Trade in Forced Labor."

71. See, for example, George E. Paulsen, "The Yellow Peril at Nogales: The Ordeal of Collector William M. Hoey," *Arizona and the West* 13 (1971): 113–28.

72. Branigin, "Report to Clinton."

73. From 1993 to 1997, the INS investigated sixty-five cases of Border Patrol agents allegedly involved in corruption, including bribery, extortion, and immigrant smuggling. Nancy San Martin, "Ranks of Border Agents Swell: U.S. Keeping Eye on Quality during Recruiting Effort," *Dallas Morning News*, May 24, 1998; Dane Schiller, "Border Agent Pleads Guilty," *San Antonio Express News*, November 3, 1999.

74. Ben Fox, "INS Officer Says He Didn't Smuggle," *Associated Press*, August 3, 1999; Tim Steller, "Bribe-Taking INS Inspectors Let Coke, Aliens In, Feds Say," *Arizona Daily Star* (Tucson), February 3, 1999; Michelle Mittelstadt, "INS, Customs Chiefs Deny Systemic Corruption in Their Ranks," *Associated Press*, April 22, 1999.

75. General Accounting Office, *Drug Control: INS and Customs Can Do More to Prevent Drug-Related Employee Corruption*, Chapter Report, 03/30/99, GAO/GGD-99-31 (Washington, D.C.: U.S. Government Printing Office, 1999).

76. The murder of José Ángel Martínez, commander of the Grupo Beta along Mexico's border with Guatemala and a man described as "profoundly honest," is believed to have been in retaliation for a report he made accusing senior government officials (including family members of a former Tabasco governor), prominent business leaders, and federal police of involvement in the illegal trafficking of drugs, migrants, and weapons. Molly Moore, "Hostility, Violence Threaten Rights Defenders in Mexico," *Washington Post*, December 26, 1999.

77. The allegations were based on a year-long investigation by the director of the Center for Human Rights in Tijuana. Shortly afterward, a top immigration official and two of his deputies were removed from office by Mexico's interior minister, Jorge Virgilio. Gregory Katz, "Mexican Immigration Unit Tied to Smugglers," *Sacramento Bee*, July 23, 1994.

78. Jo Ann Zúñiga, "Houstonians Charged in International Immigrant Smuggling Ring," *Houston Chronicle*, March 10, 1996; Sam Dillon, "Asian Aliens Now Smuggled from Mexico," *New York Times*, May 29, 1996; U.S. Immigration and Naturalization Service, "Progress Reports: Cracking Down on Alien Smuggling," in *Welcome to Public Affairs*, at www.ins.usdoj.gov/public_affairs/progress_reports/index.html, 1997.

79. Anthony M. DeStefano, "Immigrant Smuggling Through Central America and the Caribbean," in Smith, *Human Smuggling*; Anthony M. DeStefano, "People Pipeline: Officials Try to Stop Flow of Illegals through Honduras," *Newsday*, June 2, 1996.

80. Arthur H. Rotstein, "Violent Muggings of Illegal Entrants along Border Increasing," *Associated Press*, April 28, 1999.

81. William B. Kolender, "Remarks Regarding Illegal Aliens," in *The Police Yearbook 1978*, International Association of Chiefs of Police (Gaithersburg, Md.: International Association of Chiefs of Police, 1978).

82. Lee Romney, "Belated Honors for Celebrated Border Unit," *Los Angeles Times*, August 29, 1992.

83. Sebastian Rotella, "Watching from the Shadows: An Elite Mexican Police Unit Is Keeping an Eye on Migrants and the People Who Victimize Them," *Los Angeles Times*, March 8, 1992; Romney, "Belated Honors."

84. Personal interviews with members of the unit, July 1996.

85. "Stemming the Border Carnage," *San Diego Tribune*, June 11, 1990; U.S. Congress, House of Representatives, Committee on Foreign Affairs, Subcommittee on Human Rights and International Organizations, *Allegations of Violence along the U.S.–Mexico Border*, Hearings, 101 Cong., 2d Sess. (Washington, D.C.: U.S. Government Printing Office, 1990).

86. Teresa Simmons, "'Illegals' Are Back in Full Force: So Much for the '86 Immigration Act," *Sacramento Bee*, October 7, 1990; Martin Wisckol, "Crime in the Hills: Overtones of Racism Apparent," *Times-Advocate*, January 14, 1990.

87. Ernesto Portillo, Jr., "Burgreen Seeks Tijuana Help in Drive against Border Crime," *San Diego Union*, June 14, 1990; Ernesto Portillo, Jr., "86 Arrested in Tijuana Border Sweep," *San Diego Union*, June 16, 1990.

88. Valenzuela had been a student activist in the 1960s, a university professor for ten years, and a community organizer with indigenous peoples for eight years. He was appointed to the Interior Ministry by President Salinas in 1988. Personal interviews with U.S. government and academic sources in San Diego. See also Rotella, "Watching from the Shadows" and "Reducing the Misery at the Border: Immigration: Grupo Beta Is an Elite Mexican Multi-Agency Force with the Task of Protecting Migrants. It Has Cut Violence and Improved Relations between U.S. and Mexico," *Los Angeles Times*, March 10, 1992. Also, Arthur Golden, "Grupo Beta Seen as Law Enforcement's Shining Light," *San Diego Union-Tribune*, February 10, 1997.

89. The new unit was located in the Immigration Service with Valenzuela as its commander. It consisted of forty-five men and women carefully chosen from the federal immigration police, the Baja California state judicial police, and the Tijuana municipal police. Officers were psychologically screened and given extensive training, a salary of $1,000 per month (about three times that of the municipal police and twice that of the state police), a life insurance policy, and fifteen days off every six months.

90. "They [Grupo Beta] reduced crime by the bandits by 85 to 90 percent," according to Roberto Martínez, director of the American Friends Service Committee in San Diego. Tim Golden, "Mexico Is Now Acting to Protect Border Migrants from Robbery and Abuse," *New York Times (International)*, June 28, 1992.

91. It assisted in many drug seizures that year by using radio communications with the Border Patrol to coordinate efforts. Marijuana and cocaine seizures were up. In two months the Border Patrol seized more than five times the amount taken the previous year. More than 60 percent of the seizures occurred near the border in joint operations with Grupo Beta. See Chet Barfield, "Seizures of Cocaine Soar Here: New Border Fence, Mexican Aid Help Snare Smugglers," *San Diego Union-Tribune*, December 5, 1991; Lisa Petrillo, "60 Pounds of Cocaine Is Seized," *San Diego Union-Tribune*, December 7, 1991.

92. At the 12th Annual Border Law Enforcement Conference in San Diego in March 1992, San Diego Chief of Police Bob Burgreen praised Grupo Beta for helping to bring down crime at the border. Fernando Romero, "Neutral Border Site Sought for Crime Testimony," *San Diego Union-Tribune*, March 27, 1992.

93. Sebastian Rotella, "Walking a Tightrope at the Border," *Los Angeles Times*, September 15, 1993.

94. Rotella, "Watching from the Shadows."

95. In February 1992, about 250 to 300 people a day were making the runs. Seventeen illegal immigrants were killed in accidents on the freeway near the border in 1990, and fourteen in 1991. Sebastian Rotella, "Mexico Puts Brakes on I–5 Border Runs: Immigration: INS Drops Its Plan to Shut I–5 Lanes as Mexican Agents All But Halt Those Who Were Running across the Border into the U.S. at San Ysidro," *Los Angeles Times*, February 6, 1992; Rotella, "Walking a Tightrope at the Border."

96. Motorists speeding down the freeway into Tijuana would suddenly encounter dozens of men, women, and children running toward them. The runners would head to the median strip where smugglers waited with vehicles to whisk them away. The tactic succeeded because U.S. officials declined to chase them, for fear that pursuit would cause accidents. Gregory Gross and Fernando Romero, "New Danger Lurks at Border Gates: Smugglers Send Migrants Racing into U.S. against Freeway Traffic," *San Diego Union-Tribune*, February 4, 1992; Rotella, "Mexico Puts Brakes on I–5 Border Runs."

97. Since the 1990s Mexico has cracked down on immigrant smuggling. It has engaged Grupo Beta and also the Federal Judicial Police and the military officers assigned to them. The first killing of a Mexican federal officer operating against migrant smugglers occurred in August 1997; the officer died as the result of a shoot-out at a safe house. Gregory Gross, "Mexican Agent Dies of Wounds from Shootout," *San Diego Union-Tribune*, August 12, 1997.

98. Gross and Romero, "New Danger Lurks at Border Gates."

99. Rotella, "Reducing the Misery at the Border," and "Walking a Tightrope at the Border." See also, United States Commission on Civil Rights, *Federal Immigration Law Enforcement in the Southwest: Civil Rights Impacts on Border Communities*, Report of the Arizona, California, New Mexico, and Texas Advisory Committees to the United States Commission on Civil Rights (Washington, D.C.: U.S. Commission on Civil Rights, 1997).

100. Rotella, "Walking a Tightrope at the Border."

101. Howard LaFranchi, "Mexican 'Mod Squad' Seeks to Protect Migrants," *Christian Science Monitor*, June 25, 1996.

102. Personal interviews. In 1994 a reputed alien smuggler, Rafael Miranda, filed a complaint with the federal government claiming that he had been extorted by Mexican federal officials, including Grupo Beta officers. Gregory Gross, "Mexico Targets Top Migrant Smugglers: Aim Is to End Mafias, Reveal Corrupt Officials," *San Diego Union-Tribune*, July 25, 1994.

103. Alejandro Carrillo Castro, "Beta Group Yields Excellent Results," *Mexico City News*, February 7, 2000.

104. Anna Cearley, "Mexico Strips Grupo Beta of Its Powers to Police," *San Diego Union-Tribune*, August 7, 2001; Mary Jordan, "Mexico Investigating Immigration Passageway," *Washington Post*, July 22, 2001; Mary Jordan, "Mexico's Highway Robbery: High-Level Informer Details Shakedowns, Abuse of U.S.–Bound Immigrants by Officials and Police," *Washington Post*, July 5, 2001.

16

Fostering a Culture of Lawfulness on the Mexico–U.S. Border: Evaluation of a Pilot School-Based Program

Roy Godson and Dennis Jay Kenney

With the advent of the North American Free Trade Agreement (NAFTA) in 1994 and the subsequent opening of the U.S.–Mexico border, there has been increased awareness about crime and corruption on both sides of this international frontier. Noting an apparent rise in the smuggling of drugs, illegal aliens, and counterfeit and hazardous products from Mexico—and comparable increases in the movement of weapons, stolen vehicles, and other contraband from the United States—many specialists in the region and in their respective capitals have become concerned about security and governability in the region.[1] Despite enhanced law enforcement by both countries, the size and scope of border crime shows little sign of abatement.

In response, in 1998 the Ministry of Education of Baja California, Mexico, and the San Diego County Office of Education—in collaboration with specialists from the National Strategy Information Center (NSIC), a public policy and education center in Washington, D.C.—began to cooperate in a long-term community-oriented educational effort to prevent crime and corruption on both sides of the border. Its initial phase comprised a formal school-based program to reach the next generation of young adults and their parents. The program sought to improve children's knowledge of crime while strengthening their support for the rule of law and a culture of lawfulness.

The project's initial classroom teaching consisted of an experimental 36–lesson course on the rationale for rules, laws, and a culture of lawfulness; the temptation and workings of crime, organized crime, and corruption; and methods for resisting involvement in crime and furthering the culture of lawfulness in the border region. More than eight hundred experimental and control students in eleven public schools—eight in Mexico and three in the United States—participated in the project. In each experimental school, the course was incorporated into the ninth grade curriculum (*secundaria* 3 in Tijuana).

The results of this pilot project indicated that this is a promising methodology for preventing crime and corruption. In contrast to many other school-based approaches to preventing violence, drug abuse, and delinquency, this particular school-based intervention appears to be effective in influencing knowledge and attitudes. This chapter draws on a more extensive report that describes and evaluates the first pilot project and compares and contrasts it with other approaches to school-based crime prevention efforts.[2]

While the notion of the community role in furthering a lawful culture is at the heart of community policing in some parts of the United States, the foundation for this project in Tijuana and San Diego County can be found in similar efforts undertaken in Palermo, Sicily, and Hong Kong. In those efforts, educators began with the premise that knowledge of the law, attitudes toward the law, and law-abiding behavior are linked because:

- those who know the law and the reasons for laws will be less likely to break them out of ignorance;
- knowledge will lead to greater awareness of the consequences of law-breaking and law-abiding behavior; and
- greater knowledge about crime, corruption, and their consequences will increase moral support for the law.[3]

In the Hong Kong effort, "moral education" packages were produced beginning in the 1970s to help students develop "proper attitudes towards money and fair play, and to acquire appropriate knowledge and values that contribute to the development of good citizenship." According to Wing Lo, the program was intended to create a "counterculture" to challenge what was perceived as declining moral standards.[4] Although the program is generally considered to have succeeded, annual surveys of its students did not always indicate that the program was as effective or extensively implemented as intended. Wing Lo explains that "the full implementation of this moral education is restrained by competing priorities in the school curricula and tense examination pressure."[5] Other counter-effects which he cites include negative influences from the mass media, the competitive social environment in which the children live, and weakening family structures able to reinforce socially appropriate behaviors.[6]

Meanwhile, in Palermo and other towns in western Sicily that were Mafia strongholds, the anticrime focus arose in response to a particularly violent struggle among Mafia "families" that resulted in the murder of elected officials, judges, policemen, and leaders of civil society. As the anti-Mafia movement grew, reformers used legislation from the 1980s enacted to fund anti-Mafia projects in elementary, middle, and high schools. Materials for the classroom focused on promoting principles of citizenship, opposing the old systems of clientelism, and resisting the tendencies to harbor grudges and vindicate wrongs on one's own. Lessons on the nineteenth-century origins of the Mafia and the role of contemporary organized crime in international narcotics trafficking were added to school curricula.

Students also were guided by their teachers to prepare poster art and photo exhibits protesting violence, to perform concerts and plays with pro-democracy content, and to participate in school marches as part of the anti-Mafia movement. By 1996, schoolchildren from eighty Palermo schools also honored Sicily's anti-Mafia heroes by adopting, studying, and helping to restore historic buildings and monuments in their honor. Parents and community members then were led on tours by student guides who provided information about the structures that had been saved and the persons to whom they were dedicated.[7]

While recognizing the significance of what has been accomplished, some observers have questioned the long-term viability of the "Renaissance" in Palermo and other towns in western Sicily. As evidence, they cite interviews with a sample of families whose children attend the middle schools in four such neighborhoods where continued importance was found for clientelism in obtaining work and in voting. In addition, many of those interviewed blamed the area's unemployment on a slowdown in the construction industry caused by "too much legality."[8] Although Leoluca Orlando, recently mayor of Palermo, agrees that much work remains, he pointed out: "The Mafia doesn't control the minds of the populace like it once did.... Ten years ago, there were 240 murders a year in Palermo alone. Last year [1998], we had only seven—and none was Mafia related."[9] Orlando also noted that Moody's Investors Service now rates Palermo as AA3, as safe as San Francisco and Boston.

Hoping to contribute to similar results, in September 1999 the school systems of Tijuana and San Diego County began a similar effort to develop and test their own school-based education program to help prevent crime and corruption. The project's initial program of "School-Based Education to Counter Crime and Corruption," implemented in the fall of 1999, consisted of a 36–lesson course organized into three separate but related components:

- Values, Self-Esteem, and a Culture of Lawfulness,
- Organized Crime and Corruption, and
- Furthering the Rule of Law, Resistance Techniques, and What Students Can Do.

The course itself was a collaborative product developed by teachers from both Mexico and the United States with support from NSIC's curriculum and criminal justice specialists. Its overall stated goals were to "produce measurable changes in children's knowledge and attitudes and to facilitate efforts to prevent crime and corruption."[10] The evaluation reported here is based on the resulting curriculum that was taught in eleven schools in Tijuana, Mexico, and San Diego County, California. After describing the characteristics of the school systems on both sides of the border, the results of the pilot program's impact are examined.

SCHOOL SYSTEMS AND ZONES IN BAJA CALIFORNIA

The school system in Mexico differs considerably from its counterpart in the United States. Schools in the state of Baja California, for example, are not divided into school districts. Instead, "school zones" have been established, with the number of schools distributed to each being dependent upon both geographic and demographic factors. Further, although public schools generally are established locally to meet a demonstrated demand, they may be financed and administered by the municipality, the state, or federal authorities. Regardless, the basic curriculum taught in each type of school is established by the federal Ministry of Education. The main purpose of this structural division, it appears, has been a desire to balance and share the costs of school maintenance. At the time the pilot project was delivered, the Baja California Secretariat of Education and Social Welfare (SEBS) administered 256 basic education institutions, including 103 secondary schools distributed in 37 school zones.[11]

In Tijuana, where the population is in continual flux due largely to domestic migration and population shifts, many schools have been created on demand by specific communities. Irregular neighborhoods on the outskirts of cities like Tijuana, for example, are begun by settlers building makeshift houses on unoccupied lots. Once sufficient numbers of people have moved into the space (regardless of its existing ownership), they begin to fight for property rights and demand basic services such as sewerage, electricity, roads, and schools.

To illustrate, in February 1999 Tijuana was able to meet the demand for basic education at every school level. By August, however, another 1,500 children had settled into the area. The parents of these children demanded that additional schools be created close to their places of residence, quickly raising the need for more classroom space.[12] As the school year progressed, newcomers continued to swell the numbers of students in existing classrooms, severely complicating the state's ability to plan for even basic school needs.

The precarious economic situation of many Tijuana families compels many children to drop out of school in order to help support their households. Unfortunately, the education they receive during their elementary and secondary school years often is insufficient to provide them with the tools needed for the mostly technical jobs they seek. In response, the federal and state school systems created "technical" secondary schools where children can learn basic skills such as typing, mechanics, electrical work, and carpentry. More recently, these programs have added courses in computer science.

With the introduction of new laws protecting children's right to a free education and regulating child labor at ages below 18 years, schools have focused increasingly on providing technical education in a more balanced way by blending skills training into the regular curriculum. In this sense, technical secondary schools are not significantly different from other public schools, and attending a technical school no longer implies that a student will fail to receive a general education. Indeed, technical secondary schools are now little more than an alternative to regular classrooms but where students are encouraged to learn extra skills.

For the pilot school-based crime prevention project, eight secondary schools were selected in Tijuana—four to serve as experimental settings and four serving as control sites. Although three of the eight were technical schools, there was no significant difference in the students.

In Tijuana (as in the rest of Mexico), the class cohort formed during the first year of secondary school typically changes little. This means that students generally remain in the same class for three years until graduation, a system that has both advantages and disadvantages. For example, students get to know each other well, creating a safe environment where they can support one another and feel a sense of "group" within the school. Unpopular students, however, can suffer the rejection of their classmates throughout the three years of middle school—a rejection that undoubtedly impacts those students' self-esteem and behavior. Each class also has a pre-assigned classroom. It is the teachers, rather than the students, who change classrooms each hour. This allows students to set specific rules for their classroom and to decorate it with their own work—and to be held accountable for damage done to the chairs and walls.

Of the eight schools in the pilot program, all but one (Secundaria #51) have both morning sessions (typically running from 7 AM to 1:30 PM) and an evening shift running from 2 PM to either 7:20 or 9 PM, depending on their location and the dangers students might face going home.[13] Regardless of the session, students have from six to eight different subjects each day in 50-minute classes, with a 20-minute break in the middle of the school day. Also, every Monday morning students participate in a mandatory civil ceremony where they pay their respects to the national flag and listen to any important announcements given by the school principal.

According to the pilot project's teachers, the students differ considerably by shift. Morning-shift students, for example, are usually better supervised by their parents. They are younger and have better grades, more social behavior, and a lower dropout rate.[14] In contrast, students from the evening group cause more trouble in school and are more likely to become involved with gangs. These students' parents usually work all day, so they have less communication with their parents and less supervision of their schoolwork and school performance. It should be noted that when the morning shift is full, some students are assigned to the evening shift. Most parents, however, try to get their children into a morning schedule, and if unsuccessful, they often transfer to another school.

Finally, it is important to remember that students in Tijuana's public schools are among the poorest in the city. The project's teachers estimate that as many as 80 percent of them walk or use public transportation to get to school. Nearly all wear uniforms (school uniforms are generally mandatory in Mexico), and makeup and dramatic hairdos or hair color are prohibited. This code is strictly enforced, and students face penalties—ranging from low grades for neatness and presentation to an attention call to parents—for infractions.

SCHOOLS IN SAN DIEGO COUNTY, CALIFORNIA

The U.S. portion of the pilot was conducted in the Sweetwater Union High School District, a section of the San Diego County school system. Sweetwater is an ethnically diverse area located in the southeast portion of the county. With a predominately Hispanic enrollment (64 percent Hispanic during the 1997–98 school year), the district's 28,495 students are distributed among ten middle schools and nine high schools.

During the past several years, the Sweetwater District has experienced considerable transition among its student population. The total district enrollment grew by more than 30 percent during the previous decade, and the ethnic composition grew increasingly Hispanic. Anglo students currently make up less than 18 percent of the student body, a significant and steady decline since 1985. Small numbers of African American (4.8 percent), Asian (2.3 percent), Filipino (9.6 percent), Native American (0.6 percent), and Pacific Islander (0.8 percent) students complete the district's enrollment.

Adopting a fairly traditional approach, the Sweetwater District has focused its recent efforts on three clearly defined priorities: student literacy, educational technology, and School-to-Career programs. In addition, individual schools have been encouraged to establish and expand relations with local businesses. The district's superintendent reported, in fact, that, district-wide, as many as ninety businesses and other organizations have partnered with schools to provide volunteers, donate goods and services, and arrange internships and business tours for students participating in School-to-Career activities. Three-fourths of the parents surveyed by the district report that they believe their children are receiving a quality education in Sweetwater's schools.[15]

Beyond their outreach to the local business community, during the 1997–98 school year, the district received fifty-four grants totaling more than $5.7 million. As a result, programs in literacy, marine science, substance abuse prevention, and travel and tourism were introduced, and additional support and assessment services for new teachers were made available. In turn, more seniors completed both the University of California's eligibility courses and the SAT exam. In addition, five Sweetwater schools placed among the forty-six California nominees for the National Blue Ribbon School award. One district junior high school received the 1997 California School Boards Association's Golden Bell Award, another received the California Title 1 Achieving Schools Award for improvement in English language–arts test scores, and one high school was among five state schools honored nationally for improvement in both math and English language–arts test scores. Moreover, the *San Diego Business Journal* gave special recognition to the district for leadership and employee and community relations.[16]

METHODS

The pilot curriculum was taught as a quasi-experiment designed to collect measures of effect on participating students. In keeping with the program's stated goals, specific changes were expected in the students' general knowledge of crime and organized crime (including gang-related crime) and corruption issues; their approach to legal reasoning; and their overall attitudes concerning belief in rules, peer associations, self-concept, and interpersonal competency. To identify these impacts, measures were collected in two waves—first in August and September 1999, at the beginning of the project semester, and later, in December 1999, at the conclusion of the course. A quasi-experimental approach was selected because it permitted comparisons between schools that taught the pilot curriculum with those that did not.

In this project, impact data were collected from more than eight hundred students attending eleven public high schools—eight in Mexico and three in the United States. In each setting, the project's participants were ninth grade students (*secundaria* 3 in Tijuana) attending mandatory classes into which the crime and corruption curriculum had been incorporated. In the United States those included the Introduction to Social Sciences classes at Southwest and Castle Park high schools. In Mexico, the test curriculum was incorporated into regular social science classes. In each setting, control schools were selected by school officials with input on the selection criteria by the evaluation staff. With the data collected, comparisons among individual students—as well as between classes, schools, and the U.S. and Mexican school systems—were possible.

Three techniques were used to measure the impact of the program: (1) a two-part, multiple-choice survey instrument, in combination with (2) a series of focus group interviews with eight groups of students (approximately thirty students each) and (3) interviews with the eight participating teachers. Students, with assistance from their teachers, were given full class periods to complete their answers. Due to the differences in class length, however, the actual process of administration differed between the two countries. In the United States, where classroom periods are more rigid, the instrument's sections were administered over two class periods. In Tijuana, both sections of the instrument were administered during a single class period. Because anonymity was provided to all participating students, it is not possible to compare a specific student's responses to the instrument's separate component parts.

The instrument itself comprised forty-eight questions constructing five scales from the Effective School Battery (ESB)—a published, standardized survey that measures school climate and safety issues. To assess school climate, the instrument requires students to answer questions not only about their school and school environment but also about themselves, their peers, and their own fears, attitudes, and expectations.[17] Although questions from the ESB can be examined individually, the instrument also is designed to allow items to be combined to produce scales reflecting specific student attitudes and characteristics. Among the more relevant student scales available to this project are:

- *Positive Peer Associations*, which describes peer relations for the average student. High scores on this index indicate that students are associating with peers who value school and tend to stay out of trouble. Low scores indicate students reporting that their friends dislike school and are more likely to get into trouble.
- *Belief in Rules*, a scale measuring the extent to which students believe in the validity of conventional social rules.
- *Interpersonal Competency*, which measures the degree to which the average student feels competent in interpersonal relationships. Research suggests that a student's "social competency"—including his or her assertiveness, problem-solving ability, and communications skills—is related to resistance techniques and the ability to avoid or resist negative influences and behaviors.[18]
- *Positive Self-Concept*, a scale that captures how students describe themselves. According to Gottfredson, high scores on this scale imply high self-esteem in students who regard themselves as conventional, rule-abiding individuals.[19] Low scores are indicative of students who

see themselves in disparaging ways or consider themselves to be troublemakers. Low scorers should be expected to have significantly greater disciplinary problems.

The ESB was derived and validated on more than seven thousand students from approximately seventy middle and high schools at sixteen locations throughout the United States.

Supplementing the Effective School Battery, an additional twenty-two self-report questions were added to the students' survey to learn about their involvement in deviant acts as well as the extent that rule-breaking behavior evokes remorse. The deviance ranged from minor actions, such as cheating on tests and lying about age to buy alcohol, to serious crimes such as robbery, auto theft, and aggravated assault. Specific rule-breaking questions dealt with students' likely reactions after violations of local laws as well as rules set by teachers, parents, and the police.

Project consultants also developed thirty-nine subject matter questions intended to measure the extent to which students learned the lessons taught. Complementing these measures were the individual course and activity grades each student received from his or her teacher during the semester.

Finally, seven items were included in Part 2 of the evaluation instrument to measure the students' conceptions of rules, laws, rights, and responsibilities. Each of these questions presented the student with three levels of legal reasoning. At the preconventional or first level, students are governed in their actions by fear. Reasoning focuses on the external consequences of violating behavior. At this level, laws and rules have no inherent goodness or value; they are to be obeyed (unless they can be avoided) only because of the negative consequences that might result from disobedience. The second level of reasoning is the conventional level. Here, students are concerned with law and order, and conformity with role expectations and their fulfillment. In short, individuals at this level follow rules primarily because they want to be accepted as a member of a particular group or society. The postconventional level is reached by students who understand the need for social systems while being able to differentiate between the values of a given social order and universal ethics. The goal in this program, of course, is to assist students in progressing from the initial level—often defined as "law obeying"—to the higher levels of "law maintaining" or "law making."[20]

COMPARING THE SITES

Baja California

As described above, the pilot in Tijuana was conducted in eight schools—four designated as experimental sites and four as controls for comparison.

Table 16.1 **Baja California Schools Participating in the Pilot Project to Create a Culture of Lawfulness**

EXPERIMENTAL SCHOOLS

School	Students	Physical Facilities	Teachers	Neighborhood	Crime Problems	Project Participants
Escuela Técnica #36	1,000, distributed in 24 groups (2 shifts)	11 classrooms, 4 workshops (poorly equipped), basketball court	37 (15 females, 22 males)	Unpaved streets, no public transportation within a mile of school, threatening neighbors.	Vandalism, graffiti, gangs	2 evening shifts (21 boys, 26 girls). Majority born in Tijuana from middle- or lower-income families.
Escuela Técnica #51	360 in morning shift	11 classrooms, basketball court	15 (9 females, 6 males)	On top of mountain near a cliff, unpaved streets, no public transportation. School difficult to access.	Mugging while walking home	32 students (7 boys, 25 girls). Majority born in Tijuana, from middle- or lower-income families.
Escuela Secundaria Técnica #5	1,100 in morning and evening shifts	Gardens, well-built classroom, basketball court	53 (27 females, 26 males)	Safe middle-class neighborhood	Street gangs, harassment, muggings	22 (15 boys, 7 girls) from one evening shift. Majority recently moved to Tijuana and are from middle- or lower-income families.
Escuela Secundaria Técnica #37	970 students in morning and evening shifts	Poor facilities. Some classrooms have closed because of the risk of collapse.	25	Close to a railroad track, mostly unpaved roads, public transportation marginal.	Gangs, harassment, muggings	225 students. Came to Tijuana from other parts of Mexico.

CONTROL SCHOOLS

School	Students	Physical Facilities	Teachers	Neighborhood	Crime Problems	Project Participants
Escuela Secundaria Técnica #33	500 in morning and evening shifts	Library, functional workshops, center patio for sports		Considerable construction, close to inhabited mountain, busy and chaotic streets.	Street gang, drunks, drug addicts in neighbor-hood	
Escuela Secundaria Estatal #101	634 in morning and afternoon shifts	13 classrooms, poor lighting, unpaved outside patio	26	Relatively isolated, unpaved streets, irregular water and electrical services.	Little graffiti or crime	
Secundaria Técnica #6	1,500 in morning and afternoon shifts	Well-built classrooms, library, 7 workshops	82 (45 females, 37 males)	Well populated, public transportation, near historic setting, homeless shelter.	Drugs and light weapons	
Escuela Secundaria Estatal #25				Street crime	Gangs, graffiti and vandalism, light weapons	

In all, nine class groups received the project's curriculum during both morning (four classes) and afternoon (five classes) sessions. Data on the participating schools are reported in table 16.1. Unfortunately, the project's control schools are not ideally matched for the quasi-experimental design. For example, the experimental students were significantly more often males and were slightly older than their control group counterparts. Interestingly, at the project's inception the experimental students also perceived their friends to be significantly more likely to believe that getting good grades was important and less likely to "think of school as a pain." Similarly, the experimental students' friends got in trouble with the police less often, and those friends who did get in trouble did so less frequently. The experimental students also were less willing to lie to protect friends who were in police trouble and were less likely to agree that it is "all right to avoid following the law if you can." Table 16.2 reports comparisons of the control and experimental schools.

Table 16.2 **Experimental and Control Group Comparisons–Tijuana (percentages)**

	Students	
Item[a]	Experimental	Control
Gender: Male	49%	39%
Female	51	61
Age: 13 years	9	24
14 years	53	42
15 years	28	28
16 years	8	7
Others think of you as a good or very good student	78	89
Friends think getting good grades is important	90	82
My friends think that school is a pain	23	33
Best friend gets in trouble with the police	2	7
Number of friends picked up by police:		
Unknown	32	26
None	43	38
One or more	25	36
Would like to help friends in trouble with police:		
Yes	9	18
Don't know	61	41
Believes that it is all right to "get around" the law	13	21

[a] Differences in all items are significant at .05 or above.

Beyond these demographic and attitudinal items, differences also exist in the subject matter knowledge of the experimental and control students. For example, control group students were significantly better able to define the concept of corruption, and they showed greater awareness of the importance of self-esteem for one's ability to resist the attractions of deviance. In addition, the control students showed increased understanding of the gradual erosive effects of criminal environments and influences, of the elements of a "culture of law*less*ness," and of the roles of problem solving and planning for the future as life skills.

As for their self-reported behavior, although the control group students reported greater regularity in cheating on exams (during the previous two months, 25 percent of control and 16 percent of experimental students cheated three or more times), few other differences were found. This may be attributable to the consistently small numbers of students from either group who reported involvement in any of the acts described that were crimes. This is consistent with the generally lower levels of remorse that control students reported feeling after breaking their teachers' rules (32 percent of control versus 25 percent of experimental students would "never" or "almost never" feel bad or guilty).

San Diego County

Eight schools participated in the pilot in Tijuana, but only three were available in the San Diego area—two designated as experimental sites and one as a control. All are located in the county's Sweetwater Union High School District, which serves twenty-one middle, junior, and senior high schools with a combined population of 33,000 students in five southern San Diego County communities. The Hispanic influence is especially strong in Sweetwater, which is located only a few miles from the U.S.–Mexico border, and the vast majority of the district's students describe themselves as Mexican or Mexican American.

Unlike their counterparts in Mexico, the participating Sweetwater District schools operate on a single shift schedule (8:00 AM to 3:30 PM) with six 50–minute class periods. Given that class selection can vary considerably among students, cohorts of students are far less well defined in the United States, where students typically change teachers and classrooms for each class period. In all, ten different class groups, taught by four teachers, received this project's curriculum. Each of the participating schools is described in table 16.3.

Compared to their Mexican counterparts, the experimental and control schools in the Sweetwater District were a better, though not perfect, match. For example, while the proportion of males and females in each group was nearly equal and little difference was found in students' ages,

Table 16.3 **San Diego County Schools Participating in the Pilot Project to Create a Culture of Lawfulness**

EXPERIMENTAL SCHOOLS

School	Students	Student Ethnicity	Student Academic Standing	Physical Facilities	Neighborhood
Castle Park High School	2,200 students (52% males, 48% females)	79% Hispanic, 10% Anglo, 5% African American, 4% Filipino, 1% Asian, 1% American Indian, 1% Pacific Islander	2.2 average GPA (4.0 scale). 96% attend school daily.	Well-equipped classrooms, 2 computer labs, library, media resource center, school psychologist, clubs and community programs.	Middle-income neighborhood
Southwest High School	2,100 (52% males, 49% females), 80% from homes where English is not spoken.	84% Hispanic, 11% Filipino, 5% Anglo, 3% African American, 1% Asian	2.28 average GPA. 9% have perfect attendance.	Fully equipped classrooms, trained school counselors, speech and language therapists, school psychologists, after-school tutoring.	Middle- to lower-income neighborhood

CONTROL SCHOOL

School	Students	Student Ethnicity	Student Academic Standing	Physical Facilities	Neighborhood
Mar Vista High School	2,000 students			Well-equipped classrooms, extracurricular activities, computer labs, library, media resource center.	

the experimental classes had a significantly larger proportion of Hispanic students (table 16.4). In addition, the control school students were significantly more likely to report that their peers saw them at least somewhat as troublemakers. The experimental students, meanwhile, felt that their friends were more interested in school and planned to go to college. Although few students in either group reported having a friend who belonged to a gang, the control school students' friends more often get into trouble with the police.

Table 16.4 **Experimental and Control Group Comparisons–San Diego (Sweetwater District) (percentages)**

Item	Students	
	Experimental	Control
Gender: Male	58%	58%
Female	42	42
Ethnicity[a]: Hispanic	77	58
Anglo	6	22
African American	6	5
Biracial	5	9
Other	6	7
Others think of you as a troublemaker[a]	42	57
Best friend is interested in school[a]	75	61
I am able to make it if I try[a]	95	88
Believe that:		
People who leave things deserve them stolen	29	36
Taking from stores doesn't hurt anyone	18	24
It is okay to take advantage of a wimp or sucker	11	16
Teachers who get hassled usually had it coming	42	50
It is all right to "get around" the law	25	31

[a] Differences in each are significant at .05 or above.

The experimental students were significantly more likely to see themselves as able to "make it"—that is, to succeed—if they try, as having clear pictures of what they are like as individuals, and as confident in their own abilities to explain things. Conversely, although the differences were not significant, the control students more often reported a belief that people who leave things around deserve to have them taken, and that it is acceptable to take advantage of a "wimp or a sucker." These students also reported more frequently that teachers who "get hassled by students usually have it coming." With those views in mind, it is not surprising that the control students were considerably more likely to report having stolen a motor vehicle, dealt with stolen goods, sold drugs, and cheated on a test in the previous two months than were their experimental group peers.

Beyond their attitudinal differences, in the pretest the control group students also showed less understanding of the concepts of free will and self-esteem, as well as the meaning of law as the formalized rule-making role of government. Further, they were less sure of the reasons for joining gangs, what constituted corruption, and the broad impact of both crime and corruption. Finally, these students were less willing to see problem solving as an activity in which everyone engages.

No meaningful differences were found between experimental and control students in terms of the remorse they reported they would feel after breaking rules set by their parents, school, or society, or in the levels of their legal reasoning.

Cross-Border Comparison

Some of the more interesting aspects of the pilot were the differences among the students and school systems in Mexico and the United States, as shown in table 16.5. For example, although the participating students from both countries were almost exclusively in the ninth grade (generally between twelve and fourteen years old), the Mexican students were significantly older. In fact, 37 percent of the students from Tijuana reported themselves as being fifteen years old or older, compared to only 14 percent of the San Diego children. This may result in part from differences in the students' school performance, since only 24 percent of the Tijuana students reported that they received either A's or B's in their studies, compared to 60 percent of the San Diego students. Even so, 53 percent of the Mexican students, but only 24 percent of the U.S. students, reported being "very satisfied" with their current school performance.

The two countries' students varied significantly in other important aspects as well. When asked how their peers in school might perceive them, for example, the students from San Diego were far more likely to report self-perceptions as both a good student and as successful (table 16.6). Even so, they added that they were also more likely to be considered troublemakers, to some degree. As for their own friends, two-thirds of the California students reported that their friends see school as "a pain," and far fewer felt that their friends were interested in school. Despite this, the U.S.

Table 16.5 **Demographic Differences between Tijuana and San Diego (Sweetwater District) Students (percentages)**

	Students	
Item[a]	Tijuana	San Diego
Gender: Male	46%	58%
Female	54	42
Age: 13 years	14	13
14 years	49	74
15 years or older	37	14
Current grades[b]*:* A student	2	13
B student	22	47
C student	60	33
D student	16	5
F student	0	2
Satisfied with school performance:		
Very satisfied	52	24
Somewhat satisfied	37	62
Somewhat or very dissatisfied	11	14
Father's education level:		
Eighth grade or less	48	11
Some high school	7	16
Finished high school	11	23
Attended or completed college	12	22
Mother's education level:		
Eighth grade or less	58	12
Some high school	8	15
Finished high school	11	25
Attended or completed college	6	28

[a] Differences in each are significant at .000.

[b] Grades for Mexican students converted from a 10-point to a 4-point scale.

Table 16.6 **Differences in Peer Perceptions and Self-Perceptions between Tijuana and San Diego (Sweetwater District) Students (percentages)**

Item[a]	Students: Tijuana	Students: San Diego
Others think of you as:		
A very good student	6%	24%
Very successful	8	24
Somewhat a troublemaker	28	43
<u>About Their Friends</u>		
My friends think school is a pain:	26	66
Best friend:		
Is interested in school	93	71
Plans to go to college	80	87
Belongs to a gang	4	8
Gets in trouble with the police	4	10
Number of friends picked up by police:		
Unknown	30	26
None	41	22
One or more	28	52
<u>About Themselves</u>		
Would like to help friends in trouble with police:		
Yes	12	32
Don't know	55	42
I don't have much to lose by causing trouble at school	90	75
I don't mind stealing from someone	2	8
Believe that:		
People who leave things deserve them stolen	8	31
Taking from stores doesn't hurt anyone	89	19
It is okay to take advantage of a wimp or sucker	3	13
Teachers who get hassled usually had it coming	13	44
It is all right to "get around" the law	16	28

[a] Differences in each are significant at .02 or above.

students had higher expectations that their friends would go on to college. Still, those same friends were more often reported to belong to a gang and to get in trouble with the police. Further, the San Diego children were nearly twice as likely as their Mexican peers to have friends who had been "picked up" by the police.

Students from the Sweetwater schools also exhibited far less investment in lawful behavior. Although they were less likely to agree that they had little to lose by causing trouble at school, the San Diego students nonetheless were significantly more likely to agree that they would lie to help a friend in trouble with the police, that they did not mind stealing from others, and that it was all right to "get around the law." It was only when the theft involved stealing from stores that the Mexican students showed a greater willingness to break the law, with a surprising 89 percent reporting that such crimes do not hurt anyone. In keeping with these views, as noted above, the U.S. students expressed less empathy for others; more of them agreed that it is acceptable to take advantage of "a wimp or sucker," that people who leave things around deserve to have them stolen, and that teachers who "get hassled" by students usually had it coming. Even so, the San Diego students continued to see themselves more often as able to make it if they try, as able to talk with all kinds of people, and as having much to be proud of.

Given the overall attitudes prevailing among the U.S. students, it was not surprising that, prior to the course, they were more likely to report having been suspended from school and having participated in various status and drug offenses, crimes against property, and crimes against persons (see table 16.7). In fact, it was only when asked if they had cheated on school tests that the Mexican students fared worse, with nearly 73 percent reporting that they had cheated at least once in the previous two months in school. The San Diego students less often showed remorse for the violations of laws and rules that did occur (table 16.8). Interestingly, both groups of students reported that they would be most concerned about violations of their parents' rules. Students from Tijuana, meanwhile, cared least about their friends' rules, while students from the Sweetwater District rated their teachers' rules as least important.

Finally, although few meaningful differences were noted in the students' knowledge of subject matter, the San Diego students did show greater understanding of the concepts of free will, self-esteem, and the role of law as a formalized function of government. The Tijuana students, on the other hand, more accurately defined the impact of crime on victims and showed greater knowledge of the concept of corruption. The Mexican students also were more willing to attribute membership in criminal organizations to a desire for money, whereas the U.S. students gave greater weight to the needs to belong and to gain respect. Similarly, the U.S. students were more comfortable with the role of problem solving in everyday life and the elements of successful problem solving. Even so, the level of legal reasoning was consistently higher among the Mexican students.

Table 16.7 **Differences in the Frequency of Proscribed Behaviors between Tijuana and San Diego (Sweetwater District) Students (percentages)**

Item[a]	Students	
	Tijuana	San Diego
Students who have self-reported the following as having occurred one or more times during the past two months in school:		
Status or School Violations		
Been suspended	12%	32%
Lied about age to break rules	15	34
Been loud or rowdy in public places	29	46
Cheated on a school test	73	54
Crimes against Property		
Avoided paying for things	7	38
Destroyed others' property	21	29
Committed minor theft	15	37
Committed major theft	2	16
Bought, sold, or held stolen goods	9	21
Took a vehicle without permission	4	13
Stole (or tried to steal) a motor vehicle	1	7
Crimes against Persons		
Been in fights	35	51
Carried a weapon	12	21
Used force to get money or things	1	8
Attacked someone to hurt them	8	13
Drug Violations		
Sold marijuana	2	14
Sold other drugs	<1	7

[a] Differences in each are significant at .00 or above.

RESULTS OF THE PILOT PROJECT

As discussed earlier, the curriculum developed for this pilot project was administered quasi-experimentally in four experimental schools in Tijuana and two experimental schools in the Sweetwater School District in San Diego County. The curriculum was first tested during the final semester of the 1998–99 school year, and, after minor modifications, it was delivered during the first semester of 1999–2000. Data were collected from both experimental and control group students as a pretest during August and September 1999, and again as a posttest during December 1999, after the 36–section course was complete. Despite the inexact match between the experimental and control groups, which makes it necessary to apply considerable interpretive caution, there are a number of significant findings, reported below.

Table 16.8 **Differences in Attitudes toward Law Breaking and Rule Breaking between Tijuana and San Diego (Sweetwater District) Students (percentages)**

	Students	
Item[a]	Tijuana	San Diego
Would you feel bad if you broke:		
The law?		
Always or almost always	44%	30%
Never or almost never	29	37
Your teacher's rules?		
Always or almost always	37	20
Never or almost never	28	45
A police officer's orders?		
Always or almost always	42	32
Never or almost never	29	43
Your parents' rules?		
Always or almost always	69	39
Never or almost never	11	31
Your friends' rules?		
Always or almost always	32	32
Never or almost never	41	34

[a] Differences in each are significant at .00 or above.

Impact on Students' Knowledge

To examine the extent to which students learned the lessons taught in the curriculum to counter crime and corruption, 39 subject matter questions were developed and administered to students during each wave of testing. The first wave served as a pretest to establish students' existing knowledge base; the second wave, administered at the completion of curriculum, measured the extent to which new knowledge had been acquired. These measures were then complemented with the individual course and activity grades each student received during the semester. The control schools, of course, were included to assess the extent to which students' subject matter knowledge increased independently of the course.

San Diego County

The knowledge base of the students in the participating Sweetwater schools was clearly advanced as a result of the classes they attended (table 16.9). For example, prior to the project, the students' ability to define the concepts of crime, corruption, human nature, and free will was uncertain. In each case, however, by the posttest wave of questioning, the proportion of students correctly defining these concepts had improved significantly; no change (or a negative change) was found among the control students. Interestingly, much of the improvement in results appeared to have occurred among students who had previously answered "I don't know" to each question.

Beyond simple definitions, however, students were asked to make distinctions between laws and customs, demonstrate an understanding of victimization and the impact of crime and corruption, and indicate the characteristics of cultures of both lawfulness and law*less*ness. For each item, the improvements among the experimental students were both obvious and dramatic, while little change was noted among the comparison students (table 16.10). Here, too, much of the change within both groups involved students who had responded that they did not know the answers to our queries.

Following the general lessons on the importance of lawful living, the project's curriculum focused more specifically on organized crime, the activities of criminal groups, and the impacts of these crimes on social order and a free society. To measure these lessons, questions dealing more specifically with gangs and organized crime, as well as the reasons that people might join criminal groups, were also included. Here, too, the San Diego students showed significant improvement in their subject matter knowledge (table 16.11). For example, when asked to identify a general definition of organized crime, fewer than half of the students in both the experimental and control groups could do so during the pretest. Following the crime and corruption course, more than two-thirds of the experimental students provided accurate responses, compared to slightly more than one-fourth of the control students. Similar shifts in knowledge followed on questions about the businesses of organized crime, the reasons for and processes of joining organized crime, and the role of gangs as a form of organized crime. For each of these questions, either no change or a negative change occurred in the control group students.

Table 16.9 **Pretest/Posttest Comparison of San Diego (Sweetwater District) Students on the Basic Concepts of Crime and Corruption (percentages)**

	Experimental		Control	
Item	Pretest	Posttest	Pretest	Posttest
Percent of students defining:				
Crime[a]				
Defined correctly	53%	65%	49%	42%
Don't know	12	5	15	24
Corruption[a]				
Defined correctly	38	67	26	28
Don't know	18	6	17	28
Human nature[a]				
Defined correctly	44	54	37	35
Don't know	20	12	20	30
Free will[a]				
Defined correctly	58	71	48	36
Don't know	17	10	23	31

[a] Differences among experimental students are significant at .01 or above.

Finally, for questions about techniques for resisting the lure of organized criminal activities, the crime and corruption curriculum apparently had little impact on students' ability to define the concept of self-esteem, but it had a significant impact on how they applied the concept to themselves and their friends (table 16.12). For example, when asked what factors they might include in assessing a person's worth, students who believed material possessions should be excluded as a factor increased from slightly more than one-half during the pretest to nearly three-fourths following the classroom lessons. No meaningful changes occurred, however, among the control students. Similar outcomes were found when

Table 16.10 **Pretest/Posttest Comparison of San Diego (Sweetwater District) Students on the Concepts of Law, Lawfulness, and the Impacts of Crime (percentages)**

Item	Experimental		Control	
	Pretest	Posttest	Pretest	Posttest
Percent of students defining:				
Meaning of law[a]				
Defined correctly	54%	59%	47%	49%
Don't know	10	9	12	27
Meaning of customs[b]				
Defined correctly	35	52	29	23
Don't know	15	9	19	36
Elements of victimization[b]				
Defined correctly	69	80	51	46
Don't know	8	6	17	25
Elements of a culture of lawfulness[b]				
Defined correctly	21	37	25	20
Don't know	45	29	40	40
Elements of a culture of lawlessness[b]				
Defined correctly	31	43	22	14
Don't know	42	21	42	46
General impacts of crime and corruption[a/b]				
Defined correctly	44	55	35	23
Don't know	18	12	27	31
Specific impacts of corruption[a/b]				
Defined correctly	13	38	14	16
Don't know	42	26	42	54
Personal impacts of criminal involvement[b]				
Defined correctly	59	70	43	36
Don't know	9	3	18	27

[a] Differences among control students are significant at .04 or above.
[b] Differences among experimental students are significant at .00 or above.

Table 16.11 **Pretest/Posttest Comparison of San Diego (Sweetwater District) Students on the Concepts and Practices of Organized Crime (percentages)**

Item	Experimental Pretest	Experimental Posttest	Control Pretest	Control Posttest
Percent of students defining:				
Organized crime[a]				
Defined correctly	41%	68%	33%	28%
Don't know	31	16	32	39
Primary businesses of organized crime[a]				
Defined correctly	49	70	40	33
Don't know	22	8	29	32
Reasons for joining organized crime[a]				
Defined correctly	52	71	42	39
Don't know	6	2	14	20
Process of becoming a criminal[a]				
Defined correctly	54	82	53	52
Don't know	15	6	20	29
Role of nations hosting organized crime[a/b]				
Defined correctly	14	42	11	21
Don't know	43	18	37	46
Gangs as crime and corruption[a/b]				
Defined correctly	80	86	74	63
Don't know	9	7	14	26
Gang operations and definitions[a]				
Defined correctly	42	53	32	29
Don't know	21	12	23	37
Role of violence in organized crime[a]				
Defined correctly	46	56	34	33
Don't know	14	6	14	30

[a] Differences among experimental students are significant at .00 or above.
[b] Differences among control students are significant at .04 or above.

students were asked about the importance of self-esteem in resisting bad behavior and the difficulties of resisting the temptations of criminal associations. Still, little change occurred in the students' understanding of the consequences of making bad decisions or their acceptance and understanding of problem solving and its role in everyday decision making. These latter outcomes, however, may reflect the students' already high understanding of these concepts at the project's pretest stage. This is especially likely when we consider the significant increase that did occur in their ability to relate why problem solving is an important "life skill."

As for the difficulties in dealing with crime and corruption, the students far more often recognized the importance of personal intimidation, personal gain, and corrupt officials as contributors to organized crime's success. Further, they more readily identified an understanding of consequences, especially as they relate to present actions and future outcomes. In that light, they were significantly clearer about the importance of planning for the future as a "life skill," as well as the meaning of personal goals.

Although the San Diego students collectively demonstrated increased subject matter knowledge, when examined individually, the classes of the four participating experimental teachers reveal important differences. For example, of the four teachers' classes, three groups of students showed consistent improvement, while there was far less impact on the fourth group. There are readily apparent explanations for this outcome. The group with the most consistently positive results, for instance, was an advanced-placement academic honors class. In such a setting, increased subject matter performance should be expected, and the present finding is consistent with other school-based intervention projects.[21]

Conversely, during a focus group session following the completion of the course, students from the class with the poorest performance reported that a large proportion of them had friends who were in gangs. Further, they added, the course had had no effect on their external behaviors. When pressed to explain why, these students focused on the neighborhoods in which they live and expressed fear of others in their neighborhood and of not being accepted or of not fitting in. These students seemed to lack confidence and had difficulty explaining their role in the world around them. This outcome suggests that, for use with similar students in the future, the course sections on individual responsibility may require strengthening. Preliminary observations during data collection and subsequent informal conversations with several students from this group also suggested that this class might have difficulties with attendance and concentration. Verification of these concerns from school attendance and performance records was not available.

Results from the classes of the remaining two teachers are far more difficult to explain. Although comparable in performance, these groups

Table 16.12 **Pretest/Posttest Comparison of San Diego (Sweetwater District) Students on Self-Esteem and the Resistance of Crime and Criminal Association (percentages)**

	Experimental		Control	
Item	Pretest	Posttest	Pretest	Posttest
Percent of students defining:				
Self-esteem				
Defined correctly	65%	67%	58%	50%
Don't know	8	8	19	21
Excluding material possessions as a factor in personal worth[a]				
Defined correctly	58	74	50	48
Don't know	14	8	16	26
Role of self-esteem in resistance of bad behavior[a]				
Defined correctly	78	87	60	61
Don't know	10	6	17	28
Difficulty in resisting criminal association[a/b]				
Defined correctly	67	81	62	56
Don't know	18	10	14	33
Importance of problem solving as life skill[a]				
Defined correctly	21	33	14	12
Don't know	16	14	25	29
Impact of present actions on future outcomes[a]				
Defined correctly	30	49	28	18
Don't know	29	16	26	33
Importance of planning as a life skill[a]				
Defined correctly	41	52	37	28
Don't know	13	10	19	32

[a] Differences among experimental students are significant at .00 or above.

[b] Differences among control students are significant at .04 or above.

were dramatically different in size and demeanor. One teacher's class was small and quiet, while the other teacher's classes were large and boisterous. One of this teacher's classes, in fact, may reasonably be described as chaotic. Still, each of these groups showed improvements in their subject matter performance, with no obvious differences between them.

Unfortunately, when the evaluation instrument was divided into distinct parts to facilitate classroom administration, demographic information was not added to the subject matter sections. As such, additional differences among student participants cannot be determined.

Baja California

The subject matter knowledge base of the Mexican students who received the crime and corruption curriculum also improved, although far less dramatically than it did among their San Diego counterparts. Although the Tijuana students' ability to define the basic concepts of crime, corruption, free will, and human nature was increased, the improvements were far smaller than those realized in the Sweetwater schools (table 16.13). In fact, with regard to selecting the appropriate phrases to define crime, the change in students' knowledge from the pretest to the posttest did not reach statistical significance. For the concepts of corruption and human nature, the differences were far greater. It was only with the concept of free will that the students appeared to gain significant new knowledge, with 50 percent selecting the correct definition (compared to 30 percent during the pretest).

Beyond these basic conceptual terms, the evaluation also measured students' understanding of law, lawfulness, and the impacts of crime and corruption. Here the change in students' knowledge was more obvious. For example, after completing the crime and corruption curriculum, students were significantly better able to identify the appropriate reasons for societal rules, and they showed an increased understanding of the meaning of law (table 16.14). In addition, their knowledge of the elements of victimization—as well as law*ful*ness and law*less*ness—increased considerably, while their awareness of the impact of crime and corruption was enhanced. For most items, the improvements in the Tijuana students' scores were equal to or greater than those of their San Diego peers.

When asked to define organized crime, the Tijuana students' scores, both before and after receiving the curriculum, were similar to those of the San Diego students. Their responses as to why people might join criminal organizations, however, were far more varied (table 16.15). In fact, even after receiving the curriculum, these students were less sure of such motivations than the San Diego students were *prior* to the project. Still, their increase in knowledge was significant. It could be argued that these motivations are more varied in the Mexican students' communities, which might make a single "correct" answer less obvious for them. Nonetheless, their awareness of how many people experience a "slow descent" into crime was greatly enhanced during the course, as was their knowledge of gangs' criminal involvement, their ability to identify descriptions of gang methods and operations, and their understanding of the role of violence for criminal organizations.

Table 16.13 **Pretest/Posttest Comparison of Tijuana Students on the Basic Concepts of Crime and Corruption (percentages)**

	Experimental		Control	
Item	Pretest	Posttest	Pretest	Posttest
Percent of students defining:				
Crime				
Defined correctly	46%	52%	51%	52%
Don't know	13	7	7	8
Corruption[a/b]				
Defined correctly	46	49	62	43
Don't know	24	8	16	12
Human nature[a]				
Defined correctly	30	38	28	32
Don't know	19	13	17	18
Free will[a]				
Defined correctly	30	50	25	34
Don't know	35	18	41	37

[a] Differences among experimental students are significant at .00 or above.
[b] Differences among control students are significant at .00 or above.

The students in Tijuana also showed significant improvement in recognizing the elements of self-esteem and the role of positive self-esteem in resisting negative influences and bad behavior. Coupled with that awareness, participation in the project's curriculum also appears to have contributed to these students' understanding that present actions have future consequences, thereby reinforcing the need for planning as a "life skill." Still, the majority of these students continued to disagree with the everyday role of problem solving in the average person's life—despite an improved understanding of the problem-solving process itself. By the end of the course, participating Tijuana students expressed an increased

Table 16.14 **Pretest/Posttest Comparison of Tijuana Students on the Concepts of Law, Lawfulness, and the Impacts of Crime (percentages)**

Item	Experimental		Control	
	Pretest	Posttest	Pretest	Posttest
Percent of students defining:				
Societal need for rules[a]				
Defined correctly	25%	35%	39%	38%
Don't know	30	18	16	19
Meaning of law[a]				
Defined correctly	40	51	38	43
Don't know	19	11	18	16
Elements of victimization[a]				
Defined correctly	72	85	81	70
Don't know	9	6	4	11
Elements of a culture of lawfulness[b]				
Defined correctly	12	26	21	22
Don't know	53	35	39	45
Elements of a culture of lawlessness[a/b]				
Defined correctly	33	42	40	41
Don't know	43	28	30	36
General impacts of crime and corruption				
Defined correctly	35	42	40	26
Don't know	22	15	15	24
Specific impacts of corruption[a]				
Defined correctly	15	30	19	21
Don't know	50	35	42	45
Personal impacts of criminal involvement[a]				
Defined correctly	41	53	43	46
Don't know	3	6	4	6

[a] Differences among experimental students are significant at .00 or above.
[b] Differences among control students are significant at .00 or above.

Table 16.15 **Pretest/Posttest Comparison of Tijuana Students on the Concepts and Practices of Organized Crime (percentages)**

Item	Experimental		Control	
	Pretest	Posttest	Pretest	Posttest
Percent of students defining:				
Organized crime[a]				
Defined correctly	46%	70%	53%	49%
Don't know	36	15	30	29
Primary businesses of organized crime[a]				
Defined correctly	56	61	62	53
Don't know	15	10	9	10
Reasons for joining organized crime[a]				
Defined correctly	26	43	29	34
Don't know	18	9	10	8
Process of becoming a criminal[a]				
Defined correctly	49	60	57	60
Don't know	26	15	21	22
Role of nations hosting organized crime[a]				
Defined correctly	25	37	29	31
Don't know	49	23	37	40
Gangs as crime and corruption[a]				
Defined correctly	85	90	87	82
Don't know	7	6	6	11
Gang operations and definitions[a]				
Defined correctly	18	32	18	22
Don't know	24	14	18	19
Role of violence in organized crime[a]				
Defined correctly	29	42	30	36
Don't know	23	11	17	18

[a] Differences among experimental students are significant at .05 or above.

recognition that it is possible, though difficult, to resist the temptations of criminal association, and that the success of crime and corruption is dependent on intimidation, public participation, and corrupt officials.

While the overall improvement in the Mexican students' knowledge base about crime and corruption was impressive, the results achieved by the individual teachers varied considerably. The students of teachers #1 and #4, for example, consistently achieved the most dramatic proportional improvement from pretest to posttest in terms of correct answers to the subject matter questions. On nearly every question examined, however, teacher #1's students had the highest scores on the pretest, while teacher #3's students were almost always near the bottom. Comparisons are further complicated because teacher #2 had far more students participating in the project, and his was the most difficult school environment; moreover, his students scored lowest on at least 60 percent of all questions in the pretest. Teacher #4's students, meanwhile, showed steady, though not spectacular, improvement in the number of questions answered correctly. These results, along with the differing impacts among teachers in the Sweetwater District, should be explored more fully in the project's future process evaluations to identify student characteristics—and styles of teaching and classroom management—that may be effective in maximizing the project's impact.

Impact on Student Attitudes

Although the students may have learned their lessons well, there is little evidence that the project's classes changed the views of either San Diego or Tijuana students. Curriculum exposure appears to have had little impact on the students' stated likelihood of staying out of trouble in the future or on their self-reported deviant actions. Nor does it appear that participating students' views of their friends, attitudes about self, empathy toward others, or remorse about their own rule-violating behavior have changed. The variability that was noted among these individual items cannot automatically be attributed to the curriculum's impact because the movement is inconsistent and seldom statistically significant. Moreover, similar results were sometimes found among the control students as well. Still, combining the items to form the Effective School Battery's scales reveals more subtle effects.

Baja California

Interestingly, considerable evidence emerged that some of Tijuana's participating students experienced significant reductions in their positive peer associations during the course of the pilot. This was especially so among female students and students who were fourteen years old at the time of the project (see table 16.16). Sixteen-year-olds also reported substantial, although not statistically significant, reductions. How this change is related to the project is difficult to determine. It may be, for example, that participation in the crime and corruption course caused these children to be more aware of their friends' activities, leading them to reassess existing friendships in light of the lessons they had learned. Equally plausible is that the students' friends became less supportive or even directly challenging to the project students as a result of the their involvement in the course. A third option might be that the project students' friends actually engaged in less positive activities during the semester.

Unfortunately, the individual items that comprise this scale only add to the speculation, because there was little variability between the pretests and posttests when students were asked if their friends get in trouble with the police or try to get them to do things the teacher won't like. And further, students in several important groupings (both males and females, fourteen- and fifteen-year-olds, and students who are very satisfied or very dissatisfied with their school performance) increased their estimates of the number of friends who had been picked up by the police. No meaningful changes on this scale were noted among the control students.

Table 16.16 **Pretest/Posttest Comparison of Tijuana Experimental Students on Positive Peer Associations and Belief in Rules (mean scores)**

	Positive Peers[a]		Belief in Rules	
Item (n =)	Pretest	Posttest	Pretest	Posttest
Gender:				
Males (276)	.86	.86	.79	.79
Females (280)[a]	.87	.82	.76	.77
Age:				
13 years (31)	.87	.89	.79	.80
14 years (279)[b]	.87	.84	.78	.78
15 years (173)	.85	.85	.77	.78
16 years (63)[b]	.85	.80	.73	.80
Satisfaction in school:				
Very satisfied (282)	.89	.87	.78	.79
Somewhat satisfied (218)	.84	.82	.78	.78
Somewhat dissatisfied (48)	.86	.77	.78	.78
Very dissatisfied (8)	.62	.81	.70	.72

[a] Differences among experimental students are significant at .00 or above.
[b] Differences among experimental students are significant at .05 or above.

Perhaps partially as a result of these peer influences, few changes in the students' reported belief in rules occurred following completion of the crime and corruption course. A common goal of many school-based intervention programs is to strengthen the extent to which students believe in the moral validity of social rules. It is hoped that this increased belief, coupled with added peer pressure developed during the intervention, will result in positive changes in students' behavior. Unfortunately, with the exception of the sixteen-year-olds, neither of these impacts appears to have occurred among the Tijuana students. And even there, the increased belief was not broadly held because the majority of the change occurred on a single question: whether teachers who get hassled "usually had it coming." No meaningful differences were found in these students' self-reported deviance or the degree to which they would "feel bad" about breaking laws or the rules of their teachers, parents, friends, or police officers. Further, no changes were found among the control students on this scale.

Although the desired changes in students' belief in rules may have been less than hoped for, the project's effect on their interpersonal competency was not. In an educational setting, the concept of interpersonal competency generally refers to a student's social skills independent of the more complex issues of psychological well-being and neuroticism.[22] As such, it often is used to examine students' confidence in self and their security in interactions with others. In this context, improvements in students' interpersonal competency indicated that they began to learn skills necessary to internalize and implement the substantive lessons learned about resisting lawlessness.

The curriculum's impact on the interpersonal competency of the Tijuana students was not apparent at first glance (table 16.17). There was a general improvement in the students' mean scores on this index, but it did not reach statistical significance. Nevertheless, when examined further, it was not the mean score so much as the collective scores (or distribution of scores) that had changed. That is, although the mean and median scores of Tijuana students may not have varied significantly, the range and variability clearly did, with an overall clustering of higher, or more positive, results. Finally, the impact of the crime and corruption course on the Tijuana students' positive self-concept appears to have been minimal.

San Diego County

The impact of the crime and corruption course on the attitudes and behaviors of the San Diego students was quite subtle, as was the case with their Tijuana counterparts. In fact, although generally positive trends were found, on each of the attitudinal scales some changes in students' responses were inconsistent, many failed to achieve statistical significance, and a few were offset by similar differences in the control students. A few observations are important, however.

Table 16.17 **Pretest/Posttest Comparison of Tijuana Experimental Students on Interpersonal Competency and Positive Self-Concept (mean scores)**

	Interpersonal Competency		Self-Concept	
Item	Pretest	Posttest	Pretest	Posttest
Gender:				
Males	.78	.79	.67	.68
Females	.76	.79	.70	.72
Age:				
13 years	.75	.80	.73	.71
14 years	.79	.80	.69	.70
15 years	.74	.78	.66	.69
16 years	.79	.75	.69	.72
Satisfaction in school:				
Very satisfied	.82	.83	.72	.74
Somewhat satisfied	.72	.75	.69	.68
Somewhat dissatisfied	.69	.74	.54	.54
Very dissatisfied	.76	.73	.42	.56

There were some indications that participating students actually increased their involvement in minor deviant activities, including petty theft, vandalism, and disorderly conduct (table 16.18). Beyond this, however, there were no indications of changes in the attitudes of these students or their friends concerning membership in gangs, getting into trouble with the police, or engaging in acts of which their teacher disapproves. Even so, some increase was found during the posttest period among students who reported that they were unsure if they would lie to protect a friend in trouble with the police. This uncertainty appeared to be offset by a reduction in the number of male students who agreed that it is all right to sidestep the law if possible and that people who leave things around deserve to have them stolen. Once again, caution is advised in interpreting these results. Although similar results were not found among the control students, none of the differences observed among the experimental students was statistically significant.

Table 16.18 **Pretest/Posttest Comparison of San Diego Experimental Students on Self-Reported Acts of Minor Deviance (percentages)**

Item	Property Damage		Stole < $5	
	Pretest	Posttest	Pretest	Posttest
Gender:				
Males				
Never	65%	54%	64%	56%
One or more times	35	46	36	44
Females				
Never	80	80	64	69
One or more times	20	20	36	31
Age:				
14 years				
Never	71	65	61	61
One or more times	29	35	39	39
15 years[a]				
Never	75	59	85	59
One or more times	25	41	15	41

[a] Significant at .05.

When students' responses are combined to form attitudinal scales, even less variation can be found. As with their Tijuana peers, there appears to have been some reduction in the San Diego students' positive peer associations (see table 16.19), especially among Anglos, fifteen-year-olds, and students who are very satisfied with the their current school performance. This is partially offset by a significant increase in positive associations by those students who report being very dissatisfied with their own schoolwork. The importance of these findings, however, is unknown because reductions in positive peer associations among African American students in the control group were found as well.

There were smaller, though noticeable, changes in the San Diego students' belief in rules. Specifically, male and fourteen-year-old students both reported views suggesting a strengthening of such beliefs at the conclusion of the project. Because the differences for both groups approached statistical significance and because no similar changes were noted among the control students, these results probably can be accepted without much concern.

With the exception of students who reported that they were somewhat dissatisfied with their own school performance, few meaningful differences were found between the students' pretest and posttest scores on the interpersonal competence or positive self-concept scales. No changes were identified among the control students.

Table 16.19 **Pretest/Posttest Comparison of San Diego Experimental Students on Positive Peer Associations and Belief in Rules (mean scores)**

	Positive Peers[a]		Belief in Rules	
Item	Pretest	Posttest	Pretest	Posttest
Gender:				
Males	.74	.72	.69	.73
Females	.79	.78	.83	.82
Age:				
14 years	.74	.75	.74	.78
15 years	.81	.73	.75	.76
Ethnicity:				
Hispanic/Mexican	.75	.75	.75	.76
Anglo[b]	.82	.67	.82	.75
African American	.75	.72	.74	.72
Satisfaction in school:				
Very satisfied	.82	.76	.79	.74
Somewhat satisfied	.77	.76	.76	.79
Somewhat dissatisfied[a]	.60	.72	.66	.75

[a] Significant at .01.
[b] Significant at .04.

CONCLUSION

This first pilot project consisted of a 36–lesson curriculum on: (a) the rationale for rules, laws, and a culture of lawfulness; (b) the temptation and workings of crime, organized crime, and corruption; and (c) methods of resisting involvement in crime and furthering the culture of lawfulness. The curriculum was developed collaboratively by local teachers from both sides of the border and substantive specialists in other regions.

The specific purpose of the pilot was to offer a classroom approach that would enable school administrators and teachers to produce measurable changes in children's knowledge and attitudes in a relatively short time period. It was hoped that this first application of a curriculum—tailored to local needs and taught by local teachers—would achieve meaningful results. It also was expected that the pilot would reveal subjects and methods that needed to be strengthened in subsequent iterations of the course in order to increase the effectiveness of school-based education to foster a local culture of lawfulness. It was not assumed that one relatively short course on its own would "solve" the problems endemic in the culture.

The logic of the pedagogy was as follows: by improving thirteen- to fifteen-year-old students' understanding of the need for the rule of law, the way in which young people become involved in criminal activities, and ways to resist such involvement, students would gain more "tools" with which to resist such involvement, and they would be more sympathetic to crime prevention efforts and the rule of law. Further, building on other school-based prevention efforts, the curriculum sought to further develop students' interpersonal skills and problem-solving capabilities so that they could better internalize and reinforce the lessons about resisting lawlessness.

Data gathered during the pilot's testing period as well as observations of the concluding lessons and the focus groups with students and teachers clearly indicate that the curriculum was effective and had a positive impact. Students in both Baja California and southern California demonstrated a strong interest in the course that translated into significant improvements in knowledge of and ability to resist crime and corruption. After only thirty-six lessons, this improvement can be seen in measures of student knowledge of both lawful and lawless behavior. Following the course, students could more accurately define the concepts of crime, corruption, human nature, and free will. They also could explain the elements of victimization, the negative impact of crime and corruption on the individuals involved and society as a whole, and the workings of organized crime and the process of becoming involved in organized crime and corruption.

Indeed, for some concepts, correct anonymous responses increased by 190 percent following the course. This knowledge provides students with a heightened level of defense to help them avoid being drawn inadvertently into criminal and corrupt activities.

Some students also benefited from improvement in a second line of defense. Interpersonal competency (which often is associated with self-esteem) and problem-solving capability showed improvements among the Mexican students, giving them the skills necessary to internalize and implement the substantive lessons about resisting lawlessness.

Many students also came to view material possessions as less important in establishing personal worth and pride. They also became more aware of life choices and the importance of planning for the future to improve quality of life. Interestingly, the pilot's results share some similarities with other school-based programs developed and tested in past decades. Yet it differs—and is not directly comparable to other efforts—because, almost without exception, these other programs focused on reducing substance abuse, alcohol or tobacco consumption, deviant behaviors (especially in school), or conflicts on campus. Some comparisons are possible, nonetheless, because the pilot shares assumptions that are common to most school-based prevention approaches. For example, as Gottfredson (1999) notes, most efforts are guided by the general notion that different problem behaviors are highly related, and different problem behaviors share common antecedents.

These common antecedents are the risk and protective factors that research has shown to be correlates of problem behavior; therefore, prevention efforts aimed at these factors can impact the problem behaviors generally. As such, although the behavior and attitudes that this pilot attempts to address are more broadly defined than the problem behavior targeted by most intervention efforts, it is likely that they share those common antecedents that are the risk and protective factors of interest. If so, then the lessons learned there become applicable in interpreting the current results and revising this pilot's approach to maximize its impact.

Taken together, evaluations of various school-based programs implemented to date enable us to identify a few general findings:

- Approaches that rely on fear arousal, simple information dissemination, and moral appeal generally are ineffective at achieving their stated objectives. In the United States, D.A.R.E. is the best known of these programs.
- Basic resistance training to increase students' knowledge about the influences of deviance and the specific skills they might use to resist those influences does appear to be successful. Yet the effects are small and may be short-lived unless continuing instruction is provided.
- More comprehensive social competency programs that involve cognitive-behavioral feedback, behavioral rehearsal, and systematic reinforcement show the greatest promise (Gottfredson 1999).

These conclusions, when combined with the results from the pilot evaluation, suggest revisions to the project's curriculum. Although the knowledge portion of the course can be further improved, subsequent versions of the curriculum should focus on the more complex subjects of internalizing the rationale and legitimacy of rule and law making, the moral and ethical bases of the rule of law, and the sense of rewards and remorse for law-abiding and law-breaking behaviors. These revisions are currently being made to the curriculum, and further testing is scheduled in the border area over the next few years.

Notes

The authors would like to acknowledge the assistance of the following persons in the research and preparation of this essay: Dr. Delores Jones-Brown, John Jay College of Criminal Justice; and Jeffrey Berman, Adriana Kocornik-Mina, and Cristine Maglieri at the National Strategy Information Center.

1. J. Bailey and Roy Godson, eds., *Organized Crime and Democratic Governability: Mexico and the U.S.–Mexican Borderlands* (Pittsburgh: University of Pittsburgh Press, 2000).

2. Roy Godson and Dennis Jay Kenney, *School-Based Education to Counter Crime and Corruption—Evaluation of the Initial Pilot Curriculum* (Washington, D.C.: National Strategy Information Center, 2000).

3. J. Finckenauer, "Legal Socialization: Experiences from the United States and Russia," in *Furthering a Culture of Lawfulness* (Strasbourg, France: CIVITAS International, 1998).

4. T. Wing Lo, "Pioneer of Moral Education: Anticorruption Education in Hong Kong," in *Furthering a Culture of Lawfulness.*

5. Wing Lo, "Pioneer of Moral Education," 7.

6. T. Wing Lo, "Pioneer of Moral Education: Independent Commission Against Corruption (ICAC)," *Trend in Organized Crime* 4 (2): 19–29 [1998]. See also, R. La Magna, "Changing a Culture of Corruption: How Hong Kong's Independent Commission Against Corruption Succeeded in Furthering a Culture of Lawfulness," *Trends in Organized Crime* 5 (1): 121–37 [1999].

7. J. Schneider, "Educating against the Mafia: A Report from Sicily," in *Furthering a Culture of Lawfulness.* See also, Sicilian Renaissance Institute, *Creating a Culture of Lawfulness: The Palermo, Sicily Renaissance* (Palermo, 2000).

8. J. Schneider, "Educating against the Mafia: A Report from Sicily," *Trends in Organized Crime* 4 (2): 7–18 [1998].

9. T. Eaton, "Civic Leaders Take on Mexican Mafia by Involving Teens in Anti-Crime Project" (*Dallas Morning News,* May 30,1999). See also, L. Orlando, *Fighting the Mafia and Renewing Sicilian Culture* (San Francisco, Calif.: Encounter Books, 2001).

10. Curriculum Development Council, *Guidelines on Civic Education in Schools* (Wanchai, Hong Kong: Education Department, 1996).

11. Basic education includes elementary and secondary or middle school.

12. Moreover, unlike many of their counterparts in the United States, students in Tijuana may choose to attend any school, even if it is not in their neighborhood or municipality.

13. The exit time varies from 1:15 to 2:00 PM, depending on the school, the number of classes taught each day (usually six to eight), and the time the evening schedule begins.

14. The number of students leaving school appears to be mainly a function of transfers—either to another school or shift at the parents' request—or of families leaving Tijuana. In both experimental and control schools, the dropout rate in the morning shift was minimal.

15. E. Brand, *Sweetwater Union High School District: 1998 Annual Report* (Chula Vista, Calif., 1998).

16. Ibid.

17. G. Gottfredson, *The Effective School Battery: User's Manual* (Odessa, Fla.: Psychological Assessment Resources, 1991).

18. M. Rotheram, "Social Skills Training with Underachievers, Disruptive, and Exceptional Children," *Psychology in the Schools* 19 (1982): 532–39.

19. Ibid.

20. J. Tapp and F. Levine, "Legal Socialization: Strategies for an Ethical Legality," *Stanford Law Review*, 1974. See also, D. Jones-Brown, "Race and Legal Socialization" (Ph.D. dissertation, Rutgers University, 1996).

21. D. Kenney and S. Watson. *Crime in the Schools: Reducing Fear and Disorder with Student Problem Solving* (Washington, D.C.: Police Executive Research Forum, 1998).

22. Gottfredson, *The Effective School Battery: User's Manual.*

17

Conclusions and Recommendations: Toward Better Knowledge, Communication, and Confidence

John Bailey and Jorge Chabat

Inadequate public security ranks near the top of Mexico's political agenda and has become a central issue shaping U.S.–Mexico relations. There is considerable debate about the definition of the concept "public security," especially about where to draw the boundaries between public security and closely related issues such as poverty, inequality, popular culture, morality, and the like. A rather different debate concerns the relationships between "public" security and "national" security. While recognizing the significance of such issues, the focus in this volume is on the core problems of crime, corruption, violence, and defective law enforcement. The circumstances of public security differ significantly in Mexico and the United States. Mexico is undergoing a fundamental transition from an authoritarian regime and a relatively closed economic system to a democratic system and a more open economy. Although the data are inadequate, crime and violence spiked upward in the mid–1990s but may have leveled off in 1999–2000. If we set aside the decision calculations that operate at the individual level, causes of crime appear to include economic factors—especially income inequality and slow growth—and institutional factors—especially the lack of an effective police and judicial system.[1] Crime rates also show an inertial quality in the sense that significant increases tend to perpetuate themselves over time. The key public security priority for Mexico is the physical safety of its citizens through the construction of effective police and judicial institutions and the cultivation of the rule of law in government and society. At the same time, and on a parallel track, sustained economic growth and job creation will be crucial to long-term improvement in public security.

For the United States, crime increased significantly in the 1960s and persisted at comparatively high levels for some thirty years, beginning its decline only in the mid–1990s. A variety of factors, including a lengthy period of economic growth, virtually full employment, and an aging population, together with an aggressive law enforcement strategy, appear connected to the trends. The priorities for the United States concern gun-related violence and the reduction of drug abuse. However, a major gap remains between the growing recognition that demand reduction requires greater attention and the creation and implementation of programs that have been scientifically shown to be effective.

Problems of corruption afflict both countries. For the United States, decentralization and professionalism, among other factors, tend to contain corruption at the state and local levels and in more fragmented and isolated forms. In contrast, due to pronounced centralization, the absence of professional career services, and the lack of a competitive party system over many decades, corruption has penetrated more deeply into the Mexican polity and society. Corruption in the police and judicial system more broadly is a fundamental factor in the public's sense of insecurity.

Each country will address its own security priorities in the context of its individual political and social systems. Institutional reform is a top priority in Mexico, and the government that took office on December 1, 2000, is proposing an extensive agenda of reforms to combat crime and corruption. With respect to the illegal drug problem, which is the most pressing priority for the United States, the U.S. government recognizes that long-term solutions must emphasize demand reduction. Given a robust market, producers and traffickers, both domestic and foreign, can introduce far more illicit product into the United States than that needed to satisfy demand. Even so, important dimensions of the domestic drug abuse problem are driven by transnational criminal groups that traffic in drugs. Similarly, transnational criminal organizations are key to trafficking in weapons, which is a priority concern for Mexico, and in undocumented migrants, a chronic problem for the United States. Binational and international cooperation is needed to repress these criminal organizations.

In this regard we find that bilateral communication and cooperation have rather consistently improved over the past decade, at least at the top levels of government, despite occasional episodes of friction and continuing areas of contention. The U.S.–Mexico High Level Contact Group, created in 1996, has served a useful purpose to focus discussion among relevant principals on seeking joint diagnoses and prescriptions to security problems. Progress has been made in the key areas of drug trafficking and arms smuggling. It is less apparent, however, that communication and cooperation between the two countries have improved at the middle and lower levels of the relevant agencies.

Improving cooperation requires an agenda of actions to be taken and of actions to be avoided. Among the priority items to be sought are improved knowledge, communications, cooperation, and mutual confidence. The items to be avoided include unilateral initiatives in areas of shared efforts. The recommendations that flow from the conclusions fit in these broad categories.

Governmental actions and public policy can go only part way toward providing solutions to problems of public security. Civil society, taken to mean private groups and organizations of various types, should be involved in shaping, implementing, and monitoring public policy. Governments and civil society organizations should work together to promote a culture of lawfulness through means such as formal schooling as well as public information campaigns. The mass media, more professionalized and better informed by greater access to government information, can contribute positively to improve awareness. In the long term, a culture of lawfulness is essential to creating and maintaining public security. A culture of lawfulness and the involvement of civil society are the most important ingredients in crime prevention, which is the keystone of a strategy to promote public security.

Although crime and corruption generate a sense of insecurity among the citizenry in Mexico, the more pressing problem is impunity. That is, the greater source of insecurity is a sense that police, security forces, and the judiciary do not operate effectively to protect the public. Even worse, there is a widespread belief—substantiated by numerous documented cases—that police and security forces in some circumstances cooperate with criminals to prey upon the public, or even that some police officers operate as criminals. Further, corruption and inefficiency in the judicial process means that a comparatively small proportion of the complaints officially registered are actually resolved. Thus impunity means that crimes can be committed with relative assurance that the criminals will escape punishment. One implication that follows is that the relative certainty of punishment for criminal acts is more important than the severity of the punishment. That is, the hardening of penalties for crimes is a less effective strategy than improving the effectiveness of law enforcement. And improving law enforcement is not simply, or even primarily, adding more police officers. Priority also goes to improving judicial administration and the corrections system.

Institutional reforms and administrative reorganizations can be significant components of a governmental initiative to address insecurity. Similarly, government initiatives in communications and public relations—for example, to communicate what government is doing to protect the public—can be useful. Taken together, these types of initiatives can contribute to break out of a vicious circle of distrust and disengagement by the public and to create a virtuous circle of greater trust and involvement.

In many countries, military forces perform a variety of tasks, including internal order and law enforcement. U.S. military forces assist law enforcement agencies with, for example, communications, surveillance, and drug interdiction support. At the same time, long-standing doctrines, such as *posse comitatus,* limit the role of the military in direct law enforcement. The Mexican military has long played a role in securing public order, for example, by maintaining a presence in rural areas and by carrying out drug-crop eradication. In recent years, faced with increasing problems of crime, the Mexican military have taken on extensive roles as police forces. Such new roles, which may be necessary in the absence of effective civilian police, often create serious problems, such as human rights abuses, ineffective civilian control of law enforcement, and corruption of the national defense forces. In all, the military acting as a police force against its own population is a recipe for serious problems. It follows that well-trained, professional civilian police forces should be developed as quickly as feasible in order to reduce the role of the army in internal policing.

Professional intelligence capabilities are needed in order to acquire and process the information relevant to criminal activities. Such information relates to tactical operations as well as to longer-term strategic responses to crime. The essential requirements are an effective framework law that distinguishes among the types of intelligence to be gathered (criminal, political, strategic, tactical, domestic, international, and the like), along with the administrative framework needed to separate and manage the different tasks, and the institutional and procedural controls that will guarantee citizens' rights to privacy and will hold intelligence-gathering accountable to democratically elected or appointed authorities.

The U.S. government claims to pursue a strategy that balances supply and demand reduction to contain the drug problem. It appears true that substantial resources are invested in demand reduction, and demand overall has leveled off in recent years. But several important dynamics operate here. First, the U.S. emphasis on punishment and incarceration for drug trafficking and abuse is strongly rooted in a public opinion that advocates a hard-line antidrugs strategy. At the same time, despite the enormous sums of money spent on incarceration, it is relatively rare that federal or state prisons have effective programs designed to reduce demand. Furthermore, the hard-line approach tends to preclude a meaningful dialogue on demand reduction approaches. Second, much of the demand reduction activity takes place at the state and local levels, and we do not have a current, comprehensive picture of the programs being implemented or the quantities of resources being invested. Third, and related, while numerous different types of demand reduction programs are ongoing in a variety of settings, the lack of systematic, rigorous evaluations of the programs hampers the improvement of effectiveness. Put another way, the vast majority of demand reduction programs are not evaluated scientifically, and so it is not clear what approaches work best. Finally, because demand reduction programs are relatively low profile and not well evaluated, neither the Mexican nor U.S. public is sufficiently aware of the scope and weight of efforts invested in this aspect of the drug problem.

Extradition continues to be a source of friction between the United States and Mexico. In principle, the United States should routinely extradite individuals—including U.S. citizens—sought by the Mexican government. In practice, U.S. courts deny many extradition requests, often due to problems perceived in the Mexican criminal justice system. Mexico encounters constitutional-legal obstacles to extraditing Mexican nationals sought by the United States. In practice, however, Mexican courts have increasingly found grounds to extradite to the United States their own nationals accused of serious crime. The decision by the Mexican Supreme Court in January 2001 authorizing the extradition of a Mexican citizen to be tried for drug-related crimes in a U.S. court may mark an important change. Extraditions in the first months of the Fox administration support that impression. Given the rapid rates of integration of the economies and societies, an efficient means of binational cooperation is needed in order to apprehend and prosecute individuals who commit crimes in one country and flee to the other to avoid prosecution. An alternative to extradition is foreign prosecution, a process by which Mexican nationals, under certain conditions, can be prosecuted in Mexican courts for crimes committed in the United States. In order for foreign prosecution to serve as an effective alternative to extradition, however, the Mexican court system must improve its effectiveness. Another instrument that may prove useful in facilitating cooperation is temporary extradition whereby an individual who has already been tried in one country may be temporarily extradited to the other country to testify or to stand trial.

Though its dimensions are not known, weapons trafficking from the United States to Mexico contributes to violence and public insecurity in the latter country. There may be connections as well between gun smuggling and drug trafficking, although the linkage is unclear. Gun smuggling is one of several areas where the cultural and legal-constitutional orders of the two countries create tensions. The U.S. Bill of Rights, specifically the second amendment to the Constitution, guarantees the right for U.S. citizens to keep and bear arms. This is not an unlimited right, however, and numerous laws and regulations restrict the manufacture, sale, and use of firearms. The reality, however, is that guns in the United States, and especially in the states along the border, are fairly easy to obtain and smuggle into Mexico. A number of technical-institutional problems complicated cooperation between the two governments in repressing gun smuggling. Even so, with the formation of the Bi-National Firearms Trafficking Working Group in 1997, cooperation has improved.

Illegal migration from Mexico to the United States continues to be an irritant in the bilateral relationship. Here, as in weapons trafficking, legal-constitutional issues come into play. The Mexican Constitution guarantees its citizens freedom of movement within the country. Thus the Mexican government legally should not interfere with its citizens moving into the immediate border region. The issue for the United States is that undocumented entry into its territory is a crime, and reentry following forced repatriation is a serious crime. Although illegal migration is a continuing irritant, in reality the more pressing priority for bilateral cooperation is the suppression of transnational criminal groups that traffic in undocumented migrants. This is because such groups contribute to increased violence in the border region. In many cases they are responsible for abuses against, and even the deaths of, migrants. They also violate Mexico's sovereignty by trafficking third-country migrants through Mexican territory.

The shared border region is a rapidly growing area, which—in important respects—sets the tone of the bilateral relationship. We should look to the border for opportunities to promote cooperation between the countries. For example, the Arizona/Sonora Juvenile Justice Procedure Task Force project demonstrated that much can be gained through attempts by state and local governments on both sides of the border to solve a shared problem. In that case, the ability to deal effectively in Arizona with juveniles from Sonora required cross-border initiatives to integrate the criminal and juvenile services of Arizona with the social and human resources services of Sonora. The border serves simultaneously as a bridge and a barrier. As such there is tension between the goals of facilitating legal traffic of commodities while blocking illegal commodities. The border's role as a barrier means that corruption and violence are intensified in the border region as criminal organizations operate to control turf and penetrate border controls.

By and large, interagency cooperation by federal, state, and local entities generally improved on both sides of the border in the 1990s. Experience, along with the introduction of the High Intensity Drug-Trafficking Area mechanism, has facilitated federal-state-local agency cooperation in the U.S. border region. The centralization of the Mexican system and the designation of certain types of crime (including drug smuggling and weapons violations) as federal offenses to be dealt with by federal police complicates cooperation between federal and local authorities. Even so, such cooperation has improved somewhat in the past few years.

Also, there has been some improvement in cross-border cooperation between Mexican and U.S. authorities. There has not emerged, however, a broader set of dialogues among government authorities and civil society groups in order to define a common sense of what might promote public safety in the border zone. Related to this, while cross-border cooperation has improved to one or another degree at different points or within various "corridors" along the 2,000–mile border, still lacking is an effective communication and coordination among the border communities.

As noted, our recommendations fit into two broad categories. First, in order to formulate better policies, we need better information and communications. Thus some priorities for future study are recommended, along with steps to improve communications. Second, the key goal is to improve cooperation and deepen confidence, and steps toward these goals are suggested.

TO IMPROVE KNOWLEDGE AND COMMUNICATIONS

- Studies should be undertaken to better understand the causes of crime specifically in the two countries and the border region. Especially important is a better understanding of the relationships among types of crime—common or "opportunity" crime (assault, petty larceny); miscellaneous organized crime (cargo hijacking, bank robbery); and transnational organized crime (traffickers in drugs, undocumented migrants, stolen vehicles, and the like, whose organization and activities transcend the borders of a single country). We do not know, for example, the ways in which criminal groups organize themselves to conduct different types of criminal activity or the linkages they form with the political system or with licit economy and society. Nor do we know the extent to which criminal gangs tend to specialize in one or another form of crime. A priority question is the relationship between gun smuggling and drug trafficking. Understanding of these relationships is needed to craft long-term, cooperative strategies to prevent and contain crime. Also, this knowledge is crucial so that citizens in both countries can begin to comprehend the linkages among various types of criminality and thus understand and support cooperative strategies.

- With respect to drug trafficking in the United States, a key missing link in knowledge is a better understanding of the nature of the criminal organizations that operate at the wholesale level—that is, the groups that transport drug shipments from points of entry to various locales within the country, distribute the product for street-level sales, and launder the profits through various means. Such studies are needed to address a concern frequently expressed by Mexican citizens that U.S. officials and citizens unfairly emphasize the involvement of foreign nationals in U.S. crime and minimize involvement by "home-grown" U.S. criminal organizations. In congressional testimonies, for example, U.S. officials emphasize the involvement of Mexican and other foreign gangs in both smuggling and large-scale distribution.[2]

- Mexico should implement periodic national victimization studies, following accepted international standards. As in most countries, much criminal activity goes unreported for various reasons: the crimes may be so petty as to not merit complaint; complainants may not expect an effective response from the police; or, worse, complainants may fear contact with police and legal authorities. Whatever the mix of reasons, the lack of useful information about patterns of criminal activities hinders the development of effective anticrime strategies. Crime control programs thus become reactive rather than preventive.[3]

- Easily accessible, updated, comprehensive surveys of each country's constitutional, political, legal, and security systems should be prepared by both governmental and nongovernmental (academic and professional, for example) organizations and disseminated widely in both languages (through CDs, Web sites, easily obtainable documents, and so on). The surveys should: (1) summarize the main constitutional and institutional features of each system, (2) summarize key legal concepts and procedures, (3) describe the organization, duties, and functions of security forces and judicial bodies, (4) update periodically the more important trends and developments in public safety, and (5) note the principal civil society organizations involved in crime prevention and law enforcement.

- The U.S. government should give higher priority to rigorous, scientific evaluations of drug abuse prevention and reduction programs, so that resources can be channeled to those programs that show results. Related to this, better data are needed on resources invested in drug abuse prevention and reduction at the state and local levels in public and private facilities.

- With respect to better communications, dialogues should be promoted within and between the communities in the corridors along the border in order to diagnose the specific, local problems of public safety and recommend responses; communities should be understood in the broad sense of civil society and governmental actors.

- Dialogues in the border region can be facilitated by the creation of Web sites that include pertinent data such as the names and contact information of law enforcement, judicial officers, lawyers' associations, social services departments, and relevant civil society organizations in the communities along the border.

TO IMPROVE COOPERATION AND CONFIDENCE

- The Mexican government should give top priority to the creation of career professional services in law enforcement and judicial administration. The absence of career services in Mexico has been a major impediment to binational cooperation. U.S. officials are frequently frustrated by rapid turnover in personnel in counterpart positions. Improvement in technical and professional training is obviously important, but efforts to prevent or root out corruption are crucial as well.

- Multiple forms of societal involvement in both countries to promote public security should be encouraged, such as school-based education to provide understanding of the importance of lawfulness and the costs and dangers of criminality. Put another way, it is mistaken, even dangerous, to believe that public security can be managed by government alone. Over the long term, civil society and political culture are the keys to success.[4]

- A senior national official should be appointed in each country to take charge of border communication and coordination among the corridors along the border and with state and federal officials. Such an office was created by the Fox administration, and a U.S. counterpart is needed. The office should serve to promote communication and coordination across local, state, and federal jurisdictions, and it should be provided a staff and necessary resources in order to promote continuity.

- A high priority concern is the protection of human rights of all persons in the border region. The most serious current issue involves the physical safety of undocumented migrants, whether due to crimes inflicted by other persons or to suffering resulting from climate and terrain. The United States and Mexico should appoint a high-level commission to investigate the current problems of human rights violations and make appropriate recommendations to their governments.

- A binational group of informed specialists should be created to serve as a clearinghouse for questions concerning public security. The main function of the group would be to answer questions or refer questioners to appropriate sources of information. Given the capacity and potentials of the Internet, such a group could be fairly easily assembled.

- The annual inter-parliamentary meeting between U.S. and Mexican legislators should be complemented by improved direct linkages between congressional staffs and agencies (such as the Congressional Research Service) concerned with public security.

- The annual drug certification process by the U.S. government is a unilateral measure that exacts greater costs in goodwill and cooperation than benefits in accurately assessing efforts to repress drug production, consumption, and trafficking. It should be replaced by a bilateral or multilateral mechanism. One such mechanism is the Memorandum of Mutual Evaluation being developed by the Organization of American States.

- Both the United States and Mexico should ratify the protocols to the current extradition treaty and work to strengthen extradition procedures and to avoid the politicization of the issue.

THE CASE FOR GUARDED OPTIMISM

The editors and contributors have painted a fairly somber picture throughout the volume, scenes that suggest that policy strategies should be couched in the long term, in periods measured by decades and generations. The continued reduction of drug abuse in the United States and the construction of effective police and judicial institutions in Mexico, to illustrate, will require decades. The promotion of a civic culture of lawfulness in both countries is a long-term, continuing task. Solutions to Mexico's problems of sustainable economic growth and reduction of deep-seated and pervasive inequalities, clearly root causes of crime and violence, will require decades to achieve.

Even so, there is a basis for guarded optimism on at least four grounds. First, Mexico's democratic transition appears firmly on track. Democratic dynamics by their nature strengthen citizen participation and reinforce pressures for public accountability. This, along with more aggressive mass media, will create incentives for government at various levels to pursue more effective strategies to reform the administration of justice and to promote public security in tandem with increased citizen involvement.

Second and related, there is a new climate of frankness and candor. Problems of public security are being addressed in more transparent and constructive ways in both countries. The topic of corruption in Mexico, for example, which was (non)treated almost ritualistically in former times, is being addressed more frontally. While discussions about drug abuse remain in the policy box of illegality and punishment, we see more candor. Presidents Bill Clinton and George W. Bush have both frankly acknowledged that the root causes of drug trafficking and abuse are demand-driven by the United States. Political movements in several states are pressing for the decriminalization of less serious forms of drug use. Mexican authorities recognize the growing drug abuse problem within their borders.

Third, the habits of bilateral consultation and cooperation at the top levels of government put down solid roots in the late 1980s and throughout the 1990s. The progress in cooperation accelerated in the first months of the new administrations of Presidents Fox and Bush. True, the cooperative ethos still lags behind at the working levels of law enforcement. Even here, however, there is basis for optimism in the growing diversity and pluralism in the Mexican system as seen, for example, in growing numbers of mayors and governors from various parties who are themselves gaining resources and independence through policies that promote decentralization.

Finally, the forces of economic and social integration between the United States and Mexico have gained impressive momentum since the late 1980s and especially since the implementation of the North American Free Trade Agreement in 1994. Flows of trade, investment, and migration have linked core political interests of Mexican and U.S. elites. One implication is that issues of public safety, law enforcement, and judicial process will receive increasing attention on the bilateral agenda as leaders seek ways to harmonize policies or promote practical methods of cooperation. By no means do we suggest that issues of sovereignty will lose relevance; rather, the self-interest of both countries in pursuing collaboration will place sovereignty in a new perspective.

Notes

1. See James Q. Wilson and Richard J. Herrnstein, *Crime and Human Nature: The Definitive Study of the Causes of Crime* (New York: Free Press, 1985), and Robert Klitgaard, *Controlling Corruption* (Berkeley: University of California Press, 1988) for excellent examples of rational-actor approaches).

2. See, for example, Thomas Constantine, Administrator of DEA, Testimony before the Senate Caucus on International Narcotics Control Regarding United States and Mexico Counterdrug Efforts, Washington, D.C., February 24, 1999.

3. The various victimization surveys done to date in Mexico generally have been limited to specific cities or regions or have employed questionable methodologies. They have given diverse results that have tended to create confusion. See, for example, Rafael Ruiz Harrell's critique of a national-level survey done by the Office of the President; "Cifra negrerrima," *Reforma*, July 7, 2001 (Internet edition). Ruiz notes that Mexico lags behind most other countries in Latin America in doing regular national surveys.

4. Recent reforms to state-level police practices in Baja California and Jalisco have increased the role of citizen participation on oversight panels. These reforms should be evaluated with an eye to their use elsewhere.

The Contributors

Peter Andreas is Assistant Professor of Political Science at Brown University. He is the author of *Border Games: Policing the U.S.–Mexico Divide;* co-author of *Drug War Politics: The Price of Denial;* and co-editor of *The Wall around the West: State Borders and Immigration Controls in North America and Europe.*

W. Carsten Andresen is a doctoral candidate in the School of Criminal Justice at Rutgers–Newark. His major area of interest encompasses comparative and international drug policies.

Sigrid Arzt has worked in the Technical Secretariat of former Mexican attorney general Antonio Lozano and at the Centro de Investigación y Docencia Económicas (CIDE) in Mexico City. In 1998 she was a Visiting Scholar at Georgetown University and the Woodrow Wilson Center. Her research focuses on issues of national security in U.S.–Mexican relations. She is currently a doctoral candidate in international relations at the University of Miami.

John Bailey is Professor of Government and Director of the Mexico Project at the Center for Latin American Studies, Georgetown University. From 1980 to 1991 he chaired the Advanced Area Seminar on Mexico at the U.S. Department of State's Foreign Service Institute, and he has twice served as director of Georgetown's Latin American Studies Program. He recently co-edited *Organized Crime and Democratic Governability* (with Roy Godson).

Fernando Castillo focuses his research in the areas of narco-trafficking, national security, and public safety. He has served as adviser to the Office of the President and the Attorney General's Office in Mexico. Castillo was the first planning director of the Sistema Nacional de Seguridad Pública, co-author of the National Public Security Law, and an architect of Mexico's National Public Security Program (PNSP) and National Crime Prevention Program (Programa Nacional de Prevención del Delito).

Jorge Chabat is Associate Professor in the Department of International Studies at the Centro de Investigación y Docencia Económicas (CIDE) in Mexico City. He is an expert on U.S.–Mexico relations, drug trafficking, and national security issues. He is a regular political commentator for Mexican newspapers and television.

Leonardo Curzio is Research Professor in the Political Science Department of the Universidad Nacional Autónoma de México (UNAM) in Mexico City.

Graham Farrell is Associate Professor of Criminal Justice at the University of Cincinnati. He has worked for the United Nations International Drug Control Programme and the Police Foundation in Washington, D.C. He has authored publications across a range of areas relating to crime and drug policy.

José Z. García is Associate Professor of Government at New Mexico State University and Director of the university's Center for Latin American Studies. He has published extensively on politics, civil-military relations, and Latin American foreign affairs. From 1989 to 1991, he was a Visiting Scholar at the U.S. Army School of the Americas.

Roy Godson is Professor of Government at Georgetown University and directs the National Strategy Information Center in Washington, D.C. He has published extensively on issues of trans-state relations, security studies, and strategic approaches to countering transnational organized crime. He has also served as a consultant to the United Nations and to the U.S. and other governments. He is currently developing societal/cultural approaches to complement law enforcement and regulatory approaches to preventing crime and corruption.

Dennis Jay Kenney is Director of Planning and Research for the Savannah, Georgia Police and Associate Director and Research Director of the Police Executive Research Forum in Washington, D.C. He is the co-author of *Crime in the Schools: Reducing Conflict with Student Problem Solving*, among other works.

Brian Latell is Adjunct Professor in the School of Foreign Service of Georgetown University. Until 1998 he was a Latin America specialist at the Central Intelligence Agency, where he served as Director of the Center for the Study of Intelligence. Dr. Latell is co-editor of *Eye in the Sky: The Story of the Corona Spy Satellites.*

Ernesto López Portillo Vargas is Professor of Law at the Universidad Nacional Autónoma de México (UNAM) in Mexico City. He has been an adviser to the federal Attorney General's Office and has served as technical secretary of the Public Safety Commission in the Mexican Senate. He has conducted research on police institutions throughout South America and Europe and is the co-author of *Seguridad Pública en México.*

Viviana Macías has served in the planning department of Mexico's Centro de Planeación para el Control de las Drogas (CENDRO) and worked as a staff member of Mexico's National Security Council. She is currently pursuing graduate study at Massey University in New Zealand.

William F. McDonald is Professor of Sociology and Director of the Law Institute and Criminal Procedures in Georgetown University. His interests include immigration, community policies, transnational crime, and criminal law.

José M. Ramos is a Researcher at the Colegio de la Frontera Norte (COLEF) in Tijuana, Mexico, where he works on topics related to public administration, cross-border cooperation in public policy making, regional development, and U.S.–Mexico bilateral relations.

Jorge Regalado Santillán is a member of the faculty of the Centro Universitario de Ciencias Sociales y Humanidades at the Universidad de Guadalajara. He has written extensively on issues of public security and civil society in Mexico.

Graham H. Turbiville, Jr. is Director of the Foreign Military Studies Office in Fort Leavenworth, Kansas, and editor of the journal *Low-Intensity Conflict and Law Enforcement*. He has also authored several articles about the global dimensions of crime.

Bruce Zagaris is an Adjunct Professor at the Washington College of Law, American University, and the Fordham University Law School, where he teaches international business and criminal law. He is also a partner in the Washington, D.C., law firm of Berliner, Corcoran & Rowe.

Guillermo Zepeda Lecuona is Associate Researcher at the Centro de Investigación para el Desarrollo (CIDAC) in Mexico City and a doctoral candidate in law at the Universidad Nacional Autónoma de México. A practicing attorney, he specializes in institutional development, judicial reform, and criminal justice. In 1999, he was the recipient of Mexico's National Prize in Law and Economics. He has published several books and articles and is a contributor to the newspaper *El Economista.*

International Advisory Council
of the Center for U.S.–Mexican Studies
University of California, San Diego

Arturo Alvarado
El Colegio de México

John Bailey
Georgetown University

Vivienne Bennett
California State University San Marcos

Miguel Centeno
Princeton University

Carlos Elizondo
Centro de Investigación y Docencia Económicas

Agustín Escobar Latapí
CIESAS-Occidente (Guadalajara)

Federico Estévez
Instituto Tecnológico Autónomo de México

Jonathan Fox
University of California, Santa Cruz

Mercedes González de la Rocha
CIESAS-Occidente (Guadalajara)

Merilee Grindle
Harvard University

Gordon Hanson
University of California, San Diego

Gilbert Joseph
Yale University

Alan Knight
Oxford University

Gail Mummert
El Colegio de Michoacán

Peter Ward
University of Texas at Austin

Laurence Whitehead
Oxford University

Publication of important new research on Mexico and U.S.–Mexican relations is a major activity of the Center for U.S.–Mexican Studies. Statements of fact and opinion appearing in Center publications are the responsibility of the authors alone and do not imply endorsement by the Center for U.S.–Mexican Studies, the International Advisory Council, or the University of California.

Publications Program
Center for U.S.–Mexican Studies
University of California, San Diego
9500 Gilman Drive, Dept. 0510
La Jolla, CA 92093-0510
TEL 858.534.1160 FAX 858.534.6447
EMAIL usmpubs@ucsd.edu WEB http://usmex.ucsd.edu